Contents

Maps

Fodor's 7th Edition

W9-AAV-307

Maine, Vermont, New Hampshire

The complete guide, thoroughly up-to-date

Packed with details that will make your trip

The must-see sights, off and on the beaten path

What to see, what to skip

Mix-and-match vacation itineraries

City strolls, countryside adventures

Smart lodging and dining options

Essential local do's and taboos

Transportation tips, distances and directions

Key contacts, savvy travel tips

When to go, what to pack

Clear, accurate, easy-to-use maps

Excerpted from *Fodor's New England*

Fodor's Travel Publications • New York, Toronto, London, Sydney, Auckland
www.fodors.com

Fodor's Maine, Vermont, New Hampshire

EDITORS: Matt Hayes, William Travis

Editorial Contributors: Andrew Collins, Hilary M. Nangle, Bill Scheller, Kay Scheller

Editorial Production: Ira-Neil Dittersdorf

Maps: David Lindroth, *cartographer*; Rebecca Baer and Bob Blake, *map editors*

Design: Fabrizio La Rocca, *creative director*; Guido Caroti, *art director*; Jolie Novak, *senior picture editor*

Cover Design: Pentagram

Production/Manufacturing: Colleen Ziemba

Cover Photograph: Peter Guttman *(Marshall's Point Lighthouse, Near Owl's Head on the Maine Coast)*

Copyright

Important Tip

Although all prices, opening times, and other details in this book are based on information supplied to us at press time, changes occur all the time in the travel world, and Fodor's cannot accept responsibility for facts that become outdated or for inadvertent errors or omissions. So **always confirm information when it matters,** especially if you're making a detour to visit a specific place.

Special Sales

Fodor's Travel Publications are available at special discounts for bulk purchases for sales promotions or premiums. Special editions, including personalized covers, excerpts of existing guides, and corporate imprints, can be created in large quantities for special needs. For more information, contact your local bookseller or write to Special Markets, Fodor's Travel Publications, 280 Park Avenue, New York, NY 10017. Inquiries from Canada should be directed to your local Canadian bookseller or sent to Random House of Canada, Ltd., Marketing Department, 2775 Matheson Boulevard East, Mississauga, Ontario L4W 4P7. Inquiries from the United Kingdom should be sent to Fodor's Travel Publications, 20 Vauxhall Bridge Road, London SW1V 2SA, England.

PRINTED IN THE UNITED STATES OF AMERICA

10 9 8 7 6 5 4 3 2 1

CONTENTS

ON THE ROAD WITH FODOR'S

THE MORE YOU KNOW before you go, the better your trip will be. The most fascinating antiques store or the finest seafood restaurant in Maine, New Hampshire, or Vermont could be just around the corner from your hotel, but if you don't know it's there, it might as well be on the other side of the globe. That's where this book comes in. It's a great step toward making sure your next trip lives up to your expectations. As you plan, check out the Web as well. Guidebooks have been helping smart travelers find the special places for years; the Web is one more tool. Whatever reference you consult, be savvy about what you read, and always consider the source. Images and language can be massaged to make places appear better than they are. And one traveler's quaint is another's grimy. Here at Fodor's, and at our on-line arm, fodors.com, our focus is on providing you with information that's not only useful but accurate and on target. Every day Fodor's editors put enormous effort into getting things right, beginning with the search for the right contributors—people who have objective judgment, broad travel experience, and the writing ability to put their insights into words. There's no substitute for advice from a like-minded friend who has just come back from where you're going, but our writers, having seen all corners of Maine, New Hampshire, and Vermont, are the next best thing. They're the kind of people you'd poll for tips yourself if you knew them.

Hilary M. Nangle, formerly travel editor for a daily newspaper in Maine, is now a freelancer based in the state's scenic mid-coast. Her Fodor's beat is Maine, and she writes regularly about travel, food, and skiing for publications in the United States and Canada.

Former Fodor's editor and New England native **Andrew Collins,** who updated and expanded the New Hampshire chapter, is the author of several book on travel in New England including handbooks on Connecticut and Rhode Island.

Kay and Bill Scheller, who revised and expanded the Vermont chapter as well as the Berkshires and Pioneer Valley sections of Massachusetts, have a total of more than 30 years' experience as contributors to Fodor's guides. They are the authors of several books on travel in New England and the Northeast. The Schellers live in northern Vermont.

Don't Forget to Write

Your experiences—positive and negative—matter to us. If we have missed or misstated something, we want to hear about it. We follow up on all suggestions. Contact the Maine, Vermont, New Hampshire editor at editors@fodors.com or c/o Fodor's, 280 Park Avenue, New York, New York 10017. And have a fabulous trip!

Karen Cure
Editorial Director

Maine, Vermont, and New Hampshire

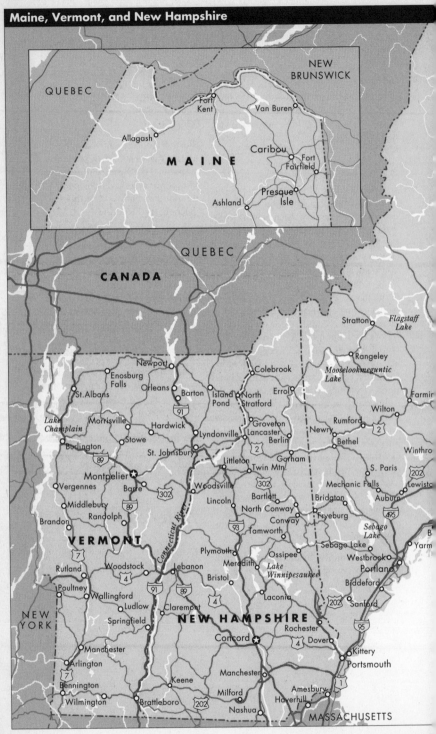

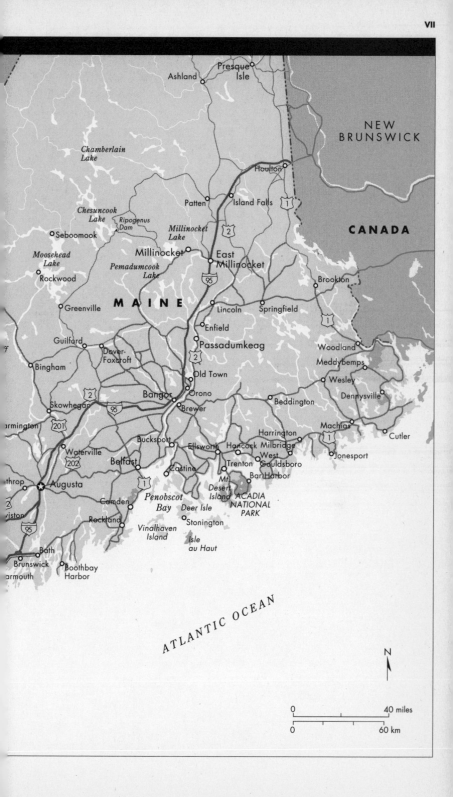

Ashland
Presque Isle

NEW BRUNSWICK

Chamberlain Lake

Houlton

Patten
Island Falls

CANADA

Chesuncook Lake
Ripogenus Dam
Millinocket Lake

Seboomook

Moosehead Lake

Rockwood

Millinocket

Pemadumcook Lake

East Millinocket

Brookton

MAINE

Greenville

Lincoln
Springfield

Enfield

Guilford

Dover-Foxcroft

Passadumkeag

Woodland

Bingham

Meddybemps

Old Town

Wesley

Bangor
Orono

Beddington

Dennysville

Skowhegan

Brewer

Machias

Cutler

armington

Harrington

Buckport

Ellsworth
Hancock Milbridge

Jonesport

Waterville

Belfast

Castine

West Gouldsboro

Trenton

throp

Augusta

Camden

Penobscot Bay

Deer Isle

Mt. Desert Island
Bar Harbor
ACADIA NATIONAL PARK

iston

Rockland

Stonington

Vinalhaven Island

Isle au Haut

Bath

Brunswick
Boothbay Harbor

armouth

ATLANTIC OCEAN

N

0   40 miles
0   60 km

The United States

ONTARIO
CANADA
QUÉBEC
NEW BRUNSWICK

Québec
Fredericton

MAINE
95

MINNESOTA
Duluth
Augusta

WISCONSIN
MICHIGAN
Lake Superior

Montréal
Montpelier
95

St. Paul
Green Bay
Lake Huron

Ottawa
VT.
Concord
N.H.
Boston

Minneapolis
Madison
Milwaukee
Lansing
Toronto
Lake Ontario
Buffalo
NEW YORK
Albany
Hartford
MASS.
Providence
R.I.

IOWA
Chicago
Detroit
Cleveland
PENNSYLVANIA
CONN.
New York

Des Moines
Springfield
INDIANA
Columbus
OHIO
Pittsburgh
Harrisburg
Trenton
N.J.
Philadelphia

Omaha
Indianapolis
WEST VIRGINIA
Baltimore
Dover
DEL.
Annapolis
MD.
Washington, D.C.

Topeka
St. Louis
Cincinnati
Louisville
Frankfort
Charleston
Richmond

Kansas City
Jefferson City
KENTUCKY
VIRGINIA
Norfolk

MISSOURI
Nashville
Raleigh

Tulsa
ARKANSAS
Memphis
TENNESSEE
NORTH CAROLINA

Little Rock
Birmingham
Atlanta
Columbia
SOUTH CAROLINA

MISSISSIPPI
GEORGIA
Savannah

Jackson
ALABAMA
Montgomery
Jacksonville

Baton Rouge
Mobile
Tallahassee
FLORIDA
Orlando

Houston
LOUISIANA
New Orleans

Gulf of Mexico

ATLANTIC OCEAN

Bahama Islands
Miami
Nassau

N

0   500 miles
0   800 km

SMART TRAVEL TIPS A TO Z

Basic Information on Traveling in Maine, Vermont, and New Hampshire; Savvy Tips to Make Your Trip a Breeze; and Companies and Organizations to Contact

AIR TRAVEL

Most travelers will head for a major gateway and then rent a car to enjoy the sights. The northern New England states form a fairly compact region, with few important destinations more than six hours apart by car, and intra-regional air transportation facilities are mainly patronized by business travelers. Should you wish to fly, be advised that intraregional fares can be high and flights limited.

BOOKING

When you book **look for nonstop flights** and **remember that "direct" flights stop at least once.** Try to avoid connecting flights, which require a change of plane. For more booking tips and to check prices and make on-line flight reservations, log on to www.fodors.com.

CARRIERS

➤ MAJOR AIRLINES: **American** (☎ 800/433-7300). **Continental** (☎ 800/525-0280). **Delta** (☎ 800/221-1212). **Northwest** (☎ 800/225-2525). **Southwest** (☎ 800/435-9792). **Sun Country** (☎ 800/359-5786). **TWA** (☎ 800/221-2000). **United** (☎ 800/241-6522). **US Airways** (☎ 800/428-4322).

➤ REGIONAL AIRLINES: **Midway** (☎ 800/446-4392).

➤ FROM THE U.K.: **American** (☎ 0345/789-789). **British Airways** (☎ 0345/222-111). **Virgin Atlantic** (☎ 01293/747-747).

➤ FROM AUSTRALIA AND NEW ZEALAND: **Qantas** (from Australia, ☎ 13-1313, 0800/808-767, or 09/357-8900; from New Zealand, outside Auckland, ☎ 0800/808-767; from Auckland area, ☎ 09/357-8900).

CHECK-IN & BOARDING

Assuming that not everyone with a ticket will show up, airlines routinely overbook planes. When everyone does, airlines ask for volunteers to give up their seats. In return, these volunteers usually get a certificate for a free flight and are rebooked on the next flight out. If there are not enough volunteers, the airline must choose who will be denied boarding. The first to get bumped are passengers who checked in late and those flying on discounted tickets, so **get to the gate and check in as early as possible,** especially during peak periods.

Always **bring a government-issued photo I.D. to the airport;** a passport is best. You may be asked to show it before you are allowed to check in.

CUTTING COSTS

The least expensive airfares to New England must usually be purchased in advance and are non-refundable. It's smart to **call a number of airlines, and when you are quoted a good price, book it on the spot**—the same fare may not be available the next day. Always **check different routings** and look into using different airports. Travel agents, especially low-fare specialists (☞ Discounts & Deals), are helpful.

Consolidators are another good source. They buy tickets for scheduled international flights at reduced rates from the airlines, then sell them at prices that beat the best fare available directly from the airlines, usually without restrictions. Sometimes you can even get your money back if you need to return the ticket. Carefully read the fine print detailing penalties for changes and cancellations, and **confirm your consolidator reservation with the airline.**

➤ CONSOLIDATORS: **Cheap Tickets** (☎ 800/377-1000). **Discount Airline Ticket Service** (☎ 800/576-1600). **Unitravel** (☎ 800/325-2222). **Up & Away Travel** (☎ 212/889-2345). **World Travel Network** (☎ 800/409-6753).

ENJOYING THE FLIGHT

For more legroom, **request an emergency-aisle seat.** Don't sit in the row in front of the emergency aisle or in front of a bulkhead, where seats may not recline. If you have dietary concerns, **ask for special meals when booking.** These can be vegetarian, low-cholesterol, or kosher, for example. On long flights, try to maintain a normal routine, to help fight jet lag. At night, **get some sleep.** By day, **eat light meals, drink water** (not alcohol), and **move around the cabin** to stretch your legs. For additional jet-lag tips consult *Fodor's FYI: Travel Fit & Healthy* (available at bookstores everywhere).

All flights within the U.S. are strictly nonsmoking, as are international flights on American-based carriers. Smoking regulations vary among non-U.S.–based carriers, so call if this is important to you. It is uncommon for U.S. airports to allow smoking, although a few permit it in specially designated areas.

FLYING TIMES

Flying time to Boston is 1 hour from New York, 2 hours and 15 minutes from Chicago, 6 hours from Los Angeles, 4 hours from Dallas, and 8 hours from London. Flying time from Sydney, Australia, to Boston (via Los Angeles) is 20 hours; flying time from Auckland, New Zealand, to Boston (via Los Angeles) is 17 hours.

HOW TO COMPLAIN

If your baggage goes astray or your flight goes awry, complain right away. Most carriers require that you **file a claim immediately.**

➤ AIRLINE COMPLAINTS: U.S. Department of Transportation **Aviation Consumer Protection Division** (✉ C-75, Room 4107, Washington, DC 20590, ☎ 202/366–2220, 🖥 www.dot.gov/airconsumer). **Federal Aviation Administration Consumer Hotline** (☎ 800/322–7873).

AIRPORTS

The main gateway to New England is Boston's Logan International Airport (BOS), the region's largest. Additional New England airports served by

major carriers include Manchester Airport (MHT) in Manchester, New Hampshire (a rapidly growing, lower-cost alternative to Boston); Portland International Jetport (PWM) in Maine; and Burlington International Airport (BTV) in Vermont. Another regional airport is in Bangor, Maine.

➤ AIRPORT INFORMATION: **Burlington International Airport** (☎ 802/863–1889). **Logan International Airport** (☎ 800/235–6426). **Manchester Airport** (☎ 603/624-6539). **Portland International Jetport** (☎ 207/774–7301).

BIKE TRAVEL

Cyclists favor New England because overnight destinations are seldom far apart. Inns and B&Bs are plentiful, and some operators offer guided inn-to-inn tours. In general, northern (except for far northern Maine) and western New England have the best cycling opportunities, with plenty of lightly traveled secondary roads and pleasant small towns to explore en route. Make sure you're in shape if you plan to tackle the hills of Vermont and New Hampshire, and **consider a mountain bike** if you're going to be on dirt roads. Both mountain and touring bikes are available for rent in resort areas and in most larger towns and cities for as little as $20 a day.

BIKES IN FLIGHT

Most airlines accommodate bikes as luggage, provided they are dismantled and boxed. Airlines sell bike boxes, which are often free at bike shops, for about $5 (it's at least $100 for bike bags). International travelers can sometimes substitute a bike for a piece of checked luggage at no charge; otherwise, the cost is about $100. Domestic and Canadian airlines charge $25–$50.

BOAT & FERRY TRAVEL

Ferry routes provide access to many islands off the Maine coast. In addition, ferries cross Lake Champlain between Vermont and upstate New York. International service between Portland and Bar Harbor, Maine, and Yarmouth, Nova Scotia, is also available. With the exception of the Lake Champlain ferries, which are first-come, first-served, car reservations are always advisable.

BUS TRAVEL

All New England states have bus service; fares are generally moderate and buses normally run on schedule, although service can be infrequent and travel time can be long due to traffic and frequent stops. Smoking is not permitted on buses.

CUTTING COSTS

Greyhound offers Ameripass, which allows riders to travel throughout New England at discounted fares for varying lengths of time from 7 to 60 days.

➤ BUS INFORMATION: **Bonanza Bus Lines** (☎ 800/556–3815). **Concord Trailways** (☎ 800/639–3317). **Greyhound** (☎ 800/231–2222; 888/454–7277 for Ameripass). **Peter Pan Bus Lines** (☎ 800/343–9999). **Vermont Transit** (☎ 800/642-3133 in Vermont; 800/552-8737 elsewhere).

BUSINESS HOURS

Banks in New England are generally open weekdays from 9 AM until 3 PM, with longer hours on Thursdays and Fridays. Post offices are open weekdays between 8 AM and 5 PM; many branches operate Saturday morning hours. Business hours tend to be weekdays from 9 to 5. Banks and post offices close on all national holidays; retail businesses generally close only on Thanksgiving, Christmas, New Year's Day, and Easter. Convenience stores, especially in urban areas, are often open 365 days a year.

GAS STATIONS

Except along major highways, gas stations frequently close at around 10 or 11 PM and reopen at 5 or 6 AM.

MUSEUMS & SIGHTS

While some major museums and attractions are open daily—at least during peak tourist season—Monday closings are common. In resort areas, museums and attractions are frequently closed or on significantly reduced schedules from mid-October to late May. Hours of sights and attractions are denoted throughout this book by the clock icon, ☉.

SHOPS

Many stores may not open until 10 or 11, but they remain open until 6 or 7; most carry on brisk business on Saturday and Sunday as well. Suburban shopping malls are generally open seven days a week, with evening hours every day except Sunday. All across New England, so-called convenience stores sell food and sundries until about 11 PM. Along the highways and in major cities you can usually find all-night diners, supermarkets, drugstores, and convenience stores.

CAMERAS & PHOTOGRAPHY

Seascapes and fall foliage are the most commonly photographed subjects in New England. Both can make for memorable images, provided you remember that saltwater and autumn leaves photograph better when there's something else included in the picture. Include a lighthouse or fog-shrouded sailboat in your ocean shots, and look for that covered bridge or church steeple tucked among the birches and maples. The *Kodak Guide to Shooting Great Travel Pictures* (available at bookstores everywhere) is loaded with tips.

➤ PHOTO HELP: **Kodak Information Center** (☎ 800/242–2424).

EQUIPMENT PRECAUTIONS

Don't pack film and equipment in checked luggage, where it is much more susceptible to damage. X-ray machines used to view checked luggage are becoming much more powerful and therefore are much more likely to ruin your film. Always **keep film and tape out of the sun.** Carry an extra supply of batteries, and **be prepared to turn on your camera or camcorder** to prove to security personnel that the device is real. Always **ask for hand inspection of film,** which becomes clouded after repeated exposure to airport X-ray machines, and **keep videotapes away from metal detectors.**

Be careful on sailboat cruises—saltwater can corrode metal camera parts. Remember to **stock up on film at home or in big cities.** Prices are a lot higher in airports, resort areas, and small towns, and the film options are often limited.

CAR RENTAL

Rates in New England begin at around $35 a day and $220 per week for an economy car with air-conditioning, an automatic transmission, and unlimited mileage. This rate does not include taxes and surcharges that can add as much as 25% if you rent a car at the airport.

➤ MAJOR AGENCIES: **Alamo** (☎ 800/ 327–9633; 020/8759–6200 in the U.K.). **Avis** (☎ 800/331–1212; 800/ 879–2847 in Canada; 02/9353–9000 in Australia; 09/525–1982 in New Zealand; 0870/606–0100 in the U.K.). **Budget** (☎ 800/527–0700; 0144/227–6266 in the U.K., through affiliate Europcar). **Dollar** (☎ 800/ 800–4000; 0124/622–0111 in the U.K., where it is known as Sixt Kenning; 02/9223–1444 in Australia). **Hertz** (☎ 800/654–3131; 800/263– 0600 in Canada; 020/8897–2072 in the U.K.; 02/9669–2444 in Australia; 09/256–8690 in New Zealand). **National Car Rental** (☎ 800/227–7368; 0845/722–2525 in the U.K., where it is known as National Europe).

CUTTING COSTS

To get the best deal, **book through a travel agent who will shop around.** Also **price local car-rental companies,** although the service and maintenance may not be as good as those of a major player. Remember to ask about required deposits, cancellation penalties, and drop-off charges if you're planning to pick up the car in one city and leave it in another. If you're traveling during a holiday period, also make sure that a confirmed reservation guarantees you a car.

INSURANCE

When driving a rented car you are generally responsible for any damage to or loss of the vehicle as well as for any property damage or personal injury that you may cause. Before you rent, see what coverage your personal auto-insurance policy and credit cards provide.

For about $15 to $20 per day, rental companies sell protection, known as a collision- or loss-damage waiver (CDW or LDW), that eliminates your liability for damage to the car.

However, **make sure you have enough coverage to pay for the car.** If you do not have auto insurance or an umbrella policy that covers damage to third parties, purchasing liability insurance and a CDW or LDW is highly recommended.

REQUIREMENTS & RESTRICTIONS

In New England you must be 21 to rent a car, and rates may be higher if you're under 25. You'll pay extra for child seats (about $3 a day), which are compulsory for children under five, and for additional drivers (about $2 per day). Non-U.S. residents need a reservation voucher (for prepaid reservations that were made in the traveler's home country), a passport, a driver's license, and a travel policy that covers each driver, when picking up a car.

SURCHARGES

Before you pick up a car in one city and leave it in another, **ask about drop-off charges or one-way service fees,** which can be substantial. Note, too, that some rental agencies charge extra if you return the car before the time specified in your contract. To avoid a hefty refueling fee, **fill the tank just before you turn in the car,** but be aware that gas stations near the rental outlet may overcharge.

CAR TRAVEL

Because public transportation is spotty or completely lacking in the outer reaches of New England, a car is the most convenient means of transportation. The region is well served by the interstate highway system, on which you can expect to average 60 mph, except near major metropolitan areas. On other federal and state highways, your average will more likely be 40–50 mph. In northern New England, east–west travel is notoriously slow, due to several mountain ranges and no limited-access highways.

GASOLINE

Self-service gas stations are the norm in New England, though in some of the less-populated regions you'll find stations with one or two pumps and a friendly attendant who provides full service (pumping your gas, checking your tires and oil, washing your windows). Stations are plentiful. Most stay open late (24 hours along large highways and in big cities), except in rural areas, where Sunday hours are limited and where you may drive long stretches without a refueling opportunity. At press time, rates for unleaded regular gas at self-service stations in New England were about $1.55 per gallon; rates at full-service stations are often slightly more.

ROAD CONDITIONS

Federal and state highways throughout New England are maintained in excellent condition and are promptly plowed and salted in winter. Secondary roads maintained by local municipalities are sometimes in poor repair, especially in spring, when frost heaves—bumps and dips in the pavement—are caused by melting ground frost. Northern New England has many miles of unpaved roads, but these are usually well graded and pleasant to travel, except in mud season in late March and early April. Far northern Maine is crisscrossed by privately owned logging roads, for which a pass is frequently required (pay at gates at entrances to logging company lands).

City traffic can be particularly trying in New England, as many streets were laid out centuries ago.

ROAD MAPS

All three states make available a free map that has directories, mileage, and other useful information—contact the state offices of tourism (☞ Visitor Information). Delorme publishes topographical atlases of Maine, New Hampshire, and Vermont that include most back roads and many outdoor recreation sites. The maps are widely available in the state.

RULES OF THE ROAD

The speed limit in much of New England is 65 mph on interstate and some limited-access highways (55 mph in densely populated areas), and 50 mph on most other roads (25–30 mph in towns and cities). Speed limits are stringently enforced throughout the region, particularly in populated areas. Fines can easily exceed $100 for driving 15–20 miles in excess of the speed limit. In New England, drivers can turn right at a red light (unless signs indicate otherwise) providing they come to a full stop and check to see that the intersection is clear first.

There is zero tolerance for drunk driving. The blood alcohol content that defines legal intoxication for adults varies between .08 and .10 percent, depending on the state, and penalties are severe.

CHILDREN IN NEW ENGLAND

In New England, there's no shortage of things to do with children. Major museums have children's sections, and you'll find children's museums in cities large and small. Many tourist areas have roadside attractions, and miniature golf courses are easy to come by. Attractions such as beaches and boat rides, parks and planetariums, lighthouses and llama treks can be fun for youngsters, as can special events such as crafts fairs and food festivals.

Be sure to plan ahead and **involve your youngsters** as you outline your trip. When packing, include things to keep them busy en route. On sightseeing days try to schedule activities of special interest to your children. If you are renting a car, don't forget to **arrange for a car seat** when you reserve. For general advice about traveling with children, consult *Fodor's FYI: Travel with Your Baby* (available in bookstores everywhere).

FLYING

If your children are two or older, **ask about children's airfares.** As a general rule, infants under two not occupying a seat fly at greatly reduced fares or even for free.

Experts agree that it's a good idea to use safety seats aloft for children weighing less than 40 pounds. Airlines set their own policies: U.S. carriers usually require that the child be ticketed, even if he or she is young enough to ride free, since the seats must be strapped into regular seats. Do **check your airline's policy about using safety seats during takeoff and landing.** And since safety seats are not allowed everywhere in the plane, get your seat assignments early.

When reserving, **request children's meals or a freestanding bassinet** if you need them. But note that bulkhead seats, where you must sit to use the bassinet, may lack an overhead bin or storage space on the floor.

LODGING

Chain hotels and motels welcome children, and New England has many family-oriented resorts with lively children's programs. You'll also find farms that accept guests and can be lots of fun for children. Rental houses and apartments abound, particularly around ski areas; off-season, these can be economical as well as comfortable touring bases. Some country inns, especially those with a quiet, romantic atmosphere and those furnished with antiques, are less enthusiastic about little ones, so **be up front about your traveling companions** when you reserve.

Most hotels allow children under a certain age to stay in their parents' room at no extra charge; others charge them as extra adults; be sure to **find out the cutoff age for children's discounts.**

Most lodgings that welcome infants and small children will be glad to provide a crib or cot, but **be sure to give advance notice** so that one will be available for you. Most resort and hotels with extended amenities will also arrange to have a baby-sitter come to your room. Many family resorts make special accommodations for small children during meals. Be sure to ask in advance.

SIGHTS & ATTRACTIONS

Places that are especially appealing to children are indicated by a rubber-duckie icon (☺) in the margin.

TRANSPORTATION

Each New England state has specific requirements regarding age and weight requirements for children in car seats. If you're renting a car, **be sure to ask about the state(s) you're planning to drive in.** If you will need a car seat, make sure the agency you select provides them and **reserve well in advance.**

CONSUMER PROTECTION

Whenever shopping or buying travel services in New England, **pay with a major credit card,** if possible, so you can cancel payment or get reimbursed if there's a problem. If you're doing business with a particular company for the first time, **contact your local Better Business Bureau and the attorney general's offices** in your state and (for U.S. businesses) the company's home state as well. Have any complaints been filed? Finally, if you're buying a package or tour, always **consider travel insurance** that includes default coverage (☞ Insurance).

➤ BBBs: **Council of Better Business Bureaus** (✉ 4200 Wilson Blvd., Suite 800, Arlington, VA 22203, ☎ 703/276–0100, ℻ 703/525–8277, ⓦ www.bbb.org).

➤ CRUISE LINES: **American Canadian Caribbean Line** (☎ 800/556–7450). **Clipper Cruise Line** (☎ 800/325–0010). **Royal Caribbean International** (☎ 800/327–6700).

CUSTOMS & DUTIES

IN AUSTRALIA

Australian residents who are 18 or older may bring home $A400 worth of souvenirs and gifts (including jewelry), 250 cigarettes or 250 grams of tobacco, and 1,125 ml of alcohol (including wine, beer, and spirits). Residents under 18 may bring back $A200 worth of goods. Prohibited items include meat products. Seeds, plants, and fruits need to be declared upon arrival.

➤ INFORMATION: **Australian Customs Service** (Regional Director, ✉ Box 8, Sydney, NSW 2001, Australia, ☎ 02/9213–2000, ℻ 02/9213–4000, ⓦ www.customs.gov.au).

IN CANADA

Canadian residents who have been out of Canada for at least seven days may bring home C$500 worth of goods duty-free. If you've been away fewer than seven days but more than 48 hours, the duty-free allowance drops to C$200; if your trip lasts 24–48 hours, the allowance is C$50. You may not pool allowances with family members. Goods claimed under the C$500 exemption may follow you by mail; those claimed under the lesser exemptions must accompany you. Alcohol and tobacco products may be included in the seven-day and 48-hour exemptions but not in the 24-hour exemption. If you meet the age requirements of the province or territory through which you reenter Canada, you may bring in, duty-free, 1.14 liters (40 imperial ounces) of wine or liquor *or* 24 12-ounce cans or bottles of beer or ale. If you are 16 or older you may bring in, duty-free, 200 cigarettes and 50 cigars. Check ahead of time with Revenue Canada or the Department of Agriculture for policies regarding meat products, seeds, plants, and fruits.

You may send an unlimited number of gifts worth up to C$60 each duty-free to Canada. Label the package UNSOLICITED GIFT—VALUE UNDER $60. Alcohol and tobacco are excluded.

➤ INFORMATION: **Revenue Canada** (✉ 2265 St. Laurent Blvd. S, Ottawa, Ontario K1G 4K3, Canada, ☎ 613/993–0534; 800/461–9999 in Canada, FAX 613/991–4126, WEB www.ccra-adrc.gc.ca).

IN NEW ZEALAND

Homeward-bound residents 17 or older may bring back $700 worth of souvenirs and gifts. Your duty-free allowance also includes 4.5 liters of wine or beer; one 1,125-ml bottle of spirits; and either 200 cigarettes, 250 grams of tobacco, 50 cigars, or a combination of the three up to 250 grams. Prohibited items include meat products, seeds, plants, and fruits.

➤ INFORMATION: **New Zealand Customs** (Custom House, ✉ 50 Anzac Ave., Box 29, Auckland, New Zealand, ☎ 09/300–5399, FAX 09/359–6730), WEB www.customs.govt.nz.

IN THE U.K.

From countries outside the EU, including the U.S., you may bring home, duty-free, 200 cigarettes or 50 cigars; 1 liter of spirits or 2 liters of fortified or sparkling wine or liqueurs; 2 liters of still table wine; 60 ml of perfume; 250 ml of toilet water; plus £136 worth of other goods, including gifts and souvenirs. If returning from outside the EU,

prohibited items include meat products, seeds, plants, and fruits.

➤ INFORMATION: **HM Customs and Excise** (✉ Dorset House, Stamford St., Bromley, Kent BR1 1XX, U.K., ☎ 020/7202–4227, WEB www.hmce.gov.uk).

DINING

Thoughts of dining in New England center on seafood, and the coast and many inland locations have restaurants specializing in lobster, clams, scallops, and fresh fish. Restaurants in New England's cities have an impressive variety of menus and price ranges. The best dining in rural areas is often to be found in country inns, the larger of which are often quite proud of their chefs and their commitment to using local meats and produce.

Restaurant prices in New England are generally on a par with those elsewhere in the country, but travelers may experience sticker shock at even more modest seafood restaurants. Catch limits on many favorite ocean species, as well as the premium charged for lobster and other shellfish, have sent prices soaring. Lobsters are sold by the pound ("market price" is the phrase that appears on many menus), and a $20 lobster dinner or a $10 lobster roll is not uncommon.

The restaurants we list are the cream of the crop in each price category. Properties indicated by an ✕🏠 are lodging establishments whose restaurant warrants a special trip. Following is the price chart used in this book; note that prices do not include tax, which is 5% in Maine (7% on alcohol), 8% in New Hampshire, and 9% in Vermont (10% on alcohol).

CATEGORY	COST*
$$$$	over $25
$$$	$17–$25
$$	$9–$16
$	under $9

*per person, for a main course dinner

MEALTIMES

In general, the widest variety of mealtime options in New England is in larger cities and at resort areas.

For an early breakfast, pick places that cater to a working clientele. City, town, and roadside establishments specializing in breakfast for the busy often open their doors at 5 or 6 AM. At country inns and B&Bs, breakfast is seldom served before 8; if you need to get an earlier start, ask ahead of time if your host or hostess can accommodate you.

Unless otherwise noted, the restaurants listed in this guide are open daily for lunch and dinner. Lunch in New England generally runs from around 11 to 2:30; dinner is usually served from 6 to 9 (many restaurants have early-bird specials beginning at 5). Only in the larger cities will you find full dinners being offered much later than 9, although you can usually find a bar or bistro serving a limited menu late into the evening in all but the smallest towns.

Many restaurants in New England are closed on Mondays, although this is never true in resort areas in high season. However, resort-town eateries often shut down completely in the off-season.

Credit cards are accepted for meals throughout New England, in all but the most modest establishments.

RESERVATIONS & DRESS

Reservations are always a good idea: we mention them only when they're essential or not accepted. Book as far ahead as you can, and reconfirm as soon as you arrive. We mention dress only when men are required to wear a jacket or a jacket and tie.

SPECIALTIES

Clam favorites include chowder, made with big, meaty quahogs (and featuring milk or cream, unlike the tomato-based Manhattan version); fried clams; and steamers. Some lobster classics include plain boiled lobster—a staple at "in the rough" picnic-bench-and-paper-plate spots along the Maine coast—and lobster rolls, a lobster meat and mayo (or just melted butter) preparation served in a hot dog bun. The leading fin fish is scrod—young cod or haddock—best sampled baked or broiled.

Inland specialties run to the plain and familiar dishes of old-fashioned Sunday-dinner America—pot roast, roast turkey, baked ham, hefty stacks of pancakes (with local maple syrup, of course), and apple pie. One regional favorite is Indian pudding, a long-boiled cornmeal and molasses concoction that's delicious with vanilla ice cream. As for ethnic menus, New England has welcomed Chinese, Thai, Middle Eastern, and all the other international cuisines popular in America. The region's deeper ethnic traditions have produced the pork pie (*tortière*) and pea soup of northern New England's French-Canadians.

WINE, BEER & SPIRITS

In recent years, New England has been in the forefront of the micro-brew revolution. The granddaddy of New England's independent beermakers is Boston's Samuel Adams, producing brews available throughout the region. Following the Sam Adams lead in offering hearty English-style ales and special seasonal brews are breweries such as Vermont's Long Trail and Catamount; Maine's Shipyard; and New Hampshire's Old Man Ale.

New England is beginning to earn some respect as a wine-producing region. Vermont is getting into the act with the new Snow Farm Vineyard in the Lake Champlain Islands and Boyden Valley Winery in Cambridge.

Although a patchwork of state and local regulations affects the hours and locations of places that sell alcoholic beverages, New England licensing laws are fairly liberal. State-owned or -franchised stores sell hard liquor in New Hampshire, Maine, and Vermont; many travelers have found that New Hampshire offers the region's lowest prices. Look for state-run liquor "supermarkets" on interstate highways in the southern part of the state; these also have good wine selections.

DISABILITIES & ACCESSIBILITY

➤ LOCAL RESOURCES: The New Hampshire Office of Travel and Tourism Development (☞ Visitor

Information) *New Hampshire Guide Book* includes accessibility ratings for lodgings and restaurants. **Vermont Chamber of Commerce** (☞ Visitor Information) includes accessibility codes for attractions in the *Vermont Traveler's Guidebook.*

RESERVATIONS

When discussing accessibility with an operator or reservations agent, **ask hard questions.** Are there any stairs, inside *or* out? Are there grab bars next to the toilet *and* in the shower/tub? How wide is the doorway to the room? To the bathroom? For the most extensive facilities meeting the latest legal specifications, **opt for newer accommodations.**

SIGHTS & ATTRACTIONS

In Kennebunkport, as in many of Maine's coastal towns south of Portland, travelers with mobility impairments will have to cope with crowds as well as with narrow, uneven steps and sporadic curb cuts. L.L. Bean's outlet in Freeport is fully accessible, and Acadia National Park has some 50 accessible mi of carriage roads that are closed to motor vehicles. In New Hampshire, many of Franconia Notch's natural attractions are accessible.

TRANSPORTATION

Many major rental agencies provide special cars for people with disabilities on request. Most ask that you provide your own handicapped sticker or plate, which will be honored throughout the region. Be sure to reserve well in advance.

➤ COMPLAINTS: **Aviation Consumer Protection Division** (☞ Air Travel) for airline-related problems. **Civil Rights Office** (✉ U.S. Department of Transportation, Departmental Office of Civil Rights, S-30, 400 7th St. SW, Room 10215, Washington, DC 20590, ☎ 202/366–4648, ℻ 202/366–9371, 🌐 www.dot.gov/ost/docr/index.htm) for problems with surface transportation. **Disability Rights Section** (✉ U.S. Department of Justice, Civil Rights Division, Box 66738, Washington, DC 20035-6738, ☎ 202/514–0301 or 800/514–0301; 202/514–0383 TTY; 800/514–0383 TTY,

℻ 202/307–1198, 🌐 www.usdoj.gov/crt/ada/adahom1.htm) for general complaints.

TRAVEL AGENCIES

In the United States, the Americans with Disabilities Act requires that travel firms serve the needs of all travelers. Some agencies specialize in working with people with disabilities.

➤ TRAVELERS WITH MOBILITY PROBLEMS: **Access Adventures** (✉ 206 Chestnut Ridge Rd., Scottsville, NY 14624, ☎ 716/889–9096, dltravel@prodigy.net), run by a former physical-rehabilitation counselor. **Accessible Vans of America** (✉ 9 Spielman Rd., Fairfield, NJ 07004, ☎ 877/282–8267, ℻ 973/808–9713, 🌐 www.accessiblevans.com). **CareVacations** (✉ 5-5110 50th Ave., Leduc, Alberta T9E 6V4, Canada, ☎ 780/986–6404 or 877/478–7827, ℻ 780/986–8332, 🌐 www.carevacations.com), for group tours and cruise vacations. **Flying Wheels Travel** (✉ 143 W. Bridge St., Box 382, Owatonna, MN 55060, ☎ 507/451–5005 or 800/535–6790, ℻ 507/451–1685, 🌐 www.flyingwheelstravel.com).

➤ TRAVELERS WITH DEVELOPMENTAL DISABILITIES: **Sprout** (✉ 893 Amsterdam Ave., New York, NY 10025, ☎ 212/222–9575 or 888/222–9575, ℻ 212/222–9768, 🌐 www.gosprout.org).

DISCOUNTS & DEALS

Be a smart shopper and **compare all your options** before making decisions. A plane ticket bought with a promotional coupon from travel clubs, coupon books, and direct-mail offers or on the Internet may not be cheaper than the least expensive fare from a discount ticket agency. And always keep in mind that what you get is just as important as what you save.

DISCOUNT RESERVATIONS

To save money, **look into discount reservations services** with toll-free numbers, which use their buying power to get a better price on hotels, airline tickets, even car rentals. When booking a room, always **call the hotel's local toll-free number** (if one is available) rather than the central reservations number—you'll often get a better price. Always ask about special packages or corporate rates.

➤ AIRLINE TICKETS: ☎ 800/FLY–ASAP.

➤ HOTEL ROOMS: **Accommodations Express** (☎ 800/444–7666, WEB www.accommodationsexpress.com). **Central Reservation Service (CRS)** (☎ 800/548–3311). **Players Express Vacations** (☎ 800/458–6161, WEB www.playersexpress.com). **RMC Travel** (☎ 800/245–5738, WEB www.rmcwebtravel.com). **Steigenberger Reservation Service** (☎ 800/223–5652, WEB www.srs-worldhotels.com). **Turbotrip.com** (☎ 800/473–7829, WEB www.turbotrip.com).

PACKAGE DEALS

Don't confuse packages and guided tours. When you buy a package, you travel on your own, just as though you had planned the trip yourself. Fly/drive packages, which combine airfare and car rental, are often a good deal.

GAY & LESBIAN TRAVEL

As one of the country's most socially and politically progressive regions, New England is almost invariably accepting of gay and lesbian travelers. Some exceptions might be found in some areas less frequented by visitors, but in general, people in the tourism business here are hospitable to travelers regardless of sexual orientation.

➤ GAY- & LESBIAN-FRIENDLY TRAVEL AGENCIES: **Different Roads Travel** (✉ 8383 Wilshire Blvd., Suite 902, Beverly Hills, CA 90211, ☎ 323/651–5557 or 800/429–8747, FAX 323/651–3678). **Kennedy Travel** (✉ 314 Jericho Turnpike, Floral Park, NY 11001, ☎ 516/352–4888 or 800/237–7433, FAX 516/354–8849, WEB www.kennedytravel.com). **Now Voyager** (✉ 4406 18th St., San Francisco, CA 94114, ☎ 415/626–1169 or 800/255–6951, FAX 415/626–8626, WEB www.nowvoyager.com). **Skylink Travel and Tour** (✉ 1006 Mendocino Ave., Santa Rosa, CA 95401, ☎ 707/546–9888 or 800/225–5759, FAX 707/546–9891, WEB www.skylinktravel.com).

HEALTH

LYME DISEASE

Lyme disease, so named for its having been first reported in the town of Lyme, Connecticut, is a potentially debilitating disease carried by deer ticks, which thrive in dry, brush-covered areas, particularly on the coast. Always **use insect repellent;** outbreaks of Lyme disease all over the East Coast make it imperative that you protect yourself from ticks from early spring through summer. To prevent bites, **wear light-colored clothing and tuck pant legs into socks.** Look for black ticks about the size of a pin head around hairlines and the warmest parts of the body. If you have been bitten, **consult a physician, especially if you see the telltale bull's-eye bite pattern.** Influenza-like symptoms often accompany a Lyme infection. Early treatment is imperative. Also **ask your physician about Lymerix;** it takes three shots and 12 months to be 80% effective but is worth considering.

PESTS & OTHER HAZARDS

New England's two greatest insect pests are black flies and mosquitoes. The former are a phenomenon of late spring and early summer and are generally a problem only in the densely wooded areas of the far north. Mosquitoes, however, can be a nuisance just about everywhere in summer—they're at their worst following snowy winters and wet springs. The best protection against both pests is repellant containing DEET; if you're camping in the woods during black fly season, you'll also want to **use fine mesh screening in eating and sleeping areas, and even wear mesh headgear.** A particular pest of coastal areas, especially salt marshes, is the greenhead fly. Their bite is nasty, and they are best repelled by a liberal application of Avon Skin So Soft.

SHELLFISHING

Coastal waters attract seafood lovers who enjoy harvesting their own clams, mussels, and even lobsters; permits are required, and casual harvesting of lobsters is strictly forbidden. Amateur clammers should be aware that New England shellfish beds are periodically visited by red tides, during which microorganisms can render shellfish poisonous. To keep abreast of the situation, inquire when you apply for a license (usually at town halls or police stations) and pay attention to red tide postings as you travel.

HOLIDAYS

Expect banks and post offices to be closed on all national holidays, but not much else—except on Thanksgiving, Christmas, New Year's Day, and Easter, when the majority of businesses close. Exceptions are restaurants and hotels, which, depending on location, may be even busier at holiday times. Christmas in ski country, for instance, will require early advance dining and lodging reservations. Public transportation schedules will also be affected on major holidays; in general, schedules will be similar for those of normal Sundays.

Major national holidays include New Year's Day (Jan. 1); Martin Luther King, Jr. Day (3rd Mon. in Jan.); President's Day (3rd Mon. in Feb.); Memorial Day (last Mon. in May); Independence Day (July 4); Labor Day (1st Mon. in Sept.); Thanksgiving Day (4th Thurs. in Nov.); Christmas Day (Dec. 25); and New Year's Eve (Dec. 31).

INSURANCE

The most useful travel-insurance plan is a comprehensive policy that includes coverage for trip cancellation and interruption, default, trip delay, and medical expenses (with a waiver for preexisting conditions).

Without insurance you will lose all or most of your money if you cancel your trip, regardless of the reason. Default insurance covers you if your tour operator, airline, or cruise line goes out of business. Trip-delay covers expenses that arise because of bad weather or mechanical delays. Study the fine print when comparing policies.

Always **buy travel policies directly from the insurance company**; if you buy them from a cruise line, airline, or tour operator that goes out of business you probably will not be covered

for the agency or operator's default, a major risk. Before making any purchase, **review your existing health and home-owner's policies** to find what they cover away from home.

➤ Travel Insurers: In the U.S.: **Access America** (✉ 6600 W. Broad St., Richmond, VA 23230, ☎ 804/285–3300 or 800/284–8300, FAX 804/673–1586), **Travel Guard International** (✉ 1145 Clark St., Stevens Point, WI 54481, ☎ 715/345–0505 or 800/826–1300, FAX 800/955–8785, WEB www.noelgroup.com).

FOR INTERNATIONAL
TRAVELERS

For information on customs restrictions, *see* Customs & Duties, *above*.

CONSULATES & EMBASSIES

➤ Australia: **Consulate** (✉ 150 East 42nd St., 34th Floor New York NY 10017, ☎ 212/351–6500).

➤ Canada: **Consulate** (✉ 3 Copley Pl., Suite 400, Boston, Massachusetts 02216, ☎ 617/262–3760).

➤ United Kingdom: **Consulate** (✉ 600 Atlantic Ave., Boston, MA 02210, ☎ 617/248–9555).

CURRENCY

The dollar is the basic unit of U.S. currency. It has 100 cents. Coins include the copper penny (1¢); the silvery nickel (5¢), dime (10¢), quarter (25¢), and half-dollar (50¢); and the golden $1 coin, replacing a now-rare silver dollar. Bills are denominated $1, $5, $10, $20, $50, and $100, all green and identical in size; designs vary. The exchange rate at press time was US$1.40 per British pound, $.65 per Canadian dollar, $.57 per Australian dollar, and $.47 per New Zealand dollar. The European Union Euro was at $.85 Euro to the dollar.

CAR TRAVEL

Interstate highways—limited-access, multilane highways whose numbers are prefixed by "I—"—are the fastest routes. Interstates with three-digit numbers beginning with an even digit encircle urban areas; those beginning with an odd digit lead into central cities. The region also has other limited-access expressways, freeways, and parkways. Tolls may be levied on limited-access highways. So-called U.S. highways and state highways are not necessarily limited-access but may have several lanes.

Along larger highways, roadside stops with rest rooms, fast-food restaurants, gasoline, and sundries stores are well spaced. State police and tow trucks patrol major highways and lend assistance. If your car breaks down on an interstate, pull onto the shoulder and wait for help, or have your passengers wait while you walk to an emergency phone. If you carry a cell phone, dial *55, noting your location on the small green roadside mileage markers.

Driving in the United States is on the right. **Obey speed limits** posted along roads and highways. Watch for lower limits in small towns and on back roads.

Book stores, gas stations, convenience stores, and rest stops sell maps (about $3) and multiregion road atlases (about $10).

For more information, *see* Car Travel.

ELECTRICITY

The U.S. standard is AC, 110 volts/60 cycles. Plugs have two flat pins set parallel to each other.

EMERGENCIES

For police, fire, or ambulance, **dial 911** (0 in rural areas).

INSURANCE

Britons and Australians need extra medical coverage when traveling overseas.

➤ INSURANCE INFORMATION: In the U.K.: **Association of British Insurers** (✉ 51–55 Gresham St., London EC2V 7HQ, U.K., ☎ 020/7600–3333, FAX 020/7696–8999, WEB www.abi.org.uk). In Australia: **Insurance Council of Australia** (✉ Level 3, 56 Pitt St., Sydney NSW 2000, ☎ 03/9614–1077, FAX 03/9614–7924). In Canada: **RBC Insurance** (✉ 6880 Financial Dr., Mississauga, Ontario L5N 7Y5, Canada, ☎ 905/816–2400 or 800/668–4342 in Canada, FAX 905/816–2498, WEB www.

royalbank.com). In New Zealand: **Insurance Council of New Zealand** (✉ Box 474, Wellington, New Zealand, ☎ 04/472–5230, FAX 04/473–3011, WEB www.icnz.org.nz).

MAIL & SHIPPING

You can buy stamps and aerograms and send letters and parcels in post offices. Stamp-dispensing machines can occasionally be found in airports, bus and train stations, office buildings, drugstores, and the like. You can also deposit mail in the stout, dark blue, steel bins at strategic locations everywhere and in the mail chutes of large buildings; pickup schedules are posted.

For mail sent within the United States, you need a 34¢ stamp for first-class letters weighing up to 1 ounce (23¢ for each additional ounce) and 21¢ for domestic postcards. For overseas mail, you pay 80¢ for 1-ounce airmail letters, 70¢ for airmail postcards, and 35¢ for surface-rate postcards. For Canada and Mexico you need a 60¢ stamp for a 1-ounce letter and 50¢ for a postcard. For 70¢ you can buy an aerogram—a single sheet of lightweight blue paper that folds into its own envelope, stamped for overseas airmail.

To receive mail on the road, have it sent c/o General Delivery at your destination's main post office (use the correct five-digit zip code). You must pick up mail in person within 30 days and show a driver's license or passport.

PASSPORTS & VISAS

When traveling internationally, **carry your passport** even if you don't need one (it's always the best form of I.D.) and **make two photocopies of the data page** (one for someone at home and another for you, carried separately from your passport). If you lose your passport, promptly call the nearest embassy or consulate and the local police.

Visitor visas are not necessary for Canadian citizens, or for citizens of Australia and the United Kingdom who are staying fewer than 90 days.

SMART TRAVEL TIPS A TO Z

➤ AUSTRALIAN CITIZENS: **Australian Passport Office** (☎ 131–232). **U.S. Office of Australia Affairs** (✉ MLC Centre, 19-29 Martin Pl., 59th floor, Sydney NSW 2000, Australia).

➤ CANADIAN CITIZENS: **Passport Office** (☎ 819/994–3500; 800/567–6868 in Canada).

➤ NEW ZEALAND CITIZENS: **New Zealand Passport Office** (☎ 04/494–0700 for application procedures; 0800/225–050 in New Zealand for application-status updates). **U.S. Office of New Zealand Affairs** (✉ 29 Fitzherbert Terr., Thorndon, Wellington, New Zealand).

➤ U.K. CITIZENS: **London Passport Office** (☎ 0870/521–0410) for application procedures and emergency passports. **U.S. Embassy Visa Information Line** (☎ 01891/200–290). **U.S. Embassy Visa Branch** (✉ 5 Upper Grosvenor Sq., London W1A 1AE, U.K.); send a self-addressed, stamped envelope. **U.S. Consulate General** (✉ Queen's House, Queen St., Belfast BTI 6EO, Northern Ireland).

TELEPHONES

All U.S. telephone numbers consist of a three-digit area code and a seven-digit local number. Within most local calling areas, dial only the seven-digit number. Within the same area code, dial "1" first. To call between area-code regions, dial "1" then all 10 digits; the same goes for calls to numbers prefixed by "800," "888," and "877"—all toll-free. For calls to numbers preceded by "900" you must pay—usually dearly.

For international calls, dial "011" followed by the country code and the local number. For help, dial "0" and ask for an overseas operator. The country code is 61 for Australia, 64 for New Zealand, 44 for the United Kingdom. Calling Canada is the same as calling within the United States. Most local phone books list country codes and U.S. area codes. The country code for the United States is 1.

For operator assistance, dial "0". To obtain someone's phone number, call directory assistance, 555–1212

or occasionally 411 (free at public phones). To have the person you're calling foot the bill, phone collect; dial "0" instead of "1" before the 10-digit number.

At pay phones, instructions are usually posted. Usually you insert coins in a slot (10¢–35¢ for local calls) and wait for a steady tone before dialing. When you call long-distance, the operator will tell you how much to insert; prepaid phone cards, widely available in various denominations, are easier. Call the number on the back, punch in the card's personal identification number when prompted, then dial your number.

LODGING

Hotel and motel chains provide standard rooms and amenities in major cities and at or near traditional vacation destinations. At small inns, where each room is different and amenities vary in number and quality, price isn't always a reliable indicator; fortunately, when you call to make reservations, most hosts will be happy to give all manner of details about their properties, down to the color scheme of the handmade quilts—so **ask all your questions before you book.** Also **ask if the property has a Web site**; sites can have helpful information and pictures, although it's always wise to confirm how up-to-date the information is. The rooms in the lodgings reviewed here have private baths unless otherwise indicated.

The lodgings we list are the cream of the crop in each price category. We always list the facilities that are available—but we don't specify whether they cost extra. When pricing accommodations, always ask what's included and what costs extra. Lodgings are indicated in the text by a little house icon, 🏠 ; lodging establishments whose restaurants warrant a special trip, by ✗🏠 . Following is the price chart used in this book; note that prices do not include tax, which is 12% in Connecticut, 5% in Maine, 5% state tax plus up to 7% local tax in some cities in Massachusetts, 8% in New Hampshire, 5% in Rhode Island, and 9% in Vermont.

CATEGORY	COST*
$$$$	over $180
$$$	$130–$180
$$	$80–$130
$	under $80

*All prices are for a standard double room during peak season and do not include tax or gratuities. Some inns add a 15% service charge.

Assume that hotels operate on the **European Plan** (EP, with no meals) unless we specify that they use the **Continental Plan** (CP, with a Continental breakfast), **Breakfast Plan** (BP, with a full breakfast), **Modified American Plan** (MAP, with breakfast and dinner), or the **Full American Plan** (FAP, with all meals).

APARTMENT & VILLA RENTALS

If you want a home base that's roomy enough for a family and comes with cooking facilities, **consider a furnished rental.** These can save you money, especially if you're traveling with a group. Home-exchange directories sometimes list rentals as well as exchanges. In New England, you are most likely to find a house, apartment, or condo rental in areas in which ownership of second homes is common, such as beach resorts and ski country. A good strategy is to **inquire about rentals in what would be the off-season** for those resort areas—for instance, it's fairly easy to rent ski chalets during the summer. Home-exchange directories sometimes list rentals as well as exchanges. Another good bet is to **contact real estate agents in the area in which you are interested.**

➤ INTERNATIONAL AGENTS: **Hideaways International** (⊠ 767 Islington St., Portsmouth, NH 03801, ☎ 603/430–4433 or 800/843–4433, FAX 603/430–4444, WEB www.hideaways.com; membership $129).

B&BS & INNS

The bed-and-breakfasts and small inns of New England offer some of the region's most distinctive lodging experiences. Some are homey and casual, others provide a stay in a historic property in a city or out in the country, and still others are modern and luxurious. At even the posh-est country inns, rooms frequently lack telephones or televisions; many proprietors feel that their guests are actively escaping from the modern world. These properties are also not likely to feature air-conditioning, which is often superfluous in New England's mountains or seashore. Most inns offer breakfast—hence the name bed-and-breakfast—yet this formula varies; at one B&B you may be served muffins and coffee, at another a multicourse feast with fresh flowers on the table. In keeping with the preferences of their guests, most inns and B&Bs prohibit smoking, and some of the inns with antiques or other expensive furnishings do not allow children. Almost all say no to pets. Always be sure to **ask about any restrictions** when you're making a reservation. It's also necessary to **inquire about minimum stays;** many inns require a two-night stay on weekends, for example.

CAMPING

The state offices of tourism (☞ Visitor Information) supply information about privately operated campgrounds and ones in parks run by state agencies and the federal government.

HOME EXCHANGES

If you would like to exchange your home for someone else's, **join a home-exchange organization,** which will send you its updated listings of available exchanges for a year and will include your own listing in at least one of them. It's up to you to make specific arrangements.

➤ EXCHANGE CLUBS: **HomeLink International** (⊠ Box 47747, Tampa, FL 33647, ☎ 813/975–9825 or 800/638–3841, FAX 813/910–8144, WEB www.homelink.org; $98 per year). **Intervac U.S.** (⊠ Box 590504, San Francisco, CA 94159, ☎ 800/756–4663, FAX 415/435–7440, WEB www.intervacus.com; $93 yearly fee includes one catalogue and on-line access).

HOSTELS

No matter what your age, you can **save on lodging costs by staying at hostels.** In some 5,000 locations in more than 70 countries around the

SMART TRAVEL TIPS A TO Z

world, Hostelling International (HI), the umbrella group for a number of national youth-hostel associations, offers single-sex, dorm-style beds and, at many hostels, rooms for couples and family accommodations. Membership in any HI national hostel association, open to travelers of all ages, allows you to stay in HI-affiliated hostels at member rates; one-year membership is about $25 for adults (C$26.75 in Canada, £9.30 in the U.K., $30 in Australia, and $30 in New Zealand); hostels run about $10–$25 per night. Members have priority if the hostel is full; they're also eligible for discounts around the world, even on rail and bus travel in some countries.

➤ ORGANIZATIONS: **Hostelling International—American Youth Hostels** (✉ 733 15th St. NW, Suite 840, Washington, DC 20005, ☎ 202/783–6161, FAX 202/783–6171, WEB www. hiayh.org). **Hostelling International—Canada** (✉ 400–205 Catherine St., Ottawa, Ontario K2P 1C3, Canada, ☎ 613/237–7884, FAX 613/237–7868, WEB www.hostellingintl.ca). **Youth Hostel Association of England and Wales** (✉ Trevelyan House, 8 St. Stephen's Hill, St. Albans, Hertfordshire AL1 2DY, U.K., ☎ 0870/8708808, FAX 01727/844126, WEB www.yha.org. uk). **Australian Youth Hostel Association** (✉ 10 Mallett St., Camperdown, NSW 2050, Australia, ☎ 02/9565–1699, FAX 02/9565–1325, WEB www. yha.com.au). **Youth Hostels Association of New Zealand** (✉ Box 436, Christchurch, New Zealand, ☎ 03/379–9970, FAX 03/365–4476, WEB www. yha.org.nz).

HOTELS

Hotel and motel chains are amply represented in New England. Some of the large chains, such as Holiday Inn, Hilton, Hyatt, Marriott, and Ramada, operate all-suites, budget, business-oriented, or luxury resorts, often variations on the parent corporation's name (Courtyard by Marriott, for example). Though some chain hotels and motels may have a standardized look to them, this "cookie-cutter" approach also means that you can rely on the same level of comfort and efficiency at all proper-

ties in a well-managed chain, and at a chain's premier properties—its so-called flagship hotels—the decor and services may be outstanding.

New England is liberally supplied with small, independent motels, which run the gamut from the tired to the tidy. Don't overlook these mom-and-pop operations; they frequently offer cheerful, convenient accommodations at lower rates than the chains.

While reservations are always a good idea, they are particularly recommended in summer and winter resort areas; in college towns during September and at graduation time in the spring; and at areas renowned for autumn foliage.

Most hotels and motels will hold your reservation until 6 PM; **call ahead if you plan to arrive late.** All will hold a late reservation for you if you guarantee your reservation with a credit-card number.

When you call to make a reservation, **ask all the necessary questions up front.** If you are arriving with a car, ask if there is a parking lot or covered garage and whether there is an extra fee for parking. If you like to eat your meals in, ask if the hotel has a restaurant or whether it has room service (most do, but not necessarily 24 hours a day—and be forewarned that it can be expensive). Most hotels and motels have in-room TVs, often with cable movies, but verify this if you like to watch TV. If you want an in-room crib for your child, there will probably be an additional charge.

All hotels listed have private bath unless otherwise noted.

➤ TOLL-FREE NUMBERS: **Best Western** (☎ 800/528–1234, WEB www. bestwestern.com). **Choice** (☎ 800/221–2222, WEB www.hotelchoice.com). **Clarion** (☎ 800/252–7466, WEB www. hotelchoice.com). **Colony** (☎ 800/777–1700, WEB www.colony.com). **Comfort** (☎ 800/228–5150, WEB www. comfortinn.com). **Days Inn** (☎ 800/325–2525, WEB www.daysinn.com). **Doubletree and Red Lion Hotels** (☎ 800/222–8733, WEB www. doubletree.com). **Embassy Suites** (☎ 800/362–2779, WEB www.

embassysuites.com). **Fairfield Inn**
(☎ 800/228–2800, WEB www.marriott.
com). **Hilton** (☎ 800/445–8667,
WEB www.hilton.com). **Holiday Inn**
(☎ 800/465–4329, WEB www.
basshotels.com). **Howard Johnson**
(☎ 800/654–4656, WEB www.hojo.
com). **Hyatt Hotels & Resorts** (☎ 800/
233–1234, WEB www.hyatt.com). **La
Quinta** (☎ 800/531–5900, WEB www.
laquinta.com). **Marriott** (☎ 800/228–
9290, WEB www.marriott.com). **Quality Inn** (☎ 800/228–5151, WEB www.
qualityinn.com). **Radisson** (☎ 800/
333–3333, WEB www.radisson.com).
Ramada (☎ 800/228–2828, WEB www.
ramada.com). **Sheraton** (☎ 800/325–
3535, WEB www.starwood.com). **Sleep
Inn** (☎ 800/753–3746, WEB www.
sleepinn.com). **Westin Hotels & Resorts** (☎ 800/228–3000, WEB www.
westin.com).

MAIL AND SHIPPING

➤ OVERNIGHT SERVICES: **FedEx** (☎ 800/
463–3339). **UPS** (☎ 800/742–5877).

MEDIA

NEWSPAPERS & MAGAZINES

The New York Times and the national *USA Today* are available in all
but the most remote regions of New
England; of the two, the *Times* is by
far the more thorough and is considered the U.S. newspaper of record.
The *Boston Globe,* a respected morning daily, is also available throughout
the region. Most cities with 10,000 or
more inhabitants generally have their
own daily newspapers, many of which
carry comprehensive listings of local
events at least once a week. Larger
cities and college towns often have at
least one alternative publication that
provides extensive coverage on the local cultural and social scene. Among
regional magazines, the most noteworthy are *Yankee, Vermont Life,*
and *Down East* (Maine).

RADIO & TELEVISION

As in the rest of the U.S., talk shows
are usually found on AM radio stations, while FM stations are devoted
primarily to music. National Public
Radio (NPR), which has FM affiliates
in each New England state, offers a
combination of both, including *Morning Edition* and *All Things Consid-*

ered, the most comprehensive radio
news programs in the U.S.

Although New England's half-dozen
or so major metropolitan areas each
have their own local television stations and public television affiliates,
cable and satellite TV bring dozens of
channels to most hotels and motels.
Cable News Network (CNN) offers
comprehensive national and international news coverage. Boston's public
television affiliate, WGBH, is a flagship station of the U.S. Public Television Network.

MONEY MATTERS

It costs about the same to travel in
New England as it does throughout
the rest of the northeastern United
States. As a rule, this is slightly more
expensive than touring just about
anywhere else in the country, with the
exception of metropolitan California
and major resort areas. In the countryside, or in lesser metropolitan
centers, you'll find consistent good
value, with the exception of times
such as fall foliage season (along the
well-traveled routes of western and
northern New England).

British, Australian, and New Zealand
travelers will find hotel and restaurant
tariffs comparable to those they're
familiar with at home; Canadians,
however, may be in for a bit of sticker
shock due to the prevailing exchange
rate between the two currencies. However, a number of hotel and resort
operators, and places frequented by
Canadian travelers, often offer exchange rates at or close to par as a
promotional come-on.

Unless you're out slumming or delib-
erately going posh, figure on paying
about $1 for a cup of coffee in New
England, $2–$3 for a draft beer, and
$4 for a ham sandwich with a few
pickles and chips. A 1-mi ride in a
Boston taxi will set you back $5,
including tip; admission to a major
museum will average about $10.

Prices throughout this guide are given
for adults. Substantially reduced fees
are almost always available for children, students, and senior citizens.
For information on taxes, *see* Taxes.

ATMS

Automatic teller machines (ATMs) are a useful way to obtain cash. A debit card, also known as a check card, deducts funds directly from your checking account and helps you stay within your budget. When you want to rent a car, though, you may still need an old-fashioned credit card. Although you can always *pay* for your car with a debit card, some agencies will not allow you to *reserve* a car with a debit card.

ATMs are located just about everywhere in New England, from big-city banks to Vermont general stores.

CREDIT CARDS

Using a credit card on the road allows you to delay payment and gives you certain rights as a consumer (☞ Consumer Protection).

Throughout this guide, the following abbreviations are used: **AE,** American Express; **D,** Discover; **DC,** Diner's Club; **MC,** MasterCard; and **V,** Visa.

➤ REPORTING LOST CARDS: To report lost or stolen credit cards, call the following toll-free numbers: **American Express** (☎ 800/327–2177); **Discover Card** (☎ 800/347–2683); **Diner's Club** (☎ 800/234–6377); **MasterCard** (☎ 800/307–7309); and **Visa** (☎ 800/847–2911).

NATIONAL PARKS

National parks and forests offer a broad range of visitor facilities, including campgrounds, picnic grounds, hiking trails, nature walks, boating, and ranger programs. For more information on any of these, contact the state tourism offices or specific national park or forest headquarters.

Look into discount passes to save money on park entrance fees. The National Parks Pass ($50) gets you and your companions free admission to all parks for one year. (Camping and parking are extra.) A percentage of the proceeds from sales of the pass will fund National Parks projects. Both the Golden Age Passport ($10), for those 62 and older, and the Golden Access Passport (free), for travelers with disabilities, entitle holders to free entry to all national parks, plus 50%

off fees for the use of many park facilities and services. You must show proof of age and of U.S. citizenship or permanent residency (such as a U.S. passport, driver's license, or birth certificate) and, if requesting Golden Access, proof of disability. The Golden Age and Golden Access passes are available at all national parks wherever entrance fees are charged. The National Parks Pass is available by mail or through the Internet.

➤ PASSES BY MAIL: **National Park Service** (✉ National Park Service/Department of Interior, 1849 C St. NW, Washington, DC 20240, ☎ 202/208–4747, WEB www.nps.gov). **National Parks Pass** (✉ 27540 Ave. Mentry, Valencia, CA 91355, ☎ 888/GO–PARKS, WEB www.nationalparks.org).

OUTDOORS & SPORTS

State information offices (☞ Visitor Information,) have further information about New England's sporting opportunities. For information about skiing, *see* Portrait of New England in Chapter 5.

BEACHES

Long, wide beaches edge the New England coast from southern Maine to southern Connecticut; the most popular in northern New England are on Maine's York County coast and the coastal region of New Hampshire. Many are maintained by state and local governments and have lifeguards on duty; they may have picnic facilities, rest rooms, changing facilities, and concession stands. Depending on the locale, you may need a parking sticker to use the lot. The waters are at their warmest in August, though they're cold even at the height of summer along much of the Maine coast. Inland, there are small lake beaches, most notably in New Hampshire and Vermont.

BIKING

Cycling is popular in the New Hampshire Lakes Region and Vermont's Green Mountains and Champlain Valley. Biking in Maine is especially scenic in and around Kennebunkport, Camden, Deer Isle, and the Schoodic Peninsula. The carriage paths in Acadia National Park are ideal. Many ski resorts allow mountain bikes during the summer months.

➤ BIKING: **Vermont Bicycle Touring** (Box 711, Bristol, VT 05443, ☎ 802/453–4811 or 800/245–3868) operates tours throughout the region.

BOATING

Along many of New England's larger lakes, sailboats, rowboats, canoes, and outboards can be rented at local marinas. Sailboats are available for rent at a number of seacoast locations; you may be required to demonstrate competence. Lessons are also frequently available. Maine's Penobscot Bay draws boaters, including windjammers. Lakes in New Hampshire and Vermont are splendid for all kinds of boating. Maine's Allagash Wilderness Waterway is one of the region's premier places to canoe.

FISHING

Anglers will find sport aplenty throughout the region—surf-casting along the shore; deep-sea fishing in the Atlantic on party and charter boats; fishing for trout in streams; and angling for bass, landlocked salmon, and other fish in freshwater lakes. Maine's Moosehead and Rangeley Lakes regions are draws for serious anglers, as are Vermont's Lakes Champlain and Memphremagog and the Connecticut Lakes of far northern New Hampshire. Sporting-goods stores and bait-and-tackle shops are reliable sources for licenses—necessary in fresh waters—and for leads to the nearest hot spots.

GOLF

The region has an ample supply of public and semi-private courses, many of which are attached to distinctive resorts or even ski areas. One dilemma facing golfers is keeping their eyes on the ball instead of the scenery: in Manchester, Vermont, the Gleneagles Course at the Equinox Hotel is ringed by mountain splendor, as are the links at the Balsams Grand Resort in Dixville Notch, New Hampshire, and the nearby course at the splendid old Mount Washington Hotel in Bretton Woods. During prime season, make sure you reserve ahead for tee times, particularly near urban areas and at resorts.

HIKING

Probably the most famous trails are the 255-mi Long Trail, which runs north–south through the center of Vermont, and the Maine-to-Georgia Appalachian Trail, which runs through New England on both private and public land. The Appalachian Mountain Club (AMC) maintains a system of staffed huts in New Hampshire's Presidential Range, with bunk space and meals available by reservation. You'll find good hiking in many state parks throughout the region.

➤ HIKING: **Audubon Society of New Hampshire** (3 Silk Farm Rd., Concord, NH 03301, ☎ 603/224–9909). **Appalachian Mountain Club** (Box 298, Gorham, NH 03581, ☎ 603/466–2725). **Green Mountain Club** (Box 650, Rte. 100, Waterbury, VT 05677, ☎ 802/244–7037). **White Mountain National Forest** (719 North Main St., Laconia, NH 03246, ☎ 603/528–8721).

PACKING

The principal rule on weather in New England is that there are no rules. A cold, foggy morning in spring can and often does become a bright, 60° afternoon. A summer breeze can suddenly turn chilly, and rain often appears with little warning. Thus, the best advice on how to dress is to **layer your clothing** so that you can peel off or add garments as needed for comfort. Showers are frequent, so **pack a raincoat and umbrella.** Even in summer you should bring long pants, a sweater or two, and a waterproof windbreaker, for evenings are often chilly and sea spray can make things cool.

Casual sportswear—walking shoes and jeans or khakis—will take you almost everywhere, but swimsuits and bare feet will not: shirts and shoes are required attire at even the most casual venues. Dress in restaurants is generally casual, except at some of the distinguished restaurants Maine coast towns such as Kennebunkport and a number of inns in the Berkshires. Upscale resorts will, at the very least, re-

SMART TRAVEL TIPS A TO Z

quire men to wear collared shirts at dinner, and jeans are often frowned upon.

In summer, **bring a hat and sunscreen.** Remember also to **pack insect repellent**; to prevent Lyme disease you'll need to guard against ticks from early spring through the summer (☞ Health).

In your carry-on luggage, **pack an extra pair of eyeglasses or contact lenses and enough of any medication** you take to last the entire trip. You may also ask your doctor to write a spare prescription using the drug's generic name, since brand names may vary from country to country. In luggage to be checked, **never pack prescription drugs or valuables.** To avoid customs delays, carry medications in their original packaging. And don't forget to carry with you the addresses of offices that handle refunds of lost traveler's checks. Check *Fodor's How to Pack* (available in bookstores everywhere) for more tips.

CHECKING LUGGAGE

How many carry-on bags you can bring with you is up to the airline. Most allow two, but not always, so make sure that everything you carry aboard will fit under your seat or in the overhead bin, and get to the gate early. Note that if you have a seat at the back of the plane, you'll probably board first, while the overhead bins are still empty.

If you are flying internationally, note that baggage allowances may be determined not by piece but by weight— generally 88 pounds (40 kilograms) in first class, 66 pounds (30 kilograms) in business class, and 44 pounds (20 kilograms) in economy.

Airline liability for baggage is limited to $1,250 per person on flights within the United States. On international flights it amounts to $9.07 per pound or $20 per kilogram for checked baggage (roughly $640 per 70-pound bag) and $400 per passenger for unchecked baggage. You can buy additional coverage at check-in for about $10 per $1,000 of coverage, but it excludes a rather extensive list of items, shown on your airline ticket.

Before departure, **itemize your bags' contents** and their worth, and label the bags with your name, address, and phone number. (If you use your home address, cover it so potential thieves can't see it readily.) Inside each bag, **pack a copy of your itinerary.** At check-in, **make sure that each bag is correctly tagged** with the destination airport's three-letter code. If your bags arrive damaged or fail to arrive at all, file a written report with the airline before leaving the airport.

PASSPORTS & VISAS

For information on passports for non-U.S. citizens, *see* For International Travelers.

PASSPORT OFFICES

The best time to apply for a passport or to renew is in fall and winter. Before any trip, check your passport's expiration date, and, if necessary, renew it as soon as possible.

➤ U.S. CITIZENS: **National Passport Information Center** (☎ 900/225–5674 or 888/362-8668, WEB www. travel.state.gov/passport services; calls to the 900 number are 35¢ per minute for automated service, $1.05 per minute for operator service); calls to the 888 number, for Visa, MC, or AE card holders, are billed at a flat rate of $4.95.

SAFETY

Rural New England is one of the country's safest regions, so much so that residents often leave their doors unlocked. In the cities, observe the usual precautions. It's worth noting, however, that crime rates have been dropping in metropolitan areas. You should avoid out-of-the-way or poorly lit areas at night; clutch handbags close to your body and don't let them out of your sight; and be on your guard in subways, not only during the deserted wee hours but in crowded rush hours, when pickpockets are at work. Keep your valuables in hotel safes. Try to use ATMs in busy, well-lighted places such as bank lobbies.

If your vehicle breaks down in a rural area, **pull as far off the road as possible,** tie a handkerchief to your radio antenna (or use flares at night—check if your rental agency can provide them), and stay in your car with the doors locked until help arrives. Don't pick up hitchhikers. If you're planning to leave a car overnight to make use of off-road trails or camping facilities, **make arrangements for a supervised parking area** if at all possible. Cars left at trailhead parking lots are subject to theft and vandalism.

The universal telephone number for crime and other emergencies throughout New England is 911.

SENIOR-CITIZEN TRAVEL

To qualify for age-related discounts, **mention your senior-citizen status up front** when booking hotel reservations (not when checking out) and before you're seated in restaurants (not when paying the bill). When renting a car, ask about promotional car-rental discounts, which can be cheaper than senior-citizen rates.

➤ EDUCATIONAL PROGRAMS: **Elderhostel** (✉ 11 Ave. de Lafayette, Boston, MA 02111-1746, ☎ 877/426–8056, 𝔽𝔸𝕏 877/426–2166, 𝖶𝖤𝖡 www.elderhostel.org). **Interhostel** (✉ University of New Hampshire, 6 Garrison Ave., Durham, NH 03824, ☎ 603/862–1147 or 800/733–9753, 𝔽𝔸𝕏 603/862–1113, 𝖶𝖤𝖡 www.learn.unh.edu).

SHOPPING

Antiques, crafts, maple syrup and sugar, fresh produce, and clothing and housewares lure shoppers to New England's factory outlet stores, flea markets, shopping malls, bazaars, yard sales, country stores, and farmers' markets.

KEY DESTINATIONS

Particularly in the Monadnock region of New Hampshire, dealers abound in barns and home stores strung along back roads—along Route 119, from Fitzwilliam to Hinsdale; Route 101, from Marlborough to Wilton; and in the towns of Hopkinton, Hollis, and Amherst. In southern New Hampshire, the stretch of U.S. 4 between Durham and Concord is another mecca. In Vermont, antiques shops and barns are scattered just about everywhere

but are especially concentrated along the southern portions of U.S. 7 and along Route 30, particularly in and around Newfane. In Maine, antiques shops are clustered in Wiscasset and Searsport and along U.S. 1 between Kittery and Scarborough.

In Vermont, galleries in Burlington, Middlebury, and Windsor sell work by some of the best of the state's craftspeople, although artisans have set up shop throughout the state. The League of New Hampshire Craftsmen operates seven fine shops, including locations in Concord, Exeter, and North Conway. On Maine's Deer Isle, Haystack Mountain School of Crafts attracts internationally renowned craftspeople to its summer institute. The Schoodic Peninsula is home to many skilled artisans. Passamaquoddy baskets can be found in Eastport.

For outlet stores, in Maine, shop along the coast in Kittery, Freeport, and Ellsworth; in New Hampshire, North Conway; and in Vermont, Manchester.

Opportunities abound for obtaining fresh farm produce from the source; some farms allow you to pick your own strawberries, raspberries, blueberries, and apples. October in Maine is prime time for pumpkins and potatoes. There are maple-syrup producers who demonstrate the process to visitors, most notably in Vermont. Maple syrup is available in different grades; while Grade AA, "fancy," is the lightest in color and the most refined, many Vermonters prefer grade B, which has a deeper flavor and is often used in cooking. Grade A, medium amber in color, has a light caramel flavor and is often used with pancakes and hot cereals.

SMART SOUVENIRS

Some distinctive items are Blue Hill pottery, sturdy, brightly colored tableware made in Blue Hill, Maine, and available at several shops in the area; Bennington Pottery, attractive, utilitarian items made in the Vermont town (Bennington Potters North in Burlington sells inexpensive seconds); moccasins of moose and deer hide made by Maine Native Americans and sold throughout the state; and whimsical animal prints by Woody Jackson (cows) and Stephen Huneck (dogs), available at several Vermont galleries.

WATCH OUT

When you're looking for pure maple syrup, a sugarhouse can be the most or the least expensive place to shop, depending on how tourist-oriented it is. Wherever you buy, remember that the smallest containers are the most expensive; you're much better off buying a gallon and freezing what you don't use right away. Small grocery stores are often a good source of less-expensive syrup. **Look for the word "pure" and the state designation;** much artificially flavored sugarcane syrup is sold as "maple."

With any crafts item, always **be aware that some vendors substitute mass-produced imports** for the real thing; if the price seems too good to be true, it probably is.

As the U.S. is signatory to treaties involving trade and products made from endangered animal species, you won't need to worry about purchasing souvenirs that you won't be able to bring into your home country. Visitors to New Hampshire should be aware that one item for sale in this state—fireworks, found at many roadside stands—is strictly forbidden as airline baggage and cannot be imported into most countries.

STUDENTS IN NEW ENGLAND

Most major attractions throughout New England offer discount admissions to students.

➤ I.D.s & SERVICES: **Council Travel** (CIEE; ✉ 205 E. 42nd St., 15th floor, New York, NY 10017, ☎ 212/822–2700 or 888/268–6245, FAX 212/822–2699, WEB www.councilexchanges.org) for mail orders only, in the U.S. **Travel Cuts** (✉ 187 College St., Toronto, Ontario M5T 1P7, Canada, ☎ 416/979–2406 or 800/667–2887 in Canada, FAX 416/979–8167, WEB www.travelcuts.com).

TAXES

See Dining *and* Lodging for information about taxes on restaurant meals and accommodations.

SALES TAX

Sales taxes are as follows: Maine 5%; Vermont 5% (with an exemption on purchase of one clothing item of up to $110). No sales tax is charged in New Hampshire. Some states and municipalities levy an additional tax (from 1% to 10%) on lodging or restaurant meals. Alcoholic beverages are sometimes taxed at a higher rate than that applied to meals.

TIME

New England is in the Eastern time zone.

TIPPING

At restaurants, a 15% tip is standard for waiters; up to 20% is expected at more expensive establishments. The same goes for taxi drivers, bartenders, and hairdressers. Coat-check operators usually expect $1; bellhops and porters should get $1 per bag; hotel maids should get about $1.50 per day of your stay. Hotel concierges should be tipped if you utilize their services; the amount varies widely depending on the nature of service. On package tours, conductors and drivers usually get $10 per day from the group as a whole; check whether this has already been figured into your cost. For local sightseeing tours, you may individually tip the driver-guide $1–$5, depending on the length of the tour and the number of people in your party, if he or she has been helpful or informative.

TOURS & PACKAGES

Because everything is prearranged on a prepackaged tour or independent vacation, you spend less time planning—and often get it all at a good price.

BOOKING WITH AN AGENT

Travel agents are excellent resources. But it's a good idea to collect brochures from several agencies as some agents' suggestions may be influenced by relationships with tour and package firms that reward them for volume sales. If you have a special interest, **find an agent with expertise in that area**; the American Society of Travel Agents (ASTA) (☞ Travel Agencies) has a database of specialists worldwide.

Make sure your travel agent knows the accommodations and other services of the place they're recommending. Ask about the hotel's location, room size, beds, and whether it has a pool, room service, or programs for children, if you care about these. Has your agent been there in person or sent others whom you can contact?

Do some homework on your own, too: local tourism boards can provide information about lesser-known and small-niche operators, some of which may sell only direct.

BUYER BEWARE

Each year consumers are stranded or lose their money when tour operators—even large ones with excellent reputations—go out of business. So **check out the operator.** Ask several travel agents about its reputation, and try to **book with a company that has a consumer-protection program.** (Look for information in the company's brochure.) In the United States, members of the National Tour Association and the United States Tour Operators Association are required to set aside funds to cover your payments and travel arrangements in the event that the company defaults. It's also a good idea to choose a company that participates in the American Society of Travel Agents' Tour Operator Program (TOP); ASTA will act as mediator in any disputes between you and your tour operator.

Remember that the more your package or tour includes the better you can predict the ultimate cost of your vacation. Make sure you know exactly what is covered, and **beware of hidden costs.** Are taxes, tips, and transfers included? Entertainment and excursions? These can add up.

➤ TOUR-OPERATOR RECOMMENDATIONS: **American Society of Travel Agents** (☞ Travel Agencies). **National Tour Association** (NTA; ✉ 546 E. Main St., Lexington, KY 40508, ☎ 859/226–4444 or 800/682–8886, WEB www.ntaonline.com). **United States Tour Operators Association** (USTOA; ✉ 342 Madison Ave., Suite 1522, New York, NY 10173, ☎ 212/599–6599 or 800/468–7862, FAX 212/599–6744, WEB www.ustoa.com).

TRAIN TRAVEL

Amtrak offers frequent daily service along its Northeast Corridor route from Washington and New York to Boston. Amtrak's new high-speed *Acela* trains now link Boston and Washington, with a stop at Penn Station in New York.

Other Amtrak services include the *Vermonter* between Washington, D.C., and St. Albans, Vermont; and the *Ethan Allen* between New York and Rutland, Vermont; and the *Lake Shore Limited* between Boston and Chicago, with stops at Worcester and Springfield, Massachusetts. These trains run on a daily basis. Amtrak sells passes good for travel within specific regions for a set period of time and also has a schedule of reduced children's fares. Overnight accommodations exist on only one New England train, the *Lake Shore Limited*. Reservations are required for certain trains and for all overnight accommodations.

Private rail lines have scenic train trips throughout New England, particularly during fall foliage season. Several use vintage steam equipment; the most notable is the Cog Railway to Mt. Washington in New Hampshire.

➤ TRAIN INFORMATION: **Amtrak** (☎ 800/872–7245, WEB www.amtrak.com).

TRANSPORTATION AROUND NEW ENGLAND

If you plan to travel around a sizable portion of New England, a car or car rental will be a *must*. Frequent rail connections between major cities exist only within Amtrak's Northeast Corridor, and regional travel by air is expensive. Buses connect major cities and towns, but schedules are often inconvenient and routes are generally not the most scenic. Since one of New England's primary attractions is its picturesque countryside and innumerable small villages, only the automobile traveler (or bicyclist) can really appreciate all the region has to offer.

TRAVEL AGENCIES

A good travel agent puts your needs first. Look for an agency that has been in business at least five years, emphasizes customer service, and has someone on staff who specializes in your destination. In addition, **make sure the agency belongs to a professional trade organization.** The American Society of Travel Agents (ASTA), with more than 26,000 members in some 170 countries, is the largest and most influential in the field. Operating under the motto "Without a travel agent, you're on your own," it maintains and enforces a strict code of ethics and will step in to help mediate any agent-client disputes if necessary. ASTA also maintains a Web site that includes a directory of agents. (If a travel agency is also acting as your tour operator, *see* Buyer Beware *in* Tours & Packages.)

➤ LOCAL AGENT REFERRALS: American Society of Travel Agents (ASTA; ☎ 800/965–2782 24-hr hot line, FAX 703/739–7642, WEB www.astanet. com). Association of British Travel Agents (✉ 68–71 Newman St., London W1T 3AH, U.K., ☎ 020/7637–2444, FAX 020/7637–0713, WEB www. abtanet.com). Association of Canadian Travel Agents (✉ 130 Albert St., Ste. 1705, Ottawa, Ontario K1P 5G4, Canada, ☎ 613/237–3657, FAX 613/237–7502, WEB www.acta.net). Australian Federation of Travel Agents (✉ Level 3, 309 Pitt St., Sydney NSW 2000, Australia, ☎ 02/9264–3299, FAX 02/9264–1085, WEB www.afta. com.au). Travel Agents' Association of New Zealand (✉ Box 1888, Wellington 10033, New Zealand, ☎ 04/499–0104, FAX 04/499–0827, WEB www. taanz.org.nz).

VISITOR INFORMATION

Each New England state offers a helpful free information kit, including a guidebook, map, and listings of attractions and events. All include listings and/or advertisements for lodging and dining establishments. Each state also has an official Web site with material on sights and lodgings; most of these sites have a calen-

dar of events and other special features.

➤ TOURIST INFORMATION: **Maine Tourism Association** (✉ 325B Water St., Box 2300, Hallowell, ME 04347, ☎ 207/623–0363 or 888/624–6345, WEB www.visitmaine.com). **New Hampshire Office of Travel and Tourism Development** (✉ Box 1856, Concord, NH 03302, ☎ 603/271–2343; 800/258–3608 seasonal events; 800/386–4664 brochures, WEB www. visitnh.gov). **Vermont Department of Tourism and Marketing** (✉ 134 State St., Montpelier, VT 05602, ☎ 802/828–3237; 800/837–6668 brochures). **Vermont Chamber of Commerce, Department of Travel and Tourism** (✉ Box 37, Montpelier, VT 05601, ☎ 802/223–3443, WEB www.1-800-vermont.com).

➤ IN THE U.K.: **Discover New England** (✉ Admail 4 International, Greatness La., Sevenoaks TN14 5BQ, ☎ 01732/742777).

WEB SITES

Do check out the World Wide Web when planning your trip. You'll find everything from weather forecasts to virtual tours of famous cities. Be sure to **visit Fodors.com** (www.fodors.com), a complete travel-planning site. You can research prices and book plane tickets, hotel rooms, rental cars, vacation packages, and more. In addition, you can post your pressing questions in the Travel Talk section and, in the site's Rants & Raves section, read comments about some of the restaurants and hotels in this book—and chime in yourself. Other planning tools include a currency converter and weather reports, and there are loads of links to travel resources.

MAINE

The site of Ski Maine (www.skimaine. com) has information about alpine snow sports. Maine's Nordic Ski Council provides cross-country info at www.mnsc.com.

NEW HAMPSHIRE

For information on downhill and cross-country skiing, www.skinh.com is the site of Ski New Hampshire.

VERMONT

The Vermont Ski Areas Association covers the downhill scene at www.skivermont.com. Up-to-date foliage reports are given at www.1-800-vermont.com.

GENERAL INTEREST

Visit New England (www.visitnewengland.com) covers the entire region. The Great Outdoor Recreation Page (www.gorp.com) is arranged into three easily navigated categories: attractions, activities, and locations; within most of the "locations" are links to the state parks office. The National Park Service site (www.nps.gov) lists all the national parks and has extensive historical, cultural, and environmental information.

WHEN TO GO

Maine, Vermont, and New Hampshire are largely year-round destinations. But you might want to **stay away from rural areas during mud season in April and black-fly season from mid-May to mid-June.** Many smaller museums and attractions are open only from Memorial Day to mid-October, at other times by appointment only.

Memorial Day is the start of the migration to the beaches and the mountains, and summer begins in earnest on July 4. Those who are driving to the Maine coast in July or August should know that Friday and Sunday are the days weekenders clog the coast and its feeder roads, I–95 and U.S. 1.

Fall is the most colorful season in New England, a time when many inns and hotels are booked months in advance by foliage-viewing visitors. New England's dense hardwood forests explode in color as the diminishing hours of autumn daylight signal trees to stop producing chlorophyll. As green is stripped away from the leaves of maples, oaks, birches, beeches, and other deciduous species, a rainbow of reds, oranges, yellows, purples, and other vivid hues is revealed. The first scarlet and gold colors emerge in mid-September in northern areas; "peak" color occurs at different times from year to year.

Generally, it's best to **visit the northern reaches in late September and early October** and move southward as October progresses.

All leaves are off the trees by Halloween, and hotel rates fall as the leaves do, dropping significantly until ski season begins. November and early December are hunting season in much of New England; those who venture into the woods should wear bright orange clothing.

Winter is the time for downhill and cross-country skiing. New England's major ski resorts are well equipped with snowmaking equipment if nature falls short. Along the coast, bed-and-breakfasts that remain open will often rent rooms at far lower prices than in summer.

In spring, despite mud season, maple sugaring goes on in Maine, New Hampshire, and Vermont, and the fragrant scent of lilacs is never far away.

CLIMATE

In winter, coastal New England is cold and damp; inland temperatures may be lower, but generally drier conditions make them easier to bear. Snowfall is heaviest in the interior mountains and can range up to several hundred inches per year in northern Maine, New Hampshire, and Vermont. Spring is often windy and rainy; in many years it appears as if winter segues almost immediately into summer. Coastal areas can be quite humid in summer, making even moderate temperatures uncomfortable. One of the delights of inland northern New England, particularly at higher elevations, is the prevalence of cool summer nights. Autumn temperatures can be quite mild in more southerly areas well into October, although northern portions of the region can be quite cold by Columbus Day. In some years, a period of unseasonably mild weather occurs in late October and early November.

➤ FORECASTS: **Weather Channel Connection** (☎ 900/932–8437), 95¢ per minute from a Touch-Tone phone.

SMART TRAVEL TIPS A TO Z

BURLINGTON, VT

Jan.	29F	– 2C	May	67F	19C	Sept.	74F	23C
	11	–12		45	7		50	10
Feb.	31F	– 1C	June	77F	25C	Oct.	59F	15C
	11	–12		56	13		40	4
Mar.	40F	4C	July	83F	28C	Nov.	45F	7C
	22	6		59	15		31	– 1
Apr.	54F	12C	Aug.	79F	26C	Dec.	31F	– 1C
	34	1		58	14		16	– 9

PORTLAND, ME

Jan.	31F	– 1C	May	61F	16C	Sept.	68F	20C
	16	– 9		47	8		52	11
Feb.	32F	0C	June	72F	22C	Oct.	58F	14C
	16	– 9		54	15		43	6
Mar.	40F	4C	July	76F	24C	Nov.	45F	7C
	27	– 3		61	16		32	0
Apr.	50F	10C	Aug.	74F	23C	Dec.	34F	1C
	36	2		59	15		22	– 6

1 DESTINATION: MAINE, VERMONT, NEW HAMPSHIRE

DEEP ROOTS IN STONY SOIL

BACK IN THE 1940S photographer Paul Strand took two pictures that capture the essence of northern New England. One photograph, "Susan Thompson, Cape Split Maine," shows a late-middle-aged woman standing perfectly still at the entrance to her barn. She stands, as if pausing in her work, with her worn hands resting at her sides and her wistful, rather tired eyes just averted from the camera. Susan Thompson has the composure of a person who has lived long and hard in a single place.

The second picture, "Side Porch, New England," is a stark, almost abstract composition. Broad, rough-sawn, white boards frame the porch. A ladder-back chair with a cane seat (unoccupied) stands on the cracked, weathered boards of the porch floor. A broom and a wire rug-beater hang from nails on the wall. The scene is one of poverty, but not of neglect. The broom has obviously swept the porch clean that very morning, and, though the house has not been painted in years, one imagines that the rugs inside receive regular and thorough beatings.

Susan Thompson is gone, and so, most likely, is the old farmhouse with the clean-swept side porch. But even today, you don't have to travel far off the interstates that knife through Maine, Vermont, and New Hampshire before you run across people and houses and landscapes that are hauntingly similar to those Paul Strand photographed 50 years ago. The serenity, the austere beauty, the reverence for humble objects, the unassuming pride in place, the deep connection between man and landscape—all of these remain very much alive in northern New England.

In northern New England, the people and the land (and in Maine, the sea) seem bound by a marriage that has withstood many hardships. The relationship derives its character in part from the harsh climate. Spring witholds its flowers until mid-May, winter blows through in November, and a summer sunny spell is interrupted by rainstorms before it's had time to settle in properly. (There's a saying that there are two seasons in the north country—winter and July.)

There is a heritage here of self-reliance: the hardship of scratching out a living in small farms; the loneliness of sailing onto the cold northern waters to fish. In some places, isolation and hardship breed suspicion and meanness of spirit; in northern New England, they have engendered patience, endurance, a shrewd sardonic humor, and bottomless loyalty.

People sink deep roots in the thin, stony soil. They forgive the climate its cruelty. The north has a way of taking hold of the body and the spirit, as if weaving a kind of spell. It's not just the residents who are susceptible; summer visitors who have endured years of humid, overcast Julys and fog-shrouded Augusts keep coming back.

Distinct as they are in landscape, geology, and feeling, Maine, Vermont, and New Hampshire are linked by their northerness. There is something pure and fine and mystical about the North, just as there is something lush and soft and voluptuous about the South. You can feel the spirit of the North in the very light. The sun seems to burn more sharply and cleanly in the north country: It scours the rocks on the Maine coast, fills Vermont valleys with powdered gold in September, and turns the new snow of January into sapphires and diamonds.

Even more evocative than the light are the sounds of the North: the mournful, five-note whistle of the white-throated sparrow piercing the stillness of a June morning; the slap of lake water against a sandy shore; or the more insistent murmur of the sea reaching into a cove.

The explosions of warfare have not sounded in northern New England since the War of 1812, but throughout the 19th century the explosions of the industrial revolution ripped through the rural quiet in parts of these three states, particularly in southern New Hampshire. But eventually the noise of this revolution subsided. For the first half of the 20th century, the history of northern New England was primarily a history of decline. Mills and quarries were closed. Farms were abandoned. Fishing villages dwindled to a handful of old folks. Fields were overgrown by maple and spruce.

It was only when Americans began to have the time, money, and inclination to travel that the region had a resurgence. Motor courts popped up along Maine's coastal Route 1 during the 1950s. Ski chalets peeked above the pines in Vermont and New Hampshire. Artists, teachers, and urban professionals snatched up the old farmhouses, and hippies set up communes in southern Vermont.

In the 1970s and '80s gentrification began to alter the towns and villages of the North. Second homes and condominiums went up in record numbers on the shores of Lake Winnepesaukee, alongside Maine's Casco and Linekin bays, and throughout the green countryside of southern Vermont.

Gentrification looks lovely compared with some of the other changes that have overtaken northern New England in the past couple of decades. Strip development has swallowed long stretches of Vermont's Route 4, especially around Rutland; and a good deal of southern New Hampshire has a distinctly suburban cast. Factory-outlet fever has reached epidemic proportions in Maine and New Hampshire. It used to be that tourists came to northern New England to buy a jug of maple syrup or a little pillow stuffed with balsam needles—now it's a pair of Bass shoes or Calvin Klein jeans.

Equally distressing are the crowds that have brought urban headaches into the heart of the northern wilderness. An endless caravan of leaf peepers crawls along the Kancamagus Highway in late September. The lift lines at Mt. Snow or Killington can be long enough to make you want to trade skiing for shopping at Manchester's boutiques and outlets. I have found few vacation experiences more depressing than slogging up the long, increasingly steep trail of Vermont's Camel's Hump mountain only to find the summit mobbed with fellow hikers. "Do we seat ourselves, or should we wait for the maitre d'?" one hiker remarked as he surveyed the scores of picnickers who had beat him to the top.

But even in the midst of the changes and crowding of the present, the eternal images, tastes, and experiences of the North endure. The steam of boiling maple sap still rises from sugarhouses all over the Green and White mountains every March. In May, lilacs bloom in fragrant, extravagant mounds beside seemingly every old farmhouse in the North. Loons flapping through the dawn mist rising off a lake, a scarlet-maple branch blazing beside a white church, sows grazing on a lush, green hillside—these images have become cliches, but they are nonetheless stirring and satisfying.

Whenever I feel the first chill of autumn in the air, whenever I see a flock of geese winging north, whenever I come upon a stand of spruce and white pine rising at the end of a freshly mown hay field, I feel the tug of northern New England. The drive north from my home outside New York City is long and dull, and, on the way up, there always comes a moment of doubt: Will it be worth the time and money? Will it have changed? Will it rain or fog the entire time?

Then I see the first ramshackle house with a side porch, the first rough pasture strewn with stones and humps of grass, the first kind wistful face, and I know it will be all right.

— David Laskin

David Laskin has written for the New York Times *and* Travel and Leisure.

WHAT'S WHERE

Maine

Maine is by far the largest state in New England. At its extremes it measures 300 mi by 200 mi; all other New England states could fit within its perimeters. Because of overdevelopment, Maine's southernmost coastal towns won't give you the rugged, "down-east" experience, but the Kennebunks will: classic townscapes, rocky shorelines punctuated by sandy beaches, quaint downtown districts. Purists hold that the Maine coast begins at Penobscot Bay, where the vistas over the water are wider and bluer, the shore a jumble of granite boulders. Beautiful Acadia National Park is Maine's principal tourist attraction; and in Freeport, numerous outlet stores and specialty shops have sprung up around the famous outfitter L.L. Bean. The vast north woods is a destination for outdoors enthusiasts. Tourism has supplanted fishing, logging, and potato farming as Maine's number one industry: The visitor seeking an untouched fishing village with locals gathered around a potbellied stove in the general store may be sadly disappointed; that innocent age had passed in all but the most remote of villages.

Vermont

Southern Vermont has farms, freshly starched New England towns, quiet back roads, bustling ski resorts, and even some strip-mall sprawl. Central Vermont's trademarks include famed marble quarries, just north of Rutland, and large dairy herds and pastures that create the quilted patchwork of the Champlain Valley. The heart of the area is the Green Mountains and the surrounding wilderness of the Green Mountain National Forest. Both the state's largest city (Burlington) and the nation's smallest state capital (Montpelier) are in northern Vermont, as are some of the most rural and remote areas of New England. Much of the state's logging, dairy farming, and skiing take place in the north. With Montréal only an hour from the border, the Canadian influence is strong, and Canadian accents and currency common.

New Hampshire

Portsmouth, the star of New Hampshire's 18-mi coastline, has great shopping, restaurants, music, theater and one of the best historic districts in the nation. Exeter, on the Exeter River, is New Hampshire's enclave of Revolutionary War history. The Lakes Region, rich with historic landmarks, also has good restaurants, several golf courses, hiking trails, and antiquing. People go to the White Mountains to hike and climb, to photograph the dramatic vistas and the vibrant sea of foliage, and to ski. More than a mile high, Mt. Washington's peak claims some of the harshest winds and lowest temperatures ever recorded. Western and central New Hampshire is the unspoiled heart of the state: This region has managed to keep the water slides and the outlet malls at bay. Beyond the museums and picture-perfect greens, this area offers Lake Sunapee and Mt. Monadnock, the second-most-climbed mountain in the world. Much of the western and central part of the state is also an

informal artists' colony where people come to write, paint, and weave in solitude.

PLEASURES AND PASTIMES

Dining

Seafood is king throughout New England. Clams, quahogs, lobster, and scrod are prepared here in an infinite number of ways, some fancy and expensive, others simple and moderately priced. One of the best ways to enjoy seafood is in the rough—off paper plates on a picnic table at a clamboil or clambake—or at one of the many shacklike eating places along the coast, where you can smell the salt air.

At inland resorts and inns, traditional fare dominates many menus, although an increasing number of innovative chefs are bringing contemporary regional fare to the table. Among the quintessentially New England dishes are Indian pudding, clam chowder, fried clams, and cranberry anything. You can also find multicultural variations on themes, such as Portuguese Chouriço (a spicy red sausage that transforms a clamboil into something heavenly) and the mincemeat pie made with pork in the tradition of the French Canadians who populate the northern regions.

National and State Parks and Forests

Many parks provide a variety of visitor facilities for enjoying the great outdoors, including campgrounds, picnic grounds, hiking trails, boating, and ranger programs. State forests are usually somewhat less developed.

MAINE➤ Acadia National Park, which preserves fine stretches of shoreline and high mountains, covers much of Mount Desert Island and more than half of Isle au Haut and Schoodic Point on the mainland.

Baxter State Park comprises more than 200,000 acres of wilderness surrounding Katahdin, Maine's highest mountain. Hiking and moose-watching are major activities. The Allagash Wilderness Waterway is a 92-mi corridor of lakes and rivers surrounded by vast commercial forest property.

VERMONT➤ The 275,000-acre Green Mountain National Forest extends south from the center of the state to the Massachusetts border. Hikers treasure the miles of trails; canoeists work its white water; and campers and anglers find plenty to keep them happy. Among the most popular spots are the Falls of Lana and Silver Lake near Middlebury; Hapgood Pond between Manchester and Peru; and Chittenden Brook near Rochester.

NEW HAMPSHIRE➤ The White Mountain National Forest covers 770,000 acres of northern New Hampshire. New Hampshire parklands vary widely, even within a region. Major recreation parks are at Franconia Notch, Crawford Notch, and Mt. Sunapee. Rhododendron State Park (near Fitzwilliam in the Monadnock region) has a singular collection of wild rhododendrons; Mt. Washington Park (White Mountains) is on top of the highest mountain in the Northeast.

Outdoor Activities

Whether you want to cast a line, ski down a snowy mountainside, or just relax on a beach, options abound throughout northern New England. Biking is a wonderful way to explore such areas as the lakes of New Hampshire or Vermont's Champlain Valley, and hikers can be challenged by the Appalachian Trail or hundreds of other trails in numerous parks. Fishing choices vary from a secluded lake in Maine to the lure of the open Atlantic. Kayakers and canoeists will find challenging white water as well as more tranquil lakes and rivers, and Maine is known for windjamming cruises and fine sailing. Outdoor fun does not stop in the winter, either. Skiers have been drawn to the softly rounded peaks of New England for a full century; the New England Ski Museum in Franconia, New Hampshire, tells the story. Today resorts from small to large cater to both beginners and experts.

Shopping

It's hard to resist doing some kind of shopping in this region. Antiques stores hold enticing pieces of the area's rich past, from maple furniture to china and old maps and prints. Artists and craftspeople of all kinds have settled here, so you can discover everything from traditional landscapes and seascapes to handblown con-temporary glassware and colorful pottery. If bargain hunting is your passion, outlet centers from Freeport, Maine, to Manchester, Vermont, will tempt you with designer fashions, practical sporting goods, and trendy housewares. Shoppers who appreciate the joys of serendipity can explore the area's many flea markets, bazaars, and yard sales. Don't overlook specialty food items such as maple syrup and Vermont cheese. For further shopping tips, see Shopping in Smart Travel Tips.

GREAT ITINERARY

Kancamagus Trail

This circuit takes in some of the most spectacular parts of the White and Green mountains, along with the upper Connecticut River valley. In this area the antiques hunting is exemplary and the traffic is often almost nonexistent. The scenery evokes the spirit of Currier & Ives.

DURATION➤ 3–6 days

1–3 DAYS➤ From the New Hampshire coast, head northwest to Wolfeboro, perhaps detouring to explore around Lake Winnipesaukee. Take Route 16 north to Conway, then follow Route 112 west along the scenic Kancamagus Pass through the White Mountains to the Vermont border.

1–2 DAYS➤ Head south on Route 10 along the Connecticut River, past scenic Hanover, New Hampshire, home of Dartmouth College. At White River Junction, cross into Vermont. You may want to follow Route 4 through the lovely town of Woodstock to Killington, then travel along Route 100 and I-89 to complete the loop back to White River Junction. Otherwise, simply proceed south along I–91, with stops at such pleasant Vermont towns as Putney and Brattleboro.

1–2 DAYS➤ Take Route 119 east to Rhododendron State Park in Fitzwilliam, New Hampshire. Nearby is Mt. Monadnock, the most-climbed mountain in the United States; in Jaffrey take the trail to the top. Dawdle along back roads to visit the preserved villages of Harrisville, Dublin, and Hancock, then continue east along Route 101 to return to the coast.

FODOR'S CHOICE

Even with so many special places in New England, Fodor's writers and editors have their favorites. Here are a few that stand out.

Dining

⭐ **White Barn Inn, Kennebunkport, ME.** One of Maine's best restaurants, the White Barn combines superb dining with unblemished service in a rustic setting. $$$$

⭐ **Fore Street, Portland, ME.** From the open kitchen here, two of Maine's best chefs create culinary magic in dishes such as roasted lobster and applewood-grilled swordfish. $$–$$$

⭐ **Round Pond Lobstermen's Co-op, Round Pond, ME.** For lobster-in-the-rough, you can't beat this dockside takeout with views over Round Pond Harbor. $

⭐ **The Balsams Wilderness, Dixville Notch, NH.** The summer buffet lunch is heaped upon a 100-ft-long table; dinners might include chilled strawberry soup spiked with Grand Marnier and poached salmon with caviar sauce. $$$$

⭐ **Porto Bello Ristorante Italiano, Portsmouth, NH.** Pure Italian food from grilled calamari to spinach gnocchi is served up at a family-run establishment downtown. $$

⭐ **Hemingway's, Killington, VT.** Superb seasonal cuisine that focuses on local game and fresh seafood has won this restaurant a reputation as one of the state's best. $$$$

⭐ **Prince and the Pauper, Woodstock, VT.** A Colonial dining room is the setting for creative French and American dishes that come with Vermont accents. $$$–$$$$

⭐ **Villa Tragara, Stowe, VT.** Italian tapas and dishes such as roasted quail have won this romantic northern Italian eatery a devoted following. $$–$$$

Lodging

⭐ **Lodge at Moosehead Lake, Greenville, ME.** This lumber baron's mansion overlooking Moosehead Lake is as luxurious as it gets in the North Woods. All rooms have whirlpool baths, fireplaces, and four-poster beds; most have lake views. $$$–$$$$

⭐ **Ullikana, Bar Harbor, ME.** Hidden within this staid Tudor mansion is a riot of color and art. Fireplaces, private decks, water views, and gourmet breakfasts make it a real treat. $$$–$$$$

⭐ **Manor on Golden Pond, Holderness, NH.** The rooms in this English-style manor on exclusive Squam Lake are filled with luxurious touches. $$$$

⭐ **Snowvillage Inn, Snowville, NH.** Rooms in this book-filled inn near North Conway are named after authors; the nicest, with 12 windows that look out over the Presidential Range, is a tribute to Robert Frost. $$$–$$$$

⭐ **West Mountain Inn, Arlington, VT.** A former farmhouse from the 1840s has a llama ranch on the property and sits on 150 acres with glorious views. $$$$

⭐ **Inn at Shelburne Farms, Shelburne, VT.** This is storybook land: A Tudor-style inn built for William Seward and Lila Vanderbilt Webb sits on the edge of Lake Champlain and has views of the Adirondack Mountains. $$$–$$$$

Ski Resorts

⭐ **Big Squaw Mountain, ME.** A down-home, laid-back atmosphere prevails at Squaw, which overlooks Moosehead Lake. This is no frills, big mountain skiing at bargain basement prices.

⭐ **Sugarloaf/USA, ME.** At 2,820 ft, Sugarloaf/USA's vertical drop is greater than that of any other New England ski peak except Killington.

⭐ **Sunday River, ME.** Good snowmaking and reliable grooming ensure great snow from November to May at this resort, the flagship of the American Skiing Company empire.

⭐ **Attitash Bear Peak, NH.** There's always something innovative happening here—demo days, special events, race camps, and more.

⭐ **Jay Peak, VT.** Jay gets the most natural snow of any Vermont ski area. Because of its proximity to Québec, this resort attracts many Montréalers, giving it an international ambience.

⭐ **Mad River Glen, VT.** The apt motto at this area owned by a skiers cooperative is "Ski It If You Can."

★ **Smugglers' Notch, VT.** With its 1,150-ft vertical, Morse Mountain at Smugglers' is tops for beginners.

★ **Sugarbush, VT.** Sugarbush is an overall great place to ski; it has beginner runs, intermediate cruisers, and formidable steeps. There's a with-it attitude, but nearly everyone will feel comfortable.

Memorable Sights

★ **Sunrise from Cadillac Mountain, Mount Desert Island, ME.** From the summit you have a 360° view of the ocean, islands, jagged coastline, woods, and lakes.

★ **Yacht-filled Camden Harbor, ME, from the summit of Mt. Battie.** Mt. Battie may not be very tall, but it has a memorable vista over Camden Harbor, which shelters a large fleet of windjammers.

★ **Early October views, Kancamagus Highway, NH.** The classic White Mountain vistas on this popular 34-mi drive burst into fiery color each fall.

★ **The trip up Mt. Washington, NH.** Whether you hike, drive the toll road, or take the Mt. Washington Cog Railway, the journey up the Northeast's tallest mountain yields spectacular panoramas.

★ **The Appalachian Gap, Route 17, VT.** Views from the top and on the way down this mountain pass near Bristol are a just reward for the challenging drive.

★ **Village green, Woodstock, VT.** The spirit of New England's past is preserved in the lovely Federal homes that surround the green in this handsome town.

FESTIVALS AND SEASONAL EVENTS

WINTER

DEC.➤ Historic **Strawbery Banke** (NH) has a Christmas Stroll, with carolers, through nine historic homes. **Christmas Prelude** in Kennebunkport (ME) celebrates winter with concerts, caroling, and special events. The final day of the year is observed with festivals, entertainment, and food in many locations during **First Night Celebrations.** Some of the major cities hosting First Nights are Portland (ME) and Burlington, Montpelier, and St. Johnsbury (all in VT).

JAN.➤ The Bethel (ME) **Winter Festival** has snowshoe and cross-country races, sleigh rides, and a snowman contest. Stowe's (VT) festive **Winter Carnival** heats up late in the month. Brookfield (VT) holds its **Ice Harvest Festival,** one of New England's largest. The weeklong **Winter Carnival** in Jackson (NH) includes ski races and ice sculptures. The University of Vermont **Lane Series,** in Burlington, showcases internationally known performers in music, dance, and theater throughout the winter.

FEB.➤ The Camden Snow Bowl in Camden (ME) is the site of the **U.S. National Toboggan Championships.** On tap at the **Brattleboro Winter Carnival** (VT), held during the last week of the month, are jazz concerts and an ice fishing derby. The **Mad River Valley Winter Carnival** (VT) is a week of winter festivities, including dogsled races and ski races and fireworks; Burlington's **Vermont Mozart Festival** showcases the Winter Chamber Music Series.

SPRING

MAR.➤ This is the season for **maple-sugaring festivals and events:** throughout the month and into April, New England sugarhouses demonstrate procedures from maple-tree tapping to sap boiling. During **Maine Maple Sunday** Maine sugarhouses open for tours and tastings. Maine's Moosehead Lake has a renowned **Ice-Fishing Derby.** Rangeley's **New England Sled Dog Races** attract more than 100 teams. Stratton Mountain (VT) hosts the **U.S. Open Snowboarding Championships.**

APR.➤ During **Reggae Weekend** at Sugarloaf/USA (ME), Caribbean reggae bands play outdoors and inside. At Sunday River's (ME) annual **Bust 'n' Burn Mogul Competition,** professional and amateur bump skiers test their mettle. You can gorge on sea grub at Boothbay Harbor's (ME) **Fishermen's Festival,** held on the third weekend in April. At the **Maple Festival,** held early each April in St. Albans (VT), you can try Sugar on Snow, a taffylike treat.

MAY➤ The Shelburne Museum in Shelburne (VT) is awash in purple glory in mid-May, when the **Lilac Festival** blossoms. If you want to see a moose, visit Greenville (ME) during **Moosemania,** which runs from mid-May to mid-June. Events include moose safaris and mountain bike and canoe races.

SUMMER

JUNE➤ In Vermont, you can listen to jazz at Burlington's **Discover Jazz Festival. Lake Champlain International Fishing Derby** entices anglers to try their fishing skills. The **Vermont Canoe and Kayak Festival** is held each year in Stowe. The **Boothbay Harbor Windjammer Days** starts the high season for Maine's boating set. Burlington, Vermont's **Green Mountain Chew Chew** offers a variety of entertainment including outdoor music and comedy. During the **Strawberry Festival** in Wiscasset (ME), you can get your fill of strawberry goodies.

JULY➤ **Independence Day** is celebrated with concerts, family entertainment, an art show, a parade, and fireworks in Bath (ME). Exeter (NH) holds a **Revolutionary War Festival** at the American Independence Museum with battle reenactments and period crafts and antiques. The **Marlboro Music Festival** presents classical music at Marlboro College (VT). The **Bar Harbor Festival** (ME) hosts classical, jazz, and popular music concerts into August. The **Bowdoin Summer Music Festival** (ME) is a six-week series of chamber music concerts.

Glorious outdoor concert sites and sumptuous picnics are sidelines to fine music at the **Vermont Mozart Festival**, held throughout central and northern Vermont in July and August. The two-day **Stoweflake Hot Air Balloon Festival** in Stowe is one of Vermont's most popular events. Admire the furnishings of homes during **Open House Tours** in Camden (ME). The **Yarmouth Clam Festival** (ME) is more than a seafood celebration—expect continuous entertainment and a crafts show throughout the three-day event.

AUG.➣ Stowe (VT) hosts a popular **Antique and Classic Car Rally**. The **Southern Vermont Crafts Fair** in Manchester (VT) features popular arts, crafts, and antiques. Sellers and collectors throng to the **Maine Antiques Festival** in Union. The **Fair of the League of New Hampshire Craftsmen** at Mt. Sunapee State Park in Newbury exhibits the works of some of the state's finest artisans. There's a **Lobster Festival** in Rockland (ME). Everything's coming up blueberries at the **Wild Maine Blueberry Festival** in Machias (ME).

In Rangeley Lake (ME), the blueberry is king at the annual **Blueberry Festival.** Brunswick's **Maine Festival** is a four-day celebration of Maine arts. Maine's **Annual Maine Highland Games** features traditional Scottish athletic events and music entertainment.

SEPT.➣ New England's Labor Day fairs include the **Vermont State Fair** in Rutland, with agricultural exhibits and entertainment. The **International Seaplane Fly-In Weekend,** sets Moosehead Lake (ME) buzzing. The **Champlain Valley Fair,** in Burlington (VT), has all the features of a large county fair. Many of the country's finest fiddlers compete at the **National Traditional Old-Time Fiddler's Contest** in Barre (VT). Folk music is the highlight at the **Rockport Folk Festival** in Rockport (ME). In Stratton (VT), artists and performers gather for the **Stratton Arts Festival.** The **Common Ground Country Fair** in

Unity (ME) is an organic farmer's delight. The **Deerfield Fair** (NH) is one of New England's oldest agricultural fairs. The six small Vermont towns of Walden, Cabot, Plainfield, Peacham, Barnet, and Groton host the weeklong **Northeast Kingdom Fall Foliage Festival**. The **Eastport Salmon Festival** (ME), the first Sunday after Labor Day, hosts entertainers and crafts artists. At the **Annual Seafood Festival** in Hampton Beach (NH), you can sample seafood specialties, dance to live bands, and watch fireworks.

OCT.➣ The **Fryeburg Fair** (ME) presents agricultural exhibits, harness racing, and a pig scramble. **Hildene Farm, Food and Crafts Fair** in Manchester (VT) has farm activities, entertainment, and lots of events for kids.

NOV.➣ The **International Film Festival** presents films dealing with environmental, human rights, and political issues for a week in Burlington (VT). The **Bradford Wild Game Supper** (VT) draws thousands to taste large and small game animals and birds.

2 MAINE

At its extremes Maine measures 300 miles
by 200 miles; all the other states in New
England could fit within its ample perimeters.
The Kennebunks hold classic townscapes,
rocky shorelines, sandy beaches, and quaint
downtown districts. Portland has the state's
best selection of restaurants, shops, and
cultural offerings, and Freeport is a mecca
for outlet shoppers. North of Portland, sandy
beaches give way to rocky coast and
treasures such as Acadia National Park.
Outdoors enthusiasts head to inland Maine's
lakes, mountains, and the vast North Woods.

By Hilary M.
Nangle

ON THE MAINE–NEW HAMPSHIRE BORDER is a sign that plainly announces the philosophy of the region: WELCOME TO MAINE: THE WAY LIFE SHOULD BE. Local folk say too many cars are on the road when you can't make it through the traffic signal on the first try. Romantics luxuriate in the feeling of a down comforter on an old, yellowed pine bed or in the sensation of the wind and salt spray on their faces while cruising in a historic windjammer. Families love the unspoiled beaches and safe inlets dotting the shoreline and the clear inland lakes. Hikers and campers are revived by the exalting and exhausting climb to the top of Katahdin, and adventure seekers get their thrills rafting the Kennebec or Penobscot River.

There is an expansiveness to Maine, a sense of distance between places that hardly exists elsewhere in New England, and along with the sheer size and spread of the place there is a tremendous variety of terrain. People speak of "coastal" Maine and "inland" Maine, as though the state could be summed up under the twin emblems of lobsters and pine trees. Yet the topography and character in this state are a good deal more complicated.

Even the coast is several places in one. Portland may be Maine's largest city, but its attitude is decidedly more big town than small city. South of this rapidly gentrifying city, Ogunquit, Kennebunkport, Old Orchard Beach, and other resort towns predominate along a reasonably smooth shoreline. North of Portland and Casco Bay, secondary roads turn south off U.S. 1 onto so many oddly chiseled peninsulas that it's possible to drive for days without retracing your route. Slow down to explore the museums, galleries, and shops in the larger towns and the antiques and curio shops and harborside lobster shacks in the smaller fishing villages on the peninsulas. Freeport is an entity unto itself, a place where numerous name-brand outlets and specialty stores have sprung up around the retail outpost of famous outfitter L. L. Bean. And no description of the coast would be complete without mention of popular Acadia National Park, with its majestic mountains, and the rugged scenery of the less-visited towns that lie way Down East.

Inland Maine likewise defies easy characterization. For one thing, a lot of it is virtually uninhabited. This is the land Henry David Thoreau wrote about in *The Maine Woods* more than 150 years ago; aside from having been logged over several times, much of it hasn't changed since Thoreau and his Native American guides passed through. Ownership of vast portions of northern Maine by forest-products corporations has kept out subdivision and development; many of the roads here are private, open to travel only by permit.

Wealthy summer visitors, or "sports," came to Maine beginning in the late 1800s to hunt, fish, and play in the clean air and clean water. The state's more than 6,000 lakes and more than 3,000 mi of rivers and streams still attract such people, and more and more families, for the same reasons. Sporting camps still thrive around Greenville, Rangeley, and in the Great North Woods.

Logging in the north created the culture of the mill towns, the Rumfords, Skowhegans, Millinockets, and Bangors that lie at the end of the old river drives. The logs arrive by truck today, but Maine's harvested wilderness still feeds the mills and the nation's hunger for paper.

The hunger for potatoes has given rise to an entirely different Maine culture, in one of the most isolated agricultural regions of the country. Northeastern Aroostook County is where the Maine potatoes

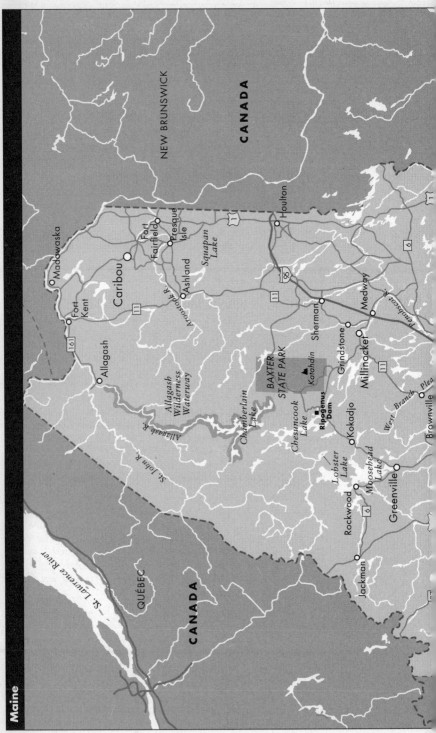

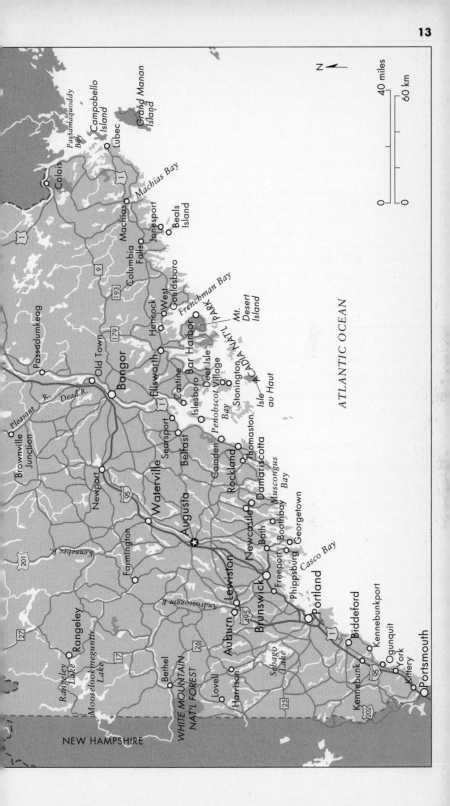

come from. This place is also changing. In what was once called the Potato Empire, farmers are as pressed between high costs and low prices as any of their counterparts in the Midwest, and a growing national preference for Idaho baking potatoes to small, round Maine boiling potatoes has only compounded Aroostook's troubles.

If you come to Maine seeking an untouched fishing village with locals gathered around a potbellied stove in the general store, you'll likely come away disappointed; that innocent age has passed in all but the most remote villages. Tourism has supplanted fishing, logging, and potato farming as Maine's number one industry, and most areas are well equipped to receive the annual onslaught of visitors. But whether you are stepping outside a motel room for a walk or watching a boat rock at its anchor, you can sense the infinity of the natural world. Wilderness is always nearby, growing to the edges of the most urbanized spots.

Pleasures and Pastimes

Dining

Lobster and Maine are synonymous. As a general rule, the closer you are to a working harbor, the fresher your lobster will be. Aficionados eschew ordering lobster in restaurants, preferring to eat them "in the rough" at classic lobster pounds, where you select your dinner out of a pool and enjoy it at a waterside picnic table. Shrimp, scallops, clams, mussels, and crabs are also caught in the cold waters off Maine. Restaurants in Portland and in resort towns prepare shellfish in creative combinations with lobster, haddock, salmon, and swordfish. Wild blueberries are grown commercially in Maine, and local cooks use them generously in pancakes, muffins, jams, pies, and cobblers. In 1999, Maine passed a law prohibiting smoking in restaurants.

For price-category information, *see* Dining *in* Smart Travel Tips.

Lodging

The beach communities in the south beckon visitors with their weathered look. Stately digs can be found in the classic inns of Kennebunkport. Bed-and-breakfasts and Victorian inns furnished with lace, chintz, and mahogany have joined the family-oriented motels of Ogunquit, Boothbay Harbor, Bar Harbor, and the Camden–Rockport region. Although accommodations tend to be less luxurious away from the coast, Bethel, Carrabassett Valley, and Rangeley have sophisticated hotels and inns. Greenville and Rockwood have the largest selection of restaurants and accommodations in the North Woods region. Lakeside sporting camps, which range from the primitive to the upscale, are popular around Rangeley and the North Woods. Many have cozy cabins heated with woodstoves and serve three hearty meals a day. At some of Maine's larger hotels and inns with restaurants, rates may include breakfast and dinner during the peak summer season.

For price-category information, *see* Lodging *in* Smart Travel Tips.

Outdoor Activities and Sports

BOATING

Maine's long coastline is justifiably famous: all visitors should get on the water, whether on an excursion headed for Monhegan Island for the day or on a windjammer for a relaxing vacation. Windjammer trips last from just a few hours to a full week. Longer trips include hearty, home-style meals and a traditional lobster bake often held on a remote island. Windjammers may sail past long, craggy fingers of land that jut into a sea dotted with more than 2,000 islands. Sail among these islands and you'll see hidden coves, lighthouses, boat-filled harbors, and quiet fishing villages. Some windjammers, traditional two- or three-masted tall ships, are historic vessels that have been modified to carry human cargo while others have more modern amenities. Most windjammers depart from Rockland, Rockport, or Camden, all ports on Penobscot Bay. Boating trips, including whale-watching, run in season, mid- to late May through September or mid-October.

HIKING

From seaside rambles to backwoods hikes, Maine has a walk for everyone. This state's beaches are mostly hard packed and good for walking. Many coastal communities, such as York, Ogunquit, and Bar Harbor, have shoreside paths for people who want to keep sand out of their shoes yet enjoy the sound of the crashing surf and the cliff-top views of inlets and coves. Those who like to walk in the woods will not be disappointed: 90% of the state is forested land. Acadia National Park has more than 150 mi of hiking trails, and within Baxter State Park are the northern end of the Appalachian Trail and Katahdin. At nearly 1 mi high, Katahdin is the tallest mountain in the state.

SKIING

Weather patterns that create snow cover for Maine ski areas may come from the Atlantic or from Canada, and Maine may have snow when other New England states do not—and vice versa. Sunday River and Sugarloaf, both operated by the American Skiing Co., are the state's largest ski areas. Both are full-service destination resorts with a choice of lodging, dining, and shopping as well as more than enough terrain to keep skiers and riders content for days. It's worth the effort to get to Sugarloaf, which provides the only above-tree-line skiing in New England and also has a lively base village.

Saddleback, in Rangeley, has big-mountain skiing at little-mountain prices. Its lift system is sorely out of date, but many would have it no other way, preferring its down-home, wilderness atmosphere. Squaw Mountain in Greenville is similar in character. Its remote location ensures few crowds, and its low prices make it an attractive alternative to other big mountains.

WHITE-WATER RAFTING

From early May through September, Maine has consistent white-water rafting on three dam-controlled, Class III–V rivers: the Kennebec, the Penobscot, and the Dead. About a dozen outfitters are based in and around the Forks, Maine's white-water capital, where the Kennebec and the Dead rivers meet. Both are good day trips, with the Kennebec being the most popular—like a white-water roller coaster; big thrills but few chills. The Penobscot, which flows near Baxter State Park in the shadow of Mt. Katahdin, provides a remote trip with challenging white water and beautiful views of the mountain. It's not uncommon to see moose or deer while on the river. Most outfitters have facilities in this area, and most offer both day and overnight trips.

Exploring Maine

Maine is a large state that offers many different experiences. The York County Coast, in the southern portion of the state, is easily accessible and has long sand beaches, historic homes, and good restaurants. The coastal geography changes in Portland, the economic and cultural center of southern Maine. North of the city, long fingers of land jut into the sea, sheltering fishing villages. Penobscot Bay is famed for its rock-bound coast, sailing, and numerous islands. Mount Desert Island lures crowds of people to Acadia National Park, which is filled with stunning natural beauty. Way down east, beyond Acadia, the tempo changes; fast-food joints and trinket shops all but disappear, replaced by family-style restaurants and artisans' shops. Inland, the western lakes and mountains provide an entirely different experience. Summer camps, ski areas, and small villages populate this region. People head to Maine's North Woods to escape the crowds and to enjoy the great outdoors by hiking, rafting, camping, or canoeing.

Numbers in the text and in the margin correspond to numbers on the maps: Southern Maine Coast, Portland, Penobscot Bay, Mount Desert Island, Way Down East, Western Maine, and the North Woods.

Great Itineraries

You can spend days exploring just the coast of Maine, as these itineraries indicate, so plan ahead and decide whether you want to ski and dogsled in the western mountains, raft or canoe in the North Woods, or simply meander up the coast, stopping at museums and historic sites, shopping for local arts and crafts, and exploring coastal villages and lobster shacks. Trying to see everything in one visit is complicated by the lack of east–west roads in the state and heavy traffic on popular routes, such as U.S. 1 and U.S. 302. Build extra time into your schedule and relax. You'll get there eventually, and in the meantime, enjoy the view.

IF YOU HAVE 2 DAYS

A two-day exploration of the southern coast provides a good introduction to different aspects of the Maine coast. Begin in **Ogunquit** ③ with a morning walk along the Marginal Way. Then head north to **Kennebunkport** ⑥, allowing at least two hours to wander through the shops and historic homes around Dock Square. Relax on the beach for an hour or so before heading to ⛴ **Portland** ⑧–⑬. If you thrive on arts and entertainment, spend the night here. Otherwise, continue north to ⛴ **Freeport** ⑯, where you can shop all night at L. L. Bean. On day two, head north, stopping in **Bath** ⑱ to tour the Maine Maritime Museum, and finish up with a lobster dinner on **Pemaquid Peninsula** ㉑.

IF YOU HAVE 4 DAYS

A four-day tour of midcoast Maine up to Acadia National Park is one of New England's classic trips. From New Harbor on **Pemaquid Peninsula** ㉑, take the boat to ⛴ **Monhegan Island** ㉕ for a day of walking the trails and exploring the artists' studios and galleries. The next day, continue northeast to **Rockland** ㉖ and ⛴ **Camden** ㉗. On day four, visit the Farnsworth Museum in Rockland, hike or drive to the top of Mt. Battie in Camden, and meander around Camden's boat-filled harbor. Or bypass midcoast Maine in favor of ⛴ **Mount Desert Island** ㉟–㊷ and Acadia National Park. To avoid sluggish traffic on U.S. 1, from Freeport, stay on I–95 to Augusta and the Maine Turnpike; then take Route 3 to Belfast and pick up U.S. 1 north there.

IF YOU HAVE 8 DAYS

An eight-day trip allows time to see a good portion of the coast. Spend two days wandering through gentrified towns and weather-beaten fishing villages from ⛴ **Kittery** ① to ⛴ **Portland** ⑧–⑬. On your third day explore Portland and environs, including a boat ride to **Eagle Island** ⑮ or one of the other Casco Bay islands and a visit to Portland Head Light and Two Lights in Cape Elizabeth. Continue working your way up the coast, letting your interests dictate your stops: outlet stores in **Freeport** ⑯, Maine Maritime Museum in ⛴ **Bath** ⑱, antiques shops in **Wiscasset** ⑲, fishing villages and a much-photographed lighthouse on **Pemaquid Peninsula** ㉑. Allow at least one day in the **Rockland** ㉖ and ⛴ **Camden** ㉗ region before taking the leisurely route to **Bar Harbor** ㉞ via the **Blue Hill** ㉛ peninsula and ⛴ **Deer Isle Village** ㉜. Finish up with two days on ⛴ **Mount Desert Island** ㉟–㊷.

When to Tour Maine

From July to September is the choice time for a vacation in Maine. The weather is warmest in July and August, though September is less crowded. In warm weather, the arteries along the coast and lakeside communities inland are clogged with out-of-state license plates, campgrounds are filled to capacity, and hotel rates are high. Midweek is less busy, and lodging rates are often lower then than on weekends.

Fall foliage can be brilliant in Maine and is made even more so by its reflection in inland lakes or streams or off the ocean. Late September is peak season in the north country, while in southern Maine the prime viewing dates are usually around October 5 to 10. In September and October the days are sunny and the nights crisp.

In winter, the coastal towns almost completely close down. If the sidewalks could be rolled up, they probably would be. Maine's largest ski areas usually open in mid-November and, thanks to excellent snowmaking facilities, provide good skiing often into April.

Springtime is mud season here, as in most other rural areas of New England. Mud season is followed by spring flowers and the start of wildflowers in meadows along the roadsides. Mid-May to mid-June is the main season for black flies, especially inland. It's best to schedule a trip after mid-June if possible, though this is prime canoeing time.

YORK COUNTY COAST

Maine's southernmost coastal towns, most of them in York County, won't give you the rugged, wind-bitten "Down East" experience, but they are easily reached from the south, and most have the sand beaches that all but vanish beyond Portland. These towns are highly popular in summer, an all-too-brief period. Crowds converge and gobble up rooms and dinner reservations at prime restaurants. You'll have to work a little harder to find solitude and vestiges of the "real" Maine here. Still, even day-trippers who come for a few fleeting hours will appreciate the magical warmth of the sand along this coast.

North of Kittery, the Maine coast has long stretches of hard-packed white-sand beach, closely crowded by nearly unbroken ranks of beach cottages, motels, and oceanfront restaurants. The summer colonies of York Beach and Wells Beach have the crowds and ticky-tacky shorefront overdevelopment, but quiet wildlife refuges and land reserves promise an easy escape. York's historic district is on the National Register of Historic Places. Ogunquit is more upscale and offers much to do, from shopping to taking a cliff-side walk.

More than any other region south of Portland, the Kennebunks—and especially Kennebunkport—provide the complete Maine-coast experience: classic townscapes where white clapboard houses rise from manicured lawns and gardens; rocky shorelines punctuated by sandy beaches; quaint downtown districts packed with gift shops, ice cream stands, and visitors; harbors where lobster boats bob alongside yachts; lobster pounds and well-appointed dining rooms. Continuing north, the scents of french fries, pizza, and cotton candy hover in the air above Coney Island-like Old Orchard Beach, known for its amusement pier and 7-mi-long shoreline. These towns are best explored on a leisurely holiday of two days—more if you require a fix of solid beach time. U.S. 1 travels along the coast. Inland, the Maine Turnpike (I–95) is the fastest route if you want to skip some towns.

Kittery

❶ *55 mi north of Boston, MA, 5 mi north of Portsmouth, NH.*

Kittery, which lacks a large sand beach of its own, hosts a complex of factory outlets that make it a popular destination. As an alternative to shopping, drive north past the outlets and go east on Route 103 for a peek at the hidden Kittery most people miss. There are hiking and biking trails and, best of all, great views of the water. Along this winding stretch are two forts, both open in summer.

Built in 1872, **Ft. Foster** (✉ Pocahontas Rd., Kittery Point, ☎ 207/439–3800) was an active military installation until 1949. **Ft. McClary** (✉ Rte. 103, Kittery Point, ☎ 207/384–5160), which dates from 1715, was staffed during five wars.

Dining and Lodging

$$–$$$ ✕ **Warren's Lobster House.** A local institution, this waterfront restaurant specializes in seafood and has a huge salad bar. In season, you can dine outdoors overlooking the water. ✉ *U.S. 1 and Water St.,* ☎ *207/439–1630. AE, MC, V.*

$$$ 🏨 **The Inn at Portsmouth Harbor.** This brick Victorian built in 1889 on the old Kittery town green overlooks the Piscataqua River and Portsmouth Harbor. An easy walk over the bridge takes you to nearby Portsmouth, NH. English antiques and Victorian watercolors decorate the no-smoking inn, and all rooms have cable TV as well as phones with voice mail. ✉ *6 Water St., 03904,* ☎ *207/439–4040,* FAX *207/438–9286,* WEB *www.innatportsmouth.com. 5 rooms. Air-conditioning, in-room data ports. AE, MC, V. BP.*

Nightlife and the Arts

Hamilton House (✉ 40 Vaughan's La., South Berwick, 20 mi northwest of Kittery, ☎ 603/436–3205), the Georgian home featured in Sarah Orne Jewett's historical novel *The Tory Lover,* presents "Sundays in the Garden" in July, a series of concerts ranging from classical to folk music. Concerts ($5) begin at 4. You can also visit **Jewett's home** (✉ 5 Portland St. South Berwick, ☎ 207/436–3205) in South Berwick during summer.

Shopping

Kittery has more than 120 outlet stores. Along a several-mi stretch of U.S. 1 you can find just about anything, from hardware to underwear. Among the stores are Crate & Barrel, Eddie Bauer, Jones New York, Esprit, Waterford/Wedgwood, Lenox, Ralph Lauren, Tommy Hilfiger, DKNY, and J. Crew.

The Yorks

❷ *4 mi north of Kittery.*

The Yorks—York Village, York Harbor, York Beach, and Cape Neddick—are typical of small-town coastal communities in New England and are smaller than most. Many of their nooks and crannies can be explored in a few hours. The beaches are the big attraction here.

Most of the 18th- and 19th-century buildings within the **York Village Historic District** are clustered along York Street and Lindsay Road in York Village; seven are owned by the Old York Historical Society and charge admission. You can buy tickets for all the buildings at the **Jefferds Tavern** (✉ U.S. 1A at Lindsay Rd.), a restored late-18th-century inn. The **Old York Gaol** (1720) was once the King's Prison for the Province of Maine; inside are dungeons, cells, and the jailer's quarters. The 1731 **Elizabeth Perkins House** reflects the Victorian style of its last

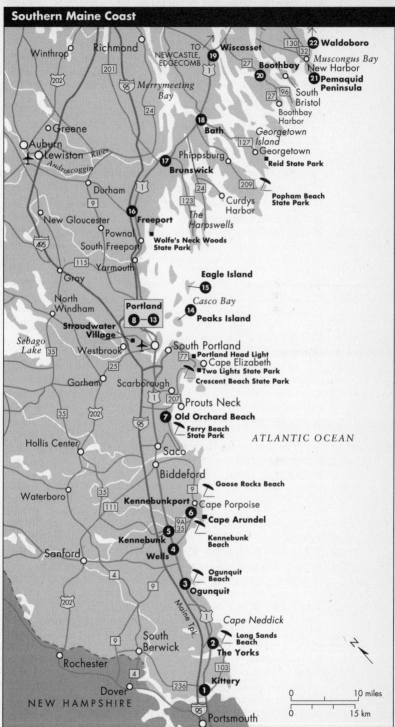

Southern Maine Coast

Winthrop

Richmond

TO
NEWCASTLE,
EDGECOMB **19** **Wiscasset**

130 **22** **Waldoboro**

32

27 **Boothbay** *Muscongus Bay*

20 New Harbor

21 **Pemaquid**
Peninsula

201

95 *Merrymeeting
Bay*

27 96 South
Bristol

Boothbay
Harbor

24

Greene

18 **Bath** *Georgetown
Island*

Auburn
Lewiston *River*

127 Georgetown

Androscoggin

Phippsburg **17** **Brunswick**

• Reid State Park

Durham

1

209 ☂

Popham Beach
State Park

New Gloucester

9

123 Curdys
Harbor

24

16 **Freeport**

Pownal *The
Harpswells*

South Freeport

■ Wolfe's Neck Woods
State Park

115

495

Yarmouth

Eagle Island

15

Gray

Casco Bay

North
Windham

Portland **14** **Peaks Island**

8 **13**

**Stroudwater
Village**

*Sebago
Lake*

35

Westbrook

25

South Portland

77 ■ Portland Head Light

○ Cape Elizabeth

■ Two Lights State Park

Gorham

Scarborough

■ Crescent Beach State Park

1

207 Prouts Neck

35

202

7 **Old Orchard Beach**

Ferry Beach
State Park

Hollis Center

95

Saco

ATLANTIC OCEAN

Biddeford

9 ☂ Goose Rocks Beach

35

Kennebunkport ■ Cape Porpoise

Waterboro

111

6 ■ **Cape Arundel**

9A
35

5

Kennebunk Kennebunk
Beach

Sanford

4 **Wells**

4

☂ Ogunquit
Beach

9

3 **Ogunquit**

202

Cape Neddick

South
Berwick

2 Long Sands
Beach

9

The Yorks

Rochester

Maine Tpk.

1

103

1 **Kittery**

4

236

Dover

95

NEW HAMPSHIRE

Portsmouth

0   10 miles

0   15 km

occupants, the prominent Perkins family. Members of the Old York Historical Society lead tours. ☎ *207/363–4974.* 🎫 *$7 for all buildings.* ☉ *Mid-June–mid-Oct., Tues.–Sat. 10–5, Sun. 1–5.*

The waterfront **Sayward-Wheeler House** (1718) mirrors the fortunes of a coastal village in the transition from trade to tourism. Jonathan Sayward prospered in the West Indies trade in the 18th century; by 1860 his descendants had opened the house to the public to share the story of their Colonial ancestors. The house, accessible only by guided tour, reflects both these eras. ⊠ *79 Barrell La., York Harbor,* ☎ *603/436–3205.* 🎫 *$4.* ☉ *June–mid-Oct., weekends 11–5; tours on the hr 11–4.*

If you drive down Nubble Road from U.S. 1A and go to the end of Cape Neddick, you can park and gaze out at the **Nubble Light** (1879), which sits on a tiny island just offshore. The keeper's house is a tidy Victorian cottage with gingerbread woodwork and a red roof.

Dining and Lodging

$$$ ✕ **Cape Neddick Inn.** The American bistro-style menu at this restaurant and art gallery changes with the seasons. Past offerings have included entrées such as sage-roasted quail and poached Atlantic salmon on lobster succotash. ⊠ *U.S. 1, Cape Neddick,* ☎ *207/363–2899. D, MC, V. Closed Mon. and mid-Oct.–May. No lunch.*

$–$$$ ✕ **Cape Neddick Lobster Pound.** There's something for everyone at this casual harborside restaurant. Lobster, all kinds of seafood, and steaks appear on the menù. A children's menu and outdoor dining are available. ⊠ *Shore Rd., Cape Neddick,* ☎ *207/363–5471. MC, V. Closed Jan.–Mar.*

$$–$$$$ ✕🏨 **York Harbor Inn.** A mid-17th-century fishing cabin with dark
★   timbers and a fieldstone fireplace forms the heart of this inn, to which wings and outbuildings have been added over the years. The rooms are furnished with antiques and country pieces; many have decks overlooking the water, and a few have whirlpool tubs or fireplaces. Rooms in the Harbor Cliffs next door have the intimate appeal of a classic Maine cottage. In the Harbor Hill building, all the rooms have fireplaces, whirlpool tubs, and ocean views. The dining room (no lunch off-season) has great ocean views. For dinner, start with Maine crab cakes and then try the lobster-stuffed chicken breast or the angel-hair pasta with shrimp and scallops. ⊠ *Box 573, U.S. 1A, York Harbor 03911,* ☎ *207/363–5119 or 800/343–3869,* 𝔽𝔸𝕏 *207/363–7151,* 🆆🅴🅱 *www.yorkharborinn.com. 45 rooms, 2 suites. Restaurant, pub. AE, DC, MC, V. CP.*

$$–$$$ 🏨 **Edward's Harborside.** This turn-of-the-century B&B sits on the harbor's edge and is just a two-minute walk from the beach. Rooms share baths, are spacious, and have big windows to take in the water views. One room has a whirlpool tub. ⊠ *Box 866, Stage Neck Rd., York Harbor 03911,* ☎ *207/363–3037,* 𝔽𝔸𝕏 *207/363–1544,* 🆆🅴🅱 *www.edwardsharborsideinn.com. 4 rooms without bath, 3 suites. Dock. MC, V. CP.*

$$–$$$ 🏨 **Union Bluff.** This fortress-like modern white structure, with balconies across the front and turrets on the ends, sits right across from Short Sands Beach with views to forever. The best rooms are in the front of the inn, but many on the north side, which cost less, also have ocean views. The front rooms in the adjacent motel have ocean views, but the motel has fewer services. ⊠ *Box 1860, 8 Beach St., York Beach 03910,* ☎ *207/363–1333 or 800/833–0721,* 𝔽𝔸𝕏 *207/363–1381,* 🆆🅴🅱 *www.unionbluff.com. 36 rooms, 6 suites in inn, 21 rooms in motel. Restaurant, pub. AE, D, MC, V.*

$$ ⛉ **The Riverbed.** An oasis of calm, this clapboard home dating from before the American Revolution provides a nice counterpoint to busy York Beach, a short walk away. Each room is carefully furnished with antiques and family pieces and has a private deck; there's also a private sitting room for guests. The shared back deck, with hot tub, slopes gently down to the Cape Neddick River. ✉ *154 Rte. 1A, 03910,* ☎ *207/363–3630. 3 rooms. Outdoor hot tub, boating. MC, V. Closed Columbus Day–Memorial Day weekend. BP.*

Nightlife and the Arts
Inn on the Blues (✉ 7 Ocean Ave., York Beach, ☎ 207/351–3221) is a hopping blues club that attracts national bands.

Outdoor Activities and Sports
U.S. 1A runs right behind **Long Sands Beach,** a 1½-mi stretch of sand in York Beach that has roadside parking and a bathhouse. **Short Sands Beach** in York Beach has a bathhouse and is convenient to restaurants and shops. **Capt. Tom Farnon** (✉ Rte. 103, Town Dock No. 2, York Harbor, ☎ 207/363–3234) takes passengers on lobstering trips, weekdays 10–2.

Ogunquit

❸ *10 mi north of the Yorks, 39 mi southwest of Portland.*

Probably more than any other south-coast community, Ogunquit combines coastal ambience, style, and good eating. The village became a resort in the 1880s and gained fame as an artists' colony. A mini Provincetown, Ogunquit has a gay population that swells in summer; many inns and small clubs cater to a primarily gay and lesbian clientele. Families love the protected beach area and friendly environment. Shore Road, which takes you into downtown, passes the 100-ft **Bald Head Cliff,** with views up and down the coast. On a stormy day the surf can be quite wild here.

Perkins Cove, a neck of land connected to the mainland by Oarweed Road and a pedestrian drawbridge, has a jumble of sea-beaten fish houses. These have largely been transformed by the tide of tourism to shops and restaurants. When you've had your fill of browsing and jostling

★ the crowds at Perkins Cove, stroll out along the **Marginal Way,** a mile-long footpath that hugs the shore of a rocky promontory known as Israel's Head. Benches along the route give walkers an opportunity to stop and appreciate the open sea vistas, flowering bushes, and million-dollar homes.

The small but worthwhile **Ogunquit Museum of American Art,** dedicated to 20th-century American art, overlooks the ocean and is set amid a 3-acre sculpture garden. Inside are works by Henry Strater, Marsden Hartley, Winslow Homer, Edward Hopper, Gaston Lachaise, Marguerite Zorach, and Louise Nevelson. The huge windows of the sculpture court command a superb view of cliffs and ocean. ✉ *183 Shore Rd.,* ☎ *207/646–4909.* 🎟 *$4.* ☉ *July 1–Oct. 15, Mon.–Sat. 10:30–5, Sun. 2–5.*

Dining and Lodging
$$$$ ✕ **Arrows.** Elegant simplicity is the hallmark of this restaurant in an 18th-century farmhouse, 2 mi up a back road. Grilled salmon and radicchio with marinated fennel and baked polenta, and Chinese-style duck glazed with molasses are typical entrées on the daily-changing menu. The Maine crabmeat mousse and lobster risotto appetizers and desserts such as strawberry shortcake with Chantilly cream are also beautifully

executed. ⊠ *Berwick Rd.,* ☎ *207/361–1100. Reservations essential. MC, V. Closed Mon. and mid-Dec.–mid-Apr. No lunch.*

$$$$ 🏨 **Cliff House.** Elsie Jane Weare opened the Cliff House in 1872, and her granddaughter Kathryn now presides over this sprawling ocean-front resort atop Bald Head Cliff. The complex is undergoing a renovation and expansion slated for completion in 2002: a new resort center will house a spa dining area, full health spa, 32 guest rooms, and new pools. This place has a loyal following, so reserve well in advance; be sure to call for updates on the construction. ⊠ *Box 2274, 2 East Shore Rd., 03907,* ☎ *207/361–1000,* 🖷 *207/361–2122,* 🌐 *www.cliffhousemaine.com. 178 rooms, 14 suites. 2 restaurants, 1 indoor and 1 outdoor pool, hot tub, sauna, spa, 2 tennis courts, health club. AE, D, MC, V. Closed mid-Dec.–late Mar.*

$$$–$$$$ ✕ **Gypsy Sweethearts.** The multi-ethnic fare at this popular bistro ranges from creole shrimp to chile-crusted rack of lamb to Jamaican jerk-rubbed chicken. In the dining area, cobalt-blue glassware accents the white-draped tables ⊠ *10 Shore Rd.,* ☎ *207/646–7021. MC, V. Closed Mon. and Jan.–Apr. No lunch.*

$$$–$$$$ ✕ **Hurricane.** Don't let the weather-beaten exterior or the frenzied atmosphere deter you—this small seafood bar and grill with spectacular views of the crashing surf turns out first-rate dishes. Start with lobster chowder or a chilled fresh-shrimp spring roll. Entrées may include lobster cioppino, rack of lamb, and fire-roasted veal chop. ⊠ *Oarweed La., Perkins Cove,* ☎ *207/646–6348 or 800/649–6348. AE, D, DC, MC, V. Closed early Jan.*

$$$–$$$$ ✕ **98 Provence.** Country French ambiance provides a fitting backdrop
★   for Chef Pierre Gignac's French fare. Begin with the duck foie gras or country-style rabbit pâté, and follow it up with gigot of lotte roasted with a fresh herb crust or medallion of veal tenderloin with a wild mushroom cream sauce. ⊠ *104 Shore Rd.,* ☎ *207/646–9898. Reservations essential. MC, V.*

$$–$$$ 🏨 **The Rockmere.** Midway along Ogunquit's Marginal Way, this shingle-style Victorian cottage is an ideal retreat from the hustle and bustle of Perkins Cove. All the rooms have corner locations and are large and airy, and all but one have ocean views. You'll find it easy to laze the day away on the wraparound porch or in the gardens. ⊠ *Box 278, 40 Stearns Rd., 03907,* ☎ *207/646–2985,* 🖷 *207/646–6947,* 🌐 *www.rockmere.com. 8 rooms. AE, D, V. CP.*

Nightlife and the Arts

Much of the nightlife in Ogunquit revolves around the precincts of Ogunquit Square and Perkins Cove, where people stroll, often enjoying an after-dinner ice cream cone or espresso. Ogunquit is popular with gay and lesbian visitors, and its club scene reflects this. **Jonathan's Restaurant** (⊠ 2 Bourne La., ☎ 207/646–4777) has live entertainment, usually blues, in season.

The **Ogunquit Playhouse** (⊠ U.S. 1, ☎ 207/646–5511), one of America's oldest summer theaters, mounts plays and musicals with name entertainment from late June to Labor Day.

Outdoor Activities and Sports

Ogunquit Beach, a 3-mi-wide stretch of sand at the mouth of the Ogunquit River, has snack bars, a boardwalk, rest rooms, and, at the Beach Street entrance, changing areas. Families gravitate to the ends; gay visitors camp at the beach's middle. The less-crowded section to the north is accessible by footbridge and has portable rest rooms, all-day paid parking, and trolley service.

Finestkind (⊠ Perkins Cove, ☎ 207/646–5227) operates cocktail cruises, lobstering trips, and cruises to Nubble Light.

Wells

❹ *5 mi north of Ogunquit, 34 mi southwest of Portland.*

This family-oriented beach community has 7 mi of densely populated shoreline, along with nature preserves where you can explore salt marshes and tidal pools and see birds and waterfowl.

Extensive trails in the **Wells Reserve** lace the 1,600 acres of meadows, orchards, fields, and salt marshes, as well as two estuaries and 9 mi of seashore. Laudholm Farm, an 18th-century saltwater farm, houses the visitor center, where an introductory slide show is screened. Five rooms have exhibits. In winter, cross-country skiing is permitted. ⊠ *342 Laudholm Farm Rd.,* ☎ *207/646–1555.* ☞ *$2 July–Aug. and weekends Sept.–mid-Oct.* ☉ *Grounds daily 8–5. Visitor center May–Dec., Mon.–Sat. 10–4, Sun. noon–4; Jan.–Apr., Sat. 10–4, Sun. noon–4.*

Rachel Carson National Wildlife Refuge (⊠ Rte. 9, ☎ 207/646–9226) has a mi-long loop nature trail through a salt marsh. The trail borders the Little River and a white-pine forest where migrating birds and waterfowl of many varieties are regularly spotted.

☙ A must for motor fanatics and youngsters, the **Wells Auto Museum** has 70 vintage cars, antique coin games, and a restored Model T you can ride in. ⊠ *U.S. 1,* ☎ *207/646–9064.* ☞ *$5.* ☉ *Memorial Day–Columbus Day, 10–5.*

Dining and Lodging

$–$$ ✕ **Billy's Chowder House.** Visitors and locals head to this simple restaurant in a salt marsh for the generous lobster rolls, haddock sandwiches, and chowders. ⊠ *216 Mile Rd.,* ☎ *207/646–7558. AE, D, MC, V. Closed mid-Dec.–mid-Jan.*

$–$$ ✕🖾 **Grey Gull Inn.** This century-old Victorian inn has views of the open sea and rocks on which seals like to sun themselves. The unpretentious rooms, most with ocean views, have shared or private baths. The restaurant ($$–$$$) serves excellent seafood dishes such as softshell crabs almandine and regional fare like Yankee pot roast or chicken breast rolled in walnuts. ⊠ *475 Webhannet Dr., at Moody Point,* ☎ *207/646–7501,* FAX *207/646–0938,* WEB *www.thegreygullinn.com. 5 rooms, 4 with bath. Restaurant. AE, D, MC, V. CP, MAP.*

$$ 🖾 **Haven by the Sea.** One block from the beach, this 1920s church was renovated in 1998 and now comforts guests with spacious rooms, some with marsh views, and four common areas, one with a fireplace. ⊠ *59 Church St., 04090,* ☎ *207/646–4194,* FAX *207/646–6883,* WEB *www.havenbythesea.com. 6 rooms, 2 suites, 1 apt.. AE, MC, V. BP.*

Outdoor Activities and Sports

Kayaking is popular along the coast, and **World Within Sea Kayaking** (☎ 207/646–0455) offers guided tours with lessons.

Shopping

Douglas N. Harding Rare Books (⊠ 2152 Post Rd. [U.S. 1], ☎ 207/646–8785) has more than 100,000 old books, maps, and prints. The **Lighthouse Depot** (⊠ U.S. 1, ☎ 207/646–0608) calls itself the world's largest lighthouse gift store. **R. Jorgensen** (⊠ 502 Post Rd. [U.S. 1], ☎ 207/646–9444) stocks 18th- and 19th-century formal and country antiques from the British Isles, Europe, and the United States.

Kennebunk

❺ *5 mi north of Wells, 29 mi southwest of Portland.*

Handsome white clapboard homes with shutters give Kennebunk, a shipbuilding center in the first half of the 19th century, a quintessential New England look. The historic town is a fine place for a stroll.

The cornerstone of the **Brick Store Museum,** a block-long preservation of early 19th-century commercial buildings, is **William Lord's Brick Store.** Built as a dry-goods store in 1825 in the Federal style, the building has an open-work balustrade across the roof line, granite lintels over the windows, and paired chimneys. Walking tours of Kennebunk's National Historic Register District depart from the museum on Friday at 1 and Wednesday at 10 from June to October. ⊠ *117 Main St.,* ☎ *207/985–4802.* ⊡ *$5.* ☉ *Tues.–Sat. 10–4:30, Wed. 10–8.*

The **Taylor-Barry House** house, owned by the Brick Store Museum, is an early 19th-century sea captain's home that's open for tours. ⊠ *24 Summer St.,* ☎ *207/985–4802.* ⊡ *$4.* ☉ *July–Oct., Tues.–Fri. 1–4:30.*

The **Wedding Cake House** (⊠ 104 Summer St./Rte. 35) has long been a local landmark. The legend behind this confection in fancy wood fretwork is that its builder, a sea captain, was forced to set sail in the middle of his wedding; the house was his bride's consolation for the lack of wedding cake. The home, built in 1826, is not open to the public.

Lodging

$ 🏨 **St. Anthony's Franciscan Monastery Guest House.** Individuals and families in search of a quiet, contemplative retreat may want to choose one of the unadorned, motel-style rooms in a former dormitory on the grounds of a riverside monastery. The guest house is private yet within walking distance of Dock Square and the beach. The landscaped grounds, open to the public, have trails and shrines. The monks live in a Tudor mansion on the property, where Mass is said daily. This place is not recommended for those uncomfortable with Christian symbolism, although no religious participation is required. ⊠ *28 Beach Ave., 04043,* ☎ *207/967–2011. 60 rooms. Saltwater pool. No credit cards. Closed Sept. 10–June 10.*

Outdoor Activities and Sports
Kennebunk Beach has three parts: Gooch's Beach, Mother's Beach, and Kennebunk Beach. Beach Road, with its cottages and old Victorian boardinghouses, runs right behind them. Gooch's and Kennebunk attract teenagers; Mother's Beach, which has a small playground and tidal puddles for splashing, is popular with families. For parking permits (a fee is charged in summer), go to the **Kennebunk Town Office** (⊠ 1 Summer St., ☎ 207/985–2102).

Shopping
Tom's of Maine Natural Living Store (⊠ U.S. 1, ☎ 207/985–3874) sells all-natural personal-care products. **Marlow's Artisans Gallery** (⊠ 39 Main St., ☎ 207/985–2931) carries a large and eclectic collection of crafts.

Kennebunkport

❻ *5 mi east of Kennebunk, 10 mi northeast of Ogunquit.*

When George Bush was president, Kennebunkport was his summer White House. But long before Bush came into the public eye, visitors were coming to Kennebunkport to soak up the salt air, seafood, and sunshine. This is a picture-perfect town with manicured lawns, elaborate flower beds, freshly painted homes, and a small-town wholesomeness. People flock to Kennebunkport mostly in summer; some come in early December when the **Christmas Prelude** is celebrated on two weekends. Santa arrives by fishing boat and the Christmas trees are lighted as carolers stroll the sidewalks.

Route 35 merges with Route 9 in Kennebunk and takes you right into Kennebunkport's **Dock Square,** the busy town center. Boutiques, T-shirt shops, art galleries, crafts stores, and restaurants encircle the square and spread out along side streets and alleys. Although many businesses close in winter, the best bargains often are had in December. Walk onto the drawbridge to admire the tidal Kennebunk River.

The **Nott House,** known also as White Columns, is an imposing Greek Revival mansion with Doric columns that rise the height of the house. The 1853 house is furnished with the belongings of four generations of the Perkins-Nott family. It is a gathering place for village walking tours; call for schedule. ⊠ *8 Maine St.,* ☎ *207/967–2751.* ⌑ *$5.* ☉ *Mid-June–mid-Oct., Tues.–Fri. 1–4, Sat. 10–1.*

Ocean Avenue follows the Kennebunk River from Dock Square to the sea and winds around the peninsula of **Cape Arundel.** Parson's Way, a small and tranquil stretch of rocky shoreline, is open to all. As you round Cape Arundel, look to the right for the entrance to George Bush's summer home at Walker's Point.

★ ☾ The **Seashore Trolley Museum** displays streetcars built from 1872 to 1972 and includes trolleys from major metropolitan areas and world capitals—Boston to Budapest, New York to Nagasaki, and San Francisco to Sydney—all beautifully restored. Best of all, you can take a trolley ride for nearly 4 mi over the tracks of the former Atlantic Shoreline trolley line, with a stop along the way at the museum restoration shop, where trolleys are transformed from junk into gems. Both guided and self-guided tours are available. ⊠ *195 Log Cabin Rd.,* ☎ *207/967–2800,* ⊞ *www.trolleymuseum.org.* ⌑ *$7.* ☉ *Late May–mid-Oct., daily 10–4:30; reduced hrs in spring and fall.*

Intown Trolley (☎ 207/967–3686) offers 45-minute sightseeing tours.

Dining and Lodging

$$$–$$$$ ✕ **Seascapes.** The emphasis is on seafood at this pretty harborfront restaurant where the view takes center stage. You can begin with lobster spring rolls, then move on to roasted lobster or try the rack of lamb. Accompany it all with a selection from the excellent wine list. ⊠ *77 Pier Rd., Cape Porpoise Harbor, Cape Porpoise,* ☎ *207/967–8500. AE, D, DC, MC, V. Closed late Oct.–Apr.*

$$$–$$$$ ✕ **Windows on the Water.** Big windows frame Dock Square and the working harbor of Kennebunkport—almost every window in the airy dining room shares the view. Lobster ravioli and rack of lamb are two noteworthy entrées. ⊠ *12 Chase Hill Rd.,* ☎ *207/967–3313. Reservations essential. AE, D, DC, MC, V.*

$–$$$ ✕ **Cape Pier Chowder House.** You can watch the surf crash over distant ledges near the Goat Island lighthouse and see lobster boats returning with their day's catch at this oceanfront lobster shack. Seating is on the deck or inside. The fare includes lobster, clams, and fried foods. ⊠ *15 Pier Rd., Cape Porpoise,* ☎ *207/967–0123 or 800/967–4268. MC, V. Closed early Nov.–mid-Apr.*

$$$$ ✕⌂ **Cape Arundel Inn.** This shingle-style inn commands a magnificent ocean view that takes in the Bush estate at Walker's Point. The spacious rooms are furnished with country-style furniture and antiques, and most have sitting areas with ocean views. You can relax on the front porch or in front of the living-room fireplace. In the candlelit dining room ($$$–$$$$), open to the public for dinner, every table has a view of the surf. The menu changes seasonally. ⊠ *208 Ocean Ave., 04046,* ☎ *207/967–2125,* ⊠ *207/967–1199,* ⊞ *www.capearundelinn.com. 14 rooms. Restaurant, kitchenettes. AE, D, MC, V. Closed Jan. 15–Mar. 15.*

$$$$ ✕⌨ **White Barn Inn.** For a romantic overnight stay or a superb meal,
★ you need look no further than the exclusive White Barn Inn, known
for its attentive, pampering service. The meticulously appointed rooms
have luxurious baths and are decorated with a blend of hand-painted
pieces and period furniture; some rooms have fireplaces and whirlpool
baths. Regional New England fare is served at the rustic but elegant
dining room ($$$$; jacket required), one of the region's best. The fixed-
price menu, which changes weekly, might list steamed Maine lobster
nestled on fresh fettuccine with carrots, ginger, and snow peas. ⊠ *Box
560C, 37 Beach Ave., 04046,* ☎ *207/967–2321,* ⅨⅩ *207/967–1100,*
ⱳ₤₧ *www.whitebarninn.com. 16 rooms, 9 suites. Restaurant, pool, bicycles. AE, MC, V. CP.*

$$$$ ⌨ **The Seaside.** This handsome seaside property has been in the hands
of the Severance family since 1667. The modern motel units, all with
cable TVs and sliding-glass doors that open onto private decks or patios (half with ocean views), are appropriate for families; so are the
cottages with one to four bedrooms. ⊠ *80 Beach Ave., 04046,* ☎ *207/
967–4461,* ⅨⅩ *207/967–1135,* ⱳ₤₧ *www.kennebunkbeach.com. 22
rooms, 10 cottages. No-smoking rooms, beach, playground, laundry
service. AE, MC, V. Cottages closed Nov.–Apr. CP.*

$$$–$$$$ ⌨ **Captain Lord Mansion.** Of all the mansions in Kennebunkport's his-
toric district that have been converted to inns, the 1812 Captain Lord
Mansion is the most stately and sumptuously appointed. The three-
story Federal-style inn is topped with a widow's walk that has views
of the town and harbor, just three blocks away. Distinctive architec-
ture, including a suspended elliptical staircase and gas fireplaces in 15
rooms, and near–museum quality accoutrements make for a formal but
not stuffy atmosphere. Five rooms have whirlpool tubs. The extrava-
gant suite has two fireplaces, a double whirlpool, a hydro-massage body
spa, a TV/VCR and stereo system, and a king-size canopy bed. ⊠ *Box
800, Pleasant and Green Sts., 04046,* ☎ *207/967–3141,* ⅨⅩ *207/967–
3172,* ⱳ₤₧ *www.captainlord.com. 15 rooms, 1 suite. D, MC, V. BP.*

$$$ ⌨ **Bufflehead Cove.** On the Kennebunk River at the end of a winding
dirt road, this gray-shingle B&B amid quiet country fields and apple
trees is only five minutes from Dock Square. Rooms in the main house
have white wicker and flowers hand-painted on the walls. The Hideaway Suite, with a two-sided gas fireplace, king-size bed, and large whirlpool tub, overlooks the river. The Garden Studio has a fireplace and
offers the most privacy. ⊠ *Box 499, 18 Bufflehead Cove Rd., 04046,*
☎ ⅨⅩ *207/967–3879,* ⱳ₤₧ *www.buffleheadcove.com. 2 rooms, 3 suites,
1 cottage. Dock, boating. D, MC, V. BP.*

Outdoor Activities and Sports

BEACHES

Three-mi-long **Goose Rocks,** a few minutes' drive north of town off
Route 9, is a favorite of families with small children. You can pick up
a **parking permit** ($5 a day, $15 a week) at the Chamber of Commerce
(⊠ 17 Western Ave., Lower Village, ☎ 207/967–0857).

BIKING

Cape-Able Bike Shop (⊠ Townhouse Corners, ☎ 207/967–4382) rents
bicycles.

BOATING AND FISHING

Deep Water II (⊠ Kennebunkport Marina, ☎ 207/967–5595) offers
scenic cruises. **First Chance** (⊠ Arundel Wharf, Lower Village, ☎ 207/
967–5507 or 800/967–2628) gives whale-watching cruises and guarantees sightings in season. **Maritime Productions** (⊠ Kennebunkport
Marina, ☎ 207/641–2313) takes passengers on sunset theater cruises
that feature tales of intrigue and horror performed by a costumed actor.

Old Orchard Beach

❼ *15 mi north of Kennebunkport, 18 mi south of Portland.*

Old Orchard Beach, a few mi north of Biddeford on Route 9, is a 7-mi strip of sand beach with an amusement park that resembles a small Coney Island. Despite the summertime crowds and fried-food odors, the atmosphere can be captivating. During the 1940s and '50s, in the heyday of the Big Band era, the pier had a dance hall where stars of the era performed. Fire claimed the end of the pier, but booths with games and candy concessions still line both sides. Plans are underway to extend the pier and offer dinner/gaming cruises. In summer the town sponsors fireworks (usually on Thursday night). The many places to stay run the gamut from cheap motels to cottage colonies to full-service seasonal hotels. You won't find free parking anywhere in town, but there are ample lots. Amtrak has a seasonal stop here.

A world away in atmosphere from the beach scene is **Ocean Park** (☎ 207/934–9068), on the southwestern edge of town. This vacation community was founded in 1881 as a summer assembly, following the example of Chautauqua, New York. Today the community still has a wide range of cultural happenings, including movies, concerts, workshops, and religious services. Most are presented in the Temple, which is on the National Register of Historic Places.

Ⓒ   **Palace Playland** (⊠ 1 Old Orchard St., ☎ 207/934–2001), open from Memorial Day to Labor Day, has rides, booths, and a roller coaster
Ⓒ   that drops almost 50 ft. **Funtown/Splashtown** (⊠ U.S. 1, Saco, ☎ 207/284–5139 or 800/878–2900) has more than 30 rides and amusements, including miniature golf, water slides, a wave pool, and Excalibur, a wooden roller coaster.

Dining and Lodging

$$$–$$$$ ✕ **Joseph's by the Sea.** Big windows frame the ocean beyond the dunes at this fine restaurant, which offers outdoor dining in season. Appetizers may include goat cheese terrine and lobster potato pancake; try the Grilled Tuscan swordfish or crabmeat napoleon for your main course. ⊠ *55 W. Grand Ave.,* ☎ *207/934–5044. MC, V.*

$$ 🏠 **Old Orchard Beach Inn.** Dating from 1730, this is Old Orchard Beach's oldest inn. It was saved from demolition in 1997 and was completely renovated. The spacious guest rooms are furnished with antiques, area rugs cover the pine floors, quilts brighten the beds, and lace curtains frame the windows. Many have views over the town to the shimmering Atlantic. ⊠ *6 Portland Ave., 04064,* ☎ *207/934–5834 or 877/700–6624,* 𝖥𝖠𝖷 *207/934–0782,* 𝖶𝖤𝖡 *www.oldorchardbeachinn.com. 17 rooms, 1 suite. Air-conditioning, in-room data ports. AE, D, MC, V. CP.*

Nightlife and the Arts

In season, weekly concerts are held in Town Square every Monday and Tuesday night at 7. Fireworks light the sky Thursdays at 9:30 from late June through Labor Day. Concerts are held most Sunday evenings in Ocean Park.

Outdoor Activities and Sports

Ferry Beach State Park (⊠ Rte. 9, Saco, ☎ 207/283–0067) comprises 117 acres of beach, bike paths, and nature trails. The **Maine Audubon Society** (⊠ Rte. 9, Scarborough, ☎ 207/781–2330; 207/883–5100 from mid-June to Labor Day) operates guided canoe trips and rents canoes in Scarborough Marsh, the largest salt marsh in Maine. Programs at Maine Audubon's Falmouth headquarters (north of Portland) include nature walks and a discovery room for children.

York County Coast A to Z

To research prices, get advice from other travelers, and book travel arrangements, visit www.fodors.com.

AIR TRAVEL
Portland International Jetport is 35 mi northeast of Kennebunk.

CAR TRAVEL
U.S. 1 from Kittery is the shopper's route north; other roads hug the coastline. Interstate 95 is usually faster for travelers headed to towns north of Ogunquit, but be forewarned that the Maine Turnpike/I–95 is in the midst of a widening project that will result in slowdowns and stops until completion in 2004. For information, call 877/682–9433.

The exit numbers can be confusing: as you go north from Portsmouth, Exits 1–3 lead to Kittery and Exit 4 leads to the Yorks. After the toll-booth in York, the Maine Turnpike begins, and the numbers start over again, with Exit 2 for Wells and Ogunquit and Exit 3 (and Route 35) for Kennebunk and Kennebunkport. Route 9 goes from Kennebunkport to Cape Porpoise and Goose Rocks. Parking is tight in Kennebunkport in peak season. Possibilities include the municipal lot next to the Congregational Church ($2 an hour from May to October) and 30 North St. (free year-round).

EMERGENCIES
➤ HOSPITALS AND EMERGENCY SERVICES: **Maine State Police** (✉ Gray, ☎ 207/793–4500 or 800/482–0730). **Kennebunk Walk-in Clinic** (✉ U.S. 1 N, ☎ 207/985–6027). **Southern Maine Medical Center** (✉ Rte. 111, Biddeford, ☎ 207/283–7000; 207/283–7100 emergency room). **York Hospital** (✉ 15 Hospital Dr., ☎ 207/351–2157, 800/283–7234, 207/351–2157, or 800/283–7234; (☎ 207/351–2157, 800/283–7234, 207/351–2157, or 800/283–7234 Tel-A-Nurse).

TOURS
Gone with the Wind schedules guided kayak and windsurfing trips. Van tours of southern Maine are offered by Seacoast Tours. Routes include Portland, Ogunquit, Kittery and York, and Kennebunkport; tours are 1¼–4 hours.
➤ TOUR-OPERATORS: **Gone with the Wind** (✉ Biddeford, ☎ 207/283–8446). **Seacoast Tours** (✉ Perkins Cove, Ogunquit, ☎ 207/646–6326 or 800/328–8687).

TRAIN TRAVEL
Amtrak offers rail service from Boston to Portland, with seasonal stops in Wells and Old Orchard Beach.
➤ TRAIN INFORMATION: **Amtrak** (☎ 800/872–7245, WEB www.amtrak. com).

TRANSPORTATION AROUND YORK COUNTY COAST
Trolleys ($1–$3) serve several areas. A trolley circulates among the Yorks from June to Labor Day. Eight trolleys serve the major tourist areas and beaches of Ogunquit, including four that connect with Wells from mid-May to mid-October. The trolley from Dock Square in Kennebunkport to Kennebunk Beach runs from Memorial Day to Columbus Day.

VISITOR INFORMATION
➤ CONTACTS: **Maine Tourism Association & Visitor Information Center** (✉ U.S. 1 and I–95, Kittery 03904, ☎ 207/439–1319). **Kennebunk-Kennebunkport Chamber of Commerce** (✉ 17 Western Ave., Kennebunk 04043, ☎ 207/967–0857). **Kittery-Eliot Chamber of Commerce** (✉

191 State Rd., Kittery 03904, ☎ 207/439–7574 or 800/639–9645).
Ogunquit Chamber of Commerce (✉ Box 2289, U.S. 1, Ogunquit
03907, ☎ 207/646–2939). **Old Orchard Beach Chamber of Commerce**
(✉ Box 600, 1st St., Old Orchard Beach 04064, ☎ 207/934–2500 or
800/365–9386). **Wells Chamber of Commerce** (✉ Box 356, Wells
04090, ☎ 207/646–2451). The **Yorks Chamber of Commerce** (✉ 571
U.S. 1, York 03903, ☎ 207/363–4422).

PORTLAND TO WALDOBORO

This south–mid-coast area provides an overview of Maine: a little bit
of urban life, a little more coastline, and a nice dollop of history and
architecture. Maine's largest city, Portland, holds some pleasant sur-
prises, including the Old Port, among the finest urban renovation pro-
jects on the East Coast. Freeport, north of Portland, was made famous
by its L. L. Bean store, whose success led to the opening of scores of
other clothing stores and outlets. Brunswick is best known for Bowdoin College. Bath has been a shipbuilding center since 1607; the
Maine Maritime Museum preserves its history. Wiscasset contains
many antiques shops and galleries.

The Boothbays—the coastal areas of Boothbay Harbor, East Boothbay, Linekin Neck, Southport Island, and the inland town of Boothbay—attract hordes of vacationing families and flotillas of pleasure craft.
The Pemaquid peninsula juts into the Atlantic south of Damariscotta
and just east of the Boothbays. Near Pemaquid Beach you can view
the objects unearthed at the Colonial Pemaquid Restoration.

Portland

*105 mi northeast of Boston, MA, 320 mi northeast of New York City,
215 mi southwest of St. Stephen, New Brunswick.*

Portland's role as a cultural and economic center for the region has
given the gentrifying city of 65,000 a variety of attractions that make
it well worth a day or two of exploration. Its restored Old Port bal-
ances modern commercial enterprise and salty waterfront character in
an area bustling with restaurants, shops, and galleries. Water tours of
the harbor and excursions to islands of Casco Bay depart from the piers
of Commercial Street. Downtown Portland, in a funk for years, is now
a burgeoning arts district connected to the Old Port by a revitalized
Congress Street, where L. L. Bean operates a factory store.

Portland's first home was built on the peninsula now known as Munjoy
Hill in 1632. The British burned the city in 1775, when residents re-
fused to surrender arms, but it was rebuilt and became a major trading center. Much of Portland was destroyed on July 4 in the Great Fire
of 1866, when a boy threw a celebration firecracker into a pile of wood
shavings; 1,500 buildings burned to the ground. Poet Henry Wadsworth
Longfellow said at the time that his city reminded him of the ruins of
Pompeii. The Great Fire started not far from where people now wander the streets of the Old Port.

Congress Street runs the length of the peninsular city from alongside
the Western Promenade in the southwest to the Eastern Promenade on
Munjoy Hill in the northeast, passing through the small downtown area.
A few blocks southeast of downtown, the bustling Old Port sprawls
along the waterfront. Below Munjoy Hill is India Street, where the Great
Fire of 1866 started.

❽ The **Portland Observatory** on Munjoy Hill reopened in 2000 after a
major restoration. Built in 1807 by Capt. Lemuel Moody, a retired sea

Portland

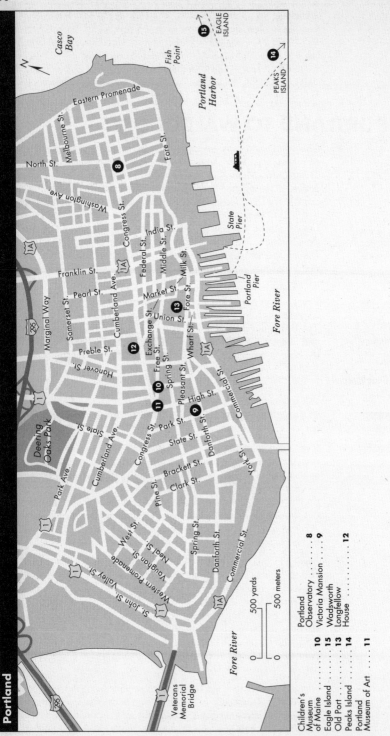

Casco Bay

N

Eastern Promenade

Fish Point

Portland Harbor

EAGLE ISLAND
15

14
PEAKS ISLAND

Melbourne St.

North St.

Washington Ave.

8

Fore St.

State Pier

Congress St.

India St.

Federal St.

Middle St.

Milk St.

Portland Pier

Franklin St.

Cumberland Ave.

Pearl St.

Market St.

13

Fore St.

Fore River

Somerset St.

Union St.

Wharf St.

Marginal Way

Preble St.

Exchange St.

12

1A

Hanover St.

Free St.

Spring St.

10

High St.

Deering Oaks Park

State Ave.

11

9

Congress St.

Park St.

Pleasant St.

Commercial St.

Cumberland Ave.

State St.

Danforth St.

Park Ave.

Brackett St.

Clark St.

York St.

Pine St.

Spring St.

Danforth St.

West St.

Vaughan St.

Western Promenade

Neal St.

Commercial St.

St. John St.

Valley St.

1A

295

Fore River

Veterans Memorial Bridge

1

0   500 yards

0   500 meters

Children's
Museum
of Maine **10**
Eagle Island **15**
Old Port **13**
Peaks Island **14**
Portland
Museum of Art **11**

Portland
Observatory **8**
Victoria Mansion **9**
Wadsworth
Longfellow
House **12**

HOW TO USE THIS GUIDE

Great trips begin with great planning, and this guide makes planning easy. It's packed with everything you need—insider advice on hotels and restaurants, cool tools, practical tips, essential maps, and much more.

COOL TOOLS

Fodor's Choice Top picks are marked throughout with a star.

Great Itineraries These tours, planned by Fodor's experts, give you the skinny on what you can see and do in the time you have.

Smart Travel Tips A to Z This special section is packed with important contacts and advice on everything from how to get around to what to pack.

Good Walks You won't miss a thing if you follow the numbered bullets on our maps.

Need a Break? Looking for a quick bite to eat or a spot to rest? These sure bets are along the way.

Off the Beaten Path Some lesser-known sights are worth a detour. We've marked those you should make time for.

POST-IT® FLAGS

Dog-ear no more!

"Post-it" is a registered trademark of 3M.

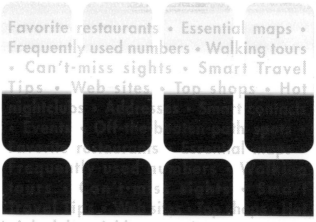

ICONS AND SYMBOLS

Watch for these symbols throughout:

★	Our special recommendations
✕	Restaurant
⊡	Lodging establishment
✕⊡	Lodging establishment whose restaurant warrants a special trip
↻	Good for kids
☞	Sends you to another section of the guide for more information
✉	Address
☎	Telephone number
FAX	Fax number
WEB	Web site
☞	Admission price
☉	Opening hours
$-$$$$	Lodging and dining price categories, keyed to strategically sited price charts. Check the index for locations.
①❶	Numbers in white and black circles on the maps, in the margins, and within tours correspond to one another.

ON THE WEB

Continue your planning with these useful tools found at **www.fodors.com**, the Web's best source for travel information.

"Rich with resources." —*New York Times*

"Navigation is a cinch." —*Forbes* "Best of the Web" list

"Put together by people bursting with know-how."
—*Sunday Times* (London)

Create a Miniguide Pinpoint hotels, restaurants, and attractions that have what you want at the price you want to pay.

Rants and Raves Find out what readers say about Fodor's picks—or write your own reviews of hotels and restaurants you've just visited.

Travel Talk Post your questions and get answers from fellow travelers, or share your own experiences.

On-Line Booking Find the best prices on airline tickets, rental cars, cruises, or vacations, and book them on the spot.

About our Books Learn about other Fodor's guides to your destination and many others.

Expert Advice and Trip Ideas From what to tip to how to take great photos, from the national parks to Nepal, Fodors.com has suggestions that'll make your trip a breeze. Log on and get informed and inspired.

Smart Resources Check the weather in your destination or convert your currency. Learn the local language or link to the latest event listings. Or consult hundreds of detailed maps—all in one place.

captain, it is the last remaining signal tower in the country and is held in place by 122 tons of ballast. After visiting the small museum at the base, you can climb to the Orb deck and take in views of Portland, the islands, and inland to the White Mountains. ⊠ *138 Congress St.,* ☎ *207/774–5561.* ⊡ *$3.* ☉ *Memorial Day–Columbus Day, Mon.–Sat. 10–6 and Sun. 1–5.*

★ ❾ The Italianate-style Morse-Libby Mansion, known as **Victoria Mansion,** was built between 1858 and 1860 and is widely regarded as the most sumptuously ornamented dwelling of its period remaining in the country. Architect Henry Austin designed the house for hotelier Ruggles Morse and his wife, Olive; the interior design—everything from the plasterwork to the furniture (much of it original)—is the only surviving commission of noted New York designer Gustave Herter. The elegant brownstone exterior of this National Historic Landmark is understated compared to the interior, which has colorful frescoed walls and ceilings, ornate marble mantelpieces, gilded gas chandeliers, stained-glass windows, and a freestanding mahogany staircase; guided tours cover all the details. ⊠ *109 Danforth St.,* ☎ *207/772–4841,* WEB *www. portlandarts.com/victoriamansion.* ⊡ *$7.* ☉ *May–Oct., Tues.–Sat. 10–4, Sun. 1–5; special Christmas hours.*

♺ ❿ Touching is okay at the relatively small but fun **Children's Museum of Maine,** where kids can pretend they are fishing for lobster or are shopkeepers or computer experts. The majority of the museum's exhibits, many of which have a Maine theme, are best for children 10 and younger. Camera Obscura, an exhibit about optics that provides fascinating panoramic views of the city, charges a separate admission fee ($3); call for times. ⊠ *142 Free St.,* ☎ *207/828–1234.* ⊡ *$5, $6 for combination ticket with Camera Obscura.* ☉ *Memorial Day–Labor Day and school vacations, Mon.–Sat. 10–5, Sun. noon–5; early Sept.– mid-June, Wed.–Sat. 10–5, Sun. noon–5.*

★ ⓫ The **Portland Museum of Art,** Maine's largest public art institution, has a number of strong collections, including fine seascapes and landscapes by Winslow Homer, John Marin, Andrew Wyeth, Edward Hopper, Marsden Hartley, and other painters. Homer's *Pulling the Dory* and *Weatherbeaten,* two quintessential Maine-coast images, are here; the museum owns 17 paintings by Homer. The Joan Whitney Payson Collection of Impressionist and Postimpressionist art includes works by Monet, Picasso, and Renoir. Harry N. Cobb, an associate of I. M. Pei, designed the strikingly modern Charles Shipman Payson building. The renovated McLellan-Sweat House is expected to open in fall 2002 with additional galleries housing the museum's 19th-century collection and decorative art as well as interactive educational stations. ⊠ *7 Congress Sq.,* ☎ *207/775–6148; 800/639–4067 recorded information,* WEB *www.portlandmuseum.org.* ⊡ *$6; free Fri. evenings 5–9.* ☉ *Columbus Day–Memorial Day, Tues.–Wed. and weekends 10–5, Thurs.–Fri. 10–9; Memorial Day–Columbus Day, Mon.–Wed. and weekends 10– 5, Thurs.–Fri. 10–9; tours daily at 2.*

⓬ The **Wadsworth Longfellow House,** the boyhood home of the poet and the first brick house in Portland, is particularly interesting because most of the furnishings are original to the house. The late-Colonial-style structure, built in 1785, sits back from the street and has a small portico over its entrance and four chimneys surmounting the hip roof. The house is part of the Center for Maine History, which includes the adjacent Maine History Gallery and a research library; the gift shop has a good selection of books about Maine. ⊠ *489 Congress St.,* ☎ *207/ 879–0427 or 207/774–1822,* WEB *www.mainehistory.org.* ⊡ *$6;*

Center $4. ⊙ *House and Maine History Gallery, June–Oct., daily 10–5; Library Tues.–Sat., 10–3.*

★ ⑬ The **Old Port** bridges the gap between the city's 19th-century commercial activities and those of today. Like the Customs House, the brick buildings and warehouses of the Old Port were built following the Great Fire of 1866 and were intended to last for ages. When the city's economy slumped in the mid-20th century, however, the Old Port declined and seemed slated for demolition. Then artists and craftspeople began opening shops in the late 1960s, and restaurants, boutiques, and bookstores followed. Allow a couple of hours to wander at leisure on Market, Exchange, Middle, and Fore streets. You can park your car at the city garage on Fore Street (between Exchange and Union streets) or opposite the U.S. Customs House at the corner of Fore and Pearl streets.

OFF THE
BEATEN PATH
CAPE ELIZABETH – This upscale Portland suburb juts out into the Atlantic. Take Route 77 south and east from Portland and follow signs to Two Lights State Park, home to Two Lights, one of the cape's three lighthouses. You can wander through old World War II bunkers and picnic on the rocky coast. Stay on Two Lights Road to the end, where you'll find another lighthouse, privately owned, and the Lobster Shack, a seafood-in-the-rough restaurant. Return to the center of Cape Elizabeth and turn right on Shore Road, which winds along the coast to Portland.

Historic **Portland Head Light,** familiar to many from photographs and Edward Hopper's painting, was commissioned by George Washington in 1791. Besides a harbor view, the park has walking paths and picnic facilities. The keeper's house is now the Museum at Portland Head Light. The lighthouse is about 2 mi from town center in Fort Williams Park. *Museum:* ⊠ *1000 Shore Rd.,* ☎ *207/799–2661.* ⊡ *$2. ⊙ June–Oct., daily 10–4.*

Dining and Lodging

$$$–$$$$ ✕ **Gabriel's.** Hand-painted wall murals let you view the sea as you savor such appetizers as confit of calamari and entrées such as whole roasted rainbow trout with sweet corn and fresh herbs. The menu changes seasonally. An upstairs dining room is quieter and also has a copper-topped bar for casual dining. ⊠ *47 Middle St.,* ☎ *207/775–1510. AE, D, DC, MC, V. Closed Sun. and Mon. No lunch.*

$$–$$$ ✕ **Fore Street.** Two of Maine's best chefs, Sam Hayward and Dana Street,
★ opened this restaurant in a renovated, cavernous warehouse on the edge of the Old Port. Every table in the two-level main dining room has a view of the enormous brick oven and hearth and the open kitchen, where creative entrées such as roasted Maine lobster, applewood-grilled Atlantic swordfish loin, and wood-oven–braised cassoulet are prepared. ⊠ *288 Fore St.,* ☎ *207/775–2717. AE, MC, V. No lunch.*

$$–$$$ ✕ **Street and Co.** Fish and seafood are the specialties here, and you won't
★ find any better or fresher. You enter through the kitchen, with all its wonderful aromas, and dine, amid dried herbs and shelves of staples, at one of a dozen copper-topped tables (so your waiter can place a skillet of steaming seafood directly in front of you). There's a beer and wine bar in one of the dining rooms. Some good choices are lobster diavolo for two, scallops in Pernod and cream, and sole Française. A vegetarian dish is the only alternative to seafood. ⊠ *33 Wharf St.,* ☎ *207/775–0887. AE, MC, V. No lunch.*

$$ ✕ **Aubergine.** This casual bistro and wine bar has staked out a prime downtown location, across the street from L. L. Bean and down the street from the Portland Museum of Art. The French-inspired menu changes daily but might list appetizers such as Swiss onion soup with fresh tarragon or duck liver pâté and entrées such as spiced duck

breast with fennel sauce or crispy salmon with spinach and Pernod. Wines by the glass are chosen to complement the dishes. ⌧ *555 Congress St.,* ☎ *207/874–0680. MC, V. Closed Sun.–Mon. No lunch.*

$–$$ ✕ **Portland Public Market.** Nibble your way through this handsome, airy market where 20 locally owned businesses sell fresh foods, organic produce, and imported specialty items, including fresh baked goods, soups, smoked seafood, rotisserie chicken, aged cheeses, and German meats. In 2000, celebrity chef Matthew Kenney opened **The Commissary** (☎ 207/228–2057. MC, V.), which serves entrées such as wood-roasted free-range chicken stuffed with foie gras and pears, or poached Maine lobster with citrus and local blue potatoes. The market is open Monday–Saturday 9–7, Sunday 10–5; some vendors open at 7. ⌧ *25 Preble St.,* ☎ *207/228–2000.*

$$$$ ✕⌂ **Inn by the Sea.** This all-suites inn welcomes families and dogs. All the spacious suites include kitchens and overlook the Atlantic, and it's just a short walk down a private boardwalk to sandy Crescent Beach, a popular family spot. The Audubon dining room($$–$$$), open to nonguests, serves fine seafood and regional dishes. Dogs are welcomed with a room-service pet menu, evening turn-down treats, and oversized beach towels. The cottage-style architecture throughout is typical New England. ⌧ *40 Bowery Beach Rd., Cape Elizabeth 04107 (7 mi south of Portland),* ☎ *207/799–3134 or 800/888–4287,* ⻫ *207/799–4779,* ⻬ *www.innbythesea.com. 25 suites, 18 cottage condominiums. Restaurant, pool, tennis court, croquet, bicycles. AE, D, MC, V.*

$$$$ ⌂ **Black Point Inn.** Toward the tip of the peninsula that juts into the ocean at Prouts Neck stands this stylish shingled, tastefully updated old-time resort with spectacular views up and down the Maine coast. Most rooms capture an old-fashioned seaside ambiance and are decorated with floral patterns and gauzy white curtains. The extensive grounds contain beaches, trails, and sports facilities; you can also use the tennis courts and golf course of the country club a few minutes' walk away. The Cliff Walk runs along the Atlantic headlands that Winslow Homer (his studio is nearby) often painted. The inn is 12 mi south of Portland and about 10 mi north of Old Orchard Beach by road. ⌧ *510 Black Point Rd., Scarborough 04074,* ☎ *207/883–4126 or 800/258–2500,* ⻫ *207/883–9976,* ⻬ *www.blackpointinn.com. 68 rooms, 12 suites. Restaurant, bar, 1 indoor and 1 outdoor pool, hot tub, golf privileges, croquet, volleyball, boating, bicycles. AE, D, MC, V. BP, MAP.*

$$$$ ⌂ **Portland Regency Hotel.** The only major hotel in the center of the Old Port, the brick Regency building was Portland's armory in the late 19th century. Rooms have four-poster beds, tall standing mirrors, floral curtains, and love seats. You can walk to shops, restaurants, and museums from the hotel. ⌧ *20 Milk St., 04101,* ☎ *207/774–4200 or 800/727–3436,* ⻫ *207/775–2150,* ⻬ *www.theregency.com. 87 rooms, 8 suites. Restaurant, massage, sauna, steam room, health club, nightclub, meeting room. AE, D, DC, MC, V.*

$$$–$$$$ ⌂ **Inn on Carleton.** After a day of exploring Portland's museums and shops, you'll find a quiet retreat at this elegant brick town house on the city's Western Promenade. Built in 1869, it is furnished throughout with period antiques as well as artwork by contemporary Maine artists. The entryway features a restored trompe l'oeil painting by Charles Schumacher, and more of his work has been uncovered in the back dining room. ⌧ *46 Carleton St., 04102,* ☎ *207/775–1910 or 800/ 639–1779,* ⻫ *207/761–0956,* ⻬ *www.innoncarleton.com. 6 rooms. D, MC, V. BP.*

$$$–$$$$ ⌂ **Pomegranate Inn.** The classic architecture of this handsome inn in the architecturally rich Western Promenade area gives no hint of the surprises within. Vivid hand-painted walls, floors, and woodwork combine with contemporary artwork to create an ambience that is both stimulating and comforting. Rooms are individually decorated, but all have telephones and TVs, and five have fireplaces. Room 8, in the carriage house, has a private garden terrace. ✉ *49 Neal St., 04102,* ☎ *207/772–1006 or 800/356–0408,* FAX *207/773–4426,* WEB *www.pomegranateinn.com. 7 rooms, 1 suite. In-room data ports. MC, V. BP.*

$$–$$$ 🛏 **Inn at St. John.** This gem of a small hotel was built by railroad tycoon John Deering in 1897. Rooms are decorated with a Victorian flair, with a mix of traditional and antique furnishings, and no two are alike. It's an uphill walk to downtown attractions from here. ✉ *939 Congress St., 04102,* ☎ *207/773–6481 or 800/636–9127,* FAX *207/756–7629,* WEB *www.innatstjohn.com. 37 rooms. In-room data ports. AE, D, DC, MC, V. CP.*

Nightlife and the Arts

NIGHTLIFE

Asylum (✉ 121 Center St., ☎ 207/772–8274) has live entertainment, dancing, and eight large screens for sports viewing. **Brian Boru** (✉ 57 Center St., ☎ 207/780–1506) is an Irish pub with occasional entertainment and an outside deck. **Gritty McDuff's—Portland's Original Brew Pub** (✉ 396 Fore St., ☎ 207/772–2739) brews fine ales and serves British pub fare and seafood dishes. **Stone Coast Brewery** (✉ 14 York St., ☎ 207/773–2337) is a brew pub with billiards and occasional live entertainment. For blues, head to the **Big Easy** (✉ 55 Market St., ☎ 207/871–8817).

THE ARTS

Portland Performing Arts Center (✉ 25A Forest Ave., ☎ 207/761–0591) presents music, dance, and theater performances. **Cumberland County Civic Center** (✉ 1 Civic Center Sq., ☎ 207/775–3458) hosts concerts, sporting events, and family shows. **Portland City Hall's Merrill Auditorium** (✉ 20 Myrtle St., ☎ 207/874–8200) is home to the Portland Symphony Orchestra and Portland Concert Association and the site of numerous theatrical and musical events. On most Tuesdays from mid-June to September, organ recitals ($5 donation) are given on the auditorium's huge 1912 Kotzschmar Memorial Organ. **Mad Horse Theatre Company** (✉ 92 Oak St., ☎ 207/797–3338) performs classic, contemporary, and original works. **Portland Stage Company** (✉ 25A Forest Ave., ☎ 207/774–0465) mounts productions year-round at the Portland Performing Arts Center.

Outdoor Activities and Sports

BALLOON RIDES

Balloon Rides (✉ 17 Freeman St., ☎ 207/772–4730) operates scenic flights over southern Maine.

BASEBALL

The Class AA **Portland Sea Dogs** (☎ 207/879–9500), a farm team of the Florida Marlins, play at Hadlock Field (✉ 271 Park Ave.). Tickets cost $4–$6.

BEACHES

Crescent Beach State Park (✉ Rte. 77, Cape Elizabeth, ☎ 207/767–3625), about 8 mi south of Portland, has a sand beach, picnic tables, a seasonal snack bar, and a bathhouse. Popular with families with young children, it charges a nominal fee for admittance.

BOAT TRIPS

For tours of the harbor, Casco Bay, and the scenic nearby islands, try **Bay View Cruises** (✉ Fisherman's Wharf, ☎ 207/761–0496). **Casco Bay Lines,** (✉ Maine State Pier, ☎ 207/774–7871) provides narrated cruises and transportation to Casco Bay Islands. **Eagle Island Tours** (✉ Long Wharf, ☎ 207/774–6498) offers daily cruises to Eagle Island and seal-watching cruises. **Old Port Mariner Fleet** (✉ Long Wharf, ☎ 207/775–0727, 207/642–3270, or 800/437–3270) has scenic cruises and whale-watching and fishing trips. **Palawan Sailing** (✉ Old Port, ☎ 207/774–2163) offers cruises on a catamaran.

HOCKEY

The **Portland Pirates,** the farm team of the Washington Capitals, play home games at the Cumberland County Civic Center (✉ 85 Free St., ☎ 207/828–4665). Tickets cost $10–$14.

Shopping

For a city its size, Portland has a satisfying variety of locally owned stores and art and crafts galleries, particularly those in or near the Old Port; trendy Exchange Street is great for browsing.

ART AND ANTIQUES

Abacus (✉ 44 Exchange St., ☎ 207/772–4880), an appealing crafts gallery, has unusual gift items in glass, wood, and textiles, plus fine modern jewelry. **Greenhut Galleries** (✉ 146 Middle St., ☎ 207/772–2693) shows contemporary art and sculpture by Maine artists. **F. O. Bailey Antiquarians** (✉ 141 Middle St., ☎ 207/774–1479), Portland's largest retail showroom, carries antique and reproduction furniture and jewelry, paintings, rugs, and china. The **Pine Tree Shop & Bayview Gallery** (✉ 75 Market St., ☎ 207/773–3007 or 800/244–3007) has original art and prints by prominent Maine painters. Representing 100 American artists, the spacious **Stein Gallery** (✉ 195 Middle St., ☎ 207/772–9072) showcases decorative and sculptural contemporary glass.

BOOKS

Carlson and Turner (✉ 241 Congress St., ☎ 207/773–4200) is an antiquarian book dealer with an estimated 70,000 titles. Besides new and used books, many of regional interest, **Emerson Books, Maps, and Prints** (✉ 18 Exchange St., ☎ 207/874–2665) stocks antique maps, botanical and bird prints, and old posters and magazine covers.

CLOTHING

Family-owned **Casco Bay Wool Works** (✉ 10 Moulton St., ☎ 207/879–9665) sells beautiful handcrafted wool capes and shawls, blankets, and scarves.

FURNITURE

Made locally, the handsome cherry-wood pieces at **Green Design Furniture** (✉ 267 Commercial St., ☎ 207/775–4234; 800/853–4234 orders) have a classic feel—somewhat Asian, somewhat Mission; a unique system of joinery enables easy assembly after shipping.

MALL

Maine Mall (✉ 364 Maine Mall Rd., ☎ 207/774–0303), 5 mi south of Portland, has 145 stores, including Sears, Filene's, JCPenney, and Macy's.

Casco Bay Islands

The islands of Casco Bay are also known as the Calendar Islands because an early explorer mistakenly thought there was one for each day of the year (in reality there are only 140). The brightly painted ferries of Casco Bay Lines are the islands' lifeline. There is frequent service to the most-populated ones, including Peaks, Long, Little Diamond, and Great Diamond. A ride on the bay is a great way to experience the Maine coast.

⓮ **Peaks Island,** nearest to Portland, is the most developed of the Calendar Islands, but you can still commune with the wind and the sea, explore an old fort, and ramble along the alternately rocky and sandy shore. The trip to the island by boat is particularly enjoyable at or near sunset. Order a lobster sandwich or cold beer on the outdoor deck of **Jones' Landing** restaurant, steps from the dock. A circle trip without stops takes about 90 minutes. On the far side of the island you can stop on the rugged shoreline and have lunch. A small museum with Civil War artifacts, open in summer, is maintained in the **Fifth Maine Regiment** building. When the Civil War broke out in 1861, Maine was asked to raise only a single regiment to fight, but the state raised 10 and sent the 5th Maine Regiment into the war's first battle at Bull Run.

⓯ **Eagle Island,** owned by the state and open to the public for day trips in summer, was the home of Admiral Robert E. Peary, the American explorer of the North Pole. Peary built a stone-and-wood house on the 17-acre island as a summer retreat in 1904 but made it his permanent residence. Filled with Peary's stuffed Arctic birds, the quartz he brought home and set into the fieldstone fireplace, and other objects, the house remains as it was when Peary lived in it. A boat ride here offers a classic Maine experience as you pass by forested islands, and the island has a rocky beach and some trails to explore. The *Kristy K.* and *Fish Hawk* depart from Long Wharf in Portland and make four-hour narrated tours; there are also tours of Portland Head Light and seal-watching cruises. You can also visit the island from Freeport. ✉ *Long Wharf,* ☎ *207/774–6498.* 🎟 *$8–$15, depending on tour.* ☉ *Departures late May–Labor Day, daily beginning 10 AM.*

Freeport

⓰ *17 mi northeast of Portland, 10 mi southwest of Brunswick.*

Freeport, on U.S. 1, has charming back streets lined with historic buildings and old clapboard houses, and the pretty little harbor on the Harraseeket River in South Freeport is a relaxing place to linger. Most people, however, come here simply to shop—L.L. Bean is the store that put Freeport on the map, and plenty of outlets and some specialty stores have settled here. Still, if you choose, you can stay awhile and sample both parts of the Freeport experience: shopping along the town streets and easy access to nearby historic sites and outdoor activities.

ℭ At the **Desert of Maine,** a 40-acre desert, a safari coach tours the sand dunes and you can walk nature trails, hunt for gemstones, and watch sand artists at work. Poor agricultural practices in the late 18th century combined with massive land clearing and overgrazing uncovered this desert, which was actually formed by a glacier during the last Ice Age. ✉ *95 Desert Rd. (I–95, Exit 19),* ☎ *207/865–6962,* WEB *www.desertofmaine.com.* 🎟 *$7.50.* ☉ *Early May–Oct. 15.*

Dining and Lodging

$–$$ ✕ **Harraseeket Lunch & Lobster Co.** Seafood baskets and lobster dinners are what this bare-bones place beside the town landing in South Freeport is all about. You can eat outside on picnic tables in good weather. ✉ *On the pier, end of Main St.,* ☎ *207/865–4888. Reservations not accepted. No credit cards. Closed mid-Oct.–Apr.*

$$$$ ✕🏨 **Harraseeket Inn.** Despite modern appointments such as elevators and whirlpool baths in some rooms, this 1850 Greek Revival home and newer (1989 and 1997) additions provide a pleasantly old-fashioned country-inn experience just a few minutes' walk from L. L. Bean. Afternoon tea is served in the paneled drawing room, and guest rooms have print fabrics and reproductions of Federal quarter-canopy beds.

The formal Maine Dining Room ($$–$$$) specializes in contemporary American regional cuisine such as lamb ragout ravioli and pan-roasted halibut with potato chowder. The more casual Broad Arrow Tavern ($–$$$), serves heartier fare. ⊠ *162 Main St., 04032,* ☎ *207/865–9377 or 800/342–6423,* FAX *207/865–1684,* WEB *www.stayfreeport.com. 82 rooms, 2 suites. 2 restaurants, air-conditioning, indoor pool, croquet, meeting room. AE, D, DC, MC, V. BP.*

$$–$$$ 🏠 **Isaac Randall House.** On a 5-acre lot within walking distance to downtown shops, this circa-1829 inn is a quiet retreat. Victorian antiques and country pieces fill the rooms. A red caboose in the backyard has been turned into a room that's ideal for families. Two rooms are in the town's former police station, now moved to the property. ⊠ *10 Independence Dr., 04032,* ☎ *207/865–9295 or 800/865–9295,* FAX *207/865–9003,* WEB *www.isaacrandall.com. 12 rooms, 1 suite. Ice-skating, playground. AE, D, MC, V. BP.*

$–$$$ 🏠 **Atlantic Seal Bed & Breakfast.** The nautical decor of this 1850 waterfront Cape Cod home complements the pleasant water views from all three of its rooms. Owner Capt. Thomas Ring creates a welcoming setting, including homemade quilts, antiques, and down comforters for each room; he also offers boat trips. ⊠ *25 Main St. (Box 146), South Freeport 04078,* ☎ *207/865–6112 or 877/285–7325. 3 rooms. AE, MC, V. BP.*

$ 🏠 **Maine Idyll Motor Court.** The third and fourth generations of the Marsteller family operate this simple 1932 cottage colony. The tidy white cabins are shaded by towering pines and popular with families. Each cabin has a rustic feel, with wood floors and paneling. Baths are tiny. ⊠ *325 Rte. 1, 04032,* ☎ *207/865–4201. 20 1- to 3-bedroom cottages, 14 with fireplace, 3 with air-conditioning. In-room refrigerators, 2 playgrounds. No credit cards. Closed mid-Nov.–mid-Apr. CP.*

Outdoor Activities and Sports

Atlantic Seal Cruises (⊠ South Freeport, ☎ 207/865–6112) operates day trips to Eagle Island and evening seal and osprey watches that are a good way to experience the coast.

L.L. Bean's year-round **Outdoor Discovery Schools** (⊠ Freeport, ☎ 888/552–3261) include half- and one-day classes, as well as longer trips, that teach canoeing, kayaking, fly-fishing, cross-country skiing, and other sports. Classes are for all skill levels; it's best to sign up several months in advance if possible.

STATE PARKS

Bradbury Mountain State Park has moderate trails to the top of Bradbury Mountain, which has views of the sea. A picnic area and shelter, a ball field, a playground, and 41 campsites are among the facilities. ⊠ *Rte. 9, Pownal (I–95, 5 mi from Freeport-Durham exit),* ☎ *207/688–4712.* 🎫 *$2 Memorial Day–Labor Day, $1 off-season.*

Wolfe's Neck Woods State Park has 5 mi of good hiking trails along Casco Bay, the Harraseeket River, and a fringe salt marsh. Naturalists lead walks. The park has picnic tables and grills but no camping. ⊠ *Wolfe's Neck Rd. (follow Bow St. opposite L. L. Bean off U.S. 1),* ☎ *207/865–4465.* 🎫 *$2 Memorial Day–Labor Day, $1 off-season.*

Shopping

The big names of designer outlets are here, from Coach, Brooks Brothers, Polo Ralph Lauren, and Cole-Haan to Hartmann and Dansk. Don't overlook the specialty stores: crafts galleries such as Abacus and Edgecombe Potters, and shops selling unique items such as the Maine Reading Pillow or Claire Murray's hand-hooked rugs. The *Freeport Visitors Guide* (☎ 207/865–1212; 800/865–1994 for a copy) lists the more than 100 shops and factory outlet stores that can be found on Main Street, Bow Street, and elsewhere.

Cuddledown of Maine (⊠ 237 U.S. 1, ☎ 207/865–1713) has a selection of down comforters, pillows, and luxurious bedding. Head upstairs for discounted merchandise. Kids get their chance to shop at the educational toy store **Play and Learn** (⊠ 140 Main St., ☎ 207/865–6434). **Thos. Moser Cabinetmakers** (⊠ 149 Main St., ☎ 207/865–4519) carries high-quality handmade furniture with clean, classic lines.

Founded in 1912 as a mail-order merchandiser of products for hunters, guides, and anglers, **L. L. Bean** (⊠ 95 Main St. [U.S. 1], ☎ 800/341–4341) attracts 3½ million shoppers a year to its giant store (open 24 hours a day) in the heart of Freeport's shopping district. You can still find the original hunting boots, along with cotton, wool, and silk sweaters; camping and ski equipment; comforters; and hundreds of other items for the home, car, boat, or campsite. The **L. L. Bean Factory Store** (⊠ Depot St., ☎ 800/341–4341) has seconds and discontinued merchandise at discount prices. **L. L. Bean Kids** (⊠ 8 Nathan Nye St., ☎ 800/341–4341) specializes in children's merchandise and has a climbing wall and other activities that appeal to kids.

Harrington House Museum Store (⊠ 45 Main St., ☎ 207/865–0477) is a restored 19th-century merchant's home owned by the Freeport Historical Society; all the period reproductions that furnish the rooms are for sale, as well as books, rugs, jewelry, crafts, Shaker items, and kitchen utensils. You can obtain a brochure with a good walking tour of Freeport here, too. **Green Design Furniture** (⊠ 45 Main St., ☎ 207/865–0342), in an 1830 carriage house near Harrington House, sells Maine-designed solid cherry-wood furniture that can be shipped.

Brunswick

⑰ *10 mi north of Freeport.*

Lovely brick and clapboard homes and structures are the highlights of the town's Federal Street Historic District, which includes Federal Street and Park Row and the stately campus of Bowdoin College. Pleasant Street, in the center of town, is the business district. Harriet Beecher Stowe wrote *Uncle Tom's Cabin* while living in Brunswick.

The 110-acre campus of **Bowdoin College** (⊠ Maine, Bath, and College Sts., off east end of Pleasant St.) holds an enclave of distinguished architecture, gardens, and grassy quadrangles, along with several museums. Campus tours (☎ 207/725–3000) depart daily except Sunday from the admissions office in Chamberlain Hall. Nathaniel Hawthorne and the poet Henry Wadsworth Longfellow attended Bowdoin.

Bowdoin's imposing neo-Gothic Hubbard Hall holds the **Peary–MacMillan Arctic Museum,** with photographs, navigational instruments, and artifacts from the first successful expedition to the North Pole, in 1909, by two of Bowdoin's most famous alumni, Admiral Robert E. Peary and Donald B. MacMillan. Changing exhibits document conditions in the Arctic. ☎ *207/725–3416.* ☒ *Free.* ☉ *Tues.–Sat. 10–5, Sun. 2–5.*

The **Bowdoin College Museum of Art,** in a splendid Renaissance Revival–style building designed by Charles F. McKim in 1894, has small but good collections that encompass Assyrian and classical art and works by Dutch, Italian, French, and Flemish old masters; a superb gathering of Colonial and Federal paintings, notably Gilbert Stuart portraits of Madison and Jefferson; and a Winslow Homer Gallery of engravings, etchings, and memorabilia (open in summer only). The museum's collection also includes 19th- and 20th-century American painting and sculpture, with works by Mary Cassatt, Andrew Wyeth, and Robert Rauschenberg. ⊠ *Walker Art Bldg.,* ☎ *207/725–3275.* 🖾 *Free.* ☉ *Tues.–Sat. 10–5, Sun. 2–5.*

The **General Joshua L. Chamberlain Museum** displays memorabilia and documents the life of Maine's most celebrated Civil War hero. The general, who played an instrumental role in the Union army's victory at Gettysburg, was elected governor in 1867. From 1871 to 1883 he served as president of Bowdoin College. ⊠ *226 Main St.,* ☎ *207/729–6606.* 🖾 *$4.* ☉ *June 1–Oct. 31, Tues.–Sat. 10–4.*

OFF THE
BEATEN PATH

THE HARPSWELLS – A side trip from Bath or Brunswick on Route 123 or Route 24 takes you to the peninsulas and islands known collectively as the Harpswells. Small coves along Harpswell Neck shelter the boats of lobstermen, and summer cottages are tucked away amid the birch and spruce trees. Along Route 123, signs with blue herons mark the studios and galleries of the Harpswell Craft Guild. For lunch, follow the signs off Route 123 to **Dolphin Marina** restaurant (⊠ End of Basin Point Rd., off Ash Point Rd.) and try the delicious fish stew and a blueberry muffin.

Dining and Lodging

$$ ✕ **The Great Impasta.** You can match your favorite pasta and sauce to create your own dish at this storefront restaurant, a good choice for lunch, tea, or dinner. The seafood lasagna is tasty, too. ⊠ *42 Maine St.,* ☎ *207/729–5858. Reservations not accepted. D, DC, MC, V.*

$ ✕ **Fat Boy Drive-In.** Put your lights on for service at this old-fashioned drive-in restaurant renowned for its BLTs made with Canadian bacon, frappés (try the blueberry), and onion rings. ⊠ *Bath Rd.,* ☎ *207/729–9431. No credit cards. Closed mid-Oct.–mid-Mar.*

$$$ ⛱ **Captain Daniel Stone Inn.** This Federal-style inn overlooks the Androscoggin River and Route 1. No two rooms are furnished identically, but all contain executive-style comforts and many have whirlpool baths, queen-size beds, and pullout sofas. A guest parlor, a breakfast room, and excellent service in the Narcissa Stone Restaurant (no lunch on Saturday) make this an upscale escape from college-town funkiness. ⊠ *10 Water St., 04011,* ☎ 🆋 *207/725–9898,* 🆆🅴🅱 *www.netquarters. net/cdsi. 34 rooms, 4 suites. Restaurant. AE, DC, MC, V. CP.*

$$–$$$ ⛱ **Captain's Watch Bed and Breakfast and Sail Charter.** Built in 1862 and originally known as the Union Hotel, the Captain's Watch is the oldest surviving hotel on the Maine coast. Although much smaller than originally built, this National Historic Register property retains its distinctive octagonal cupola and a homey, old-fashioned feel. Two guest rooms share access to the cupola. Others have less-inspired but still-pleasant water views. Guests can arrange to go on a day sail aboard the inn's 37-ft sloop, *Symbion.* ⊠ *2476 926 Cundy's Harbor Rd., Harpswell, 04079,* ☎ *207/725–0979,* 🆆🅴🅱 *www.gwi.net/~cwatch. 4 rooms. MC, V for deposit only. BP.*

$–$$$ ⛱ **Harpswell Inn.** Spacious lawns and neatly pruned shrubs surround the stately white clapboard Harpswell Inn, built in 1761. The three-story inn was the center of a shipbuilding operation on Lookout Point, and the living room faces Middle Bay and Birch Island. Half the rooms have water views, as do the three carriage-house suites, one with a whirlpool. The inn is no-smoking. ⊠ *108 Lookout Point Rd., Harpswell 04079,* ☎ *207/833–5509 or 800/843–5509,* 🆆🅴🅱 *www.gwi.net/~harpswel. 9 rooms, 7 with bath, 1 with half bath; 3 suites. MC, V. BP.*

Nightlife and the Arts

Bowdoin Summer Music Festival (☎ 207/725–3322 information; 207/725–3895 tickets) is a six-week concert series featuring performances by students, faculty, and prestigious guest artists. **Maine State Music Theater** (⊠ Pickard Theater, Bowdoin College, ☎ 207/725–8769) stages musicals from mid-June to September. **Theater Project of Brunswick** (⊠ 14 School St., ☎ 207/729–8584) performs semiprofessional, children's, and community theater.

Outdoor Activities and Sports

H2Outfitters (⊠ Rte. 24, Orr's Island, ☎ 207/833–5257) provides seakayaking instruction and rentals and conducts day and overnight trips.

Shopping

ICON Contemporary Art (⊠ 19 Mason St., ☎ 207/725–8157) specializes in modern art. **O'Farrell Gallery** (⊠ 58 Maine St., ☎ 207/729–8228) represents artists such as Neil Welliver, Marguerite Robichaux, and Sheila Geoffrion. **Wyler Craft Gallery** (⊠ 150 Maine St., ☎ 207/729–1321) carries an intriguing selection of crafts, jewelry, and clothing.

Tontine Fine Candies (⊠ Tontine Mall, 149 Maine St., ☎ 207/729–4462) has chocolates and other goodies. A **farmer's market** takes place on Tuesday and Friday from May to October, on the town mall between Maine Street and Park Row.

Bath

⑱ *11 mi northeast of Brunswick, 38 mi northeast of Portland.*

Bath has been a shipbuilding center since 1607, so it's appropriate that a museum here explores the state's rich maritime heritage. These days the Bath Iron Works turns out guided-missile frigates for the U.S. Navy and merchant container ships. It's a good idea to avoid Bath and U.S. 1 on weekdays between 3:15 and 4:30 PM, when BIW's major shift change occurs. The massive exodus can tie up traffic for miles.

★ At the **Maine Maritime Museum,** displays in the Maritime History Building and in the buildings of the former Percy & Small shipyard examine the world of shipbuilding and the relationship between Mainers and the sea. The history building contains themed exhibits with maritime paintings, ship models, journals, photographs, artifacts, and videos. From May to November, one-hour tours (call for times) of the shipyard explain how wooden ships were built; at other times you can visit the buildings on your own. You can also watch boatbuilders wield their tools on classic Maine boats in the boatshop and learn about lobstering in a special exhibit building. In summer boat tours sail the scenic Kennebec River (extra charge); a number of boats, including the 142-ft Grand Banks fishing schooner *Sherman Zwicker,* are on display when in port. The museum has a fine gift shop and bookstore, and you can picnic on the grounds. ⊠ *243 Washington St.,* ☎ *207/443–1316.* ☜ *$9; tickets valid for 2 consecutive days.* ⊙ *Daily 9:30–5.*

The **Chocolate Church Arts Center** offers guided walking tours of private homes and historic buildings from mid-June to mid-September. Call for schedule and fees.

Reid State Park (☎ 207/371–2303), on Georgetown Island, off Route 127, has 1½ mi of sand on three beaches. Facilities include bathhouses, picnic tables, fireplaces, and a snack bar. Parking lots fill by 11 AM on summer Sundays and holidays; admission is charged.

OFF THE   **POPHAM** - Follow Route 209 south from Bath to Popham, the site of the
BEATEN PATH   short-lived 1607 Popham Colony, where the *Virginia,* the first English
               ship built in the Northeast, was launched. Benedict Arnold set off from
               Popham in 1775 on his ill-fated march against the British in Québec.
               Granite-walled **Ft. Popham** (⊠ Phippsburg, ☎ 207/389–1335) was

built in 1861. **Popham State Park,** at the end of Route 209, has a sand beach, a marsh area, bathhouses, and picnic tables; admission is charged.

Dining and Lodging

$$$–$$$$ ✕ **Robinhood Free Meetinghouse.** Chef Michael Gagne, one of Maine's
★ best, finally has a restaurant that complements his classic and creative multiethnic cuisine. The 1855 Greek Revival–style meetinghouse has cream-color walls, pine floorboards, cherry Shaker-style chairs, and white table linens. You might begin with the artichoke strudel; veal saltimbocca and confit of duck are two entrées. Finish up with Gagne's signature "Obsession in Three Chocolates." ⊠ *Robinhood Rd., Georgetown,* ☎ *207/371–2188. AE, D, MC, V. Closed some weeknights mid-Oct.–mid-May. No lunch.*

$$–$$$ ✕ **Kristina's Restaurant & Bakery.** This restaurant in a frame house with a front deck prepares some of the finest pies, pastries, and cakes on the coast. The satisfying new American cuisine served for dinner usually includes fresh seafood and grilled meats. All meals can be packed to go. ⊠ *160 Centre St.,* ☎ *207/442–8577. D, MC, V. Closed Jan. No dinner Sun. Call ahead in winter.*

$$$–$$$$ 🏨 **Sebasco Harbor Resort.** This family resort sprawls over 575 oceanfront acres at the foot of the Phippsburg peninsula. The owners have retained the resort's old-fashioned feel while updating and renovating the facilities. A new all-suites building is scheduled to open in 2002. Children's programs are offered in peak season. ⊠ *Route 217, Sebasco Estates 04565,* ☎ *207/389–1161 or 800/225–3819,* 🖷 *207/389–2004,* 🕸 *www.sebasco.com. 57 rooms, cottages. 3 restaurants, lounge, in-room data ports, saltwater pool, hair salon, sauna, 9-hole golf course, 3-hole practice course, 2 tennis courts, bowling, health club, Ping-Pong, dock, boating, bicycles, shop, recreation room, children's programs, playground, airport shuttle. AE, D, MC, V. Nov.–Apr. MAP available.*

$$–$$$$ 🏨 **The Inn at Bath.** Filled with antiques, this handsome 1810 Greek Revival inn in the town's historic district makes a convenient and comfortable base for exploring Bath on foot. All rooms are air-conditioned, five have wood-burning fireplaces, and two have two-person whirlpool tubs. ⊠ *969 Washington St., 04530,* ☎ *207/443–4294,* 🖷 *207/443–4295,* 🕸 *www.innatbath.com. 9 rooms. AE, D, MC, V. BP.*

$$–$$$ 🏨 **1774 Inn.** On the National Register of Historic Places, the 1774 Inn is a pre-Revolutionary mansion with handsome interior detailing and magnificent antiques. The inn, on a bend in the Kennebec River, has large corner guest rooms in the main house, two with fireplaces. In the attached ell is a room with a deck overlooking the river. A four-bedroom cottage on the river is available for longer stays. ⊠ *44 Parker Head Rd., Phippsburg Center 04562,* ☎ *207/389–1774,* 🖷 *207/389–9076. 7 rooms, 1 cottage. No credit cards. BP.*

Nightlife and the Arts

Chocolate Church Arts Center (⊠ 804 Washington St., ☎ 207/442–8455) hosts folk, jazz, and classical concerts, theater productions, and performances for children. The gallery exhibits works in various media by Maine artists.

Shopping

On Front and Centre streets in the heart of Bath's historic downtown district, antiques shops and intriguing specialty shops invite browsing. The **Montsweag Flea Market** (⊠ U.S. 1 between Bath and Wiscasset, ☎ 207/443–2809) is a roadside attraction with trash and treasures. It's open on weekends from May to October and also on Wednesday (for antiques) and Friday during the summer. **West Island Gallery,** ⊠ 11 Centre St., ☎ 207/443–9625) carries contemporary Maine art and quality crafts.

Wiscasset

19 *10 mi north of Bath, 46 mi northeast of Portland.*

Settled in 1663 on the banks of the Sheepscot River, Wiscasset fittingly bills itself as Maine's Prettiest Village. Stroll through town and you'll pass by elegant sea captains' homes (many now antiques shops or galleries), old cemeteries, churches, and public buildings.

The **Nickels-Sortwell House,** maintained by the Society for the Preservation of New England Antiquities, is an outstanding example of Federal architecture. ⊠ *12 Main St.,* ☎ *207/882–6218.* ☞ *$4.* ☉ *June–mid-Oct., Wed.–Sun. 11–5; tours on the hr 11–4.*

The 1807 **Castle Tucker,** is known for its extravagant architecture, Victorian decor, and freestanding elliptical staircase. It's run by the Society for the Preservation of New England Antiquities. ⊠ *Lee and High Sts.,* ☎ *207/882–7364.* ☞ *$4.* ☉ *June–mid-Oct., Wed.–Sun. 11–5; tours on the hr 11–4.*

★ The 1852 **Musical Wonder House,** formerly a sea captain's home, houses a private collection of thousands of antique music boxes from around the world. ⊠ *18 High St.,* ☎ *207/882–7163 or 800/336–3725,* WEB *www.musicalwonderhouse.com.* ☞ *$1 for grand hallway, ½-hr presentation on main floor $8; 1-hr presentation $15; 3-hr tour of entire house $30 by reservation only.* ☉ *Memorial Day–mid-Oct., daily 10–5; last tour usually at 4; call ahead for 3-hr tours.*

Dining and Lodging

$$–$$$ ✕ **Le Garage.** The best tables at this automotive garage turned casual restaurant are on the glassed-in porch overlooking the Sheepscot River and Wiscasset's harbor. Entrées include homemade chicken pie, sea scallops au gratin, charbroiled lamb and vegetable kebabs, and pastas and salads. ⊠ *Water St.,* ☎ *207/882–5409. MC, V. Closed Jan.*

$$ 🏨 **Marston House.** Two carriage-house rooms provide a quiet retreat from the bustle of Main Street but are just a stone's throw from the action. Both have private entrances and fireplaces and are simply furnished with Shaker- and Colonial-style pieces. The rooms can be joined by opening a door between them. A hearty Continental breakfast is delivered to your room. ⊠ *101 Main St. (Box 517),* ☎ *207/882–6010,* FAX *207/882–6965. 2 rooms. AE, MC, V. Closed Nov.–Apr. CP.*

Shopping

The Wiscasset area rivals Searsport as a destination for antiquing. Shops line Wiscasset's main and side streets and extend over the bridge into Edgecomb. The **Butterstamp Workshop** (⊠ 55 Middle St., ☎ 207/882–7825) carries handcrafted folk-art designs from antique molds. The **Maine Art Gallery** (⊠ Warren St., ☎ 207/882–7511) presents the works of local artists. **Marston House American Antiques** (⊠ Main St. at Middle St., ☎ 207/882–6010) specializes in 18th- and 19th-century painted furniture and "smalls" (small objects), homespun textiles, and antique garden accessories and tools. The **Wiscasset Bay Gallery** (⊠ Main St., ☎ 207/882–7682) has a fine collection of the works from 19th- and 20th-century American and European artists. **Treats** (⊠ Main St., ☎ 207/882–6192) is a good place to pick up fancy foods for a picnic at Waterfront Park.

Boothbay

20 *10 mi southeast of Wiscasset, 60 mi northeast of Portland, 50 mi southwest of Camden.*

When Portlanders want a break from city life, many come north to the Boothbay region, which comprises Boothbay proper, East Boothbay, and Boothbay Harbor. This part of the shoreline is a craggy stretch of inlets where pleasure craft anchor alongside trawlers and lobster boats. Commercial Street, Wharf Street, the By-Way, and Townsend Avenue are filled with shops, galleries, and ice cream parlors. Excursion boats leave from the piers off Commercial Street. From the harbor, you can catch a boat to Monhegan Island.

At the **Boothbay Railway Village,** about 1 mi north of Boothbay, you can ride 1½ mi on a narrow-gauge steam train through a re-creation of a century-old New England village. Among the 24 buildings is a museum with more than 50 antique automobiles and trucks. ⊠ *Rte. 27,* ☎ *207/633–4727,* WEB *www.railwayvillage.org.* ☞ *$7.* ☺ *Early June–Columbus Day, daily 9:30–5; special Halloween and Christmas schedules.*

The **Department of Marine Resources Aquarium** has a shark you can pet, touch tanks, and rare blue and multiclawed lobsters. ⊠ *194 McKown Point Rd., West Boothbay Harbor,* ☎ *207/633–9559.* ☞ *$2.50.* ☺ *Memorial Day–late Sept., daily 10–5.*

Dining and Lodging

$$–$$$ ✕ **Christopher's Boathouse.** You can't beat the harbor view or the stylish food at this restaurant in a renovated boathouse where you can watch the chefs at work. The lobster and mango bisque with spicy lobster wontons is noteworthy. Some main-course options are lobster succotash and Asian-spiced tuna steak with Caribbean salsa; finish off with the raspberry almond flan. ⊠ *25 Union St., Boothbay Harbor,* ☎ *207/633–6565. DC, MC, V. Closed Mar. and Mon.–Wed. in Jan. and Feb.*

$ ✕ **Lobstermen's Coop.** Crustacean lovers and landlubbers alike will find something to satisfy their cravings at this dockside working lobster pound. Lobster, steamers, hamburgers, and sandwiches are on the menu. Eat indoors or outside to watch the lobstermen at work. ⊠ *Atlantic Ave., Boothbay Harbor,* ☎ *207/633–4900. Closed mid-Oct.–mid-May.*

$$$–$$$$ ✕⌂ **Spruce Point Inn.** Escape the hubbub of Boothbay Harbor at this sprawling resort, which is a short shuttle ride from town, yet a world away. Guest rooms are in the main inn, including 39 suites added in 2000. Most are comfortable but not fancy and have ocean views. Some guests complain about inconsistent service and the nearby fog horn, which blows in inclement weather. ⊠ *Box 237, Atlantic Ave., Boothbay Harbor 04538,* ☎ *207/633–4152 or 800/553–0289,* FAX *207/633–7138,* WEB *www.sprucepointinn.com. 21 rooms, 39 suites, 7 cottages. Lounge, pool, saltwater pool, spa, 2 tennis courts, exercise room, dock. AE, D, DC, MC, V. Closed mid-Oct.–mid-May.*

$$$ ⌂ **Admiral's Quarters Inn.** This renovated 1830 sea captain's house is ideally situated for exploring Boothbay Harbor by foot. The air-conditioned rooms have private decks, many overlooking the harbor, and on rainy days you can relax by the woodstove in the solarium. ⊠ *71 Commercial St., Boothbay Harbor 04538,* ☎ *207/633–2474,* FAX *207/633–5904,* WEB *www.admiralsquartersinn.com. 2 rooms, 4 suites. D, MC, V. Closed Dec.–mid-Feb. BP.*

$$–$$$ ⌂ **Welch House.** This 1873 sea captain's house sits high on a hill, a few minutes' walk from the center of town. Antiques, artwork, and bric-a-brac from the owner's worldwide travels adorn the rooms. From the shared third-floor deck, you can take in the 180-degree views of the harbor. ⊠ *36 McKown St., 04538,* ☎ *207/633–3431 or 800/279–7313,* WEB *www.welchhouse.com. 16 rooms. MC, V. Dec. 1–Mar. 31. BP.*

$$ \quad \boxed{\Xi} \text{ } \textbf{Hodgdon Island Inn.} \text{ Every room in this 1810 inn, which is within}$$

walking distance of a lobster pound and a botanical garden, has a view of the water; two rooms open unto a shared deck. Inside, artwork from New England and the Caribbean graces the walls. ⊠ *Barters Island Road, 04571,* ☎ *207/633–7474. 6 rooms. Pool. D, MC, V. BP.*

Outdoor Activities and Sports

BOAT TRIPS

Balmy Day Cruises (⊠ Pier 8, 62 Commercial St., Boothbay Harbor, ☎ 207/633–2284 or 800/298–2284) operates day boat trips to Monhegan Island and tours of the harbor. **Cap'n Fish's Boat Trips** (⊠ Pier 1, Boothbay Harbor, ☎ 207/633–3244 or 800/636–3244) runs regional sightseeing cruises, including puffin-watching excursions, lobster-hauling and whale-watching rides, and trips to Damariscove Harbor, Pemaquid Point, and up the Kennebec River to Bath.

KAYAKING

Tidal Transit Ocean Kayak Co. (☎ 207/633–7140) offers guided tours and rentals.

Shopping

BOOTHBAY HARBOR

You can browse for hours in the trinket and T-shirt shops, crafts galleries, clothing stores, and boutiques that line the streets around the harbor. **Gleason Fine Art** (⊠ 7 Oak St., ☎ 207/633–6849) showcases fine art—regional and national, early 19th century and contemporary. **House of Logan** (⊠ 20 Townsend Ave., ☎ 207/633–2293) stocks upscale casual and fancy attire for men and women. Beautiful housewares and attractive children's clothes can be found at the **Village Store & Children's Shop** (⊠ 34 Townsend Ave., ☎ 207/633–2293).

EDGECOMB

Highly reputable **Edgecomb Potters** (⊠ Rte. 27, ☎ 207/882–6802) sells stylish glazed porcelain pottery and other crafts at rather high prices; some discontinued items or seconds are discounted. There's a store in Freeport if you miss this one. **Sheepscot River Pottery** (⊠ U.S. 1, ☎ 207/882–9410) has hand-painted pottery as well as a large collection of American-made crafts, including jewelry, kitchenware, furniture, and home accessories.

Pemaquid Peninsula

㉑ *8 mi southeast of Wiscasset.*

A detour off U.S. 1 via Routes 130 and 32 leads to the Pemaquid Peninsula and a satisfying microcosm of coastal Maine. Art galleries, country stores, antiques and crafts shops, and lobster shacks dot the country roads that meander to the tip of the point, where you'll find a much-photographed lighthouse perched on an unforgiving rock ledge, as well as a pleasant beach. Exploring here reaps many rewards, including views of salt ponds, the ocean, and boat-clogged harbors. The twin towns of Damariscotta and Newcastle anchor the region, but small fishing villages such as Pemaquid, New Harbor, and Round Pond give the peninsula its purely Maine flavor.

At what is now the **Colonial Pemaquid Restoration,** on a small peninsula jutting into the Pemaquid River, English mariners established a fishing and trading settlement in the early 17th century. The excavations at Ft. William Henry, begun in the mid-1960s, have turned up thousands of artifacts from the Colonial settlement, including the remains of an old customs house, a tavern, a jail, a forge, and homes. Some items are from even earlier Native American settlements. The state operates a museum displaying many of the artifacts. ⊠ *Off Rte. 130, New Harbor,* ☎ *207/677–2423.* ☜ *$2.* ☉ *Memorial Day–Labor Day, daily 9:30–5.*

★ Route 130 terminates at the **Pemaquid Point Light,** which looks as though it sprouted from the ragged, tilted chunk of granite that it commands. The former lighthouse-keeper's cottage is now the Fishermen's Museum, with photographs, models, and artifacts that explore commercial fishing in Maine. Here, too, is the Pemaquid Art Gallery, which mounts exhibitions from July to Labor Day. ⊠ *Museum: Rte. 130,* ☎ *207/677–2494.* ☜ *$1.* ☉ *Memorial Day–Columbus Day, Mon.–Sat. 10–5, Sun. 11–5.*

Dining and Lodging

$ ✕ **Round Pond Lobstermen's Co-op.** Lobster doesn't get much rougher, ★ any fresher, or any cheaper than what's served at this no-frills dockside takeout. The best deal is the dinner special: a 1-pound lobster, steamers, and corn-on-the-cob, with a bag of chips. Regulars often bring beer, wine, bread, and salads. Settle in at a picnic table and breathe in the fresh salt air while you drink in the view over dreamy Round Pond Harbor. ⊠ *Round Pond Harbor, off Rte. 32, Round Pond,* ☎ *207/ 529–5725. MC, V.*

$$–$$$$ ✕🏨 **Newcastle Inn.** This classic country inn with a riverside location and an excellent dining room attracts guests year-round. All the rooms are filled with country pieces and antiques; some rooms have fireplaces and whirlpool baths. Breakfast is served on the back deck in fine weather. The four-course dinners ($$$$) at the inn, open to the public by reservation, emphasize local seafood. ⊠ *60 River Rd., Newcastle 04553,* ☎ *207/563–5685 or 800/832–8669,* FAX *207/563–6877,* WEB *www.newcastleinn.com. 11 rooms, 3 suites. Dining room, pub. AE, MC, V. BP.*

$$ 🏨 **Mill Pond Inn.** A quiet residential street holds this circa-1780 inn, which is on a mill pond across the street from Damariscotta Lake. Loons, otters, and bald eagles reside on the lake, and you can arrange a trip with the owner, a Registered Maine Guide, on the inn's 17-ft antique lapstrake boat. The rooms are warm and inviting and there's a pub for guests, though you may find it hard to tear yourself away from the hammocks-for-two overlooking the pond. ⊠ *50 Main St., off Rte. 215 N, Nobleboro 04555,* ☎ *207/563–8014,* WEB *www.millpondinn.com. 6 rooms, 1 suite. Horseshoes, boating, bicycles. No credit cards. BP.*

$–$$ 🏨 **Briar Rose.** Round Pond is a sleepy harborside village with an old-fashioned country store, two lobster co-ops, a nice restaurant, and a handful of antiques and crafts shops. The mansard-roof Briar Rose commands a ship captain's view over it all. Antiques and whimsies decorate the airy rooms. ⊠ *1442 Rte. 32 (Box 27), Round Pond 04564,* ☎ *207/529–5478. 2 rooms, 1 suite. No credit cards. BP.*

$–$$ 🏨 **Hotel Pemaquid.** This turn-of-the-century inn is less than 500 ft from the lighthouse at Pemaquid Point. The main building is Victorian in style; cottages and bungalow units have a more contemporary feel; and the carriage house suite is ideal for honeymooners or others seeking a romantic retreat. ⊠ *3098 Bristol Rd. (Rte. 130), New Harbor 04554,* ☎ *207/677–2312,* WEB *www.hotelpemaquid.com. 21 rooms, 17 with bath; 4 suites, 3 cottages, 1 apt. No credit cards. Closed mid-Oct.–mid-May.*

Nightlife and the Arts

Round Top Center for the Arts (⊠ Business Rte. 1, Damariscotta, ☎ 207/563–1507) has a gallery with rotating exhibits and a performance hall where classical, folk, operatic, and jazz concerts are held.

Outdoor Activities and Sports

Pemaquid Beach Park (✉ Off Rte. 130, New Harbor, ☎ 207/677–2754) has a sand beach, a snack bar, changing facilities, and picnic tables overlooking John's Bay; admission is charged.

Shopping

Of the villages on and near the Pemaquid Peninsula, downtown Damariscotta offers boutiques, a book shop, clothing stores, and galleries. New Harbor and Round Pond have crafts and antiques shops as well as artisans' studios. Antiques shops dot the main thoroughfares in the region.

Bramble's (✉ Main St., Damariscotta, ☎ 207/563–2800) is a paradise for gardeners, with tools, sculpture, pots, artwork, and topiary. **Granite Hill Store** (✉ Backshore Rd., Round Pond, ☎ 207/529–5864) has penny candy, kitchen goodies, baskets, and cards on the first floor, antiques and books on the second, and an ice cream window on the side. The work of more than 50 Maine artisans is displayed in the 15 rooms of the **Pemaquid Craft Co-op** (✉ Rte. 130, New Harbor, ☎ 207/677–2077). You never know what you'll find at **Reny's** (✉ Rte. 1A, Damariscotta, ☎ 207/563–5757)—perhaps merchandise from L. L. Bean or a designer coat. This bargain chain has outlets in many Maine towns, but this is its hometown, and there are two outlets: one for clothes, the other for everything else. The **Victorian Stable Gallery** (✉ Water St., Damariscotta, ☎ 207/563–1991) is a barn with fine Maine crafts, paintings, and prints by more than 100 artisans.

Waldoboro

㉒ *10 mi. northeast of Damariscotta.*

Veer off of U.S. 1 onto Main Street or down Rtes. 220 or 32, and you'll discover a seafaring town with a proud ship-building past. The **Waldoborough Historical Society Museum** comprises the one-room Boggs Schoolhouse, built in 1857, the Town Pound, built in 1819, and a barn and museum filled with artifacts and antiques, including hooked rugs, old toys, tools, clothing, and housewares. ✉ *Route 220,* ☎ *No phone.* 🎟 *Free* ☉ *July–Labor Day, daily 1–4:30.*

One of the three oldest churches in Maine, the **Old German Church** was built in 1772 on the eastern side of the Medomak River, then moved across the ice to its present site in 1794. Inside you'll find box pews and a 9-ft-tall chalice pulpit. ✉ *Rte. 32,* ☎ *207/832–5639.* ☉ *July–Aug., daily 1–3.*

The **Fawcett's Toy Museum** delights adults and children with collectible toys, from Betty Boop and Charlie Brown to Mickey Mouse and Popeye, and original comic art. ✉ *3506 Rte. 1,* ☎ *207/832–7398.* 🎟 *$3* ☉ *Early July–Columbus Day, Thurs.–Mon., 10–3:30; fall and winter, Sat. and Sun., 12–3:30; spring most weekends and by chance.*

Dining and Lodging

$–$$$ ✕ **Pine Cone Cafe.** Paintings by local painter Eric Hopkins hang on
★ the walls of this cozy restaurant which serves up hearty soups, salads, and a mix of home-style and creative entrées. Try the corn-fried soft-shell crab tower or turkey pot pie; the crème brulée is a good choice for dessert. In favorable weather ask for a table on the back deck overlooking the river. ✉ *13 Friendship St.,* ☎ *207/832–6337. MC, V.*

$ ✕ **Moody's Diner.** Settle into one of the well-worn wooden booths or snag a counter stool at this old-style diner for home-cooking fare. Breakfast is served all day; don't miss the legendary walnut pie. ✉ *Rte. 1,* ☎ *207/832–5362. D, MC, V.*

$ ⊞ **La Va Tout.** An 1830 Cape Cod houses a simply decorated bed-and-breakfast and the Eliza Sweet Gallery, which shows work by contemporary Maine artists. Relax in the inn's gardens or the Swedish sauna. ⊠ *218 Kalers Corner/Rte. 32 04572,* ☎ *207/832–4969,* WEB *www. midcoast.com/lavatout. 5 rooms, 3 with bath. Hot tub, sauna. MC, V. BP.*

Nightlife and the Arts

The **Waldo Theatre** (⊠ 916 Main St., ☎ 207/832–6060), a Greek Revival-style cinema with an Art Deco interior, stages concerts, plays, lectures, and other performances.

Shopping

The **Waldoboro 5 & 10/Fernald's General Store** (⊠ 17 Friendship St., ☎ 207/832–4624) is the oldest, continually operated 5 & 10 in the country. It has an old-fashioned soda fountain, which serves sandwiches, soups, and ice cream; there's even a penny candy counter. **Glockenspiel Imports** (⊠ U.S. 1, ☎ 207/832–8000) sells traditional German lace. For a taste of authentic German sauerkraut, visit **Morse's Sauerkraut** (⊠ 3856 Washington Rd./Rte. 220 north, ☎ 207/832–5569). The **Roserie at Bayfields** (⊠ Rte. 32, ☎ 207/832–6330) specializes in roses. The gardens here have sweeping views over the Medomak River.

Portland to Waldoboro A to Z

To research prices, get advice from other travelers, and book travel arrangements, visit www.fodors.com.

BOAT & FERRY TRAVEL

Casco Bay Lines provides ferry service from Portland to the islands of Casco Bay.

➤ BOAT & FERRY INFORMATION: **Casco Bay Lines** (☎ 207/774–7871).

BUS TRAVEL TO & FROM PORTLAND

Greater Portland's Metro runs seven bus routes in Portland, South Portland, and Westbrook. The fare is $1; exact change ($1 bills accepted) is required. Buses run from 5:30 AM to 11:45 PM.

➤ BUS INFORMATION: **Greater Portland's Metro** (☎ 207/774–0351).

CAR TRAVEL

Congress Street leads from I–295 into the heart of Portland; the Gateway Garage on High Street, off Congress, is a convenient place to leave your car downtown. North of Portland, I–95 takes you to Exit 20 and U.S. 1, Freeport's Main Street, which continues on to Brunswick and Bath. East of Wiscasset you can take Route 27 south to the Boothbays, where Route 96 is a good choice for further exploration. To visit the Pemaquid region, take Route 129 off Business Route 1 in Damariscotta; then pick up Route 130 and follow it down to Pemaquid Point. Return to Waldoboro and U.S. 1 on Route 32 from New Harbor.

EMERGENCIES

➤ HOSPITALS: **Maine Medical Center** (⊠ 22 Bramhall St., Portland, ☎ 207/871–0111). **Mid Coast Hospital** (⊠ 1356 Washington St., Bath, ☎ 207/443–5524; ⊠ 58 Baribeau Dr., Brunswick, ☎ 207/729–0181). **Miles Memorial Hospital** (⊠ Bristol Rd., Damariscotta, ☎ 207/563–1234). **St. Andrews Hospital** (⊠ 3 St. Andrews La., Boothbay Harbor, ☎ 207/633–2121).

TOURS

BUS TOURS

In Portland, the informative van tours of Mainely Tours cover the city's historical and architectural highlights (with a stop at Portland Head

Light, too) from Memorial Day through October. Other tours combine a city tour with a bay cruise or take visitors to four lighthouses.
➤ TOUR OPERATOR: **Mainely Tours** (✉ 5½ Moulton St., ☎ 207/774–0808).

WALKING TOURS
Greater Portland Landmarks offers 1½-hour walking tours of the city from July through September; tours begin at the Convention and Visitors Bureau and cost $8.
➤ TOUR OPERATORS: **Greater Portland Landmarks** (✉ 165 State St., ☎ 207/774–5561). **Convention and Visitors Bureau** (✉ 305 Commercial St., ☎ 207/772–5800).

VISITOR INFORMATION
➤ CONTACTS: **Boothbay Harbor Region Chamber of Commerce** (✉ Box 356, Boothbay Harbor 04538, ☎ 207/633–2353). **Chamber of Commerce of the Bath/Brunswick Region** (✉ 45 Front St., Bath 04530, ☎ 207/443–9751; ✉ 59 Pleasant St., Brunswick 04011, ☎ 207/725–8797). **Convention and Visitors Bureau of Greater Portland** (✉ 305 Commercial St., Portland 04101, ☎ 207/772–5800 or 877/833–1374). **Greater Portland Chamber of Commerce** (✉ 145 Middle St., Portland 04101, ☎ 207/772–2811). **Damariscotta Region Chamber of Commerce** (✉ Box 13, Damariscotta 04543, ☎ 207/563–8340). **Freeport Merchants Association** (✉ Box 452, Freeport 04032, ☎ 207/865–1212 or 877/865–1212). **Maine Tourism Association** (✉ U.S. 1 [I–95, Exit 17], Yarmouth 04347, ☎ 207/846–0833).

PENOBSCOT BAY

Purists hold that the Maine coast begins at Penobscot Bay, where the vistas over the water are wider and bluer; the shore a jumble of broken granite boulders, cobblestones, and gravel punctuated by small sand beaches; and the water numbingly cold. Port Clyde in the southwest and Stonington in the southeast are the outer limits of Maine's largest bay, 35 mi apart across the bay waters but separated by a drive of almost 100 mi on scenic but slow two-lane highways. From Pemaquid Point at the western extremity of Muscongus Bay to Port Clyde at its eastern extent, it's less than 15 mi across the water, but it's 50 mi for the motorist, who must return north to U.S. 1 to reach the far shore. A relaxing sail on a windjammer is a great way to explore the area.

Thomaston, on the western edge of the region, has a fine collection of sea captains' homes. Rockland, the largest town on the bay, is a growing arts center, home of the Maine Lobster Festival, and the port of departure for trips to Vinalhaven, North Haven, and Matinicus islands. The Camden Hills, looming green over Camden's fashionable waterfront, turn bluer and fainter as you head toward Castine, the small town across the bay. In between Camden and Castine are Belfast and the antiques and flea-market mecca of Searsport. Deer Isle is connected to the mainland by a slender, high-arching bridge, but Isle au Haut, accessible from Deer Isle's fishing town of Stonington, can be reached by passenger ferry only: More than half of this steep, wooded island is wilderness, the most remote section of Acadia National Park.

The most promising shopping areas are Main Street in Rockland, Main and Bay View streets in Camden, and the Main Streets in Belfast, Blue Hill, Stonington. Antiques shops are clustered in Searsport and scattered around the outskirts of villages, in farmhouses and barns. Yard sales abound in summer.

Thomaston

㉓ *10 mi northeast of Waldoboro, 72 mi northeast of Portland.*

The Maine State Prison that has loomed over Thomaston for decades is slated to be replaced by a new facility in Warren in late 2001. Plans call for the dreary monstrosity to be razed and replaced with a park. Prison aside, this is a delightful town, full of beautiful sea captains' homes and dotted with antiques and specialty shops. A National Historic District encompasses parts of High, Main, and Knox streets.

Montpelier: General Henry Knox Museum was built in 1930 as a replica of the late-18th-century mansion of Major General Henry Knox, a general in the Revolutionary War and secretary of war in Washington's Cabinet. Antiques and Knox family possessions fill the interior. Architectural features of note include an oval room and a double staircase. ⊠ *U.S. 1 and Rte. 131,* ☎ *207/354–8062,* WEB *www.generalknoxmuseum.org.* 🎫 *$5.* ☉ *Memorial Day–late Sept., Tues.–Sat. 10–4, Sun. 1–4; tours are offered on the hour and half-hour, 10–3.*

Dining

$–$$ ✕ **Thomaston Cafe & Bakery.** This small café is a popular spot for lunch. Entrées may include haddock cakes or grilled Black Angus. ⊠ *154 Main St.,* ☎ *207/354–8589. MC, V. No dinner Sun.–Thurs.*

Shopping

Maine authors frequently sign books at the **Personal Bookstore** (⊠ 144 Main St., ☎ 207/354–8058 or 800/391–8058); a small gallery is upstairs. The **Maine State Prison Showroom Outlet** (⊠ Main St., ☎ 207/354–2535) carries crafts, furniture, and woodwork made by prisoners.

Tenants Harbor

㉔ *13 mi south of Thomaston.*

Tenants Harbor is a quintessential Maine fishing town, its harbor dominated by lobster boats, its shores rocky and slippery, its center full of clapboard houses, a church, and a general store. The fictional Dunnet Landing of Sarah Orne Jewett's classic *The Country of the Pointed Firs* (1896) is based on this region. It's a favorite with artists, too, and galleries and studios invite browsing.

The keeper's house at the **Marshall Point Lighthouse** has been turned into a museum containing memorabilia from the town of St. George (a few miles north of Tenants Harbor). The setting has inspired Jamie Wyeth and other artists. You can stroll the grounds and watch the boats go in and out of Port Clyde. ⊠ *Marshall Point Rd., Port Clyde,* ☎ *207/372–6450.* 🎫 *Free.* ☉ *June–Sept., weekdays 1–5 and Sat. 10–5.*

Dining and Lodging

$$–$$$ ✕🏨 **East Wind Inn & Meeting House.** Overlooking the harbor and the islands, the East Wind has unadorned but comfortable rooms, suites, and apartments in three buildings, including the main inn, the Meeting House (a converted sea captain's house), and the Wheeler Cottage; some accommodations have fireplaces. The inn is open to the public for dinner, breakfast, and Sunday brunch. Dinner options include prime rib, boiled lobster, and baked stuffed haddock. A take-out restaurant on the wharf offers lobster, clams, and lighter fare and picnic-style dining. You get a credit for breakfast at the restaurant. ⊠ *Mechanic St., 04860,* ☎ *207/372–6366 or 800/241–8439,* FAX *207/372–6320,* WEB *www.eastwindinn.com. 18 rooms, 12 with bath; 3 suites; 4 apartments. 2 restaurants. AE, D, MC, V. Closed Dec.–Apr. BP.*

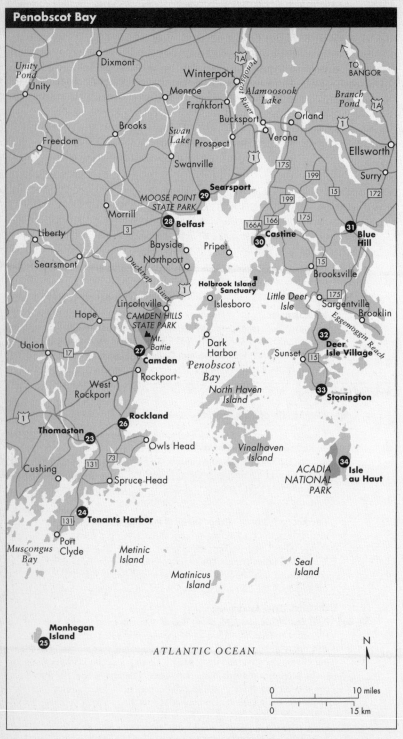

Penobscot Bay

Unity Pond
Dixmont
Unity
Freedom
Monroe
Winterport
1A
to Penobscot River
Alamoosook Lake
Branch Pond
1A
TO BANGOR
Frankfort
Bucksport
Orland
1
Brooks
Prospect
Verona
Ellsworth
Swan Lake
Swanville
175
Surry
172
Morrill
Searsport
29
199
15
MOOSE POINT STATE PARK
199
28 **Belfast**
166A **166**
175
31 **Blue Hill**
3
Bayside
Pripet
Castine
30
Liberty
Northport
15
Brooksville
Searsmont
Ducktrap River
1
Holbrook Island Sanctuary
Little Deer Isle
175
Sargentville
Brooklin
Lincolnville
Islesboro
Hope
CAMDEN HILLS STATE PARK
Eggemoggin Reach
Union
▲ *Mt. Battie*
Dark Harbor
32
Deer Isle Village
17
27
Camden
Sunset
15
West Rockport
Rockport
Penobscot Bay
33
Stonington
North Haven Island
1
Rockland
26
Thomaston
23
Owls Head
Vinalhaven Island
ACADIA NATIONAL PARK
34
Isle au Haut
Cushing
131 **73**
Spruce Head
24 **Tenants Harbor**
131
Port Clyde
Metinic Island
Seal Island
Muscongus Bay
Matinicus Island
25
Monhegan Island
ATLANTIC OCEAN
N

0   10 miles
0   15 km

Shopping

Gallery-by-the-Sea (⊠ Port Clyde Village, Port Clyde, ☎ 207/372–8631) carries works by a dozen local artists including Leo Brooks, Lawrence Goldsmith, and Emily Muir.

Monhegan Island

★ ㉕ *East of Pemaquid Peninsula, 10 mi south of Port Clyde.*

Remote Monhegan Island, with its high cliffs fronting the open sea, was known to Basque, Portuguese, and Breton fishermen well before Columbus "discovered" America. About a century ago Monhegan was discovered again by some of America's finest painters, including Rockwell Kent, Robert Henri, A. J. Hammond, and Edward Hopper, who sailed out to paint its meadows, savage cliffs, wild ocean views, and fishermen's shacks. Tourists followed, and today three excursion boats dock here. The village bustles with activity in summer, when many artists open their studios. You can escape the crowds on the island's 17 mi of hiking trails, which lead to the lighthouse and to the cliffs. Those who overnight here have a quieter experience, since lodging is limited. Day visitors should bring lunch, as restaurants can have long waits at lunchtime.

The **Monhegan Museum,** in an 1824 lighthouse and an adjacent, newly built assistant keeper's house, has wonderful views of Manana Island and the Camden Hills in the distance. Inside, artworks and displays depict island life and local flora and birds. ⊠ *White Head Rd.,* ☎ *no phone.* ⊡ *Donations accepted.* ☉ *July–mid-Sept., daily 11:30–3:30.*

Lodging

$$–$$$$ ⊞ **Island Inn.** This three-story inn, which dates from 1807, has a commanding presence on Monhegan's harbor. The waterside rooms, though mostly small, are the nicest, with sunset views over the harbor and stark Manana Island. Some of the meadow-view rooms have the distinct disadvantage of being over kitchen vents. New owners are gradually updating and redecorating the property, which includes the main inn, the adjacent Pierce Cottage, a small bakery-café, and a good dining room that serves breakfast, lunch, and dinner. ⊠ *Box 128, 04852,* ☎ *207/ 596–0371,* FAX *207/594–5517,* WEB *www.islandinnmonhegan.com. 30 rooms, 11 with bath; 4 suites in 2 buildings. Restaurant, café. MC, V. Closed Columbus Day–Memorial Day. BP.*

Outdoor Activities and Sports

Port Clyde, a fishing village at the end of Route 131, is the point of departure for the **Laura B.** (☎ 207/372–8848 schedules), the mail boat that serves Monhegan Island. The **Balmy Days** (☎ 207/633–2284 or 800/298–2284) sails from Boothbay Harbor to Monhegan on daily trips in summer. **Hardy Boat Cruises** (☎ 207/677–2026 or 800/278–3346) leave daily from Shaw's Wharf in New Harbor.

Rockland

㉖ *4 mi northeast of Thomaston, 14 mi northeast of Tenants Harbor.*

Once a place to pass through on the way to tonier ports like Camden, Rockland now attracts attention on its own, thanks to the expansion of the Farnsworth Museum. Specialty shops and galleries line Main Street and the side streets, and new restaurants and inns continue to open. A large fishing port and the commercial hub of this coastal area, with working boats moored alongside yachts and windjammers, Rockland still holds on to its working-class flavor, but it's fading.

Day trips to Vinalhaven and North Haven islands and distant Matinicus depart from the harbor, the outer portion of which is bisected by a nearly mile-long granite breakwater. At the end of the breakwater is a late-19th-century lighthouse, one of the best places in the area to watch the many windjammers sail in and out of Rockland Harbor. Owl's Head Lighthouse, off Route 73, is also a good vantage point.

★ The **Farnsworth Art Museum,** an excellent small museum of American art, contains works by Andrew, N. C., and Jamie Wyeth; Fitz Hugh Lane; George Bellows; Frank W. Benson; Edward Hopper; Louise Nevelson; and Fairfield Porter. The **Wyeth Center** is devoted to Maine-related works of the Wyeth family. Some works from the personal collection of Andrew and Betsy Wyeth include *The Patriot, Adrift, Maiden Hair, Dr. Syn, The Clearing,* and *Watch Cap.* In 2000, the **Jamien Morehouse Wing** opened, doubling the museum's gallery space. Shown here are new works by living Maine artists. The **Farnsworth Homestead,** a handsome circa-1852 Greek Revival dwelling that is part of the museum, retains its original lavish Victorian furnishings. The museum also operates the **Olson House** (⊠ Hathorn Point Rd., Cushing), which was depicted in Andrew Wyeth's famous painting *Christina's World.* ⊠ *356 Main St.,* ☎ *207/596–6457,* WEB *www.farnsworthmuseum.org.* 🎫 *$9; Olson House only, $4.* ☉ *Museum Memorial Day–Columbus Day, daily 9–5; Columbus Day–Memorial Day, Tues.–Sat. 10–5, Sun. 1–5. Homestead Memorial Day–Columbus Day, daily 10–4. Olson House Memorial Day–Columbus Day, daily 11–4.*

🐚 The **Shore Village Museum** displays many lighthouse and Coast Guard artifacts and has exhibits of maritime and Civil War memorabilia. ⊠ *104 Limerock St.,* ☎ *207/594–0311,* WEB *www.lighthouse.cc/shorevillage.* 🎫 *Donation suggested.* ☉ *June–mid-Oct., daily 10–4; rest of yr by chance or appointment..*

🐚 **Owls Head Transportation Museum** displays antique aircraft, cars, and engines and stages air shows every other weekend May–October. ⊠ *117 Museum Lane, off Rte. 73, Owls Head (3 mi south of Rockland),* ☎ *207/594–4418, www.ohtm.org.* 🎫 *$6.* ☉ *Apr.–Oct., daily 10–5; Nov.–Mar., daily 10–4.*

....

OFF THE
BEATEN PATH
VINALHAVEN – You can take the ferry from Rockland to this island for a pleasant day of bicycling or walking. A number of parks are within walking distance of the ferry dock, including Armbrust Hill, the site of an abandoned quarry, and Lane's Island Preserve, a 40-acre site of moors, granite shoreline, tide pools, and beach. You can learn about the island's quarrying history at the Historical Society Museum on High Street and even take a dip in the cool, clear waters of two quarries. Lawson's is 1 mi out on the North Haven Road; Booth Quarry is 1½ mi out East Main Street. Neither has changing facilities, so go prepared. For ferry information, call **Maine State Ferry Service** (☎ 207/596–2202).

....

Dining and Lodging

$$–$$$ ✕ **Amalfi.** Delicious Mediterranean cuisine, a well-chosen and af-
★   fordable wine list, and excellent service have made this storefront Mediterranean bistro an immediate hit. The Amalfi fish stew and lobster risotto are especially good; the menu changes seasonally. ⊠ *421 Main St.,* ☎ *207/596–0012. D, MC, V. Closed Sun.–Mon.*

$$–$$$ ✕ **Café Miranda.** Expect to wait for a table at this cozy bistro, where the daily changing menu reflects fresh, seasonal ingredients and the chef's creative renditions of both new American and traditional home-style foods. You can make a meal from the 20 or so appetizers, many roasted in the brick oven. The two dozen entrées may include crispy

panfried softshell crabs with red bean ragout and yellow jasmine rice. The outdoor patio is a good choice on nice days. ⊠ *15 Oak St.,* ☎ *207/594–2034. MC, V. Closed Sun.–Mon. No lunch.*

$$–$$$ ✕ **Primo.** Chef Melissa Kelly and baker and pastry chef Price Kush-
★ ner opened this restaurant in 2000, serving cuisine that combines fresh Maine ingredients with Mediterranean influences. The weekly chang-ing menu may include wood-roasted black sea bass, local crab-stuffed turbot, or diver scallop and basil ravioli. ⊠ *2 South Main St.,* ☎ *207/594–0770. Reservations essential. AE, MC, V. Closed Tues.–Wed.*

$$$$ ☷ **Samoset Resort.** On the Rockland-Rockport town line next to the breakwater, this sprawling oceanside resort has excellent golf and fit-ness facilities. Plans called for all rooms and public areas to be reno-vated with new furnishings by mid-2001. Most of the spacious rooms, decorated in deep green and burgundy tones, have views of Penobscot Bay over the fairways; all have patios or decks. ⊠ *220 Warrenton St., Rockport 04856,* ☎ *207/594–2511 or 800/341–1650,* ℻ *207/594–0722,* 𝖶𝖤𝖡 *www.samoset.com. 154 rooms, 24 suites. Restaurant, air-conditioning, in-room data ports, 1 indoor and 1 outdoor pool, 18-hole golf course, 4 tennis courts, exercise room, racquetball, children's programs. AE, D, DC, MC, V.*

$$–$$$$ ☷ **Berry Manor Inn.** Built in 1898 as the residence of Charles E. Berry,
★ a prominent Rockland merchant, this Victorian shingle-style inn has been carefully restored. Guest rooms are large and elegantly furnished with antiques and reproduction pieces. All have fireplaces, five have whirlpool tubs, and TVs are available upon request. A guest pantry is stocked with sweets. ⊠ *81 Talbot Ave., 04841,* ☎ *207/596–7696 or 800/774–5692,* ℻ *207/596–9958,* 𝖶𝖤𝖡 *www.berrymanorinn.com. 8 rooms. In-room data ports, library. AE, MC, V. BP.*

$$–$$$ ☷ **Limerock Inn.** You can walk to the Farnsworth and the Shore Vil-
★ lage museums from this magnificent Queen Anne–style Victorian on a quiet residential street. The meticulously decorated rooms include Island Cottage, with a whirlpool tub and doors that open onto a pri-vate deck overlooking a garden, and Grand Manan, which has a fire-place, a whirlpool tub, and a four-poster king-size bed. ⊠ *96 Limerock St., 04841,* ☎ *207/594–2257 or 800/546–3762,* ℻ *207/594–1846,* 𝖶𝖤𝖡 *www.limerockinn.com. 8 rooms. Croquet, bicycles. D, MC, V. BP.*

$$ ☷ **Beech Street Guest House.** This cozy bed-and-breakfast provides quiet, comfortable accommodations just a few minutes walk from downtown attractions. You can browse the owners' collection of rare books for sale or arrange for an in-house massage, herbal wrap, or steam treat-ment. Breakfasts emphasize organic and natural foods. ⊠ *41 Beech St., 04841,* ☎ *207/596–7280,* 𝖶𝖤𝖡 *www.midcoast.com/~beechstr. 2 rooms. Massage, spa treatments. MC, V. CP, FP.*

Outdoor Activities and Sports

BOAT TRIPS

Bay Island Yacht Charters (⊠ 120 Tillison Ave., ☎ 207/596–5770 or 800/421–2492) operates bareboats and charters. The **Maine Windjammer Association** (⊠ Box 1144, Blue Hill 04614, ☎ 800/807–9463) repre-sents the Rockland-based windjammers *American Eagle, Heritage, Isaac H. Evans, J & E Riggin, Nathaniel Bowditch, Stephen Taber,* and *Victory Chimes,* which sail on three- to eight-day cruises. The schooner **Wendameen** (⊠ Box 252, 04841, ☎ 207/594–1751) takes passengers on overnight sails.

TOURS

Downeast Air Inc. (☎ 207/594–2171 or 800/594–2171) offers scenic flights and lighthouse tours.

Shopping

Caldbeck Gallery (✉ 12 Elm St., ☎ 207/596–5935) displays contemporary Maine works by artists such as William Thon. **Harbor Square Gallery** (✉ 374 Main St., ☎ 207/596–8700) has roomfuls of Maine-related arts and craft. The **Islands of Maine Gallery** (✉ 412 Main St., ☎ 207/596–0701) carries work created by residents of Maine's islands.

Camden

㉗ *8 mi north of Rockland, 19 mi south of Belfast.*

"Where the mountains meet the sea," Camden's longtime publicity slogan, is an apt description, as you will discover when you look up from the harbor. The town is famous not only for geography but for its large fleet of windjammers—relics and replicas from the age of sailing. At just about any hour during warm months you're likely to see at least one windjammer tied up in the harbor. The busy downtown has some of the best shopping in the region. The district's compact size makes it perfect for exploring on foot: shops, restaurants, and galleries line Main Street (U.S. 1) and Bayview, as well as side streets and alleys around the harbor.

Their height may not be much more than 1,000 ft, yet the hills in **Camden Hills State Park** are lovely landmarks for miles along the low, rolling reaches of the Maine coast. The 5,500-acre park contains 20 mi of trails, including the easy Nature Trail up Mt. Battie. Hike or drive to the top for a magnificent view over Camden and island-studded Penobscot Bay. The 112-site camping area, open from mid-May to mid-October, has flush toilets and hot showers. The entrance is 2 mi north of Camden. ✉ *U.S. 1,* ☎ *207/236–3109.* 🎫 *Trails and auto road up Mt. Battie $2.* ⊙ *Daily dawn–dusk.*

Merryspring Horticultural Nature Park is a 66-acre retreat with herb, rose, rhododendron, hosta, and children's gardens as well as woodland trails. ✉ *Conway Rd., off U.S. 1,* ☎ *207/236–2239.* 🎫 *Free.* ⊙ *Daily dawn–dusk.*

🄲 **Kelmscott Farm** is a rare-breed animal farm (sheep, pigs, horses, poultry, goats, and cows) with displays, a nature trail, children's activities, a picnic area, heirloom gardens, and special events. ✉ *Rte. 52, Lincolnville,* ☎ *207/763–4088 or 800/545–9363, www.kelmscott.org.* 🎫 *$5.* ⊙ *May 1–Oct. 31, Tues.–Sun. 10–5; Nov. 1–Apr. 30, Tues.–Sun. 10–3.*

Dining and Lodging

$$–$$$ ✕ **Waterfront Restaurant.** A ringside seat on Camden Harbor can be had here; the best view is from the outdoor deck, open in warm weather. The fare is primarily seafood: boiled lobster, scallops, bouillabaisse, or seafood risotto. Some lunchtime highlights are lobster and crabmeat rolls. ✉ *Bayview St.,* ☎ *207/236–3747. Reservations not accepted. MC, V.*

$$–$$$ ✕▥ **Whitehall Inn.** One of Camden's best-known inns, just north of town, is an 1843 white clapboard sea captain's home with a wide porch and a turn-of-the-century wing. The Millay Room, off the lobby, preserves memorabilia of the poet Edna St. Vincent Millay, who grew up in the area. The sparsely furnished rooms have dark-wood bedsteads, white bedspreads, and claw-foot tubs. The dining room, which serves traditional and creative American cuisine, is open to the public for dinner. ✉ *52 High St. (Box 558), 04843,* ☎ *207/236–3391 or 800/789–6565,* ℻ *207/236–4427,* 🕸 *www.whitehall.com. 44 rooms, 40 with bath. Restaurant, tennis court, shuffleboard. AE, MC, V. Closed mid-Oct.–mid-May. MAP.*

$$–$$$ ✕🖾 **Youngtown Inn.** Inside this white Federal-style farmhouse are a
★ French-inspired country retreat and a well-respected French restaurant
($$$). The country location guarantees quiet, and the inn is a short
walk from the Fernald Neck Preserve on Lake Megunticook. Simple,
airy rooms open to decks with views of the rolling countryside. Two
have fireplaces. The restaurant, open to the public for dinner, serves
entrées such as lobster ravioli and breast of pheasant with foie gras
mousse. 🖾 *Rte. 52 at Youngtown Rd. Lincolnville 04849,* ☎ *207/763–
4290 or 800/291–8438,* 🖾 *207/763–4078,* 🕮 *www.youngtowninn.
com. 6 rooms, 1 suite. AE, MC, V. BP.*

$$$$ 🖾 **Inn at Ocean's Edge.** Perched on the ocean's edge, this shingle-style
★ inn looks as if it has been here for decades. In actuality, the original
building dates from 1999 and the upper building from 2001. Both were
built with modern-day comforts in mind. Every room has a king-size
bed, an ocean view, a fireplace, and a whirlpool for two, and all have
TVs, VCRs, and individually controlled heat and air-conditioning. 🖾
U.S. 1, Lincolnville (Box 704, Camden 04843); ☎ *207/236–0945,* 🖾
207/236–0609, 🕮 *www.innatoceansedge.com. 26 rooms, 1 suite. In-
room data ports, exercise room, meeting room. DC, MC, V. BP.*

$$$–$$$$ 🖾 **Victorian by the Sea.** It's less than 10 minutes from downtown Cam-
den, but with a quiet waterside location well off U.S. 1, the Victorian
Inn feels a world away. Most rooms and the wraparound porch have
magnificent views over island-studded Penobscot Bay. Romantic touches
include canopy and brass beds, braided rugs, white wicker furniture,
and floral wallpapers. Six guest rooms have fireplaces, and there are
four more in common rooms, including the glass-enclosed breakfast
room. 🖾 *Sea View Dr., Lincolnville (Box 1385, Camden 04843),* ☎
207/236–3785 or 800/382–9817, 🖾 *207/236–0017,* 🕮 *www.
victorianbythesea.com. 5 rooms, 2 suites. AE, MC, V. BP.*

$$–$$$ 🖾 **Camden Maine Stay.** This 1802 clapboard inn on the National Reg-
★ ister of Historic Places is within walking distance of shops and restau-
rants. The grounds are classic and inviting, from the flowers lining the
granite walk in summer to the snow-laden bushes in winter. Fresh and
colorful, the rooms contain many pieces of Eastlake furniture; six have
fireplaces. 🖾 *22 High St., 04842,* ☎ *207/236–9636,* 🖾 *207/236–0621,*
🕮 *www.mainestay.com. 5 rooms, 3 suites. AE, MC, V. BP.*

Nightlife and the Arts

Bay Chamber Concerts (🖾 Rockport Opera House, 6 Central St., Rock-
port, ☎ 207/236–2823 or 888/707–2770) presents chamber music on
Thursday and Friday night during July and August; concerts are given
once a month from September to June. **Gilbert's Public House** (🖾 12
Bay View St., ☎ 207/236–4320) has dancing and live entertainment.
Sea Dog Tavern & Brewery (🖾 43 Mechanic St., ☎ 207/236–6863), a
popular brew pub in a converted woolen mill, has live entertainment
in season. The **Whale's Tooth Pub** (🖾 U.S. 1, Lincolnville Beach, ☎ 207/
236–3747) has folk or acoustic entertainment on weekends.

Outdoor Activities and Sports

Brown Dog Bikes (🖾 53 Camden St., ☎ 207/236–6664) delivers rental
bikes to area lodgings. **Maine Sport** (🖾 U.S. 1, Rockport, ☎ 207/236–
8797 or 800/722–0826), the best sports outfitter north of Freeport,
rents bikes, camping and fishing gear, canoes, kayaks, cross-country
skis, ice skates, and snowshoes. It also conducts skiing and kayaking
clinics and trips. The *Betselma* (🖾 Camden Public Landing, ☎ 207/
236–4446) offers one- and two-hour powerboat trips.

A voyage around the bay by windjammer, whether for an afternoon
or a week, is unforgettable. The excursions are best from June through
September. Eggemoggin Reach is a famous cruising ground for yachts,

as are the coves and inlets around Deer Isle and the Penobscot Bay waters between Camden and Castine. The **Maine Windjammer Association** (⊠ Box 1144, Blue Hill 04614, ☎ 800/807–9463) represents the Camden-based windjammers *Angelique, Grace Bailey, Lewis R. French, Mary Day,* and *Mercantile* and the Rockport-based *Timberwind.* Cruises last three to eight days.

Shopping

Shops and galleries line Camden's Bayview and Main streets and the alleys that lead to the harbor. **L. E. Leonard** (⊠ 67 Pascal Ave., Rockport, ☎ 207/236–0878) sells an intriguing mix of antiques, Asian furnishings, contemporary clothing, and fun jewelry. **Maine Coast Artists** (⊠ 162 Russell Ave., Rockport, ☎ 207/236–2875) specializes in contemporary Maine art. **Maine Gathering** (⊠ 21 Main St., ☎ 207/236–9004) has a well-chosen selection of crafts, including Passamaquoddy and Penobscot baskets. **Maine's Massachusetts House Galleries** (⊠ U.S. 1, Lincolnville, ☎ 207/789–5705) display regional art, including bronzes, carvings, sculptures, and landscapes and seascapes in pencil, oil, and watercolor. The **Owl and Turtle Bookshop** (⊠ 8 Bay View St., ☎ 207/236–4769) sells books, CDs, cassettes, and cards. The two-story shop has rooms devoted to marine and children's books. The **Pine Tree Shop & Bayview Gallery** (⊠ 33 Bay View St., ☎ 207/236–4534) specializes in original art, prints, and posters, almost all with Maine themes. The **Windsor Chairmakers** (⊠ U.S. 1, Lincolnville, ☎ 207/789–5188 or 800/789–5188) sells custom-made handcrafted beds, chests, china cabinets, dining tables, highboys, and chairs.

Ski Areas

CAMDEN SNOW BOWL

The Maine coast isn't known for skiing, but this small, lively park in a Currier & Ives setting has skiing, snowboarding, tubing, and tobogganing—plus magnificent views over Penobscot Bay. ⊠ *Box 1207, Hosmer Pond Rd., 04843,* ☎ *207/236–3438.*

Downhill. The park has a 950-ft-vertical mountain, a small lodge with cafeteria, a ski school, and ski and toboggan rentals. Camden Snow Bowl has 11 trails accessed by one double chair and two T-bars. It also has night skiing.

Other Activities. Camden Snow Bowl has a small lake that is cleared for ice-skating, a snow-tubing park, and a 400-ft toboggan run that shoots sledders out onto the lake.

CROSS-COUNTRY SKIING

There are 16 km (10 mi) of cross-country skiing trails at **Camden Hills State Park** (⊠ U.S. 1, ☎ 207/236–9849). **Tanglewood 4-H Camp** (⊠ U.S. 1, ☎ 207/789–5868), about 5 mi away in Lincolnville, has 20 km (12½ mi) of trails.

Belfast

㉘ *19 mi north of Camden, 46 mi east of Augusta.*

Like many other Maine towns, Belfast has ridden the tides of affluence and depression since its glory days in the 1800s, when it was a shipbuilding center and home to many sea captains. Today it's high-tech, namely credit-card giant MBNA, that has helped rescue the city economically. The upswing has brought the revival of the old-fashioned redbrick Victorian downtown and a lively waterfront, as well as affordable lodging and dining. The houses on Church Street are a veritable glossary of 19th-century architectural styles; pick up a map with a walking tour at the visitor center at the foot of Main Street.

A ride on the **Belfast & Moosehead Lake Railroad** (⊠ One Depot Sq., Unity, ☎ 207/948–5500 or 800/392–5500, WEB www.belfastrailroad. com), which operates from July to mid-October ($16), is especially enjoyable in the fall after the leaves begin to change colors. The railroad's timetable coordinates with a cruise boat; a discount applies if you travel on both.

Dining and Lodging

$-$$ ✕ **Darby's.** Tin ceilings and an old-fashioned bar create a comfortable atmosphere for the creative casual fare served here. The eclectic menu lists hearty soups and sandwiches as well as dishes with an international flavor, such as Moroccan lamb. ⊠ *155 High St.,* ☎ *207/338–2339. AE, D, DC, MC, V.*

$$-$$$ 🏠 **Jeweled Turret Inn.** Turrets, columns, gables, and magnificent woodwork embellish this inn, originally built in 1898 as the home of a local attorney. The inn is named for the jewel-like stained-glass windows in the stairway turret; the gem theme continues in the den, where the ornate rock fireplace is said to include rocks from every state in the Union. Elegant Victorian pieces furnish the rooms: the Opal room has a marble bath with whirlpool tub in addition to a French armoire and a four-poster. ⊠ *40 Pearl St., 04915,* ☎ *207/338–2304 or 800/696–2304,* WEB *www.bbonline.com/me/jeweledturret. 7 rooms. AE, MC, V. BP.*

$$-$$$ 🏠 **The White House.** New owners have poured their hearts and purses into renovating this fine example of Greek Revival architecture, an 1840–1842 landmark by Maine architect Calvin Ryder. An eight-side cupola tops the house; inside are ornate plaster ceiling medallions, Italian marble fireplaces, an elliptical flying staircase, and intricate moldings. Crystal chandeliers, Asian rugs, and antiques and reproduction pieces elegantly decorate the spacious rooms. Two guest rooms have whirlpool tubs. You can relax in the English garden, in the gazebo, or under the enormous copper beech tree. ⊠ *1 Church St., 04915,* ☎ *207/338–1901 or 888/290–1901,* FAX *207/338–5161,* WEB *www.mainebb.com. 4 rooms, 2 suites. D, MC, V. BP.*

Outdoor Activities and Sports

KAYAKING
Belfast Kayak Tours (⊠ Belfast City Pier, ☎ 207/338–6204) provides fully outfitted trips and instruction.

PARKS
Belfast City Park (⊠ High St., 1 mi east of downtown) has a playground, tennis courts (lighted at night), a baseball diamond, and an outdoor swimming pool with lockers and showers. Use of the park is free.

Moose Point State Park (⊠ U.S. 1 between Belfast and Searsport, ☎ 207/548–2882) is ideal for easy hikes and picnics overlooking Penobscot Bay.

TOURS
Belfast Walks (☎ 207/338–6306) offer 1.5–hour walking tours that emphasize the town's history and architecture.

Shopping

Belfast's main and side streets house an eclectic selection of shops that mirror the city's economic base. Shoppers who prefer upscale boutiques rub elbows with those who bargain-hunt in thrift stores; fancy chocolate and pastry shops are just around the corner from the Belfast Co-op, a popular natural foods store.

Searsport

❷ *11 mi northeast of Belfast, 57 mi east of Augusta.*

Searsport, Maine's second-largest deepwater port (after Portland), has a rich shipbuilding and seafaring history. In the 1880s, 10 percent of all captains under deepwater sail hailed from here. Many of the former sea captains' homes are now bed-and-breakfasts. They make an ideal base for exploring the multitude of antiques shops and flea markets lining U.S. 1 that have earned Searsport the title of Maine's Antiques Capital.

★ The fine holdings within the nine historic and five modern buildings of the **Penobscot Marine Museum** provide fascinating documentation of the region's seafaring way of life. These buildings, including a still-active church and a sea captain's house, remain in their original spots in town. The museum's outstanding collection of marine art includes the largest collection of works by Thomas and James Buttersworth in the country. Also of note are photos of 284 local sea captains, a collection of China trade articles, artifacts of the whaling industry (including lots of scrimshaw), navigational instruments, treasures collected by seafarers around the globe, and models of famous ships. The museum's newest building, a boat barn, opened in 2001 with exhibits of small craft. ⊠ *5 U.S. 1, at Church St.,* ☎ *207/548–2529,* WEB *www. penobscotmarinemuseum.org.* ⌑ *$6.* ☉ *Memorial Day–late Oct., Mon.–Sat. 10–5, Sun. noon–5.*

Dining and Lodging

$$$ ✕ **The Rhumb Line.** The upscale restaurant in this 18th-century sea captain's home delivers fine dining, with formally attired waitstaff and excellent food. Pepper-glazed pork tenderloin, orange-glazed duck with potato pancakes, and horseradish-crusted salmon are typical entrées. ⊠ *U.S. 1,* ☎ *207/548–2600. MC, V. No lunch.*

$$ 🏠 **Brass Lantern** This antiques-filled Victorian bed-and-breakfast is an elegant retreat after a day of shopping nearby flea markets and antiques shops. The multicourse breakfasts are served on china and crystal by candlelight in the tin-ceiling dining room. ⊠ *81 W. Main St. (U.S. 1), 04874,* ☎ *207/548–0150 or 800/691–0150,* FAX *207/548–0304,* WEB *www.brasslanternmaine.com. 5 rooms. D, MC, V. FB.*

$–$$ 🏠 **Homeport Inn.** This 1861 inn, a former sea captain's home, provides an opulent Victorian environment that might put you in the mood to rummage through the nearby antiques and treasure shops. The back rooms downstairs have private decks and views of the bay. Families often stay in the housekeeping cottage. ⊠ *121 E. Main St. (U.S. 1),* ☎ *207/548–2259 or 800/742–5814,* WEB *www.bnbcity.com/inns/20015. 10 rooms, 7 with bath; 2 cottages. AE, D, MC, V. BP.*

Shopping

Along U.S. 1 you'll see several dozen shops and, in season, outdoor flea markets. Museum-quality model ship kits can be found at **Bluejacket Shipcrafters** (⊠ 160 E. Main St. [U.S. 1], ☎ 207/548–9970). More than 70 dealers show their wares in the two-story **Searsport Antique Mall** (⊠ 149 E. Main St. [U.S. 1], ☎ 207/548–2640); look for everything from linens and silver to turn-of-the-century oak. **Pumpkin Patch Antiques** (⊠ 15 W. Main St. [U.S. 1], ☎ 207/548–6047) displays such items as quilts, nautical memorabilia, and painted and wood furniture from about 20 dealers. It's open April through Thanksgiving or by appointment. **Penobscot Books** (⊠ 164 W. Main St. [U.S. 1], ☎ 207/548–6490) stocks a handsome collection of used and new books on the fine arts.

Castine

30 *30 mi southeast of Searsport.*

Set on the tip of a peninsula, Castine is a quiet, peaceful place to escape most of the coastal crowds. The French, the British, the Dutch, and the Americans fought over the town from the 17th century to the War of 1812. Present-day Castine's many appealing attributes include its lively harborfront, lovely Federal and Greek Revival houses, and town common; there are two small museums and the ruins of a British fort to explore. For a nice stroll, park your car at the landing and walk up Main Street toward the white Trinitarian Federated Church, which has a tapering spire. Among the white clapboard buildings that ring the town common are the Ives House (once the summer home of the poet Robert Lowell), the Abbott School, and the Unitarian Church, capped by a whimsical belfry. Castine is also home to the Maine Maritime Academy, and its training ship often can be seen in port.

Castine's **Soldiers and Sailors Monument** (⊠ Castine Town Common) is typical of many town memorials that honor the state's participation in the Civil War. It was dedicated in May 1887 to the veterans of that conflict.

Dining and Lodging

$$–$$$ ✕☷ **Manor Inn.** Bordering a 95-acre conservation forest with trails leading to the bay, this 1895 English manor-style inn provides a quiet retreat. Yoga classes are offered in a fully equipped studio. Rooms are individually decorated, and four have fireplaces. The dining room ($$–$$$), which specializes in regional cuisine, is on the front porch and overlooks the expansive lawn and side gardens. The pub offers a lighter menu. ⊠ *15 Manor Drive, off Battle Ave. 04421,* ☎ *207/326–4861 or 877/626–6746,* ℻ *207/326–0891,* 𝚆𝙴𝙱 *www.manor-inn.com. 10 rooms, 2 suites. Restaurant, pub. AE, DC, MC, V. BP.*

$$ ✕☷ **Castine Inn.** Upholstered easy chairs and fine prints and paintings
★   are typical of the furnishings in the no-smoking inn's airy and simply decorated rooms. The third floor has the best views: the harbor over the gardens on one side, the village on the other. The dining room ($$$), decorated with a wraparound mural of Castine and its harbor, is open to the public for breakfast and dinner; the creative menu features local ingredients and entrées such as oil-poached salmon. There's a snug, English-style pub off the lobby. ⊠ *33 Main St. (Box 41), 04421,* ☎ *207/326–4365,* ℻ *207/326–4570,* 𝚆𝙴𝙱 *www.castineinn.com. 15 rooms, 4 suites. Restaurant, pub, sauna. MC, V. Closed Nov. 1–late Apr.; restaurant closed Tues. BP.*

Outdoor Activities and Sports

Castine Kayak Adventures (⊠ Dennett's Wharf, ☎ 207/326–9045) offer tours with a Registered Maine Guide. The **Steam Launch *Laurie Ellen*** (⊠ Dennett's Wharf, ☎ 207/326–9045 or 207/266–2841), the only wood-fired, steam-powered, USCG-inspected passenger steam launch in the country, offers cruises around Castine Harbor and up the Bagaduce River.

Shopping

H.O.M.E. (⊠ U.S. 1, Orland, ☎ 207/469–7961) is a cooperative crafts village with a crafts and pottery shop, weaving shop, flea market, market stand, and woodworking shop. **Leila Day Antiques** (⊠ Main St., ☎ 207/326–8786) specializes in antiques, quilts, folk art, and nautical accessories. **McGrath-Dunham Gallery** (⊠ Main St., ☎ 207/326–9175) carries paintings, sculpture, original prints, and pottery.

Blue Hill

③① *19 mi east of Castine.*

Blue Hill has a dramatic perch over the harbor. It is renowned for its pottery and is a good spot for shopping and gallery hopping.

Jonathan Fisher was the first settled minister of Blue Hill. The **Parson Fisher House,** which he built from 1814 to 1820, provides a fascinating look at his many accomplishments and talents, which included writing and illustrating books and poetry, farming, painting, furniture building, and making a camera obscura. Also on view is a wooden clock he crafted while a student at Harvard; the face holds messages about time written in English, Greek, Latin, Hebrew, and French. ✉ *Rtes. 15/176,* ☎ *No phone.* ☞ *$3.* ◔ *July–mid-Sept., Mon.–Sat., 2–5.*

Dining and Lodging

$$–$$$ ✕ **Arborvine.** This restaurant was an immediate hit when opened in 2000 by chef/owner John Hikade. The old cape has four dining areas, all tastefully decorated. Entrées may include crispy roast duckling and medallions of lamb with wild mushrooms. A take-out lunch is available at the adjacent Moveable Feasts deli. ✉ *Main St.,* ☎ *207/374–2119. MC, V. Closed Mon.; Moveable Feasts closed Sun.*

$$–$$$ ✕ **Jonathan's.** Although the ownership has changed at this in-town restaurant, chef Jonathan Chase is still in the kitchen. He's known for his use of fresh regional Maine products. Choose from Maine seacoast vegetable salad, pan-roasted mussels with potatoes, onions, and greens, or warm cranberry bread pudding, among many other delicious options. ✉ *Main St.,* ☎ *207/374–5226. MC, V.*

$$–$$$$ ☷ **Oakland House.** An inn, dining hall, and cottages are tucked among the towering pines at this sprawling oceanfront property. Owner Jim Littlefield is a fourth-generation innkeeper. The Shore Oaks seaside inn, built in 1907 in the Arts and Crafts style, retains an elegant turn-of-the-century ambience. Cottages, most with kitchenettes and fireplaces, are rustic but fully equipped. The inn has a ½ mi of ocean shorefront on Eggemoggin Reach as well as a lake beach. ✉ *435 Herrick Rd., Brooksville 04617,* ☎ *207/359–8521 or 800/359–7352,* FAX *207/359–9865,* WEB *www.oaklandhouse.com. 10 rooms, 7 with bath; 15 cottages. Dining room, lake, beaches, hiking, boating, recreation room, playground. MC, V. MAP.*

$$$ ☷ **Blue Hill Inn.** Rambling and antiques-filled, this 1830 inn is a com-
★   forting place to relax after exploring nearby shops and galleries. Original pumpkin pine and painted floors set the tone for the mix of Empire and early Victorian pieces that fill the two parlors and guest rooms; five rooms have fireplaces. ✉ *Union St. (Box 403), 04614,* ☎ *207/374–2844 or 800/826–7415,* FAX *207/374–2829,* WEB *www.bluehillinn. com. 11 rooms, 1 suite. AE, MC, V. Closed Dec.–mid-May and midweek in Nov. BP.*

Nightlife and the Arts

Kneisel Hall Chamber Music Festival (✉ Kneisel Hall, Rte. 15, ☎ 207/374–2811) has concerts on Sunday and Friday in summer.

Outdoor Activities and Sports

Holbrook Island Sanctuary (✉ off Cape Rosier Rd., Brooksville, ☎ 207/326–4012) has a gravel beach with splendid views, a picnic area, and hiking trails.

Shopping

Big Chicken Barn (✉ U.S. 1, Ellsworth, ☎ 207/374–2715) has three floors filled with books, antiques, and collectibles. **Handworks Gallery** (✉ Main St., ☎ 207/374–5613) carries unusual crafts, jewelry, and clothing. **Leighton Gallery** (⊠ Parker Point Rd., ☎ 207/374–5001) shows oil paintings, lithographs, watercolors, and other contemporary art in the gallery, and sculpture in its garden. **North Country Textiles** (⊠ Main St., ☎ 207/374–2715) specializes in fine woven shawls, place mats, throws, baby blankets, and pillows in subtle patterns and color schemes.

Mark Bell Pottery (⊠ Rte. 15, ☎ 207/374–5881) has received national acclaim for his porcelain bowls, bottles, and vases. **Rackliffe Pottery** (⊠ Rte. 172, ☎ 207/374–2297) is famous for its vivid blue pottery, including plates, tea and coffee sets, pitchers, casseroles, and canisters. **Rowantrees Pottery** (⊠ Union St., ☎ 207/374–5535) has an extensive selection of styles and patterns in dinnerware, tea sets, vases, and decorative items.

En Route   Scenic Route 15 south from Blue Hill passes through Brooksville and takes you over the graceful suspension bridge that crosses Eggemoggin Reach to Deer Isle. The turnout and picnic area at **Caterpillar Hill**, 1 mi south of the junction of Routes 15 and 175, commands a fabulous view of Penobscot Bay, hundreds of dark-green islands, and the Camden Hills across the bay.

Deer Isle Village

32   *16 mi south of Blue Hill.*

In Deer Isle Village, thick woods give way to tidal coves. Stacks of lobster traps populate the backyards of shingled houses, and dirt roads lead to summer cottages.

Haystack Mountain School of Crafts attracts internationally renowned glassblowers, potters, sculptors, jewelers, blacksmiths, printmakers, and weavers to its summer institute. You can attend evening lectures or visit artists' studios (by appointment only). ⊠ *Rte. 15, south of Deer Isle Village (turn left at Gulf gas station and follow signs for 6 mi)*, ☎ *207/ 348–2306.* ⊒ *Free.* ⊙ *June–Sept.*

Dining and Lodging

$$$$ ✕⊞ **Goose Cove Lodge.** This wooded property has a fine stretch of ocean frontage, a sandy beach, and a long sandbar that leads to a nature preserve. Cottages and suites are in secluded woodlands and on the shore. Some are attached, some have a single large room, and still others have one or two bedrooms. All but three units have fireplaces. Dinner at the restaurant ($$$$; reservations essential) is superb, and the contemporary American fare includes at least one vegetarian entrée. On Monday night in July and August, there's a lobster feast on the beach. ⊠ *Box 40, Goose Cove Rd., Sunset 04683,* ☎ *207/348–2508 or 800/728–1963,* ⅌ℵ *207/348–2624,* ⅌ℰℬ *www.goosecovelodge.com. 2 rooms, 7 suites, 13 cottages. 2 restaurants, hiking, beach, boating. AE, D, MC, V. All but 3 units closed mid-Oct.–mid-May. BP.*

$$$ ✕⊞ **Pilgrim's Inn.** A deep-red, four-story gambrel-roof house, the Pilgrim's Inn dates from about 1793 and overlooks a mill pond and harbor in Deer Isle Village. Wing chairs and Oriental rugs fill the library; a downstairs taproom has a huge brick fireplace and pine furniture. Guest rooms have English fabrics and carefully selected antiques. The dining room (reservations essential; no lunch) is in the attached barn, a rustic yet elegant space with farm implements, French oil lamps, and tiny windows. The five-course menu changes nightly but might list rack of lamb or fresh seafood. ⊠ *Bridge Rd. (Rte. 15A), 04627,* ☎ *207/ 348–6615,* ⅌ℵ *207/348–7769,* ⅌ℰℬ *www.pilgrimsinn.com. 13 rooms, 10 with bath; 2 seaside cottages. Restaurant, bicycles. MC, V. Closed mid-Oct.–mid-May. BP, MAP.*

Shopping

Blue Heron Gallery & Studio (⊠ Rte. 15, ☏ 207/348–6051) sells the work of the Haystack Mountain School of Crafts faculty. **Harbor Farm** (⊠ Rte. 15, Little Deer Isle, ☏ 207/348–7737) carries wonderful products for the home, such as pottery, furniture, dinnerware, linens, and folk art. **Nervous Nellie's Jams and Jellies** (⊠ 474A Sunshine Rd., ☏ 800/777–6825) sells jams and jellies and operates a café. The outdoor sculpture garden is a hit with kids. **Old Deer Isle Parish House Antiques** (⊠ Rte. 15, ☏ 207/348–9964) is a place for poking around in jumbles of old kitchenware, glassware, books, and linens. **Turtle Gallery** (⊠ Rte. 15, ☏ 207/348–9977) shows contemporary painting and sculpture.

Stonington

㉝ *7 mi south of Deer Isle.*

Stonington's isolation at the tip of the Deer Isle peninsula has helped it retain its fishing village flavor. This is changing now, as boutiques and galleries open in summer now line its main thoroughfare. Still, Stonington remains a working port town—the principal activity is at the waterfront, where fishing boats arrive with the day's catch. At night, the town can be rowdy. The high, sloped island that rises beyond the archipelago known as Merchants Row is Isle au Haut, which contains a remote section of Acadia National Park; it's accessible by mail boat from Stonington.

The tiny **Deer Isle Granite Museum** documents Stonington's quarrying tradition. The museum's centerpiece is an 8- by 15-ft working model of quarrying operations on Crotch Island and the town of Stonington in 1900. ⊠ *Main St.,* ☏ *207/367–6331.* 🎟 *Free.* ☉ *Memorial Day–Labor Day, Mon.–Sat. 10–5 and Sun. 1–5.*

Dining and Lodging

$$–$$$ ✕ **Cafe Atlantic.** Whether you want ice cream, tasty boiled lobster, or a fancier meal, you'll find it at this harborfront eatery. Country linens and antiques decorate the restaurant, which serves fresh seafood as well as chicken and steak. For lobster in the rough, head to the deck overhanging the water. For a quick snack, visit the ice cream window. ⊠ *Main St.,* ☏ *207/367–6373. AE, D, MC, V.*

$–$$ ✕ **Lily's.** Local artwork embellishes the three dining rooms in this old Victorian house. The bistro-style menu emphasizes fresh, seasonal foods and may include entrées such as fresh salmon with a sesame butter sauce or curried chicken. The desserts are legendary. ⊠ *Rte. 15,* ☏ *207/367–5936. MC, V. Closed Sat.–Sun.*

$$ ▥ **Inn on the Harbor.** From the front, this inn composed of four 100-year-old Victorian buildings is as plain and unadorned as Stonington itself. But out back it opens up, with an expansive deck over the harbor. Many guests take breakfast here in the morning. Rooms on the harbor side have views, and some have fireplaces and private decks. Those on the street side lack the views and can be noisy at night. ⊠ *Main St. (Box 69), 04681,* ☏ *207/367–2420 or 800/942–2420,* FAX *207/367–5165. 13 rooms, 1 suite. Coffee shop. AE, D, MC, V. CP.*

The Arts

Stonington Opera House (⊠ School St.) books live theater, music, and dance events.

Outdoor Activities and Sports

You can be a lobsterman for the day on the *Jacob Lewis* (☏ 207/367–5198), a 32-ft traditional Maine lobster boat. **Old Quarry** (☏ 207/367–8977) operates a charter and boat-taxi service, rents canoes, kayaks, and bicycles and offers guided kayak trips. Call for directions.

Shopping

Dockside Books & Gifts (✉ W. Main St., ☎ 207/367–2652) on the harborfront stocks an eclectic selection of books, crafts, and gifts. The **Clown** (✉ Main St., ☎ 207/367–6348) has fine art, antiques, a good wine selection, and specialty foods. **Eastern Bay Gallery** (✉ Main St., ☎ 207/367–6368) carries contemporary Maine crafts; summer exhibits highlight the works of specific artists. **Firebird Gallery** (✉ W. Main St., ☎ 207/367–0955) is a good choice for fine contemporary crafts.

Isle au Haut

③④ *14 mi south of Stonington.*

Isle au Haut thrusts its steeply ridged back out of the sea south of Stonington. Accessible only by passenger mail boat (☎ 207/367–5193), the island is worth visiting for the ferry ride itself, a half-hour cruise amid the tiny islands of Merchants Row, where you might see terns, guillemots, and harbor seals.

More than half the island is part of **Acadia National Park**: 17½ mi of trails extend through quiet spruce and birch woods, along beaches and seaside cliffs, and over the spine of the central mountain ridge. (For more information on the park, *see* Bar Harbor *and* Acadia National Park.) From mid-June to mid-September, the mail boat docks at **Duck Harbor** within the park. The small campground here, with five lean-tos, is open from mid-May to mid-October and fills up quickly. Reservations, which are essential, can be made after April 1 by writing to Acadia National Park (✉ Box 177, Bar Harbor 04609).

Lodging

$$$$ 🏨 **The Keeper's House.** Thick spruce forest surrounds this converted lighthouse-keeper's house on a rock ledge. There is no electricity, but everyone receives a flashlight upon registering; you dine by candlelight on seafood or chicken and read in the evening by kerosene lantern. Trails link the inn with Acadia National Park's Isle au Haut trail network, and you can walk to the village. The spacious rooms contain simple, painted-wood furniture and local crafts. A separate cottage, the Oil House, has no indoor plumbing. Access to the island is via the mail boat from Stonington. ✉ *Box 26, Lighthouse Rd., 04645,* ☎ *207/367–2261,* WEB *www.keepershouse.com. 4 rooms without bath, 1 cottage. Dock, bicycles. No credit cards. Closed Nov.–Apr. FAP.*

Penobscot Bay A to Z

To research prices, get advice from other travelers, and book travel arrangements, visit www.fodors.com.

CAR TRAVEL

U.S. 1 follows the west coast of Penobscot Bay, linking Rockland, Rockport, Camden, Belfast, and Searsport. On the east side of the bay, Route 175 (south from U.S. 1) takes you to Route 166A (for Castine) and Route 15 (for Blue Hill, Deer Isle, and Stonington). A car is essential for exploring the bay area.

EMERGENCIES

➤ HOSPITALS: **Blue Hill Memorial Hospital** (✉ Water St., Blue Hill, ☎ 207/374–2836). **Island Medical Center** (✉ Airport Rd., Stonington, ☎ 207/367–2311). **Penobscot Bay Medical Center** (✉ U.S. 1, Rockport, ☎ 207/596–8000). **Waldo County General Hospital** (✉ 56 Northport Ave., Belfast, ☎ 207/338–2500).

LODGING

Camden Accommodations provides assistance for reservations around Camden.

➤ LOCAL AGENTS: **Camden Accommodations** (☎ 207/236–6090 or 800/236–1920, FAX 207/236–6091).

VISITOR INFORMATION

➤ CONTACTS: **Belfast Area Chamber of Commerce** (✉ Box 58, 1 Main St., Belfast 04915, ☎ 207/338–5900). **Blue Hill Chamber of Commerce** (✉ Box 520, Blue Hill 04614, ☎ no phone). **Castine Town Office** (✉ Emerson Hall, Court St., Castine 04421, ☎ 207/326–4502). **Deer Isle–Stonington Chamber of Commerce** (✉ Box 459, Stonington 04681, ☎ 207/348–6124). **Rockland–Thomaston Area Chamber of Commerce** (✉ Box 508, Harbor Park, Rockland 04841, ☎ 207/596–0376 or 800/562–2529). **Rockport-Camden-Lincolnville Chamber of Commerce** (✉ Public Landing, Box 919, Camden 04843, ☎ 207/236–4404 or 800/223–5459). **Waldo County Regional Chamber of Commerce** (✉ School St., Unity 04988, ☎ 207/948–5050 or 800/870–9934).

MOUNT DESERT ISLAND

Acadia is the informal name for the area east of Penobscot Bay that includes Mount Desert Island (pronounced "dessert") as well as Blue Hill Bay and Frenchman Bay. Mount Desert, 13 mi across, is Maine's largest island, and it encompasses most of Acadia National Park, an astonishingly beautiful preserve with rocky cliffs, crashing surf, and serene mountains and ponds. Maine's number-one tourist attraction, it draws more than 4 million visitors a year. The 40,000 acres of woods and mountains, lake and shore, footpaths, carriage roads, and hiking trails that make up the park extend to other islands and some of the mainland. Outside the park, on Mount Desert's eastern shore, Bar Harbor has become a busy tourist town. Less commercial and congested are the smaller island towns, such as Southwest Harbor and Northeast Harbor, and the outlying islands.

Bar Harbor

㉟ *160 mi northeast of Portland, 22 mi southeast of Ellsworth on Rte. 3.*

An upper-class resort town in the 19th century, Bar Harbor now serves visitors to Acadia National Park with inns, motels, and restaurants. Most of its grand mansions were destroyed in a fire that devastated the island in 1947, but many surviving estates have been converted into inns and restaurants. Motels abound, yet the town retains the beauty of a commanding location on Frenchman Bay. Shops, restaurants, and hotels are clustered along Main, Mt. Desert, and Cottage streets. Take a stroll down West Street, a National Historic District, where you can see some of the grand cottages that survived the fire.

The **Bar Harbor Historical Society Museum** displays photographs of Bar Harbor from the days when it catered to the very rich. Other exhibits document the fire of 1947. ✉ *33 Ledgelawn Ave.,* ☎ *207/288–3807 or 207/288–0000.* 🎫 *Free.* ☉ *June–Oct., Mon.–Sat. 1–4 or by appointment.*

★ The **Abbe Museum,** a treasure trove of Native American artifacts, expects to be in its new downtown quarters, across from the village green, in September 2001. The museum's collections contain 50,000 objects spanning 10,000 years of Native American history, archaeology, and culture in Maine. A glass-walled archaeological laboratory will allow visitors to observe staff and volunteers working with arti-

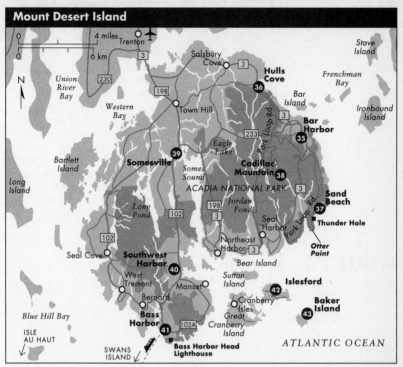

Mount Desert Island

facts found during the museum's scientific excavations. The 1893 building, the former home of the YMCA, is eligible for the National Register of Historic Places. Its facade is an example of the eclectic Shingle Style often used for coastal summer homes at the turn of the 20th century. ⊠ *26 Mt. Desert St.* ☎ *207/288–3519,* WEB *www.abbemuseum. org.* ☞ *$4.50.* ☯ *Mem. Day–June 30 and Sept. 1–mid-Oct., Mon.– Wed. 10-5 and Thurs.–Sun. 10–9; July–Aug., Mon.–Tues. 10–5, Wed.– Sun. 10–9; mid-Oct.–Mem. Day, Thurs.–Sun. 1–5.*

🖑 The small **Natural History Museum** at the College of the Atlantic has wildlife exhibits, a hands-on discovery room, interpretive programs, and a self-guided nature trail. ⊠ *Rte. 3,* ☎ *207/288–5015.* ☞ *$3.50.* ☯ *Mid-June–Labor Day, Mon.–Sat. 10–5; Labor Day–Columbus Day, Thurs.–Mon. 10–4.*

🖑 The **Acadia Zoo** has pastures, streams, and woods that shelter about 45 species of wild and domestic animals, including reindeer, wolves, monkeys, and a moose. A barn has been converted into a rain-forest habitat for monkeys, birds, reptiles, and other Amazon creatures. ⊠ *Rte. 3, Trenton, north of Bar Harbor,* ☎ *207/667–3244.* ☞ *$6.* ☯ *May– Dec., daily 9:30–dusk.*

Dining and Lodging

$$$ ✕ **The Burning Tree.** Fresh is the key word at this casual restaurant just outside town. The menu emphasizes seafood and organic produce and chicken; some typical items are pan-sautéed monkfish, Cajun lobster, crab au gratin, and chicken pot roast. There are always two or three vegetarian choices. Local contemporary art adorns the walls in the two dining rooms and on the porch. ⊠ *Rte. 3, Otter Creek,* ☎ *207/288– 9331. D, MC, V. Closed Tues. and mid-Oct.–late May.*

$$$ ✕ **George's.** Candles, flowers, and linens grace the tables, and art fills
★ the walls of the four small dining rooms in this old house. The menu's Mediterranean influences can be tasted in the phyllo-wrapped lobster;

the lamb and wild-game entrées are superb. The prix-fixe menu includes an appetizer, an entrée, and dessert. Jazz musicians perform nightly in peak season. ✉ *7 Stephen's La.,* ☏ *207/288–4505. AE, D, DC, MC, V. Closed Nov.–mid-June. No lunch.*

$$$ ✕ **Porcupine Grill.** This restaurant, named for a cluster of islets in Frenchman Bay, has a menu that changes regularly but might include starters such as pan-roasted mussels or citrus barbecued quail and main courses like grilled lobster, twin Portobello fillets, or filet mignon. Soft-green walls, antique furnishings, and Villeroy & Boch porcelain create an ambience that complements the sophisticated cuisine. ✉ *123 Cottage St.,* ☏ *207/288–3884. AE, MC, V. Closed Sun. and Nov.–May.*

$$–$$$ ✕ **Café This Way.** Jazz, unmatched tables and chairs, and a few couches provide a relaxing background for the creative, internationally inspired menu at this restaurant tucked in a back street. You might begin with crab cakes with tequila-lime sauce and then move on to cashew-crusted chicken over sautéed greens with sesame-ginger aioli or perhaps butternut squash ravioli with roasted red peppers, broccoli, and a rosemary maple cream sauce. Save room for the homemade desserts. ✉ *14½ Mt. Desert St.,* ☏ *207/288–4483. MC, V.*

$$–$$$ ✕ **Havana.** Pumpkin-colored walls, soft jazz, wood floors, and cloth-
★   covered tables set the tone at this storefront restaurant on the fringe of downtown Bar Harbor. The Latin-influenced menu emphasizes local natural and organic ingredients and changes weekly. The menu may include crab-and-roasted-corn cakes or grilled swordfish, marinated in ginger and lime and finished with a scallion vinaigrette. ✉ *318 Main St.,* ☏ *207/288–2822. Reservations essential. MC, V. Closed Sun.–Tues. late Oct.–mid-May.*

$$$–$$$$ ✕⊞ **Bar Harbor Inn.** The roots of this genteel inn date from the 1880s. Rooms are spread out over three buildings on nicely landscaped waterfront property, just a short walk from town. Most rooms have balconies, hot tubs, fireplaces, and great views. The two-level suites are a good choice for families. Rooms in the Oceanfront Lodge offer private decks or patios overlooking the ocean, while those in the Newport Lodge, behind it, are more simply furnished and smaller. The formal waterfront Reading Room serves mostly Continental fare but has some Maine specialties like lobster pie and a scrumptious Indian pudding. The more casual Terrace Grill is an outdoor restaurant on the waterfront. ✉ *Newport Dr., 04609,* ☏ *207/288–3351 or 800/248–3351,* FAX *207/288–5296,* WEB *www.barharborinn.com. 138 rooms, 15 suites. 2 restaurants, no-smoking room, exercise room, pool, business services. AE, D, DC, MC, V. CP.*

$$$$ ⊞ **Balance Rock Inn.** This grand summer cottage built in 1903 commands a prime, secluded location on the water but is only two blocks from downtown. The atmosphere is a bit stuffy, but service is thoughtful. Rooms are spacious and meticulously furnished with reproduction pieces—four-poster and canopy beds in guest rooms, crystal chandeliers and a grand piano in common rooms. Some rooms have fireplaces, saunas, steam rooms, whirlpool tubs, or porches, and most have views of the pool and gardens and of the water beyond. From the bar on the veranda, you can watch the activity in the harbor. ✉ *21 Albert Meadow, 04609,* ☏ *207/288–2610 or 800/753–0494,* FAX *207/288–5534,* WEB *www.barharborvacations.com. 13 rooms, 1 suite, 3 apartments. Bar, pool, exercise room, concierge. AE, D, MC, V. Closed late Oct.–early May. BP.*

$$$–$$$$ ⊞ **Inn at Canoe Point.** Seclusion and privacy are the main attributes
★   of this snug, 100-year-old Tudor-style house on the water at Hulls Cove, 2 mi from Bar Harbor and ¼ mi from Acadia National Park's Hulls Cove Visitor Center. The Master Suite, a large room with a gas fireplace, has French doors that open onto a waterside deck. The inn's living room has huge windows that look out on the water, a granite

fireplace, and a waterfront deck. ⊠ *Box 216, Rte. 3, 04609,* ☎ *207/ 288–9511,* FAX *207/288–2870,* WEB *www.innatcanoepoint.com. 3 rooms, 2 suites. D, MC, V. BP.*

$$$–$$$$ ⊞ **Ullikana.** Inside the stucco-and-timber walls of this traditional
★ Tudor cottage, the exuberant decor juxtaposes antiques with contemporary country pieces, vibrant color with French country wallpapers, and abstract art with folk creations. The combination not only works— it shines. Rooms are large, most have at least a glimpse of the water, many have fireplaces, and some have decks. Breakfast is an elaborate multicourse affair. The refurbished Yellow House across the drive has six additional rooms decorated in traditional Old Bar Harbor style. Ullikana is a short walk to downtown shops. ⊠ *16 The Field, 04609,* ☎ *207/288–9552,* FAX *207/288–3682,* WEB *www.ullikana.com. 16 rooms. MC, V. Closed Nov.–May. BP.*

$$ ⊞ **Seacroft Inn.** It's an easy walk to town or the Shore Path from this rambling multigabled inn, which is a good choice for families. One room has a fireplace, another a kitchen, yet another a private deck, but all have refrigerators and microwaves. A breakfast basket is delivered to your room each morning. ⊠ *18 Albert Meadow, 04609,* ☎ *207/288– 4669 or 800/824–9694. 3 rooms (1 with separate bath), 1 suite, 1 studio, 1 efficiency. Refrigerator. MC, V. CP.*

Nightlife and the Arts

For dancing, try **Carmen Verandah** (⊠ 119 Main St., upstairs, ☎ 207/ 288–2766). **Geddy's Pub** (⊠ 19 Main St., ☎ 207/288–5077) has live entertainment early in the evening followed by a DJ spinning discs. At the **Lompoc Cafe & Brewpub** (⊠ 30 Rodick St., ☎ 207/288–9513) you can relax in a garden setting and play a game of bocce. Comfortable chairs, pizza, and beer make the viewing easy at **Reel Pizza Cinerama** (⊠ 33B Kennebec Pl., ☎ 207/288–3811).

Arcady Music Festival (☎ 207/288–3151) schedules concerts (primarily classical) at locations around Mount Desert Island and at some off-island sites, year-round. **Bar Harbor Music Festival** (⊠ 59 Cottage St., ☎ 207/288–5744) arranges jazz, chamber music, string-orchestra, and pop concerts by young professionals from July to early August.

Outdoor Activities and Sports

BIKING

Acadia Bike & Canoe (⊠ 48 Cottage St., ☎ 207/288–9605 or 800/526– 8615) rents and sells mountain bikes. **Bar Harbor Bicycle Shop** (⊠ 141 Cottage St., ☎ 207/288–3886 or 800/824–2453) rents both recreational and high-performance bikes by the half or full day.

BOATING

Acadia Bike & Canoe has canoe and sea kayak rentals. For guided kayak tours, try **National Park Sea Kayak Tours** (⊠ 39 Cottage St., ☎ 207/ 288–0342 or 800/347–0940). **Coastal Kayaking Tours** (⊠ 48 Cottage St., ☎ 207/288–9605 or 800/526–8615) offers tours led by registered Maine guides. The four-mast schooner *Margaret Todd* (⊠ Bar Harbor Inn Pier, ☎ 207/288–4585) offers 1½- to 2-hour tours daily between mid-May and October.

STATE PARK

On Frenchman Bay but off Mount Desert Island, the 55-acre **Lamoine State Park** (⊠ Rte. 184, Lamoine, ☎ 207/667–4778) has a boat-launching ramp, a fishing pier, a children's playground, and a 61-site campground that's open from mid-May to mid-October.

WHALE-WATCHING

Acadian Whale Watcher (⊠ Golden Anchor Pier, 52 West St., ☎ 207/ 288–9794 or 800/421–3307) runs 3½-hour whale-watching cruises from

June to mid-October. **Bar Harbor Whale Watch Co.** (✉ 1 West St., ☎ 207/288–3322 or 800/508–1499) operates the catamaran *Friendship V,* for whale-watching and the *Katherine,* for lobster fishing and seal watching.

Shopping

Bar Harbor in summer is prime territory for browsing for gifts, T-shirts, and novelty items. For bargains, head for the outlets that line Route 3 in Ellsworth, which have good discounts on shoes, sportswear, cookware, and more.

Ben and Bill's Chocolate Emporium (✉ 66 Main St., ☎ 207/288–3281) is a chocolate-lover's nirvana, and the adventurous can try lobster ice cream here. **Birdsnest Gallery** (✉ 12 Mt. Desert St., ☎ 207/288–4054) sells fine art, paintings, and sculpture. The **Eclipse Gallery** (✉ 12 Mt. Desert St., ☎ 207/288–9048) carries handblown glass, ceramics, art photography, and wood furniture. **Island Artisans** (✉ 99 Main St., ☎ 207/288–4214) is a crafts cooperative. The **Lone Moose–Fine Crafts** (✉ 78 West St., ☎ 207/288–4229) has art glass and works in clay, pottery, wood, and fiberglass. **Songs of the Sea** (✉ 47 West St., ☎ 207/ 288–5653) sells handcrafted musical instruments.

Acadia National Park

★   *4 mi northwest of Bar Harbor (to Hulls Cove).*

There is no one Acadia. The park holds some of the most spectacular and varied scenery on the eastern seaboard: a rugged coastline of surf-pounded granite and an interior graced by sculpted mountains, quiet ponds, and lush deciduous forests. Cadillac Mountain, the highest point of land on the eastern coast, dominates the park. Although it's rugged, Acadia National Park also has graceful stone bridges, horse-drawn carriages, and the elegant Jordan Point Tea House. The 27-mi Park Loop Road provides an excellent introduction, yet to truly appreciate the park you must get off the main road and experience it by walking, biking, or taking a carriage ride on the carriage trails, by hiking or perhaps sea kayaking. If you get off the beaten path, you'll find places in the park that you can have practically to yourself, despite the millions of visitors who descend in summer.

㊱   The popular **Hulls Cove** approach to Acadia National Park, northwest of Bar Harbor on Route 3, brings you to the start of the **Park Loop Road.** Even though it is often clogged with traffic in summer, the road provides the best introduction to the park. You can drive it in an hour, but allow at least half a day or more to explore the many sites along the route. At the start of the loop, the visitor center shows a free 15-minute orientation film. Acadia Rangers lead nature walks, children's programs, mountain hikes, photography programs, and evening talks. A schedule of programs is available here. You can also pick up the *Acadia Beaver Log* (the park's free newspaper detailing guided hikes and other ranger-led programs), books, maps of hiking trails and carriage roads, the schedule for naturalist-led tours, and cassettes for drive-it-yourself tours. Traveling south on the Park Loop Road, you'll reach a small ticket booth where you pay the $10-per-vehicle entrance fee, good for seven consecutive days. ✉ *Visitor center, Park Loop Rd. off Rte. 3,* ☎ *207/288–3338,* WEB *www.nps.gov/acad.* ☉ *Park daily. Visitor center late June–Aug., daily 8–6; mid-Apr.–mid-June and Sept.–Oct., daily 8–4:30.*

㊲   **Sand Beach** is a small stretch of pink sand backed by the mountains of Acadia and the odd lump of rock known as the Beehive. The **Ocean Trail,** which runs alongside the Park Loop Road from Sand Beach to the Otter Point parking area, is an easily accessible walk with some of the most awesome scenery in Maine: huge slabs of pink granite heaped at the ocean's edge, ocean views unobstructed to the horizon, and Thunder Hole, a natural seaside cave into which the ocean rushes and roars.

★ ⓷ **Cadillac Mountain,** at 1,532 ft, is the highest point on the eastern seaboard. From the smooth, bald summit you have an awesome 360-degree view of the ocean, islands, jagged coastline, and woods and lakes of Acadia and its surroundings. You can drive or hike to the summit.

The Sieur de Monts Spring exit off the Park Loop offers two enticing sites. The original **Abbe Museum** (a new museum is expected to open in downtown Bar Harbor in late 2001) holds a treasure trove of Maine's Native American history, including arrowheads, moccasins, tools, jewelry, and a well-documented collection of baskets. ⊠ *Sieur de Monts Spring exit from Rte. 3 or Acadia National Park Loop Rd.,* ☎ *207/288–3519.* ☜ *$2.* ☼ *July–Aug., daily 9–5; late May–June 30 and Sept.–late Oct., daily 10–4.*

The **Wild Gardens of Acadia** present a miniature view of the plants that grow on Mount Desert Island. ⊠ *Rte. 3 at the Sieur de Monts Spring exit,* ☎ *207/288–3400.* ☜ *Free.* ☼ *Paths 24 hrs.*

Dining and Lodging

$$–$$$ ✕ **Jordan Pond House.** The restaurant's setting overlooking Jordan Pond is magnificent and serene. Come for tea and the oversize popovers with homemade strawberry jam and ice cream, a century-old tradition. If you choose to sit on the terrace or lawn, be forewarned that bees are more than a nuisance. The menu offers lunch and dinner items, including lobster stew, but these get mixed reviews. ⊠ *Park Loop Rd.,* ☎ *207/ 276–3316. AE, D, MC, V. Closed late Oct.–mid-May.*

$ ⚑ **Blackwoods and Seawall.** These two campgrounds with a total of 530 campsites fill up quickly during the summer. Space at Seawall is allocated on a first-come, first-served basis, starting at 8 AM. Between mid-June and mid-September, reserve a Blackwoods site within five months of a visit. No reservations are essential in the off-season. *Blackwoods:* ⊠ *Rte. 3, Northeast Harbor,* ☎ *800/365–2267.* ☼ *Year-round. Seawall:* ⊠ *Rte. 102A, Northeast Harbor,* ☎ *207/244–3600. Closed late Sept.–late May.*

Outdoor Activities and Sports
BIKING

The carriage roads that wind through the woods and fields of Acadia National Park are ideal for biking and jogging when the ground is dry and for cross-country skiing in winter. You can pick up trail maps at the Hulls Cove Visitor Center.

HIKING

Acadia National Park maintains nearly 200 mi of foot and carriage paths, from easy strolls along flatlands to rigorous climbs that involve ladders and handholds on rock faces. Among the more rewarding hikes are the Precipice Trail to Champlain Mountain, the Great Head Loop, the Gorham Mountain Trail, and the path around Eagle Lake. The Hulls Cove visitor center has trail guides and maps and will help you match a trail with your interests and abilities.

Around Acadia

There's plenty to explore on Mount Desert Island beyond the 27-mi Park Loop Road. You can continue an auto tour of the island by heading west on Route 233 for the villages on Somes Sound, a true fjord— the only one on the East Coast—that almost bisects the island.

③⑨ **Somesville,** the oldest settlement on the island (1621), is a carefully preserved New England village of white clapboard houses and churches,
neat green lawns, and bits of blue water visible behind them.

④⓪ **Southwest Harbor,** south from Somesville on Route 102, combines the
salty character of a working port with the refinements of a summer
resort community. From the town's Main Street (Route 102), turn left
onto Clark Point Road to reach the harbor.

◔ **Mount Desert Oceanarium** has exhibits in two locations on the fishing
and sea life of the Gulf of Maine, a live-seal program, a lobster hatch-
ery, and hands-on exhibits such as a touch tank. ✉ *Clark Point Rd.,
Southwest Harbor,* ☎ *207/244–7330;* ✉ *Rte. 3, Thomas Bay, Bar Harbor,* ☎ *207/288–5005.* ⊠ *Call for admission fees (combination tickets available).* ◔ *Mid-May–late Oct., Mon.–Sat. 9–5.*

Wendell Gilley Museum of Bird Carving showcases bird carvings by Gilley,
has carving demonstrations and workshops and natural-history programs, and exhibits wildlife art. ✉ *4 Herrick Rd., Southwest Harbor,*
☎ *207/244–7555,* 🖳 *www.acadia.net/gilley.* ⊠ *$3.25.* ◔ *July–Aug.,
Tues.–Sun. 10–5; June and Sept.–Oct., Tues.–Sun. 10–4; May and
Nov.–Dec., Fri.–Sun. 10–4.*

④① **Bass Harbor,** 4 mi south of Southwest Harbor (follow Route 102A when
Route 102 forks), is a tiny lobstering village with cottages for rent, inns,
a restaurant, and a gift shop. You can visit the **Bass Harbor Head lighthouse,** which clings to a cliff at the eastern entrance to Blue Hill Bay.
It was built in 1858. Also here is the **Maine State Ferry Service's** car-
and-passenger ferry (☎ 207/244–3254) to Swans Island. The ferry has
six daily runs June to mid-October, fewer the rest of the year.

Dining and Lodging

$–$$ ✗ **Beal's Lobster Pier.** You can watch lobstermen bringing in their
catch at this working lobster pound. Order lobster at one take-out window and fried foods, burgers, and dessert at another. ✉ *End of Clark
Point Rd., Southwest Harbor,* ☎ *207/244–3202, 207/244–7178, or
800/244–7178. Closed mid-Oct.–mid-May.*

$–$$ ✗ **Seaweed Café.** This unpretentious restaurant serves natural and or-
ganic seafood with an Asian touch. Entrées may include Thai jumbo
shrimp scampi and vegetables or tuna au poivre. ✉ *Rt. 102, Southwest Harbor,* ☎ *207/244–0572. Reservations essential. No credit
cards. Closed Sun.–Tues. No lunch.*

$$–$$$$ ▥ **Claremont Hotel.** Built in 1884 and operated continuously as an inn,
the Claremont calls up memories of the long, leisurely vacations of days
gone by. The yellow clapboard structure commands a view of Somes Sound.
Croquet is played on the lawn, and cocktails and lunch are served at the
Boat House in summer. Rooms are simply, some would say sparsely, dec-
orated, and the cottages have a rustic feel. The dining room, open to the
public for breakfast and dinner, has picture windows overlooking the
sound. The menu changes weekly and includes fresh fish and a vegetar-
ian entrée; reservations are essential, and a jacket is required for dinner.
✉ *Off Clark Point Rd., Box 137, Southwest Harbor 04679,* ☎ *207/
244–5036 or 800/244–5036,* 🖷 *207/244–3512,* 🖳 *www.acadia.net/
claremont. 31 rooms, 2 suites, 13 cottages. Restaurant, tennis court, cro-
quet, dock, boating, bicycles. No credit cards. Hotel and restaurant
closed mid-Oct.–mid-June; cottages closed Nov.–mid-May. BP, MAP.*

$$ ▥ **Island House.** This sweet B&B on the quiet side of the island has
four simple and bright rooms in the main house. The carriage-house
suite comes complete with a sleeping loft and a kitchenette. ✉ *Box 1006,
121 Clark Point Rd., Southwest Harbor 04679,* ☎ *207/244–5180,* 🖳
www.acadia.net/islandhouse. 4 rooms, 1 suite. MC, V. BP.

$$ ⬚ **Moorings Inn & Cottages.** Nothing is fancy here except the jaw-dropping view of Somes Sound. The Maine House dates to the late 18th century; the cottages and a small motel are more recent. Rooms in the Maine House are decorated with antiques and country touches; the motel rooms lack the atmosphere but have sliding glass doors onto decks. The homey cottage rooms offer the most privacy and have cooking facilities. Lookout Front has a fireplace, screened porch, and king-size bed. ✉ *135 Shore Rd., Manset (Box 744, Southwest Harbor 04679),* ☎ *207/ 244–5523, 207/244–3210, or 800/596–5523,* WEB *www.mooringsinn. com. 13 rooms, 5 cottages, 1 apartment. Dock. No credit cards. Closed late Oct.–late Apr. CP.*

Outdoor Activities and Sports
BIKING
Southwest Cycle (✉ Main St., Southwest Harbor, ☎ 207/244–5856) rents bicycles.

BOATING
Manset Yacht Service (✉ Shore Rd., Manset, ☎ 207/244–4040) rents power boats and sailboats. **National Park Canoe Rentals** (✉ Pretty Marsh Rd., Somesville, at the head of Long Pond, ☎ 207/244–5854) rents canoes and kayaks.

Island Cruises (✉ Shore Rd., Bass Harbor, ☎ 207/244–5785) takes passengers on a 40-ft lobster boat through the islands of Blue Hill Bay.

Shopping
E. L. Higgins (✉ Bernard Rd., off Rte. 102, Bernard, ☎ 207/244– 3983) carries antique wicker, furniture, and glassware. **Marianne Clark Fine Antiques** (✉ Main St., Southwest Harbor, ☎ 207/244–9247) has formal and country furniture, American paintings, and accessories from the 18th and 19th centuries. **Port in a Storm Bookstore** (✉ Main St., Somesville, ☎ 207/244–4114) is a book-lover's nirvana.

Excursions to the Cranberry Isles

Off the southeast shore of Mount Desert Island at the entrance to Somes Sound, the five Cranberry Isles—Great Cranberry, Islesford (or Little Cranberry), Baker Island, Sutton Island, and Bear Island—escape the hubbub that engulfs Acadia National Park in summer. Sutton and Bear islands are privately owned. The **Beal & Bunker passenger ferry** (☎ 207/244–3575) serves Great Cranberry and Islesford from Northeast Harbor. **Cranberry Cove Boating Company** (☎ 207/244–5882) serves Great Cranberry and Islesford from Southwest Harbor. Baker Island is reached by the summer cruise boats of the **Islesford Ferry Company** (☎ 207/276–3717) from Northeast Harbor.

42 **Islesford** comes closest to having a village: a collection of houses, a church, a fishermen's co-op, a market, and a post office near the ferry dock.

The **Islesford Historical Museum,** run by Acadia National Park, has displays of tools, documents relating to the island's history, and books and manuscripts of the poet Rachel Field (1894–1942), who summered on Sutton Island. ✉ *Isleford,* ☎ *207/244–9224.* ➲ *Free.* ☉ *Mid-June–late Sept., daily 10–noon and 12:30–4:30.*

43 The 123-acre **Baker Island,** the most remote of the Cranberry Isles, looks almost black from a distance because of its thick spruce forest. The Islesford Ferry cruise boat from Northeast Harbor conducts a 4½-hour narrated tour, during which you are likely to see ospreys, harbor seals, and cormorants. Because Baker Island has no natural harbor, you take a fishing dory to get to shore.

Mount Desert Island A to Z

To research prices, get advice from other travelers, and book travel arrangements, visit www.fodors.com.

BUS TRAVEL

The free Island Explorer shuttle services the entire island from mid-June through Labor Day.

➤ BUS INFORMATION: **Island Explorer** (☎ 207/667–5796).

CAR RENTAL

➤ LOCAL AGENCIES: **Avis** (✉ Bangor International Airport, 299 Godfrey Blvd., ☎ 207/947–8383 or 800/331–1212). **Budget** (✉ Hancock County Airport, Rte. 3, Trenton, ☎ 207/667–1200 or 800/527–0700). **Hertz** (✉ Bangor International Airport, 299 Godfrey Blvd., ☎ 207/942–5519 or 800/654–3131). **Thrifty** (✉ Bangor International Airport, 357 Odlin Rd., ☎ 207/942–6400 or 800/367–2277).

CAR TRAVEL

North of Bar Harbor, the scenic 27-mi Park Loop Road leaves Route 3 to circle the eastern quarter of Mount Desert Island, with one-way traffic from Sieur de Monts Spring to Seal Harbor and two-way traffic between Seal Harbor and Hulls Cove. Route 102, which serves the western half of Mount Desert, is reached from Route 3 just after it enters the island or from Route 233 west from Bar Harbor. All these island roads pass through the precincts of Acadia National Park.

EMERGENCIES

➤ CONTACTS: **Maine Coast Memorial Hospital** (✉ 50 Union St., Ellsworth, ☎ 207/667–5311). **Mount Desert Island Hospital** (✉ 10 Wayman La., Bar Harbor, ☎ 207/288–5081). **Southwest Harbor Medical Center** (✉ Herrick Rd., Southwest Harbor, ☎ 207/244–5513).

TOURS

Acadia National Park Tours operates a 2½-hour bus tour of Acadia National Park, narrated by a naturalist, from May to October. Also offered are 2½-hour, narrated trolley tours. Bar Harbor Taxi and Tours conducts half-day historic and scenic tours of the area. Downeast Nature Tours offers personalized and small group tours highlighting the island's flora and fauna.

Acadia Air, on Route 3 in Trenton, between Ellsworth and Bar Harbor at Hancock County Airport, rents aircraft and flies seven aerial sightseeing routes, from spring to fall. A Step Back in Time uses Victorian-costumed guides to lead walking tours that highlight the 1890s in Bar Harbor. Tours leave from 48 Cottage St.

➤ CONTACTS: **Acadia National Park Tours** (☎ 207/288–3327). **Bar Harbor Taxi and Tours** (☎ 207/288–4020). **Downeast Nature Tours** (☎ 207/288–8128). **Acadia Air** (☎ 207/667–5534). **A Step Back in Time** (☎ 207/288–9605).

VISITOR INFORMATION

➤ CONTACTS: **Acadia National Park** (✉ Box 177, Bar Harbor 04609, ☎ 207/288–3338). **Bar Harbor Chamber of Commerce** (✉ Box 158, 93 Cottage St., Bar Harbor 04609, ☎ 207/288–3393, 207/288–5103, or 800/288–5103). **Southwest Harbor/Tremont Chamber of Commerce** (✉ Box 1143, Main St., Southwest Harbor 04679, ☎ 207/244–9264 or 800/423–9264).

WAY DOWN EAST

East of Ellsworth on U.S. 1 is a different Maine, a place pretty much off the beaten path that seduces with a rugged, simple beauty. Red-hued blueberry barrens dot the landscape, and scraggly jack pines hug the highly accessible shoreline. The quiet pleasures include hiking, birding, and going on whale-watching and puffin cruises. Many artists live in the region; you can often purchase works directly from them.

Hancock

44 *9 mi east of Ellsworth.*

As you approach the small town of Hancock and the summer colony of cottages at Hancock Point, stunning views await, especially at sunset, over Frenchman Bay toward Mt. Desert.

Dining and Lodging

$$$$ ✕▥ **Le Domaine.** Owner-chef Nicole L. Purslow whips up classic French haute cuisine, the perfect accompaniments to which can be found amid the more than 5,000 bottles of French wine in the restaurant's cellar. Le Domaine is known primarily for its food, but its Provence-inspired guest rooms are also inviting; the two suites have fireplaces. Although the building fronts on U.S. 1, the well-equipped rooms open to private decks on porches overlooking the perennial gardens, private pond, and trails that meander the property's 100 acres, and the building is well insulated to block out road noise. ⊠ *U.S. 1 (HC 77, Box 496), 04640,* ☎ *207/422–3395 or 800/554–8498,* ℻ *207/422–2316,* WEB *www.ledomaine.com. 5 rooms, 2 suites. Restaurant, in-room data ports, hiking. AE, D, MC, V. Closed late Oct.–mid-June; restaurant closed Sun.–Mon. BP, MAP.*

$$$ ✕▥ **Crocker House Inn.** Set amid tall fir trees, this century-old shingle-style cottage is a mere 200 yards from the water and holds comfortable rooms decorated with antiques and country furnishings. The accommodations in the Carriage House, which also has a TV room and a hot tub, are best for families. The inn's dining room draws Maine residents from as far away as Bar Harbor. ⊠ *Hancock Point Rd. (HC 77, Box 171), 04640,* ☎ *207/422–6806,* ℻ *207/422–3105,* WEB *www.acadia.net/crocker. 11 rooms. Restaurant, hot tub, bicycles. AE, D, MC, V. BP.*

$$ ▥ **Sullivan Harbor Farm.** Antiques and country pieces decorate this simple bed-and-breakfast in an 1829 farmhouse built by Captain James Urann, a shipbuilder who launched his boats across the road. The house, set well back from the road, has nice views of Frenchman Bay and Mount Desert Island. Cottages can be rented by the week. You can relax on the pretty grounds or take a canoe or kayak to the cove across the way. Even if you don't stay here, stop by to purchase some of the award-winning salmon cold-smoked here in the traditional Scottish manner. ⊠ *U.S. 1 (Box 96), 04664,* ☎ *207/422–3735 or 800/422–4014,* ℻ *207/422–8229,* WEB *www.sullivanharborfarm.com. 2 rooms; 3 cottages. Boating. D, MC, V. Closed late Oct.–May. BP.*

Nightlife and the Arts

Pierre Monteux School for Conductors (⊠ off U.S. 1, ☎ 207/422–3931) presents orchestral and chamber concerts from mid-June through July.

Shopping

Hog Bay Pottery (⊠ 245 Hog Bay Rd., Franklin, ☎ 207/565–2282) sells pottery by Charles Grosjean and handwoven rugs by Susanne Grosjean. **Spring Woods Gallery** (⊠ 40A Willobrook Ln., Sullivan, ☎ 207/ 422–3006) carries contemporary art by Paul and Ann Breeden and other

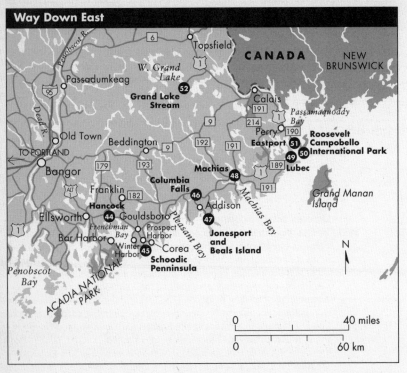

Way Down East

artists, as well as Native American pottery, jewelry, and instruments. **Sullivan Harbor Gallery** (⊠ Town Office Building, U.S. 1, ☎ no phone) shows the work of local artisans.

Schoodic Peninsula

🌑 *23 mi southeast of Hancock; 32 mi east of Ellsworth.*

The landscape of the Schoodic Peninsula makes it easy to understand why the overflow from Bar Harbor's wealthy summer population settled in Winter Harbor: the views over Frenchman's Bay to Mount Desert, the craggy coastline, and the towering evergreens. A drive through the community of Grindstone Neck shows what Bar Harbor might have been like before the Great Fire of 1947. Artists and craftspeople have opened galleries in and around Winter Harbor. No visit to Winter Harbor is complete without a stop at **Gerrish's Store** (⊠ Main St., ☎ 207/963–5575), an old-fashioned ice cream counter.

★ The Schoodic section of **Acadia National Park** (⊠ off Rte. 186, ☎ 207/288–3338), 2 mi east of Winter Harbor, has a scenic 6½-mi one-way loop that edges around the tip of the peninsula and yields views of Winter Harbor, Grindstone Neck, and Winter Harbor Lighthouse. At the tip of the point, huge slabs of pink granite lie jumbled along the shore, thrashed unmercifully by the crashing surf, and jack pines cling to life amid the rocks. The Fraser Point Day-Use Area at the beginning of the loop is an ideal place for a picnic. Work off your lunch with a hike up Schoodic Head for the panoramic views up and down the coast. Admission is free, but there is no visitor center here.

Prospect Harbor, on Route 186 northeast of Winter Harbor, is a small fishing village nearly untouched by tourism. There's little to do in **Corea,** at the tip of Route 195, other than watch the fishermen at work, pick your way over stone beaches, or gaze out to sea—and that's what makes it so special. **Petit Manan National Wildlife Refuge** (⊠ Pigeon Hill Rd. off Rte. 1, ☎ 207/546–2124) is a 2,166-acre refuge of fields, forest, and rocky shorefront on the peninsula east of Schoodic. You can explore the property on two walking trails; the wildlife viewing and bird-watching is renowned. Admission is free, parking is limited.

Dining and Lodging

$$$ ✕ **Kitchen Garden.** This restaurant just off U.S. 1 in an old Cape-style house is a wonderful surprise. The five-course, fixed-price menu emphasizes organic foods, home-grown produce, and Jamaican specialties. Bring your own wine or beer, and be sure to allow time to stroll through the gardens before dinner. ⊠ *335 Village Rd., Steuben, ☎ 207/546–2708. Reservations essential. No credit cards. Closed Mon.–Tues. and mid-Oct.–June.*

$$–$$$ ✕ **Fisherman's Inn.** New owners have greatly improved the food, service, and ambience at this ever-popular establishment. The house specialty is lobster pie, but beef, chicken, seafood, and Italian dishes also appear on the menu. ⊠ *7 Newman St., Winter Harbor, ☎ 207/963–5585. AE, D, MC, V. Closed mid-Oct.–Memorial Day.*

$–$$ ✕ **West Bay Lobsters in the Rough.** Lobsters, steamers, corn-on-the-cob, coleslaw, baked beans, and homemade blueberry pie are among the offerings. Eat at the outdoor tables or set up a picnic on nearby Schoodic Point. ⊠ *Rte. 186, Prospect Harbor, ☎ 207/963–7021. AE, D, DC, MC, V. Closed Nov.–May.*

$$–$$$ 🏠 **Oceanside Meadows.** Inspired by the ocean out the front door; fields,
★ woods, and a salt marsh out back; and moose, eagles, and other wildlife, the owners created the Institute for the Arts and Sciences, an environmental center with lectures, musical performances, art shows, and other events held weekly in the barn. Rooms, furnished with antiques, country pieces, and family treasures, are spread out among two white clapboard buildings; many have ocean views. Breakfast is an extravagant multicourse affair. In the off-season, the inn is open only by special arrangement. ⊠ *Corea Rd. (Rte. 195), Prospect Harbor 04669, ☎ 207/963–5557, FAX 207/963–5928, WEB www.oceaninn.com. 12 rooms, 3 suites. No-smoking rooms, croquet, horseshoes, hiking, beach. D, MC, V. Closed Nov. 1–May 1. BP.*

$$ 🏠 **Black Duck.** This small bed-and-breakfast has comfortable public areas and guest rooms, tastefully decorated with antiques and art. Two tiny cottages perch on the harbor. ⊠ *Crowley Island Rd., Corea 04624, ☎ 207/963–2689 or 877/963–2689, FAX 207/963–7495, WEB www.blackduck.com. 2 rooms, 1 suite; 2 cottages. MC, V. BP.*

$ 🏠 **The Pines.** This motel's location, right at the beginning of the Schoodic Point Loop, makes it a good value. New owners have remodeled, adding cottages and log cabins and updating the decor with hand-stitched quilts. Six units have kitchenettes. ⊠ *17 Rte. 186, Winter Harbor 04693, ☎ 207/963–2296, WEB www.ayuh.net. 3 rooms, 4 cottages, 2 cabins. Snack bar. MC, V.*

Outdoor Activities and Sports

Moose Look Guide Service (⊠ Rte. 186, Gouldsboro, ☎ 207/963–7720) provides kayak tours and rentals, rowboat and canoe rentals, and bike rentals; it also conducts guided fishing trips and all-terrain-vehicle tours.

Shopping

The wines sold at the **Bartlett Maine Estate Winery** (⊠ off Rte. 1, Gouldsboro, ☎ 207/546–2408) are produced from locally grown apples, pears, blueberries, and other fruit. The **Harbor Shop** (⊠ Newman St., Winter Harbor, ☎ 207/963–4117) shows the work of 80 local artisans. **Lee Art Glass Studio** (⊠ Main St., Winter Harbor, ☎ 207/963–

7004) carries fused-glass tableware and other items. **Pyramid Glass** (⊠ Rte. 186, South Gouldsboro, ☎ 207/963–2027) sells stained-glass artwork and mosaics. **U.S. Bells** (⊠ Rte. 186, Prospect Harbor, ☎ 207/963–7184) produces hand-cast bronze wind and door bells.

Columbia Falls

46 *41 mi east of Ellsworth, 78 mi west of Calais.*

Columbia Falls, founded in the late 18th century, is a small, pretty village on the Pleasant River. Once a prosperous shipbuilding center, it still has a number of stately homes dating from that era.

★ Judge Thomas Ruggles, a wealthy lumber dealer, store owner, postmaster, and Justice of the Court of Sessions, built **Ruggles House** in 1818. The house's distinctive Federal architecture, flying staircase, Palladian window, and woodwork were crafted over a period of three years by Massachusetts woodcarver Alvah Peterson with a penknife. ⊠ *Main St.,* ☎ *207/483–4637.* ⚏ *$3 donation requested.* ☉ *June 1–Oct. 15 weekdays 9:30–4:30, Sun. 11–4:30.*

Lodging

$ 🏨 **Pleasant Bay Inn and Llama Keep.** This Cape-style inn takes advantage of its riverfront location. You can stroll the nature paths on the property, which winds around a peninsula and out to Pleasant Bay; you can even take a llama with you for company. The rooms, all with water views, are decorated with antiques and have country touches. ⊠ *West Side Rd. (Box 222), Addison 04606,* ☎ *207/483–4490,* ℻ *207/483–4653,* 🕸 *www.nemaine.com/pleasantbay. 3 rooms, 1 with bath. MC, V. BP.*

Shopping

Columbia Falls Pottery (⊠ Main St., ☎ 207/483–4075) stocks stoneware and a sampling of Maine foods.

Jonesport and Beals Island

47 *12 mi south of Columbia Falls, 20 mi southwest of Machias.*

Jonesport and Beals Island, two fishing communities joined by a bridge over the harbor, are less polished than the towns on the Schoodic Peninsula. The birding here is superb. **Norton of Jonesport** (☎ 207/497–5933) takes passengers on day trips to Machias Seal Island, where there's a large puffin colony.

Great Wass Island Preserve (☎ 207/729–5181) a 1,540-acre nature conservancy at the tip of Beals Island, protects rare plants, stunted pines, and raised peat bogs. Trails lead through the woods and emerge onto the undeveloped, raw coast, where you can make your way along the rocks and boulders before retreating into the forest. To get to the preserve from Jonesport, cross the bridge over Moosabec Reach to Beals Island. Go through Beals to Great Wass Island. Follow the road, which eventually becomes unpaved, to Black Duck Cove, about 3 mi from Beals, where there is a parking area on the left. Admission is free.

Dining and Lodging

$$ ✕ **Seafarer's Wife and Old Salt Room.** These two restaurants share a central kitchen. Allow at least a couple of hours to dine at the Seafarer's Wife, where a five-course meal with main dishes such as a seafood platter and baked stuffed chicken is presented at a leisurely pace in a candlelit dining room. The casual Old Salt Room, open for lunch and dinner, specializes in fresh fish and seafood. Bring your own wine—neither restaurant has a liquor license. ⊠ *Rte. 187, Jonesport,* ☎ *207/497–2365. MC, V. No lunch at the Seafarer's Wife.*

$$ ⊡ **Harbor House.** The two spacious rooms on the third floor of this
★ harborfront building have big windows to take in the water view.
Both are tastefully furnished with Victorian touches such as cabbage
rose wallpaper and Asian-style rugs, and both have separate sleeping
and sitting areas. An alcove is stocked with books, coffee, tea, snacks,
a small refrigerator, and a telephone. Breakfast is served on the porch,
and the owners will prepare a lobster dinner if asked in advance. ⊠
*Box 468, Sawyer Sq., Jonesport 04649, ☎ 207/497–5417, FAX 207/497–
3211,* WEB *www.harborhs.com. 2 rooms. MC, V. BP.*

$ ⊡ **Raspberry Shores.** This comfortably furnished Victorian sits on
Main Street, but its backyard slopes down to a small beach on Jones-
port Harbor. Rooms in the back of the house share the view, but the
nicest room is in the turret and right on the road, which can be noisy.
Owner Nan Ellis will prepare a Continental breakfast for guests tak-
ing early morning boat trips. ⊠ *Box 409, Rte. 187, Jonesport 04649,
☎ 207/497–2463 or 877/710–3268,* WEB *www.jonesportmaine.com. 3
rooms without bath. Beach, bicycles, boating. MC, V. Closed Nov.–
Apr. BP.*

Machias

48 *20 mi northeast of Jonesport.*

Machias boasts of being the site of the first naval battle of the Revo-
lutionary War. On June 12, 1775, despite being outnumbered and
out-armed, a small group of Machias men under the leadership of
Jeremiah O'Brien captured the armed British schooner *Margaretta* in
a battle now known as the "Lexington of the Sea." The town's other
claim to fame is wild blueberries. The Machias Wild Blueberry Festi-
val, held annually during the third weekend in August, is a true com-
munity celebration complete with parade, crafts fair, concerts, and plenty
of blueberry dishes. Machias is the county seat of Washington County
and is home to a campus of the University of Maine.

★ The **Burnham Tavern Museum,** in a building dating to 1770, details
the colorful history of Job Burnham, Mary O'Brien (his wife), and other
early residents of the area. It was here that the men of Machias laid
the plans that culminated in the capture of the *Margaretta*. ⊠ *Rte. 192,
☎ 207/255–4432.* ⊡ *$2.* ☉ *Mid-June–late Sept., weekdays 9–5; late
Sept.–mid-June, by appointment.*

Although small, the **Art Galleries at the University of Maine at Machias**
have a strong selection of paintings by John Marin and other Maine
artists. Two galleries showcase rotating exhibitions of works from the
permanent collection, the Marin Foundation collection, and visiting
shows. Don't miss the William Zorach sculpture just outside the front
door. ⊠ *Powers Hall, University of Maine at Machias, 9 O'Brien
Ave., ☎ 207/255–1200.* ⊡ *Free.* ☉ *Weekdays 10–noon and 2–4.*

Built by Nathan Gates in 1810, the **Gates House** houses the Machias-
port Historical Society. It contains an extensive collection of pho-
tographs, tools, period furniture, housewares, memorabilia, and
genealogical library. ⊠ *Rte. 92, Machiasport, ☎ 207/255–8461.* ⊡
$1 donation. ☉ *Mid-June–early Sept., Tues.–Sat. 12:30–4:30.*

The **O'Brien Cemetery** dates from the late 18th century; many of
Machias' earliest settlers and heroes are buried here. ⊠ *Bad Little Falls
Park off Rte. 92, Machias (Walk through the park toward the water
and look for a stairway on your right, which leads to the path. Follow
it along the river until you see a white fence on a hill to your right. A
small, side path leads to the cemetery.)*

OFF THE
BEATEN PATH

There's no sand in sight at **Jasper Beach,** just smooth, heather-color jasper and rhyolite stones polished by the sea. ⊠ *Rte. 92, Buck's Harbor (9.5 miles south of Machias).*

Dining and Lodging

$$ ✕ **Artist's Cafe.** The white-walled dining rooms in this old house provide a simple backdrop for artwork and creative food. The menu usually has a choice of four entrées such as a catch of the day, a rib-eye steak, and "The Mex," the house vegetarian dish. You might start with Horses Standing Still, handmade Thai dumplings filled with chicken and shrimp and served with a dipping sauce. ⊠ *3 Hill St.,* ☎ *207/255–8900. MC, V. Closed Sun.–Mon.*

$$ ✕☰ **Riverside Inn & Restaurant.** The Victorian era is captured in the furnishings and linens of this restored sea captain's home overlooking the East Machias River. Suites in the guest house have balconies, and one has a full kitchen. The restaurant ($$), open to the public for dinner Thursday–Saturday, is the best in the area, serving four-course feasts of contemporary American fare by candlelight. ⊠ *U.S. 1 (Box 373), 04630,* ☎ *207/255–4134,* 𝖥𝖠𝖷 *207/255–3580,* 𝖶𝖤𝖡 *www.riversideinn-maine.com. 2 rooms, 2 suites. Restaurant. AE, MC, V. BP.*

Outdoor Activities and Sports

Machias Bay Boat Tours and Sea Kayaking (⊠ Buck's Harbor, Machiasport, ☎ 207/259–3338) operates day trips aboard the *Martha Ann* to see seals, islands and lighthouses, salmon aquaculture, and historical sites. Also offered are guided fishing and sea-kayaking trips.

Lubec

㊾ *28 mi east of Machias.*

Lubec is the first town in the United States to see the sunrise. Once a thriving shipbuilding and sardine packing site, it now attracts residents and visitors with its rural beauty. Lubec is best appreciated by those who enjoy outdoor pleasures; there are few shops and little entertainment. It also makes a good base for day trips to Campobello Island.

★ **Quoddy Head State Park,** the easternmost point of land in the United States, is marked by candy-striped West Quoddy Head Light. The mystical 2-mi path along the cliffs here yields magnificent views of Canada's Grand Manan island. Whales can often be sighted offshore. The 483-acre park has a picnic area. ⊠ *S. Lubec Rd. off Rte. 189,* ☎ *no phone.* ⌨ *$1.* ☉ *Memorial Day–mid-Oct., daily 8–sunset; Apr.– Memorial Day and mid-Oct.–Dec., weekends 9–sunset.*

㊿ **Roosevelt Campobello International Park,** a joint project of the American and Canadian governments, has hiking trails and historical displays. Neatly manicured Campobello Island has always had a special appeal for the wealthy and famous. It was here that the Roosevelt family spent its summers. The 34-room **Roosevelt Cottage** was presented to Eleanor and Franklin as a wedding gift. The island can be reached by land only by crossing the International Bridge from Lubec. Stop at the information booth for an update on tides—specifically, when you will be able to walk out to East Quoddy Head Lighthouse—and details on walking and hiking trails. Once you've crossed the bridge, you're in the Atlantic time zone. ⊠ *Rte. 774, Welshpool, Campobello Island, New Brunswick, Canada,* ☎ *506/752–2922.* ⌨ *Free.* ☉ *House mid-May–mid-Oct., daily 10–6; grounds daily.*

Dining and Lodging

$–$$ ✕🏠 **Home Port Inn.** Lubec's grandest accommodations are in this 1880 Colonial-style house atop a hill. The spacious rooms, some with water views, are furnished with antiques and family pieces. There are two sitting areas, and the living room has a fireplace and a television. The dining room ($$), the best in town, is open to the public for dinner. The weekly changing menu changes emphasizes seafood. ⊠ *45 Main St., 04652,* ☎ *207/733–2077 or 800/457–2077,* WEB *www.quoddyloop. com/hpi. 7 rooms. Restaurant. AE, D, MC, V. Closed mid-Oct.–mid-June. CP.*

$ 🏠 **Peacock House.** Four generations of the Peacock family lived in this 1860 Victorian before it was converted into an inn. A few of the simply furnished rooms have water views through lace-curtained windows; rooms on the first floor have air-conditioning. ⊠ *27 Summer St., 04652,* ☎ FAX *207/733–2403 or 888/305–0036,* WEB *www.peacockhouse. com. 2 rooms, 4 suites.. MC, V. Closed Oct. 15–May 15. BP.*

En Route The road to Eastport leads through the Pleasant Point Indian Reservation, where the **Waponahki Museum and Resource Center** explains the culture of the Passamaquoddy, or "People of the Dawn." Tools, baskets, beaded artifacts, historic photos, and arts and crafts are displayed. ⊠ *Rte. 190, Perry,* ☎ *207/853–4001.* 🔤 *Free.* ☉ *Weekdays 8:30–11 and noon–4.*

Eastport

51 *39 mi north of Lubec, 102 mi east of Ellsworth.*

Eastport is a small island connected to the mainland by a granite causeway. In the late 19th century, 14 sardine canneries operated in Eastport. The decline of that industry in the 20th century has left the city economically depressed, though a new port facility, growing aquaculture, and an increase in tourism bode well for the future. From the waterfront, you can take a ferry to Deer Island and Campobello.

The **National Historic Waterfront District** extends from the Customs House, down Water Street to Bank Square and the Peavey Library. Pick up a walking map at the **Chamber of Commerce** (⊠ 78 Water St., ☎ 207/853–4644) and wander through streets lined with historic homes and buildings. You can also take the waterfront walkway to watch the fishing boats and freighters. The tides fluctuate as much as 28 ft, which explains the ladders and steep gangways necessary to access boats.

Raye's Mustard Mill is the only remaining mill in the U.S. producing stone-ground mustard. Historically, this mill served the sardine-packing industry. You can purchase mustards made on the premises at the mill's Pantry Store; Maine-made crafts and other foods are also for sale. ⊠ *85 Washington St.,* ☎ *207/853–4451 or 800/853–1903.* 🔤 *Free.* ☉ *Jan.–Mar., weekdays 8–5; Apr.–Dec., daily 10–5. Tours on the hr Memorial Day–Labor Day; rest of year subject to guide availability.*

The short hike to **Shakford Head** (⊠ behind Washington County Technical College on Deep Cove Rd.) affords views over Passamaquoddy Bay to Campobello. From here you can see the pens for Eastport's salmon-farming industry as well as the new port facility.

Dining and Lodging

$$–$$$ ✕ **The Cannery.** Fish and seafood don't come much fresher than they do at this restaurant, where the lobsters weigh as much as 3¼ pounds. Unfortunately, neither the service nor the food is reliable. You can eat in the dining room, the downstairs pub, or out on the dock. ⊠ *167 Water St.,* ☎ *207/853–9669. MC, V. Call ahead Oct.–mid-May for hrs.*

$–$$ ✕ **WaCo Diner.** The food here is home-style Down East, with an emphasis on seafood. You can eat at the counter with the locals, in the new dining room, or on the deck overlooking the water. The service can be slow and the food quality is uneven. ⊠ *Water St. at Bank Square,* ☎ *207/853–4046. MC, V.*

$–$$ 🏠 **Brewer House.** In 1827, Captain John Nehemiah Marks Brewer built an ornate Greek Revival house across from one of his shipyards. Now a B&B, the house is distinguished by such details as carved Grecian moldings, Ionic pilasters, marble fireplaces, silver doorknobs, and an elliptical staircase. ⊠ *U.S. 1 (Box 94), Robbinston 04671,* ☎ *207/454–2385 or 800/821–2028,* 𝖥𝖠𝖷 *207/454–8770,* 𝖶𝖤𝖡 *www.brewerhouse.com. 4 rooms, 2 with bath; 1 apartment. MC, V. BP.*

$–$$ 🏠 **Weston House.** A Federal-style home built in 1810, the antiques-
★   filled Weston House overlooks Eastport and Passamaquoddy Bay from a prime in-town location. The family room, with a fireplace and a TV, is a casual place to plan the day's activities. An elegant multicourse breakfast is served in the formal dining room, and dinner is available by advance reservation. ⊠ *26 Boynton St., 04631,* ☎ *207/853–2907 or 800/ 853–2907,* 𝖥𝖠𝖷 *207/853–0981,* 𝖶𝖤𝖡 *www.virtualcities.com/me/weston-house.htm. 4 rooms without bath. No credit cards. BP.*

Outdoor Activities and Sports

East Coast Ferries, Ltd. (☎ 506/747–2159) provides ferry service between Eastport and Deer Island and Deer Island and Campobello from late June to mid-September. **Harris Whale Watching** (⊠ Harris Point Rd., ☎ 207/853–2940 or 207/853–4303) operates three-hour tours. **Tidal Trails** (⊠ Water St., ☎ 207/853–7373) offers boat charters, natural-history tours, and guided bird-watching, canoeing, sea-kayaking, and saltwater-fishing trips.

Shopping

Dog Island Pottery (⊠ 224 Water St., ☎ 207/853–4775) stocks stoneware pottery and local crafts. The **Eastport Gallery** (⊠ 69 Water St., ☎ 207/853–4166) displays works by area artists. **45th Parallel** (⊠ U.S. 1, Perry, ☎ 207/853–9600) stocks an intriguing mix of antiques, crafts, and home furnishings. **Joe's Basket Shop** (⊠ Rte. 190, Pleasant Point, ☎ 207/853–2840) has fancy and coarse (work) baskets and jewelry made by the Passamaquoddy.

Grand Lake Stream

52 *50 mi northwest of Eastport, 108 mi east of Bangor.*

This tiny community, on Grand Lake Stream between West Grand Lake and Big Lake, was once one of the largest tannery centers in the world. Today it's renowned for fishing, especially for land-locked salmon and smallmouth bass, and for the Grand Laker, a stable, square-ended, wooden canoe built specifically for use on the big and often windy lakes in this region. Outdoors-lovers will find lakes and rivers for swimming, boating, and fishing; trails for hiking; and plenty of places to spot wildlife. On the last full weekend of July, the town holds a juried folk arts festival which attracts thousands of visitors.

The tiny **Grand Lake Stream Historical Society & Museum** is jam-packed with artifacts from the town's early days. Here you can learn more about the Grand Laker canoes, the town's tannery years, and its fishing heritage. ☎ *207/796–5562.* 🎟 *Donation accepted.* ☉ *By chance or appt.*

Lodging

$$$$ 🏠 **Leen's Lodge.** Ten rustic cabins varying in size from one to four bedrooms are nestled on 23 wooded acres on West Grand Lake. Three have kitchens, and all have woodstoves or fireplaces and big windows to take in the views. A country-style breakfast and a hearty, home-style dinner are served in a central lodge, where you'll also find a TV/VCR, card tables, books, and games. The lodge can arrange guided fishing trips, wildlife or photographic safaris, and other excursions. Boat rentals are available. ✉ *Box 40, 04637,* ☎ *207/796–5575 or 800/995–3367,* WEB *www.leenslodge.com. 10 cabins. Kitchenettes (some), hiking, beach, boating, recreation room. MC, V. Closed Nov.–Apr. MAP.*

$$$$ ⌘ **Weatherby's.** Nicknamed "the fishermen's resort," Weatherby's is ideal for those who want to be in the center of the action in Grand Lake Stream. Fifteen cottages, each with an open brick or Franklin fireplace, surround the main lodge, where guests take breakfast and dinner daily. Lunch is available upon request. The main lodge also has a library, television, and piano. ✉ *Grand Lake Stream 04637,* ☎ *207/796–5558,* WEB *www.weatherbys.com, 15 cottages. MC, V. Closed mid-Oct–Apr. MAP.*

Outdoor Activities and Sports

The **Grand Lake Stream Guides Association** (☎ 506/796–5207) maintains more than 25 lunch sites on area lakes. Guides offer fishing, family, boating, hiking, photographic, and wildlife trips.

Shopping

Shamel Boat & Canoe Works (✉ Tough End Road, ☎ 207/796–8199) specializes in building canoes.

Way Down East A to Z

To research prices, get advice from other travelers, and book travel arrangements, visit www.fodors.com.

BOAT & FERRY TRAVEL

East Coast Ferries, Ltd. provides ferry service between Eastport and Deer Island and Deer Island and Campobello from late June to mid-September.

➤ BOAT & FERRY INFORMATION: **East Coast Ferries, Ltd.** (☎ 506/747–2159).

CAR TRAVEL

U.S. 1 is the primary coastal route, with smaller roads leading to the towns on the long fingers of land in this region. Route 182 is a pleasant inland route; Route 186 loops through the Schoodic Peninsula. The most direct route to Lubec is Route 189, but Route 191, between East Machias and West Lubec, is a scenic coastal drive.

TOURS

Quoddy Air has scenic flights. Scenic Island Tours offers tours of Eastport in a 1947 Dodge Woody bus. Picnic lunches with smoked salmon are available.

➤ TOUR OPERATORS: **Quoddy Air** (✉ Eastport Municipal Airport, County Rd., Eastport, ☎ 207/853–0997). **Scenic Island Tours** (✉ 37 Washington St., Eastport, ☎ 207/853–2840).

VISITOR INFORMATION

➤ CONTACTS: **Eastport Area Chamber of Commerce** (✉ Box 254, 78 Water St., 04631, ☎ 207/853–4644). **Lubec Area Chamber of Commerce** (✉ Box 123, 04652, ☎ 207/733–4522). **Machias Bay Area Chamber of Commerce** (✉ Box 606, 378 Main St., 04654, ☎ 207/255–4402). **Quoddy Coastal Tourism Association of New Brunswick and Maine** (✉ Box 1171, St. Andrews, New Brunswick, Canada E0G 2X0,

☎ 800/377–9748). **Schoodic Peninsula Chamber of Commerce** (✉ Box 381, Winter Harbor 04693, ☎ no phone).

WESTERN LAKES AND MOUNTAINS

Less than 20 mi northwest of Portland and the coast, the sparsely populated lake and mountain areas of western Maine stretch north along the New Hampshire border to Québec. In winter this is ski country; in summer the woods and waters draw vacationers.

The Sebago–Long Lake region bustles with activity in the summer. Harrison and the Waterfords are quieter. Bridgton attracts lake visitors in summer and skiers in winter, while Lovell is a dreamy escape. Kezar Lake, tucked away in a fold of the White Mountains, has long been a hideaway of the wealthy. Children's summer camps dot the region. Bethel, in the Androscoggin River valley, is a classic New England town, its town common lined with historic homes. The more rural Rangeley Lake area brings long stretches of pine, beech, spruce, and sky—and stylish inns and bed-and-breakfasts with access to golf, boating, fishing, and hiking. Snow sports, especially snowmobiling, are popular winter pastimes. Carrabassett Valley, just north of Kingfield, is home to Sugarloaf/USA, a major ski resort with a challenging golf course.

Sebago Lake

53 *17 mi northwest of Portland.*

Sebago Lake, which provides all the drinking water for Greater Portland, is Maine's best-known lake after Moosehead. Many camps and year-round homes surround Sebago, which is popular with water-sports enthusiasts. At the north end of the lake, the **Songo Lock** (☎ 207/693–6231), which permits the passage of watercraft from Sebago Lake to Long Lake, is the lone surviving lock of the Cumberland and Oxford Canal. Built of wood and masonry, the original lock dates to 1830 and was expanded in 1911; today it sees heavy traffic in summer.

The 1,300-acre **Sebago Lake State Park** on the north shore of the lake provides opportunities for swimming, picnicking, camping (250 sites), boating, and fishing (salmon and togue). ✉ *11 Park Access Rd., Casco,* ☎ *207/693–6613 May–mid-Oct.; 207/693–6231 mid-Oct.–Apr.* ✇ *$2.50.* ⊙ *Daily 9–8.*

The **Jones Museum of Glass & Ceramics** houses more than 7,000 glass, pottery, stoneware, and porcelain objects from around the world. Also on the premises are a research library and gift shop. ✉ *35 Douglas Mountain Rd., off Rte. 107. Sebago,* ☎ *207/787–3370.* ✇ *$5.* ⊙ *Mid-May–mid-Nov., Mon.–Sat. 10–5, Sun. 1–5; tours by appointment.*

OFF THE
BEATEN PATH

SABBATHDAY LAKE SHAKER MUSEUM – Established in the late 18th century, this is the last active Shaker community in the United States. Members continue to farm crops and herbs, and you can see the meetinghouse of 1794—a paradigm of Shaker design—and the ministry shop with 14 rooms of Shaker furniture, folk art, tools, farm implements, and crafts from the 18th to the early 20th century. There is also a small gift shop, but don't expect to find furniture or other large Shaker items. On the busy road out front, a farmer usually has summer and fall vegetables for sale. In autumn, he sells cider, apples, and pumpkins. ✉ *707 Shaker Rd. (Rte. 26), New Gloucester (20 mi north of Portland, 12 mi east of Naples),* ☎ *207/926–4597.* ✇ *Tour $6, extended tour $7.50.* ⊙ *Memorial Day–Columbus Day, Mon.–Sat. 10–4:30.*

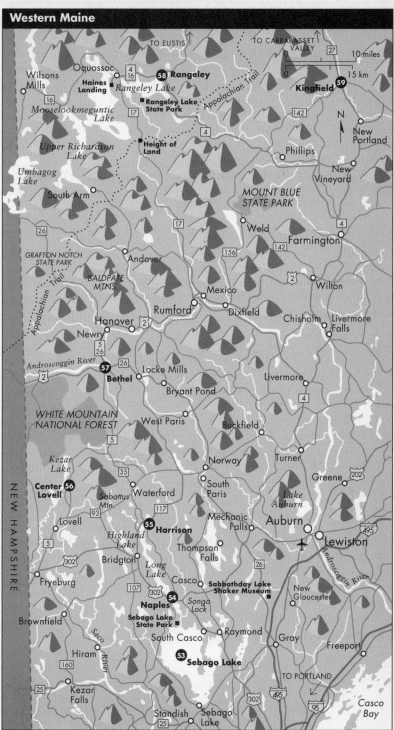

TO EUSTIS

TO CARRABASSET VALLEY

27   10 miles

0   15 km

Wilsons Mills

Oquossoc   **58 Rangeley**

4 16

Haines Landing   *Rangeley Lake*

Rangeley Lake State Park

16

Mooselookmeguntic Lake

17

Upper Richardson Lake

4

Height of Land

Umbagog Lake

South Arm

MOUNT BLUE STATE PARK

26

17

Weld

156

142

GRAFTON NOTCH STATE PARK

Andover

BALDPATE MTNS

Appalachian Trail

Hanover   Rumford   2

Newry   Mexico   Dixfield

5 26   *Androscoggin River*   26

57   Locke Mills

Bethel   Bryant Pond

2

WHITE MOUNTAIN NATIONAL FOREST   West Paris   Buckfield

5

Kezar Lake   35   Norway   Turner

Center 56 Lovell   *Sabattus Mtn.*   Waterford   South Paris   *Lake Auburn*

93

Lovell   117   Mechanic Falls   **Auburn**

5   **55 Harrison**   *Highland Lake*

Long Lake   Thompson Falls   26

302   Bridgton

Fryeburg   107   Casco   *Sabbathday Lake Shaker Museum*

302   **54**   *Songo Lock*   New Gloucester

Brownfield   **Naples**

Sebago Lake State Park   South Casco   Raymond   Gray

Hiram   160   **53 Sebago Lake**   Freeport

25   Kezar Falls   TO PORTLAND   *Casco Bay*

Standish   Sebago Lake   302   495

25   95

Kingfield **59**

142

New Portland

Phillips

New Vineyard

4

Farmington

2   Wilton

Chisholm   Livermore Falls

Livermore

4

Greene   202

495

Lewiston

Androscoggin River

NEW HAMPSHIRE

Naples

54   *32 mi northwest of Portland.*

Naples swells with seasonal residents and visitors in summer. The town occupies an enviable location between Long and Sebago lakes.

Songo River Queen II, a 92-ft stern-wheeler, takes passengers on hour-long cruises on Long Lake and longer voyages down the Songo River and through Songo Lock. ⊠ *U.S. 302, Naples Causeway,* ☎ *207/693–6861.* ▣ *Long Lake cruise $8, Songo River ride $11.* ☉ *July–Labor Day, daily at 9:45, 1, 2:30, 3:45, 7; call for spring and fall hrs.*

Dining and Lodging

$$ ✕ **Bistro du Lac.** The country French fare and reasonable fixed-price menu have made this restaurant in a big red farmhouse a popular choice. A four-course dinner for two, including a bottle of wine, is $49. Among the entrées are salmon with caramelized leeks, chicken with tarragon sauce, and filet mignon. ⊠ *U.S. 302 and Rte. 85, Raymond,* ☎ *207/655–4100. AE, D, MC, V. Closed Mon.–Wed. No lunch.*

$$$$ ▥ **Migis Lodge.** The lodge's pine-panel cottages, scattered among 100 shorefront acres, have fieldstone fireplaces and are handsomely furnished with braided rugs and handmade quilts. A warm, woodsy feeling pervades the main inn. The deck has views (marvelous at sunset) of Sebago Lake. All kinds of outdoor and indoor activities are included in the room rate, and canoes, kayaks, and sailboats are available. Guests gather in the main dining room for three fancy meals daily. ⊠ *Box 40, Migis Lodge Rd., off U.S. 302, South Casco 04077,* ☎ *207/655–4524,* FAX *207/655–2054,* WEB *www.migis.com. 29 cottages, 6 rooms. Dining room, 2 tennis courts, exercise room, beach, boating, waterskiing, fishing, playground. No credit cards. FAP.*

$$–$$$ ▥ **Augustus Bove House.** Built as the Hotel Naples in the 1820s, this rambling brick B&B sits across from the Naples Causeway and has views down Long Lake. Rooms are furnished with antiques and a television. ⊠ *Box 501, R.R. 1, U.S. 302, 04055,* ☎ *207/693–6365,* WEB *www.maineguide.com/naples/augustus. 10 rooms, 7 with bath; 1 suite. Air-conditioning, hot tub. AE, D, MC, V. BP.*

Outdoor Activities and Sports

U.S. 302 cuts through Naples, and in the center at the Naples Causeway are rental craft for fishing or cruising. Sebago, Long, and Rangeley lakes are popular areas for sailing and motorboating. For boat rentals, try **Mardon Marine** (⊠ U.S. 302, ☎ 207/693–6264). **Naples Marina** (⊠ U.S. 302 and Rte. 114, ☎ 207/693–6254) rents motorboats. **Long Lake Marina** (⊠ U.S. 302, ☎ 207/693–3159) rents fishing boats and canoes.

Shopping

The **Cry of the Loon** (⊠ U.S. 302, South Casco, ☎ 207/655–5060) complex includes a gift shop, The Nest country home-furnishings shop, and the Barn, which carries specialty foods, nautical gifts, and other items.

Harrison

55   *10 mi north of Naples, 25 mi south of Bethel.*

Harrison anchors the northern end of Long Lake but is less commercial than Naples. The combination of woods, lakes, and views makes it a good choice for leaf-peepers. The nearby towns of North Waterford, South Waterford, and tiny Waterford, a National Historic District, are ideal for outdoors-lovers who prefer to get away from the crowds.

Lodging

$$ **★** ⊡ **Bear Mountain Inn.** After swimming at the private beach on Bear Lake or hiking up Bear Mountain (across the street), it's nice to return to this rambling farmhouse inn, which the owner has meticulously decorated in a woodsy theme. The luxurious Great Grizzly Suite has a fireplace, whirlpool bath for two, and mesmerizing views, while the cozy Sugar Bear Cottage is a romantic retreat. A gourmet breakfast with an emphasis on organic ingredients is served in the dining room, which has a fieldstone fireplace and views over the lake. ⊠ *Rte. 35, South Waterford 04081,* ☎ FAX *207/583–4404,* WEB *www.bearmtninn.com. 6 rooms, 2 with bath; 3 suites; 1 cottage. Badminton, croquet, horseshoes, volleyball, beach, boating, fishing, ice-skating, cross-country skiing, snowmobiling. MC, V. BP.*

$$ ⊡ **Harrison House.** When it was built in 1867, this house at the head of Long Lake was one of the most costly and elegant residences in town. Today it charms guests with feather beds, quilts, and a porch swing. The living room, dining room, and three guest rooms have lake views. All rooms have private baths, but four of the baths are adjacent to or across the hall from the rooms. ⊠ *16 Waterford Rd., 04040,* ☎ *207/583–6564,* WEB *www.megalink.net/~hrsnbnb. 5 rooms. AE, MC, V. BP.*

$$ ⊡ **Waterford Inne.** This gold-painted house on a hilltop provides a good home base for trips to lakes, ski trails, and antiques shops. The bedrooms have lots of nooks and crannies. The Nantucket, with a whale motif, and the Chesapeake, with a private porch and a fireplace, are the nicest. A converted woodshed holds five additional rooms, and though they have less character than the rooms in the inn, four have sunny decks. ⊠ *Box 149, 258 Chadbourne Rd., Waterford 04088,* ☎ FAX *207/583–4037. 8 rooms, 6 with bath; 1 suite. Ice-skating, cross-country skiing. AE. Closed Apr. BP.*

Nightlife and the Arts

From late June through Labor Day, **Deertrees Theater and Cultural Center** (⊠ Deertrees Rd. off Rte. 117, ☎ 207/583–6747) stages musicals, dramas, dance performances, shows for children, concerts, and other events in a theater listed on the National Register of Historic Places.

Outdoor Activities and Sports

Mutiny Brook Stables (⊠ Sweden Rd., South Waterford, ☎ 207/583–6650) outfits horseback tours in the Maine woods.

Center Lovell

56 *17 mi northwest of Harrison, 28 mi south of Bethel.*

At Center Lovell you can barely glimpse the secluded Kezar Lake to the west, the retreat of wealthy and very private people. Sabattus Mountain, which rises behind Center Lovell, has a public hiking trail and stupendous views of the Presidential Range from the summit.

Dining and Lodging

$$$$ ✕⊡ **Quisisana.** Music-lovers may think they've found heaven on earth at this delightful resort on Kezar Lake. After dinner, the staff—students and graduates of some of the country's finest music schools—perform everything from Broadway tunes to concert piano pieces at the music hall. White cottages have pine interiors and cheerful decor. One night dinner might be lobster and blueberry pie; the next night the choice might be saddle of lamb with a black-olive tapenade or salmon-and-leek roulade. For most of the resort's season, a one-week stay beginning Saturday is required. ⊠ *Pleasant Point Rd., 04016,* ☎ *207/925–3500,* FAX *207/925–1004 in season,* WEB *www.quisisanaresort.com. 11* *rooms in 2 lodges, 32 cottages. Restaurant, 3 tennis courts, windsurfing, boating, waterskiing. Closed Sept.–mid-June. FAP.*

$–$$ ✕🏠 **Center Lovell Inn.** The current owners won this rambling, old-fashioned country inn in an essay contest in 1993. The eclectic decor blends furnishings from the mid-19th to mid-20th centuries in a pleasing, homey style. The best tables for dining are on the wraparound porch, which has sunset views over Kezar Lake and the White Mountains. Entrées may include veal scaloppini, chateaubriand, or chicken breast toscano. Rooms are upstairs and in the adjacent Harmon House. ✉ *Rte. 5 (Box 261) 04016,* ☎ *207/925–1575 or 800/777–2698,* WEB *www.centerlovellinn.com. 9 rooms, 4 with shared bath. Restaurant. D, MC, V. Nov.–late Dec. and Apr.–mid-May. EP, MAP.*

Outdoor Activities and Sports

BOATING AND FISHING

For guided fishing trips, call **Carl Bois** (☎ 207/925–6262) in Lovell. **Kezar Lake Marina** (✉ West Lovell Rd. at The Narrows, Lovell, ☎ 207/925–3000) rents boats.

CANOEING

Two scenic canoeing routes on the Saco River (near Fryeburg) are the gentle stretch from Swan's Falls to East Brownfield (19 mi) and from East Brownfield to Hiram (14 mi). For rentals, try **Saco River Canoe and Kayak** (✉ Rte. 5, Fryeburg, ☎ 207/935–2369).

DOGSLEDDING

Winter Journeys (☎ 207/928–2026) in Lovell operates half- and full-day dog-sledding trips.

Bethel

57 *28 mi north of Lovell, 66 mi north of Portland.*

Bethel is pure New England, a town with white clapboard houses and white-steeple churches and a mountain vista at the end of every street. The architecture here is something to behold. In winter this is ski country: Bethel is a few miles south of Sunday River in Newry. Sunday River has plenty of action in summer, too.

A stroll in Bethel should begin at the **Moses Mason House and Museum,** a Federal home of 1813. The museum, on the town common across from the Bethel Inn and Country Club, has nine period rooms and a front hall and stairway wall decorated with murals by Rufus Porter. It is part of the Bethel Regional Historical Center, which has local history exhibits. You can pick up materials here for a walking tour of Bethel Hill Village, most of which is on the National Register of Historic Places. ✉ *14 Broad St.,* ☎ *207/824–2908 or 800/824–2910.* 🎫 *$3.* ☉ *July–Labor Day, Tues.–Sun. 1–4; Labor Day–June, Tues.–Fri., 1–4.*

The **Major Gideon Hastings House** on Broad Street has a columned-front portico typical of the Greek Revival style. The severe white **West Parish Congregational Church** (1847), with an unadorned triangular pediment and a steeple supported on open columns, is on Church Street, around the common from the Major Gideon Hastings House. The campus of **Gould Academy** (✉ Church St., ☎ 207/824–7777), a preparatory school, opened its doors in 1835; the dominant style of the school buildings is Georgian.

Dining and Lodging

$$$$ ✕🏠 **Victoria Inn.** It's hard to miss this turreted inn, with its beige-, ★   mauve-, and teal-painted exterior and attached carriage house topped with a cupola. Inside, Victorian details include ceiling rosettes, stained-glass windows, elaborate fireplace mantels, and gleaming oak trim. Guest rooms vary in size and decor; most are furnished with reproductions of antiques. One-bedroom-with-loft units in the carriage house are perfect for families. The restaurant, open to the public for dinner ($$–$$$; closed Monday), has three rooms, one with a wraparound mural of Italian scenes. The menu lists entrées such as beef tenderloin au poivre and rack of lamb. A children's menu is available. Rates for inn guests include a full breakfast and four-course dinner. ⊠ *32 Main St. (Box 249) 04217,* ☎ *207/824–8060 or 888/774–1235,* FAX *207/824–3926,* WEB *www.victoria-inn.com. 15 rooms. Restaurant. MC, V. MAP.*

$–$$ ✕🏠 **Briar Lea.** Both children and pets are welcome at this Georgian-style inn. You can snuggle under a down comforter at night in rooms decorated in a warm and inviting country style. The dining room is open to the public for breakfast and dinner. Entrées ($–$$) may include pork chops, rainbow trout, and crispy roast duck. A children's menu is available. ⊠ *150 Mayville Rd./Rte. 2 04217,* ☎ *207/824–4717 or 877/311–1299,* FAX *207/824–7121. 6 rooms. Restaurant, air-conditioning, no-smoking rooms. AE, D, MC, V. Restaurant closed Tues. Nov.–late Dec. and mid-Apr.–mid-June. BP.*

$$$$ 🏠 **Bethel Inn and Country Club.** Bethel's grandest accommodation, a full-service resort that includes 40 km (25 mi) of cross-country ski trails, delivers an uneven experience. Rooms in the new wing of the main inn are spacious, many with fireplaces and whirlpool tubs in the baths. Some rooms in the main section of the inn have been completely renovated; others have been spruced up with new drapes and bedding but have tiny, old-fashioned baths and peeling paint. Housekeeping, too, could be more meticulous. Winter guests will find the clanky steam heating difficult to control. Lobster specialties and updated Continental dishes are highlights of the restaurant menu. ⊠ *Box 49, Village Common, 04217,* ☎ *207/824–2175 or 800/654–0125,* FAX *207/824–2233,* WEB *www.bethelinn.com. 49 rooms, 9 suites, 40 condo units. Restaurant, bar, pool, 18-hole golf course, tennis court, health club, cross-country skiing, meeting room. AE, D, DC, MC, V. MAP.*

$$$ 🏠 **Jordan Grand Resort Hotel.** A hit with Sunday River skiers, this condominium hotel provides ski-in, ski-out access to the Jordan Bowl trails. Most units have kitchenettes, and there's a heated outdoor pool to relax in after a day on the slopes. ⊠ *Box 450, 1 Grand Circle, off Skiway Rd. and U.S. 2, Newry 04217,* ☎ *207/824–5000 or 800/543–2754,* FAX *207/824–5399. 195 condominiums. 2 restaurants, café, pool, health club, baby-sitting, meeting room. AE, D, MC, V.*

$$$ 🏠 **Sunday River Inn.** This homey chalet on the Sunday River ski-area access road has private rooms for families and dorm rooms (bring your sleeping bag) for groups and students, all within easy access of the slopes. A hearty breakfast and dinner are served buffet-style, and a stone hearth dominates the comfortable living room. The inn operates an excellent ski-touring center. ⊠ *19 Skiway Rd., Newry 04261,* ☎ *207/824–2410,* FAX *207/824–3181,* WEB *www.sundayriverinn.com. 19 rooms; 3 with private bath; 5 dorms with shared bath. Restaurant, pool, hot tub, sauna, exercise room, cross-country skiing, downhill skiing. AE, MC, V. Closed Apr.–late Nov. MAP.*

Nightlife and the Arts

Sunday River nightlife is spread out between the mountain and downtown Bethel. For a quiet evening, head to the piano bar at the **Bethel Inn and Country Club** (⊠ Village Common, ☎ 207/824–2175). At Sunday River, the **Bumps Pub** (⊠ Whitecap Lodge, ☎ 207/824–5269) has après-ski and evening entertainment. Tuesday night is comedy night, ski movies are shown on Wednesday, and bands play on weekends and holidays. **Sunday River Brewing Company** (⊠ U.S. 2, ☎ 207/824–4253) has pub fare and live entertainment—usually progressive rock bands—

on weekends. The **Sudbury Inn** (⌂ 151 Main St., ☎ 207/824–2174) is popular for après-ski and has music that tends toward the blues.

Outdoor Activities and Sports

CANOEING

Bethel Outdoor Adventures (⌂ 121 Mayville Rd., ☎ 207/824–4224) rents canoes, kayaks, bikes, and snowmobiles.

DOGSLEDDING

Mahoosuc Guide Service (⌂ Bear River Rd., Newry, ☎ 207/824–2073) leads day and multiday dogsledding expeditions on the Maine–New Hampshire border.

HIKING

Telemark Inn & Llama Treks (⌂ King's Hwy., Mason Township, ☎ 207/836–2703) operates one- to six-day llama-supported hiking trips in the White Mountain National Forest.

NATIONAL FORESTS AND PARKS

White Mountain National Forest straddles New Hampshire and Maine. Although the highest peaks are on the New Hampshire side, the Maine section has magnificent rugged terrain, camping and picnic areas, and hiking opportunities from hour-long nature loops to a 5½-hour scramble up Speckled Mountain. ⌂ *Evans Notch Visitor Center, 18 Mayville Rd., 04217,* ☎ *207/824–2134.* ⌂ *Parking pass (good 1–7 days) $5.* ☉ *Center early May–mid-Oct., daily 8–5; mid-Oct.–early May, daily 8:30–4:30.*

At **Grafton Notch State Park** (⌂ Rte. 26, 14 mi north of Bethel, ☎ 207/824–2912) you can take an easy nature walk to Mother Walker Falls or Moose Cave and see the spectacular Screw Auger Falls, or you can hike to the summit of Old Speck Mountain, the state's third-highest peak. If you have the stamina and the equipment, you can pick up the Appalachian Trail here, hike over Saddleback Mountain, and continue on to Katahdin. The **Maine Appalachian Trail Club** (⌂ Box 283, Augusta 04330) publishes a map and trail guide.

Shopping

Bonnema Potters (⌂ 146 Lower Main St., ☎ 207/824–2821) sells plates, lamps, tiles, and vases in colorful modern designs. The **Lyons' Den** (⌂ U.S. 2, Hanover, ☎ 207/364–8634), a great barn of a place near Bethel, stocks antique glass, china, tools, prints, rugs, hand-wrought iron, and some furniture. **Mt. Mann Jewelers** (⌂ 57 Maine Street Pl., ☎ 207/824–3030) carries contemporary jewelry with unusual gems.

Ski Areas

SUNDAY RIVER

In the 1980s, Sunday River was a sleepy little ski area with minimal facilities. Today it's a sprawling resort that attracts skiers from as far away as Europe. Spread throughout the valley are three base areas, two condominium hotels, trailside condominiums, town houses, and a ski dorm. Sunday River is home to the Maine Handicapped Skiing program, which provides lessons and services for skiers with disabilities. There's plenty of summer action here, too. ⌂ *Sunday River Rd. off U.S. 2, Newry (Box 450, Bethel 04217),* ☎ *207/824–3000; 207/824–5200 snow conditions; 800/543–2754 reservations.*

Downhill. White Heat has gained fame as the steepest, longest, widest lift-served trail in the East; but skiers of all abilities will find plenty of suitable terrain, from a 5-km (3-mi) beginner run to steep glades, in-your-face bumps, and terrain parks. The area has 127 trails, the majority of them in the intermediate range. Expert and advanced runs are grouped from the peaks, and most beginner slopes are near the base.

Trails spreading down from eight peaks have a total vertical descent of 2,340 ft and are served by nine quads, four triples, and two double chairlifts and three surface lifts.

Other activities. The Entertainment Center at White Cap has a lighted halfpipe, a lighted ice-skating rink, a tubing area, a teen center, and a nightclub with live music.

Child care. There are three licensed day-care centers for children from ages 6 weeks to 6 years. Coaching for children from ages 3 to 18 is available in the Children's Center at the South Ridge base area.

Summer and year-round activities. Within the housing complexes are indoor pools, outdoor heated pools, saunas, hot tubs, and 4 tennis courts. In summer, the Mountain Adventure Center attracts families with its water slides, climbing wall, BMX park, and in-line skating park, as well as hiking and mountain biking.

CROSS-COUNTRY SKIING

Bethel Inn Touring Center (⊠ Village Common, ☎ 207/824–6276) has 40 km (25 mi) of trails and offers ski and snowshoe rentals and lessons. **Carter's Cross-Country Ski Center** (⊠ 786 Intervale Rd., ☎ 207/539–4848) offers 50 km (31 mi) for all levels of skiers; a center in Oxford has 35 km (22 mi) of trails for novice and intermediate skiing. Both centers provide lessons and snowshoe, ski, and sled rentals. **Sunday River Cross-Country Ski Center** (⊠ 23 Skiway Rd., Newry, ☎ 207/824–2410), based at the Sunday River Inn, has 40 km (25 mi) of trails; all are tracked and most have skating lanes. A special trail is designated for skiing with dogs. Lessons and rentals are available.

En Route The routes north from Bethel to the Rangeley district are all scenic, particularly in the autumn when the maples are aflame with color. In the town of Newry, make a short detour to the **Artist's Bridge** (turn off Route 26 onto Sunday River Road and drive about 3 mi), the most painted and photographed of Maine's eight covered bridges. Route 26 continues north to the gorges and waterfalls of **Grafton Notch State Park.** Past the park, Route 26 continues to Errol, New Hampshire, where Route 16 will return you east around the north shore of Mooselookmeguntic Lake, through Oquossoc, and into Rangeley. A more direct route (if marginally less scenic) from Bethel to Rangeley still allows a stop in Newry. Follow U.S. 2 north and east from Bethel to the twin towns of Rumford and Mexico, where Route 17 continues north to Oquossoc, about an hour's drive. When you've driven for about 20 minutes beyond Rumford, the signs of civilization all but vanish and you pass through what seems like untouched territory—though the lumber companies have long since tackled the virgin forests, and sporting camps and cottages are tucked away here and there. The high point of this route is **Height of Land,** about 30 mi north of Rumford, with its unforgettable views of range after range of mountains and the island-studded blue mass of Mooselookmeguntic Lake directly below. Turnouts on both sides of the highway allow you to pull over for a long look. **Haines Landing** on Mooselookmeguntic Lake lies 7 mi west of Rangeley. Here you can stand at 1,400 ft above sea level and face the same magnificent scenery you admired at 2,400 ft from Height of Land on Route 17. Boat and canoe rentals are available at Mooselookmeguntic House.

Rangeley

❺❽ *67 mi north of Bethel.*

Rangeley, north of Rangeley Lake on Route 4/16, has long lured anglers, hunters, and winter-sports enthusiasts to its more than 40 lakes and ponds and 450 square mi of woodlands. Equally popular in summer or winter, Rangeley has a rough, wilderness feel to it. Lodgings are in the woods, around the lake, and along the golf course.

The **Wilhelm Reich Museum** interprets the life and work of controversial physician-scientist Wilhelm Reich (1897–1957), who believed that a force called orgone energy was the source of neurosis. The Orgone Energy Observatory, designed for Reich in 1948, exhibits biographical materials, inventions, and the equipment used in his experiments. Also on view are Reich's library, personal memorabilia, and artwork. Trails lace the 175-acre grounds, and the observatory deck has magnificent views of the countryside. ⊠ *Dodge Pond Rd.,* ☎ *207/864–3443,* WEB *www.somtel.com/~wreic.* ⊡ *$4.* ☉ *July–Aug., Wed.–Sun. 1–5; Sept., Sun. 1–5.*

OFF THE   **SANDY RIVER & RANGELEY LAKES RAILROAD –** You can ride a mile
BEATEN PATH   through the woods along a narrow-gauge railroad on a century-old
                 train drawn by a replica of the *Sandy River No. 4* locomotive. ⊠ *Bridge
                 Hill Rd., Phillips (20 mi southeast of Rangeley),* ☎ *207/778–3621,*
                 WEB *www.srrl-rr.org.* ⊡ *$3.* ☉ *June–Oct., 1st and 3rd Sun. each month;
                 rides hourly 11–3.*

Dining and Lodging

$$–$$$ ✕ **Gingerbread House.** A big fieldstone fireplace, well-spaced tables, and an antique marble soda fountain, all with views to the woods beyond, make for a comfortable atmosphere at this gingerbread-trim house, which is open for breakfast, lunch, and dinner. Soups, salads, and sandwiches at lunch give way to entrées such as shrimp scampi, roasted cranberry-maple chicken, and Maine crab cakes. ⊠ *Rtes. 17 and 4, Oquossoc,* ☎ *207/864–3602. AE, D, MC, V. Closed Mon. No dinner Sun.*

$–$$ ✕ **Porter House Restaurant.** This popular restaurant, seemingly in the middle of nowhere, draws diners from Rangeley, Kingfield, and Canada with its good service, excellent food, and casual atmosphere. Of the 1908 farmhouse's four dining rooms, the front one downstairs, which has a fireplace, is the most intimate and elegant. The broad Continental-style menu includes entrées for diners with light appetites. On the heavier side are porterhouse steak and roast duckling. Try the boneless lamb loin and lobster Brittany casserole if they're on the menu. ⊠ *Rte. 27, Eustis (20 mi north of Rangeley)* ☎ *207/246–7932. Reservations essential. AE, D, MC, V. Closed Mon.–Tues.*

$$ ✕▥ **Country Club Inn.** Built in the 1920s on the Mingo Springs Golf Course, this retreat is favored with a secluded hilltop location and sweeping lake and mountain views. The inn's baronial living room has a cathedral ceiling, a fieldstone fireplace at each end, and game trophies. Rooms downstairs in the main building and in the motel-style wing added in the 1950s are cheerfully if minimally decorated. The glassed-in dining room ($$)—open to nonguests by reservation only—has linen-draped tables set well apart. On the menu are mostly contemporary dishes using duck, veal, fresh fish, and filet mignon. ⊠ *Box 680, Mingo Loop Rd., 04970,* ☎ *207/864–3831,* WEB *www.rangeleymaine. com/ccinn. 19 rooms. Restaurant, pub, pool, 18-hole golf course. AE, MC, V. Closed Apr.–mid-May and mid-Oct.–late Dec. BP, MAP.*

$$ ✕▥ **Rangeley Inn and Motor Lodge.** From Main Street you see only the three-story blue inn building (circa 1907), but behind it is a newer motel wing with views of Haley Pond, a lawn, and a garden. Some of the inn's sizable rooms have iron-and-brass beds and subdued wallpaper, some have claw-foot tubs, and others have whirlpool tubs. The dining room ($$$), open for dinner, has Continental-style choices in-

cluding bouillabaisse, fresh fish, and New Zealand rack of lamb. The tavern serves casual fare such as soups, sandwiches, steaks, and ribs. You can choose to include breakfast and dinner in the rate. ⊠ *Box 160, 51 Main St., 04970,* ☎ *207/864–3341 or 800/666–3687,* FAX *207/ 864–3634,* WEB *www.rangeleyinn.com. 36 inn rooms, 15 motel rooms, 2 cabins. Restaurant, bar, meeting room. AE, D, MC, V.*

$$$$ ⊡ **Grant's Kennebago Camps.** People have been roughing it in comfort at this traditional sporting camp on Kennebago Lake for more than 85 years, lured by the mountain views, excellent fly-fishing, and hearty home-cooked meals. The wilderness setting is nothing less than spectacular. The cabins, whose screened porches overlook the lake, have woodstoves and are finished in knotty pine. Meals are served in the cheerful waterfront dining room. Motorboats, canoes, sailboats, Windsurfers, and mountain bikes are available; floatplane rides and fly-fishing instruction can be arranged. ⊠ *Box 786, off Rte. 16, 04970,* ☎ *207/864–3608 in summer; 207/282–5264 in winter; 800/633–4815,* WEB *www.grantscamps.com. 18 cabins. Dining room, lake, hiking, boating, fishing, mountain bikes, baby-sitting, playground. MC, V. Closed Oct.–late May. FAP.*

$$–$$$ ⊡ **Hunter Cove on Rangeley Lake.** These lakeside cabins, which sleep from two to six people, provide all the comforts of home in a rustic setting. The interiors are unfinished knotty pine and include kitchens, full baths, and comfortable if plain living rooms. Cabin No. 1 has a fieldstone fireplace, and others have wood-burning stoves. Cabins No. 5 and No. 8 have hot tubs. Summer guests can take advantage of a sand swimming beach, boat rentals, and a nearby golf course. In winter, snowmobile right to your door or ski nearby (cross-country and downhill). ⊠ *Mingo Loop Rd.,* ☎ *207/864–3383,* WEB *www.rangeleymaine. com/hunter. 8 cabins. Beach, boating. AE.*

Nightlife and the Arts

Rangeley Friends of the Arts (⊠ Box 333, 04970, ☎ no phone) sponsors musical theater, fiddlers' contests, rock and jazz, classical, and other summer fare, mostly at Lakeside Park.

Outdoor Activities and Sports

BOATING

Rangeley and Mooselookmeguntic lakes are good for canoeing, sailing, and motorboating. For fishing and paddleboat rentals, call **Oquossoc Cove Marina** (⊠ Oquossoc, ☎ 207/864–3463). **Dockside Sports Center** (⊠ Town Cove, ☎ 207/864–2424) rents a variety of boats, canoes, and other crafts. **River's Edge Sports** (⊠ Rte. 4/16, Oquossoc, ☎ 207/864–5582) rents canoes.

FISHING

Fishing for brook trout and salmon is at its best in May, June, and September; the Rangeley area is especially popular with fly-fishers. If you'd like a fishing guide, try **Westwind Charters and Guide Service** (☎ 207/864–5437).

SNOWMOBILING

More than 100 mi of maintained trails link lakes and towns to wilderness camps in the Rangeley area. The **Maine Snowmobile Association** has information about Maine's nearly 8,000-mi trail system.

STATE PARK

On the south shore of Rangeley Lake, **Rangeley Lake State Park** (⊠ off Rte. 17, ☎ 207/864–3858) has superb lakeside scenery, swimming, picnic tables, a boat ramp, showers, and 50 campsites.

Ski Areas

SADDLEBACK SKI AND SUMMER LAKE PRESERVE

A down-home atmosphere prevails at Saddleback, where the quiet and the absence of crowds, even on holiday weekends, draw return visitors—many of them families. A dispute over the Appalachian Trail, which crosses Saddleback's summit ridge, prevented development here for nearly a quarter of a century, but a settlement in 2000 opens the door for expansion and modernization. ⊠ *Box 490, Saddleback Rd. off Rte. 4, 04970,* ☎ *207/864–5671; 207/864–3380 snow conditions; 207/864–5364 reservations,* WEB *www.saddlebackskiarea.com.*

Downhill. The terrain is short and concentrated at the top of the mountain, accessible only by a T-bar. The middle of the mountain is mainly intermediate, with a few meandering easy trails; the beginner or novice slopes are toward the bottom. Two double chairlifts and three T-bars carry skiers to the 41 trails on the 1,830 ft of vertical.

Cross-country. 40 km (25 mi) of groomed cross-country trails spread out from the base area and circle Saddleback Lake and several ponds and rivers.

Child care. The nursery takes children from ages 6 weeks to 8 years. There are ski classes and programs for kids of different levels and ages.

Summer activities. Hiking is the big sport in warm weather.

Kingfield

59 *33 mi east of Rangeley, 15 mi west of Phillips.*

In the shadows of Mt. Abraham and Sugarloaf Mountain, Kingfield has everything a "real" New England town should have: a general store, historic inns, and a white clapboard church. Sugarloaf/USA has golf and tennis in summer.

The **Stanley Museum** houses a collection of original Stanley Steamer cars built by the Stanley twins, Kingfield's most famous natives. ⊠ *40 School St.,* ☎ *207/265–2729.* ☑ *$2.* ☉ *May–Oct., Tues.–Sun. 10–4; Nov.–Apr., Mon.–Fri, 1–4.*

Nowetah's American Indian Museum displays an extensive collection of baskets as well as artifacts from native peoples of North and South America. This small museum is part of a store. ⊠ *Rte. 27, New Portland,* ☎ *207/628–4981.* ☑ *Free.* ☉ *Daily 10–5.*

Dining and Lodging

$–$$$ ✕ **Gepetto's.** An institution at the 'Loaf, Gepetto's combines efficient service with a wide-ranging menu: homemade soups, hearty salads, burgers, pizza, vegetarian pasta, and fresh seafood are all options. ⊠ *Sugarloaf Base Village, Carrabassett Valley,* ☎ *207/237–2953. MC, V.*

$$–$$$ ✕⛉ **Sugarloaf Inn Resort.** Guest rooms at this older inn could use a face-lift, but you can't beat the ski-on access to Sugarloaf/USA. Rooms range from king-size on the fourth floor to dorm-style (bunk beds) on the ground floor. A greenhouse section of the Seasons Restaurant ($$–$$$) affords views of the slopes. At breakfast the sunlight pours into the dining room, and at dinner you can watch the snow-grooming machines prepare your favorite run. The in-house brew pub is a comfortable après-ski spot. ⊠ *Box 5000, R.R. 1, Sugarloaf Access Rd., Carrabassett Valley 04947,* ☎ *207/237–6814 or 800/843–5623,* FAX *207/237–3773,* WEB *www.sugarloaf.com. 38 rooms, 4 dorm-style rooms. Restaurant, pub, health club, downhill skiing, meeting room. AE, D, MC, V.*

$ ✕⛉ **One and Three Stanley Avenue.** These sister properties, a fine-dining restaurant and a simple B&B, are in adjacent Victorian houses. The quiet neighborhood is a few minutes' walk from downtown Kingfield and about a 20-minute drive from Sugarloaf/USA. Both are decorated with period furnishings. The restaurant ($$–$$$) specializes in creative Continental fare and emphasizes fresh Maine ingredients. ⊠ Box 169, 3 Stanley Ave., 04947, ☎ 207/265–5541. 6 rooms, 3 with bath. MC, V. Restaurant closed May–Nov. BP.

$$–$$$ 🖫 **Grand Summit.** New England ambience and European-style service are combined at this six-story brick hotel at the base of the lifts at Sugarloaf/USA. Oak and redwood paneling in the main rooms is enhanced by contemporary furnishings. Valet parking, ski tuning, lockers, and mountain guides are available through the concierge. The Double Diamond Pub has a lively après-ski scene. ⊠ R.R. 1, Box 2299, Carrabassett Valley 04947, ☎ 207/237–2222 or 800/527–9879, ℻ 207/237–2874, ⓦⒺⒷ www.sugarloaf.com. 100 rooms, 19 suites. Restaurant, pub, hot tub, massage, sauna, spa, concierge. AE, D, DC, MC, V.

Nightlife and the Arts

At Sugarloaf/USA, nightlife is concentrated at the mountain's base village. Monday is blues night at the **Bag & Kettle** (☎ 207/237–2451), which is the best choice for pizza and burgers. A microbrewery on the access road called the **Sugarloaf Brewing Company** (☎ 207/237–2211) pulls in revelers who come for après-ski brewskies. **Widowmaker Lounge** (☎ 207/237–6845) frequently presents live entertainment in the base lodge.

Outdoor Activities and Sports

T.A.D. Dog Sled Services (⊠ Rte. 27, Carrabassett Valley, ☎ 207/246–4461) conducts short 1½-mi rides near Sugarloaf/USA. Sleds accommodate up to two adults and two children.

Ski Areas

SUGARLOAF/USA

Abundant natural snow, a huge mountain, and the only above-tree-line skiing in the East have made Sugarloaf one of Maine's best-known ski areas. Sugarloaf skiers like the nontrendy Maine atmosphere and the base village, which has restaurants and shops. Two slopeside hotels and hundreds of slopeside condominiums provide ski-in/ski-out access. Once you are here, a car is unnecessary—a shuttle connects all mountain operations. Summer is much quieter than winter, but you can bike, hike, golf, and fish. ⊠ R.R. 1, Box 5000, Sugarloaf Access Rd., Carrabassett Valley 04947, ☎ 207/237–2000; 207/237–6808 snow conditions; 800/843–5623.

Downhill. With a vertical of 2,820 ft, Sugarloaf is taller than any other New England ski peak except Killington in Vermont. The advanced terrain begins with the steep snowfields on top, wide open and treeless. Coming down the face of the mountain, there are black-diamond runs everywhere, often blending into easier terrain. Many intermediate trails can be found down the front face, and a couple more come off the summit. Easier runs are predominantly toward the bottom, with a few long, winding runs that twist and turn from higher elevations. The mountain has three terrain parks and a halfpipe. Serving the resort's 126 trails are two high-speed quad, two quad, one triple, and eight double chairlifts and one T-bar.

Cross-country. The Sugarloaf Ski Outdoor Center has 105 km (62 mi) of cross-country trails that loop and wind through the valley. Trails connect to the resort.

Other activities. Snowshoeing and ice skating are available at the Outdoor Center. On Wednesday and Saturday nights, a snowcat takes guests to Bullwinkles, a mid-mountain restaurant, for a multicourse dining adventure ($80 per person). Reservations are essential. (☏ 207/237–2000).

Child care. A nursery takes children from ages 6 weeks to 6 years. Children's ski programs begin at age 3. A night nursery is open on Thursday and Saturday from 6 to 10 PM by reservation. Instruction is provided on a half-day or full-day basis for children from ages 4 to 14. Nightly children's activities are free. The teen club, Avalanche, is in the base lodge.

Summer and year-round activities. The resort has a superb 18-hole, Robert Trent Jones Jr.–designed golf course and six tennis courts for public use in warmer months. The Original Golf School operates from late June to late October. You can get advice on planning mountain biking and hiking trips, and the resort has canoe and bike rentals and can arrange fly-fishing instruction. The **Sugarloaf Sports and Fitness Club** (☏ 207/237–6946) has an indoor pool, six indoor and outdoor hot tubs, racquetball courts, full fitness and spa facilities, and a beauty salon. Use of club facilities is included in all lodging packages.

Western Lakes and Mountains A to Z

To research prices, get advice from other travelers, and book travel arrangements, visit www.fodors.com.

AIR TRAVEL
Mountain Air Service provides air access to remote areas, scenic flights, and charter fishing trips. Naples Flying Service operates sightseeing flights over the lakes in summer.
➤ AIRLINES & CONTACTS: **Mountain Air Service** (✉ Rangeley, ☏ 207/864–5307). **Naples Flying Service** (✉ Naples Causeway, Naples, ☏ 207/693–6591).

CAR TRAVEL
A car is essential to tour the western lakes and mountains. To travel from town to town in the order described in this section, drive U.S. 302 to Naples, then Route 35 to Harrison and the Waterfords. Take the Sweden Road, an ideal pick for autumn due to its vistas of the White Mountains, across to Lovell and pick up Route 5 to Bethel. From there, take Rte. 26 to U.S. 2 to Route 17 to Oquossoc, then head east on Route 16 through Rangeley to Kingfield.

EMERGENCIES
➤ HOSPITALS: **Bethel Area Health Center** (✉ Railroad St., Bethel, ☏ 207/824–2193). **Mt. Abram Regional Health Center** (✉ Depot St., Kingfield, ☏ 207/265–4555). **Northern Cumberland Memorial Hospital** (✉ S. High St., Bridgton, ☏ 207/647–8841). **Rangeley Regional Health Center** (✉ Main St., Rangeley, ☏ 207/864–3303).

VISITOR INFORMATION
Bethel's Chamber of Commerce has a reservations service. For reservations at Sugarloaf/USA, contact Sugarloaf Area Reservations Service.
➤ CONTACTS: **Bethel Area Chamber of Commerce** (✉ Box 439, 30 Cross St., Bethel 04217, ☏ 207/824–2282 or 800/442–5526). **Bethel's Chamber of Commerce Reservation Service** (☏ 207/824–3585 or 800/442–5826). **Bridgton–Lakes Region Chamber of Commerce** (✉ Box 236, U.S. 302, Bridgton 04009, ☏ 207/647–3472). **Greater Windham Chamber of Commerce** (✉ Box 1015, U.S. 302, Windham 04062, ☏ 207/892–8265). **Maine Tourism Association Welcome Center** (✉ Box 1084, U.S. 2, Bethel 04217, ☏ 207/824–4582). **Naples Business Association** (✉ Box 412, Naples 04055, ☏ 888/627–5379). **Rangeley Lakes Region Chamber of Commerce** (✉ Box 317, Main St., Range-

ley 04970, ☎ 207/864–5571 or 800/685–2537). **Sugarloaf Area Chamber of Commerce** (✉ R.R. 1, Box 2151, Kingfield 04947, ☎ 207/235–2100). **Sugarloaf Area Reservations Service** (☎ 800/843–2732).

THE NORTH WOODS

Maine's North Woods, the vast area in the north-central section of the state, is best experienced by canoe or raft, hiking trail, or on a fishing trip. Some great theaters for these activities are Moosehead Lake, Baxter State Park, and the Allagash Wilderness Waterway—as well as the summer resort town of Greenville, dramatically situated Rockwood, and the no-frills outposts that connect them.

Rockwood

60 *180 mi north of Portland, 91 mi northwest of Bangor.*

Rockwood, on Moosehead Lake's western shore, is a good starting point for a wilderness trip or a family vacation on the lake. Maine's largest lake, Moosehead supplies more in the way of rustic camps, restaurants, guides, and outfitters than any other northern locale. Its 420 mi of shorefront, three-quarters of which is owned by paper manufacturers, is virtually uninhabited. Though it doesn't possess many amenities, Rockwood has the most striking location of any town on Moosehead: the dark mass of **Mt. Kineo,** a sheer cliff that rises 789 ft above the lake and 1,789 ft above sea level, looms just across the narrows (you get an excellent view just north of town on Route 6/15).

OFF THE
BEATEN PATH

KINEO – Once a thriving summer resort, the original Mount Kineo Hotel (built in 1830 and torn down in the 1940s) was accessed primarily by steamship. Today Kineo makes a pleasant day trip. You can take the Kineo Shuttle, which departs from the State Dock in Rockwood (☎ 207/534–8812), or rent a motorboat in Rockwood and make the journey across the lake in about 15 minutes. There's a small marina on the shore, in the shadow of Mt. Kineo, and a half dozen buildings dot the land. Some are for sale and others are being restored, but there is no real town here. A tavern sells cold libations to drink there or take with you. A walkway laces the perimeter of the mountain, and trails lead to the summit.

Lodging

$$$$ ▦ **Attean Lake Lodge.** The Holden family has owned and operated this island lodge about an hour west of Rockwood since 1900. Log cabins, which sleep from two to six people, provide a secluded environment. The tastefully decorated central lodge has a library and games. Look for lobster, beef, and veal at the substantial meals; cookouts and picnic lunches add variety. ✉ *Box 457, off Rte. 201, Birch Island, Jackman 04945,* ☎ *207/668–3792,* FAX *207/668–4016,* WEB *www.atteanlodge.com. 18 cabins. Beach, boating, recreation room, library. AE, MC, V. Closed Oct.–May. FAP.*

$–$$ ▦ **The Birches.** This family-oriented resort supplies the full north-country experience: Moosehead Lake, birch woods, log cabins, and boats. The century-old main lodge has guest rooms, a lobby with a trout pond, and a living room dominated by a fieldstone fireplace. Cottages have wood-burning stoves or fireplaces and sleep from 2 to 15 people. The dining room (closed in December and April) overlooking the lake is open to the public for breakfast and dinner; the fare at dinner is pasta, seafood, and steak. ✉ *Box 41, off Rte. 6/15, on Moosehead Lake, 04478,* ☎ *207/534–7305 or 800/825–9453,* FAX *207/534–8835,* WEB *www.birches.com. 4 lodge rooms without bath, 15 cottages. Dining room, hot tub, sauna, boating. AE, D, MC, V. BP.*

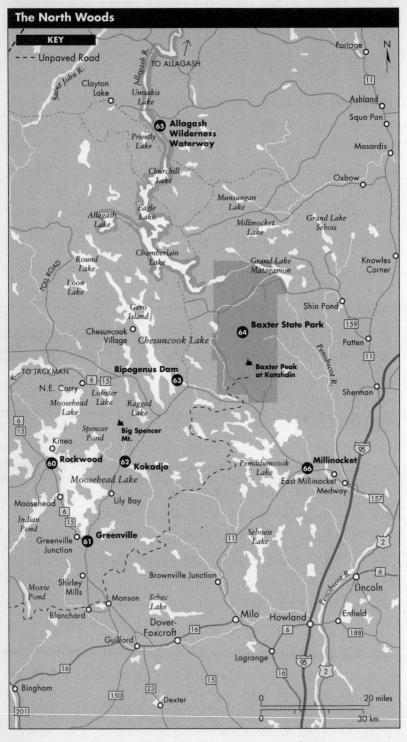

The North Woods

KEY
- - - Unpaved Road

N

Portage

TO ALLAGASH

Saint John R.

Allagash R.

Clayton
Lake

Umsakis
Lake

Ashland

Squa Pan

65 **Allagash
Wilderness
Waterway**

Priestly
Lake

Masardis

Churchill
Lake

Munsungan
Lake

Oxbow

Eagle
Lake

Allagash
Lake

Millinocket
Lake

Grand Lake
Sebois

Chamberlain
Lake

Round
Lake

Grand Lake
Matagamon

Knowles
Corner

TOLL ROAD

Loon
Lake

Gero
Island

Shin Pond

159

Chesuncook
Village

Chesuncook Lake

64 **Baxter State Park**

Patten

11

TO JACKMAN

Ripogenus Dam

63

Penobscot R.

Baxter Peak
at Katahdin

Sherman

N.E. Carry

6 15

Lobster
Lake

Moosehead
Lake

Ragged
Lake

6
15

Spencer
Pond

Big Spencer
Mt.

Kineo

60 **Rockwood**

62 **Kokadjo**

Pemadumcook
Lake

95

66 **Millinocket**

East Millinocket
Medway

Moosehead Lake

Moosehead

6
15

Lily Bay

157

Indian
Pond

11

Seboeis
Lake

2

61 **Greenville**

Greenville
Junction

Penobscot R.

6

Moxie
Pond

Shirley
Mills

Brownville Junction

Lincoln

Monson

Sebec
Lake

Enfield

Blanchard

Dover-
Foxcroft

16

Milo

Howland

188

Guilford

6

Lagrange

95

Bingham

16

15

16

2

150

23

Dexter

201

0   20 miles

0   30 km

$ ⊞ **Rockwood Cottages.** These eight white cottages on Moosehead Lake, off Route 15 and convenient to the center of Rockwood, have screened porches and fully equipped kitchens and sleep from two to seven people. There is a one-week minimum stay in July and August. ⊠ *Box 176, Rte. 15, 04478,* ☎ FAX *207/534–7725,* WEB *www.connectmaine. com/rockwood. 8 cottages. Sauna, dock, boating. MC, V. Closed Dec. 1–Apr. 30.*

Outdoor Activities and Sports

The **Birches** (☎ 207/534–7305) operates a moose cruise. **Mt. Kineo Cabins** (⊠ Rte. 6/15, ☎ 207/534–7744) rents canoes and larger boats on Moosehead Lake for the trip to Kineo. You can rent a boat or take a shuttle operated by **Rockwood Cottages** (☎ 207/534–7725) to Kineo. **Old Mill Campground** (☎ 207/534–7333) provides shuttle service to Kineo.

East Outlet of the Kennebec River, a popular Class II and III white-water run for canoeists and white-water rafters, is about 10 mi from Rockwood on Route 6/15 south. You'll come to a bridge with a dam to the left. The outlet ends at the Harris Station Dam at Indian Pond, headwaters of the Kennebec.

Greenville

Ⓖ⑴ *20 mi southeast of Rockwood, 160 mi northeast of Portland.*

Greenville, the largest town on Moosehead Lake, is an outdoorslover's paradise. Boating, fishing, and hiking are popular in summer; snowmobiling and skiing attract visitors in winter. The town has a smattering of shops, restaurants, and inns.

Moosehead Marine Museum has exhibits on the local logging industry and the steamship era on Moosehead Lake, plus photographs of the Mount Kineo Hotel. ⊠ *Main St.,* ☎ *207/695–2716.* ⊠ *$3.* ☉ *Late May–early Oct., daily 10–4.*

★ The Moosehead Marine Museum offers three- and five-hour trips on Moosehead Lake aboard the *Katahdin,* a 1914 steamship (now diesel). The 115-ft ship, called *The Kate,* carried passengers to Kineo until 1942 and then was used in the logging industry until 1975. ⊠ *Main St. (boarding is on the shoreline by the museum),* ☎ *207/695–2716,* WEB *www. katahdincruises.com.* ⊠ *$20–$26.* ☉ *July–Columbus Day.*

Dining and Lodging

$-$$ ✕ **Blue Moose Cafe.** A big moose marks this special restaurant, where fresh seafood, tenderloin, and lamb are prepared with a French accent. The small menu may include entrées such as pepper-crusted tenderloin of beef, full rack of lamb, or stuffed crèpes. ⊠ *Rte. 6/15,* ☎ *207/695–0786. MC, V. Closed Sunday; no lunch.*

$-$$ ✕ **The Black Frog.** For a fun and frivolous atmosphere and the best location on the lake, head to this downtown restaurant. The wide-ranging menu runs from burgers to filet mignon, and everything is served with a sense of humor. Specialties include barbecued baby-back pork ribs and grilled salmon steak. Grab a seat on the lakefront deck or in the dining room, where the decor runs from treasures to trash. ⊠ *Pritham Ave.,* ☎ *207/695–1100. D, DC, MC, V.*

$$$ ✕⊞ **Greenville Inn.** Built more than a century ago, this rambling structure is a block from town on a rise over Moosehead Lake. The ornate cherry and mahogany paneling, Oriental rugs, and leaded glass create an aura of masculine ease. Cottages have mountain and lake views, and some have decks. The restaurant ($$$; open May–Oct.; reservations essential; no lunch) has water views. Revised daily, the menu reflects the owners' Austrian background with choices such as spicy maple-glazed salmon fillets with potato pancakes and pork tenderloin with paprika sauce and spaetzle. ⊠ *Box 1194, Norris St., 04441,* ☎ *207/695–2206 or 888/695–6000,* ℻ *207/695–0335,* WEB *www. greenvilleinn.com. 4 rooms and 1 suite in main inn; 1 suite in carriage house; 6 cottages. Restaurant. D, MC, V. CP.*

$$$–$$$$ 🏨 **Blair Hill Inn.** Beautiful gardens and a hilltop location distinguish this 1891 estate. Guest rooms are spacious, and four have fireplaces; those in the front of the house have marvelous views over the lake. A restaurant, open to the public by reservation, serves dinner ($15–$24) from late May to mid-October on Friday and Saturday nights. ⊠ *Box 1288; Lily Bay Road, 04441,* ☎ *207/695–0224,* ℻ *207/695–4324,* WEB *www.blairhill.com, 8 rooms, 2 suites. Exercise room, outdoor hot tub, lawn games. D, MC, V. FB.*

$$$–$$$$ 🏨 **Lodge at Moosehead Lake.** This grand manor overlooking Moose-
★   head Lake is about as close as things get to luxury in the North Woods. No detail is overlooked; the service is exacting, yet the ambiance is casual. All rooms have whirlpool baths, fireplaces, and hand-carved four-poster beds; most have lake views. The carriage house suites are romantic retreats that open on to private patios. The dining room, where breakfast is served, has a spectacular view of the water. Dinners are occasionally available to guests, and dinner entrées such as pan-seared salmon with citrus and herbs have sophisticated touches. ⊠ *Box 1167, Lily Bay Rd., 04441,* ☎ *207/695–4400,* ℻ *207/695–2281,* WEB *www. lodgeatmooseheadlake.com. 5 rooms, 3 suites. D, MC, V. Closed late Oct.–late Dec. and mid-Mar.–mid-May. AP.*

$$ 🏨 **Lakeview House.** You get nearly the same sweeping views over Moosehead Lake at this small, minimally decorated B&B as you do from the more exclusive and expensive Lodge at Moosehead Lake. ⊠ *Box 1102, Lily Bay Rd., 04441,* ☎ *207/695–2229,* ℻ *207/695–2512. 2 rooms, 1 suite. Open year-round; call ahead in winter. BP.*

$ 🏨 **Chalet Moosehead.** Fifty yards off Route 6/15 and right on Moosehead Lake, this property has efficiencies (with two double beds, a living room, and a kitchenette), motel rooms, and cabins, all with picture windows to capture the view. The attractive grounds include a private beach and dock. Rooms in the new building have whirlpool tubs and private balconies overlooking the lake. ⊠ *Box 327, Rte. 6/15, Greenville Junction 04442,* ☎ *207/695–2950 or 800/290–3645,* WEB *www. mooseheadlodging.com. 19 rooms, 8 efficiencies, cabins. Horseshoes, beach, dock, boating. AE, D, MC, V.*

Outdoor Activities and Sports

Beaver Cove Marina (☎ 207/695–3526) rents boats and snowmobiles. **Kineo Kayak Guide Service** (☎ 207/474–3945 or 207/695–2896) schedules guided kayak tours and moose safaris in the Moosehead Lake and Kennebec Valley area. **Moose Country Safaris and Dogsled Trips** (☎ 207/876–4907) leads moose safaris, dogsled trips, and canoe and kayak trips. **Northwoods Outfitters** (☎ 207/695–3288) outfits a variety of sports and offers tours, moose safaris, and trail advice.

FISHING

Togue, landlocked salmon, and brook and lake trout lure thousands of anglers to the region from ice-out in mid-May until September; the hardiest return in winter to ice-fish. Call for current **information** (☎ 207/695–3756 or 800/322–9844) on water levels.

RAFTING

The Kennebec and Dead rivers and the West Branch of the Penobscot River offer thrilling white-water rafting (guides are strongly recommended). These rivers are dam-controlled, so trips run rain or shine daily from May to October (day and multiday trips are conducted). Most guided raft trips on the Kennebec and Dead rivers leave from the Forks, southwest of Moosehead Lake, on Route 201; Penobscot River trips leave from either Greenville or Millinocket. Many rafting outfitters operate resort facilities in their base towns. **Raft Maine** (☎ 800/723–8633) has lodging and rafting packages and information about outfitters.

STATE PARK

Lily Bay State Park (✉ Lily Bay Rd., ☎ 207/695–2700, 🖃 $2), 8 mi northeast of Greenville, has a good swimming beach, two boat-launching ramps, and two campgrounds with 91 sites.

Shopping

Indian Hill Trading Post (✉ Rte. 6/15, ☎ 207/695–2104) stocks just about anything you might need for a North Woods vacation, including sporting and camping equipment, canoes, and fishing licenses; there's even an adjacent grocery store. You enter **Moosehead Traders** (✉ Moosehead Center Mall, Rte. 6/15, ☎ 207/695–3806) through an antler archway; inside are books, clothing, and antiques and artifacts.

Ski Areas

BIG SQUAW MOUNTAIN RESORT

The management is modernizing this remote but pretty resort overlooking Moosehead Lake. The emphasis is on affordable family skiing—prices are downright cheap compared with those at other in-state areas. New snowmaking, new grooming equipment, and a new attitude make this a wonderful place for skiers longing to escape crowds. ✉ *Box D, Rte. 6/15, 04441,* ☎ *207/695–1000.*

Downhill. Trails are laid out according to difficulty, with the easy slopes toward the bottom, intermediate trails weaving from midpoint, and steeper runs high up off the 1,750-vertical-ft peak. The 22 trails are served by one triple and one double chairlift and two surface lifts.

Child care. The nursery takes children from infants through age 6. The ski school has daily lessons and racing classes for children of all ages.

Summer activities. The resort has a recreation program for children and two tennis courts, hiking, and lawn games.

Kokadjo

㉒ *22 mi northeast of Greenville.*

Kokadjo, population "not many," has a sign that reads KEEP MAINE GREEN. THIS IS GOD'S COUNTRY. WHY SET IT ON FIRE AND MAKE IT LOOK LIKE HELL? This is the last outpost before you enter the North Woods. As you leave Kokadjo, bear left at the fork and follow signs to Baxter State Park. A drive of 5 mi along this road (now dirt) brings you to the Sias Hill checkpoint, where from June to November a fee may be charged to travel the next 40 mi. Access is through a forest where you're likely to encounter logging trucks (which have the right of way), logging equipment, and work in progress. At the bottom of the hill after you pass the checkpoint, look to your right—there's a good chance you'll spot a moose.

Ripogenus Dam

㉓ *20 mi northeast of Kokadjo, 25 mins southeast of Chesuncook Village by floatplane.*

Ripogenus Dam and the granite-walled Ripogenus Gorge are on Ripogenus Lake, east of Chesuncook Lake. The gorge is the jumping-off point for the famous 12-mi West Branch of the Penobscot River white-water rafting trip and the most popular put-in point for Allagash canoe trips. The Penobscot River drops more than 70 ft-per-mile through the gorge, giving rafters a hold-on-for-your-life ride. The best spot to watch the Penobscot rafters is from Pray's Big Eddy Wilderness Campground, overlooking the rock-choked Crib Works Rapid (a Class V rapid). To get here, follow the main road northeast and turn left on Telos Road; the campground is about 10 yards after the bridge.

En Route   From the Pray's Big Eddy Wilderness Campground, take the main road (here called the Golden Road for the amount of money it took the Great Northern Paper Company to build it) southeast toward Millinocket. The road soon becomes paved. After you drive over the one-lane Abol Bridge and pass through the Bowater/Great Northern Paper Company's Debsconeag checkpoint, bear left to reach Togue Pond Gatehouse, the southern entrance to Baxter State Park.

Baxter State Park

★ ⑥④   *24 mi northwest of Millinocket.*

Few places in Maine are as remote or as beautiful as Baxter State Park and the Allagash Wilderness Waterway. Baxter, a gift from Governor Percival Baxter, is the jewel in the crown of northern Maine, a 204,733-acre wilderness area that surrounds Katahdin, Maine's highest mountain (5,267 ft at Baxter Peak) and the terminus of the Appalachian Trail. There are 46 mountain peaks and ridges, 18 of which exceed an elevation of 3,000 ft. Day-use parking areas fill quickly in season; it's best to arrive early, before 8 AM. The park is intersected by more than 180 mi of trails. No pets, domestic animals, oversize vehicles, all-terrain vehicles, motorboats, or motorcycles are allowed in the park, and there are no pay phones, gas stations, stores, or running water or electricity. The one visitor center is at Togue Pond, for which Millinocket is the nearest gateway. ⊠ *Mailing address: 64 Balsam Dr., Millinocket 04462,* ☎ *207/723–5140,* WEB *www.state.me.us.* ⊠ *$8 per vehicle; free to Maine residents.*

OFF THE BEATEN PATH   **LUMBERMAN'S MUSEUM –** This museum comprises 10 buildings filled with exhibits depicting the history of logging, including models, dioramas, and equipment. ⊠ *Shin Pond Rd. (Rte. 159), Patten (22 mi east of Baxter State Park),* ☎ *207/528–2650,* WEB *www.lumbermensmuseum. org.* ⊠ *$3.50.* ☉ *July–Aug., Tues.–Sun., 10–4; May 15–June 30 and Sept. 1–Columbus Day, Fri., Sat., and holiday Mon., 10–4.*

Lodging

$ ⚠ **Baxter State Park Authority.** Camping spaces at the 10 campgrounds here can be reserved only by mail or in person. Reservations can be made beginning the first working day in January—some sites are fully booked for midsummer weekends soon after that. The state also maintains primitive backcountry sites. ⊠ *64 Balsam Dr., Millinocket 04462,* ☎ *207/723–5140.*

Outdoor Activities and Sports

Katahdin, in Baxter State Park, draws thousands of hikers every year for the daylong climb to the summit and the stunning views of woods, mountains, and lakes from the hair-raising Knife Edge Trail along its ridge. The crowds can be formidable on clear summer days, so if you crave solitude, tackle one of the 45 other mountains in the park, all of which are accessible from a 150-mi network of trails. South Turner can be climbed in a morning (if you're fit)—it has a great view of Katahdin across the valley. On the way you'll pass Sandy Stream Pond, where moose are often seen at dusk. The Owl, the Brothers, and Doubletop Mountain are good day hikes.

Allagash Wilderness Waterway

⑥⑤ *22 mi north of Ripogenus Dam.*

The Allagash is a spectacular 92-mi corridor of lakes and rivers that cuts across 170,000 acres of wilderness, beginning at the northwest corner of Baxter State Park and running north to the town of Allagash, 10 mi from the Canadian border. For information, contact the **Allagash Wilderness Waterway** (✉ 106 Hogan Rd., Bangor 04401, ☎ 207/ 941–4014).

Outdoor Activities and Sports

The Allagash rapids are ranked Class I and Class II (very easy and easy), but that doesn't mean the river is a piece of cake; river conditions vary greatly with the depth and volume of water, and even a Class I rapid can hang your canoe up on a rock, capsize you, or spin you around. On the lakes, strong winds can halt your progress for days. The Allagash should not be undertaken lightly or without planning; the complete 92-mi course requires 7 to 10 days. The canoeing season along the Allagash is from mid-May to October, although it's wise to remember that the black-fly season ends about July 1. The best bet for a novice is to go with a guide; a good outfitter will help plan your route and provide your craft and transportation.

Millinocket

⑥⑥ *19 mi southeast of Baxter State Park, 70 mi north of Bangor, 90 mi northwest of Greenville.*

Millinocket, a papermill town with a population of 7,000, is a gateway to Baxter State Park. There are a number of outfitters here.

OFF THE
BEATEN PATH

KATAHDIN IRON WORKS – For a worthwhile day trip from Millinocket, take Route 11 and head southwest to a trailhead 5 mi north of Brownville Junction. Drive the gravel road 6 mi to Katahdin Iron Works, the site of a mining operation that employed nearly 200 workers in the mid-1800s; a deteriorated kiln, a stone furnace, and a charcoal-storage building are all that remain. From here, a hiking trail leads over fairly rugged terrain to **Gulf Hagas,** with natural chasms, cliffs, a 3.5-mi gorge, waterfalls, pools, exotic flora, and rock formations.

Lodging

$$$$ 🏠 **Bradford Camps.** It's tempting to laze the day away on the front porch of these lakefront log cabins or in front of the massive fieldstone fireplace in the main lodge. But alas, there are miles of trails and woods roads to explore, rivers and lakes to fish and canoe, and even the Allagash is close enough for a day trip. Rates include three hearty, home-style meals. Float plane transportation is available from Millinocket and other locations. ✉ *Box 729, Ashland, 04732,* ☎ *May 1–Nov. 30, 207/ 746–7777; Dec. 1–Apr. 30, 207/469–6364,* 🌐 *www.bradfordcamps. com. 8 cabins. Dining room, lake, hiking, boating. Late Nov.–May. AP.*

$$$$ 🏠 **Libby Camps.** Matt Libby, along with his wife, Ellen, represent the fifth generation of Libbys to run this sporting camp on Millinocket Lake, the headwaters of the Allagash and Aroostook rivers. Skylights brighten the well-kept cabins, where handmade quilts cover the beds and woodstoves keep the chill at bay. The main lodge is open and airy with a magnificent central stone fireplace. Rates include all meals as well as use of sea kayaks, canoes, sail and motor boats. ⊠ *Box 810, Ashland, 04732,* ☎ *207/435–8274 or 207/435–6233,* FAX *207/435–3230,* WEB *www.libbycamps.com. 8 cabins; 10 rustic outpost cabins. Beach, boating, fishing, hiking. MC, V. Late Nov.–May 1. MAP.*

$ ⊞ **Big Moose Inn.** There's nothing fancy about this old-fashioned inn and the cabins and campsites nestled between Ambejesus and Millinocket lakes, just 8 mi from the entrance to Baxter State Park. The inn has a big stone and brick fireplace decorated with a moose trophy and snowshoes; inn rooms are comfortably furnished with country pieces. The popular dining room, open for dinner Wednesday through Saturday, emphasizes seafood. Canoes and a store are other amenities. ⊠ *Box 98, Baxter State Park Rd., 04462,* ☎ *207/723–8391,* FAX *207/723–8199,* WEB *www.bigmoosecabins.com. 11 rooms without bath, 11 cabins, 44 campsites. Restaurant, boating. MC, V. Closed late Nov.–May. CP.*

$ ⊞ **Gateway Inn.** This new motel is just off I–95. Book a room with a deck facing Katahdin for the best views. ⊠ *Box 637, Rte. 157, Medway 04460,* ☎ *207/746–3193,* FAX *207/746–3430,* WEB *www. medwaygateway.com. 30 rooms, 8 efficiencies. Air-conditioning, no-smoking rooms, indoor pool, hot tub, sauna, exercise room. AE, D, MC, V. CP.*

Outdoor Activities and Sports

Katahdin Area Guide Service (⊠ 74 Water St., ☎ 207/723–9522 or 800/548–4355) outfits fishing, snowmobiling, canoeing, and camping expeditions. **Penobscot River Outfitters** (☎ 800/794–5267) rents canoes and offers a shuttle service. **New England Outdoor Center** (☎ 207/ 723–5438 or 800/766–7238) rents snowmobiles and offers guided trips.

The North Woods A to Z

To research prices, get advice from other travelers, and book travel arrangements, visit www.fodors.com.

AIR TRAVEL

Charter flights, usually by seaplane, from Bangor, Greenville, or Millinocket to smaller towns and remote lake and forest areas can be arranged with a number of flying services, which will transport you and your gear and help you find a guide.

➤ AIRLINES & CONTACTS: **Currier's Flying Service** (⊠ Greenville Junction, ☎ 207/695–2778). **Folsom's Air Service** (⊠ Greenville, ☎ 207/ 695–2821). **Katahdin Air Service** (⊠ Millinocket, ☎ 207/723–8378). **Scotty's Flying Service** (⊠ Shin Pond, ☎ 207/528–2626).

AIRPORTS

Bangor International Airport is the closest airport.

CAR TRAVEL

A car is essential to negotiate this vast region but may not be useful to someone spending a vacation entirely at a wilderness camp. Public roads are scarce in the north country, but lumber companies maintain private roads that are often open to the public (sometimes by permit only). When driving on a logging road, always give lumber company trucks the right of way. Be aware that loggers often take the middle of the road and will neither move over nor slow down for you.

I–95 offers the quickest access to the North Woods. U.S. 201 (I–95, Exit 36) is the major route to Jackman and to Québec. Route 15 connects Jackman to Greenville and Bangor. The Golden Road is a private, paper company–operated road that links Greenville to Millinocket.

EMERGENCIES

➤ HOSPITALS: **Charles A. Dean Memorial Hospital** (✉ Pritham Ave., Greenville, ☎ 207/695–2223 or 800/260–4000). **Mayo Regional Hospital** (✉ 75 W. Main St., Dover-Foxcroft, ☎ 207/564–8401). **Millinocket Regional Hospital** (✉ 200 Somerset St., Millinocket, ☎ 207/723–5161).

LODGING
CAMPING

Reservations for state park campsites (excluding Baxter State Park) can be made through the Bureau of Parks and Lands, which can also tell you if you need a camping permit and where to obtain one. Maine Sporting Camp Association publishes a list of its members, with details on the facilities available at each camp.

The Maine Campground Owners Association publishes a helpful annual directory of its members. The Maine Forest Service, Department of Conservation will direct you to the nearest place to get a fire permit. Maine Tourism Association publishes a listing of private campsites and cottage rentals. North Maine Woods maintains 500 primitive campsites on commercial forest land.

➤ CONTACTS: **Bureau of Parks and Lands** (✉ State House Station 22, Augusta 04333, ☎ 207/287–3821; 800/332–1501 in ME). **Maine Sporting Camp Association** (✉ Box 89, Jay 04239). **Maine Campground Owners Association** (✉ 655 Main St., Lewiston 04240, ☎ 207/782–5874). The **Maine Forest Service, Department of Conservation** (✉ State House Station 22, Augusta 04333, ☎ 207/287–2791). **Maine Tourism Association** (✉ Box 2300, 325B Water St., Hallowell 04347, ☎ 207/623–0363; 800/533–9595 outside ME). **North Maine Woods** (✉ Box 425, Ashland 04732, ☎ 207/435–6213).

OUTDOORS & SPORTS
CANOEING

Most canoe rental operations will arrange transportation, help plan your route, and provide a guide. Transport to wilderness lakes can be arranged through the flying services listed under Air Travel.

The Bureau of Parks and Lands provides information on independent Allagash canoeing and camping. Allagash Canoe Trips operates guided trips on the Allagash Waterway, plus the Moose, Penobscot, and St. John rivers. Allagash Wilderness Outfitters/Frost Pond Camps provides equipment, transportation, and information for canoe trips on the Allagash and the Penobscot rivers. Mahoosuc Guide Service conducts guided trips on the Penobscot, Allagash, and Moose rivers. North Country Outfitters operates a white-water canoeing and kayaking school, rents equipment, and leads guided canoe trips on the Allagash Waterway and the Moose, Penobscot, and St. John rivers. Sunrise County Canoe & Kayak outfits trips on eastern and northern Maine waterways. Willard Jalbert Camps has been leading guided Allagash trips since the late 1800s.

➤ CONTACTS: **Allagash Canoe Trips** (✉ Box 713, Greenville 04441, ☎ 207/695–3668). **Allagash Wilderness Outfitters/Frost Pond Camps** (✉ Box 620, Greenville 04441, ☎ 207/695–2821). **Mahoosuc Guide Service** (✉ Bear River Rd., Newry 04261, ☎ 207/824–2073). **North Country Outfitters** (✉ Box 41, Rockwood 04478, ☎ 207/534–2242 or 207/534–7305). **Sunrise County Canoe & Kayak** (✉ Cathance Lake,

Grove Post 04657, ☎ 207/454–7708 or 800/980–2300). **Willard Jalbert Camps** (✉ 6 Winchester St., Presque Isle 04769, ☎ 207/764–0494).

GUIDES

Fishing guides are available through most wilderness camps, sporting goods stores, and canoe outfitters. For assistance in finding a guide, contact North Maine Woods (☞ Visitor Information).
➤ CONTACTS: **Gilpatrick's Guide Service** (✉ Box 461, Skowhegan 04976, ☎ 207/453–6959). **Maine Guide Fly Shop and Guide Service** (✉ Box 1202, Main St., Greenville 04441, ☎ 207/695–2266). **Professional Guide Service** (✉ Box 346, Sheridan 04775, ☎ 207/435–8044).

HORSEBACK RIDING

North Woods Riding Adventures, owned by registered Maine guides Judy Cross-Strehlke and Bob Strehlke, conducts one-day, two-day, and week-long pack trips (10 people maximum) through parts of Piscataquis County. A popular two-day trip explores the Whitecap–Barren Mountain Range, near Katahdin Iron Works.
➤ CONTACTS: **North Woods Riding Adventures** (✉ 64 Garland Line Rd., Dover-Foxcroft 04426, ☎ 207/564–3451).

RAFTING

Raft Maine is an association of white-water outfitters licensed to lead trips down the Kennebec and Dead rivers and the West Branch of the Penobscot River. Rafting season begins May 1 and continues through mid-October. North Maine Woods has maps; a canoeing guide for the St. John River; and lists of outfitters, camps, and campsites.
➤ CONTACTS: **Raft Maine** (☎ 800/723–8633). **North Maine Woods** (✉ Box 425, Ashland 04732, ☎ 207/435–6213).

VISITOR INFORMATION
➤ CONTACTS: **Baxter State Park Authority** (✉ 64 Balsam Dr., Millinocket 04462, ☎ 207/723–5140). **Katahdin Area Chamber of Commerce** (✉ 1029 Central St., Millinocket 04462, ☎ 207/723–4443). **Moosehead Lake Region Chamber of Commerce** (✉ Box 581, Rte. 6/15, Greenville 04441, ☎ 207/695–2702).

MAINE A TO Z

To research prices, get advice from other travelers, and book travel arrangements, visit www.fodors.com.

AIR TRAVEL
Regional flying services, operating from regional and municipal airports, provide access to remote lakes and wilderness areas as well as to Penobscot Bay islands.

AIRPORTS
Portland International Jetport is served by Air Nova, American, Business Express, Continental, Delta, Northwest, TWA, United, and US Airways. Bangor International Airport is served by Business Express, Continental, Delta/Comair, U.S. Air, and Finnair. Hancock County Airport, 8 mi northwest of Bar Harbor, is served by US Airways Express. Knox County Regional Airport, in Owls Head, 3 mi south of Rockland, has flights to Boston and Bar Harbor on US Airways Express.
➤ AIRPORT INFORMATION: **Portland International Jetport** (✉ Westbrook St. off Rte. 9, ☎ 207/774–7301). **Bangor International Airport** (✉ Godfrey Blvd., ☎ 207/947–0384). **Hancock County Airport** (✉ Rte. 3, Trenton, ☎ 207/667–7329). **Knox County Regional Airport** (✉ off Rte. 73, ☎ 207/594–4131).

BIKE & MOPED TRAVEL

For information on bicycling in Maine and a list of companies offering tours, contact the Bicycle Coalition of Maine.

➤ CONTACTS: **Bicycle Coalition of Maine**(☎ 207/288–3028).

BOAT & FERRY TRAVEL

Northumberland/Bay Ferries operates the Cat, a high-speed car-ferry service on a catamaran, between Yarmouth, Nova Scotia, and Bar Harbor from mid-May to mid-October. The crossing takes three hours, and the Cat has everything from a casino to sightseeing decks. Prince of Fundy Cruises operates a car ferry from May to October between Portland and Yarmouth, Nova Scotia. Maine State Ferry Service provides service from Rockland, Lincolnville, and Bass Harbor to islands in Penobscot and Blue Hill bays.

➤ BOAT & FERRY INFORMATION: **Northumberland/Bay Ferries** (☎ 888/ 249–7245). **Prince of Fundy Cruises** (☎ 800/341–7540; 800/482– 0955 in Maine). **Maine State Ferry Service** (☎ 207/596–2202 or 800/ 491–4883).

BUS TRAVEL

Concord Trailways provides service between Boston and Bangor (via Portland); a coastal route connects towns between Brunswick and Searsport. Vermont Transit provides service to Augusta, Bangor, Brunswick, Lewiston, Portland, and Waterville. Vermont Transit is a subsidiary of Greyhound Lines.

➤ BUS INFORMATION: **Concord Trailways** (☎ 800/639–3317). **Vermont Transit** (☎ 207/772–6587). **Greyhound Lines** (☎ 800/231– 2222).

CAR RENTAL

Portland has a good number of car rental outlets.

➤ MAJOR AGENCIES: **Alamo** (✉ 1000 Westbrook St., ☎ 207/775– 0855; 800/327–9633 in Portland). **Avis** (✉ Portland International Jetport, ☎ 207/874–7500 or 800/831–2847). **Budget** (✉ 1128 Westbrook St., ☎ 800/848–8005). **Hertz** (✉ 1049 Westbrook St., Portland International Jetport, ☎ 207/774–4544 or 800/654–3131). **National** (✉ Portland International Jetport, ☎ 207/773–0036 or 800/227– 7368).

CAR TRAVEL

Interstate 95 is the fastest route to and through the state from coastal New Hampshire and points south, turning inland at Brunswick and going on to Bangor and the Canadian border. U.S. 1, more leisurely and scenic, is the principal coastal highway from New Hampshire to Canada. U.S. 302 is the primary access to the Sebago Lake region, while Route 26 leads to the western mountains and Route 27 leads to the Rangeley and Sugarloaf regions. U.S. 201 is the fastest route to Québec, and Route 9 is the inland route from Bangor to Calais.

The maximum speed limit is 65 mph, unless otherwise posted, on I-95 and the Maine Turnpike. Local municipalities post speed limits on roads within their jurisdictions. State law requires drivers to stop for pedestrians. Drivers can make right turns on red if no sign prohibits such turns. Note that Maine law requires drivers to turn on their lights when windshield wipers are operating.

In many areas a car is the only practical means of travel. The *Maine Map and Travel Guide,* available for a small fee from the Maine Tourism Association, is useful for driving throughout the state; it has directories, mileage charts, and enlarged maps of city areas. DeLorme's

Maine Atlas & Gazetteer, sold at local bookstores, includes enlarged, detailed maps of every part of the state.

LODGING
CAMPING
Reservations for state park campsites (excluding Baxter State Park) can be made from January until August 23 through the Bureau of Parks and Lands. Make reservations as far ahead as possible (at least seven days in advance), because sites go quickly. The Maine Campground Owners Association has a statewide listing of private campgrounds.
➤ CONTACTS: **Bureau of Parks and Lands** (☎ 207/287–3824; 800/332–1501 in ME). **Maine Campground Owners Association** (✉ 655 Main St., Lewiston 04240, ☎ 207/782–5874, FAX 207/782–4497, WEB www.campmaine.com).

OUTDOORS & SPORTS
BIRDING
The Maine Audubon Society provides information on birding in Maine and hosts field trips for novice to expert birders.
➤ CONTACTS: **Maine Audubon Society** (✉ 20 Gilsland Farm Rd., Falmouth 04105, ☎ 207/781–6180, WEB www.maineaudubon.org).

FISHING
For information about fishing and licenses, contact the Maine Department of Inland Fisheries and Wildlife.
➤ CONTACTS: **Maine Department of Inland Fisheries and Wildlife** (✉ 41 State House Station Augusta 04333, ☎ 207/287–8000. WEB www.state.me.us/ifw).

KAYAKING
A number of outfitters provide sea-kayaking instruction as well as tours along the Maine coast.
➤ CONTACTS: **Coastal Kayaking Tours** (✉ 48 Cottage St., Bar Harbor, ☎ 800/526–8615 or 207/288–9605). **Maine Island Kayak Co.** (✉ 70 Luther St., Peaks Island, ☎ 207/766–2373 or 800/796–2376). **Maine Sport Outfitters** (✉ U.S. 1, Rockport, ☎ 207/236–8797 or 800/722–0826). **Sunrise County Canoe & Kayak** (✉ Cathance Lake, Grove Post 04657, ☎ 207/454–7708 or 800/980–2300).

PARKS AND PUBLIC LANDS
The Bureau of Parks and Public Lands publishes the brochure "Outdoors in Maine," a listing of state parks, public reserved lands, state historic trails, boat access sites, snowmobile trails, and all-terrain-vehicle trails.
➤ CONTACTS: **Bureau of Parks and Public Lands** (✉ 22 State House Station, Augusta 04333, ☎ 207/287–3821, WEB www.state.me.us/doc/parks).

RAFTING
Raft Maine provides information on white-water rafting on the Kennebec, Penobscot, and Dead rivers.
➤ CONTACTS: **Raft Maine** (✉ Box 3, Bethel 04217, ☎ 800/723–8633).

SKIING
For information on alpine skiing, contact Ski Maine. For information on cross-country ski centers, shops, and lodging packages, contact the Maine Nordic Ski Council.
➤ CONTACTS: **Ski Maine** (✉ Box 7566, Portland 04112, ☎ 207/622–6983; 207/761–3774; 888/624–6345 snow conditions, WEB www.skimaine.com). **Maine Nordic Ski Council** (✉ Box 645, Bethel 04217, ☎ 207/824–3694 or 800/754–9263, WEB www.mnsc.com).

SNOWMOBILING

The Maine Snowmobile Association offers an excellent statewide trail map of about 8,000 mi of trails.

➤ CONTACTS: **Maine Snowmobile Association** (⊠ Box 77, Augusta 04332, ☎ 207/622–6983; 207/626–5717 trail conditions, WEB www. mesnow.com).

SPORTING CAMPS

Maine Sporting Camp Association publishes a directory of sporting camps throughout the state.

➤ CONTACTS: **Maine Sporting Camp Association** (⊠ Box 89, Jay 04249, WEB www.mainesportingcamps.com).

WINDJAMMING

The Maine Windjammer Association represents 13 schooners offering multiday cruises along the Maine coast.

➤ CONTACTS: **Maine Windjammer Association** (⊠ Box 1144, Blue Hill 04614, ☎ 800/807–9463, WEB www.sailmainecoast.com).

TOURS

The Maine Professional Guides Association maintains and mails out listings of its members and their specialties.

➤ TOUR-OPERATORS: **Maine Professional Guides Association** (Box 847, Augusta 04332, ☎ 207/549–5631, WEB www.maineguides.org).

TRAIN TRAVEL

Amtrak is planning to begin service from Boston to Portland in summer 2001, with stops in Saco and Wells year-round and in Old Orchard Beach in the summer.

➤ TRAIN INFORMATION: **Amtrak** (☎ 800/872–7245, WEB www.amtrak. com).

VISITOR INFORMATION

The Maine Tourism Association operates a welcome center on U.S. 2 in Bethel. State of Maine Visitor Information Centers are located on Union St. in Calais, Rte. 203 in Fryeburg, I–95 and U.S. 1 in Kittery, and on U.S. 1 in Yarmouth, I–95, Exit 17.

For a directory of members of the Maine Antique Dealer Association, send a self-addressed, stamped envelope and $3 to MADA. The Maine Antiquarian Booksellers Association publishes a directory of members throughout Maine.

For a brochure describing eight art museums along the Maine coast, write the Maine Art Museum Trail. The Maine Crafts Association publishes a "Guide to Crafts and Culture." "The Maine Archives and Museums Directory" lists museums, historical societies, archives, and historic sites statewide. Call the Maine Garden and Landscape Trail for a map and guide. *The Maine Outdoor Sculpture Guide* is available from the Maine Arts Commission. The Web site, www.mainemusic. org, lists music-related events around the state.

➤ CONTACTS: **Maine Innkeepers Association** (⊠ 305 Commercial St., Portland 04101, ☎ 207/773–7670, WEB www.maineinns.com). **Maine Tourism Association** (⊠ Box 2300, 325B Water St., Hallowell 04347, ☎ 207/623–0363 or 888/624–6345, WEB www.mainetourism.com). **Maine Office of Tourism** (⊠ 33 Stone St., Augusta 04333, ☎ 888/624–6345, WEB www.visitmaine.com). **Maine Antique Dealer Association,** (⊠ Box 352, Scarborough 04074. WEB www.maineada.com). **Maine Antique Dealer Directory** (⊠ R.R. 3, Box 1290, Winslow 04901).The

Maine Antiquarian Booksellers Association (✉ ☎ 207/645–4122, WEB www.wworx.net/maba). **Maine Art Museum Trail** (✉ 75 Russell St., Lewiston 04240 ☎ 800/782–6497. WEB www.maineartmuseums.org). **Maine Crafts Association** (✉ 15 Walton St., Portland 04103, WEB www.mainecrafts.maine.com). **"The Maine Archives and Museums Directory"** (✉ 60 Community Dr., Augusta 04330. ☎ 800/452–8786, WEB www.mainemuseums.org). **Maine Garden and Landscape Trail** (✉ ☎ 800/782–6497). **Maine Arts Commission** (✉ 25 State House Station, Augusta 04333, ☎ 207/287–2724.

3 VERMONT

Southern Vermont has manicured landscapes, immaculate villages, and summer theaters, as well as a surprisingly large chunk of wilderness in the Green Mountain National Forest. Central Vermont is home to the state's largest ski resort, Killington, along with the rolling farmland vistas of the lower Lake Champlain valley. Up north, Vermont attractions include the state's largest city, cosmopolitan and collegiate Burlington; the nation's smallest state capital, Montpelier; the legendary slopes of Stowe; and the leafy back roads of the Northeast Kingdom.

Revised and
updated by
Kay and Bill
Scheller

E VERYWHERE YOU LOOK IN VERMONT, the evidence is clear: this
is not the state it was 30 years ago. That may be true for the rest
of New England as well, but the contrasts between the present
and recent past seem all the more sharply drawn in the Green Mountain State, if only because an aura of timelessness has always been at
the heart of the Vermont image. Vermont was where all the quirks and
virtues outsiders associate with up-country New England were supposed
to reside. It was where the Yankees were Yankee-est and where there
were more cows than people.

Not that you should be alarmed if you haven't been here in a while;
Vermont hasn't become southern California, or even, for that matter,
southern New Hampshire. The state's population, which increased from
335,000 to only 390,000 from 1860 to 1960, began to climb sharply
as interstate highways and resort development made their impact. By
1990 the state had 563,000 residents; today, a population of approx-
imately 600,000 indicates some leveling off of the rate of growth. This
is still the most rural state in the Union (meaning that it has the smallest percentage of citizens living in statistically defined metropolitan areas),
and it still turns out most of New England's milk, even though there
are, finally, more people than cows. Vermont remains a place where
cars occasionally have to stop while a dairy farmer walks his herd across
a secondary road; and up in Essex County, in what George Aiken dubbed
the Northeast Kingdom, there are townships with zero population. And
the kind of scrupulous, straightforward, plainspoken politics practiced by Governor (later Senator) Aiken for 50 years has not become
outmoded in a state that still turns out on town-meeting day.

How has Vermont changed? In strictly physical terms, the most obvi-
ous transformations have taken place in and around the two major cities,
Burlington and Rutland, and near the larger ski resorts, such as Stowe,
Killington, Stratton, and Mt. Snow. Burlington's Church Street, once
a paradigm of all the sleepy redbrick shopping thoroughfares in northern New England, is now a pedestrian mall with chic bistros; outside
the city, suburban development has supplanted farms in towns where
someone's trip to Burlington might once have been an item in a weekly
newspaper. As for the ski areas, it's no longer enough simply to boast
the latest in chairlift technology. Slopeside hotels and condos have
boomed, especially in the southern part of the state, turning ski areas
into big-time resort destinations. And once-sleepy Manchester has become one of New England's factory-outlet meccas.

The real metamorphosis in the Green Mountains, however, has to do
more with style, with the personality of the place, than with development. The past couple of decades have seen a tremendous influx of outsiders—not only skiers and "leaf peepers" but people who have come
to stay year-round—and many of them are determined either to freshen
the local scene with their own idiosyncrasies or to make Vermont even
more like Vermont than they found it. On the one hand, this trans-
lates into the fact that Vermont is the only state represented in Washington by an independent socialist congressman; on the other, it means
that sheep farming has been reintroduced to the state, largely to provide a high-quality product for the hand-weaving industry.

This ties in with another local phenomenon, one best described as Made
in Vermont. Once upon a time, maple syrup and sharp cheddar cheese
were the products that carried Vermont's name to the world. The market niche that they created has since been widened by Vermonters—a
great many of them refugees from more hectic arenas of commerce—

Vermont

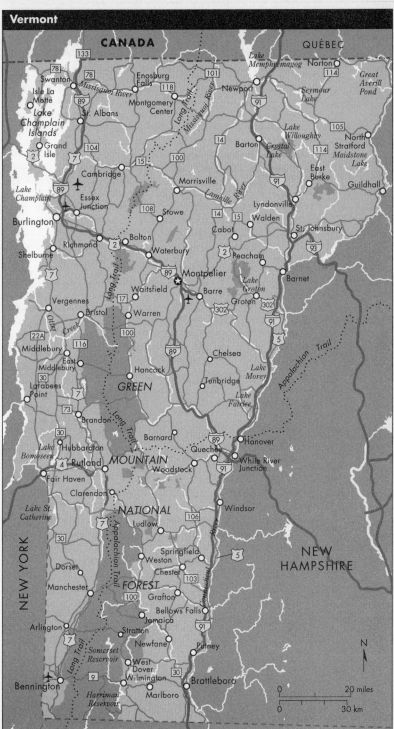

CANADA   QUÉBEC

Lake Memphremagog

133

78   Enosburg Falls   101   Norton   114

78   118   Newport   Great Averill Pond

Swanton   Mississquoi River   Montgomery Center   91   Seymour Lake

Isle La Motte   St. Albans   Lake Willoughby

89   Lake Champlain Islands   104   14   Barton   Crystal Lake   105

Grand Isle   7   15   14   91   114   North Stratford   Maidstone Lake

2   100   Morrisville   East Burke   Guildhall

Cambridge   108   Lamoille River   Lyndonville

Essex Junction   Stowe   14   15   Walden   St. Johnsbury

Lake Champlain   Bolton   Cabot   2   Peacham   93

Burlington   Richmond   2   Waterbury   Barnet

Shelburne   89   Montpelier   Lake Groton

7   Waitsfield   Barre   302   Groton   302

Vergennes   17   Warren   302   91

Bristol   100   5

22A   Otter Creek   89   Chelsea

116   Middlebury   Lake Morey

East Middlebury   Hancock   Tunbridge

30   7   GREEN   Lake Fairlee

Larabees Point   73   Barnard   89   Hanover   Appalachian Trail

Brandon   Long Trail   Quechee   White River Junction

30   MOUNTAIN   Woodstock   91

Lake Bomoseen   Hubbardton   Clarendon

4   Rutland   NATIONAL   Windsor

Fair Haven   7   106   NEW HAMPSHIRE

Lake St. Catherine   Ludlow   Springfield   5

30   Weston   103

Dorset   FOREST   Chester

Manchester   100   Grafton

Appalachian Trail   Jamaica   Bellows Falls

Arlington   7   Stratton   91

Somerset Reservoir   Newfane   Putney

NEW YORK   West Dover   30

Bennington   9   Wilmington   Brattleboro

Harriman Reservoir   Marlboro

N

0   20 miles

0   30 km

who now offer a dizzying variety of goods with the ineffable cachet of Vermont manufacture. There are Vermont wood toys, Vermont apple wines, Vermont chocolates, even Vermont gin. The most successful Made in Vermont product is Ben & Jerry's ice cream; the company has become the largest single purchaser of Vermont milk.

The character and appearance of the landscape are what most readily ignite preservationists' passions in Vermont. Farming may be changing—in addition to sheep, there are goats, llamas, emus, and even elk grazing the Green Mountain foothills—but farms are farms, valued for their open-space counterpoint to Vermont forests and villages. The Vermont Land Trust has saved thousands of acres of farmland through the purchase of development rights; meanwhile, vast tracts of northern woodlands have been preserved for wildlife habitat, recreation, and low-impact forestry. The challenge is to bring Vermont into the 21st century while making sure it still looks like Vermont. The model might be an old farmhouse, with fiber-optic cables hidden in its walls.

Pleasures and Pastimes

Dining

Over the past few years, Vermont chefs have been working hard to fulfill two distinct responsibilities. One is the need to honor the traditions of Yankee cooking, the realm of pot roast and Indian pudding, sticky buns and homemade corn relish. As travelers and residents have become more sophisticated, there has also been a demand for the ethnic cuisines, lighter adaptations of classics, and new American treatments of seasonal ingredients that now characterize urban menus.

The more ambitious restaurants and inn kitchens have not only managed to balance these two gastronomic imperatives but also have succeeded in combining them. The trick is to take an innovative approach with Vermont game and local produce, introduce fresh herbs and other seasonings, and change menus to suit the season. Look for imaginative approaches to native New England foods such as fiddlehead ferns (available only for a short time in the spring), maple syrup (Vermont is the largest U.S. producer), dairy products (especially cheese), native fruits and berries, "new Vermont" products such as salsa and salad dressings, and venison, quail, pheasant, and other game.

Your chances of finding a table for dinner vary with the season: Many restaurants have lengthy waits during peak seasons (when it's always a good idea to make a reservation) and then shut down during the slow months of April and November. Some of the best dining is found at country inns.

For price-category information, *see* Dining *in* Smart Travel Tips.

Lodging

Vermont's largest hotels are in Burlington and near the major ski resorts. There's a dearth of inns and bed-and-breakfasts in Burlington, though chain hotels provide dependable accommodations. Elsewhere you'll find a range of inns, B&Bs, and small motels. The many lovely and sometimes quite luxurious inns and B&Bs provide what many people consider the quintessential Vermont lodging experience. Rates are highest during foliage season, from late September to mid-October, and lowest in late spring and November, when many properties close. Many of the larger hotels offer package rates.

For price-category information, *see* Lodging *in* Smart Travel Tips.

National Forests

The two sections of the 355,000-acre Green Mountain National Forest (GMNF) are central and southern Vermont's primary stronghold of woodland and high mountain terrain. Like all national forests, it contains sections on which timber leases are sometimes granted, but it's possible to travel through much of this preserve without seeing significant evidence of human intrusion. In addition to the paved public highways that traverse the GMNF, many of the occasional logging roads are maintained for public use, and although unpaved, these are kept in good condition during snow-free times of the year.

The Forest Service maintains a number of picnic areas and primitive campgrounds; complete information is available from the Forest Supervisor. Fishing, subject to state laws and seasonal closings and limits, is allowed throughout the GMNF. Canoeing, cross-country skiing, and hiking are also popular; the Appalachian and Long trails run the length of the forest. Snowmobiles and other forms of motorized transportation, such as all-terrain vehicles, are permitted on marked trails, except within roadless areas designated as wilderness.

Outdoor Activities and Sports

BIKING

Vermont, especially the often deserted roads of the Northeast Kingdom, is great bicycle-touring country. Many companies lead weekend tours and weeklong trips throughout the state. If you'd like to go it on your own, most chambers of commerce have brochures highlighting good cycling routes in their area, including *Vermont Life* magazine's "Bicycle Vermont" map and guide, and many bookstores sell *25 Bicycle Tours in Vermont* by John Freidin.

FISHING

Central Vermont is the heart of the state's warm-water lake and pond fishing. Harriman and Somerset reservoirs have both warm- and cold-water species; Harriman has a greater variety. Lake Dunmore produced the state-record rainbow trout; Lakes Bomoseen and St. Catherine are good for rainbows and largemouth bass. In the east, Lakes Fairlee and Morey hold bass, perch, and chain pickerel, while the lower part of the Connecticut River contains smallmouth bass, walleye, and perch; shad are returning via the fish ladders at Vernon and Bellows Falls.

In northern Vermont, rainbow and brown trout inhabit the Missisquoi, Lamoille, Winooski, and Willoughby rivers, and there's warm-water fishing at many smaller lakes and ponds. Lakes Seymour, Willoughby, and Memphremagog and Great Averill Pond in the Northeast Kingdom are good for salmon and lake trout. The Dog River near Montpelier has one of the best wild populations of brown trout in the state. Good news is that landlocked Atlantic salmon are returning to the Clyde River following removal of a controversial dam.

Lake Champlain, stocked annually with salmon and lake trout, has become the state's ice-fishing capital; walleye, bass, pike, and channel catfish are also taken. Ice fishing is also popular on Lake Memphremagog.

SKIING

The Green Mountains run through the middle of Vermont like a bumpy spine, visible from almost every point in the state; generous accumulations of snow make the mountains an ideal site for skiing. Increased snowmaking capacity and improved, high-tech computerized equipment at many areas virtually assure a good day on the slopes. Vermont has 26 alpine ski resorts with nearly 1,000 trails and some 5,000 acres of skiable terrain. Combined, the resorts operate nearly 200 lifts and have the capacity to carry some 215,000 skiers per hour. Though grooming is sophisticated at all Vermont areas, conditions usually run to a typically Eastern hard pack, with powder a rare luxury and ice a bugbear after January thaw. The best advice for skiing in Vermont is to keep your skis well tuned.

Route 100 is also known as "Skier's Highway," passing by 13 of the state's ski areas. Vermont's major resorts are Stowe, Jay Peak, Sugarbush, Killington, Okemo, Mt. Snow, and Stratton. Midsize, less hectic areas to consider include Ascutney, Bromley, Smugglers' Notch, Pico, Mad River Glen, and Burke Mountain. In 1999, Bolton Valley Holiday Resort—long a favorite because of its proximity to Burlington and ample intermediate terrain—reopened under a new owner.

Exploring Vermont

Vermont can be divided into three regions. The southern part of the state, flanked by Bennington on the west and Brattleboro on the east, played an important role in Vermont's Revolutionary War–era drive to independence (yes, there was once a Republic of Vermont) and its eventual statehood. The central part is characterized by rugged mountains and the gently rolling dairy lands near Lake Champlain. Northern Vermont is the site of the state's capital, Montpelier, and its largest city, Burlington, yet it is also home to Vermont's most rural area, the Northeast Kingdom.

Numbers in the text correspond to numbers in the margin and on the Southern Vermont, Central Vermont, and Northern Vermont maps.

Great Itineraries

There are many ways to take advantage of Vermont's beauty—skiing or hiking its mountains, biking or driving its back roads, fishing or sailing its waters, shopping for local products, visiting its museums and sights, or simply finding the perfect inn and never leaving the front porch. Distances in Vermont are relatively short, yet the mountains and many back roads will slow a traveler's pace. You can see a representative north–south section of Vermont in a few days; if you have up to a week you can hit the highlights around the state.

IF YOU HAVE 3 DAYS

Spend a few hours in historic **Bennington** ⑤ in the southern part of Vermont; then travel north to see Hildene and stay in ⊞ **Manchester** ⑦. On your second day take Route 100 through Weston and travel north through the Green Mountains to Route 125, where you turn west to explore ⊞ **Middlebury** ㉕. On day three, enter the Champlain Valley, which has views of the Adirondack Mountains to the west. Stop at Shelburne Farms and carry on to **Burlington** ㊱; catch the sunset from the waterfront and take a walk on Church Street.

IF YOU HAVE 5 TO 7 DAYS

You can make several side trips off Route 100 and also visit the Northeast Kingdom on a trip of this length. Visit **Bennington** ⑤ and ⊞ **Manchester** ⑦ on day one. Spend your second day walking around the small towns of **Chester** ⑪ and ⊞ **Grafton** ⑫. On day three head north to explore **Woodstock** ⑳ and ⊞ **Quechee** ⑲, stopping at either the Billings Farm Museum and Marsh-Billings-Rockefeller National Historical Park or the Vermont Institute of Natural Science. Head leisurely on your fourth day toward ⊞ **Middlebury** ㉕, along one of Vermont's most inspiring mountain drives, Route 125 west of Route 100. Between Hancock and Middlebury, you'll pass nature trails and the picnic spot at Texas Falls Recreation Area, then traverse a moderately steep mountain pass. Spend day five in ⊞ **Burlington** ㊱. On day six head east to **Waterbury** ㉚ and then north to ⊞ **Stowe** ㉜ and Mt. Mansfield for a full day. Begin your last day with a few hours in **Montpelier** ㉙ on your way to **Peacham** ㊸, **St. Johnsbury** ㊶, 🚫 **Lake Willoughby** ㊷, and the serenity and back roads of the Northeast Kingdom. Especially noteworthy are U.S. 5, Route 5A, and Route 14.

When to Tour Vermont

The number of visitors and the rates for lodging reach their peaks along with the color of the leaves during foliage season, from late September to mid-October. But if you have never seen a kaleidoscope of autumn colors, it is worth braving the slow-moving traffic and paying the extra money. In summer the state is lush and green. Winter, of course, is high season at Vermont's ski resorts. Rates are lowest in late spring and November, although many properties close during these times.

SOUTHERN VERMONT

The Vermont tradition of independence and rebellion began in southern Vermont. Many towns founded in the early 18th century as frontier outposts or fortifications were later important as trading centers. In the western region the Green Mountain Boys fought off both the British and the claims of land-hungry New Yorkers—some say their descendants are still fighting. In the 19th century, as many towns turned to manufacturing, the farmers here retreated to hillier regions and, as the modern ski and summer-home booms got under way, retreated even farther.

The first thing you'll notice upon entering the state is the conspicuous lack of billboards along the highways and roads. The foresight back in the 1960s to prohibit them has made for a refreshing absence of aggressive visual clutter that allows unencumbered views of working farmland, fresh-as-paint villages, and quiet back roads—but does not hide the reality of abandoned dairy barns, bustling ski resorts, and strip-mall sprawl. Visitors who reach Vermont via the well-settled districts around Brattleboro and Bennington, though, are often surprised at the beautifully desolate woodlands that lie between these gateways. Much of the Green Mountain National Forest's southern section occupies rugged uplands where homesteads and farms thrived 450 years ago.

The towns are listed in counterclockwise order, beginning in the east, south of the junction of I–91 and Route 9 in Brattleboro, and following the southern boundary of the state toward Bennington, then north up to Manchester and Weston and south back to Newfane.

Brattleboro

❶ *60 mi south of White River Junction.*

Its downtown bustling with activity, Brattleboro, with about 13,000 inhabitants, is the center of commerce for southeastern Vermont. This town at the confluence of the West and Connecticut rivers originated as a frontier scouting post and became a thriving industrial center and resort town in the 1800s. More recently, the area has become a home to political activists and a raft of earnest counterculturists.

A former railroad station, the **Brattleboro Museum and Art Center** has replaced locomotives with works created by internationally and locally renowned artists and with exhibits that chronicle the region's rich history. The organs here were made in Brattleboro between 1853 and 1961, when the city was home to the Estey Organ Company, one of the world's largest organ manufacturers. The museum hosts a lecture and concert series. ✉ *Vernon and Main Sts.,* ☎ *802/257–0124,* WEB *www.brattleboromuseum. org.* 🎟 *$3.* ☉ *Mid-May–Oct., Tues.–Sun. noon–6.*

Southern Vermont

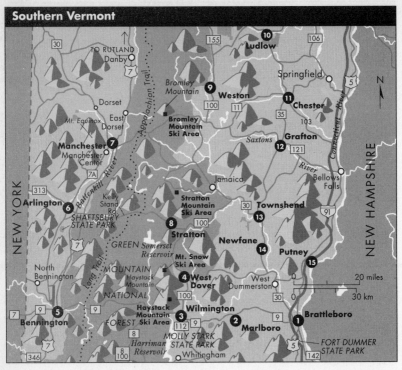

Dining and Lodging

$$$ ✕ **Peter Havens.** In a town better known for tofu than toniness, this chic little bistro knows just what to do with a filet mignon—serve it with Roquefort walnut butter, of course. Look for the house-cured gravlax made with lemon vodka and fresh seasonal seafood, which even includes a spring fling with softshell crabs. The wine list is superb. ⊠ *32 Elliot St.,* ☎ *802/257–3333. MC, V. Closed Sun. and Mon. No lunch.*

$ ✕ **Common Ground.** The political posters and concert fliers that line the staircase here attest to Vermont's progressive element. The stairs lead to loft-like, rough-hewn dining rooms. Owned cooperatively by the staff, this mostly organic vegetarian restaurant serves cashew burgers, veggie stir-fries, curries, hot soup and stew, and the humble bowl of brown rice. All the desserts, including a chocolate cake with peanut butter frosting, are made without white sugar. ⊠ *25 Elliot St.,* ☎ *802/ 257–0855. No credit cards. Closed Mon.–Wed. No lunch Thurs.*

$ ✕ **Sarkis Market.** Gail Sarkis's Lebanese grandmother gave her many of the recipes she uses to create Middle Eastern delicacies such as falafel, stuffed grape leaves, hummus, and *kibbe*—a layered meatloaf stuffed with ground lamb, pine nuts, and onions. Undecided about what to order? Go for the combination plate and finish with a wedge of home-made baklava. ⊠ *50 Elliot St.,* ☎ *802/258–4906. AE, MC, V. Closed Sun. in winter.*

$$$ 🛏 **40 Putney Road.** Expect a warm welcome at Gwen and Dan Pasco's antiques-filled French château–style estate. Rooms are furnished with antiques and have phones, TV/VCRs, robes, and air-conditioning; the suite has a gas fireplace. In warm weather, breakfast is served on the patio of the formally landscaped grounds, which lead to the shores of the West River. ⊠ *40 Putney Rd., 05301,* ☎ *802/254–6268 or 800/ 941–2413,* 🖷 *802/258–2673,* 🆆🅴🅱 *www.putney.net/40putneyrd. 3 rooms, 1 suite. Pub, in-room VCRs. AE, D, MC, V. BP.*

$–$$ ⊡ **Latchis Hotel.** Front rooms at this 1938 downtown Art Deco landmark overlook busy—and often noisy—Main Street. All the rooms have coffeemakers and are furnished comfortably, many with their original restored 1930s furniture; the suites are a bargain. Muffins arrive outside your door each morning at 8, and you can catch a movie under the zodiac ceiling of the adjoining Latchis Theater. The Latchis Grille (☏ 802/254–4747; closed Mon. and Tues., no lunch Mon.–Thurs.) is home to the Windham Brewery. ⊠ *50 Main St., 05301,* ☏ *802/254–6300,* FAX *802/254–6304,* WEB *www.brattleboro.com/latchis. 30 rooms; 3 suites. Restaurant, pub. AE, MC, V. CP.*

Nightlife and the Arts

Common Ground (⊠ 25 Elliot St., ☏ 802/257–0855) often presents live acoustic music, especially during Sunday brunch. **Mole's Eye Cafe** (⊠ 4 High St., ☏ 802/257–0771) hosts an open mike night every Thursday, and live bands Friday and Saturday (cover charge).

Outdoor Activities and Sports

BIKING

Brattleboro Bicycle Shop (⊠ 165 Main St., ☏ 802/254–8644 or 800/272–8245) rents and repairs bikes.

Burrows Specialized Sports (⊠ 105 Main St., ☏ 802/254–9430) services bikes, skis, and snowboards.

CANOEING

Vermont Canoe Touring Center (⊠ U.S. 5, ☏ 802/257–5008) has guided and self-guided tours as well as canoe and kayak rentals and a shuttle service.

SKATING

Nelson Withington Skating Rink (⊠ Memorial Park, 4 Guilford St., ☏ 802/257–2311) rents skates.

STATE PARK

The hiking trails at **Fort Dummer State Park** (⊠ S. Main St., 2 mi south of Brattleboro, ☏ 802/254–2610) afford views of the Connecticut River valley; campsites are available.

Shopping

The **Book Cellar** (⊠ 120 Main St., ☏ 802/254–6026), with two floors of volumes, carries many travel books. **Vermont Artisan Designs** (⊠ 106 Main St., ☏ 802/257–7044), one of the state's best crafts shops, displays ceramics, glass, wood, clothing, jewelry, and furniture. You can watch **Tom and Sally's Homemade Chocolates** being made just around the corner from their shop (⊠ 55 Elliott St., ☏ 802/258–3065), which also sells the famous Vermont Meadow Muffins.

Marlboro

❷ *10 mi west of Brattleboro.*

Tiny Marlboro draws musicians and audiences from around the world each summer to the Marlboro Music Festival, founded by Rudolf Serkin and joined for many years by Pablo Casals. **Marlboro College,** high on a hill off Route 9, is the center of musical activity. The college's white-frame buildings have outstanding views of the valley below, and the campus is studded with apple trees.

The **Southern Vermont Natural History Museum** houses one of New England's largest collections of mounted birds, specimens of three extinct birds, and a complete collection of mammals native to the Northeast. The museum also has weather displays and live hawk and owl exhibits. ⊠ *Rte. 9,* ☎ *802/464–0048.* 🎫 *$3.* ⊙ *Memorial Day–late Oct., daily 10–5; call for hrs rest of yr.*

Nightlife and the Arts

The **Marlboro Music Festival** (⊠ Marlboro Music Center, Marlboro College, ☎ 802/254–2394; 215/569–4690 Sept.–June) presents chamber music at weekend concerts in July and August. The **New England Bach Festival** (☎ 802/257–4523) is held at Marlboro College in October.

Wilmington

❸ *8 mi west of Marlboro.*

Wilmington is the shopping and dining center for the Mt. Snow ski area to the north. Main Street has a cohesive assemblage of 18th- and 19th-century buildings, many of them listed on the National Register of Historic Places.

For a great stroll, pick up a self-guided tour map from the **Chamber of Commerce** (⊠ Rte. 9, W. Main St., ☎ 802/464–8092 or 877-887-6884, 🌐 www.visitvermont.com).

North River Winery, which occupies a converted farmhouse and barn, produces fruit wines such as Green Mountain Apple and Vermont Pear. ⊠ *Rte. 112, 6 mi south of Wilmington, Jacksonville,* ☎ *802/368–7557.* 🎫 *Free.* ⊙ *Daily 10–5; tours late May–Dec.*

....

OFF THE
BEATEN PATH

SCENIC TOUR – To begin a scenic (though well-traveled) 35-mi circular tour with panoramic views of the region's mountains, farmland, and abundant cow population, drive west on Route 9 to the intersection with Route 8. Turn south and continue to the junction with Route 100; follow Route 100 through Whitingham (the birthplace of the Mormon prophet Brigham Young), and stay with the road as it turns north again and takes you back to Route 9.

....

Lodging

$$$–$$$$ 🏨 **White House of Wilmington.** The grand staircase in this Federal-style mansion leads to rooms with antique bathrooms and brass wall sconces. The newer section has more contemporary plumbing; some rooms have fireplaces, whirlpool tubs, and lofts. The leather wing chairs of the public rooms suggest formality, but the atmosphere is casual and comfortable. Children under 8 are welcome in the more casual Guest Cottage. The White House has a cross-country ski touring and snowshoeing center, a tubing hill, and 12 km (7 mi) of groomed trails. Guests can dine at the restaurant for a fixed price of $35. ⊠ *178 Rte. 9 E, 05363,* ☎ *802/464–2135 or 800/541–2135,* 📠 *802/464–5222,* 🌐 *www.whitehouseinn.com. 23 rooms. Restaurant, bar, 1 indoor and 1 outdoor pool, sauna, cross-country skiing. AE, D, DC, MC, V. BP.*

$$–$$$ 🏨 **Trail's End, A Country Inn.** This cozy four-season lodge is set on 10 acres 4 mi from Mt. Snow. The inn's centerpiece is its cathedral-ceiling living room with catwalk loft seating and a 21-ft fieldstone fireplace. Guest rooms are comfortable, if simple, though two suites have fireplaces, whirlpool tubs, cable TV, refrigerators, and microwaves; four other rooms also have fireplaces. Dinner is served during the holiday season only. There's a stocked trout pond on site, and cross-country ski trails nearby. ⊠ *5 Trail's End La., 05363,* ☎ *802/464–2727 or 800/859–2585,* 📠 *802/464–5532,* 🌐 *www.trailsendvt.com. 13 rooms, 2 suites. Pool, pond, game room, tennis court. AE, D, MC, V. BP.*

Nightlife and the Arts

In addition to steak and Mexican specialties, the standard fare on weekends at **Poncho's Wreck** (⊠ S. Main St., ☎ 802/464–9320) is acoustic jazz or mellow rock. **Sitzmark** (⊠ Rte. 100, ☎ 802/464–3384) hosts rock bands on weekends.

Outdoor Activities and Sports

SLEIGH RIDES

Adams Farm (⊠ 15 Higley Hill Rd., ☎ 802/464–3762) has three double-traverse sleighs drawn by Belgian draft horses. Rides include a narrated tour and hot chocolate. An indoor petting farm is open Wed.–Sun. from Nov.–Apr., and an outdoor version is open daily the rest of the year.

STATE PARK

Molly Stark State Park (⊠ Rte. 9, east of Wilmington, ☎ 802/464–5460) has campsites and a hiking trail that leads to a vista from a fire tower on Mt. Olga.

WATER SPORTS

Lake Whitingham (Harriman Reservoir), just west of Wilmington, is the largest lake in the state, with good fishing. Boat launch areas are at Wards Cove, Whitingham, Mountain Mills, and the Ox Bow. **Green Mountain Flagship Company** (⊠ Rte. 9, 2 mi west of Wilmington, ☎ 802/464–2975) runs a cruise boat on Lake Whitingham and rents canoes, kayaks, surfbikes, and sailboats from May to late October.

Shopping

Quaigh Design Centre (⊠ Rte. 9, W. Main St., ☎ 802/464–2780) sells New England crafts, artwork from Britain and New England—including works by Vermont woodcut artists Sabra Field and Mary Azarian—and Scottish woolens and tartans. **Wilmington Flea Market** (⊠ Rtes. 9 and 100 S, ☎ 802/464–3345) sells antiques on weekends from Memorial Day to mid-October.

West Dover

❹ *6 mi north of Wilmington.*

The Congregational church in small West Dover, a classic New England town, dates from the 1700s. The year-round population of about 1,000 swells on winter weekends as skiers flock to Mt. Snow/Haystack Ski Resort. The many condos, lodges, and inns at the base of the mountain accommodate them.

Dining and Lodging

$$$$ ✕▥ **Inn at Saw Mill Farm.** This elegant retreat close to Mt. Snow is
★   one of Vermont's two Relais & Châteaux inns (the other is the Pitcher Inn) and has all the upscale amenities expected at these properties. English chintzes, antiques, and dark wood set a comfortable tone in the common room. Each of the guest rooms is individually decorated, and many have sitting areas and fireplaces. The 19 landscaped acres are perfect for hiking; there's also a stocked trout pond. The inn's well-regarded restaurant ($$$$) has a seasonal menu that might include potato-crusted black sea bass with wild mushrooms and orzo or a grilled veal chop with wild mushroom risotto and rosemary sauce. The wine selection, with more than 30,000 bottles, is superb. ⊠ *Rte. 100 and Crosstown Rd., 05356,* ☎ *800/493–1133 or 802/464–8131,* ℻ *802/464–1130,* WEB *www.vermontdirect.com/sawmill. 20 rooms. Restaurant, pool, tennis court, fishing. AE, DC, MC, V. Closed Easter–late May. MAP.*

$$$–$$$$ ✕▥ **Deerhill Inn and Restaurant.** The west-facing windows at this En-
★   glish-style country inn have views of the valley below and the ski slopes across the way. A huge fireplace dominates the living room, and English hand-painted yellow wallpaper, a garden-scene mural, and

collections of antique plates accent the dining rooms. One guest room has an Asian bedroom set, several have hand-painted murals, and many have fireplaces. The three balcony rooms are the largest; they have great views. Some rooms have whirlpool baths. In the restaurant ($$$–$$$$; closed Wednesday in summer; Tues. and Wed. in winter), the upscale comfort food might include fresh fish, a veal medallion with wild mushrooms in a lemon cream sauce, or a black-pepper sirloin steak. ⊠ *Box 136, Valley View Rd., 05356,* ☎ *802/464–3100 or 800/993–3379,* FAX *802/464–5474,* WEB *www.deerhill.com. 13 rooms, 2 suites. Restaurant, pool. AE, MC, V. BP; MAP.*

$$ ✕🖭 **Doveberry Inn.** After a day's skiing, this handsome country inn just a few minutes from the slopes offers a welcome haven. The living room has a fireplace and wine bar. Guest rooms are cheerful and bright, with TVs and VCRs; one room has a fireplace. The restaurant ($$$; closed Tuesday) serves up northern Italian specialties such as wood-grilled veal chop with wild mushrooms and pan-seared salmon with herbed risotto in intimate, candlelit dining rooms. ⊠ *Rte. 100, 05356,* ☎ *802/464–5652 or 800/722–3204,* FAX *802/464–6229,* WEB *www.doveberryinn. com. 8 rooms. Restaurant, bar. AE, MC, V. BP.*

Nightlife and the Arts

Deacon's Den Tavern (⊠ Rte. 100, ☎ 802/464–9361) hosts bands on weekends from Thanksgiving through Easter. The **Snow Barn** (⊠ near the base of Mt. Snow, ☎ 802/464–1100, ext. 4693) has live music several nights a week.

Ski Areas

MT. SNOW/HAYSTACK SKI RESORT

Mt. Snow, established in the 1950s, was purchased in 1996 by the American Skiing Company, which also owns Sugarbush, Killington, and Pico. Recent developments have included the 1998 opening of the year-round Grand Summit Hotel and Conference Center; the inauguration of the Learn to Ski and Ride Center at the Perfect Turn Discovery Center, complete with its own expanded terrain, triple chairlift, and building; and increased snowmaking capability. Two new terrain parks are the Carnival minipark for kids and the Inferno for advanced snowboarders. One lift ticket lets you ski at Mt. Snow and Haystack.

Haystack—the southernmost ski area in Vermont—is much smaller than Mt. Snow but has a more personal atmosphere. A modern base lodge is close to the lifts. A free shuttle connects the two ski areas. ⊠ *400 Mountain Rd., Mt. Snow, 05356,* ☎ *802/464–3333; 800/245–7669 for lodging; 802/464–2151 for snow conditions.*

Downhill. Mt. Snow has five separate mountain faces, each with its own personality. Most of the 1,130 trails down its 1,700-ft vertical summit are intermediate, wide, and sunny. Most of the beginner slopes are toward the bottom; most of the expert terrain is on the North Face, where there's excellent fall-line skiing. The trails are served by 23 lifts, including three high-speed quads, one regular quad, 10 triple chairs, four double chairs, and three Magic Carpets (similar to an escalator). The ski school's Perfect Turn instruction program is designed to help advanced and expert skiers.

Child care. The well-organized child-care center (reservations essential) takes children from ages 6 weeks to 6 years. The center has age-appropriate toys and balances indoor play—including arts and crafts—with trips outdoors. The Pre-ski program is for 3-year-olds, and a Perfect Kids program for ages 4–12 teaches skiing and snowboarding.

Summer activities. Mt. Snow offers two- to seven-day Grand Summer Vacation packages with a variety of activities, including golf at the 18-

hole Mt. Snow Golf Course, mountain biking on ski trails and forest roads, and use of the health club, with a pool, hot tubs, and spa. The Summit Local triple chairlift transports riders to the 3,600-ft peak. Swimming, boating, and a children's water play pool are available at the resort's Snow Lake. A hiking center, in-line skating park, climbing wall, and BMX track provide other summer fun.

CROSS-COUNTRY SKIING/SNOWSHOEING

Four cross-country-trail areas within 4 mi of Mt. Snow/Haystack provide more than 150 km (90 mi) of varied terrain. The **Hermitage** (✉ Coldbrook Rd., Wilmington, ☎ 802/464–3511) has 50 km (30 mi) of groomed trails. The groomed trails at the **White House of Wilmington** (✉ Rtes. 9 and 100, ☎ 802/464–2135) cover 50 km (30 mi). **Timber Creek** (✉ Rte. 100, north of the Mt. Snow entrance, ☎ 802/464–0999) is appealingly small with 16 km (10 mi) of thoughtfully groomed trails.

Snowmobile Tours

At **Sitzmark** (✉ East Dover Rd., Wilmington, ☎ 802/464–3384) guides lead snowmobile tours across a golf course and through 50 acres of woods and fields.

Bennington

⑤ *21 mi west of Wilmington.*

Bennington, college town and commercial focus of Vermont's southwest corner, lies at the edge of the Green Mountain National Forest. It has retained much of the industrial character it developed in the 19th century, when paper mills, grist mills, and potteries formed the city's economic base. It was in Bennington, at the Catamount Tavern, that Ethan Allen organized the Green Mountain Boys, who helped capture Ft. Ticonderoga in 1775. Here also, in 1777, American general John Stark urged his militia to attack the British-paid Hessian troops across the New York border: "There are the redcoats; they will be ours or tonight Molly Stark sleeps a widow!"

A brochure available at the Chamber of Commerce describes an interesting self-guided walking tour of **Old Bennington,** a National Register Historic District west of downtown. Impressive white-column Greek Revival and sturdy brick Federal homes stand around the village green. In the graveyard of the **Old First Church,** at Church Street and Monument Avenue, the tombstone of the poet Robert Frost proclaims, "I had a lover's quarrel with the world."

The **Bennington Battle Monument,** a 306-ft stone obelisk with an elevator to the top, commemorates General Stark's victory over the British, who attempted to capture Bennington's stockpile of supplies. The battle, which took place near Walloomsac Heights in New York State on August 16, 1777, helped bring about the surrender two months later of the British commander "Gentleman Johnny" Burgoyne at Saratoga in New York. ✉ *15 Monument Ave.,* ☎ *802/447–0550.* ▱ *$1.50.* ☉ *Mid-Apr.–Oct., daily 9–5.*

The **Bennington Museum**'s rich collections include vestiges of rural life, a percentage of which are packed into towering glass cases. The decorative arts are well represented; one room is devoted to early Bennington pottery. Two rooms cover the history of American glass and contain fine Tiffany specimens. The museum displays the largest public collection of the work of Grandma Moses (1860–1961), the popular, self-taught folk artist who lived and painted in the area. Among the 30 paintings and assorted memorabilia are her only self-portrait and the famous painted caboose window. Also here are the only surviving automobile of Bennington's Martin company, a 1925 Wasp, and the Bennington Flag, one of the oldest versions of the Stars and Stripes in existence. ✉ *W. Main St./Rte. 9,* ☎ *802/447–1571,* WEB *www.benningtonmuseum. com.* ⊡ *$6.* ☽ *Nov.–May, daily 9–5; June–Oct., daily 9–6.*

Built in 1865 and home to two Vermont governors, the **Park-McCullough House** is a 35-room classic French Empire–style mansion furnished with period pieces. Several restored flower gardens grace the landscaped grounds, and a stable houses a collection of antique carriages. Call for details on the summer concert series, Victorian Christmas, and other special events. ✉ *Corner of Park and West Sts., North Bennington,* ☎ *802/442–5441,* WEB *www.park/mccullough.org.* ⊡ *$6.* ☽ *Mid-May–mid-Oct., Thurs.–Mon. 10–4; last tour at 3.*

Contemporary stone sculpture and white-frame neo-Colonial dorms surrounded by acres of cornfields punctuate the green meadows of **Bennington College**'s placid campus. The small liberal arts college, one of the most expensive to attend in the country, is noted for its progressive program in the arts. ✉ *Rte. 67A, off U.S. 7 (look for stone entrance gate),* ☎ *800/833–6845 tour information.*

Dining and Lodging

$ ✕ **Blue Benn Diner.** Breakfast is served all day in this authentic diner, where the eats include turkey hash and breakfast burritos, with scrambled eggs, sausage, and chilies, plus pancakes of all imaginable varieties. The menu lists many vegetarian selections. Lines may be long, especially on weekends. ✉ *U.S. 7 N,* ☎ *802/442–5140. No credit cards. Reservations not accepted. No dinner Sat.–Tues.*

$$$–$$$$ ☷ **South Shire Inn.** Canopy beds in lushly carpeted rooms, ornate plaster moldings, and a dark mahogany fireplace in the South Shire's library re-create the grandeur of the Victorian past; fireplaces and hot tubs in some rooms add warmth. Four freshly renovated rooms in the Carriage House have whirlpool baths. The furnishings are antique except for the reproduction beds. The South Shire is in a quiet residential neighborhood within walking distance of the bus depot and downtown stores. Breakfast is served in the burgundy-and-white dining room. ✉ *124 Elm St., 05201,* ☎ *802/447–3839,* FAX *802/442–3547,* WEB *www.southshire.com. 9 rooms. AE, MC, V. BP.*

$$ ☷ **Molly Stark Inn.** Tidy blue-plaid wallpaper, gleaming hardwood floors, antique furnishings, and a wood-burning stove in a brick alcove of the sitting room add country charm to this 1860 Queen Anne Victorian. Molly's Room, at the back of the building, gets less noise from Route 9 and has a whirlpool bath; the attic suite is the most spacious. Three cottages have fireplaces and Jacuzzis and offer more secluded accommodations. ✉ *1067 E. Main St./Rte. 9, 05201,* ☎ *802/ 442–9631 or 800/356–3076,* FAX *802/442–5224,* WEB *www.mollystarkinn. com. 6 rooms and 3 suites. AE, D, MC, V. BP.*

Nightlife and the Arts

The **Bennington Center for the Arts** (✉ Rte. 9 at Gypsy La., ☎ 802/ 442–7158), hosts a variety of cultural events, including exhibitions by local and nationally recognized artists, and of wildlife and Native American art. The **Oldcastle Theatre Co.** (☎ 802/447–0564) at the Bennington Center for the Arts, whose season runs from May through December, is one of the Northeast's finest regional theaters.

Outdoor Activities and Sports

Cutting Edge (✉ 160 Benmont Ave., ☎ 802/442–8664) rents and repairs bicycles and also sells and rents snowboards and cross-country skis. It has one of Vermont's few skateboarding parks, open Monday through Saturday 10–6, and noon–6 on Sunday.

HIKING

Four mi east of Bennington, the **Long Trail** crosses Route 9 and runs south to the top of Harmon Hill. Allot two or three hours for this hike.

STATE PARKS

Lake Shaftsbury State Park (⊠ Rte. 7A, 10½ mi north of Bennington, ☎ 802/375–9978) is one of a few parks in Vermont with group camping. It has a swimming beach, nature trails, boat and canoe rentals, and a snack bar. **Woodford State Park** (⊠ Rte. 9, 10 mi east of Bennington, ☎ 802/447–7169) has an activities center on Adams Reservoir, campsites, a playground, boat and canoe rentals, and nature trails.

Shopping

The **Apple Barn and Country Bake Shop** (⊠ U.S. 7 S, ☎ 802/447–7780) sells home-baked goodies, fresh cider, Vermont cheeses, and maple syrup. The showroom at the **Bennington Potters Yard** (⊠ 324 County St., ☎ 802/447–7531 or 800/205–8033) stocks first-quality pottery and antiques in addition to seconds from the famed Bennington Potters. On the free tour you can follow the clay through production and hear about the Potters Yard, in business for five decades. Tours begin at 10 and 2 in spring, summer, and fall. **Hawkins House Craftsmarket** (⊠ U.S. 7/ 262 North St., ☎ 802/447–0488) showcases jewelry, woodenware, glass, pottery, rugs, and clothing from more than 450 craftspeople.

Arlington

❻ *15 mi north of Bennington.*

Don't be surprised to see familiar-looking (if considerably aged) faces among the roughly 2,200 people of Arlington. The illustrator Norman Rockwell lived here from 1939 to 1953, and many of the models for his portraits of small-town life were his neighbors. First settled in 1763, Arlington was called Tory Hollow for its Loyalist sympathies— even though a number of the Green Mountain Boys lived here, too. Smaller than Bennington and more down-to-earth than upper-crust Manchester to the north, Arlington exudes a certain Rockwellian folksiness. Dorothy Canfield Fisher, a novelist popular in the 1930s and 1940s, also lived here.

There are no original paintings at the **Norman Rockwell Exhibition,** but the exhibition rooms are crammed with reproductions of the illustrator's works, arranged in every way conceivable: chronologically, by subject matter, and juxtaposed with photos of the models—several of whom work here. ⊠ *Rte. 7A/Main St.,* ☎ *802/375–6423,* WEB *www. normanrockwellexhibit.com.* ⊠ *$2.* ☉ *May–Oct., daily 9–5; Nov.–Dec. and Feb.–Apr., daily 10–4.*

Dining and Lodging

$$$$ ✕▥ **West Mountain Inn.** A former farmhouse built in the 1840s, this
★ romantic inn has a front lawn with a spectacular view of the countryside. Its 150 acres include a llama farm. Rooms 2, 3, and 4 overlook the lawn; the three small nooks of Room 11 resemble railroad sleeper berths and are perfect for kids. The children's room, brightly painted with life-size Disney characters, is stocked with games, stuffed animals, and a TV with VCR. A low-beamed candlelit dining room ($$$) is the setting for six-course prix-fixe dinners featuring updated Continental cuisine. Aunt Min's Swedish rye and other toothsome breads, as well as desserts, are all made on the premises. Try to get a table by the window. ⊠ *River Rd., off Rte. 313, 05250,* ☎ *802/375–6516,* FAX *802/375– 6553,* WEB *www.westmountaininn.com. 18 rooms, 6 suites. Restaurant, bar, hiking, cross-country skiing, meeting room. AE, D, MC, V. MAP.*

$$–$$$$ ✕🏨 **Arlington Inn.** Greek Revival columns at the entrance to this home
★   built by a railroad magnate in 1848 lend it an imposing presence, but
         the atmosphere is hardly forbidding. The inn's charm is created by linens
         that coordinate with the Victorian-style wallpaper, claw-foot tubs in
         some bathrooms, and the house's original moldings and wainscoting.
         The carriage house, built a century ago, contains country-French and
         Queen Anne furnishings. Some rooms have TVs and phones; king-size
         rooms have fireplaces and two-person hot tubs. The restaurant serves
         regional American dishes ($$$–$$$$), and polished wood floors, rose
         walls, and soft candlelight complement the food. The grounds have a
         garden, gazebo, pond, and waterfall. ✉ *Rte. 7A, 05250,* ☎ *802/375–*
         6532 or 800/443–9442, FAX *802/375–6534,* WEB *www.arlingtoninn.com.*
         17 rooms, 5 suites. Restaurant, taproom. AE, D, DC, MC, V. BP.

$$–$$$ 🏨 **Hill Farm Inn.** This homey inn on the Battenkill River has the feel
         of the country farmhouse it used to be. The fireplace in the informal
         living room, the sturdy antiques, and the spinning wheel in the upstairs
         hallway all convey a relaxed, friendly atmosphere. The Battenkill Suite
         has a beamed cathedral ceiling, and from its porch you can see Mt.
         Equinox. The rooms in the 1790 guest house are very private; the one-
         and two-bedroom cabins, open spring through fall, are charming. ✉
         458 Hill Farm Rd., off Rte. 7A, 05250, ☎ *802/375–2269 or 800/882–*
         2545, FAX *802/375–9918,* WEB *www.hillfarminn.com. 5 rooms (2 with*
         kitchenettes), 6 suites, 4 cabins. D, MC, V. BP.

Outdoor Activities and Sports

Battenkill Canoe, Ltd. (✉ Rte. 7A, ☎ 802/362–2800 or 800/421–
5268) rents canoes and offers inn-to-inn tours and day trips on the Bat-
tenkill.

Shopping

The shops at **Candle Mill Village** (✉ Old Mill Rd., between U.S. 7 and
Rte. 7A, East Arlington, ☎ 802/375–6068 or 800/772–3759) specialize
in community cookbooks from around the country, music boxes, and
candles. Listed on the National Register of Historic Places, the mill was
built in the 1760s by Remember Baker, a cohort of Ethan Allen and
one of the Green Mountain Boys. The nearby waterfall is a pleasant
backdrop for a picnic.

Equinox Valley Nursery (✉ Rte. 7A between Arlington and Man-
chester, ☎ 802/362–2610) is known for its perennials (more than
1,000 varieties) and materials for water gardens. The nursery has 17
greenhouses and a conservatory, sells 150 varieties of herbs, and car-
ries many Vermont-made products in the large gift shop.

Manchester

★ ❼ *9 mi northeast of Arlington.*

Manchester, where Ira Allen proposed financing Vermont's participa-
tion in the American Revolution by confiscating Tory estates, has been
a popular summer retreat since the mid-19th century. Manchester Vil-
lage's tree-shaded marble sidewalks and stately old homes reflect the
luxurious resort lifestyle of a century ago. Manchester Center's upscale
factory outlets appeal to the affluent 20th-century ski crowd drawn
by nearby Bromley and Stratton mountains. Warning: Shoppers come
in droves at times, giving the place the feel of a crowded mall on the
weekend before Christmas. If you're coming here from Arlington, take
pretty Route 7A, which passes directly by a number of sights.

★ **Hildene,** the summer home of Abraham Lincoln's son and onetime Pull-
man company chairman Robert Todd Lincoln, is a beautifully preserved
412-acre estate. The 24-room mansion, with its Georgian Revival

symmetry, welcoming central hallway, and grand curved staircase, is unusual in that its rooms are not roped off. When the 1,000-pipe Aeolian organ is played, the music reverberates as though from the mansion's very bones. Tours include a short film on the owner's life and a walk through the elaborate formal gardens. When snow conditions permit, you can cross-country ski on the property, which has views of nearby mountains. ⊠ *Rte. 7A,* ☎ *802/362–1788,* WEB *www.hildene.org.* 🗹 *$8.* ☉ *Mid-May–Oct., daily 9:30–5:30, visitor center daily 9–5:30. Tours on the ½ hour (first tour at 9:30, last tour at 4). Candlelight tours Dec. 27–29, 5 PM.*

The **American Museum of Fly Fishing,** which houses the largest collection of fly-fishing equipment in the world, displays more than 1,500 rods, 800 reels, 30,000 flies, and the tackle of famous people such as Winslow Homer, Bing Crosby, and Jimmy Carter. Its library of 2,500 books is open by appointment. ⊠ *Rte. 7A at Seminary Ave.,* ☎ *802/362–3300,* WEB *www.amff.com.* 🗹 *$3.* ☉ *Daily 10–4.*

The **Southern Vermont Arts Center** showcases rotating exhibits and its permanent collection of more than 700 pieces of 19th- and 20th-century American art in a 12,500-square-ft museum opened in July 2000. The Arts Center's original building, a graceful Georgian mansion set on 375 acres, is the frequent site of concerts, performances, and film screenings. In summer and fall, a pleasant restaurant with magnificent views opens for business. ⊠ *West Rd.,* ☎ *802/362–1405.* 🗹 *$6.* ☉ *May–Oct., Tues.-Sat, 10–5, Sun. noon–5; Nov.–Apr., Mon.–Sat. 10–5.* WEB *www.svac.org.*

You may want to keep your eye on the temperature gauge of your car as you drive the 5-mi toll road to the top of 3,825-ft **Mt. Equinox.** Along the way you'll see the Battenkill trout stream and the surrounding Vermont countryside. Picnic tables line the drive, and there's an outstanding view down both sides of the mountain from a notch known as the Saddle. The seasonal **Inn on Mt. Equinox** (☎ 802/362–1113 or 800/868–6843) is perched on top of the mountain. ⊠ *Off Rte. 7A, south of Manchester,* ☎ *802/362–1114.* 🗹 *$6 for car and driver, $2 each additional adult.* ☉ *May–Oct., daily 8 AM–10 PM.*

Dining and Lodging

$$$$ ✕ **Chantecleer.** Intimate dining rooms have been created in a former dairy barn that has a large fieldstone fireplace. The menu reflects the chef's Swiss background: The appetizers include *Bündnerfleisch* (airdried Swiss beef) and frogs' legs in garlic butter; among the entrées are rack of lamb, whole Dover sole filleted table-side, and veal chops. The restaurant is 5 mi north of Manchester. ⊠ *Rte. 7A, East Dorset,* ☎ *802/362–1616. Reservations essential. AE, DC, MC, V. Closed Tues. in summer, Mon. and Tues. in winter, and mid–Oct. to mid–Nov. and mid–Apr. to mid–May; No lunch.*

$$–$$$ ✕ **Bistro Henry's.** This airy restaurant on the outskirts of town attracts a devoted clientele for authentic Mediterranean fare. The menu changes often; recent highlights include merlot-braised lamb shank with balsamic-glazed onions and garlic mashed potatoes; eggplant, mushroom, and fontina terrine Provençal; and crispy sweetbreads in Armagnac cream. The wine list is extensive. ⊠ *Rte. 11/30,* ☎ *802/362–4982. AE, DC, MC, V. Closed Mon. No lunch.*

$$$$ ✕🏨 **Barrows House.** This 200-year-old Federal-style inn and mini-re-
★ sort is a favorite with those who wish to escape the bustle of Manchester (Bromley is about 8 mi away). The rooms afford great privacy; some have gas or woodburning fireplaces, and the newly refurbished Bird's Nest Suite has a fireplace and hot tub. Dinner—served in the spacious main dining room, the greenhouse room, and the tavern—includes peren-

nial favorites such as rack of lamb and filet mignon as well as nightly specials, which might include Maine crab cakes and native grilled trout. ⊠ *Box 98, Rte. 30, Dorset, 05251,* ☎ *802/867–4455 or 800/ 639–1620,* ℻ *802/867–0132,* WEB *www.barrowshouse.com. 18 rooms, 10 suites. Restaurant, pool, sauna, 2 tennis courts, bicycles, cross-country skiing. AE, D, DC, MC, V. BP, MAP.*

$$$$ ✕⌂ **The Equinox.** Even before Abe Lincoln's family began summering here, this grand white-column resort was a local fixture. The spacious, sunny rooms are furnished with reproductions of antiques. In the Marsh Tavern, richly upholstered settees, stuffed armchairs, and several fireplaces create a plush traditional ambience. There are 136 rooms (including five Presidential Suites) in the main hotel; nine one- and two-bedroom suites in the Orvis Inn next door; and 27 rooms in the Town House. The three restaurants include the elegant Colonnade, where men are requested to wear jackets, and a seasonal grill at the golf course. The woodland supper of roast duck, venison sausage, and wild mushrooms is popular, and the Sunday brunch is spectacular. ⊠ *3567 Main St., Rte. 7A, Manchester Village 05254,* ☎ *802/362–4700 or 800/362–4747,* ℻ *802/362–1595,* WEB *www.equinoxresort.com. 3 restaurants, bar, 1 indoor and 1 outdoor pool, sauna, steam room, 18-hole golf course, 3 tennis courts, croquet, health club, horseback riding, fishing, mountain bikes, ice-skating, cross-country skiing, snowmobiling. MAP, AP. AE, D, DC, MC, V.*

$$$$ ⌂ **Inn at Ormsby Hill.** During the Revolutionary War, this 1774 Fed-
   ★ eral-style building provided refuge from the British for Ethan Allen, and it later served the same purpose for slaves heading north on the Underground Railroad. When renovating, the owners created interesting public spaces and romantic bedrooms. Furnished with antiques and canopied or four-poster beds, the rooms have fireplaces that can be viewed from the bed or the two-person whirlpool tub. Some have mountain views. Breakfasts in the conservatory—entrées may include baked, stuffed French toast with an apricot brandy sauce—are sumptuous. ⊠ *1842 Main St./Rte. 7A, 05255,* ☎ *802/362–1163 or 800/ 670–2841,* ℻ *802/362–5176,* WEB *www.ormsbyhill.com. 10 rooms. D, MC, V. BP.*

$$$$ ⌂ **Wilburton Inn.** The Great Gatsby would have felt right at home at this turn-of-the-century Tudor mansion perched on a hill off the main road overlooking the Battenkill Valley. The common rooms, paneled in dark hardwoods, are elegant yet informal, and are decorated with part of the owners' vast art collection. Outdoor sculptures dot the spacious grounds. There are bedrooms and suites in the main house, and 25 rooms in outlying cottages. A buffet breakfast is served in the windowed Terrace Room, and dinner is served in the handsome Billiard Room. One note: Weddings take place here most summer weekends. ⊠ *River Rd., 05254,* ☎ *802/362–2500 or 800/648–4944,* ℻ *802/362–1107,* WEB *www.wilburton.com. 31 rooms, 4 suites. Restaurant, pool, 3 tennis courts. AE, MC, V. BP.*

$$–$$$$ ⌂ **1811 House.** At this mansion once owned by President Lincoln's grand-
   ★ daughter, the atmosphere of an English country home can be experienced without crossing the Atlantic. The pub-style bar is decorated with horse brasses, Waterford crystal is used in the dining room, and three acres of lawn are landscaped in the English floral style. Rooms contain period antiques; six have fireplaces, and many have four-poster beds. Bathrooms are old-fashioned but serviceable. ⊠ *Box 39, Rte. 7A, 05254,* ☎ *802/362–1811 or 800/432–1811,* ℻ *802/362–2443,* WEB *www. 1811house.com. 14 rooms. Dining room, bar. AE, D, MC, V. BP.*

$–$$ ⌂ **Aspen Motel.** A rare find in this area, the immaculate, family owned Aspen is set well back from the highway and is moderately priced. The

When you pack your MCI Calling Card, it's like packing your loved ones along too.

Your MCI Calling Card is the easy way to stay in touch when you travel. Use it to call to and from over 125 countries. Plus, every time you call, you can earn frequent flier miles. So wherever your travels take you, call home with your MCI Calling Card. It's even easy to get one. Just visit **www.mci.com/worldphone.**

EASY TO CALL WORLDWIDE

1. Just enter the WorldPhone® access number of the country you're calling from.

2. Enter or give the operator your MCI Calling Card number.

3. Enter or give the number you're calling.

Aruba ⁜	800-888-8
Bahamas ⁜	1-800-888-8000

Barbados ⁜	1-800-888-8000
Bermuda ⁜	1-800-888-8000
British Virgin Islands ⁜	1-800-888-8000
Canada	1-800-888-8000
Mexico	01-800-021-8000
Puerto Rico	1-800-888-8000
United States	1-800-888-8000
U.S. Virgin Islands	1-800-888-8000

⁜ Limited availability.

EARN FREQUENT FLIER MILES

SEE THE WORLD IN FULL COLOR

Fodor's Exploring Guides bring all the great sights vividly to life with hundreds of photographs, fascinating historical background, and colorful anecdotes. Detailed maps and practical information keep you headed in the right direction.

Pair a **Fodor's** Exploring Guide with your trusted Gold Guide for a complete planning package.

spacious, tastefully decorated rooms have Colonial-style furnishings, and all have cable TV, phones, and in-room coffeemakers; some have refrigerators. The social room has a fireplace. ⊠ *Rte. 7A N, 05255,* ☎ *802/362–2450,* FAX *802/362–1348,* WEB *www.thisisvermont.com/ aspen. 24 rooms, 1 cottage. Pool, playground. AE, D, MC, V.*

Nightlife and the Arts

The two pre-Revolutionary War barns of the **Dorset Playhouse** (⊠ off town green, Dorset, ☎ 802/867–5777) host a community group in winter and a resident professional troupe in summer. The **Marsh Tavern** (☎ 802/362–4700) at the Equinox has cabaret music and jazz from Wednesday to Sunday in summer and on weekends in winter. **Mulligan's** (⊠ Rte. 7A, ☎ 802/362–3663) is a popular hangout in Manchester Village, especially for the après-ski set.

Outdoor Activities and Sports

BIKING

The 20-mi Dorset-Manchester trail runs from Manchester Village north on West Street to Route 30, turns west at the Dorset village green onto West Road, and heads back south to Manchester. **Battenkill Sports** (⊠ Exit 4 off U.S. 7, at Rte. 11/30, ☎ 802/362–2734 or 800/340–2734) rents and repairs bikes and provides maps and route suggestions.

FISHING

Battenkill Anglers (☎ 802/362–3184) teaches the art and science of fly-fishing in both private and group lessons. The **Orvis Co.** (⊠ Rte. 7A, Manchester Center, ☎ 800/235–9763) hosts a nationally known fly-fishing school on the Battenkill, the state's most famous trout stream, with 2½-day courses given weekly between April and October.

HIKING

One of the most popular segments of Vermont's **Long Trail** starts at Route 11/30 west of Peru Notch and goes to the top of Bromley Mountain. The round-trip trek takes about four hours.

The **Mountain Goat** (⊠ Rte. 7A south of Rte. 11/30, ☎ 802/362–5159) sells hiking, backpacking, and climbing equipment and rents snowshoes and cross-country and telemark skis. The shop also conducts rock- and ice-climbing clinics.

STATE PARK

Emerald Lake State Park (⊠ U.S. 7, North Dorset, ☎ 802/362–1655), 9 mi north of Manchester, has campsites, a marked nature trail, an on-site naturalist, boat and canoe rentals, and a snack bar.

Shopping

ART AND ANTIQUES

Carriage Trade (⊠ Rte. 7A north of Manchester Center, ☎ 802/362–1125) contains room after room of Early American antiques and has a fine collection of ceramics. **Danby Antiques Center** (⊠ ⅛ mi off U.S. 7, Danby, ☎ 802/293–5990), 13 mi north of Manchester, has 11 rooms and a barn filled with furniture and accessories, folk art, textiles, and stoneware. Vermont-based artists have shown their oils, watercolors, and sculptures at **Gallery North Star** (⊠ Rte. 7A, ☎ 802/ 362–4541) for more than 25 years. The **Peel Gallery of Fine Art** (⊠ Peel Gallery Rd., Danby, ☎ 802/293–5230), which has celebrated its third decade in business, represents 40 professional American artists. **Tilting at Windmills Gallery** (⊠ Rte. 11/30, ☎ 802/362–3022) exhibits the works of well-known artists such as Douglas Flackman of the Hudson River School.

BOOKS

Northshire Bookstore (⊠ Main St., ☎ 802/362–2200 or 800/437–3700), a community bookstore for more than 20 years, carries many travel and children's books and sponsors readings year-round.

CLOTHING AND SPECIALTY ITEMS

Alfred Baier (⊠ Butternut La., ☎ 802/362–3371) makes and sells pipes in his studio-workshop.

Orvis Sporting Gifts (⊠ Union St., ☎ 802/362–6455), a discount outlet that carries discontinued items from the popular outdoor clothing and home furnishings mail-order company, is housed in what was Orvis's shop in the 1800s.

Anne Klein, Liz Claiborne, Donna Karan, Levi Strauss, Giorgio Armani, and Jones New York are among the shops on Route 11/30 and U.S. 7 South—a center for **designer outlet stores.**

FISHING GEAR

Orvis Retail Store (⊠ Rte. 7A, ☎ 802/362–3750), an outdoor specialty store that is one of the largest suppliers of fishing gear in the Northeast, also carries clothing, gifts, and hunting supplies.

MALLS AND MARKETPLACES

Manchester Designer Outlets (⊠ U.S. 7 and Rte. 11/30, ☎ 802/362–3736 or 800/955–7467) has such big-city names as Joan & David, Baccarat, Coach, Ralph Lauren, and Cole-Haan. At **Manchester Square** (⊠ Rte. 11/30 and Richville Rd.) you'll find outlet stores for Giorgio Armani, Yves Delorme/Palais Royal, Vermont Toy Chest, Brooks Brothers, Levi Strauss, Escada, and more.

Ski Areas

BROMLEY MOUNTAIN

The first trails at Bromley were cut in 1936. The area has a comfortable red-clapboard base lodge, built when the ski area first opened; it was later expanded. Many families appreciate the resort's convivial atmosphere. There's a large ski shop and a condominium village adjacent to the slopes. A reduced-price, two-day lift pass is available, as is a snowboard park-only lift ticket. Kids 6 and under ski free when accompanied by an adult. Eighty-four percent of the area is covered by snowmaking. ⊠ *Box 1130, Rte. 11, Manchester Center 05255, ☎ 802/824–5522 information and snow conditions; 800/865–4786 lodging,* WEB *www.bromley.com.*

Downhill. Most ski areas are laid out to face the north or east, but Bromley faces south, making it one of the warmer spots to ski in New England. Its 43 trails are equally divided into beginner, intermediate, and advanced terrain; the last is serviced by the Blue Ribbon quad chairlift on the east side. The vertical drop is 1,334 ft. Four double chairlifts, two quad lifts, a J-bar, and two surface lifts for beginners provide transportation. The high-speed quad lift takes skiers from the base to the summit in just six minutes.

Child care. Bromley is one of the region's best places to bring children. Besides a nursery for children from ages 6 weeks to 4 years, ski instruction is provided for children ages 3 to 12.

Summer activities. The area becomes a veritable playground in summer. At the DevalKart and the Alpine Slide, passengers ride up on a chairlift and come down on wheeled sleds (or ride back down on the chair). There's also Parabounce, a helium-filled, parachute-harnessed tethered balloon, a climbing wall, kiddie bumper cars, and a huge trampoline.

With 21 km (16 mi) of marked trails, the **Meadowbrook Inn** (✉ Rte. 11, Landgrove, ☎ 802/824–6444 or 800/498–6445) offers an idyllic setting for cross-country skiing and snowshoeing. The inn, which has eight guest rooms and a restaurant, has rental gear and provides lessons.

Stratton

8 *18 mi southeast of Manchester.*

Stratton, home to the famous Stratton Mountain Resort, has a self-contained town center with shops, restaurants, and lodgings clustered at the base of the slopes. There's plenty of activity year-round between skiing and summer sports.

Lodging

$$–$$$$ 🏨 **Stratton Mountain Inn and Village Lodge.** The complex includes a 120-room inn—the largest on the mountain—and a 91-room lodge of studio units equipped with microwaves, refrigerators, and small wet bars. The lodge is the only slopeside ski-in, ski-out hotel at Stratton. The inn is within walking distance of the lifts. Ski packages that include lift tickets bring down room rates. ✉ *Middle Ridge Rd., 05155,* ☎ *802/297–2500; 800/777–1700 lodgings,* FAX *802/297–1778,* WEB *www.strattonmountain.com. 120 rooms, 91 studios. Restaurant, lounge, pool, hot tub, sauna, golf course, 4 tennis courts, cross-country and downhill skiing. AE, D, DC, MC, V.*

Nightlife and the Arts

Popular **Mulligan's** (✉ Mountain Rd., ☎ 802/297–9293) serves American cuisine. Bands or DJs provide entertainment in the late afternoon and on weekends. The **Red Fox Inn** (✉ Winhall Hollow Rd., Bondville, ☎ 802/297–2488) hosts musicians in the tavern on weekends.

Ski Areas

Since its creation in 1961, Stratton has undergone physical transformations and upgrades, yet the area's sophisticated character has been retained. It has been the special province of well-to-do families and, more recently, young professionals from the New York–southern Connecticut corridor. Since the mid-'80s, an entire village, with a covered parking structure for 700 cars, has arisen at the base of the mountain. Adjacent to the base lodge are a condo-hotel, restaurants, and about 25 shops lining a pedestrian mall. Stratton is 4 mi up its own access road off Route 30 in Bondville, about 30 minutes from Manchester's popular shopping zone. ✉ *Box 145, R.R. 1, Stratton Mountain 05155,* ☎ *802/297–2200; 800/843–6867; 802/297–4211 snow conditions; 800/ 787–2886 lodging,* WEB *www.stratton.com.*

Downhill. Stratton's skiing is in three sectors. The first is the lower mountain directly in front of the base lodge-village-condo complex; several lifts reach mid-mountain from this entry point, and practically all skiing is beginner or low-intermediate. Above that, the upper mountain, with a vertical drop of 2,000 ft, has a high-speed, 12-passenger gondola, Starship XII. Down the face are the expert trails, and on either side are intermediate cruising runs with a smattering of wide beginner slopes. The third sector, the Sun Bowl, is off to one side with two quad chairlifts and two expert trails, a full base lodge, and plenty of intermediate terrain. Stratton hosts the U.S. Open Snowboarding championships; its snowboard park has a 380-ft halfpipe. A Ski Learning Park has its own Park Packages for novice skiers. In all, Stratton has 11 lifts that service 90 trails and 90 acres of glades.

Cross-country. The resort has more than 30 km (18 mi) of cross-country skiing and two Nordic centers: Sun Bowl and Country Club.

Child care. The day-care center takes children from ages 6 weeks to 5 years for indoor activities and outdoor excursions. There is a ski school for children ages 4 to 12. A junior racing program and special instruction groups are geared toward more experienced young skiers.

Summer and year-round activities. Stratton has 15 outdoor tennis courts, 27 holes of golf, horseback riding, mountain biking and hiking accessed by a gondola to the summit, and instructional programs in tennis and golf. The sports center, open year-round, contains two indoor tennis courts, three racquetball courts, a 25-meter indoor swimming pool, a hot tub, a steam room, a fitness facility with Nautilus equipment, and a restaurant. Stratton also hosts summer entertainment and family activities, including a skating park and climbing wall.

Weston

9 *20 mi northeast of Manchester.*

Although perhaps best known for the Vermont Country Store, Weston is famed as one of the first Vermont towns to have discovered its own intrinsic loveliness—and marketability. With its summer theater, pretty town green, and Victorian bandstand, as well as an assortment of shops offering variety without modern sprawl, the little village really lives up to its vaunted image.

The **Mill Museum,** down the road from the Vermont Country Store, has numerous hands-on displays depicting the engineering and mechanics of one of the town's mills. The many old tools on view kept towns like Weston running smoothly in their early days. ⊠ *Rte. 100,* ☎ *802/824–3119.* 🖃 *Donations accepted.* ☉ *July–Aug., Wed.–Sun. 1-4; Sept.–mid-Oct., Sat. and Sun. 1-4.*

Dining and Lodging

$$$$ ✕🖭 **Inn at Weston.** Country elegance best describes this 1848 village inn. Plush linens, Ralph Lauren comforters, fresh flowers, and chocolate truffles await in its luxurious rooms and suites. All rooms have phones and private baths; many have whirlpool tubs, TVs, fireplaces, and CD players. The restaurant serves contemporary regional cuisine including herb-crusted lambchops and smoked trout in a candlelit setting. Vermont cheddar cheese and Granny Smith apple omelettes are popular at breakfast. ⊠ *Rte. 100, Box 179, 05161,* ☎ *802/824–6789,* FAX *802/824–3073,* WEB *www.innweston.com. 13 rooms. Restaurant, pub. AE, MC, V. BP.*

$–$$ 🖭 **Colonial House Inn & Motel.** You'll find warmth and charm at this family friendly complex just 2 mi south of the village. Relax on comfortable furniture in the large living room or enjoy the sun in the solarium. Homey, country furnishings adorn both the inn rooms and the motel units. The complimentary breakfast features fresh goodies from the on-site bakery; there's a family-style dinner on Friday and Saturday nights. ⊠ *287 Rte. 100, 05161,* ☎ *802/824–6286 or 800/639–5033,* FAX *802/824-3934,* WEB *www.cohoinn.com. 9 motel units; 6 inn rooms, shared bath. Game room. D, MC, V. BP.*

Nightlife and the Arts

The members of the **Weston Playhouse** (⊠ Village Green, off Rte. 100, ☎ 802/824–5288), the oldest professional theater in Vermont, have produced Broadway plays, musicals, and other works since 1937. Their season runs from late June to early September.

The **Kinhaven Music School** (⊠ Lawrence Hill Rd., ☎ 802/824–3365) stages free student concerts on Fridays at 4 PM and Sundays at 2:30 in July and August.

Shopping

The **Vermont Country Store** (⊠ Rte. 100, ☎ 802/824–3184, WEB www. vtcountrystore.com; closed Sun.) sets aside one room of its old-fashioned emporium for Vermont Common Crackers and bins of fudge and other candy. For years the retail store and its mail-order catalog have carried nearly forgotten items such as Lilac Vegetal aftershave, Monkey Brand black tooth powder, Flexible Flyer sleds, and tiny wax bottles of colored syrup, but have also sold plenty of practical items such as sturdy outdoor clothing and even a manual typewriter. Nostalgia-evoking implements dangle from the store's walls and ceiling. (There's another store on Route 103 in Rockingham.)

Drury House Antiques (⊠ On the Village Green, ☎ 802/824–4395) specializes in antique clocks, fly rods, and fishing-related objects.

The **Todd Gallery** (⊠ 614 Main St., ☎ 802/824–5606) exhibits paintings, prints, and sculptures by Vermont artists and craftspeople.

Ludlow

⑩ *9 mi northeast of Weston.*

Up until just a few years ago, Ludlow was a nondescript factory town that just happened to have a major ski area—Okemo—on its outskirts. Today the old General Electric plant is gone, its premises recycled into a rambling, block-long complex of shops and restaurants, and the town seems much more integrated into the ski scene. A beautiful, often-photographed historic church overlooks the town green.

Dining and Lodging

$–$$$ ✕ **Pot Belly Pub.** Aprés-ski fun seekers pile into this popular restaurant/nightspot for house specialties such as Belly burgers, smoked ribs, steaks, applejack pork, and fresh seafood. Live entertainment—from jazz and rhythm-and-blues to swing—keeps patrons warm on winter weekends. ⊠ *130 Main St.,* ☎ *802/228–8989.*

$$$–$$$$ ✕🖾 **Governor's Inn.** This 19th-century Victorian country home on the village green is a welcome retreat for those looking for gracious accommodations and creative, contemporary fare. The second- and third-floor guest rooms are decorated with antique furnishings; the third-floor rooms, including the suite, have gaslit fire stoves. Chef/co-owner Kathy Kubec prepares prix-fixe ($45), six-course dinners Thursday through Sunday (reservations essential). An elegant breakfast is served at individual tables for two. ⊠ *86 Main St., 05149,* ☎ *802/228–8830 or 800/ 468–3766,* FAX *802/228–2961,* WEB *www.thegovernorsinn.com. 9 rooms. AE, D, MC, V. BP.*

$$$–$$$$ 🖾 **Andrie Rose Inn.** Many of the handsomely furnished, antiques-filled rooms at this lovely 1829 inn on a quiet in-town street have whirlpool tubs and views of the mountains. The inn has five buildings in all; two-person luxury suites have whirlpool tubs, fireplaces, and steam showers for two. Full-floor condo suites in the 1883 Victorian Town House sleep up to 12, and two family suites have fireplaces and kitchens. The living room, complete with fireplace, is a grand spot to enjoy a cocktail after hiking or skiing. Candlelight breakfast is served to guests staying in standard rooms; a breakfast basket is delivered to the luxury suites. A four-course dinner with a seasonal menu is prepared Friday and Saturday evenings by award-winning chef Irene B. Maston. ⊠ *13 Pleasant St., 05149,* ☎ *802/223–4846 or 800/223–4846,* FAX *802/228–*

7910, WEB *www.andrieroseinn.com. 9 rooms, 14 suites. Restaurant, bar, bicycles. AE, MC, V. BP.*

$$$–$$$$ 🏨 **Okemo Mountain Lodge.** The one-bedroom condominiums clustered around the base of Okemo's ski lifts come with kitchens, fireplaces, and decks. The restaurant is open for breakfast and lunch only. The Okemo Mountain Lodging Service also rents units in the Kettle Brook, Winterplace, and Solitude slopeside condominiums. Ski-and-stay packages are available for three or more non-holiday nights. ✉ *77 Okemo Ridge Rd., off Rte. 103, 05149,* ☎ *802/228–5571, 802/228–4041, or 800/786–5366,* FAX *802/228–2079. 55 units. Restaurant, bar, in-room VCRs, cross-country and downhill skiing. AE, MC, V.* WEB *www. okemo.com.*

Outdoor Activities and Sports

Cavendish Trail Horse Rides (✉ 20 Mile Stream Rd., Proctorsville, ☎ 802/226–7821) operates horse-drawn sleigh rides in snowy weather, wagon rides at other times, and guided trail rides from mid-May to mid-October.

Ski Areas

OKEMO MOUNTAIN RESORT

An ideal ski area for families with children, family owned Okemo has evolved into a major resort. The main attraction is a long, broad, gentle slope with two beginner lifts just above the base lodge. All the facilities at the bottom of the mountain are close together, so family members can regroup easily during the ski day. The Solitude Village Area has a triple chairlift, two new trails, and lodging. The resort offers numerous ski and snowboarding packages. ✉ *77 Okemo Ridge Rd. (Rte. 100),* ☎ *802/228–4041; 800/786–5366 lodging; 802/228–5222 snow conditions,* WEB *www.okemo.com.*

Downhill. Above the broad beginner's slope at the base, the upper part of Okemo has a varied network of trails: long, winding, easy trails for beginners; straight fall-line runs for experts; and curving, cruising slopes for intermediates. The 98 trails are served by an efficient lift system of 14 lifts, including seven quads, three triple chairlifts, and four surface lifts; 95% are covered by snowmaking. From the summit to the base lodge, the vertical drop is 2,150 ft, the highest in southern Vermont. Okemo has a self-contained snowboarding area serviced by a surface lift; the mile-long park is home to the Pipe, a massive 420-ft by 40-ft halfpipe, and a new superpipe. There's also a snowboard park for beginners.

Cross-country/Snowshoeing. The **Okemo Valley Nordic Center** (✉ Fox La., ☎ 802/228–1396) has 26 km (16 mi) of groomed trails and rents equipment.

Child care. The area's nursery, for children from ages 6 weeks to 8 years, has many indoor activities and supervised outings. Children ages 3 to 4 can get a one-hour introduction to skiing; the SnowStar program is for kids ages 4–7. Nursery reservations are essential. Okemo also offers a Kids' Night Out evening child-care program on Saturdays during the regular season and certain holiday weeks.

Summer activities. The Okemo Valley Golf Club has a new 18-hole, par-71, 6,000-yard course. Seven target greens, a putting green, a golf academy, and an indoor putting green, swing stations, and a simulator provide plenty of ways to improve your game.

Chester

① *11 mi east of Weston.*

Gingerbread Victorians frame Chester's town green. The local pharmacy on Main Street has been in continuous operation since the 1860s. The **stone village** on North Street on the outskirts of town, two rows of buildings constructed from quarried stone, was built by two brothers and is said to have been used during the Civil War as a station on the Underground Railroad.

In Chester's restored 1852 train station you can board the **Green Mountain Flyer** for a 26-mi, two-hour round-trip journey to Bellows Falls, on the Connecticut River at the eastern edge of the state. The cars that date from the golden age of railroading travel past covered bridges and along the Brockway Mills gorge. The fall foliage trips are spectacular. ⊠ *Rte. 103,* ☎ *802/463–3069 or 800/707–3530,* WEB *www.rails-vt.com.* 🖼 *$11 in summer; $12 in fall.* ☉ *Late June–early Sept., Tues.–Sun.; mid-Sept.–late Oct., daily. Train departs several times daily, call for schedule.*

Dining and Lodging

$ ✕ **Raspberries and Thyme.** Breakfast specials, homemade soups, a large selection of salads, homemade desserts, and a menu listing more than 40 sandwiches make this one of the area's most popular spots for casual dining. ⊠ *On the Green,* ☎ *802/875–4486. AE, D, MC, V. No dinner Tues.*

$$ 🏠 **Fullerton Inn.** Guest rooms with country quilts and lace curtains vary in size and amenities at this three-story, wooden 19th-century building with a big porch. Some favorites are the bright corner rooms and numbers 8 and 10, which share a private porch. The restaurant serves breakfast daily and dinner every night except Wednesday, offering morning delicacies such as lobster omelets and nightly entrées like roast duck and trout Provençal. There's live entertainment in the lounge Saturday night. A shuttle bus to local attractions and ski areas stops in front of the inn. ⊠ *40 Common St., on the Green, 05143,* ☎ *802/875–2444,* FAX *802/875–6414,* WEB *www.fullertoninn.com. 21 rooms, 3 suites. Restaurant, lounge. AE, D, MC, V. CP.*

Outdoor Activities and Sports

A 26-mi **driving or biking loop** out of Chester follows the Williams River along Route 103 to Pleasant Valley Road north of Bellows Falls. At Saxtons River, turn west onto Route 121 and follow along the river to connect with Route 35. When the two routes separate, follow Route 35 north back to Chester.

Shopping

The **National Survey Charthouse** (⊠ Main St., ☎ 802/875–2121) is a map-lover's paradise. The store is good for a rainy-day browse even if maps aren't your passion.

Grafton

★ **⑫** *8 mi south of Chester.*

Like many Vermont villages its size, Grafton enjoyed its heyday as an agricultural community well before the Civil War, when its citizens grazed some 10,000 sheep and spun their wool into sturdy yarn for locally woven fabric. Unlike most other out-of-the-way country towns, though, Grafton was born again, following a long decline, by preservationists determined to revitalize not only its centerpiece, the Old Tavern, but many other commercial and residential structures in the village center. Beginning in 1963, the Windham Foundation—Vermont's second-largest private foundation—commenced the rehabilitation of Grafton. The **Historical Society** documents the town's renewal. ⊠ *Townshend Rd.,* ☎ *802/843–2584 visitor center information.* 🎫 *$1.* ☉ *June–late Sept., weekends 1:30–4; late Sept.–Oct., daily 1:30–4.*

Dining and Lodging

$$$$ ✕🏨 **Old Tavern at Grafton.** White-column porches on both stories wrap around the main building of this commanding inn, which dates from 1801. The main building has 12 rooms; the rest are dispersed among other buildings in town. Two dining rooms ($$$), one with formal Georgian furniture and oil portraits, the other with rustic paneling and low beams, serve inspired New England fare such as grilled choice sirloin steeped in McNeil's stout and a blend of spices. Cross-country skiing is at the Grafton Ponds Cross-Country Ski Center, run by the inn. ⊠ *Rte. 121, 05146,* ☎ *802/843–2231 or 800/843–1801,* 𝐅𝐀𝐗 *802/843–2245,* 𝖶𝖤𝖡 *www.old-tavern.com. 58 rooms, 7 suites. Restaurant, bar, pond, tennis court, paddle tennis, mountain bikes, ice-skating, cross-country skiing, recreation room. AE, MC, V. Closed Apr. BP.*

Shopping

Gallery North Star (⊠ Townshend Rd., ☎ 802/843–2465) exhibits the oils, watercolors, lithographs, and sculptures of Vermont-based artists.

Townshend

⓭ *9 mi south of Grafton.*

One of a string of pretty villages along the banks of the West River, Townshend embodies the Vermont ideal of a lovely town green presided over by a gracefully proportioned church spire. The spire belongs to the 1790 Congregational Meeting House, one of the state's oldest houses of worship. Just north on Route 30 is the Scott Bridge (closed to traffic), the state's longest single-span covered bridge.

At **Townshend State Park,** you'll find a sandy beach and a trailhead for the rigorous, 2.7-mi hike to the top of Bald Mountain. Campsites are available. ⊠ *Rte. 30 N,* ☎ *802/365-7500.*

Dining and Lodging

$–$$ ✕ **Townshend Dam Diner.** Folks come from miles around to enjoy traditional fare such as Mom's meatloaf, chili, and roast beef croquettes, as well as Townshend-raised bison burgers, and creative daily specials. Breakfast, served all day everyday, includes such tasty treats as raspberry chocolate-chip walnut pancakes and homemade French toast. ⊠ *Rte. 30,* ☎ *802/874–4107. No credit cards.*

$$$$ ✕🏨 **Windham Hill Inn.** The 1825 brick farmhouse and white barn annex house the elegant accommodations that comprise this country inn. Period antiques, Oriental carpets, and locally made furniture adorn the interior. Some rooms have fireplaces, private porches and Jacuzzis; all have magnificent views of the West River valley. The Music Room has an 1888 restored Steinway piano and more than 800 CDs. A four-course candlelight dinner is served in the Frog Pond Dining Room. The seasonal menu might include marinated shiitake mushrooms and ham *en croustade* with Dijon sherry sauce. ⊠ *311 Lawrence Drive, West Townshend 05359,* ☎ *800/944–4080,* 𝐅𝐀𝐗 *802/874–4702,* 𝖶𝖤𝖡 *www.windhamhill.com. 21 rooms. Restaurant, pool, tennis court, hiking, cross-country skiing. MAP.*

$–$$ 🏨 **Boardman House.** This handsome Greek Revival home on the town green combines modern comfort with the relaxed charm of a 19th-century farmhouse. The uncluttered guest rooms are furnished with Shaker-style furniture, colorful duvets, and paintings. Both the breakfast room and front hall have *trompe l'oeil* floors. ⊠ *On the Green, 05353,* ☎ *802/ 365–4086,* WEB *www.southvermont.com/townshend/boardmanhouse, 5 rooms, 1 suite. Breakfast room, sauna. No credit cards. BP.*

Outdoor Activities and Sports

You can rent canoes, kayaks, tubes, cross-country skis, and snowshoes at **Townshend Outdoors** (⊠ Rte. 30, ☎ 802/365–7309).

Shopping

Mary Meyer Stuffed Toys Factory Store, the state's oldest stuffed toy company, offers discounts of up to 70%. (⊠ Rte. 30, ☎ 802/365–7993).

Newfane

⑭ *15 mi south of Grafton.*

With a village green surrounded by pristine white buildings, Newfane is sometimes described as the quintessential New England small town. The 1839 First Congregational Church and the Windham County Court House, with 17 green-shuttered windows and a rounded cupola, are often open. The building with the four-pointed spire is Union Hall, built in 1832.

Dining and Lodging

$$$–$$$$ ✕▥ **Four Columns.** The majestic white columns of this Greek Revival mansion, built in 1834 for a homesick southern bride, are more intimidating than the Colonial-style rooms inside. Rooms are decorated with a mix of antiques and turn-of-the-century reproductions. Most of the suites have cathedral ceilings; all have double whirlpool baths and gas fireplaces. The two newly remodeled suites on the third floor in the old section afford the most privacy. In the elegant restaurant ($$$; closed Tuesdays and part of April), chef Greg Parks prepares New American dishes; a favorite is roasted young chicken with herbs served in a chardonnay and mushroom sauce. The expanded Continental breakfast overflows with yogurts, cheeses, homemade breads, and the house special oatmeal. ⊠ *Box 278, West St., 05345,* ☎ *802/365–7713 or 800/787–6633,* FAX *802/365–0022,* WEB *www.fourcolumnsinn.com. 9 rooms, 6 suites. Restaurant, pool, hiking. AE, D, DC, MC, V. CP.*

Shopping

The **Newfane Country Store** (⊠ Rte. 30, ☎ 802/365–7916) carries many quilts (which can also be custom ordered), homemade fudge, and other Vermont foods, gifts, and crafts. Collectibles dealers from across the state sell their wares at the **Newfane Flea Market** (⊠ Rte. 30, ☎ 802/365–7771), held every weekend during summer and fall. Corncob-smoked ham and bacon and Vermont cheeses are just a few of the delectable goodies at **Lawrence's Smoke House** (⊠ Rte. 30, ☎ 802/ 365–7751).

Putney

⑮ *7 mi east of Newfane, 9 mi north of Brattleboro.*

Putney, a Connecticut River valley town just upriver from Brattleboro, was a prime destination for many of the converts to alternative rural lifestyles who swarmed into Vermont during the late 1960s and early '70s. Those who remain maintain a tradition of progressive schools, artisanship, and organic farming.

☾ **Harlow's Sugar House** (⊠ U.S. 5, ☎ 802/387–5852), 2 mi north of Putney, has a working cider mill and sugar house, as well as berry picking in summer and apple picking in autumn. You can buy cider, maple syrup, and other items in the gift shop.

Tours are given of the **Green Mountain Spinnery,** a factory-shop that sells yarn, knitting accessories, and patterns. ⊠ *Depot Rd. at Exit 4 off I–91,* ☎ *802/387–4528 or 800/321–9665.* ☒ *Tours $2.* ☉ *Tours at 1:30 on the 1st and 3rd Tues. of each month.*

Dining and Lodging

$$–$$$ ✕🖾 **Putney Inn.** The inn's main building dates from the 1790s and was later part of a seminary—the present-day pub was the chapel. Two fireplaces dominate the lobby. The spacious, modern rooms in an adjacent building have Queen Anne mahogany reproductions and are 100 yards from the banks of the Connecticut River. Regionally inspired cuisine—seafood, New England potpies, a wild-game mixed grill, and burgers with Vermont cheddar—is marked by innovative flourishes. Locally raised meat is butchered on the premises. ⊠ *Depot Rd., 05346,* ☎ *802/ 387–5517 or 800/653–5517,* ℻ *802/387–5211,* WEB *www.putneyinn. com. 25 rooms. Restaurant, lounge. AE, D, MC, V. BP.*

$$$ 🖾 **Hickory Ridge House Bed and Breakfast.** This gracious 1808 Federal mansion, listed on the National Register of Historic Places, has Palladian windows, a parlor with a Rumford fireplace, and large, comfortable guest rooms filled with antiques and country furnishings. Four rooms have wood-burning fireplaces, and one has a gas fireplace stove. A two-bedroom cottage, with a full kitchen and fireplace, can be rented as a unit, or the rooms can be rented separately. ⊠ *53 Hickory Ridge Rd., 05346,* ☎ *802/387–5709 or 800/380–9218,* ℻ *802/ 387–4328,* WEB *www.hickoryridgehouse.com. 6 rooms, 1 cottage. Hiking, cross-country skiing. AE, MC, V. BP.*

Shopping

Allen Bros. (⊠ U.S. 5 north of Putney, ☎ 802/722–3395) bakes apple pies, makes cider doughnuts, and sells Vermont foods and products.

Southern Vermont A to Z

To research prices, get advice from other travelers, and book travel arrangements, visit www.fodors.com.

BUS TRAVEL
Vermont Transit links Bennington, Manchester, and Brattleboro.
➤ BUS INFORMATION: **Vermont Transit** (☎ 800/552–8737).

CAR TRAVEL
In the south the principal east–west highway is Route 9, the Molly Stark Trail, from Brattleboro to Bennington. The most important north–south roads are U.S. 7; the more scenic Route 7A; Route 100, which runs through the state's center; I–91; and U.S. 5, which runs along the state's eastern border. Route 30 from Brattleboro to Manchester is a scenic drive.

EMERGENCIES
➤ HOSPITALS: **Brattleboro Memorial Hospital** (⊠ 9 Belmont Ave., Brattleboro, ☎ 802/257–0341). **Southwestern Vermont Medical Center** (⊠ 100 Hospital Dr., Bennington, ☎ 802/442–6361).

VISITOR INFORMATION
➤ CONTACTS: **Bennington Area Chamber of Commerce** (⊠ Veterans Memorial Dr., Bennington 05201, ☎ 802/447–3311, WEB www. bennington.com). **Brattleboro Area Chamber of Commerce** (⊠ 180 Main St., Brattleboro 05301, ☎ 802/254–4565, WEB www.brattleboro.com). **Chamber of Commerce, Manchester and the Mountains** (⊠ 5046 Main St., Manchester 05255, ☎ 802/362–2100, WEB www.manchesterandmtns.

com). **Mt. Snow Valley Chamber of Commerce** (✉ Box 3, W. Main St., Wilmington 05363, ☎ 802/464–8092 or 877/887–6884, WEB www. visitvermont.com).

CENTRAL VERMONT

Central Vermont's economy once centered on the mills and railroad yards of Rutland and the marble quarries that honeycomb nearby towns. Vermont's "second city" is still a busy commercial hub, but today, as in much of the rest of the state, it's tourism that drives the economic engine. The center of the dynamo is the massive ski-and-stay infrastructure around Killington, the East's largest downhill resort.

There's a lot more to central Vermont than high-speed chairlifts and slopeside condos, however. The protected (except for occasional logging) lands of the Green Mountain National Forest surround the spine of Vermont's central range; off to the west, the rolling dairyland of the southern Lake Champlain valley is one of the truly undiscovered corners of the state. To the east, in the Connecticut River valley, are towns as diverse as Calvin Coolidge's Plymouth, a Yankee Brigadoon, and busy, polished-to-perfection Woodstock, where upscale shops are just a short walk from America's newest national park.

The coverage of towns begins with Windsor, on U.S. 5 near I–91 at the state's eastern edge; winds westward toward U.S. 7; then continues north before heading over the spine of the Green Mountains.

Windsor

⓰ *50 mi north of Brattleboro, 42 mi east of Rutland.*

Windsor justly bills itself as the birthplace of Vermont. An interpretive exhibit on Vermont's constitution, the first in the United States to prohibit slavery and establish a system of public schools, is housed in the **Old Constitution House.** The site, where in 1777 grant holders declared Vermont an independent republic, contains 18th- and 19th-century furnishings, American paintings and prints, and Vermont-made tools, toys, and kitchenware. ✉ *N. Main St.,* ☎ *802/828–3211.* 🎫 *$1.* ☉ *Late May–mid-Oct., Wed.–Sun., 11–5.*

The firm of Robbins & Lawrence became famous for applying the "American system" (the use of interchangeable parts) to the manufacture of rifles. Although the company no longer exists, the **American Precision Museum** extols the Yankee ingenuity that created a major machine-tool industry here in the 19th century. The museum contains the largest collection of historically significant machine tools in the country and presents changing exhibits. ✉ *196 Main St.,* ☎ *802/674–6628.* 🎫 *$5.* ☉ *Memorial Day–Nov. 1, daily 10–5.*

The mission of the **Vermont State Craft Gallery,** in the restored 1846 Windsor House, is to advance the appreciation of Vermont crafts through education and exhibition. The center presents crafts exhibitions and operates a small museum. ✉ *54 Main St.,* ☎ *802/674–6729.* ☉ *Mon.–Sat. 10–5, Sun. 1–5.*

Glass blowers demonstrate their art at **Simon Pearce** (✉ U.S. 5, ☎ 802/ 674–6280 or 800/774–5277), where there's also a retail shop.

At 460 ft, the **Cornish-Windsor Covered Bridge** off U.S. 5, which spans the Connecticut River between Windsor and Cornish, New Hampshire, is the longest in the state.

Central Vermont

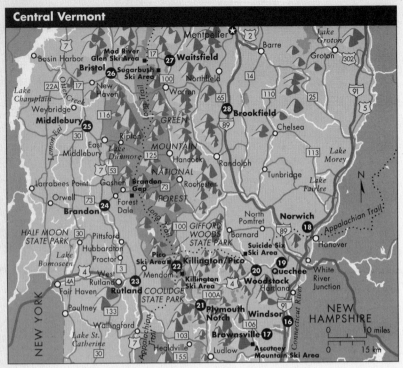

Dining and Lodging

$$ ✕ **Windsor Station.** This converted main-line railroad station serves such entrées as chicken Kiev, filet mignon, and prime rib. The booths, with their curtained brass railings, were created from the high-back railroad benches of the depot. ⊠ *Depot Ave.,* ☎ *802/674–2052. AE, MC, V. Closed Mon. in fall and winter; dinner only*

$$–$$$ ✕🏠 **Juniper Hill Inn.** An expanse of green lawn with Adirondack chairs and a garden of perennials sweeps up to the portico of this Greek Revival mansion, built at the turn of the century and now on the National Register of Historic Places. The central living room, with its hardwood floors, oak paneling, Oriental carpets, and thickly upholstered furniture, has a stately feel. Bedrooms are furnished with antiques; 11 have fireplaces. Four-course dinners ($34; reservations essential) served in the candlelit dining room at 7:00 PM Monday through Saturday may include herb-crusted rack of lamb or sautéed scallops with glazed garlic and champagne sauce. ⊠ *Box 79, Juniper Hill Rd., 05089,* ☎ *802/674–5273 or 800/359–2541,* FAX *802/674–2041,* WEB *www.juniperhillinn.com. 16 rooms. Restaurant, pool, hiking. D, MC, V. BP.*

Nightlife and the Arts

Destiny (⊠ U.S. 5, Windsor, ☎ 802/674–6671) hosts rock bands most days and has a DJ on Sunday.

Brownsville

⑰ *5 mi southwest of Windsor.*

Brownsville, a small village at the foot of Ascutney Mountain, has everything a village needs: a country store, post office, town hall, and historic grange building. The Ascutney Mountain ski area is a self-contained four-season resort.

Lodging

$$–$$$$ ⊞ **Ascutney Mountain Resort Hotel.** One of the big attractions of this five-building resort hotel-condo complex is the ski lift outside the main door. The comfortable, well-maintained suites come in different configurations and sizes—some with kitchens, fireplaces, and decks. Slopeside multilevel condos have three bedrooms, three baths, and private entrances. The Ascutney Harvest Inn, which serves Continental cuisine, is within the complex. ⊠ *Box 699, Hotel Rd., off Rte. 44, 05037,* ☎ *802/484–7711 or 800/243–0011,* FAX *802/484–3117,* WEB *www.ascutney. com. 212 units. 3 restaurants, 2 bars, 1 indoor and 1 outdoor pool, hot tub, health club, racquetball, ice-skating. AE, MC, V.*

$$ ⊞ **Mill Brook.** This Victorian farmhouse, built in 1880, is directly across from the Ascutney ski slopes. Making après-ski idleness easy are the four sitting rooms, decorated with antiques and contemporary furnishings. The honeymoon suite has a separate dressing room with a clawfoot bathtub; the other suites are perfect for families. Rates include afternoon tea. ⊠ *Box 410, Rte. 44, 05037,* ☎ *802/484–7283,* WEB *www.millbrookbb.com. 2 rooms, 3 suites. Hot tub. AE, MC, V. BP.*

Nightlife and the Arts

Crow's Nest Club (⊠ Ascutney Mountain Resort Hotel, Hotel Rd., off Rte. 44, ☎ 802/484–7711) has entertainment on weekends.

Ski Areas

ASCUTNEY MOUNTAIN RESORT

The Plausteiner family, whose patriarch, John, was instrumental in operations at Mt. Snow and White Face Mountain, in Lake Placid, New York, purchased this resort in the mid-1990s, and since then has been continually making improvements. In 2001, a mi-long high-speed quad on the North Peak was opened and snowmaking coverage was increased to 95%. The five buildings of the resort village have hotel suites and condominium units. ⊠ *Rte. 44, off I–91 (Box 699, Brownsville 05037),* ☎ *802/484–7711; 800/243–0011 lodging.*

Downhill. 56 trails with varying terrain are serviced by six lifts, including the quad, three triple chairs, one double chair, and a surface lift. Beginner and novice skiers stay toward the base, while intermediates enjoy the band that wraps the midsection. For experts, tougher black-diamond runs top the mountain. One disadvantage to Ascutney is that there is no easy way down from the summit, so novice skiers should not make the trip. Ascutney is popular with families because it offers some of the least-expensive junior lift tickets in the region.

Cross-country. The resort has 32 km (19 mi) of groomed cross-country trails and offers rentals.

Child care. Day care is available for children from ages 6 weeks to 10 years, with learn-to-ski options and rental equipment for toddlers and up. There are half- and full-day instruction programs for children ages 3 to 12; a Mini-Olympians program for ages 4 to 6; and a Young Olympians program for ages 7 to 12.

Summer and year-round activities. Ascutney Mountain Resort Hotel has a sports-and-fitness center with full-size indoor and outdoor pools, a hot tub, racquetball, aerobics facilities and classes, weight training, and massage. Summer activities include mountain biking, hiking, and tennis.

Norwich

⬤ *6 mi north of White River Junction, 22 mi north of Brownsville.*

Norwich is home to an excellent science museum. The town is across the river from Hanover, New Hampshire, home of Dartmouth College.

★ ☾   Numerous hands-on exhibits at the **Montshire Museum of Science** explore space, nature, and technology; there are also living habitats, aquariums, and many children's programs. A maze of trails winds through 100 acres of pristine woodland. An ideal destination for a rainy day, this is one of the finest museums in New England. ⊠ *Montshire Rd., Box 770,* ☎ *802/649–2200,* WEB *www.montshire.net.* ☞ *$5.50.* ☉ *Daily 10–5.*

Shopping

The shelves at **King Arthur Flour Baker's Store** (⊠ 135 Rte. 5 S, ☎ 802/649–3881) are stocked with all the tools and ingredients in the company's Baker's Catalogue, including mixes and flours, and local products. A bakery with a viewing area enables visitors to watch products being made.

Quechee

⑲   *11 mi south of Norwich, 6 mi west of White River Junction.*

Quechee is perched astride the Ottauquechee River. Quechee Gorge, 165 ft deep, is impressive, though sometimes overrun by tourists. You can see the mi-long gorge, carved by a glacier, from U.S. 4, but many people picnic nearby or scramble down one of several descents for a closer look.

More than a decade ago Simon Pearce set up **Simon Pearce,** an eponymous glassblowing factory in an old mill by a waterfall here, using the water power to drive his furnace. Today the glassblowing factory is at the heart of a handsome, upscale shopping complex that also houses a weaver (demonstrations Tuesday through Sunday) and a pottery studio. You can watch the glassblowers at work daily, and then purchase their wares in the gift shop. A restaurant overlooks the waterfall. ⊠ *The Mill, Main St.,* ☎ *802/295–2711,* WEB *www.simonpearce.com.* ☉ *Store daily 9–9.*

Dining and Lodging

$$$ ✕ **Simon Pearce.** Candlelight, sparkling glassware from the studio downstairs, contemporary dinnerware, exposed brick, and large windows that overlook the roaring Ottauquechee River create an ideal setting for contemporary American cuisine. Sesame-crusted tuna with noodle cakes and wasabi and roast duck with mango chutney sauce are house specialties; the wine cellar holds several hundred vintages. ⊠ *Main St.,* ☎ *802/295–1470. AE, D, DC, MC, V.*

$$$–$$$$ ✕🏠 **Quechee Inn at Marshland Farm.** The 1793 country home of Joseph Marsh, Vermont's first lieutenant governor, has been handsomely restored; newer additions have modern amenities yet retain a traditional feeling. Each room, decorated with Queen Anne–style furnishings and period antiques, has air-conditioning and cable TV. There are groomed cross-country ski trails, bike and canoe rentals, and a fly-fishing school, but if you run short on activities, you also have privileges at the Quechee Country Club, with two 18-hole golf courses, tennis courts, and indoor and outdoor pools. Among the dining room's ($$$$) creative offerings are entrées such as duck confit and seared sesame tuna. ⊠ *Clubhouse Rd., 05059,* ☎ *802/295–3133 or 800/235–3133,* FAX *802/295–6587,* WEB *www.pinnacle-inns.com. 22 rooms, 2 suites. Restaurant, golf privileges, fishing, bicycles, cross-country skiing, meeting room. AE, D, DC, MC, V. BP.*

$$–$$$ ✕🏠 **Parker House.** The peach-and-blue rooms of this 1857 Victorian mansion are named for former residents: Emily has a marble fireplace, Walter is the smallest room, and Joseph has a view of the Ottauquechee River. Third-floor rooms are air-conditioned. The elegant dining room

($$$) prepares sophisticated American comfort cuisine such as loin of venison with a port and balsamic vinegar sauce. Guests have access to the Quechee Country Club's first-rate golf courses, tennis courts, indoor and outdoor pool, and cross-country and downhill skiing. ⊠ *Box 0780, 1792 Quechee Main St., 05059,* ☎ *802/295–6077,* FAX *802/296–6696,* WEB *www.theparkerhouseinn.com. 7 rooms. Restaurant, golf privileges. AE, MC, V. BP.*

Outdoor Activities and Sports

FISHING

The **Vermont Fly Fishing School/Wilderness Trails** (⊠ Quechee Inn, Clubhouse Rd., ☎ 802/295–7620) leads workshops, rents fishing gear and mountain bikes, and arranges canoe and kayak trips. In winter, the company conducts cross-country and snowshoe treks.

POLO

Quechee Polo Club (⊠ Dewey's Mill Rd., ½ mi north of U.S. 4, ☎ 802/295–7152) draws hundreds of spectators on summer Saturdays to its matches near the Quechee Gorge. Admission is $3 per person or $6 per carload.

Shopping

The 40 dealers at the **Hartland Antiques Center** (⊠ U.S. 4, ☎ 802/457–4745) stock furniture, paper items, china, glass, and collectibles. More than 350 dealers sell their wares at the **Quechee Gorge Village** (⊠ U.S. 4, ☎ 802/295–1550 or 800/438–5565), an antiques and crafts mall in an immense reconstructed barn that also houses a country store and a classic diner. A merry-go-round and a small-scale working railroad operate when weather permits.

Ottauquechee Valley Winery (⊠ 5967 Woodstock Rd./U.S. 4, ☎ 802/295–9463) has a tasting room and sells fruit wines, such as apple and blueberry.

Scotland by the Yard (U.S. 4, ☎ 802/295–5351 or 800/295–5351) is the place to shop for all things Scottish, from kilts to Harris tweed jackets and tartan ties.

Woodstock

★ ⑳ *4 mi west of Quechee.*

Perfectly preserved Federal houses surround Woodstock's tree-lined village green, and streams flow around the town center, which is anchored by a covered bridge. The town owes much of its pristine appearance to the Rockefeller family's interest in historic preservation and land conservation.

Woodstock's history of conservationism dates from the 19th century: town native George Perkins Marsh, a congressman and diplomat, wrote the pioneering book *Man and Nature* in 1864 and was closely involved in the creation of the Smithsonian Institution in Washington, D.C.

☾ The **Billings Farm and Museum,** on the grounds of George Perkins Marsh's boyhood home, was founded by Frederick Billings in 1870 as a model of conservation, and is one of the oldest dairy farms in the country. Billings, a lawyer and businessman, put into practice Marsh's ideas about the long-term effects of farming and grazing. Exhibits in the reconstructed Queen Anne farmhouse, school, general store, workshop, and former Marsh homestead demonstrate the lives and skills of early Vermont settlers. ⊠ *Rte. 12, ½ mi north of Woodstock,* ☎ *802/457–2355,* WEB *www.billingsfarm.org.* ⊠ *$8.* ☾ *May–late Oct., daily 10–5; call for Thanksgiving and Dec. weekend schedules.*

The 500-acre **Marsh-Billings-Rockefeller National Historical Park,** which opened in 1998, is Vermont's only national park and the nation's first to focus on conservation and stewardship of natural resources. The park encompasses the forest lands planned by Frederick Billings according to the principles of George Perkins Marsh, as well as Billings's mansion, gardens, and carriage roads. The entire property was the gift of Laurance S. Rockefeller, who lived here with his late wife, Mary, Frederick Billings's granddaughter. It is adjacent to the Billings Farm and Museum. The residential complex is accessible by guided tour only, but you can explore the extensive network of carriage roads and trails on your own. ✉ *Rte. 12,* ☎ *802/457–3368,* WEB *www.nps.marshbillings.com.* 🎫 *Tour $6.* ⏲ *Memorial Day–Oct., daily for guided tours only (call for schedules), grounds daily dawn–dusk.*

Period furnishings of the Woodstock Historical Society fill the white clapboard **Dana House,** built circa 1807. Exhibits include the town charter, furniture, maps, and locally minted silver. The converted barn houses the Woodstock Works exhibit, an economic portrait of the town. ✉ *26 Elm St.,* ☎ *802/457–1822.* 🎫 *$2.* ⏲ *Late May–late Oct., Mon.–Sat. 10–4, Sun. noon–4; Mid-Oct.–mid-May, by appointment only.*

The Raptor Center of the **Vermont Institute of Natural Science** (VINS) houses 23 species of birds of prey, among them bald eagles, peregrine falcons, and 3-ounce saw-whet owls. There are also ravens, turkey vultures, and snowy owls. All the caged birds have been found injured and unable to survive in the wild. This nonprofit, environmental research and education center is on a 77-acre nature preserve with walking trails. ✉ *Church Hill Rd.,* ☎ *802/457–2779,* WEB *www.vinsweb.org.* 🎫 *$6.* ⏲ *Mon.–Sat., 10–4.*

Dining and Lodging

$$$–$$$$ ★ ✕ **Prince and the Pauper.** Modern French and American fare with a Vermont accent is the focus of this romantic restaurant in a candlelit Colonial setting. The grilled duck breast might have an Asian five-spice sauce; lamb and pork sausage in puff pastry comes with a honey-mustard sauce. A less-expensive bistro menu is available in the lounge. ✉ *24 Elm St.,* ☎ *802/457–1818. AE, D, MC, V. No lunch.*

$–$$ ✕ **Pane & Salute.** Authentic regional Italian breads are a specialty, but this restaurant has a whole lot more to offer. You can try homemade Tuscan pizzas and soups, sandwich specials, and pasta entrées such as penne with spinach, pine nuts, raisins, and garlic. Add a glass of Chianti and *mangia bene.* Desserts include meringues with whipped cream and raspberry sauce and fruit tarts. There's outdoor seating when weather permits. The restaurant serves breakfast and lunch daily in summer, brunch all year from 10 to 2, and dinner Thursday, Friday, and Saturday; call for winter hours. ✉ *61 Central St.,* ☎ *802/457–4882. Reservations not accepted. D, MC, V. Closed Wed..*

$$$$ ★ ✕🏨 **Kedron Valley Inn.** Two 19th-century buildings, including the 13-room Main House, and a 1968 log structure make up this inn set on 15 acres. Many rooms have a fireplace or a Franklin stove, two have decks, one has a veranda, and another has a terrace overlooking a stream. Exposed-log walls make the motel units in back more rustic than the rooms in the main inn, but they're decorated similarly, with country antiques and reproductions. The chef creates French masterpieces such as fillet of Norwegian salmon stuffed with herb seafood mousse in puff pastry, and shrimp, scallops, and lobster with wild mushrooms served with a Fra Angelico cream sauce. A terrace with views of the grounds is open in summer. ✉ *Rte. 106, 05071,* ☎ *802/457–1473 or 800/836–1193,* FAX *802/457–4469. 21 rooms, 7 suites. Restaurant, bar, pond, beach. AE, D, MC, V. Closed Apr. and 10 days before Thanksgiving. MAP, BP.*

$$$–$$$$ ✕🏠 **Jackson House Inn.** This fine property consistently wins high ac-
★ colades for both accommodations and dining. European antiques, Ori-
ental rugs, and French-cut crystal fill the formal parlor and cozy library.
There are two wings: one for suites with gas fireplaces, Anichini linens,
down duvets, and thermal massage tubs; the other, overlooking the inn's
5 acres of manicured grounds, for the cathedral-ceiling restaurant, whose
focal point is a granite, open-hearth fireplace. Herb-crusted cod with
an artichoke ragout and lamb shanks braised in red wine and port typ-
ify the lighter contemporary cuisine. You can choose from a prix-fixe,
three-course menu ($49) or the five-course chef's tasting menu ($58).
✉ *114-3 Senior La., 05091,* ☎ *802/457–2065 or 800/448–1890,* 𝔽𝔸𝕏
802/457–9290, 𝕎𝔼𝔹 *www.jacksonhouse.com. 9 rooms, 6 suites. Restau-
rant, sauna, exercise room. AE, MC, V. BP.*

$$$–$$$$ ✕🏠 **Woodstock Inn and Resort.** Country formality might sound like
an oxymoron, but it best describes the relaxed yet polished atmo-
sphere here. Resort entrepreneur Laurance Rockefeller, long a Wood-
stock resident, made this a flagship property of his Rockresorts chain.
The lobbies and lounges hold a grand piano, decorative quilts, a mon-
umental fieldstone fireplace, and bowls of shiny Vermont apples. Guest
rooms are spacious, serene, and set well back from Woodstock's often
noisy main drag. The dinner fare is nouvelle New England; the menu
might list entrées such as salmon steak with avocado beurre blanc, beef
Wellington, and prime rib. Guests can ski free midweek at the inn-owned
Suicide Six. ✉ *14 The Green, U.S. 4, 05091,* ☎ *802/457–1100 or 800/
448–7900,* 𝔽𝔸𝕏 *802/457–6699,* 𝕎𝔼𝔹 *www.woodstockinn.com. 144 rooms,
7 suites. 2 restaurants, bar, indoor lap pool, outdoor pool, sauna, 2
18-hole golf courses, 12 tennis courts, croquet, health club, racquet-
ball, squash, cross-country skiing, meeting room. AE, MC, V. MAP.*

$$$$ 🏠 **Twin Farms.** At the center of this exclusive 300-acre resort stands
the 1795 farmhouse where writers Sinclair Lewis and Dorothy Thomp-
son lived. Not that Lewis and Thompson would recognize the place:
it's been transformed into Vermont's most sumptuous—and most ex-
pensive—resort. Twin Farms' rooms and cottages are fantasy envi-
ronments, drawing their inspiration from Moorish, Scandinavian,
Japanese, and Adirondack design. There are fireplaces throughout, along
with museum-quality artworks. The rich contemporary cuisine em-
phasizes local ingredients. You can help yourself at the open bar. ✉
*Stage Rd., off Rte. 12, 8 mi north of Woodstock (Box 115, Barnard
05031);* ☎ *802/234–9999 or 800/894–6327,* 𝔽𝔸𝕏 *802/234–9990,* 𝕎𝔼𝔹
*www.twinfarms.com. 6 rooms, 8 cottages. 2 bars, dining room, Jap-
anese baths, spa, exercise room, boating, bicycles, ice-skating, cross-
country skiing, recreation room, meeting room. AE, MC, V. FAP.*

$$$ 🏠 **Shire Motel.** Some rooms in this immaculate, in-town motel have
decks overlooking the Ottauquechee River and the Billings Farm. All
have four-poster beds, wing chairs, color TVs, and telephones, and the
suites have Jacuzzi baths and fireplaces. Complimentary coffee is served
each morning. ✉ *46 Pleasant St., 05091,* ☎ *802/457–2211,* 𝔽𝔸𝕏 *802/
457–5836,* 𝕎𝔼𝔹 *www.shiremotel.com. 33 rooms, 3 suites. Refrigerators.
AE, D, MC, V.*

$$–$$$ 🏠 **Winslow House.** New owners Jeff and Kathy Bendis take great pride
★ in their beautifully restored 1872 farmhouse on U.S. 4, which has hardwood and wide pine flooring, fine architectural details, and lovely but
simple antique furnishings. The two guest rooms on the first floor include a suite with a private sitting room and a day bed; the three sec-
ond-floor accommodations include two suites with private sitting rooms
and a spacious room with a cathedral ceiling and private balcony. Breakfast is served by candlelight. ✉ *492 Woodstock Rd. (U.S. 4), 05091,* ☎
802/457–1820, 𝔽𝔸𝕏 *802/457–1820,* 𝕎𝔼𝔹 *www.scenesofvermont.com/
winslowhouse. 2 rooms, 3 suites. Refrigerators. MC, V. BP.*

$$ 🏠 **Deer Brook Inn B&B.** Each spacious, immaculate guest room at this 1820 Colonial-style farmhouse has comfortable, unpretentious furnishings. The quilts are handmade by the inn's owner, Rosemary McGinty, who brings her two golden retrievers out to meet guests on request. The Deer Brook is 5 mi from downtown Woodstock and 10 mi from Killington. ⊠ *5354 U.S. 4, 05091,* ☎ *802/672–3713,* WEB *www. bbhost.com/deerbrookinn. 4 rooms, 1 suite. AE, MC, V. BP.*

Outdoor Activities and Sports

BIKING

Cyclery Plus (⊠ 36 U.S. 4 W, West Woodstock, ☎ 802/457–3377) rents, sells, and services bikes, and also offers a free touring map of local rides.

GOLF

Robert Trent Jones Sr., designed the 18-hole, par-69 course at **Woodstock Country Club** (⊠ South St., ☎ 802/457–6674), which is run by the Woodstock Inn. Greens fees are $32–$75; cart rentals are $38.

HORSEBACK RIDING

Kedron Valley Stables (⊠ Rte. 106, South Woodstock, ☎ 802/457–2734 or 800/225–6301) gives lessons and conducts guided trail rides and excursions in a sleigh and a wagon.

STATE PARK

Coolidge State Park (⊠ Rte. 100A, 2 mi north of Rte. 100, ☎ 802/672–3612) abuts Coolidge State Forest and has campsites (log lean-tos from the 1930s).

Shopping

The **Marketplace at Bridgewater Mills** (⊠ U.S. 4, west of Woodstock, ☎ 802/672–3332) houses shops and attractions in a three-story converted woolen mill. There's an antiques and crafts center, a bookstore, Miranda Thomas pottery, and handsome Charles Shackleton furniture. Sample Vermont stocks gourmet foods and gifts.

Stephen Huneck Studio (⊠ 49 Central St., ☎ 802/457–3206) invites canines and humans to visit the artist's gallery, filled with whimsical animal carvings, prints, and furniture. **Taftsville Country Store** (⊠ U.S. 4, Taftsville, ☎ 802/457–1135 or 800/854–0013) sells an excellent selection of Vermont cheeses, moderately priced wines, and fresh-baked breads and pastries. The **Village Butcher** (⊠ Elm St., ☎ 802/457–2756) is an emporium of Vermont comestibles. **Who Is Sylvia?** (⊠ 26 Central St., ☎ 802/457–1110), in the old firehouse, sells vintage clothing and antique linens, lace, and jewelry.

Sugarbush Farm Inc. (⊠ 591 Sugarbush Farm Rd., ☎ 802/457–1757 or 800/281–1757) taps 5,000 maple trees to make syrup each spring. You can purchase syrup here and take a self-guided tour at any time of the year. The farm also makes excellent cheeses. The road here can be messy, so call for conditions and directions.

Ski Areas

SUICIDE SIX

The site of the first ski tow in the United States (1934), this resort is owned and operated by the Woodstock Inn and Resort. The inn's package plans are remarkably inexpensive, considering the high quality of the accommodations. ⊠ *Pomfret Rd., 05091,* ☎ *802/457–6661; 800/448–7900 lodging; 802/457–6666 snow conditions.*

Downhill. Despite Suicide Six's short vertical of only 650 ft, the skiing is challenging. There are steep runs down the mountain's face, intermediate trails that wind around the hill, and glade skiing. Beginner terrain is mostly toward the bottom. Two double chairlifts and one surface lift service the 23 trails and slopes. The resort also has a snowboard area with a halfpipe. Snowmaking covers 61% of the area's terrain.

Child care. The ski area has no nursery, but baby-sitting can be arranged through the Woodstock Inn if you're a guest. Lessons for children are given by the ski-school staff, and there's a children's ski-and-play park for kids ages 3 to 7.

Summer and year-round activities. Outdoor tennis courts, lighted paddle courts, croquet, and an 18-hole golf course are open in summer. The **Woodstock Health and Fitness Center** (☎ 802/457–6656), open year-round, has an indoor lap pool; indoor tennis, squash, and racquetball courts; whirlpool, steam, sauna, and massage rooms; and exercise and aerobics rooms.

CROSS-COUNTRY

The **Woodstock Ski Touring Center** (☎ 802/457–6674), headquartered at the Woodstock Country Club (⊠ Rte. 106), has 60 km (37 mi) of trails. Equipment and lessons are available.

Plymouth Notch

㉑ *14 mi southwest of Woodstock.*

U.S. president Calvin Coolidge was born and buried in Plymouth Notch, a town that shares his character: low-key and quiet. The perfectly preserved 19th-century buildings of the **Plymouth Notch Historic District** look more like a large farm than a town; in addition to the homestead there's the general store once run by Coolidge's father, a visitor center, a cheese factory (with tasty cheeses for sale), and a one-room schoolhouse. Coolidge's grave is in the cemetery across Route 100A. The Aldrich House, which mounts changing historical exhibits, is open on some weekdays during the off-season. ⊠ *Rte. 100A, 6 mi south of U.S. 4, east of Rte. 100,* ☎ *802/672–3773.* ⌂ *$5.* ☽ *Late May–mid-Oct., daily 9:30–5:30.*

Killington/Pico

㉒ *11 mi (Pico) and 15 mi (Killington) east of Rutland.*

The intersection of U.S. 4 and Route 100 is the heart of central Vermont's ski country, with the Killington, Pico, and Okemo resorts nearby. Unfortunate strip development characterizes the Killington access road, but the views from the top of the mountain are worth the drive.

Dining and Lodging

$$$$ ✕ **Hemingway's.** With a national reputation reinforced by major
★ awards and a loyal clientele, Hemingway's is as good as dining gets in central Vermont. You can tuck into the celebrated cream of garlic soup and a seasonal kaleidoscope of dishes based on native game, fresh seafood, and prime meats. Recent offerings on the prix-fixe, four- to five-course menu have included autumn vegetable strudel with hazelnuts, Arctic char with flageolet beans, and Vermont venison with pumpkin sage pudding and parsnip crisps. Desserts are spectacular, as is the five-course wine tasting menu ($75–$85), which matches each dish with an appropriate glass of wine. Request seating in either the formal, vaulted dining room or the intimate wine cellar. ⊠ *U.S. 4,* ☎ *802/422–3886. AE, D, DC, MC, V. Closed most Mon. and Tues., and early Nov. and mid-Apr.–mid-May. No lunch.*

$$$$ ✕▦ **Red Clover Inn.** Plushly elegant accommodations and fine dining
★ are the attractions at this romantic 1840s hideaway on 13 mountain acres 5 mi from Killington. Among the antiques-filled rooms in the inn

and carriage house are three with fireplaces and whirlpool tubs for two. Many rooms have mountain views. A four-course candlelight dinner, with choice of menu, is served Monday–Saturday evenings. Appetizers might be crispy eggplant, spinach, and Parmesan fritters, or duck ravioli in a wild mushroom broth; some entrée choices have been rosemary-coated rack of lamb or fire-grilled Panama shrimp. *Wine Spectator* magazine cited the inn's wine list as one of the world's most outstanding. You can also choose to include only breakfast in the rate. Pets are allowed in the carriage house. ⊠ *7 Woodward Rd., Mendon 05701,* ☎ *802/775–2290 or 800/752–0571,* FAX *802/773–0594,* WEB *www.redcloverinn.com. 14 rooms. Dining room, pool, hiking. D, MC, V. Closed Apr.–Memorial Day. MAP.*

$$$–$$$$ ✕☲ **Birch Ridge Inn.** A slate-covered carriage way leads to one of Killington's newest inns, a former executive retreat that new owners have converted into an upscale getaway, adding a new wing to the older building. Rooms are decorated in styles that range from Colonial and Shaker to Mission, and all have a sitting area and television. Six rooms have gas fireplaces, and four of these also have whirlpool baths. The intimate dining room offers a four-course meal with two glasses of wine or an à la carte menu. Typical dishes include an appetizer of wild mushroom strudel and entrée such as potato-crusted salmon or pan-seared duckling breast. ⊠ *Butler Rd., at Killington Rd., 05751,* ☎ *802/422–4293 or 800/435–8566,* FAX *802/422–3406,* WEB *www.birchridge.com. 10 rooms. Restaurant, lounge. AE, MC, V. BP, MAP.*

$$$ ☲ **Cortina Inn.** This large lodge and miniresort is comfortable and its location prime. About two-thirds of the contemporary country rooms have private balconies, though the views from them aren't spectacular. Two-room family suites have bunk beds. Horseback riding, sleigh rides, ice-skating, and guided snowmobile, fly-fishing, and mountain-biking tours are among the off-the-slopes activities. ⊠ *U.S. 4, Mendon 05751,* ☎ *802/773–3333 or 800/451–6108,* FAX *802/775–6948,* WEB *www.cortinainn.com. 89 rooms, 7 suites. 2 restaurants, bar, indoor pool, hot tub, sauna, 8 tennis courts, health club, ice-skating, sleigh rides. AE, D, DC, MC, V. BP.*

$$–$$$ ☲ **Mountain Meadows Lodge.** The accommodations at this miniresort simple and a bit worn but comfortable, and the lodge offers activities for kids and adults that should exhaust even the most stalwart. There's fishing, boating (rowboats, sailboats, and canoes), and swimming in the lake, hiking on the Appalachian Trial, yard games, and pony rides. Kids are invited to the barn to help feed the animals. In winter, the lodge has sleds and dog sleds, toboggans, Norwegian kick sleds, snowshoes, and ice skates for use; a cross-country ski center next door rents skis. Mountain Meadow Munchkins provides child care. Dinner is served Friday and Saturday nights, and a light menu is available Sunday–Thursday from noon until 7. ⊠ *285 Thundering Brook Rd., 05751,* ☎ *802/775–1010 or 800/370–4567,* FAX *802/773–4459,* WEB *www.mtmeadowslodge. com. 20 rooms, 1 suite with fireplace. Restaurant, lake, pool, sauna, hiking, boating, fishing, recreation room, children's programs. AE, D, MC, V. Closed mid-Oct.–mid-Nov. BP, MAP.*

$–$$:   ✕☲ **Summit Lodge.** Three miles from Killington Peak, this rustic two-story country lodge caters to a varied crowd of ski enthusiasts, who are warmly met by the lodge's mascots—a pair of Saint Bernards. Country decor and antiques blend with modern conveniences to create a relaxed atmosphere. The restaurant ($$) serves continental specialties such as rack of lamb and chicken Birmingham—a boneless breast of chicken with spinach, garlic, feta cheese, and sun-dried tomatoes. ⊠ *Killington Rd. 05751,* ☎ *802/422–3535 or 800/635–6343,* FAX *802/ 422–3536,* WEB *www.summitlodgevermont.com. 43 rooms, 2 suites.*

Restaurant, bar, pool, pond, hot tub, massage, sauna, ice-skating, nightclub, recreation room. AE, DC, MC, V. BP.

Nightlife and the Arts

The pub at the **Inn at Long Trail** (⊠ U.S. 4, ☎ 802/775–7181) hosts Irish music on weekends. The **Pickle Barrel** (⊠ Killington Rd., ☎ 802/422–3035), a favorite with the après-ski crowd, presents up-and-coming acts and can get pretty rowdy. The **Wobbly Barn** (⊠ Killington Rd., ☎ 802/422–3392), with dancing to blues and rock, is open during ski season.

Outdoor Activities and Sports

FISHING

Gifford Woods State Park's Kent Pond (⊠ Rte. 100, ½ mi north of U.S. 4, ☎ 802/775–5354) is a terrific fishing hole. Campsites are available.

GOLF

The 18-hole, par 71 **Green Mountain National Golf Course** (⊠ Rte. 100 N, Sherburne, ☎ 802/422–4653) has earned accolades as one of the state's best. Greens fees are $52 mid week and $57 weekends in May and June; $57 midweek and $62 weekends from late June through fall. Cart rental is $18 per person.

ICE-SKATING

Cortina Inn has an ice-skating rink and offers sleigh rides; you can also skate on Summit Pond.

Ski Areas

KILLINGTON

"Megamountain," "Beast of the East," and plain "huge" are apt descriptions of Killington. The American Skiing Company operates Killington and its neighbor Pico and over the past several years has improved lifts, snowmaking capabilities, and lodging options. A project is under way to join Pico and Killington by interconnecting trails and lifts, Green Mountain College at Killington is scheduled to open in winter 2002, and future plans call for the creation of a giant alpine village at the complex. The resort has the longest ski season in the East and some of the best package plans, as well as several new terrain parks. Killington's après-ski activities are plentiful and have been rated best in Vermont by the national ski magazines. With a single call to Killington's hot line or a visit to their Web site, skiers can plan an entire vacation: choose accommodations; book air or railroad transportation; and arrange for rental equipment and ski lessons. Killington ticket holders can also ski at Pico. ⊠ *400 Killington Rd., 05751,* ☎ *802/422–8763; 800/621–6867 lodging; 802/422–3261 snow conditions.* WEB www.killington.com.

Downhill. It would probably take several weeks to test all 200 trails on the seven mountains of the Killington complex, even though all except Pico interconnect. About 70% of the 1,123 acres of skiing terrain can be covered with machine-made snow. Transporting skiers to the peaks of this complex are 32 lifts, including two gondolas, 12 quads (including six high-speed express quads), six triples, and a Magic Carpet. The K-1 Gondola goes to the area's highest elevation, at 4,241 ft off Killington Peak, and a vertical drop of 3,091 ft to the base of the Skyeship, the world's fastest and first heated eight-passenger lift, complete with piped-in music. The Skyeship base station has a rotisserie, food court, and a coffee bar. The skiing includes everything from Outer Limits, one of the steepest and most challenging trails anywhere in the country, to the 6½-mi Great Eastern Trail. In the Fusion Zones, underbrush and low branches have been cleared away to provide tree skiing. The Terrain Park has the longest run in the east.

Child care. Nursery care is available for children from 6 weeks to 6 years old. There's a one-hour instruction program for youngsters from ages 3 to 8; those from 6 to 12 can join an all-day program.

Summer activities. The Killington/Pico complex has a host of activities, including rides up the mountain on the Killington Skyeship or K1 Express Gondola (☎ 802/422–6200), an alpine slide, a "Bungee Thing" ride, and a swimming pool. The resort rents mountain bikes and advises hikers.

PICO SKI RESORT

Although it's only 5 mi down the road from Killington, Pico—one of the state's first ski areas—has long been a favorite among people looking for old New England–style skiing, with lots of glades and winding and narrow trails. When modern lifts were installed and a village square was constructed at the base, some feared a change in atmosphere might occur, but the condo-hotel, restaurants, and shops have not altered the essential nature of the area. ⊠ *2 Sherburne Pass, Rutland 05701,* ☎ *802/422–3333; 800/621–6867 lodging; 802/422–3261 snow conditions.*

Downhill. Many of the 42 trails are advanced to expert, with two intermediate bail-out trails for the timid. The rest of the mountain's 2,000 ft of vertical terrain is mostly intermediate or easier. The mountain has nine lifts including two high-speed quads, two triples, and three double chairs and has 85% snowmaking coverage. Snowboarding is permitted everywhere on Pico, and there is a Terrain Park. For instruction of any kind, head to the Alpine Learning Center.

Child care. Pico's nursery takes children from ages 6 months to 6 years and provides indoor activities and outdoor play. The ski school has full- and half-day instruction programs for children ages 3 to 12.

Summer and year-round activities. A sports center (☎ 802/773–1786) at the base of the mountain has fitness facilities, a 75-ft pool, whirlpool tub, saunas, and a massage room. You can also take advantage of activities at Killington.

CROSS-COUNTRY SKIING

Mountain Meadows (⊠ Thundering Brook Rd., ☎ 802/775–7077 or 800/221–0598) has 57 km (34½ mi) of groomed trails and 10 km (6 mi) of marked outlying trails. You can also access 500 acres of backcountry skiing. **Mountain Top Inn and Resort** ☎ 802/483–6089 or 800/445–2100) is mammoth, with 120 km (72 mi) of trails, 80 km (49 mi) of which are groomed.

Rutland

㉓ *15 mi southwest of Killington, 32 mi south of Middlebury, 31 mi west of Woodstock, 47 mi west of White River Junction.*

On and around U.S. 7 in Rutland are strips of shopping centers and a seemingly endless row of traffic lights, although the mansions of the marble magnates who made the town famous still command whatever attention can be safely diverted from the traffic. Rutland's compact downtown, one of only a handful of urban centers in Vermont, has experienced a modest revival and is worth an hour's stroll. The area's traditional economic ties to railroading and marble, the latter an industry that became part of such illustrious structures as the central research building of the New York Public Library in New York City, have been rapidly eclipsed by the growth of the Pico and Killington ski areas to the east. If you're planning to visit more than one of the area's attractions, ask about the "One Great Day" admission at the Vermont Marble Exhibit, New England Maple Museum, or Wilson Castle.

The **Chaffee Center for the Visual Arts** (✉ 16 S. Main St., ☎ 802/775–0356; closed Tues.) exhibits and sells the output of more than 250 Vermont artists who work in various media.

The highlight of the Rutland area, the **Vermont Marble Exhibit** includes a sculptor-in-residence who transforms stone into finished works of art or commerce (you can choose firsthand the marble for a custom-built kitchen counter). The gallery illustrates the many industrial and artistic applications of marble—there's a hall of presidents and a replica of Leonardo da Vinci's *Last Supper* in marble—and depicts the industry's history via exhibits and a video. Factory seconds and foreign and domestic marble items are for sale. ✉ *62 Main St., Proctor (4 mi north of Rutland, off Rte. 3),* ☎ *802/459–2300 or 800/427–1396.* 🎟 *$6.* ⏲ *Mid-May–Oct., daily 9–5:30.*

A 32-room mansion built in 1888 by a doctor, **Wilson Castle** comes complete with turrets, towers, stained glass, and 13 fireplaces. It's magnificently furnished with European and Asian objets d'art. Head west out of Rutland on Route 4A and follow signs. ✉ *West Proctor Rd., Proctor,* ☎ *802/773–3284,* WEB *www.wilsoncastle.com.* 🎟 *$7.* ⏲ *Late May–mid-Oct., daily 9–5:30.*

Dining and Lodging

$$ ✕ **The Palms.** This Rutland landmark, which opened its doors on Palm Sunday in 1933, was the first restaurant in the state to serve pizza. It's still owned by the same family. The menu is primarily southern Italian, with specialties such as fried mozzarella; antipasto Neapolitan (with provolone, pepperoni, mild peppers, anchovies, and house dressing); and the chef's personal creation, veal à la Palms—veal scallops topped with mushrooms, two kinds of cheese, and a special tomato sauce. Dessert choices are fairly pedestrian. ✉ *36 Strongs St.,* ☎ *802/773–2367. AE, DC, MC, V. Closed Sun. No lunch.*

$$$$ ✕🏨 **Mountain Top Inn and Resort.** One of the state's most spectacular family resorts occupies 500 lofty acres overlooking secluded Chittenden Reservoir and the Green Mountain National Forest. It's essentially an outdoorsperson's inn, with an equestrian center, swimming and canoeing, fishing, trap and skeet shooting, and a golf school with a five-hole pitch-and-putt course and driving range. Winter brings cross-country skiing on more than 70 mi of trails, sleigh rides, and skating. The dinner menu ($$$) runs to uncomplicated American fare such as rack of lamb and roast pork tenderloin and unadventurous French fare such as sole meunière. A tip: Opt for the more-expensive deluxe rooms, which are larger and have spectacular views. If you wish, breakfast and dinner can be included in the rate. ✉ *195 Mountaintop Rd., Chittenden 05737,* ☎ *802/483–2311 or 800/445–2100,* FAX *802/483–6373,* WEB *www.mountaintopinn.com. 35 rooms, 6 cottages, 6 chalets. Restaurant, pool, driving range, horseback riding, beach, boating, fishing, ice-skating, cross-country skiing, sleigh rides. AE, MC, V. Closed late Oct.–late Dec. and mid-Mar.–mid-May.*

$$–$$$ 🏨 **Inn at Rutland.** One alternative to Rutland's chain motel and hotel accommodations is this renovated Victorian mansion. The ornate oak staircase lined with heavy embossed gold and leather wainscoting leads to rooms that blend modern bathrooms with late 19th-century touches such as elaborate ceiling moldings and frosted glass. The two large common rooms, one with a fireplace, have views of surrounding mountains and valleys. The meal plan varies. ✉ *70 N. Main St., 05701,* ☎ *802/773–0575 or 800/808–0575,* FAX *802/775–3506,* WEB *www.innatrutland.com. 11 rooms. AE, D, MC, V. BP, CP.*

Nightlife and the Arts

Crossroads Arts Council (⊠ 39 E. Center St., ☎ 802/775–5413) presents music, opera, dance, jazz, and theater year-round at venues throughout the region.

Outdoor Activities and Sports

Half Moon State Park's principal attraction is Half Moon Pond (⊠ Town Rd., 3½ mi off Rte. 30, west of Hubbardton, ☎ 802/273–2848). The park has nature trails, campsites, and boat and canoe rentals.

Shopping

Tuttle Antiquarian Books (⊠ 28 S. Main St., ☎ 802/773–8229) has a large collection of books on Asia. The store stocks rare and out-of-print books, genealogies, local histories, and miniature books.

Brandon

㉔ *15 mi northwest of Rutland.*

Straddling busy U.S. 7, Brandon nevertheless has broad side streets lined with gracious Victorian houses, lodging at the landmark Brandon Inn or at smaller B&Bs, and ready access to the mountain scenery and recreation of nearby Brandon Gap.

The **Stephen A. Douglas Birthplace** commemorates the "Little Giant" (he stood only 5 ft, 2 in tall), best known for his debates with Abraham Lincoln in 1858. Douglas, who became a U.S. representative and senator from Illinois, was born here on April 23, 1813. His boyhood home and a monument to his memory are just north of the village, next to the Baptist church. ⊠ *U.S. 7.* ☎ *802/247–6569 or 802/247–6332.* ☞ *Free.* ☉ *June–Labor Day, Thurs. 2–5, or by appointment.*

Maple syrup is Vermont's signature product, and the **New England Maple Museum and Gift Shop** explains the history and process of turning maple sap into syrup with murals, exhibits, and a slide show. ⊠ *U.S. 7, Pittsford (9 mi south of Brandon),* ☎ *802/483–9414.* ☞ *$1.75 museum.* ☉ *Late May–Oct., daily 8:30–5:30; Nov.–Dec. and mid-Mar.–late May, daily 10–4.*

Dining and Lodging

$$$$ ✕📷 **Blueberry Hill Inn.** If you're looking for total peace and quiet, this is the place. In the Green Mountain National Forest and 5½ mi off a mountain pass on a dirt road, Blueberry Hill is an idyllic spot with lush gardens, a stream, and a pond with a wood-fired sauna on its bank. Many rooms have views of the mountains; all are furnished with antiques, quilts, and hot-water bottles to warm winter beds. Three rooms have lofts (good for families), and the Moosalamoo Room is in a private cottage. The restaurant menu has dishes such as garlic fish soup with mussels and venison fillet with cherry sauce. A ski-touring center with 80 km (50 mi) of marked trails focuses on hiking in the summer. Rates include breakfast and dinner, but you can choose breakfast only on weekdays. ⊠ *Forest Rd. 32, Goshen 05733,* ☎ *802/247–6735 or 800/448–0707,* ℻ *802/247–3983,* ☒ *www.blueberryhillinn.com. 11 rooms and 1 cottage. Restaurant, sauna, hiking, volleyball, crosscountry skiing, mountain bikes. MC, V. MAP.*

$$$ 📷 **Lilac Inn.** The bridal suite at this Greek Revival mansion, which bills itself as a romantic retreat, is one of the most-elegant inn rooms in Vermont, with a pewter canopy bed, whirlpool bath for two, and fireplace. The other rooms, all uniquely furnished and with claw-foot tubs and handheld European shower heads, are also charming. Breakfast is served on the patio or in the bright, gleaming dining room, both of which overlook the lovely gardens with 15 varieties of lilacs. The inn

is a popular spot for weddings on summer weekends, and is home to two cats. ⊠ *53 Park St./Rte. 73, 05733,* ☎ *802/247–5463 or 800/221–0720,* ⎕ⱯⱯ *802/247–5499,* ⎕ⱤⱤ *www.lilacinn.com. 9 rooms. Restaurant. AE, D, MC, V. Restaurant closed Nov.–Apr. BP.*

Outdoor Activities and Sports

Moosalamoo (☎ 800/448–0707) is the name given by a partnership of public and private entities to a 20,000-acre chunk of Green Mountain National Forest land (along with several private holdings) just northeast of Brandon. More than 60 mi of trails take hikers, mountain bikers, and cross-country skiers through some of Vermont's most gorgeous mountain terrain. Attractions include Branbury State Park, on the shores of Lake Dunmore; secluded Silver Lake, a trout-fishing mecca; and sections of both the Long Trail and Catamount Trail (the latter is a Massachusetts-to-Québec ski trail). Both the Blueberry Hill Inn and Churchill House Inn (☎ 802/247–3078) have direct public access to trails.

GOLF

Neshobe Golf Club (⊠ Rte. 73, east of Brandon, ☎ 802/247–3611) has 18 holes of par-72 golf on a bent-grass course totaling nearly 6,500 yards. The Green Mountain views are terrific. Several local inns offer golf packages.

HIKING

About 8 mi east of Brandon on Route 73, a trail that takes an hour to hike starts at Brandon Gap and climbs steeply up **Mt. Horrid.** South of Lake Dunmore on Route 53, a large turnout marks a trail (a hike of about two hours) to the **Falls of Lana.** Four trails—two short ones of less than a mile each and two longer ones—lead to the old abandoned Revolutionary War fortifications at **Mt. Independence**; to reach them, take the first left turn off Route 73 west of Orwell and go right at the fork. The road will turn to gravel and once again will fork; take a sharp left-hand turn toward a small marina. The parking lot is on the left at the top of the hill.

Shopping

The **Warren Kimble Gallery & Studio** (⊠ Off Rte. 73 E, ☎ 802/247–3026 or 800/954–6253) is the workplace, gallery, and gift shop of the nationally renowned folk artist.

Middlebury

★ ㉕ *17 mi north of Brandon, 34 mi south of Burlington.*

In the late 1800s Middlebury was the largest Vermont community west of the Green Mountains: an industrial center of river-powered wool, grain, and marble mills. This is Robert Frost country; Vermont's late poet laureate spent 23 summers at a farm east of Middlebury. Otter Creek, the state's longest river, traverses the town center. Still a cultural and economic hub amid the Champlain Valley's serene pastoral patchwork, the town and countryside invite a day of exploration.

Smack in the middle of town, **Middlebury College** (☎ 802/443–5000), founded in 1800, was conceived as a more godly alternative to the worldly University of Vermont. The college has no religious affiliation today, however. The early-19th-century stone buildings contrast provocatively with the postmodern architecture of the Center for the Arts and the sports center. Music, theater, and dance performances take place throughout the year at the **Wright Memorial Theatre** and **Center for the Arts.**

The **Middlebury College Museum of Art** has a permanent collection of paintings, photography, works on paper, and sculpture. ⊠ *Center for* *the Arts, Rte. 30,* ☎ *802/443–5007.* 🎫 *Free.* ☉ *Tues.–Fri. 10–5, weekends noon–5. Closed major holidays and last 2 wks of Aug.*

The **Vermont Folklife Center** exhibits photography, antiques, folk paintings, manuscripts, and other artifacts and contemporary works that examine facets of Vermont life. The center is in the basement of the restored 1801 home of Gamaliel Painter, the founder of Middlebury College. ✉ *3 Court St.,* ☎ *802/388–4964.* 🎫 *Donations accepted.* ☉ *Gallery May–Dec., Tues.–Sat. 11–4. Oral history archive weekdays 10–4.*

The **Sheldon Museum,** an 1829 marble merchant's house, is the oldest community museum in the country. The period rooms contain Vermont-made textiles, furniture, toys, clothes, kitchen tools, and paintings. ✉ *1 Park St.,* ☎ *802/388–2117.* 🎫 *$4.* ☉ *Mon.–Sat. 10–5; open occasional Sundays.*

More than a crafts store, the **Vermont State Craft Center at Frog Hollow** mounts changing exhibitions and displays exquisite work in wood, glass, metal, clay, and fiber by more than 250 Vermont artisans. The center, which overlooks Otter Creek, sponsors classes taught by some of those artists. There are other centers in Burlington and Manchester. ✉ *1 Mill St.,* ☎ *802/388–3177,* WEB *www.froghollow.com.* ☉ *Call for hrs.*

The Morgan horse—the official state animal—has an even temper, good stamina, and slightly truncated legs in proportion to its body. The University of Vermont's **UVM Morgan Horse Farm,** about 2½ mi west of Middlebury, is a breeding and training center where in summer you can tour the stables and paddocks. ✉ *74 Battell Dr., off Horse Farm Rd. (follow signs off Rte. 23), Weybridge,* ☎ *802/388–2011.* 🎫 *$4.* ☉ *May–Oct., daily 9–5 (last tour at 4).*

About 10 mi east of town on Route 125 (1 mi west of Middlebury College's Bread Loaf campus), the easy ¾-mi **Robert Frost Interpretive Trail** winds through quiet woodland. Plaques along the way bear quotations from Frost's poems. A picnic area is across the road from the trailhead.

OFF THE BEATEN PATH

LAKE CHAMPLAIN MARITIME MUSEUM – A replica of Benedict Arnold's Revolutionary War gunboat is part of this museum, which documents centuries of activity on the historically significant lake. The museum commemorates the days when steamships sailed along the coast of northern Vermont carrying logs, livestock, and merchandise bound for New York City. Among the 13 exhibit areas is a blacksmith's shop. A one-room stone schoolhouse built in the late 1810s houses historic maps, nautical prints, and maritime objects. Also on site are a nautical archaeology center, a conservation laboratory, and a restaurant. ✉ *Basin Harbor Rd., Basin Harbor (14 mi west of Bristol, 7 mi west of Vergennes),* ☎ *802/475–2022.* 🎫 *$7.* ☉ *Late May–Oct., daily 10–5.*

Dining and Lodging

$$–$$$ ✕ **Fire & Ice.** A 55-item salad bar (with peel-and-eat shrimp), prime rib, steak, fish, and a house specialty—homemade mashed potatoes—are all choices at this family friendly spot. Although large, the space is divided into several rooms (each with a different theme) and has numerous intimate nooks and crannies for diners who seek privacy. Families may want to request a table next to the "children's corner," which is outfitted with cushions and a VCR. Sunday dinner begins at 1. ✉ *26 Seymour St.,* ☎ *802/388–7166 or 800/367–7166. AE, D, DC, MC, V. No lunch Mon.*

$$–$$$ ✕ **Roland's Place.** Chef Roland Gaujac prepares classic French and
★ American dishes, elegantly served in a house built in 1796. He opened
his restaurant overlooking the Adirondacks after working as a chef in
various parts of the world, including the French dining room in Los
Angeles's Four Seasons Hotel. Some dishes use locally raised lamb, turkey,
and venison; shrimp with chipotle and roasted garlic vinaigrette on fried
ravioli is one entrée. A prix-fixe menu is available, and a special menu
served daily from 5 to 6 lists numerous à la carte dishes for just $9.
The restaurant has three moderately priced guest rooms upstairs; the
rate includes a full breakfast. ⊠ U.S. 7, New Haven, ☎ 802/453–6309.
AE, DC, MC, V. Closed Mon. No dinner Sun. Nov.–Apr.

$$–$$$ ✕ **Woody's.** In addition to cool jazz, diner-deco light fixtures, and ab-
stract paintings, Woody's has a view of Otter Creek below. Seafood
and Vermont lamb are the specialties—some folks say the Caesar salad
is the best in the state. Sunday brunch is a popular event. ⊠ 5 Bakery
La., ☎ 802/388–4182. AE, MC, V.

$$–$$$$ ☷ **Middlebury Inn.** Gracious New England–style hospitality is served
up along with traditional Yankee fare in this three-story, brick Geor-
gian building, which has been an inn since 1827. The property now
encompasses a contemporary motel (decorated, like the rooms in the
inn, with Early American-style furnishings) and the Victorian-era
Porter House Mansion. Rooms have phones, TVs, and hair dryers; those
facing the lovely town green are subject to the noise of passing traffic.
Plan to arrive between 3 and 4 for the inn's complimentary afternoon
tea, served daily except holidays. In nice weather, you can have lunch
on the wicker-furnished porch. Dinner can be included in the price. ⊠
14 Courthouse Sq., 05753, ☎ 802/388–4961 or 800/842–4666, FAX
802/388–4563, WEB www.middleburyinn.com. 75 rooms. Restaurant.
AE, D, MC, V. CP.

$$–$$$ ☷ **Swift House Inn.** The main building at Swift House, the Georgian
★ home of a 19th-century governor and his philanthropist daughter,
contains white-panel wainscoting, mahogany and marble fireplaces, and
cherry paneling in the dining room. The rooms—most with Oriental
rugs and nine with fireplaces—have period reproductions such as
canopy beds, curtains with swags, and claw-foot tubs. Some bathrooms
have double whirlpool tubs. Rooms in the gatehouse suffer from street
noise but are charming; a carriage house holds six luxury accommo-
dations. ⊠ 25 Stewart La., 05753, ☎ 802/388–9925, FAX 802/388–9927,
WEB www.swifthouseinn.com. 21 rooms. Pub, sauna, steam room. AE,
D, DC, MC, V. CP.

$$ ☷ **Lemon Fair.** This tidy, unfussy bed-and-breakfast occupies a building dating from 1796; it was tiny Bridport's first church before it was
moved to its present location overlooking the town green in 1819. Furnishings are Early American in style, the grounds are spacious, and the
entire establishment is kid-friendly. The common room is a cozy spot
in which to curl up by the fireplace. Lemon Fair is just 8 mi from downtown Middlebury and 4 mi from Lake Champlain. The owners live next
door and will rent out the entire house. ⊠ Crown Point Rd., Bridport
05734, ☎ 802/758–9238, FAX 802/758–2135, WEB www.limewalk.com/
lemonfair. 3 rooms; 1 suite. Pool. No credit cards. BP.

Outdoor Activities and Sports
The **Bike and Ski Touring Center** (⊠ 74 Main St., ☎ 802/388–6666)
has rentals and repairs.

HIKING

On Route 116, about 5½ mi north of East Middlebury, a U.S. Forest
Service sign marks a dirt road that forks to the right and leads to the
start of the two- to three-hour hike to **Abbey Pond,** which has a beaver
lodge and dam as well as a view of Robert Frost Mountain.

Shopping

Historic Marble Works (⊠ Maple St., ☎ 802/388–3701), a renovated marble manufacturing facility, is a collection of unique shops set amid quarrying equipment and factory buildings. **De Pasquale's** (☎ 802/388–3385) prepares subs and fresh fried fish platters for take-out and sells imported Italian groceries and wines. **Danforth Pewterers** (☎ 802/388–0098) sells handcrafted pewter vases, lamps, and tableware. **Holy Cow** (⊠ 44 Main St., ☎ 802/388–6737) is where Woody Jackson sells his Holstein cattle–inspired T-shirts, memorabilia, and paintings.

Bristol

❷❻ *13 mi northeast of Middlebury.*

At the northeastern threshold of the Green Mountain National Forest, where the rolling farmlands of the Champlain Valley meet the foothills of Vermont's main mountain chain, Bristol has a redbrick 19th-century Main Street that reflects the town's prosperous heyday as the center of a number of wood-products industries. Almost overshadowing the still-busy little downtown are the brooding heights of the Bristol Cliffs Wilderness Area, a section of national forest that has been assured permanent status as a primitive, roadless tract.

Dining

$–$$ ✕ **Mary's at Baldwin Creek.** This restaurant and B&B in a 1790 farmhouse provides a truly inspired culinary experience. The "summer kitchen" has a fireplace and rough-hewn barn-board walls, and the main dining room is done in pastels. The innovative fare includes a superb garlic soup, Vermont rack of lamb with a rosemary-mustard sauce, and duck cassis smoked over applewood. Farmhouse dinners on Wednesdays in summer highlight Vermont products. Four guest rooms ($$–$$$) above the restaurant have simple, comfortable furnishings. ⊠ *Rte. 116,* ☎ *802/453–2432. AE, MC, V, DC. Closed Mon. and Tues. in winter. No lunch.*

Outdoor Activities and Sports

A challenging 32-mi bicycle ride starts in Bristol. Take North Street from the traffic light in town and continue north to Monkton Ridge and on to Hinesburg. To return, follow Route 116 south through Starksboro and back to Bristol.

Shopping

Folkheart (⊠ 18 Main St., ☎ 802/453–4101) carries unusual jewelry, toys, and crafts from around the world.

En Route   From Bristol, Route 17 winds eastward up and over the **Appalachian Gap,** one of Vermont's most panoramic mountain passes. The views from the top and on the way down the other side toward the ski town of Waitsfield are a just reward for the challenging drive.

Waitsfield

❷❼ *20 mi east of Bristol, 55 mi north of Rutland, 32 mi northeast of Middlebury, 19 mi southwest of Montpelier.*

Although in close proximity to Sugarbush and Mad River Glen ski areas, the Mad River valley towns of Waitsfield and Warren have maintained a decidedly low-key atmosphere. The gently carved ridges cradling the valley and the swell of pastures and fields lining the river seem to keep further notions of ski-resort sprawl at bay. With a map from the Sugarbush Chamber of Commerce you can investigate back roads off Route 100 that have exhilarating valley views.

Dining and Lodging

$$$–$$$$ ✕ **Spotted Cow.** Jay and Renate Young, who were previously involved in running the Sugarbush Inn, are attracting a steady clientele to their intimate dining room decorated with contemporary furnishings and warm woods. Lunch features items such as a fresh spinach salad with fried oysters and Bermuda codfish cakes (Mr. Young's family owns the Lantana Colony Club in Bermuda). For dinner, try a ragout of seafood in puff pastry or grilled breast of duckling with foie gras. Sunday brunch is served from 10:30–3. ⊠ *Bridge St.,* ☎ *802/496–5151. MC, V. Closed Mon.*

$$–$$$ ✕ **Common Man.** Although the chef is Parisian, he occasionally sneaks in dishes such as *pescespada de merida* (grilled New England swordfish steak) and ravioli *alla calabrese.* Otherwise, expect to find classics such as *entrecôte maison* (sirloin steak with an herb and garlic butter sauce), rack of lamb, and roast duck. The restaurant, a local institution since 1972, is housed in a mid-1800s barn with hand-hewn rafters and crystal chandeliers. Dinner is served by candlelight. ⊠ *German Flats Rd., Warren,* ☎ *802/583–2800. AE, D, MC, V. No lunch. Closed Mon. Easter–Christmas.*

$ ✕ **American Flatbread.** For ideologically and gastronomically sound pizza, you won't find a better place in the Green Mountains than this modest haven between Waitsfield and Warren. Organic flour and produce fuel mind and body, and Vermont hardwood fuels the earth-and-stone oven. The "punctuated equilibrium flatbread," made with olive-pepper goat cheese and rosemary, is a dream, as are more traditional pizzas. It's open Monday–Thursday 7:30 AM–8 PM for take-out, and Friday and Saturday 5:30–9 for dinner as well. ⊠ *Rte. 100,* ☎ *802/496–8856. Reservations not accepted. MC, V. Closed Sun.*

$$$$ ✕🏨 **Pitcher Inn.** In 1997, four years after burning to the ground, this
★ local institution was reborn in an incarnation of *haute luxe.* Designed by architect David E. Sellers, each guest room has its own motif. In the Mallard, a curved ceiling gives the illusion of a duck blind, and the windows are etched and frosted in the likeness of the banks of a marsh. The Mountain Suite has a mountain mural, and a unique slate and mirror combination renders the effect of a waterfall. All rooms have original Vermont-inspired artwork, stereos, and a TV/VCR; most have fireplaces and steam showers. The formal dining room focuses on locally grown produce and wild game; you can also dine in the private wine cellar, one of the state's finest. Arrangements for activities such as skiing and hiking can be made here. ⊠ *Box 347, 275 Main St., Warren 05674,* ☎ *802/496–6350 or 888/867–4824,* 🅵🅰🆇 *802/496–6354,* 🆆🅴🅱 *www.pitcherinn.com. 9 rooms, 2 suites. Restaurant, billiard room, in-room data ports. AE, MC, V. BP.*

$$–$$$$ 🏨 **Inn at the Round Barn Farm.** Art exhibits have replaced cows in the big round barn here (one of only eight in the state), but the Shaker-style building still dominates the farm's 215 acres. The inn's guest rooms are in the 1806 farmhouse, where books line the walls of the cream-colored library. The rooms are sumptuous, with eyelet-trimmed sheets, elaborate four-poster beds, rich-colored wallpapers, and brass wall lamps for easy bedtime reading. Seven have fireplaces, four have whirlpool tubs, and five have steam showers. The inn offers snowshoe packages and tours. ⊠ *1661 E. Warren Rd., 05673,* ☎ *802/496–2276,* 🅵🅰🆇 *802/496–8832,* 🆆🅴🅱 *www.innatroundbarn.com. 12 rooms. Indoor pool, cross-country skiing, recreation room, library. AE, D, MC, V. BP.*

$$–$$$$ 🏨 **Tucker Hill Lodge.** The 1940s lodge has a new owner and a new look. Local innkeeper David Jackson purchased the property in 1999 and modernized the rooms; all have country-casual furnishings, antiques, phones, and TV/VCRs. There are fireplaces in the living room, dining

room, and pub. The menu at the Steak Place includes a 24-ounce steak and barbecue ribs, as well as fish and vegetarian choices. Lighter fare is served in the pub area for late-night patrons. Dinner can be included in the room rate if desired. ⊠ *Rte. 17, 05673,* ☎ *802/496–3983 or 800/543–7841,* FAX *802/496–3203,* WEB *www.tuckerhill.com. 18 rooms, 1 suite. Restaurant, bar, in-room data ports, pool, tennis court, hiking. AE, MC, V. CP.*

$$ 🏠 **Beaver Pond Farm Inn.** This small 1840 farmhouse less than a mile from Sugarbush overlooks rolling meadows and is next door to Sugarbush Golf Course. Guest rooms are decorated simply, and bathrooms are ample; the inn's focal point is the huge deck. The hearty breakfast might include orange-yogurt pancakes; other meals may be provided at guests' requests. The inn has a limited practice driving range, and the innkeeper is a fly-fishing guide. ⊠ *1225 Golf Course Rd., Warren 05674,* ☎ *802/583–2861,* FAX *802/583–2860,* WEB *www.beaverpondfarminn. com. 5 rooms. Dining room, driving range. MC, V. Closed Jan.–mid-May. BP.*

Nightlife and the Arts

The Back Room at **Chez Henri** (⊠ Sugarbush Village, ☎ 802/583–2600) has a pool table and is popular with the après-ski and late-night dance crowds. Local bands play music at **Gallagher's** (⊠ Rtes. 100 and 17, ☎ 802/496–8800).

The **Green Mountain Cultural Center** (⊠ Inn at the Round Barn Farm, E. Warren Rd., ☎ 802/496–7722), a nonprofit organization, brings concerts and art exhibits, as well as educational workshops, to the Mad River valley. The **Valley Players** (⊠ Rte. 100, ☎ 802/496–9612) present musicals, dramas, follies, and holiday shows.

Outdoor Activities and Sports

BIKING

The popular 14-mi Waitsfield–Warren loop begins when you cross the covered bridge in Waitsfield. Keep right on East Warren Road to the four-way intersection in East Warren; continue straight, then bear right, riding down Brook Road to the village of Warren. Return by turning right (north) on Route 100 back toward Waitsfield.

Clearwater Sports (⊠ Rte. 100, ☎ 802/496–2708) rents canoes, kayaks, and camping equipment, and offers guided river trips and white-water instruction in the warm months; in the winter, the store leads snowshoe tours and rents telemark equipment, snowshoes, and one-person Mad River Rocket sleds.

GOLF

Great views and challenging play are the trademarks of the Robert Trent Jones–designed 18-hole, par-72 course at **Sugarbush Resort** (⊠ Golf Course Rd., ☎ 802/583–6727). The greens fee runs from $32 to $52; a cart (sometimes mandatory) costs $17.

SLEIGH RIDES

The 100-year-old sleigh of the **Lareau Farm Country Inn** (⊠ Rte. 100, ☎ 802/496–4949) cruises along the banks of the Mad River.

Shopping

ART AND ANTIQUES

Luminosity Stained Glass Studios (☎ 802/496–2231), inside the converted Old Church on Rte. 100, specializes in stained glass, custom lighting, and art glass. **Cabin Fever Quilts** (⊠ Rte. 100, ☎ 802/496–2287), which shares a building with Luminosity Stained Glass Studios, sells fine new handmade quilts.

CRAFTS

All Things Bright and Beautiful (⊠ Bridge St., ☎ 802/496–3997) is a 12-room Victorian house jammed to the rafters with stuffed animals of all shapes, sizes, and colors as well as folk art, prints, and collectibles. **Warren Village Pottery** (⊠ Main St., Warren, ☎ 802/496–4162) sells handcrafted wares from its retail shop and specializes in functional stoneware pottery.

Ski Areas

MAD RIVER GLEN

In 1995, Mad River Glen became the first ski area to be owned by a cooperative formed by the skiing community. The hundreds of share-holders are dedicated, knowledgeable skiers devoted to keeping ski-ing what it used to be—a pristine alpine experience. Mad River's unkempt aura attracts rugged individualists looking for less-polished terrain: the area was developed in the late 1940s and has changed rel-atively little since then. It remains one of only four resorts in the coun-try that bans snowboarding. ⊠ *Rte. 17, 05673,* ☎ *802/496–3551; 800/ 850–6742 cooperative office; 802/496–2001 snow conditions,* WEB *www.madriverglen.com.*

Downhill. Mad River is steep, with natural slopes that follow the con-tours of the mountain. The terrain changes constantly on the 45 in-terconnected trails, of which 30% are beginner, 35% are intermediate, and 35% are expert. Intermediate and novice terrain is regularly groomed. Five lifts, including a single 1940s chairlift that may be the only lift of its vintage still carrying skiers, service the mountain's 2,037-ft vertical drop. Most of Mad River's trails (85%) are covered only by natural snow.

Telemark. The "Mecca of Free-Heel Skiing" sponsors telemark pro-grams through the season and each March hosts the North America Telemark Organization, which attracts up to 1,200 skiers.

Child care. The nursery is for children ages 3 weeks to 6 years. The ski school runs classes for little ones ages 4 to 12. Junior racing is avail-able weekends and during holidays.

SUGARBUSH

In the Warren-Waitsfield ski world, Sugarbush is Mad River Glen's alter ego. Sugarbush's current owner, the American Skiing Company, has spent millions to keep the resort on the cutting edge. The Slide Brook Express quad connects the two mountains, Sugarbush South and Sug-arbush North. A computer-controlled system for snowmaking has in-creased coverage to nearly 70%. At the base of the mountain is a village with condominiums, restaurants, shops, bars, and a sports center. ⊠ *Box 350, Sugarbush Access Rd., accessible from Rte. 100 or Rte. 17, Warren 05674,* ☎ *802/583–6300; 800/537–8427 lodging; 802/583– 7669 snow conditions,* WEB *www.sugarbush.com.*

Downhill. Sugarbush is two distinct, connected mountain complexes. The Sugarbush South area is what old-timers recall as Sugarbush Mountain: with a vertical of 2,400 ft, it is known for formidable steeps toward the top and in front of the main base lodge. Sugarbush North offers what South has in short supply—beginner runs. North also has steep fall-line pitches and intermediate cruisers off its 2,600 vertical ft. There are 115 trails in all: 23% beginner, 48% intermediate, 29% expert. The resort has 18 lifts: seven quads (including four high-speed versions), three triples, four doubles, and four surface lifts.

Child care. The Sugarbush Day School accepts children from ages 6 weeks to 6 years; older children have indoor play areas and can go on outdoor excursions. There's half- and full-day instruction available for children from ages 4 to 11. Kids have their own Magic Carpet lift. Sugarbear Forest, a terrain garden, has fun bumps and jumps.

Summer and year-round activities. The Sugarbush Mountain Biking & Technical Hiking Center (☎ 802/583–6572) has bike rentals and miles of terrain; it provides guided tours and instruction. Open year-round, the Sugarbush Health and Racquet Club (☎ 802/583–6700), near the ski lifts, has Nautilus and Universal equipment; tennis, squash, and racquetball courts; a whirlpool, a sauna, and steam rooms; one indoor pool; and a 30-ft-high climbing wall.

CROSS-COUNTRY SKIING

Blueberry Lake Cross-Country Ski Area (⊠ Plunkton Rd., Warren, ☎ 802/496–6687) has 30 km (18 mi) of groomed trails through thickly wooded glades. **Ole's** (⊠ Airport Rd., Warren, ☎ 802/496–3430) runs a cross-country center and small restaurant out of the tiny Warren airport; it has 60 km (37 mi) of groomed European-style trails that span out into the surrounding woods from the landing strips.

Brookfield

28 *26 mi southeast of Waitsfield, 15 mi south of Montpelier.*

The residents of secluded Brookfield have voted several times to keep the town's roads unpaved and even turned down an offered I–89 exit when the interstate highway was being built in the '60s. Route 14 east of town is a scenic road. Crossing the nation's only **floating bridge** (⊠ Rte. 65 between Rtes. 12 and 14) feels like driving on water. The bridge, supported by nearly 400 barrels, sits at water level. It's the scene of the annual ice-harvest festival in January, though it's closed to traffic in winter.

Lodging

$$–$$$ 🏨 **Green Trails Inn.** The enormous fieldstone fireplace that dominates
★ the living and dining area at Green Trails is symbolic of the stalwart hospitality of the innkeepers. Antique clocks fill the common areas, and the comfortably elegant rooms in two historic buildings have antiques and Oriental rugs. One room has a fireplace, and two rooms have whirlpool tubs. Vegetarians are happily accommodated. The inn overlooks Sunset Lake and is a tranquil place for a walk down a tree-shaded country road. In winter, dinner can be included in the room rate. ⊠ *Main St., 05036,* ☎ *802/276–3412 or 800/243–3412,* WEB *www.greentrailsinn.com. 13 rooms, 9 with bath. Dining room, lake, boating, cross-country skiing, ski shop, sleigh rides. D, MC, V. BP.*

Central Vermont A to Z

To research prices, get advice from other travelers, and book travel arrangements, visit www.fodors.com.

BUS TRAVEL

Vermont Transit links Rutland, White River Junction, Burlington, and many smaller towns.

➤ BUS INFORMATION: **Vermont Transit** (☎ 800/552–8737).

CAR TRAVEL

The major east–west road is U.S. 4, which stretches from White River Junction in the east to Fair Haven in the west. Route 125 connects Middlebury on U.S. 7 with Hancock on Route 100; Route 100 splits the region in half along the eastern edge of the Green Mountains. Route 17 travels east–west from Waitsfield over the Appalachian Gap through

Bristol and down to the shores of Lake Champlain. I–91 and the parallel U.S. 5 follow the state's eastern border; U.S. 7 and Route 30 are the north–south highways in the west. I–89 links White River Junction with Montpelier to the north.

EMERGENCIES

➤ HOSPITALS: **Porter Hospital** (✉ South St., Middlebury, ☎ 802/388–7901). **Rutland Medical Center** (✉ 160 Allen St., Rutland, ☎ 802/775–7111; 800/649–2187 in Vermont).

LODGING

Sugarbush Reservations and the Woodstock Area Chamber of Commerce provide lodging referral services.
➤ RESERVATION SERVICES: **Sugarbush Reservations** (☎ 800/537–8427). **Woodstock Area Chamber of Commerce** (☎ 802/457–3555 or 888/496–6378).

TOURS

Country Inns Along the Trail offers self-guided and guided hiking and skiing trips, and self-guided biking trips from inn to inn in Vermont. The Vermont Icelandic Horse Farm conducts year-round guided riding expeditions on easy-to-ride Icelandic horses. Full-day, half-day, and hourly rides, weekend tours, and inn-to-inn treks are available.
➤ TOUR-OPERATOR RECOMMENDATIONS: **Country Inns Along the Trail** (✉ 834 Van Cortland Rd., Brandon 05733, ☎ 802/247–3300 or 800/838–3301). **Vermont Icelandic Horse Farm** (✉ N. Fayston Rd., Waitsfield 05673, ☎ 802/496–7141).

VISITOR INFORMATION

➤ TOURIST INFORMATION: **Addison County Chamber of Commerce** (✉ 2 Court St., Middlebury 05753, ☎ 802/388–7951 or 800/733–8376, WEB www.midvermont.com). **Quechee Chamber of Commerce** (✉ P.O. Box 106, 1789 Quechee St., Quechee 05059, ☎ 802/295–7900 or 800/295–5451, WEB www.quechee.com). **Rutland Region Chamber of Commerce** (✉ 256 N. Main St., Rutland 05701, ☎ 802/773–2747 or 800/756–8880, WEB www.rutlandvermont.com). **Sugarbush Chamber of Commerce** (✉ Box 173, Rte. 100, Waitsfield 05673, ☎ 802/496–3409 or 800/828–4748, WEB www.madrivervalley.com). **Woodstock Area Chamber of Commerce** (✉ Box 486, 18 Central St., Woodstock 05091, ☎ 802/457–3555 or 888/496–6378, WEB www.woodstockvt.com).

NORTHERN VERMONT

Vermont's northernmost region reveals the state's greatest array of contrasts. To the west, along Lake Champlain, Burlington and its Chittenden County suburbs have grown so rapidly that rural wags now say that Burlington's greatest advantage is that it's "close to Vermont." The north country also harbors Vermont's tiny capital, Montpelier, and its highest mountain, Mt. Mansfield, site of the famous Stowe ski slopes. To the northeast of Burlington and Montpelier spreads a sparsely populated and heavily wooded territory, the domain of loggers as much as farmers, where French spills out of the radio and the last snows melt toward the first of June.

You'll find plenty to do in the region's cities (Burlington, Montpelier, St. Johnsbury, and Barre), in the bustling resort area of Stowe, in the Lake Champlain Islands, and—if you like the outdoors—in the wilds of the Northeast Kingdom.

The coverage of towns in this area begins in the state capital, Montpelier; moves west toward Waterbury, Stowe, and Burlington; then goes

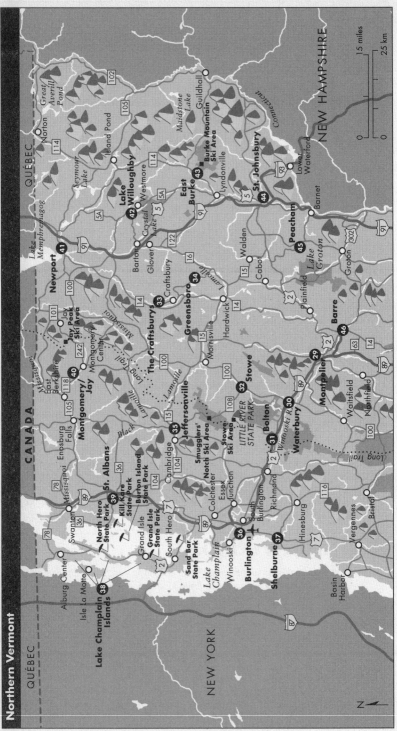

Northern Vermont

north through the Lake Champlain Islands, east along the boundary with Canada toward Jay Peak and Newport, and south into the heart of the Northeast Kingdom before completing the circle in Barre.

Montpelier

㉙ *38 mi southeast of Burlington, 115 mi north of Brattleboro.*

With only about 8,000 residents, Montpelier is the country's least populous state capital. The intersection of State and Main streets is the city hub, bustling with the activity of state and city workers during the day. It's a pleasant place to spend an afternoon shopping and browsing; in true small-town Vermont fashion, though, the streets become deserted at night.

The **Vermont State House**—with a gleaming gold dome and columns of Barre granite 6 ft in diameter—is impressive for a city this size. The goddess of agriculture tops the dome. The Greek Revival building dates from 1836, although it was rebuilt after a fire in 1859; the latter year's Victorian style was adhered to in a lavish 1994 restoration. Interior paintings and exhibits make much of Vermont's sterling Civil War record. ⊠ *115 State St.,* ☎ *802/828–2228.* ⌨ *Free.* ☉ *Weekdays 8–4; tours July–mid-Oct. weekdays every ½ hr 10–3:30 (last tour begins at 3:30), also Sat. 11–3 (last tour begins at 2:30). Self-guided tours available when building is open.*

Perhaps you're wondering what the last panther shot in Vermont looked like? Why New England bridges are covered? What a niddy-noddy is? Or what Christmas was like for a Bethel boy in 1879? ("I skated on my new skates. In the morning Papa and I set up a stove for Gramper.") The **Vermont Museum,** on the ground floor of the Vermont Historical Society offices in Montpelier, satisfies the curious with intriguing and informative exhibits. ⊠ *109 State St.,* ☎ *802/828–2291,* 〖WEB〗 *www.state.vt.us/vhs.* ⌨ *$3.* ☉ *Tues.–Fri. 9–4:30, Sat. 9–4, Sun. noon–4.*

Dining and Lodging

$$–$$$ ✕ **Chef's Table.** Nearly everyone working here is a student at the New
★ England Culinary Institute. Although this is a training ground, the quality and inventiveness are anything but beginner's luck. The menu changes daily. The atmosphere is more formal than that of the sister operation downstairs, the Main Street Bar and Grill (open daily for lunch and dinner). A 15% gratuity is added to the bill. ⊠ *118 Main St.,* ☎ *802/229–9202; 802/223–3188 grill. AE, D, DC, MC, V. Closed Sun. No lunch Sat.*

$$–$$$ ✕ **Sarducci's.** Legislative lunches have been a lot more leisurely ever since Sarducci's came along to fill the trattoria void in Vermont's capital. These bright, cheerful rooms alongside the Winooski River are a great spot for pizza fresh from wood-fired ovens, wonderfully textured homemade Italian breads, and imaginative pasta dishes such as pasta pugliese, which marries penne with basil, black olives, roasted eggplant, Portobello mushrooms, and sun-dried tomatoes. ⊠ *3 Main St.,* ☎ *802/ 223–0229. Reservations not accepted. AE, MC, V. No lunch Sun.*

$$–$$$ ☷ **Inn at Montpelier.** This inn built in the early 1800s was renovated with the business traveler in mind, but the architectural detailing, antique four-poster beds, Windsor chairs, and the classical guitar on the stereo attract the leisure trade as well. The formal sitting room has a Federal feel to it, and the wide wraparound Colonial Revival porch is perfect for reading a good book or watching the townsfolk stroll by. The rooms in the annex, also a 19th-century building, are equally spiffy. ⊠ *147 Main St., 05602,* ☎ *802/223–2727,* 〖FAX〗 *802/223–0722,* 〖WEB〗 *www.innatmontpelier. com. 19 rooms. Meeting room. AE, D, DC, MC, V. CP.*

Waterbury

③⓪ *12 mi northwest of Montpelier.*

The face of Waterbury's compact downtown is changing as coffee shops, restaurants, and galleries begin to move into the brick buildings that once housed tired-looking furniture and hardware stores. But the anchor here remains the huge state office complex that formerly served as a hospital. The little red train station comes to life only when Amtrak's *Vermonter* stops in town, once a day in each direction. The principal draws for visitors, however, are north of I–89, along Route 100.

Ben & Jerry's Ice Cream Factory is the mecca, nirvana, and Valhalla for ice cream lovers. Ben and Jerry began selling ice cream from a renovated gas station in Burlington in the 1970s. Famous for their social and environmental consciousness, the boys do good works while living off the butterfat of the land. The tour only skims the surface of the behind-the-scenes goings-on at the plant—a flaw forgiven when the free samples are offered. ✉ *Rte. 100, 1 mi north of I–89,* ☎ *802/244–8687,* WEB *www.benjerry.com.* ✑ *Tour $2.* ☉ *June, daily 9–5; July–Aug., daily 9–8; Sept.–Oct., daily 9–6; Nov.–May, daily 10–5. Tours every ½ hr in winter, more frequent in summer.*

Dining and Lodging

$$–$$$ ✕ **Mist Grill Cafe, Bakery, Roastery.** The fare is best described as country bistro, and the atmosphere casual contemporary, at this handsome restaurant in a renovated grist mill overlooking Thatcher Brook Falls just a minute from downtown. The café serves premium roasted coffee and handmade breakfast treats every day; some lunch choices are a ploughman's lunch and *panini* (Italian rolls) with Gorgonzola and greens. Traditional dinner offerings such as grilled rib steak and pork spare ribs are on the menu Friday and Saturday evenings, and on Sunday "supper" is served—a selection of comfort foods, plus delicious desserts. ✉ *92 Stowe St.,* ☎ *802/244–2233. MC, V.*

$$–$$$ ✕ **Villa Tragara.** Intimate and creative, this northern Italian restaurant
★ with Vermont farmhouse decor consistently wins recognition as one of the state's best dining spots. Besides entrées such as the mixed grill (lamb chop, veal cutlet, and quail) and *risotto con quaglie* (roast quail stuffed with toasted bread, prosciutto, sun-dried tomatoes, sage, and Asiago cheese), the owner-chef prepares a five-course tasting menu for $40. The Italian tapas—smaller portions of some popular offerings—are moderately priced to allow patrons to pick and share dishes. (There's a $12 minimum charge per person for the tapas.) The restaurant has live entertainment Friday evenings and a popular seasonal dinner theater. ✉ *Rte. 100, Waterbury, south of Stowe,* ☎ *802/244–5288. AE, MC, V. Closed Tues. No lunch.*

$$$ ✕🛏 **Thatcher Brook Inn.** Twin gazebos poised on both ends of the front porch of this sprawling 1899 inn define its space on busy Route 100. Three buildings hold comfortable guest rooms in a variety of sizes, with modern bathroom fixtures and Laura Ashley–style floral wallpaper. Some rooms have fireplaces and whirlpool tubs. The pine-paneled tavern is a popular socializing spot, and classic French cuisine is served in the dining room. ✉ *Rte. 100, 05676,* ☎ *802/244–5911 or 800/292–5911,* FAX *802/244–1294,* WEB *www.thatcherbrook.com. 22 rooms. Restaurant, pub. AE, D, DC, MC, V. BP.*

Outdoor Activities and Sports

Mt. Mansfield State Forest and Little River State Park (✉ U.S. 2, 1½ mi west of Waterbury, ☎ 802/244–7103) have extensive trail systems for hiking, including one that reaches the headquarters of the Civilian Conservation Corps unit that was stationed here in the 1930s. At Little

River State Park, there are campsites, boat rentals, and trails leading to Mt. Mansfield and Camel's Hump.

Shopping

The **Cold Hollow Cider Mill** (⊠ Rte. 100, 3 mi north of I–89, ☎ 802/244–8771 or 800/327–7537) sells cider, baked goods, Vermont produce, and specialty foods. Tastes of fresh-pressed cider are offered while you watch how it is made. **Green Mountain Chocolate Complex** (⊠ Rte. 100, 2½ mi north of I–89, ☎ 802/244–1139) houses gourmet and specialty shops including the Cabot Cheese Annex Store (☎ 802/244–6334) and Shimmering Glass Studio and Gallery (☎ 802/244–8134). The **Vermont Clay Studio & Gallery** (⊠ Rte. 100, ☎ 802/244–1126) displays works by artists from around the country.

Bolton

③ *8 mi northwest of Waterbury, 20 mi northwest of Montpelier, 20 mi southeast of Burlington.*

There isn't much to the town of Bolton itself, but Bolton Valley Holiday Resort bustles with activity.

Lodging

$$$ 🏠 **Black Bear Inn.** Teddy bears in all shapes and sizes decorate this mountaintop inn near the Bolton resort and overlooking the Green Mountains. Twelve rooms have glass-door firestoves and balconies, and six have private hot tubs. Grilled Atlantic salmon with a maple-Dijon mustard glaze is a typical dish at the restaurant. ⊠ *Bolton Access Rd., 05477,* ☎ *802/434–2126; 800/395–6335 outside VT,* 🆁🅰🆇 *802/434–5161,* 🆆🅴🅱 *www.blkbearinn.com. 24 rooms. Restaurant, pool, outdoor hot tub. MC, V. BP, MAP.*

$$$ 🏠 **Bolton Resort Hotel and Condominiums.** This slopeside complex includes completely renovated rooms with unexciting but functional contemporary decor, all with mountain views and most with balconies. Studios and suites with kitchens and fireplaces are available, as are condominiums. The newer rooms tend to be more spacious. Guests can use the resort's sports center, including a pool, sauna, and indoor tennis courts. Ski packages are available. ⊠ *Mountain Rd., 05477,* ☎ *802/434–3444 or 877/926–5866,* 🆁🅰🆇 *802/434–2131,* 🆆🅴🅱 *www.boltonvalleyvt.com. 60 rooms, 50 suites, 100 condominiums. AE, MC, V.*

Ski Areas

BOLTON VALLEY HOLIDAY RESORT

With new owners and a multimillion-dollar face-lift, Bolton is well on the way to its goal of becoming a four-season destination. The minivillage at the base of the mountain encompasses a completely renovated hotel as well as several restaurants, a wine and cheese shop, and a sports shop. The major attraction, however, is the downhill ski facility. ⊠ *Bolton Access Rd., 05477,* ☎ *802/434–3444 or 877/926–5866.*

Downhill. Bolton's six lifts include a quad chair, four double chairs, and a surface lift, which service 51 trails covering 157 acres of skiable terrain. The majority of the trails are rated for intermediates; the longest is the 2½-mi Cobrass Run. The vertical drop is 1,625 ft. The resort has 60% snowmaking coverage and offers top to bottom night skiing Monday–Saturday until 10 PM. There's a 1,500-ft terrain park for snowboarders.

Cross-country. A Nordic center offers cross-country ski, telemark, and snowshoe rentals and lessons. The resort has 35 km (22 mi) of groomed trails and 65 km (40 mi) of natural trails, including some where dogs are permitted.

Child care. The licensed Honey Bear Child Care Center provides care for children from six weeks to six years of age. There are ski programs for ages 3–15.

Summer and year-round activities. The resort has a mountain bike center that offers rentals; indoor and outdoor tennis courts; and hiking trails. A chairlift transports hikers to the top of the mountain, but not down. The sports center, open year-round, houses the indoor tennis courts and a pool, sauna, whirlpool, and weight room.

Stowe

★ ㉜ *16 mi northeast of Bolton, 22 mi northwest of Montpelier, 36 mi east of Burlington.*

Ever since the Civilian Conservation Corps cut the first downhill trails on Mt. Mansfield, ever since Austrian instructors first told weekenders to "bend mit der knees," Stowe has been the spiritual home of Vermont skiing. The village itself is tiny, just a few blocks of shops and restaurants clustered around a snow-white church spire—but it serves as the anchor for the Mountain Road, which leads north past more places to dine, stay, and shop on its way to those fabled slopes.

To many, Stowe rings a bell as the place where the von Trapp family, of *Sound of Music* fame, chose to settle after fleeing Austria. Set amid acres of pastures that fall away and allow for wide-angle panoramas of the mountains beyond, the **Trapp Family Lodge** (✉ Luce Hill Rd., ☎ 802/253–8511 or 800/826–7000) is the site of a popular outdoor music series in summer and an extensive cross-country ski-trail network in winter.

For more than a century the history of Stowe has been determined by the town's proximity to **Mt. Mansfield,** at 4,393 ft the highest elevation in the state. As early as 1858, visitors were trooping to the area to view the mountain, which has a shape that suggests the profile of the face of a man lying on his back. If hiking to the top isn't your idea of a good time, in summer you can take the 4½-mi toll road to the top for a short scenic walk and a magnificent view. ✉ *Mountain Rd., 7 mi from Rte. 100,* ☎ *802/253–3000.* 🎫 *Toll road $14.* ☉ *Mid-May–mid-Oct., daily 10–5.*

Mt. Mansfield's upper reaches are accessible by the eight-seat gondola that shuttles continuously up to the area of "the Chin" and the Cliff House Restaurant (☎ 802/253–3000, ext. 237), where lunch is served daily from 11–2:30. ✉ *Mountain Rd., 8 mi off Rte. 100,* ☎ *802/253–3000.* 🎫 *Gondola $14.* ☉ *Mid-June–mid-Oct., daily 10–5; early Dec.–late Apr., daily 8–4 for skiers.*

Dining and Lodging

$$$–$$$$ ✕ **Chelsea Grill.** Stowe's newest "in" spot successfully blends the accoutrements of a traditional Vermont country restaurant with the glitz and ambition of a big city dining room. The chef describes his cuisine as "refined country comfort food," with such appetizers as a deviled fried-oyster salad with smoked bacon and lemon parsley vinaigrette, and entrées such as grilled rack of lamb with roasted peppers and pan-roasted sea bass with citrus couscous. The homemade desserts are every bit as creative. ✉ *Mountain Road,* ☎ *802/253–3075. MC, V. No lunch Mon.–Thurs.*

$$$–$$$$ ✕ **Mes Amis.** Carole Fisher, who built her reputation as chef at the Isle
★ de France up the road, opened her own place a few years ago and has the locals queuing up for house specialties such as fresh oysters, lobster bisque, braised lamb shanks, roast duck (secret recipe), and ba-

nanas Foster. Opt for the patio on a warm summer's night. ⊠ *311 Mountain Rd.,* ☎ *802/253–8669. Reservations not accepted. D, MC, V. Closed Mon.*

$–$$ ✕ **Miguel's Stowe Away.** Miguel's serves up all the Tex-Mex standards along with tasty surprises such as coconut-fried shrimp, Cajun lamb fajitas, and a Yankee-flavored maple flan. Steaks and burgers round out the gringo menu. The cozy front room has a pool table (no quarters required) and a bar stocked with frosty Corona beer. Miguel's has an outpost on the Sugarbush Access Road in Warren (☎ 802/583–3858). ⊠ *3148 Mountain Rd.,* ☎ *802/253–7574 or 800/245–1240. AE, D, MC, V. No lunch Apr., Nov.*

$$$$ ✕🖼 **Edson Hill Manor.** This French-Canadian–style manor built in 1940
★ sits atop 225 acres of rolling hills. Oriental rugs accent the dark wide-board floors, and a tapestry complements the burgundy-patterned sofas that face the huge stone fireplace in the living room. The guest rooms are pine-paneled and have fireplaces, canopy beds, and down comforters. The dining room ($$$; no lunch; closed Sun.–Thurs. Apr.–May), the heart of the place, has walls of windows allowing contemplation of the inspiring view, wildflower paintings, and vines climbing to the ceiling. The highly designed contemporary cuisine might include rack of lamb or pan-seared salmon. ⊠ *1500 Edson Hill Rd., 05672,* ☎ *802/253–7371 or 800/621–0284,* ℻ *802/253–4036,* ⓌⒺⒷ *www.stowevt.com. 25 rooms. Restaurant, pool, hiking, horseback riding, cross-country skiing, sleigh rides. AE, D, MC, V. BP, MAP.*

$$$$ ✕🖼 **Topnotch at Stowe Resort and Spa.** One of the state's poshest resorts occupies 120 acres overlooking Mt. Mansfield. Floor-to-ceiling windows, a freestanding circular stone fireplace, and cathedral ceilings distinguish the lobby. Country-decorated rooms have thick carpeting and accents such as painted barn-board walls or Italian prints. The large European spa offers 22 massage-treatment rooms and a fitness program. Maxwell's restaurant serves contemporary Continental cuisine. ⊠ *Mountain Rd., 05672,* ☎ *802/253–8585 or 800/451–8686,* ℻ *802/253–9263,* ⓌⒺⒷ *www.topnotch-resort.com. 77 rooms, 13 suites, 20 town houses. 2 restaurants, bar, 1 indoor and 1 outdoor pool, 10 tennis courts (4 indoor), massage, sauna, spa, horseback riding, cross-country skiing, sleigh rides. AE, D, DC, MC, V. MAP.*

$$$$ 🖼 **Stone Hill Inn.** Innkeepers Hap and Amy Jordan have combined the amenities of a fine hotel with the intimacy of a B&B. Each elegantly decorated (and soundproof) guest room has a king-size bed, sitting area, and two-person whirlpool bath in front of a fireplace. Common areas include a sitting room and a game room, and the 10 acres of grounds are beautifully landscaped with gardens and waterfalls. For skiers there's overnight boot and glove drying service, and you can use the inn's toboggan and snowshoes. Rates include evening hors d'oeuvres. ⊠ *89 Houston Farm Rd., 05672,* ☎ *802/253–6282,* ℻ *802/253–7415,* ⓌⒺⒷ *www.stonehillinn.com. 9 rooms. Breakfast room, outdoor hot tub, golf privileges, hiking, recreation room. AE, DC, MC, V. BP.*

$$$ 🖼 **Stoweflake Mountain Resort and Spa** You'll find scenic mountain views and a range of accommodations here, from comfortable, country-inn rooms to luxurious suites with fireplaces, wet bars, refrigerators, and balconies. This full service resort also has one- to three-bedroom, fully equipped town houses and hosts Stowe's annual Hot Air Balloon Festival. ⊠ *1746 Mountain Rd. (Box 69), 05672,* ☎ *802/253–7355,* ℻ *802/253–6858,* ⓌⒺⒷ *www.stoweflake.com. 94 rooms; 30 town houses. 2 restaurants, kitchenettes (some), indoor-outdoor pools, hair salon, spa, sauna, driving range, putting green, 2 tennis courts, bicycles, sleigh rides, recreation room, business services, meeting rooms. AE, D, DC, MC, V. BP, MAP.*

$$ ☷ **Inn at Turner Mill.** Families will feel particularly welcome at this simple inn tucked well off the main road. Accommodations range from a one-bedroom unit to a two-bedroom apartment with two private baths, full kitchen, and fireplace; most units have kitchens. The inn is close to the ski area, a short walk from a swimming hole, and just across the road from miles of hiking trails. You can rent snowshoes here or purchase a pass to a nearby health club. ⊠ *56 Turner Mill La., 05672,* ☎ *802/253–2062 or 800/992–0016,* WEB *www.turnermill.com. 5 units. AE, MC, V. BP.*

$–$$$ ☷ **Sunset Motor Inn.** Strategically located among northern Vermont's big-three ski areas, this family owned, family friendly motel has clean and comfortable accommodations. Rooms numbered 70–87 in the newer section are larger and have whirlpool baths and refrigerators; the best are the ones facing the back of the motel. There's a restaurant next door. ⊠ *Junction of Rtes. 15 and 100, Morrisville 05661,* ☎ *802/ 888–4956 or 800/544–2347,* FAX *802/888–3698,* WEB *www.gostowe.com/ members/sunset. 55 rooms. Pool. AE, D, MC, V. CP.*

Nightlife and the Arts

NIGHTLIFE

The **Matterhorn Night Club** (⊠ Mountain Rd., ☎ 802/253–8198) has live music and dancing on weekends, DJs during the week. Live weekend entertainment takes place at **Stoweflake Mountain Resort and Spa.** Entertainers perform at the **Topnotch at Stowe** lounge on weekends.

THE ARTS

Stowe Performing Arts (☎ 802/253–7792) sponsors a series of classical and jazz concerts during July in the Trapp Family Lodge meadow. **Stowe Theater Guild** (⊠ Town Hall Theater, Main St., ☎ 802/253– 3961, summer only) performs musicals in July and August.

Outdoor Activities and Sports

A **recreational path** begins behind the Community Church in the center of town and meanders for 5⅓ mi along the river valley. There are many entry points along the way; whether you're on foot, skis, bike, or in-line skates, it's a tranquil spot to enjoy the outdoors.

BIKING

The junction of Routes 100 and 108 is the start of a 21-mi tour with scenic views of Mt. Mansfield; the course takes you along Route 100 to Stagecoach Road, to Morristown, over to Morrisville, and south on Randolph Road. The **Mountain Sports and Bike Shop** (⊠ Mountain Rd., ☎ 802/253–7919 or 800/682–4534 outside Stowe area) supplies equipment and rents bicycles.

CANOEING AND KAYAKING

Umiak Outdoor Outfitters (⊠ 849 S. Main St./Rte. 100, just south of Stowe Village, ☎ 802/253–2317) specializes in canoes and kayaks, rents them for day trips, and leads overnight excursions. The store also operates a rental outpost at Lake Elmore State Park in Elmore, and on the Winooski River off Route 2 in Waterbury.

FISHING

The **Fly Rod Shop** (⊠ Rte. 100, 3 mi south of Stowe, ☎ 802/253–7346 or 800/535–9763) provides a guiding service; gives fly-tying, casting, and rod-building classes in winter; rents fly tackle; and sells equipment, including classic and collectible firearms.

GOLF

Stowe Country Club (⊠ Mountain Rd., ☎ 802/253–4893) has a scenic 18-hole, par-72 course, a driving range, and a putting green. Greens fee is $35–$65; cart rental is $16.

An ascent of **Mt. Mansfield** makes for a scenic day hike. Trails lead from Route 108 (the Mountain Road) to the summit ridge, where they meet the north-to-south Long Trail. An option is to take the gondola at Stowe to the top and walk down along a ski trail. Views from the summit take in New Hampshire's White Mountains, New York's Adirondacks across Lake Champlain, and southern Québec. The Green Mountain Club has a trail guide.

For the two-hour climb to **Stowe Pinnacle,** go 1½ mi south of Stowe on Route 100 and turn east on Gold Brook Road opposite the Nichols Farm Lodge; turn left at the first intersection, continue straight at an intersection by a covered bridge, turn right after 1.8 mi, and travel 2.3 mi to a parking lot on the left. The trail crosses an abandoned pasture and takes a short, steep climb to views of the Green Mountains and Stowe Valley.

Jackson Arena (⊠ Park St., ☎ 802/253–6148 or 802/253–4402) is a public ice-skating rink. Skate rental is available.

Charlie Horse Sleigh and Carriage Rides (⊠ Mountain Rd., ☎ 802/253–2215) operates rides daily from 11 to 7; reservations are suggested for evening rides.

Topnotch at Stowe Resort and Spa has 10 outdoor and 4 indoor courts. Public courts are located at Stowe's elementary school.

Shopping

Mountain Road is lined with shops from town up toward the ski area.

Ski Areas

To be precise, the name of the village is Stowe and the name of the mountain is Mt. Mansfield, but to generations of skiers, the area, the complex, and the region are just plain Stowe. The resort is a classic that dates from the 1930s. Even today the area's mystique attracts as many serious skiers as social skiers. In recent years, on-mountain lodging, improved snowmaking, new lifts, and free shuttle buses that gather skiers from lodges, inns, and motels along Mountain Road have added convenience to the Stowe experience. Yet the traditions remain: the Winter Carnival in January, the Sugar Slalom in April, ski weeks all winter. Three base lodges provide the essentials, including two on-mountain restaurants. Expansion plans over the next few years include the construction of a new slopeside village with shops and accommodations. ⊠ *5781 Mountain Rd., 05672,* ☎ *802/253–3000; 800/253–4754 lodging; 802/253–3600 snow conditions.*

Downhill. Mt. Mansfield, with a vertical drop of 2,360 ft, is one of the giants among Eastern ski mountains and the highest in Vermont. The mountain's symmetrical shape allows skiers of all abilities long, satisfying runs from the summit. The famous Front Four (National, Liftline, Starr, and Goat) are the intimidating centerpieces for tough, expert runs, yet there is plenty of mellow intermediate skiing, with 59% of the runs rated at that level. One long beginner trail, the Toll Road Trail, is 3.7 mi. Mansfield's satellite sector is a network of intermediate trails and one expert trail off a basin served by a gondola. Spruce Peak, separate from the main mountain, is a teaching hill and a pleasant experience for intermediates and beginners; it also has a mountaintop trail that connects with slopes at neighboring resort Smugglers' Notch.

In addition to the high-speed, eight-passenger gondola, Stowe has 10 lifts, including a quad, one triple, and six double chairlifts, plus one handle tow, to service its 47 trails. Night-skiing trails are accessed by the gondola. The resort has 73% snowmaking coverage. Snowboard facilities include a halfpipe, quarterpipe, and two terrain parks—one for beginners, at the base of Spruce Peak, and one for experts on the Mt. Mansfield side.

Cross-country. The resort has 35 km (22 mi) of groomed cross-country trails and 40 km (24 mi) of backcountry trails. There are four interconnecting cross-country ski areas with more than 150 km (90 mi) of groomed trails within the town of Stowe.

Child care. The child-care center takes children from ages 6 weeks to 6 years, with kids' ski-school programs for ages 6 to 12. A center on Spruce Peak is headquarters for programs for children from ages 3 to 12, and there's another program for teenagers 13 to 17.

Summer activities. The resort offers mountain biking, hiking, in-line skating, an alpine slide, gondola rides, and an 18-hole golf course.

The Craftsburys

③③ *27 mi northeast of Stowe.*

The three villages of the Craftsburys—Craftsbury Common, Craftsbury, and East Craftsbury—are among Vermont's finest and oldest towns. Handsome white houses and barns, the requisite common, and terrific views make them well worth the drive. **Craftsbury General Store** in Craftsbury Village is a great place to stock up on picnic supplies and local information. The rolling farmland hints at the way Vermont used to be: the area's sheer distance from civilization and its rugged weather have kept most of the state's development farther south.

Lodging

$$$$ ✕🏠 **Inn on the Common.** All the rooms at this inn—actually a complex made of three Federal-style buildings—contain antique reproductions and contemporary furnishings; deluxe rooms have generous seating areas and fireplaces. Cocktails and hors d'oeuvres are offered in one house's cozy library. Five-course dinners (reservations essential) are served in the dining room, which overlooks the inn's gardens. The inn has an excellent wine cellar, and a dining deck open in summer. Guests have access to the facilities at the Craftsbury Sports Center and Albany's Wellness Barn, which has a lap pool, aerobics machines, a sauna, and a whirlpool. Cross-country ski trails connect with those at the Craftsbury Nordic Center. ✉ *On the common, 05827,* ☎ *802/586–9619 or 800/521–2233,* FAX *802/586–2249,* WEB *www.innonthecommon.com. 15 rooms, 1 suite. Dining room, lounge, pool, tennis court, library, cross-country skiing. AE, MC, V. MAP.*

$$–$$$ 🏠 **Craftsbury Outdoor Center.** This outdoors-enthusiasts' haven has standard accommodations and sporting packages. Because of a long season of snowcover—it's white here when the rest of Vermont is green—the cross-country skiing is terrific on the 135 km (80 mi) of trails (85 km/50 mi groomed) on the property and through local farmland. During the rest of the year, sculling and running camps are held. Guests and nonguests alike can ski, mountain bike, and canoe at day-use rates; equipment rental is available. The buffet-style meals include soups, stews, and homemade breads and desserts. In winter, rates include use of trails. ✉ *Box 31, Lost Nation Rd., 05827,* ☎ *802/586–7767 or 800/729–7751,* FAX *802/586–7768,* WEB *www.craftsbury.com. 49 rooms, 10 with bath, 3 cottages, 2 efficiencies. Dining room, boating, mountain bikes, cross-country skiing. MC, V. AP.*

$ ⊞ **Craftsbury Bed & Breakfast.** Craftsbury's longest operating traditional B&B is a lovely place to unwind. Owner Margaret Ramsdell creates an air of peaceful informality at her farmhouse, right down to the absence of a TV. Common rooms include a spacious country kitchen with a wood-stove and a living room. In summer, relax on lawn chairs in the big yard; in winter, ski on the property's cross-country ski trails, which are part of a 105 km (65 mi) network. ⊠ *Wylie Hill, 05827,* ☎ *802/586–2206, 6 rooms without bath. MC, V. BP.* WEB *www.scenesofvermont.com/ craftsburybb.*

Greensboro

③④ *10 mi southeast of Craftsbury Common.*

Greensboro is an idyllic small town with a long history as a vacation destination.

Lodging

$$$$ ⊞ **Highland Lodge.** Tranquillity reigns at this 1860 house, which over-looks a pristine lake. The lodge's 120 acres of rambling woods and pas-tures are laced with hiking and skiing trails (ski rentals available). Widely known for its great front porch, this quiet family resort is part refined el-egance and part casual country of the summer-camp sort. The comfort-able guest rooms have Early American–style furnishings. Most rooms have views of the lake; the one- to three-bedroom cottages are more private (four with gas stoves stay open in winter). The traditional dinner menu, which incorporates Vermont foods, might include entrées such as roasted leg of lamb and grilled Black Angus sirloin. ⊠ *E. Craftsbury Rd., 05841,* ☎ *802/533–2647,* FAX *802/533–7494. 11 rooms, 11 cottages. Restaurant, lake, tennis court, hiking, boating, cross-country skiing, recreation room. D, MC, V. Closed mid-Mar.–late May and mid-Oct.–mid-Dec. MAP.*

Shopping

The **Miller's Thumb** (⊠ Main St., ☎ 802/533–2960 or 800/680–7886) sells Italian pottery, Vermont furniture, crafts and antiques, and April Cornell clothing and linens. **Willey's Store** (⊠ Main St., ☎ 802/533–2621), with wooden floors and tin ceilings, warrants exploration. Foodstuffs, baskets, candy, kitchen paraphernalia, and more are packed to the rafters.

Jeffersonville

③⑤ *36 mi west of Greensboro, 18 mi north of Stowe, 28 mi northeast of Burlington.*

Mt. Mansfield and Madonna Peak tower over Jeffersonville, whose ac-tivities are closely linked with those of Smugglers' Notch Ski Resort.

Boyden Valley Winery (⊠ Junction of Rtes. 15 and 104, Cambridge, ☎ 802/644–8151) conducts tours of its microwinery and also show-cases an excellent selection of Vermont specialty products and local handicrafts, including fine furniture. The winery is closed Monday.

Lodging

$$$$ ⊞ **Smugglers' Notch Resort.** Most of the condos at this large year-round resort have fireplaces and decks. The resort is known for its many fam-ily programs. Rates include lift tickets and ski lessons in season, and kids 6 weeks to 2 years of age get free care if parents stay three or more nights. ⊠ *Rte. 108, 05464,* ☎ *802/644–8851 or 800/451–8752,* FAX *802/644–1230,* WEB *www.smugs.com. 502 condominiums. 3 restaurants, bar, indoor-outdoor pools, hot tub, sauna, 6 tennis courts, exercise room, ice-skating, downhill skiing, recreation room, baby-sitting, children's programs (ages 3–17), nursery, playground. AE, DC, MC, V.*

$ 🏨 **Deer Run Motor Inn.** This well-kept, comfortable motel may be the north country's best bargain. Although it's right on busy Route 15, the units are set fairly well back (second-floor rooms with queen-size beds face the rear), and each has a coffeemaker, deck, sliding glass doors, and cable TV. A swing set and grills are other amenities. ✉ *80 Deer Run Loop, 05464,* 🕾 *802/644–8866 or 800/354–2728. 25 units. Picnic area, refrigerator, pool. AE, D, MC, V.*

Outdoor Activities and Sports

Applecheek Farm (✉ 567 McFarlane Rd., Hyde Park, 🕾 802/888–4482) offers daytime and evening (by lantern) hay and sleigh rides, llama treks, and farm tours. **Smugglers' Notch State Park** (✉ Rte. 108, 10 mi north of Mt. Mansfield, 🕾 802/253–4014) is good for picnicking and hiking on wild terrain among large boulders. **Northern Vermont Llamas** (✉ 766 Lapland Rd., Waterville, 🕾 802/644–2257) offers half- and full-day treks from May through October along the cross-country ski trails of Smugglers' Notch. The llamas carry everything, including snacks and lunches. Advance reservations essential. **Vermont Horse Park** (✉ Rte. 108 🕾 802/644–5347) conducts rides on authentic horse-drawn sleighs as well as trail rides when weather permits.

Shopping

ANTIQUES

The **Buggy Man** (✉ Rte. 15, 7 mi east of Jeffersonville, 🕾 802/635–2110) sells American furniture and collectibles including horse-drawn vehicles. **Mel Siegel** (✉ Rte. 15, 7 mi east of Jeffersonville, 🕾 802/635–7838) specializes in 19th-century American furniture and glassware.

CLOTHING

Johnson Woolen Mills (✉ Main St., Johnson, 9 mi east of Jeffersonville, 🕾 802/635–2271) is an authentic factory store with deals on woolen blankets, yard goods, and the famous Johnson outerwear.

CRAFTS

Vermont Rug Makers (✉ Rte. 100C, East Johnson, 10 mi east of Jeffersonville, 🕾 802/635–2434) weaves imaginative rugs and tapestries from fabrics, wools, and exotic materials. Its International Gallery displays rugs and tapestries from countries throughout the world. The shop has a branch on Main Street in Stowe.

Ski Areas

SMUGGLERS' NOTCH RESORT

This sprawling resort complex consistently wins accolades for its family programs. Its children's ski school is one of the best in the country—and possibly *the* best. But skiers of all levels come here (in 1996, Smugglers' became the first ski area in the East to designate a triple-black-diamond run—the Black Hole). All the essentials are available at the base of the lifts. A three-phase plan, which will allow snowmaking top to bottom on all three mountains is scheduled to be completed by 2002. ✉ *Rte. 108, 05464,* 🕾 *802/644–8851 or 800/451–8752,* 🌐 *www.smuggs.com.*

Downhill. Smugglers' has three mountains. The highest, Madonna, with a vertical drop of 2,610 ft, is in the center and connects with a trail network to Sterling (1,500-ft vertical). The third mountain, Morse (1,150-ft vertical), is adjacent to Smugglers' "village" of shops, restaurants, and lodgings; it's connected to the other peaks by trails and a shuttle bus. The wild, craggy landscape lends a pristine, wilderness feel to the skiing experience on the two higher mountains. The tops of each of the mountains have expert terrain—a couple of double-black diamonds make Madonna memorable. Intermediate trails fill the lower sections. Morse has many beginner trails, including the new Morse Bowl, with a double chair that services five new trails for beginners and advanced beginners. Smugglers' 67 trails are served by nine lifts, including five chairs and four surface lifts. Top-to-bottom snowmaking on all three mountains allows for 62% coverage. A trail at the top of Sterling Mountain connects to Spruce Peak at the Stowe Mountain Resort. There are several terrain parks for snowboarders, including Prohibition Park, at 3,500 ft one of the longest in Vermont.

Cross-country. The area has 37 km (23 mi) of groomed and tracked cross-country trails.

Other activities. The self-contained village has ice-skating and sleigh rides. The numerous snowshoeing programs include family walks and backcountry trips. The FunZone at SmuggsCentral has an indoor pool, playground, slides, miniature golf, a hot tub, ice-skating rink, and Nordic Center. A Teen Center is open from 5 PM until midnight.

Child care. The state-of-the-art Alice's Wonderland Child Care Center accepts children from ages 6 weeks to 6 years. Ski camps for kids ages 3–17 offer excellent instruction, plus movies, games, and other activities.

Summer and year-round activities. Smugglers' has a full roster of summertime programs, including a pool, complete with waterfalls and water slides, the Giant Rapid River Ride (the longest water ride in the state), lawn games, and mountain biking and hiking programs. It also has an indoor sports center, the FunZone. Horseback riding is available in summer and fall.

Burlington

★ ❸❻ *31 mi southwest of Jeffersonville, 76 mi south of Montréal, 349 mi north of New York City, 223 mi northwest of Boston, MA.*

Cited in survey after survey as one of America's most livable small cities, Burlington has the vibrant character of a college town in which a lot of the graduates have stayed behind to put down roots. The largest population center in Vermont, the city was founded in 1763 and is now the center of a rapidly growing suburban area. It has held its own against highway malls by cleverly positioning itself in the "festival marketplace" retail style, as well as by trading on its incomparable location on Lake Champlain. The Burlington area's eclectic population includes many transplants from larger urban areas as well as roughly 20,000 students from the area's five colleges. For years it was the only city in America with a socialist mayor—now the nation's sole socialist congressional representative.

The **Church Street Marketplace**—a pedestrian mall of boutiques, restaurants, sidewalk cafés, crafts vendors, and street performers—is an animated downtown focal point.

Crouched on the shores of Lake Champlain, which shimmers in the shadows of the Adirondacks to the west, Burlington's revitalized waterfront teems with outdoor enthusiasts who stroll along its recreation path and ply the waters in sailboats and motorcraft in summer. A 500-passenger, three-level cruise vessels, *The Spirit of Ethan Allen II,* takes people on narrated cruises on the lake and, in the evening, dinner and sunset sailings that drift by the Adirondacks and the Green Mountains. ✉ *Burlington Boat House, College St. at Battery St.,* ☎ *802/862–8300.* ☞ *$8.* ☉ *Cruises late May–mid-Oct., daily 10–9.*

Part of the waterfront's revitalization and still a work in progress, the
Ⓒ **Lake Champlain Basin Science Center** aims to educate the public about

the ecology, history, and culture of the lake region. From looking at plankton through a "kidscope" to dragging a net off the University of Vermont research boat docked on the property, there are activities for the whole family. ⊠ *1 College St.,* ☎ *802/864–1848,* WEB *www.lakechamplaincenter.org.* 🎟 *$3.* ☉ *Mid-June–Labor Day, daily 11–5; Labor Day–mid-June, weekends and school vacations 12:30–4:30.*

Crowning the hilltop above Burlington is the campus of the **University of Vermont** (☎ 802/656–3480), known simply as UVM for the abbreviation of its Latin name, Universitas Viridis Montis—the University of the Green Mountains. With more than 10,000 students, UVM is the state's principal institution of higher learning. The most architecturally interesting buildings face the Green, which contains some of the grandest surviving specimens of the elm trees that once shaded virtually every street in Burlington, as well as a statue of UVM founder Ira Allen, Ethan's brother. The Robert Hull Fleming Art Museum (⊠ Colchester Ave., ☎ 802/656–0750), just behind the Ira Allen Chapel, houses American portraits and landscapes, including works by Sargent, Homer, and Bierstadt; two Corots and a Fragonard; and an Egyptian mummy. Contemporary Vermont works are also exhibited.

Burlington's **Intervale,** once home to Abenaki and early colonial pioneers, encompasses 700 acres of open land along the Winooski River. You can rent canoes, bicycle the 2-mi trail (which connects with Burlington's 10-mi Cycle the City loop), take a river tour, or hike the trails. The project is under the auspices of Gardener's Supply Company (⊠ 128 Intervale Rd., ☎ 802/660-3505 WEB www.gardeners.com), a major direct mail gardening company, with greenhouses and outdoor display gardens. The company provides maps, information, and a schedule of the many seasonal events held there. One of the earliest residents of the Intervale was Ethan Allen, Vermont's Revolutionary-era guerrilla fighter, who remains a captivating figure. Exhibits at the visitor center at the **Ethan Allen Homestead** answer questions about his flamboyant life. The house contains frontier hallmarks like rough saw-cut boards and an open hearth for cooking. A re-created Colonial kitchen garden resembles the one the Allens would have had. After the tour, you can stretch your legs on scenic trails along the Winooski River. ⊠ *North Ave. off Rte. 127, north of Burlington,* ☎ *802/865–4556,* WEB *www.ethanallentogether.com.* 🎟 *$5.* ☉ *Call for schedule.*

OFF THE BEATEN PATH

GREEN MOUNTAIN AUDUBON NATURE CENTER – This is a wonderful place to discover Vermont's outdoor wonders. The center's 300 acres of diverse habitats are a sanctuary for all things wild, and the 5 mi of trails provide an opportunity to explore the workings of differing natural communities. Events include dusk walks, wildflower and birding rambles, nature workshops, and educational activities for kids and adults. The center is 18 mi southeast of Burlington. ⊠ *Huntington-Richmond Rd., Richmond,* ☎ *802/434–3068.* 🎟 *Donations accepted.* ☉ *Grounds dawn–dusk, center weekdays (and some Sat.) 8–4.*

Dining and Lodging

$$–$$$ ✕ **Isabel's.** An old lumber mill on Lake Champlain houses this restaurant with high ceilings, exposed-brick walls, and knockout views. The menu is seasonal; past dishes, all presented with an artistic flair, have included Thai seafood pasta and vegetable Wellington. Lunch and Sunday brunch are popular; be sure to dine on the outdoor patio on warm days. ⊠ *112 Lake St.,* ☎ *802/865–2522. AE, D, DC, MC, V.* *Mon.; Nov.–Apr., lunch only and closed Mon. and Sat.*

$$–$$$ ✕ **Trattoria Delia.** Didn't manage to rent that villa in Umbria this year?
★ The next best thing, if your travels bring you to Burlington, is this superb Italian country eatery just around the corner from City Hall Park.
Local game and produce are the stars, as in roast rabbit marinated in
herbs, wine, and olive oil. The chef's passion for the truly homemade
extends to wild boar sausage, salami, and fresh mozzarella. Wood-grilled
items are a specialty. ⊠ *152 St. Paul St.,* ☎ *802/864–5253. AE, D,
DC, MC, V. No lunch.*

$$ ✕ **NECI Commons.** The initials stand for New England Culinary Institute,
the respected Montpelier academy whose students and teachers run this
all-under-one-roof café, bakery, market, restaurant, and bar. The deli
counter can get a little pricey, but everything is fresh and tasty. It's open
daily for lunch and dinner and on Sundays for brunch. Mornings, home-
made pastries and muffins are served in the market area. ⊠ *25 Church
St.,* ☎ *802/862–6324. AE, D, MC, V.*

$$ ✕ **Old Heidelberg German Restaurant.** This chef-owned restaurant, gra-
ciously appointed with linens and fresh flowers, serves such tasty Teu-
tonic standards as *sauerbraten,* pork and veal *schnitzels,* and homemade
bratwurst; hearty homemade *goulash* and potato soups round out the
luncheon and appetizer menus. German cuisine is the original "comfort food"—perfect for a cold northern Vermont winter night. German
beers and wines are available. ⊠ *1016 Shelburne Rd. (Rt. 7),* ☎ *802/
865–4423. AE, D, DC, MC, V. Closed Mon.*

$$ ✕ **Parima Thai Restaurant.** Chef's specials such as crispy roasted duck
in tamarind sauce and seafood *phuket* (shrimp, mussels, cod, and
squid sautéed in basil sauce) join a menu of traditional Thai including
curries and *pad thai* (stir-fried noodles with shrimp or chicken). This
handsomely appointed restaurant has one of the most elegant bars in
town. ⊠ *185 Pearl St.,* ☎ *802/864–7917. AE, D, DC, MC, V. No lunch
Nov.–Apr.*

$$$–$$$$ ✕🏠 **Basin Harbor Club.** Owned by the Beach family since 1886, this
★ outstanding resort sprawls over 700 acres of prime real estate over-
looking Lake Champlain. Luxurious accommodations, a full roster of
amenities including an 18-hole Geoffrey Cornish golf course, boating
(with a 40-ft tour boat), and daylong children's programs make Basin
Harbor a popular spot for families. Some rooms have fireplaces, decks,
or porches. The restaurant menu is classic American, the wine list ex-
cellent. Coats and ties are required in common areas after 6 PM from
mid-June through Labor Day. ⊠ *Basin Harbor Rd., Vergennes 05491,*
☎ *802/475–2311 or 800/622–4000,* FAX *802/475–6545,* WEB *www.bas-
inharbor.com. 36 rooms, 2 suites in 3 guest houses, 77 cottages. 2 restau-
rants, pool, 18-hole golf course, 5 tennis courts, health club, bicycles,
boating, children's programs (ages 3–15). MC, V. Closed mid-Oct.–
mid-May. MAP, AP, BP available spring and fall.*

$$$–$$$$ ✕🏠 **Inn at Essex.** About 10 mi from downtown Burlington, near Essex
Outlet Fair, is a state-of-the-art inn and conference center dressed in
country clothing. Rooms with flowered wallpaper and reproduction
period desks lend the place some character, and many of the rooms have
fireplaces. The two restaurants are run by the New England Culinary
Institute. Butlers serves dishes such as sweet dumpling squash with gin-
ger-garlic basmati rice, and lobster in yellow-corn sauce with spinach
pasta. Five-onion soup, burgers, and daily flatbread pizza specials are
among the highlights at the Tavern. ⊠ *70 Essex Way, off Rte. 15, Essex
Junction 05452,* ☎ *802/878–1100 or 800/288–7613,* FAX *802/878–0063
or 800/727–4295,* WEB *www.innatessex.com. 97 rooms. 2 restaurants,
bar, pool, billiards, library, business services, meeting rooms. AE, D,
DC, MC, V. CP.*

$$–$$$$ ★   ⊞ **Willard Street Inn.** High in the historic hill section of Burlington, this grand house with an exterior marble staircase and English gardens incorporates elements of Queen Anne and Colonial–Georgian Revival styles. The stately foyer, paneled in cherry, leads to a more formal sitting room with velvet drapes. The solarium is bright and sunny with marble floors, many plants, and big velvet couches for contemplating views of Lake Champlain. All the rooms have down comforters and phones; some have lake views and canopied beds. Orange French toast is among the breakfast favorites. ⊠ *349 S. Willard St., 05401,* ☎ *802/651–8710 or 800/577–8712,* FAX *802/651–8714,* WEB *www.willard-streetinn.com. 14 rooms. AE, D, MC, V. BP.*

Nightlife and the Arts

NIGHTLIFE

Name and local musicians come to **Higher Ground** (⊠ 1 Main St., Winooski, ☎ 802/654–8888). The music at the **Metronome** (⊠ 188 Main St., ☎ 802/865–4563) ranges from cutting-edge sounds to funk, blues, and reggae. The band Phish got its start at **Nectar's** (⊠ 188 Main St., ☎ 802/658–4771). This place is always jumping to the sounds of local bands and never charges a cover. **Ri Ra** (123 Church St., ☎ 802/860–9401) hosts live entertainment with an Irish flair and dishes up Irish and American fare. **Vermont Pub and Brewery** (⊠ 144 College St., ☎ 802/865–0500) makes its own beer and fruit seltzers and is arguably the most popular spot in town. Folk musicians play here regularly.

THE ARTS

Burlington City Arts (☎ 802/865–7166; 802/865–9163 24-hr Artsline) has up-to-date arts-related information. **Flynn Theatre for the Performing Arts** (⊠ 153 Main St., ☎ 802/652–4500 information; 802/863–5966 tickets), a grandiose old structure, is the cultural heart of Burlington; it schedules the Vermont Symphony Orchestra, theater, dance, big-name musicians, and lectures. The **Lyric Theater** (☎ 802/658–1484) puts on musical productions in the fall and spring at the Flynn Theatre. **St. Michael's Playhouse** (⊠ St. Michael's College, Rte. 15, Colchester, ☎ 802/654–2281 box office; 802/654–2617 administrative office) performs in the McCarthy Arts Center Theater. The **UVM Lane Series** (☎ 802/656–4455 programs and times; 802/656–3085 box office) sponsors classical as well as folk music concerts in the Flynn Theatre, Ira Allen Chapel, and the UVM Recital Hall. The **Vermont Symphony Orchestra** (☎ 802/874–5741 or 800/876–9203) performs throughout the state year-round, and at the Flynn from October through May.

Outdoor Activities and Sports

BEACHES

The **North Beaches** are on the northern edge of Burlington: North Beach Park (⊠ off North Ave., ☎ 802/864–0123), Bayside Beach (⊠ Rte. 127 near Malletts Bay), and Leddy Beach (⊠ Leddy Park Rd., off North Ave.), which is popular for sailboarding.

BIKING

Burlington's 10-mi Cycle the City loop runs along the waterfront, connecting several city parks and beaches. It also passes the Lake Champlain Basin Science Center and the Community Boathouse, and runs within several blocks of downtown restaurants and shops. **North Star Cyclery** (⊠ 100 Main St., ☎ 802/863–3832) rents bicycles and provides maps of bicycle routes. **Ski Rack** (⊠ 81 Main St., ☎ 802/658–3313 or 800/882–4530) rents and services bikes, and provides maps.

Marina services are available north and south of Burlington. **Malletts Bay Marina** (⊠ 228 Lakeshore Dr., Colchester, ☎ 802/862–4072) has facilities for mooring, sells gasoline, and repairs boats. **Point Bay Marina** (⊠ 1401 Thompson's Point Rd., Charlotte, ☎ 802/425–2431) provides full service and repairs. **Burlington Community Boathouse** (⊠ Foot of College St., Burlington Harbor, ☎ 802/865–3377) rents Jet Skis, sailboats, sailboats from 13 ft to 40 ft, and motorboats (some captained); the boathouse also gives lessons. **Marble Island Resort** (⊠ Colchester, ☎ 802/864–6800) has a marina and a nine-hole golf course.

Shopping

ANTIQUES

Architectural Salvage Warehouse (⊠ 53 Main St., ☎ 802/658–5011) is a great place to hunt for claw-foot tubs, stained-glass windows, mantels, andirons, and other similar items. The large rhinoceros head bursting out of the **Conant Custom Brass** (⊠ 270 Pine St., ☎ 802/658–4482) storefront may tempt you in to see the custom work; the store specializes in decorative lighting and bathroom fixtures.

CRAFTS

In addition to its popular pottery, **Bennington Potters North** (⊠ 127 College St., ☎ 802/863–2221 or 800/205–8033) stocks interesting gifts, glassware, furniture, and other housewares. **Vermont State Craft Center** (⊠ 85 Church St., ☎ 802/863–6458) displays contemporary and traditional crafts by more than 200 Vermont artisans. **Yankee Pride** (⊠ Champlain Mill, E. Canal St., Winooski, ☎ 802/655–0500) has a large inventory of quilting fabrics and supplies as well as Vermont-made quilts.

MALLS AND MARKETPLACES

Burlington Square Mall (⊠ Church St., ☎ 802/658–2545) has a large Filene's department store and a few dozen other shops. The **Champlain Mill** (⊠ U.S. 2/7, northeast of Burlington, ☎ 802/655–9477), a former woolen mill on the banks of the Winooski River, holds three floors of stores, including a bookstore and clothing shops, and several restaurants. **Church Street Marketplace** (⊠ Main St.–Pearl Sts., ☎ 802/863–1648), a pedestrian thoroughfare, is lined with boutiques, cafés, and street vendors. **University Mall** (⊠ Dorset St., ☎ 802/863–1066), home to Sears, Bon Ton, and JCPenney, continues to expand. Look for bargains at the rapidly growing **Essex Outlet Fair** (⊠ Rte 15, at Rte. 289, Essex, ☎ 802/657–2777); you'll find outlets for Brooks Brothers, Polo Ralph Lauren, and Levi's, among others.

Shelburne

🐠 *5 mi south of Burlington.*

Once a village surrounded by small farms and lakeshore estates, Shelburne is now largely a bedroom community for Burlington. It's distinguished by one of the nation's premier repositories of Americana and by a tycoon's gilded-age fiefdom that has become a model farm and agricultural education center.

A few miles south of Burlington, the Champlain Valley gives way to fertile farmland, affording stunning views of the rugged Adirondacks across the lake. You can trace much of New England's history simply ★ by wandering the 45 acres and 37 buildings of the **Shelburne Museum.** The outstanding 80,000-object collection of Americana consists of 18th- and 19th-century period homes and furniture, fine and folk art, farm tools, more than 200 carriages and sleighs, Audubon prints, an old-fashioned jail, and even a private railroad car from the days of steam. The museum also has an assortment of duck decoys, an old stone cottage, and a display of early toys—as well as the *Ticonderoga*, an old side-wheel steamship, grounded amid lawn and trees. The newest exhibit is an interactive period house from the 1950s. ⊠ *U.S. 7,* ☎ *802/ 985–3346 or 802/985–3344,* WEB *www.shelburnemuseum.org.* ☑ *$17.50 for 2 consecutive days.* ☉ *June–mid-Oct., daily 10–5; mid.-Oct.– Dec. and Apr.–late May, daily 1–4.*

★ ☺ **Shelburne Farms** has a history of improving the farmer's lot by developing new agricultural methods. Founded in the 1880s as a private estate, the 1,400-acre property is an educational and cultural resource center with, among other things, a working dairy farm, a Children's Farmyard, and a spot for watching the farm's famous cheddar cheese being made. Frederick Law Olmsted, co-creator of New York's Central Park, designed the magnificent grounds overlooking Lake Champlain. For an additional charge of $5, you can tour the 1891 breeding barn. ⊠ *West of U.S. 7 at Harbor and Bay Rds.,* ☎ *802/985–8686,* WEB *www. shelburnefarms.org.* ☑ *Day pass $5, tour an additional $5.* ☉ *Visitor center and shop daily 10–5; tours mid-May–mid-Oct. (last tour at 3:30); mid-Oct.–mid-May, walking trails open, weather permitting.*

☺ On the tour of the **Vermont Teddy Bear Company,** you'll hear more puns than you ever thought possible and learn how a few homemade bears, sold from a cart on Church Street, have turned into a multimillion-dollar business. A children's play tent is set up outdoors in summer, and you can wander the beautiful 57-acre property. ⊠ *2236 Shelburne Rd.,* ☎ *802/985–3001.* ☑ *Tour $1.* ☉ *Tours Mon.–Sat. 9:30–4, Sun. 10:30–4; store Mon.–Sat. 9–6, Sun. 10–5.*

At the 6-acre **Vermont Wildflower Farm,** the display along the flowering pathways changes constantly: violets in the spring, daisies and black-eyed Susans for summer, and for fall, flowers with colors that rival those of the trees' foliage. You can buy wildflower seeds, crafts, and books here. ⊠ *U.S. 7, Charlotte, 5 mi south of the Shelburne Museum,* ☎ *802/425–3641,* WEB *www.americanmeadows.com.* ☑ *$3.* ☉ *Early May–late Oct., daily 10–5.*

Dining and Lodging

$$$–$$$$ ✕ **Café Shelburne.** One of the area's most popular restaurants has been
★ serving creative French bistro cuisine for more than 30 years. Some specialties are sweetbreads in a port wine and mushroom sauce in puff pastry and homemade fettuccine with prunes. Desserts such as the sweet chocolate layered terrine and maple syrup mousse with orange terrine are fabulous. ⊠ *U.S. 7,* ☎ *802/985–3939. AE, MC, V. Closed Sun.– Mon. No lunch.*

$$$–$$$$ ✕🖫 **Inn at Shelburne Farms.** This is storybook land. Built at the turn
★ of the century as the home of William Seward and Lila Vanderbilt Webb, the Tudor-style inn perches on Saxton's Point overlooking Lake Champlain, the distant Adirondacks, and the sea of pastures that make up this 1,400-acre working farm. Each room is different, from the wallpaper to the period antiques. The dining room ($$$–$$$$) defines elegance, and the seasonal contemporary menu makes clever use of local ingredients. Sunday brunch (not served in May) is one of the area's best. The inn's profits help support the farm's environmental education programs for local schools. ⊠ *Harbor Rd., 05482,* ☎ *802/985– 8498,* FAX *802/985–8123,* WEB *www.shelburnefarms.org. 24 rooms, 17 with bath. Restaurant, lake, tennis court, hiking, boating, fishing, billiards. AE, D, DC, MC, V. Closed mid-Oct.–mid-May.*

Outdoor Activities and Sports

A moderately easy 18½-mi bike trail begins at the blinker on U.S. 7 in
Shelburne and follows Mt. Philo Road, Hinesburg Road, Route 116,
and Irish Hill Road.

Shopping

When you enter **Shelburne Country Store** (⊠ Village Green, off U.S.
7, ☎ 802/985–3657) you'll step back in time. Walk past the potbellied stove and take in the aroma emanating from the fudge neatly piled
behind huge antique glass cases. The store specializes in candles,
weather vanes, glassware, and local foods.

Lake Champlain Islands

38 *20 mi northwest of Shelburne, 15 mi northwest of Burlington.*

South Hero, North Hero, Isle La Motte, and the Alburg peninsula compose the elongated archipelago that stretches southward from the
Canadian border. Because of their temperate climate, the islands are
home to several apple orchards and numerous state parks and are a
center of water recreation in summer and ice fishing in winter. A scenic
drive through the islands on U.S. 2 begins at I–89 and travels north to
Alburg Center; Route 78 takes you back to the mainland.

Snow Farm Vineyard and Winery offers self-guided tours, a tasting room,
and free concerts on the lawn for 10 Thursday evenings, beginning in
mid-June. ⊠ *190 W. Shore Rd., South Hero,* ☎ *802/372–9463.* ☞ *Free.*
☉ *May–Dec., daily 10–5, tours at 11 and 2.*

Hyde Log Cabin, built in 1783 on South Hero, is often cited as the country's oldest surviving log cabin. ⊠ *U.S. 2, Grand Isle,* ☎ *802/828–3051.*
☞ *$3.* ☉ *July 4–Labor Day, Thurs.–Mon. 11–5*

The **Royal Lippizaner Stallions,** descendants of the noble white horses
bred in Austria since the 16th century, perform intricate dressage ma-
neuvers at their summer home on the islands. ⊠ *U.S. 2, North Hero,*
☎ *802/372–5683.* ☞ *Barn visits free between performances; shows
$15–$18; Fridays, children free.* ☉ *July–Aug.; Thurs. and Fri. at 6 PM.;
Sat. and Sun. at 2:30 PM.*

St. Anne's Shrine marks the site where French soldiers and Jesuits put
ashore in 1665 and built a fort, creating Vermont's first European settlement. The state's first Roman Catholic Mass was celebrated here
on July 26, 1666. ⊠ *W. Shore Rd., Isle La Motte,* ☎ *802/928–3362.*
☞ *Free.* ☉ *Mid-May–mid-Oct., daily 9–7.*

On the mainland east of the Alburg Peninsula, the **Missisquoi National Wildlife Refuge** (⊠ Off Rte. 78, Swanton, 36 mi north of Burlington, ☎ 802/868–4781) consists of 6,300 acres of federally protected
wetlands, meadows, and woods. It's a beautiful setting for bird-watching, canoeing, or walking nature trails.

Dining and Lodging

$–$$ ✕ **Ruthcliffe Lodge & Restaurant.** Good food and a fabulous setting
make this off-the-beaten-path motel and restaurant overlooking Lake
Champlain worth the drive. Owner-chef Mark Infante specializes in
Italian pasta, fish, and meat dishes; save room for the homemade
desserts. Fixed-price dinners include soup, salad, bread, starch, and coffee or tea. All rooms at the seven-unit motel have waterfront views.
⊠ *Old Quarry Rd., Isle La Motte,* ☎ *802/928–3200. MC, V. Closed
Columbus Day–mid-May. No lunch mid-May–June and Sept.–Columbus Day.*

$$–$$$$ ☷ **North Hero House Inn and Restaurant.** A classic country inn, North Hero House overlooks Lake Champlain and has four buildings, including the 1891 Colonial Revival main house with nine guest rooms, the restaurant, a pub room, library, and sitting room. Many rooms have water views, and each is decorated with country furnishings and antiques. Dinner is served in the informal glass greenhouse or Colonial-style dining room, or on the glassed-in veranda. Friday evenings in summer there's a lobster bake on the beach. ✉ *U.S. 2, North Hero 05474,* ☎ *802/372–4732 or 888/525–3644,* FAX *802/372–3218,* WEB *www. northherohouse.com. 26 rooms. Restaurant, pub, lake, hot tub, library. MC, V. CP.*

$$–$$$ ☷ **Shore Acres Inn and Restaurant.** This lakefront motel well off the main road offers clean, comfortable rooms overlooking the water and ½ mi of private lakeshore. Breakfast and dinner are served in the restaurant overlooking the lake. The 9-hole, par-3 golf course is free to guests. ✉ *U.S. 2, North Hero 05474,* ☎ *802/372–8722,* WEB *www. shoreacres.com. 23 rooms. Restaurant, 2 tennis courts, 9-hole golf course, beach, lawn games. AE, MC, V. Most rooms closed Nov.–Apr.; 4 rooms in annex open year-round..*

Outdoor Activities and Sports

BIKING

Hero's Welcome (✉ U.S. 2, North Hero, ☎ 802/372–4161 or 800/372–4376) rents bicycles. **Bike Shed Rentals** (✉ W. Shore Rd., Isle La Motte, ☎ 802/928–3440) rents bicycles.

BOATING

Apple Island Resort (✉ U.S. 2, South Hero, ☎ 802/372–3922) rents sailboats, rowboats, canoes, and motorboats. **Henry's Sportsman's Cottages** (✉ 218 Poor Farm Rd., Alburg, ☎ 802/796–3616) rents motorboats. **Hero's Welcome** (✉ U.S. 2, North Hero, ☎ 802/372–4161 or 800/372–4376) has canoes and kayaks for rent.

Sea Trek Charters (✉ Tudhope Sailing Center, U.S. 2, Grand Isle, ☎ 802/372–5391) on South Hero Island offers full-day fishing and sightseeing trips aboard a 25-ft cruiser.

STATE PARKS

Alburg Dunes State Park, one of the state's newest parks, has a sandy beach and some fine examples of rare flora and fauna along the hiking trails. ✉ *Off U.S. 2, Alburg,* ☎ *802/893–2825.* ☜ *$2.* ☉ *Late May–Labor Day, dawn–dusk.*

Grand Isle State Park has a fitness trail, hiking trails, and boat rentals. ✉ *U.S. 2, Grand Isle,* ☎ *802/372–4300.* ☜ *$2.* ☉ *Late May–Labor Day, dawn–dusk.*

North Hero State Park's 400 acres hold a swimming beach, nature trail, and campsites. You can rent rowboats and canoes. ✉ *North Hero, North Hero,* ☎ *802/372–8727.* ☜ *$2.* ☉ *Late May–Labor Day, dawn–dusk.*

Sand Bar State Park, with one of Vermont's best swimming beaches, has a snack bar, changing room, and boat rental concession. ✉ *U.S. 2, South Hero,* ☎ *802/372–8240.* ☜ *$2.* ☉ *Late May–Labor Day, dawn–dusk.*

Shopping

Open July–December, **Allenholm Farm** (✉ 111 South St., South Hero, ☎ 802/372–5566) has a farm store that stocks local produce.

St. Albans

③ *18 mi south of Alburg Center.*

Don't let the suburban sprawl on the outskirts of St. Albans fool you. The city's compact Victorian downtown, built during its heyday as a bustling railroad center, is very much alive with shops, restaurants, and cafés. St. Albans' centerpiece is Taylor Park, a broad green space graced with an ornate bronze fountain and lined with churches and municipal buildings in an array of imposing 19th-century styles. St. Albans was the scene of the northernmost action of the Civil War, an 1864 robbery of the city's banks by a band of Confederate soldiers disguised as civilians. The **St. Albans Historical Museum** is inside an 1861 three-story brick house (Church Street ☎ 802/527–7933)

Dining and Lodging

$$$ ✕ **Jeff's Maine Seafood.** Jeff's Fish Market and Deli has long been one of the area's best spots for seafood. The market is still here, but now there's an attractive adjoining dining room, a welcoming spot to enjoy a glass of wine and sample the creatively prepared cuisine. Appetizers include crispy salmon potato cakes topped with sour cream and caviar; for entrées, try the sautéed sea scallops, plum tomatoes and scallions in an artichoke Parmesan sauce over linguine, or pan-seared tuna steak glazed with pesto and topped with fresh plum tomatoes. Meat eaters can always find a steak here, too. A Light Fare menu is available Tuesday, Wednesday, and Thursday evenings. ⊠ *65 North Main St.,* ☎ *802/524–6135. AE, DC, MC, V.*

$–$$$ ✕ **Chow! Bella.** This narrow, handsomely decorated Victorian parlor of the former St. Albans Opera House complements chef/owner Connie Jacobs Warden's culinary creations. Pastas, individual flatbreads such as Bella Greek Shrimp with tomatoes, calamata olives and spinach, and Black Angus N.Y. strip steak with Gorgonzola Berkshire shiitake sauce are all worth sampling. For dessert, try the baklava cheesecake or Italian walnut tort. ⊠ *28 N. Main St.,* ☎ *802/524–1405. AE, D, MC, V.*

$ ✕ **Kept Writer Book Shop & Café.** Pairing soft classical music and the aroma of freshly brewed coffee with a fine selection of used tomes, this bookstore and café warms with ambience. The menu includes light fare like sandwich croissants and spanikopita (spinach pie), locally baked goodies, and moderately priced wine and beer. It's a cozy retreat perfect for curling up with a good book or the newspaper. ⊠ *5 Lake St.,* ☎ *802/527–6242. Closed Mon.*

$ ⊡ **Old Mill River Place.** The first owner of this 1799 five-bay Federal home was a niece of Vermont patriot Ethan Allen. When Anna Neville's family bought the home in 1926, her mother hung out a ROOMS TO RENT sign (Anna still has the sign), becoming one of the first lodging establishments in the area to take in tourists. Antiques and objets d'art her family has collected in their world travels adorn the house. The three second-floor bedrooms with shared bath are spacious and neat. There's a TV/VCR on the second floor with children's movies, and Ridley, the family dog, is apt to curl up and enjoy the show. ⊠ *Georgia Shore Rd., 05478,* ☎ *802/524–7211. 3 rooms, with shared baths. Closed Nov.–Apr. No credit cards. BP.*

Shopping

Rail City Market (⊠ 8 South Main St.,) has an excellent selection of natural foods, teas, spices and coffees, and body creams and soaps.

Montgomery/Jay

40   *51 mi northeast of Burlington.*

Montgomery is a small village near the Canadian border and Jay Peak ski resort. Amid the surrounding countryside are seven historic covered bridges. **Kilgore's Store** (⊠ Main St., Montgomery Center, ☎ 802/326–3058), an old-time country store with an antique soda fountain, is a great place to stock up on picnic supplies, eat a hearty bowl of soup and an overstuffed sandwich, and check out local crafts.

Lodging

$$$ 🏨 **Hotel Jay & Jay Peak Condominiums.** Unlike a lot of other lodging places, this ski-in, ski-out hotel manages to combine cheerful simplicity, convenience, and attractive prices. Rooms on the southwest side have a view of Jay Peak, and those on the north overlook the valley; upper floors have balconies. The condominiums (most slopeside) have fireplaces, one to three bedrooms, modern kitchens, and washers and dryers; some are quite luxurious. In winter, a minimum two-night stay is required, and lift tickets and some meals are included in the rates. The summer rates are low. The meal plan varies during the year; breakfast and dinner are included in ski season. ⊠ *Rte. 242, 05859,* ☎ *802/988–2611 or 800/451–4449 outside Vermont,* FAX *802/988–4049,* WEB *www.jaypeakresort.com. 48 rooms, 120 condominiums. Restaurant, bar, pool, hot tub, sauna, 2 tennis courts, downhill skiing, recreation room. AE, D, DC, MC, V. CP, MAP.*

$$ 🏨 **Black Lantern.** Built in 1803 as a hotel for mill workers, the inn has been providing bed and board ever since. Though the feeling is country, touches of sophistication abound: Provençal-print wallpaper in the dining room, a subtle rag-roll finish in the rooms in the renovated building next door. All the suites have whirlpools, and most have fireplaces. An outdoor hot tub, sheltered by a gazebo, overlooks the mountains. The restaurant menu ($$–$$$) includes pan-seared salmon with a red pepper sauce and rack of lamb. ⊠ *Rte. 118, Montgomery Village 05470,* ☎ *802/326–4507 or 800/255–8661,* FAX *802/326–4077,* WEB *www.blacklantern.com. 10 rooms, 6 suites. Restaurant, outdoor hot tub. AE, D, MC, V. BP, MAP.*

$$ 🏨 **Inn on Trout River.** The large stove is often the center of attention in the two-tier living and dining area of this 100-year-old inn, though the piano, the library, and the pub with a U-shape bar are also eye-catching. Guest rooms are decorated in either English country cottage style or country Victorian, and all have down quilts and flannel sheets in winter. The back lawn rambles down to the river, and llama treks are available for groups. The restaurant specializes in American and Continental fare with a heart-healthy emphasis. ⊠ *Main St., Montgomery Center 05471,* ☎ *802/326–4391 or 800/338–7049,* FAX *802/326–3194,* WEB *www.troutinn.com. 9 rooms, 1 suite. Restaurant, pub, library. AE, D, MC, V. BP, MAP.*

Ski Areas

JAY PEAK

Sticking up out of the flat farmland, Jay averages 332 in of snowfall a year—more than any other Vermont ski area. Its proximity to Québec attracts Montréalers and discourages eastern seaboarders; hence, the prices are moderate and the lift lines shorter than at other resorts. The big news is the upgrading of the aerial tram: new cars offer good visibility and a superior sound system. ⊠ *Rte. 242, Jay 05859,* ☎ *802/988–2611; 800/451–4449 outside VT,* WEB *www.jaypeakresort.com.*

Downhill. Jay Peak is in fact two mountains with 74 trails, the highest reaching nearly 4,000 ft with a vertical drop of 2,153 ft. The area is served by seven lifts, including Vermont's only tramway, which transports skiers to the top of the mountain in just seven minutes, and the longest detachable quad in the East. The area also has a quad, a triple, and a double chairlift, and two T-bars. The smaller mountain has more straight-fall-line, expert terrain, and the tram-side peak has many curving and meandering trails perfectly suited for intermediate and beginning skiers. Jay, highly rated for gladed skiing by major ski-ing publications, has 19 gladed trails. The longest trail, Ullr's Dream, is 3 mi. Every morning at 9 AM the ski school offers a free tour, from the tram down one trail. Jay has 75% snowmaking coverage. The area has a halfpipe and snowboard terrain for snowboarders.

Cross-country. A touring center at the base of the mountain has 20 km (12 mi) of groomed cross-country trails. There is a $5 trail fee. A net-work of 200 km (124 mi) of trails is in the vicinity.

Other activities. Snowshoes can be rented, and guided walks are led by a naturalist. Telemark rentals and instruction are available.

Child care. The child-care center for youngsters ages 2–7 is open from 9 AM to 9 PM. Guests of the Hotel Jay and the Jay Peak Condomini-ums receive this nursery care free, as well as free skiing for children ages 6 and under, evening care, and supervised dining at the hotel. In-fant care is available on a fee basis with advanced reservations. Chil-dren ages 5–10 can participate in a daylong Mountain Explorers program, which includes lunch; a Minirider program for snowboard-ers aged 5–10 is also available.

Summer activities. Jay Peak offers tram rides to the summit from mid-June through September ($10) and rents mountain bikes.

CROSS-COUNTRY SKIING

Hazen's Notch Cross Country Ski Center and B & B (⊠ Rte. 58, ☎ 802/ 326–4708), delightfully remote at any time of the year, has 50 km (31 mi) of marked and groomed trails and rents equipment and snow shoes.

En Route The descent from Jay Peak on Route 101 leads to Route 100, which can be the beginning of a scenic loop tour of Routes 14, 5, 58, and back to 100, or it can take you east to the city of Newport on Lake Memphremagog. You will encounter some of the most unspoiled areas in all Vermont on the drive south from Newport on either U.S. 5 or I–91 (I–91 is faster, but U.S. 5 is prettier). This region, the Northeast King-dom, is named for the remoteness and stalwart independence that have helped preserve its rural nature.

Newport

🔆 *20 mi east of Jay Peak.*

From its rough-and-tumble days as a logging town, Newport passed through a long stretch of doldrums and decline before discovering that revitalization lay in taking advantage of its splendid location on the southern shores of Lake Memphremagog, Vermont's second-largest lake (only the southern 3 mi of the lake lie within the state; the northern 30 mi are in Canada). Only a block from the waterfront, downtown's main street has evolved into a busy shopping district. The waterfront has a handsome new public boat house where tours of the lake begin. One of the best ways to explore the lake on both sides of the border is aboard the 49-passenger **Stardust Princess,** which sails from the City Dock from Memorial Day through Labor Day. ⊠ *Newport City Dock,* ☎ *802/334–6617.*

Dining and Lodging

$$ ✕ **The East Side.** With an outdoor deck that overlooks the lake, this popular spot serves American fare such as beef stew and prime rib and specialties such as crab chicken—a boneless breast of chicken stuffed with crabmeat and napped with lobster sauce. Homemade soups and desserts also share the menu, and daily specials include a variety of over-stuffed sandwiches. ✉ *Lake St.,* ☎ *802/334–2340. D, MC, V. No breakfast Mon.–Fri.*

$ 🏨 **Newport City Motel.** Rooms at this reasonably priced, two-story motel, a short distance from the center of town, are clean, modern, and nicely furnished, and have cable TV and air-conditioning. ✉ *444 E. Main St., 05855,* ☎ *800/338–6558,* 🕿 *802/334–6557. 64 rooms, 1 suite. Indoor pool, fitness center, hot tub.*

Outdoor Activities and Sports

The Great Outdoors of Newport (✉ 177 Main St., ☎ 802/334–2831) rents boats, kayaks, and canoes, as well as cross-country skis and snowshoes. The store sells fishing supplies and bicycles.

Shopping

Bogner Haus Factory Outlet (✉ 150 Main St., ☎ 802/334–0135) sells first-quality men's and women's skiwear and golf apparel as well as snowboarding and activewear.

Lake Willoughby

42 *30 mi southeast of Montgomery (summer route; 50 mi by winter route), 28 mi north of St. Johnsbury.*

Flanking the eastern and western shores of Lake Willoughby, the cliffs of surrounding Mts. Pisgah and Hor drop to water's edge, giving this glacially carved, 500-ft-deep lake a striking resemblance to a Norwegian fjord. The beautiful lake is popular for summer and winter recreation, and the trails to the top of Mt. Pisgah reward hikers with glorious views.

The **Bread and Puppet Museum** is a ramshackle barn that houses a surrealistic collection of props used in past performances by the world-renowned Bread and Puppet Theater. The troupe, whose members live communally on the surrounding farm, have been performing social and political commentary with the towering (they're supported by people on stilts), eerily expressive puppets for about 30 years. ✉ *Rte. 122, Glover, 1 mi east of Rte. 16,* ☎ *802/525–3031.* 🎟 *Donations accepted.* ☽ *June–Oct., daily 9–5; other times by appointment.*

Lodging

$$–$$$ 🏨 **WilloughVale Inn.** Few Vermont inns can claim a more spectacular location than this waterfront property at the northern end of Lake Willoughby. The main building, with a wraparound veranda, has six spacious and nicely furnished rooms overlooking the lake. The lakefront dining room is open for dinner to guests on Friday and Saturday in winter, and Thurs.–Mon. in summer. An even better bet are the cottages on Willoughby's shore. They come with fully equipped kitchens, fireplaces, screened porches, and private docks and sleep up to four persons. Pets weighing 50 lbs or less are welcome in the cottages. Canoes and kayaks are available. ✉ *Rte. 5A, Westmore 05860,* ☎ *802/525–4123 or 800/594–9102,* 🕿 *802/525–4514,* 🌐 *www.willoughvale. com. 6 rooms, 4 cottages. Dining room, boating. AE, MC, V. CP.*

East Burke

43 *17 mi south of Lake Willoughby.*

A jam-packed general store, a post office, and a couple of great places to eat are in the center of East Burke, near the Burke Mountain ski area. A major attraction are the 100 mi of old logging, fire, and country roads, which are good for self-guided hiking, mountain biking, cross-country skiing, and snowshoeing. The **Kingdom Trails Association** (✉ Box 204, East Burke 05832, ☎ 802/626–0737 WEB www.kingdomtrails. org) manages the trails and provides information.

Dining and Lodging

$$–$$$ ✕ **River Garden Café.** You can eat outdoors on the enclosed porch or the patio and view the perennial gardens that rim the grounds; the café is bright and cheerful on the inside as well. The fare includes lamb tenderloin, warm artichoke dip, bruschetta, pastas, and fresh fish. A lighter menu is offered nightly. ✉ *Rte. 114, East Burke,* ☎ *802/626–3514. AE, D, MC, V. Closed Mon., 1 wk Apr., and month of Nov.*

$$$ ✕⌂ **Inn at Mountain View Creamery.** The 1890 redbrick Georgian-style creamery at this former gentleman's farm has been modernized as an elegant hostelry. Set high on a hilltop amid 440 acres of rolling hills and meadows, the inn has second-floor guest rooms handsomely furnished with country antiques and handmade quilts. Miles of cross-country ski, snowshoe, hiking, and mountain biking trails are right at the doorstep, and hay and sleigh rides provide a grand way to enjoy the scenery. The menu at Darling's Country Bistro ($$–$$$; dinner Thursday through Sunday) lists hearty dishes such as beef carbonnade with caramelized onions as well as fish and vegetarian fare. ✉ *Darling Hill Rd., 05832,* ☎ *802/626–9924 or 800/572–4509,* WEB *www.innmtnview. com. 10 rooms. Restaurant, hiking, cross-country skiing. Closed Apr., Nov. AE, MC, V. BP.*

$$ ✕⌂ **Wildflower Inn.** The hilltop views are breathtaking at this ram-★ bling complex of old farm buildings on 500 acres. Guest rooms in the restored Federal-style main house and four other buildings are decorated with reproductions and contemporary furnishings. Rooms in the carriage house are somewhat dark and cramped; they have kitchenettes and bunk beds. In warm weather, the inn is family oriented: there's a petting barn, planned children's activities, and a kids' swimming pool. The inn quiets down in winter when it caters more to cross-country skiers. The restaurant serves gourmet fare, with dishes such as a seasonal tricolor peppercorn cognac breast of duck, and a blackened prime rib from their own herd of Belted Galloways. ✉ *Darling Hill Rd., west of East Burke, Lyndonville 05851,* ☎ *802/626–8310 or 800/627–8310,* FAX *802/626–3039,* WEB *www.wildflowerinn.com. 10 rooms, 11 suites. Restaurant, pool, hot tub, sauna, tennis court, soccer, fishing, ice-skating, skiing, sleigh rides, tobogganing, recreation room. MC, V. Closed Apr., Nov. BP.*

$ ✕⌂ **Old Cutter Inn.** A small converted farmhouse only ½ mi from the Burke Mountain base lodge offers quaint inn rooms in the main building, as well as comfortable if less charming accommodations in an annex. The restaurant ($$–$$$) serves fare that reflects the Swiss chef-owner's heritage, as well as superb, good-value Continental cuisine including osso buco, chateaubriand, and veal piccata. You can choose to include breakfast and dinner in the price. ✉ *143 Pinkham Rd., 05832,* ☎ *802/ 626–5152 or 800/295–1943,* WEB *www.pbpub.com/cutter.htm. 9 rooms, 5 with bath; 1 suite. Restaurant, bar, pool, hiking, bicycles, cross-country skiing. D, MC, V. Closed Wed., Apr., Nov.*

Outdoor Activities and Sports

Village Sport Shop (⊠ 4 Broad St., Lyndonville, ☎ 802/626–8448) rents canoes, kayaks, bikes, Rollerblades, paddleboats, snowshoes, and cross-country and downhill skis.

Shopping

Bailey's & Burke, Inc. (⊠ Rte. 114, ☎ 802/626–9250), an institution, sells baked goods, pizza and sandwiches, wine, clothing, and sundries.

Trout River Brewing Co. brews all-natural premium ales and lagers and has six styles on tap daily. The tasting room is open Wed.–Sun. from 11 AM to 6 PM. (⊠ Main St., Route 114, ☎ 802/626–3984 or 888/296–2739).

Ski Areas

BURKE MOUNTAIN

This low-key, moderately priced resort has plenty of terrain for beginners, but intermediate skiers, experts, racers, telemarkers, and snowboarders will find time-honored narrow New England trails. Many packages at Burke are significantly less expensive than those at other Vermont areas. ⊠ *Mountain Rd., East Burke 05832,* ☎ *802/626–3302; 802/626–4069 snow conditions,* WEB *www.skiburke.com.*

Downhill. With a 2,000-ft vertical drop and 43 trails and glades, Burke is something of a sleeper among the larger Eastern ski areas. It has greatly increased its snowmaking capability (75%), which is enhanced by the mountain's northern location and exposure, assuring plenty of natural snow. There is a 5-acre snowboard park (with a halfpipe and snowmaking capabilities) for all levels. Burke has one quad, one double chairlift, and two surface lifts. Lift lines, even on weekends and holidays, are light to nonexistent.

Cross-country. Burke Ski Touring Center has more than 80 km (50 mi) of trails (65 km/39 mi groomed); some lead to high points with scenic views. There's a snack bar at the center.

Child care. In the Children's Center, the nursery takes children from ages 6 months to 6 years on weekends and holidays. SKIwee and MINIriders lessons through the ski school are available to children from ages 4 to 16.

Summer activities. Hiking, biking (rentals are available), and a children's swing are summer options.

St. Johnsbury

44 *16 mi south of East Burke, 39 mi northeast of Montpelier.*

St. Johnsbury is the southern gateway to the Northeast Kingdom. Though the town was chartered in 1786, its identity was not firmly established until 1830, when Thaddeus Fairbanks invented the platform scale, a device that revolutionized weighing methods that had been in use since the beginning of recorded history. Because of the Fairbanks family's philanthropic bent, this city with a distinctly 19th-century industrial feel has a strong cultural and architectural imprint.

Opened in 1891, the **Fairbanks Museum and Planetarium** attests to the Fairbanks family's inquisitiveness about all things scientific. The red-brick building in the squat Romanesque Revival architectural style of H. H. Richardson houses Vermont plants and animals, as well as ethnographic and natural history collections from around the globe. There's also a 50-seat planetarium and a hands-on exhibit room for kids. On the third Saturday in September, the museum sponsors the

Festival of Traditional Crafts, with demonstrations of early American household and farm skills such as candle and soap making. ⊠ *Main and Prospect Sts.,* ☎ *802/748–2372,* WEB *www.fairbanksmuseum.org.* ⊡ *$5; planetarium $2.* ⊙ *July–Aug., Mon.–Sat. 10–6, Sun. 1–5; Sept.– June, Mon.–Sat. 10–4, Sun. 1–5. Planetarium shows July–Aug., daily at 11 and 1:30; Sept.–June, weekends at 1:30.*

★   The **St. Johnsbury Athenaeum,** with its dark rich paneling, polished Victorian woodwork, and ornate circular staircases that rise to the gallery around the perimeter, is one of the oldest art galleries in the country. The gallery at the back of the building specializes in Hudson River School paintings and has the overwhelming *Domes of Yosemite* by Albert Bierstadt. ⊠ *1171 Main St.,* ☎ *802/748–8291,* WEB *www. stjathenaeum.org.* ⊡ *Free.* ⊙ *Mon. and Wed. 10–8, Tues. and Thurs.– Fri. 10–5:30, Sat. 9:30–4.*

Dog Mountain is artist–dog lover Stephen Huneck's newly constructed art gallery (works are for sale) and sculpture garden, complete with a chapel where humans and their canine companions can meditate. ⊠ *Off Spaulding Rd.,* ☎ *802/748–2700 or 800/449–2580,* WEB *www.huneck. com.* ⊡ *Free.* ⊙ *June–Oct., Mon.–Sat. 10–5 and Sun. 11–4, and by appointment.*

OFF THE
BEATEN PATH

CABOT CREAMERY – The biggest cheese producer in the state, a dairy cooperative, has a visitor center with an audiovisual presentation about the dairy and cheese industry. You can taste samples, purchase cheese, and tour the plant. The center is midway between Barre and St. Johnsbury. ⊠ *2870 Main St./Rte. 215, 3 mi north of U.S. 2, Cabot,* ☎ *802/563–3393; 800/639–4031 orders only.* ⊡ *$1.* ⊙ *June–Oct., daily 9–5; Nov.–Dec. and Feb.–May, Mon.–Sat. 9–4; call ahead to check cheese-making days.*

Dining and Lodging

$$$$ ✕⛉ **Rabbit Hill Inn.** Each of the guest rooms at this classic, white-
★   columned rural inn is different: the Loft, with an 8-ft Palladian window, a king canopy bed, a double whirlpool bath, and a corner fireplace, is one of the most requested. Rooms facing front have views of the Connecticut River and New Hampshire's White Mountains. Common areas, from porches to sitting rooms, make it easy to unwind. The intimate, candlelit dining room serves a five-course fixed price dinner ($40) featuring regional dishes such as grilled sausage of Vermont pheasant with pistachios or smoked chicken and red-lentil dumplings. Meat and fish are smoked on the premises, and the herbs and vegetables often come from gardens out back. ⊠ *Rte. 18, Lower Waterford, 11 mi south of St. Johnsbury, 05848,* ☎ *802/748–5168 or 800/762–8669,* FAX *802/ 748–8342,* WEB *www.rabbithillinn.com. 16 rooms, 5 suites. Restaurant, pub, hiking, cross-country skiing. AE, MC, V. Closed 1st 3 wks of Apr., 1st 2 wks of Nov. MAP.*

$$ ⛉ **Emergo Farm.** Bebo and Lori Webster rent out three guest rooms in their 1890, 15-room farmhouse on a 240-acre dairy farm that has been in the Webster family for five generations. Lori collects antiques, which are liberally sprinkled throughout the house and in the second-floor guest rooms. One room has its own bath. The other two, which share a bath, have a kitchen and can be rented out as a suite to sleep up to six. The view from the hilltop picnic grove is spectacular. ⊠ *261 Webster Hill Rd., Danville 05828,* ☎ *802/684–2215. 3 rooms, 1 with bath. BP.*

Peacham

㊺ *10 mi southwest of St. Johnsbury.*

Tiny Peacham's stunning scenery and 18th-century charm have made it a favorite with urban refugees, artists seeking solitude and inspiration, and movie directors looking for the quintessential New England village. *Ethan Frome,* starring Liam Neeson, was filmed here.

Gourmet soups and hearty lamb and barley stew are among the seasonally changing take-out specialties at the **Peacham Store** (⊠ Main St., ☎ 802/592–3310). You can browse through the locally made crafts while waiting for your order.

Barre

㊻ *7 mi southeast of Montpelier, 35 mi southwest of St. Johnsbury.*

Barre has been famous as the source of Vermont granite ever since two men began working the quarries in the early 1800s; the number of immigrant laborers attracted to the industry made the city prominent in the early years of the American labor movement. Downtown, at the corner of Maple and North Main, look for the statue of a representative Italian stonecutter of a century ago. On Route 14, just north of Barre, stop at **Hope Cemetery** to see spectacular examples of carving.

The attractions of the **Rock of Ages granite quarry** range from the awe-inspiring (the quarry resembles the Grand Canyon in miniature) to the mildly ghoulish (you can consult a directory of tombstone dealers throughout the country). You might recognize the sheer walls of the quarry from *Batman and Robin,* the film starring George Clooney and Arnold Schwarzenegger. At the crafts center, skilled artisans sculpt monuments; at the quarries themselves, 25-ton blocks of stone are cut from sheer 475-ft walls by workers who clearly earn their pay. ⊠ *Exit 6 off I–89, follow Rte. 63,* ☎ *802/476–3119.* ▣ *Tour of active quarry $4, craftsman center and self-guided tour free.* ☉ *Visitor center May–Oct., Mon.–Sat. 8:30–5, Sun. noon–5; narrated tours every 45 mins 9:15–3 weekdays June–mid-Oct.*

Dining and Lodging

$–$$ ✗ **A Single Pebble.** Devotees of Chinese food have been making pilgrimages to this restaurant since it opened in 1997. Chef and co-owner Steve Bogart has been cooking creative, authentic Asian dishes for more than 30 years. He prepares traditional clay-pot dishes as well as wok specialties such as sesame catfish and kung po chicken. The dry fried green beans (sautéed with flecks of pork, black beans, preserved vegetables, and garlic) and mock eel (thinly sliced shiitake mushrooms) are house specialties. All dishes can be made without meat. ⊠ *135 Barre-Montpelier Rd.,* ☎ *802/476–9700. D, MC, V. Reservations essential. Closed Sun.–Mon. No lunch.*

$–$$ ▣ **Autumn Harvest Inn.** You'll be tempted to spend the whole day on the porch that graces the front of this casual inn, built in 1790. It sits atop a knoll overlooking a 46-acre workhorse farm and the surrounding valley. Rooms in the older part of the house have more character; all have phones and TVs with VCRs. Prime rib and veal dishes are among the highlights of the seasonal country menu at the restaurant (no lunch), where dinner is served by candlelight Wednesday through Saturday. ⊠ *118 Clark Rd., Williamstown 05679,* ☎ *802/433–1355,* ☒ *802/433–5501,* ⓦⓔⓑ *www.central-vt.com/web/autumn. 18 rooms. Restaurant, bar, pond, horseback riding, cross-country skiing. AE, MC, V. BP, MAP.*

Northern Vermont A to Z

To research prices, get advice from other travelers, and book travel arrangements, visit www.fodors.com.

BOAT & FERRY TRAVEL

Lake Champlain Ferries, in operation since 1826, operates three ferry crossings during the summer months and one—between Grand Isle and Plattsburgh, New York—in winter through thick lake ice. Ferries leave from the King Street Dock in Burlington, Charlotte, and Grand Isle. This is a convenient means of getting to and from New York State, as well as a pleasant way to spend an afternoon.

➤ BOAT & FERRY INFORMATION: **Lake Champlain Ferries** (☎ 802/864–9804).

BUS TRAVEL

Vermont Transit links Burlington, Waterbury, Montpelier, St. Johnsbury, and Newport.

➤ BUS INFORMATION: **Vermont Transit** (☎ 800/552–8737).

CAR TRAVEL

In north-central Vermont, I–89 heads west from Montpelier to Burlington and continues north to Canada. Interstate 91 is the principal north–south route in the east, and Route 100 runs north–south through the center of the state. North of I–89, Routes 104 and 15 provide a major east–west transverse. From Barton, near Lake Willoughby, U.S. 5 and Route 122 south are beautiful drives. Strip-mall drudge bogs down the section of U.S. 5 around Lyndonville.

EMERGENCIES

➤ HOSPITALS AND EMERGENCY SERVICES: **Fletcher Allen Health Care** (⊠ 111 Colchester Ave., Burlington, ☎ 802/847–2434, 24-hour emergency health care information). **Copley Hospital** (⊠ Washington Hwy., Morrisville, ☎ 802/999–4231). **Northeastern Vermont Regional Hospital** (⊠ Hospital Dr., St. Johnsbury, ☎ 802/748–8141).

OUTDOORS & SPORTS

HIKING

The Green Mountain Club maintains the Long Trail—the north–south border-to-border footpath that runs the length of the spine of the Green Mountains—as well as other trails nearby. The club headquarters sells maps and guides, and experts dispense advice.

➤ CONTACTS: The **Green Mountain Club** (⊠ Rte. 100, Waterbury, ☎ 802/244–7037).

TOURS

P.O.M.G. Bike Tours of Vermont leads weekend and five-day adult camping-bike tours. True North Kayak Tours operates a guided tour of Lake Champlain and a natural-history tour and will arrange a custom multiday trip. The company also coordinates special trips for kids.

➤ TOUR-OPERATOR RECOMMENDATIONS: **P.O.M.G. Bike Tours of Vermont** (⊠ Richmond, ☎ 802/434–2270). **True North Kayak Tours** (⊠ 53 Nash Pl., Burlington, ☎ 802/860–1910).

TRAIN TRAVEL

The *Champlain Valley Weekender* runs between Middlebury and Burlington, with stops in Vergennes and Shelburne. The views from the coach cars, which date from the 1930s, are of Lake Champlain, the valley farmlands, and surrounding mountains. (*$12 round-trip. July–early Sept., weekends, 2 trips per day; call for foliage season schedule.*) The new *Champlain Flyer,* developed to ease traffic into and out

of Burlington, transports passengers on weekdays between Burlington
and Charlotte—with a stop in Shelburne—in just 25 minutes.
➤ TRAIN INFORMATION: *Champlain Valley Weekender* (☎ 802/463–
3069 or 800/707–3530). *Champlain Flyer* (☎ 802/951–4010).

VISITOR INFORMATION

➤ TOURIST INFORMATION: **Lake Champlain Regional Chamber of Com**
merce (✉ 60 Main St., Suite 100, Burlington 05401, ☎ 802/863–3489
or 877/686–5253, WEB www.champlainislands.com). **Northeast King**
dom Chamber of Commerce (✉ 357 Western Ave., St. Johnsbury 05819,
☎ 802/748–3678 or 800/639–6379, WEB www.vermontnekchamber.
org). **Northeast Kingdom Travel and Tourism Association** (✉ Box 465,
Barton 05822, ☎ 802/525–4386 or 888/884–8001, WEB www.
travelthekingdom.com). **Smugglers' Notch Area Chamber of Com**
merce (✉ Box 364, Jeffersonville 05464, ☎ 802/644–2239, WEB www.
smugnotch.com). The **Stowe Area Association** (✉ Main St., Box 1320,
Stowe 05672, ☎ 802/253–7321 or 800/247–8693, WEB www.stoweinfo.
com). **Vermont North Country Chamber of Commerce** (✉ The Causeway, Newport 05855, ☎ 802/334–7782 or 800/635–4643, WEB www.
vtnorthcountry.com).

VERMONT A TO Z

To research prices, get advice from other travelers, and book travel ar
rangements, visit www.fodors.com.

AIRPORTS & TRANSFERS

Continental, Delta, United, and US Airways fly into Burlington International Airport. Rutland State Airport has daily service to and from
Boston on US Airways Express. West of Bennington and convenient
to southern Vermont, Albany International Airport in New York State
is served by 10 major U.S. carriers.
➤ AIRPORT INFORMATION: **Burlington International Airport** (✉ Airport
Dr., 4 mi east of Burlington off U.S. 2, ☎ 802/863–2874). **Rutland State**
Airport (✉ 1002 Airport Rd., North Clarendon, ☎ 802/786–8881).
Albany International Airport (✉ 737 Albany Shaker Rd., Albany, ☎
518/869–3021).

AIRPORT TRANSFERS

Aircraft charters are available at Burlington International Airport from
Valet Air Services. Mansfield Heliflight provides helicopter transportation throughout New England.
➤ SHUTTLES: **Valet Air Services** (☎ 802/863–3626 or 800/782–0773).
Mansfield Heliflight (✉ Milton, ☎ 802/893–1003 or 800/872–0884).

BUS TRAVEL

Bonanza Bus Lines connects New York City and Providence with Bennington. Vermont Transit connects Bennington, Brattleboro, Burlington, Rutland, and other Vermont cities and towns with Boston, Springfield,
Albany, New York, Montréal, and cities in New Hampshire.
➤ BUS INFORMATION: **Bonanza Bus Lines** (☎ 800/556–3815). **Ver**
mont Transit (☎ 800/552–8737).

CAR TRAVEL

Interstate 91, which stretches from Connecticut and Massachusetts in
the south to Québec in the north, reaches most points along Vermont's
eastern border. I–89, from New Hampshire to the east and Québec to
the north, crosses central Vermont from White River Junction to
Burlington. Southwestern Vermont can be reached by U.S. 7 from
Massachusetts and U.S. 4 from New York.

The official speed limit in Vermont is 50 mph, unless otherwise posted; on the interstates it's 65 mph. Right turns are permitted on a red light unless otherwise indicated. You can get a state map, which has mileage charts and enlarged maps of major downtown areas, free from the Vermont Department of Tourism and Marketing. The *Vermont Atlas and Gazetteer,* sold in many bookstores, shows nearly every road in the state and is great for driving on the back roads.

EMERGENCIES

➤ HOT LINES: **Ambulance, fire, police** (☎ 911). **Vermont State Police** (☎ 800/525–5555).

LODGING

The Vermont Chamber of Commerce (☞ Visitor Information) publishes the *Vermont Travelers' Guidebook,* which is an extensive list of lodgings, and additional guides to country inns and vacation rentals. The Vermont Department of Tourism and Marketing (☞ Visitor Information) has a brochure that lists lodgings at working farms.

CAMPING

Call Vermont's Department of Forests, Parks, and Recreation for a copy of the "Vermont Campground Guide," which lists state parks and other public and private camping facilities. Call the following numbers from the second Tuesday in January through May 1; after that, call the individual parks. Between Labor Day and January, reservations not accepted.

➤ CONTACTS: Department of Forests, Parks, and Recreation (☎ 802/241–3655). ☎ 802/885–8891 or 800/299–3071 in southeastern Vermont; ☎ 802/483–2001 or 800/658–1622 in southwestern Vermont; ☎ 802/879–5674 or 800/252–2363 in northwestern Vermont; ☎ 802/479–4280 or 800/658–6934 in northeastern Vermont.

NATIONAL PARKS

Vermont state parks open during the last week in May and close after the Labor Day or Columbus Day weekend, depending on location. Day-use charges are $2 per person for ages 14 and up, $1.50 for ages 4 to 13; children under 4 are free. Call individual parks or the Department of Forests, Parks, and Recreation for information.

➤ CONTACTS: **Department of Forests, Parks, and Recreation** (☎ 802/241–3655).

Outdoors & Sports

A hot line has tips on peak viewing locations and times and up-to-date snow conditions.

➤ CONTACTS: **Foliage and Snow Hot Line** (☎ 802/828–3239).

CANOEING

Umiak Outdoor Outfitters has shuttles to nearby rivers for day excursions and customized overnight trips. Vermont Canoe Trippers/Battenkill Canoe, Ltd. organizes canoe tours (some are inn-to-inn) and fishing trips.

➤ CONTACTS: **Umiak Outdoor Outfitters** (✉ 849 S. Main St., Stowe, ☎ 802/253–2317. **Vermont Canoe Trippers/Battenkill Canoe, Ltd.** (✉ River Rd., off Rte. 7A, Arlington, ☎ 802/362–2800).

FISHING

For information about fishing, including licenses, call the Vermont Fish and Wildlife Department. Strictly Trout will arrange a fly-fishing trip on any Vermont stream or river, including the Battenkill.

➤ CONTACTS: **Vermont Fish and Wildlife Department** (☎ 802/241–3700). **Strictly Trout** (☎ 802/869–3116).

HIKING

The Green Mountain Club publishes hiking maps and guides. The club also manages the Long Trail, the north–south trail that traverses the entire state.

➤ CONTACTS: **Green Mountain Club** (✉ Rte. 100, Waterbury, ☎ 802/244–7037).

HORSEBACK RIDING

Kedron Valley Stables has one- to six-day riding tours with lodging in country inns.

➤ CONTACTS: **Kedron Valley Stables** (✉ South Woodstock, ☎ 802/457–1480 or 800/225–6301).

SKIING

For information, contact Ski Vermont/Vermont Ski Area Association.

➤ CONTACTS: **Ski Vermont/Vermont Ski Area Association** (✉ Box 368, 26 State St., Montpelier 05601, ☎ 802/223–2439, WEB www.skivermont.com).

TOURS

Bicycle Holidays helps you plan your own inn-to-inn tour by providing route directions and booking your accommodations. Vermont Bicycle Touring leads numerous tours in the state and the region. New England Hiking Holidays leads guided walks with lodging in country inns. North Wind Hiking and Walking Tours conducts guided walking tours through Vermont's countryside.

➤ TOUR-OPERATOR RECOMMENDATIONS: **Bicycle Holidays** (✉ Munger St., Middlebury, ☎ 802/388–2453 or 800/292–5388). **Vermont Bicycle Touring** (✉ Monkton Rd., Bristol, ☎ 802/453–4811 or 800/245–3868). **New England Hiking Holidays** (✉ North Conway, NH, ☎ 603/356–9696 or 800/869–0949). **North Wind Hiking and Walking Tours** (✉ Waitsfield, ☎ 802/496–5771 or 800/496–5771).

TRAIN TRAVEL

Amtrak's *Vermonter* is a daytime service linking Washington, D.C., with Brattleboro, Bellows Falls, White River Junction, Montpelier, Waterbury, Essex Junction, and St. Albans. The *Adirondack,* which runs from Washington, D.C., to Montréal, serves Albany, Ft. Edward (near Glens Falls), Ft. Ticonderoga, and Plattsburgh, allowing relatively convenient access to western Vermont. The *Ethan Allen Express* connects New York City with Fair Haven and Rutland.

➤ TRAIN INFORMATION: **Amtrak** (☎ 800/872–7245, WEB www.amtrak.com).

VISITOR INFORMATION

➤ TOURIST INFORMATION: **Forest Supervisor, Green Mountain National Forest** (✉ 231 N. Main St., Rutland 05701, ☎ 802/747–6700). **Vermont Chamber of Commerce** (✉ Box 37, Montpelier 05601, ☎ 802/223–3443). **Vermont Department of Tourism and Marketing** (✉ 134 State St., Montpelier 05602, ☎ 802/828–3237 or 800/837–6668). There are **state information centers** on the Massachusetts border at I–91, the New Hampshire border at I–89, the New York border at Route 4A, and the Canadian border at I–89.

4 NEW HAMPSHIRE

The seacoast, majestic mountains, and peaceful villages are all part of New Hampshire. Along the coast is a short stretch of towns with sandy beaches, as well as the engaging city of Portsmouth. The Lakes Region is a summer and fall haven for fishing, swimming, and boating. Up north, the majestic White Mountains attract people who come to gaze on Mt. Washington, the tallest peak in the East, to ski and snowboard, to hike, and to shop at North Conway's outlet stores. Western and central New Hampshire have a string of cities along I-93 and a large unspoiled area of small towns, each with its own historic district and town green.

By Andrew
Collins

CRUSTY, INDEPENDENT-MINDED NEW HAMPSHIRE is often defined more by what it is not than by what it is. It lacks the folksy charm of neighboring Vermont, nor does it have the miles of awe-inspiring rocky coast of Maine, its neighbor to the east. And New Hampshire's politics tend toward conservative (with a distinctly libertarian slant), unlike the decidedly more liberal Massachusetts.

Whether in spite of or because of its differences, New Hampshire has been welcoming visitors for centuries. The first hiker to reach the top of Mt. Washington was Darby Field, in 1642. The first summer home appeared on one of the state's many lakes in 1763. Ralph Waldo Emerson, Henry David Thoreau, Nathaniel Hawthorne, and Louisa May Alcott all visited and wrote about the state, sparking a strong literary tradition that continues today. Filmmaker Ken Burns, writer J. D. Salinger, and poet Donald Hall all make their homes here.

New Hampshire's independent spirit nourishes other branches of the arts as well. Portsmouth has several theater groups, both cutting-edge and mainstream. New Hampshire's oldest professional theater, Tamworth's Barnstormers, claims the son of a president (Francis Cleveland) as founder. Throughout the state, a large number of stores display the work of local artisans. On back roads and in small towns, you can find makers of fine furniture and museum-quality pewter, glassblowers and potters, weavers and woodworkers. The League of New Hampshire Craftsmen operates eight stores around the state and runs the nation's oldest crafts fair each year in early August.

But it was the mountain peaks, clear air, and sparkling lakes that attracted most of New Hampshire's early visitors, the same things that draw people today. You can ski, snowboard, hike, and fish, or explore on snowmobiles, sailboats, and mountain bikes. Rock climbing and snowshoeing are popular, too. The diversity of the state's natural resources make it a popular spot with everyone from avid adventurers to young families looking for easy access to nature.

New Hampshire natives have no objection to others enjoying the natural beauty of the state as long as they leave some of their money behind. The state has long resisted both sales and income taxes, so tourism adds much-needed revenue to the state coffers.

Taxes are only one hotly debated topic in the politically minded Granite State. New Hampshire was the first colony to declare itself independent from Great Britain, the first to adopt a state constitution, and the first to require that constitution to be referred to the people for approval. From the start, New Hampshire residents took their hard-won freedoms seriously. Twenty years after the Revolutionary War's Battle of Bennington, New Hampshire native General John Stark, who led the troops to that crucial victory, wrote a letter to be read at the reunion he was too ill to attend. In it, he reminded his men, "Live free or die; death is not the worst of evils." The first half of that sentiment is now the state's motto, appearing even on its license plates. Nothing symbolizes those freedoms more than voting, and residents relish their role as host of the nation's earliest presidential primary.

With a few of its cities consistently rated among the most livable in the nation, New Hampshire has seen considerable growth over the past decade or two. Even as growth has leveled in the rest of New England, New Hampshire's population continues upward, fueled mainly by transplants seeking a higher quality of life and lower costs of living.

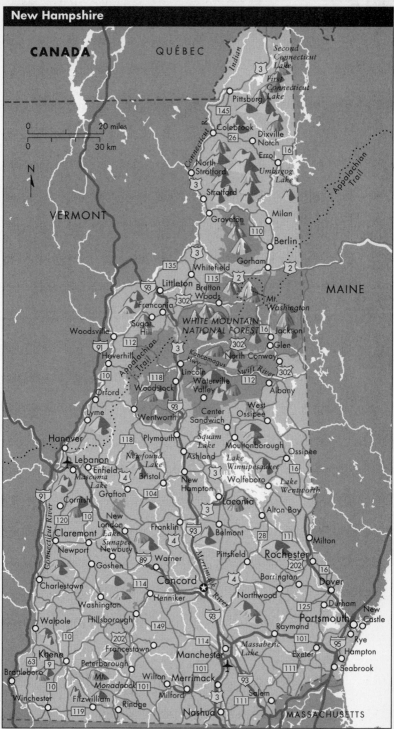

New Hampshire

CANADA — QUÉBEC

Second Connecticut Lake
First Connecticut Lake

Pittsburg

145

Colebrook
26
Dixville Notch
Errol
16

North Stratford
3
Stratford

Umbagog Lake

VERMONT

Milan
Groveton
110
Berlin

Gorham
3
2

135
Whitefield
115
2
MAINE

93 Littleton
Bretton Woods
302
Mt. Washington

Franconia

Sugar Hill
WHITE MOUNTAIN NATIONAL FOREST
16 Jackson

Woodsville
112
3
302
Glen
North Conway
302

91
Haverhill
Kancamagus Hwy.
Swift River

10
118
Lincoln
112
Albany

Orford
Woodstock
Waterville Valley

Lyme
93
Center Sandwich
West Ossipee

Hanover
Wentworth
Squam Lake

118
Plymouth
Ashland
Moultonborough
Ossipee

Lebanon
Newfound Lake
Lake Winnipesaukee
16

Enfield
Mascoma Lake
4
Bristol
New Hampton
3
Wolfeboro
Lake Wentworth

Cornish
Grafton
104
Laconia

91
Alton Bay

120
New London
Franklin
93
Belmont
28
11
Milton

Claremont
Sunapee Lake
4
Pittsfield
Rochester

Newport
Newbury
89
Warner
202
16

Goshen
Concord
Barrington
Dover

Charlestown
114
Northwood
125
Durham

Henniker
New Castle

Washington
Portsmouth

Walpole
Hillsborough
149
Raymond
101
95

10
Francestown
114
Massabesic Lake
Rye

63
202
Manchester
101
Exeter
Hampton

Keene
9
Peterborough
Mt. Monadnock
101
Merrimack
111
Seabrook

Brattleboro
Wilton
Milford
93
Salem

10
Fitzwilliam
Rindge
3
111

Winchester
119
Nashua
MASSACHUSETTS

0   20 miles
0   30 km

N

Much of this population boom is in the southern section of the state, and longtime residents worry that New Hampshire will soon take on two distinct personalities: one driven by the upwardly cities of the southeast, such as Nashua, Derry, and Londonderry, and the other by the small towns and villages that make up the western and northern tiers of the state. Only time will tell how New Hampshire will cope. But while the influx of newcomers has brought inevitable change, the independent nature of the people and the state's natural beauty continue to please newcomers and locals alike.

Pleasures and Pastimes

Dining

New Hampshire prides itself on seafood, not just lobster but also salmon pie, steamed mussels, fried clams, and seared tuna steaks. Across the state you'll find country inns with upscale Continental and American menus, many of them embracing regional ingredients and cutting-edge preparations of the day. In the past two or three years, several hip contemporary eateries have opened up, especially in the southern half of the state, alongside such state traditions as greasy-spoon diners, excellent pizza restaurants, and pubs and taverns serving hearty comfort fare (especially in the ski and boating areas).

For price-category information, *see* Dining *in* Smart Travel Tips.

Lodging

In the mid-19th century, wealthy Bostonians would pack up and move to their grand summer homes in the countryside for two- or three-month stretches. Many of these homes have been restored and converted into the handsome country inns that are so strongly identified with the region. The smallest have only a couple of rooms; typically, they're done in period style. The largest contain 30 or more rooms, with in-room fireplaces and even hot tubs. Pampering amenities seem to increase each year at some properties, but others remain stuck in an earlier time, appealing for their retro value but perhaps in need of updating.

Bed-and-breakfasts and inns dominate New Hampshire's lodging scene, but you'll also find a great many well-kept, often family-owned motor lodges—particularly in the White Mountains and Lakes regions. A few of the grand old resorts still stand, with their world-class cooking staffs and tradition of top-notch service. In the Merrimack River valley, as well as along major highways, chain hotels and motels dominate the lodging scene.

For price-category information, *see* Lodging *in* Smart Travel Tips.

National and State Parks and Forests

The awesome White Mountain National Forest, the jewel of the state's park areas, covers 770,000 acres in northern New Hampshire. Major recreation parks are at Franconia Notch, Crawford Notch, and Mt. Sunapee. Rhododendron State Park, in Fitzwilliam in the Monadnock region, has a singular collection of wild rhododendrons. Mt. Washington Park crowns the highest mountain in the Northeast. Numerous state recreation areas offer camping, picnicking, hiking, boating, fishing, swimming, biking, and winter sports.

Outdoor Activities and Sports

BEACHES AND LAKES

New Hampshire makes the most of its 18-mi coastline with several good beaches, among them Hampton Beach and Wallis Sands in Rye. For warmer, fresh waters, head to pristine Lake Winnipesaukee, Lake Sunapee, Squam Lake, and Newfound Lake.

BIKING

A safe, scenic route along New Hampshire's seacoast is the bike path along Route 1A, for which you can park at Odiorne Point and follow the road 14 mi south to Seabrook. Some bikers begin at Prescott Park and take Route 1B into New Castle, but beware of the traffic. Another pretty route is from Newington Town Hall to the Great Bay Estuary. Excellent routes in the White Mountains are detailed in the mountain-bike guide map "The White Mountain Ride Guide," sold at area sports and book shops. There's also a bike path in Franconia Notch State Park at the Lafayette Campground and a mountain-biking center, Great Glen Trails, at the base of Mt. Washington. Many ski areas offer lift-serviced mountain biking in summer.

FISHING

Lake trout and salmon swim in Lake Winnipesaukee, trout and bass in smaller lakes, and trout in streams all around the Lakes Region. Alton Bay has an "Ice Out" salmon derby in spring. In winter, ice fishing takes place on all the lakes from huts known as "ice bobs." In the Sunapee region, you can fish for brook, rainbow, and lake trout; smallmouth bass; pickerel; and horned pout. The Monadnocks have more than 200 lakes and ponds stocked with a similar range of species.

SKIING AND SNOW SPORTS

Scandinavian settlers who came to New Hampshire's high, handsome, rugged peaks in the late 1800s brought their skis with them. Skiing got its modern start in the Granite State in the 1920s with the cutting of trails on Cannon Mountain; you can now ski or snowboard at nearly 20 areas, from the old, established slopes (Cannon, Cranmore, Wildcat) to more contemporary ones (Attitash, Loon, Waterville Valley). Promotional packages assembled by the ski areas allow you to sample different resorts. There's Ski 93 (referring to resorts along I–93), Ski the Mt. Washington Valley, and more.

Shopping

The absence of sales tax makes New Hampshire a hugely popular destination for shopping. Outside the outlet meccas of North Conway and Tilton, this pastime revolves around antiques and local crafts, which are plentiful and high in quality. Depression glass, silverware, and china abound, with furniture becoming scarcer and more expensive. Look for pottery, jewelry, furniture, and wooden boxes as well.

In the southern Lakes Region and in Hampton Beach, tacky souvenir shops are the norm. Summertime fairs, such as the one operated by the League of New Hampshire Craftsmen at Mt. Sunapee State Park, are a good way to see some of the state's best arts and crafts. The densest clusters of antiques shops are along U.S. 4, between Route 125 and Concord; along Route 119, from Fitzwilliam to Hinsdale; along Route 101, from Marlborough to Wilton; and in the towns of North Conway, North Hampton, Hopkinton, Hollis, and Amherst. In the Lakes Region, most shops are along the eastern side of Winnipesaukee, near Wolfeboro. Particularly in the Monadnock region, stores in barns and homes along back roads are "open by chance or by appointment."

Exploring New Hampshire

New Hampshire can be divided into four regions. The main attraction of the coast is bustling, historic Portsmouth; several somewhat quieter communities such as Durham and Exeter lie a bit further inland. The Lakes Region, in east-central New Hampshire, has good hiking trails, antiques shops, and, of course, water sports. People go to the White Mountains in the north to hike, ski, and photograph vistas and vibrant foliage.

Southwestern New Hampshire is the unspoiled quiet corner of the state, hemmed in to the east by the central Merrimack Valley, which contains a string of fast-growing communities along I–93 and U.S. 3.

Numbers in the text and in the margin correspond to numbers on the maps: New Hampshire Coast, New Hampshire Lakes, The White Mountains, Dartmouth–Lake Sunapee, and Monadnock Region and Central New Hampshire.

Great Itineraries

Some people come to New Hampshire to hike or ski the mountains, fish and sail the lakes, or cycle along the back roads. Others prefer to drive through scenic towns, visiting museums and shops. Although New Hampshire is a small state, roads curve around lakes and mountains, making distances longer than they appear. You can get a taste of the coast, lake, and mountain areas of the state in three to five days; eight days gives you time to make a comprehensive loop.

IF YOU HAVE 3 DAYS

Drive along Route 1A to see the coast or take a boat tour of the Isles of Shoals before exploring ☷ **Portsmouth** ①. The next day visit ☷ **Wolfeboro** ㉒, on the eastern edge of Lake Winnipesaukee, good for an overnight stop. The following morning drive across the scenic **Kancamagus Highway** ㊲ from Conway to **Lincoln** ㉕ to see the granite ledges and mountain streams of the White Mountains.

IF YOU HAVE 5 DAYS

After visiting ☷ **Portsmouth** ① and ☷ **Wolfeboro** ㉒, explore Squam and Ossipee lakes and the charming towns near them: **Moultonborough** ⑱, **Center Harbor** ⑮, and **Tamworth** ⑲. Spend your third night in the White Mountains town of ☷ **Jackson** ㉝, which is equally beautiful in the winter, when cross-country skiing is popular, and in the summer, when hiking is the main activity. After crossing the **Kancamagus Highway** ㊲ to **Lincoln** ㉕, tour the western part of the White Mountain National Forest via Route 112 to Route 118. Take Route 25A and then Route 10 south through the upper Connecticut River valley to reach ☷ **Hanover** ㊺, home of Dartmouth College, for an overnight. Follow I–89 back by way of **Newbury** ㊸ and the Lake Sunapee region.

When to Tour New Hampshire

In summer, people flock to seaside beaches, mountain hiking trails, and lake boat ramps. In the cities, festivals bring music and theater to the forefront. Fall brings leaf-peepers, especially to the White Mountains and along the Kancamagus Highway. Skiers take to the slopes in winter, when Christmas lights and carnivals brighten the long, dark nights. April's mud season, the black fly season in late May, and unpredictable weather keep visitor numbers low in spring, but the season has its joys, not the least of which is the appearance of New Hampshire's state flower, the purple lilac, from mid-May to early June.

THE COAST

New Hampshire's brief, shining 18-mi stretch of coastline packs in a wealth of scenery and diversions, from beaches to the historic and cultural pleasures of Portsmouth. The honky-tonk of Hampton Beach gets plenty of attention, good and bad, but first-timers are often surprised by the significant chunk of shoreline that remains pristine and unspoiled—especially through the town of Rye. This tour begins in the regional hub, Portsmouth; cuts down the coast to the beaches; branches inland to the quintessential prep school town Exeter; and then runs back up north through charming Dover, Durham (home to the University of New Hampshire), and Rochester. From here it's a short drive to the Lakes Region.

Portsmouth

★ ❶ *47 mi southeast of Concord; 50 mi southwest of Portland, ME; 56 mi north of Boston, MA.*

Originally settled in 1623 as Strawbery Banke, Portsmouth became a prosperous port before the Revolutionary War. Abundant with grand residential architecture spanning the 18th- through early 20th centuries, Portsmouth has numerous historic house-museums, including the collection of buildings that make up the Strawbery Banke Museum. The energetic downtown brims with trendy eateries and both quirky and upscale shops, plus theaters and music venues. You can walk to most of these attractions from Market Square.

The **Portsmouth Harbour Trail** passes more than 70 18th- and 19th-century homes and buildings downtown, through the South End, and along State and Congress streets. You can purchase a tour map ($2.50) at the information kiosk on Market Square, the Chamber of Commerce, and at several house-museums. A guided walk can be enjoyed year-round. ☎ 603/436–3988, WEB *www.seacoastnh.com/harbourtrail* ☜ *$7,* ☉ *Thurs.–Mon.*

The **Portsmouth Black Heritage Trail** (☎ 603/431–2768, WEB www. seacoastnh.com/blackhistory)—established in 1999—is a self-guided walk that visits sites important to black history in Portsmouth. Included are the **New Hampshire Gazette Printing Office**, where skilled slave Primus Fowle operated the paper's printing press for some 50 years beginning in 1756, and the city's 1866 **Election Hall**, outside of which the city's black citizens held annual celebrations of the Emancipation Proclamation. The yellow, hip-roof **John Paul Jones House** was a boarding house when the Revolutionary War hero lived here during his tenure in Portsmouth supervising shipbuilding for the Continental Navy. The 1758 structure, now the headquarters of the **Portsmouth Historical Society**, contains furniture, costumes, glass, guns, portraits, and documents from the late 18th century. ✉ *43 Middle St.,* ☎ *603/ 436–8420,* WEB *www.seacoastnh.com/touring/jpjhouse.html.* ☜ *$4.* ☉ *June–mid-Oct., Mon.–Sat. 10–4, Sun. noon–4.*

The period interior of the **Moffatt-Ladd House,** built in 1763, tells the story of Portsmouth's merchant class through portraits, letters, and fine furnishings. The Colonial Revival garden includes a horse chestnut tree, believed to be one of New Hampshire's oldest trees, planted by General William Whipple when he returned home after signing the Declaration of Independence in 1776. ✉ *154 Market St.,* ☎ *603/436–8221.* ☜ *$5.* ☉ *Mid-June–mid-Oct., Mon.–Sat. 11–5, Sun. 1–5.*

| NEED A BREAK? | For some midday noshing, drop by **Annabelle's Natural Ice Cream** (✉ 49 Ceres St., ☎ 603/436–3400) for a dish of Ghirardelli chocolate chip or Almond Joy ice cream. **Cafe Brioche** (✉ 14 Market Sq., ☎ 603/430–9225), right on Market Square, serves coffees, thick deli sandwiches, and fresh-baked pastries. |

The first English settlers named the area around today's Portsmouth for the wild strawberries abundant along the shore of the Piscataqua ★ River. **Strawbery Banke Museum,** the city's largest and most-impressive museum, now uses the name. This attractive 10-acre outdoor museum with period gardens, exhibits, and craftspeople holds 46 buildings that date from 1695 to 1820. Ten furnished homes represent 300 years of history in one continuously occupied neighborhood. Half the interior of the **Drisco House,** built in 1795, depicts its history as a colonial dry-goods store, while the living room and kitchen are decorated as they were in the 1950s, showing how buildings are adapted. The **Shapiro House** has been restored to reflect the life of the Russian Jewish immigrant family who lived in the home in the early 1900s. Perhaps the most opulent house, decorated in decadent Victorian style, is the 1860 **Goodwin Mansion,** former home of Governor Ichabod Goodwin. ⊠ *Marcy St.,* ☎ *603/433–1100,* WEB *www.strawberybanke.org.* ⊟ *$6.* ☺ *May–Oct., daily 10–5; Nov.–Apr., Wed.–Sat. 10–4.*

Picnicking is popular in **Prescott Park,** on the waterfront between Strawbery Banke Museum and the Piscataqua River. A large formal garden with fountains is perfect for whiling away an afternoon. The park also contains **Point of Graves,** Portsmouth's oldest burial ground, and two 17th-century warehouses.

Ⓒ Nineteen hands-on exhibits at the **Children's Museum of Portsmouth** explore lobstering, sound and music, computers, space travel, and other subjects. The museum is best for kids under 11. Some programs require reservations. ⊠ *280 Marcy St.,* ☎ *603/436–3853,* WEB *www. childrens-museum.org.* ⊟ *$4.* ☺ *Tues.–Sat. 10–5, Sun. 1–5; also Mon. 10–5 in summer and during school vacations.*

The **Wentworth-Coolidge State Historic Mansion,** a National Historic Landmark that's now part of **Little Harbor State Park,** was originally the residence of Benning Wentworth, New Hampshire's first Royal Governor (1753–1770). Notable among the period furnishings in the house is the carved pine mantelpiece in the council chamber. Wentworth's imported lilac trees, believed to be the oldest in North America, bloom each May. The visitor center stages lectures and exhibits. ⊠ *Little Harbor Rd., near South Street Cemetery,* ☎ *603/436–6607.* ⊟ *$2.50.* ☺ *Grounds, daily year-round; mansion, June–Sept., Tues., Thurs.–Sat. 10–3, Sun. noon–5.*

Docked at the **Port of Portsmouth Maritime Museum** in Albacore Park is the USS *Albacore,* built here in 1953. You can board this prototype submarine, which was a floating laboratory assigned to test a new hull design, dive brakes, and sonar systems for the navy. The nearby **Memorial Garden** and its reflecting pool are dedicated to those who lost their lives in submarine service. ⊠ *600 Market St.,* ☎ *603/436–3680.* ⊟ *$4.* ☺ *Daily 9:30–5:30.*

The **Redhook Ale Brewery,** visible from the Spaulding Turnpike, conducts tours that end with a beer tasting of three to four samples. If you don't have time to tour, you can stop in the Cataqua Public House to sample the fresh ales and have a bite to eat (open daily, lunch and dinner). ⊠ *Pease International Tradeport, 35 Corporate Dr.,* ☎ *603/ 430–8600,* WEB *www.redhook.com.* ⊟ *$1.* ☺ *Tours weekdays 11 AM, weekends 1, 3, and 5.*

Dining and Lodging

$$$ ✕ **Dunfey's Aboard the *John Wanamaker*.** Portsmouth's floating restaurant, on a restored tugboat, prepares creative delicacies such as roasted rack of New Zealand lamb with thyme and asparagus and roasted-garlic mashed red bliss potatoes. You can watch the river from the bar, enjoy the bistro-like atmosphere of the main dining room, or relax in the romantic Captain's Room. The upper-level deck is a favorite on starry summer nights for light meals, a glass of wine, or dessert and cappuccino. ⊠ *1 Harbour Pl.,* ☎ *603/433–3111. Reservations essential on weekends. AE, MC, V.*

$$–$$$ ✕ **Blue Mermaid World Grill.** The chefs at Blue Mermaid prepare innovative, globally influenced fare on a wood-burning grill. Specialties include lobster-and-shrimp pad Thai, pan-seared cod with a coconut cream sauce and plantain chips, and grilled spiced pork chops with a rhubarb-ginger-cranberry chutney. In summer you can eat on a deck that overlooks the historic Hill neighborhood. Entertainers perform (outdoors in summer) on Friday and Saturday. ⊠ *409 Hanover St.,* ☎ *603/427–2583. AE, D, DC, MC, V.*

$$–$$$ ✕ **Ciento: A Tapas Bar.** Whether nibbling on tapas or digging into substantial platters of pan-Mediterranean fare, lively yupsters and beautiful people fill Ciento nightly. The grilled flat bread sandwich with sautéed rock shrimp, applewood-smoked bacon, and citrus aioli are hard to resist. You can also try three kinds of paella. ⊠ *409 Hanover St.,* ☎ *603/427–2583. AE, D, DC, MC, V.*

$$–$$$ ✕ **Library at the Rockingham House.** Most of this Portsmouth landmark, a former luxury hotel, has been converted to condominiums, but the restaurant retains the hand-carved mahogany paneling, a marbletop bar, and bookcases on every wall. Although the kitchen churns out some lighter fare such as risotto primavera, the mainstays are traditional dishes such as veal marsala and baked stuffed shrimp. The check arrives between the pages of a vintage best-seller. ⊠ *401 State St.,* ☎ *603/431–5202. Reservations essential. AE, DC, MC, V.*

$$ ✕ **Porto Bello Ristorante Italiano.** This family-run restaurant brings the
★ tastes of Naples to downtown Portsmouth. In the second-story dining room overlooking the harbor, you can savor daily antipasto specials ranging from grilled calamari to stuffed baby eggplant. Pastas include spinach gnocchi and homemade ravioli. A house specialty is veal *carciofi*—a 6-ounce cutlet served with artichokes. ⊠ *67 Bow St.,* ☎ *603/ 431–2989. Reservations essential. AE, D, MC, V. Closed Mon.–Tues.*

$–$$ ✕ **Muddy River Smokehouse.** Red-check tablecloths and murals of trees and meadows create the look of an outdoor summer barbecue joint— even when the weather turns cold. Roll up your sleeves and dig into platters of ribs, homemade corn bread, and molasses baked beans. Chicken, blackened catfish, exceptional burgers, and other dishes are on the menu, but devotees swear by the "pig city" platter of St. Louis– grilled ribs, with smoked sweet sausage and pulled pork. ⊠ *21 Congress St.,* ☎ *603/430–9582. AE, MC, V.*

$$$ 🏨 **Sheraton Harborside Portsmouth Hotel.** Portsmouth's only luxury hotel, this five-story redbrick building is within easy walking distance of shops and attractions. Suites have full kitchens and living rooms. ⊠ *250 Market St., 03801,* ☎ *603/431–2300 or 800/325–3535,* ℻ *603/ 431–7805,* WEB *www.sheraton.com. 179 rooms, 24 suites. 2 restaurants, bar, room service, indoor pool, sauna, health club, nightclub, business services, meeting room. AE, D, DC, MC, V.*

$$$ 🏨 **Sise Inn.** Each room at this Queen Anne town house in Portsmouth's historic district is decorated in Victorian style, with special fabrics, antiques, and reproductions of antiques. Some rooms have hot tubs and about half are in a 1980s addition that blends well with the older section. It's close to the Market Square area. ⊠ *40 Court St., 03801,* ☎ ℻ *603/433–1200 or* ☎ *877/747–3466. 26 rooms, 8 suites. In-room VCRs, meeting room. AE, DC, MC, V. CP.*

$$ 🏨 **Martin Hill Inn.** Two buildings downtown—one dating from 1815,
★ and another from 1850—hold a charming inn that's within walking distance of the historic district and the waterfront. Extensive perennial gardens enhance the B&B. The quiet rooms, furnished with antiques, are decorated in formal Colonial or country-Victorian style. The Greenhouse suite has a private solarium facing the water garden. The inn is no-smoking. ⊠ *404 Islington St.,* ☎ *603/436–2287,* WEB *www. portsmouthnh.com/martinhillinn. 4 rooms, 3 suites. MC, V. BP.*

Nightlife and the Arts

NIGHTLIFE

The **Portsmouth Gas Light Co.** (✉ 64 Market St., ☎ 603/430–9122) is a popular brick-oven pizzeria and restaurant that hosts local rock bands in its courtyard in summer and in the lounge at other times. People come from as far away as Boston and Portland to hang out at the **Press Room** (✉ 77 Daniel St., ☎ 603/431–5186), which showcases folk, jazz, blues, and bluegrass performers.

THE ARTS

The **Prescott Park Arts Festival** (✉ 105 Marcy St., ☎ 603/436–2848) presents theater, dance, and musical events outdoors during June, July, and August. Beloved for its acoustics, the 1878 **Music Hall** (✉ 28 Chestnut St., ☎ 603/436–2400; 603/436–9900 film line) brings the best touring events to the seacoast—from classical and pop concerts to dance and theater. The hall also hosts an ongoing art-house film series. The **Players' Ring** (✉ 105 Marcy St., ☎ 603/436–8123) highlights more than 15 original and well-known plays and performances by local theater groups from September through June. The **Pontine Movement Theatre** (✉ 135 McDonough St., ☎ 603/436–6660) presents dance performances in a renovated warehouse—the company also tours throughout the year around New Hampshire and northern New England. The **Seacoast Repertory Theatre** (✉ 125 Bow St., ☎ 603/433–4472 or 800/639–7650) offers a year-round schedule of musicals, classic dramas, and works by up-and-coming playwrights, as well as a youth theater.

Outdoor Activities and Sports

Portsmouth doesn't have any beaches, but the **Seacoast Trolley** (☎ 603/431–6975) departs from Market Square on the hour (daily 10–5), servicing a continuous loop between Portsmouth sights and area beaches. You can get a schedule for the trolley, which operates from mid-June to Labor Day, at the information kiosk in Market Square or by visiting WEB www.locallink.com/seacoasttrolley. The **Urban Forestry Center** (✉ 45 Elwyn Rd., ☎ 603/431–6774) has gardens and marked trails appropriate for short hikes on its 180 acres.

Just inland from Portsmouth, the **Great Bay Estuarine Research Reserve** preserves one of southeastern New Hampshire's most precious assets: its shoreline on the Great Bay estuary. Blue herons, ospreys, and snowy egrets, all of which are especially conspicuous during spring and fall migrations, can be found among the 4,471 acres of tidal waters, mud flats, and about 48 mi of inland shoreline that compose the reserve. New Hampshire's largest concentration of winter eagles also lives here. The best public access is via **Sandy Point Discovery Center** (✉ 89 Depot Rd., off Rte. 101, Stratham, ☎ 603/778–0015, WEB www.greatbay.org). This excellent facility contains both outdoor and indoor exhibits, a 1,700-ft boardwalk and other trails through both mudflats and upland forest, and a library and bookshop; interpretive programs are offered year-round. The center, about 15 mi southeast of Durham and 6 mi west of exit 3 from I–95 in Portsmouth, distributes maps and information and has trails for walking. ✉ *Information: New Hampshire Fish & Game Dept., 37 Concord Rd., Durham, 03824,* ☎ *603/868–1095.* ▣ *Free.* ☉ *Daily dawn–dusk.*

Shopping

Market Square, in the center of town, has gift and clothing boutiques, book and card shops, and exquisite crafts stores.

Byrne & Carlson (✉ 121 State St., ☎ 888/559–9778) produces handmade chocolates in the finest European tradition. **Kumminz Gallery** (✉ 65 Daniel St., ☎ 603/433–6488) carries pottery, jewelry, and fiber art

by New Hampshire artisans. **N. W. Barrett** (⊠ 53 Market St., ☎ 603/
431–4262) specializes in leather, jewelry, pottery, and fiber and other
arts and crafts. It also sells furniture, including affordable steam-bent
oak pieces and one-of-a-kind lamps and rocking chairs. **Pierce Gallery**
(⊠ 105 Market St., ☎ 603/436–1988) has prints and paintings of the
Maine and New Hampshire coasts. The **Portsmouth Bookshop** (⊠ 1–
7 Islington St., ☎ 603/433–4406) carries old and rare books and
maps. At **Salamandra Glass Studios** (⊠ 7 Commercial Alley, ☎ 603/
743–6553), you'll find hand-blown glass vases, bowls, and other items;
you can also peruse their wares at the **Salamandra Gallery** (⊠ 67 Bow
St., ☎ 603/436–1038).

Isles of Shoals

❷ *10 mi southeast of Portsmouth, by ferry.*

Many of these nine small, rocky islands (eight at high tide)—like Hog
Island, Smuttynose, and Star Island—retain the earthy names given them
by the transient 17th-century fishermen. A colorful history of piracy,
murder, and ghosts surrounds the archipelago, long populated by an
independent lot who, according to one writer, hadn't the sense to winter on the mainland. Not all the islands lie within the New Hampshire
border: after an ownership dispute between Maine and New Hampshire, they were divvied up between the two states (five went to Maine,
four to New Hampshire).

Celia Thaxter, a native islander, romanticized these islands with her
poetry in *Among the Isles of Shoals* (1873) and celebrated her garden
in *An Island Garden* (1894; now reissued with the original color il-
lustrations by Childe Hassam). In the late 19th century, **Appledore Island** became an offshore retreat for Thaxter's coterie of writers,
musicians, and artists. The island is now used by the Marine Laboratory of Cornell University. **Star Island** contains a nondenominational
conference center and is open to those on guided tours.

New Castle

❸ *3 mi south of Portsmouth.*

Though it consists of a single square mi of land, the small island of New
Castle was once known as Great Island. The narrow roads lined with
pre-Revolutionary houses and upscale condos and homes make the island, which is accessible from the mainland by car, perfect for a stroll.

Wentworth by the Sea, the last of the state's great seaside resorts, is
impossible to miss as you approach New Castle on Route 1B. Empty
these days, it was the site of the signing of the Russo-Japanese Treaty
in 1905, a fact that attracts many Japanese tourists. The current owners and the town have reached a tentative agreement to bring this grand
hotel back to life; renovations begin late in 2001.

Fort Constitution was originally built in 1631 and then rebuilt in 1666
as Fort William and Mary, a British stronghold overlooking Portsmouth
Harbor. Various additions and improvements were made over the
decades, but the site earned notoriety when Rebel patriots raided the
fort in 1774 in one of revolutionary America's first overt acts of defi-
ance against King George III. The rebels later used the captured mu-
nitions against the British at the Battle of Bunker Hill. Panels throughout
the fort explain its history. ⊠ *Rte. 1B at the Coast Guard Station,* ☎
603/436–1552, WEB *www.geocities.com/Pentagon/Barracks/6402/Fort
Constitution.* 🎫 *Free.* ☉ *Mid-June–Labor Day, daily 9–5; Labor Day–
mid-June, weekends 9–5.*

Rye

❹ *8 mi south of Portsmouth.*

In 1623 the first European settlers landed at Odiorne Point in what is now the largely undeveloped and picturesque town of Rye, making it the birthplace of New Hampshire. Today the area's main draws are a lovely state park, oceanfront beaches, and the view from Route 1A.

★ ⊙ **Odiorne Point State Park** encompasses more than 330 acres of protected land, on the site where David Thomson established the first permanent European site in what is now New Hampshire. Stroll several nature trails with interpretive panels describing the park's military history or simply enjoy the vistas of the nearby Isles of Shoals. The rocky shore's tide pools—considered the best in New England—shelter crabs, periwinkles, and sea anemones. Throughout the year, the Seacoast Science Center conducts guided nature walks and interpretive programs, has exhibits on the area's natural history, and traces the social history of Odiorne Point back to the Ice Age. The facility's tide-pool touch tank and the 1,000-gallon Gulf of Maine deepwater aquarium is popular with kids. Day camp is offered for grades K–8 throughout the summer and during school vacations. ⊠ *570 Rte. 1A, north of Wallis Sands, Rye State Beach,* ☎ *603/436–8043 science center, 603/436–1552 park.* 🎟 *Science center $1 ($4 for guided walks and some interpretive programs); park Memorial Day–Columbus Day and on weekends $2.50.* ⊙ *Science center daily 10–5, park daily 8 AM–dusk. www.seacentr.org.*

Dining and Lodging

$$–$$$ ✕ **Saunders at Rye Harbor.** Locals and visitors have been lazing about on the waterfront deck at sunset or over lunch since this festive spot opened in the 1920s. Fresh-caught lobster, Asian-seared salmon, and baked-stuffed shrimp are among the house specialties, which also include several chicken and steak dishes. ⊠ *175 Harbor Rd.,* ☎ *603/964–6466. Closed Tues. AE, D, MC, V.*

$$–$$$$ 🏠 **Rock Ledge Manor.** Built out on a point, this mid-19th-century, gambrel-roof summer house with a wraparound porch anchored a resort colony. The rooms have water views; the family suite has a private balcony. Owners Stan and Stella Smith serve breakfast in the sunny dining room overlooking the Atlantic. This no-smoking B&B has a two-night minimum on weekends and holidays, and children must be over age 11. ⊠ *1413 Ocean Blvd., 03870,* ☎ *603/431–1413,* WEB *www.rockledgemanor.com. 2 rooms, 1 suite. No credit cards. BP.*

Outdoor Activities and Sports

BEACHES

Good for swimming and sunning, **Jenness State Beach,** on Route 1A, is a favorite with locals. The facilities include a bathhouse, lifeguards, and metered parking. **Wallis Sands, Rye State Beach,** on Route 1A, is a swimmers' beach with bright white sand and a bathhouse. Parking is ample and costs $8 on weekends, $5 weekdays.

FISHING

Between April and October, deep-sea anglers head out for cod, mackerel, and bluefish. For a full- or half-day charter, try **Atlantic Fishing Fleet** (⊠ Rye Harbor, ☎ 603/964–5220 or 800/942–5364).

Shopping

Although Rye is not known for its shopping, **Antiques at Rye Center** (⊠ 655 Wallis Rd., ☎ 603/964–8999) is worth searching out for well-presented antiques from hand-painted porcelain to early toys.

En Route   On Route 1A as it winds south through Rye to North Hampton, you'll pass a group of late-19th- and early-20th-century mansions known as

Millionaires' Row. Because of the way the road curves, the drive south along this route is especially breathtaking.

Hampton Beach

❺ *8 mi south of Rye.*

Hampton Beach, from Route 27 to where Route 1A crosses the causeway, is an authentic seaside amusement center—the domain of fried dough stands, loud music, arcade games, palm readers, parasailing, and bronzed bodies. An estimated 150,000 people visit the town and its free public beach on the Fourth of July, and it draws plenty of people until late September, when things close up. The 3-mi boardwalk, where kids can play games and see how saltwater taffy is made, looks as if it were snatched out of the 1940s; in fact, the whole community remains remarkably free of modern franchise eateries and chain shops. Free outdoor concerts are held on many evenings in summer, and once a week there's a fireworks display. Talent shows and karaoke performances take place in the Seashell Stage, right on the beach.

Each summer locals hold a children's festival in August and celebrate the end of the season with a huge seafood feast on the weekend after Labor Day. For a quieter time, stop by for a sunrise stroll, when only seagulls and the occasional jogger interrupt the serenity.

Away from the beach crowds, you'll find **Fuller Gardens,** a late-1920s estate garden (the original mansion was razed in 1961) designed in the Colonial Revival style by Arthur Shurtleff, with a 1938 addition by the Olmsted brothers. With 2,000 rosebushes, a hosta garden, an annual display garden, a tropical conservatory, and a Japanese garden, it blooms all summer long. The Fuller Foundation is currently restoring the gardens to original blueprints, which were recently discovered—note that certain sections may be closed off during this process. ⊠ *10 Willow Ave., North Hampton,* ☏ *603/964–5414,* WEB *www.fullergardens. org.* 🎟 *$5.* ☉ *Early May–mid-Oct., daily 10–6.*

Dining and Lodging

$$–$$$$ ✕ **Ron's Landing at Rocky Bend.** Nestled in among the motels lining Ocean Boulevard is this casually elegant restaurant, which prepares fresh seafood, pasta, beef, and veal dishes. Specialties include smoked Virginia oysters and filet mignon topped with fresh horseradish sauce. In summer, you can dine on the second-floor screened porch, which has a sweeping view of the Atlantic. ⊠ *379 Ocean Blvd.,* ☏ *603/929–2122. AE, D, DC, MC, V.*

$$–$$$$ ✕🏨 **Ashworth by the Sea.** This family-owned hotel was built across the street from Hampton Beach in 1912; most rooms have private decks, and the furnishings vary from period to contemporary. Beachside rooms have breathtaking ocean views, and the others look out onto the pool or the quiet street. The Ashworth Dining Room ($$–$$$) serves steaks, poultry, and fresh seafood—including seven lobster variations. ⊠ *295 Ocean Blvd., 03842,* ☏ *603/926–6762 or 800/345–6736,* FAX *603/926–2002. 105 rooms. 3 restaurants, pool. AE, D, DC, MC, V.*

$$$ 🏨 **D. W.'s Oceanside Inn.** The square front and simple awnings of this oceanfront inn look much the same as those on all the other buildings lining Ocean Boulevard. Inside, though, carefully selected antiques and collectibles, individually decorated rooms, a cozy living room and library with a fireplace, and a second-floor veranda for watching the waves give the Oceanside the feel of a late-19th-century home. Should the resort's crush of people and noise begin to overwhelm, you'll appreciate the soundproofing that makes this inn seem like a calm port in a storm. A separate three-bedroom cottage sleeps up to six guests

and has a kitchen. ⊠ *365 Ocean Blvd., 03842,* ☎ *603/926–3542,* 🆀🆇
603/926–3542, 🆆🅴🅱 *www.oceansideinn.com. 9 rooms, 1 cottage. In-room
safes. AE, D, MC, V. Closed mid-Oct.–mid-May. BP.*

Nightlife and the Arts

The **Hampton Beach Casino Ballroom** (⊠ 169 Ocean Blvd., ☎ 603/
929–4100), despite the name, is not a gambling casino but a late 19th-
century, 2,000-seat performance venue that has hosted everyone from
Janis Joplin to Jerry Seinfeld to Everclear. Performances are scheduled
weekly April through October.

Outdoor Activities and Sports

BEACHES

Hampton Beach State Park (⊠ Rte. 1A, ☎ 603/926–3784) is a quieter stretch of the same beach that shares its name with the town. The
park, on the southwestern edge of town at the mouth of the Hampton River, has picnic tables, a store (seasonal), parking ($8 on summer
weekends, $5 weekdays), and a bathhouse.

FISHING

Between April and October, deep-sea anglers head out for cod, mack-
erel, and bluefish. There are rentals and charters offering half- and full-
day cruises, as well as some night fishing. Most leave from the Hampton
State Pier on Route 1A. **Al Gauron Deep Sea Fishing** (☎ 603/926–2469)
maintains a fleet of four boats for whale-watching cruises and fishing
charters. **Eastman Fishing Fleet** (⊠ Seabrook, ☎ 603/474–3461) offers whale-watching and fishing cruises, with evening and morning charg-
ers. **Smith & Gilmore** (☎ 603/926–3503) hosts deep-sea fishing
expeditions, cruises, and whale watches.

Hampton

❻ *3 mi west of Hampton Beach; 11 mi south of Portsmouth; 45 mi north
of Boston, MA.*

One of New Hampshire's first towns, Hampton was settled in 1638. Its
name in the 17th century was Winnacunnet, which means "beautiful place
of pines." Today busy U.S. 1 defines the center of town and makes it a
crossroads for anyone traveling along the seacoast. The center of the early
town was **Meeting House Green,** where 42 stones represent the found-
ing families. It is still a tranquil place surrounded by pine trees.

Tuck Museum, across from Meeting House Green, contains displays on
the town's early history. The grounds also include a 19th-century
schoolhouse, a farm museum, and a fire-fighting museum. ⊠ *40 Park
Ave.,* ☎ *603/929–0781; 603/926–3840 for appointments.* 🆓 *Free.* 🕒
June–Sept., Tues.–Fri. and Sun. 1–4 PM; and by appointment.

At 400-acre **Applecrest Farm Orchards**—the oldest and largest apple
orchard in the region—you can pick your own apples and berries or
buy fresh fruit pies and cookies from the bakery. Fall brings cider pressing, hay rides, pumpkins, and music on weekends. In winter a cross-
country ski trail traverses the orchard. ⊠ *133 Rte. 88, Hampton Falls,*
☎ *603/926–3721,* 🆆🅴🅱 *www.applecrest.com.* 🕒 *Daily 9–5.*

☾ At the **Seabrook Science & Nature Center,** adjacent to the Seabrook
Station nuclear power plant 4 mi south of Hampton, you can tour exhibits on the science of power, see control-room operators in training,
walk through a replica of a cooling tunnel, and pedal a bike to create
electricity. The center maintains the ¾-mi Owascoag Nature Trail, a
touch pool for kids, and several large aquariums of local sea life. ⊠
Lafayette Rd., Seabrook, ☎ *603/474–9521 or 800/338–7482.* 🆓 *Free.*
🕒 *Weekdays 10–4.*

Lodging

$$–$$$ 🏨 **Hampton Falls Inn.** Intricate Burmese wall hangings and leather furniture decorate the lobby of this modern motel only 3½ mi from Hampton Beach. The bright, airy rooms and mini-suites (with mini-refrigerators and wet bars) are large, and many have a view of the neighboring farm; all have microwave ovens. An enclosed porch by the indoor pool looks out over the woods and fields. ⊠ *11 Lafayette Rd., 03844,* ☎ *603/926–9545 or 800/356–1729,* FAX *603/926–4155,* WEB *www.hamptonfallsinn. com. 33 rooms, 15 suites. Restaurant, pool, hot tub, meeting room. AE, D, DC, MC, V.*

$$ 🏨 **Victoria Inn.** Easygoing innkeepers Ron and Marina Mansfield run this romantic B&B a ½ mi from Hampton Beach. Built as a carriage house in 1875, this upscale inn is decorated with plush Victorian antiques and fabrics, augmented with such modern amenities as central air-conditioning and heat, cable TV, and in-room phones. A large wraparound porch and a gazebo are perfect spots for relaxing with a book on a warm summer afternoon. Savor breakfast in the inn's dining room, which overlooks the former summer home of President Franklin Pierce. ⊠ *430 High St., 03842,* ☎ *603/929–1437 or 800/291–2672,* FAX *603/929–0747,* WEB *www.thevictoriainn.com. 3 rooms, 2 suites. Dining room, bicycles. MC, V. BP.*

$ ⚠️ **Tidewater Campground.** This camping area has 170 sites, a large playground, a pool, a game room, and a basketball court. ⊠ *160 Lafayette Rd., 03842,* ☎ *603/926–5474. MC, V. Closed mid-Oct.–mid-May.*

Nightlife and the Arts

From July to September, the **Hampton Playhouse** (⊠ 357 Winnacunnet Rd., ☎ 603/926–3073) brings familiar Hollywood movie and New York theater actors to the coast for five musicals, plus Saturday children's shows.

Shopping

Antiques shops line U.S. 1 (Lafayette Rd.) in Hampton and neighboring Hampton Falls. The more than 50 dealers at **Antiques at Hampton Falls** (☎ 603/926–1971) have all types of antiques and collectibles. **Antiques New Hampshire** (☎ 603/926–9603) is a group shop with 35 dealers and a range of items. **Antiques One** (☎ 603/926–5332) carries everything but furniture, including books and maps. The prodigious **Barn at Hampton Falls** (☎ 603/926–9003) is known for American and European furniture.

Exeter

❼   *9 mi northwest of Hampton, 52 mi north of Boston, MA, 47 mi southeast of Concord.*

In Exeter's center, contemporary shops mix well with the buildings of the esteemed Phillips Exeter Academy, which opened in 1783, and other equally historic buildings. During the Revolutionary War, Exeter was the state capital, and it was here that the first state constitution and the first Declaration of Independence from Great Britain were put to paper.

The **American Independence Museum,** adjacent to Phillips Exeter Academy in the Ladd-Gilman House, celebrates the birth of our nation. The story of the Revolution unfolds during each guided tour, on which you'll see drafts of the U.S. Constitution and the first Purple Heart. Other items include letters and documents written by George Washington and the household furnishings of John Taylor Gilman, one of New Hampshire's early governors. The museum also hosts a Revolutionary War Festival in June. ⊠ *1 Governor's La.,* ☎ *603/772–2622,*

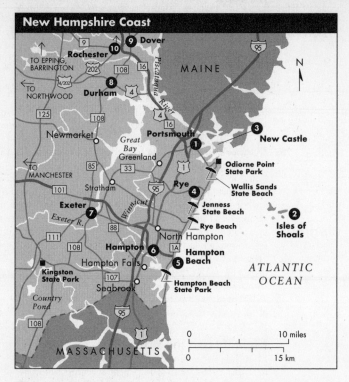

New Hampshire Coast

WEB *www.independencemuseum.org.* ⊠ *$5.* ⊙ *May–Oct., Wed.–Sun. noon–5 (last tour at 4).*

Dining and Lodging

$ ✕ **Loaf and Ladle.** Hearty chowders, soups, and stews and huge sandwiches on homemade bread are served cafeteria-style at this understated eatery overlooking the river. Check the blackboard for the ever-changing rotation of chef's specials, breads, and desserts, and don't miss the fresh salad bar. The café is near the shops, galleries, and historic houses along Water Street. ⊠ *9 Water St.,* ☎ *603/778–8955. Reservations not accepted. AE, D, DC, MC, V.*

$$–$$$ ✕🖼 **Exeter Inn.** This brick Georgian-style inn on the campus of Phillips Exeter Academy has been the choice of visiting parents for the past half century. It is furnished with antique and reproduction pieces and possesses plenty of modern amenities. Among the Terrace Restaurant's specialties are a fillet of salmon wrapped in a pastry crust and stuffed with wild mushrooms and onions, and a napoleon of grilled vegetables with layers of Boursin cheese. On Sunday, the line forms early for a brunch with more than 40 options. ⊠ *90 Front St., 03833,* ☎ *603/ 772–5901 or 800/782–8444,* 𝔽𝔸𝕏 *603/778–8757. 47 rooms. Restaurant, meeting room. AE, D, DC, MC, V.*

$$–$$$$ 🖼 **Inn by the Bandstand.** Common rooms in this 1809 Federal mansion, including a 1909 large addition, are decorated in period style. Seven guest rooms have working fireplaces; some have hot tubs, marble baths, and curtained four-poster beds. After a day of sightseeing, you can relax with a glass of complimentary sherry either in the privacy of your guest room or in one of the inviting common areas. ⊠ *4 Front St., 03833,* ☎ *603/772–6352,* 𝔽𝔸𝕏 *603/778–0212,* WEB *www.innbythe-bandstand.com. 5 rooms, 4 suites. AE, D, MC, V. CP.*

$ ⚠ **Exeter Elms Family Campground.** This 50-acre campground has 202 sites (some riverfront), a swimming pool, a playground, canoe rentals, and a recreation program. ⊠ *188 Court St., 03833,* ☎ 𝔽𝔸𝕏 *603/778–*

7631, WEB *www.ucampnh.com/exeterelms. MC, V. Closed mid-Sept.–mid-May.*

Shopping

The **Exeter League of New Hampshire Craftsmen** shop (⊠ 61 Water St., ☎ 603/778–8282) sells original jewelry, woodworking, and pottery. **A Picture's Worth a Thousand Words** (⊠ 65 Water St., ☎ 603/778–1991) stocks antique and contemporary prints, old maps, town histories, and rare books. **Water Street Artisans** (⊠ 20 Water St., ☎ 603/778–6178) carries fine crafts including jewelry, fiber arts, and pottery.

The **Travel and Nature Bookshop** (⊠ 59 Water St., ☎ 603/772–5573) has a wide selection of travel books including guides to New Hampshire hiking spots and other specialized titles. **Water Street Books** (⊠ 125 Water St., ☎ 603/778–9731) carries new fiction and nonfiction with an emphasis on New Hampshire authors.

Durham

❽ *12 mi north of Exeter, 11 mi northwest of Portsmouth.*

Settled in 1635 and home of General John Sullivan, a Revolutionary War hero and three-time New Hampshire governor, Durham was where Sullivan and his band of rebel patriots stored the gunpowder they captured from Fort William and Mary. Easy access to Great Bay via the Oyster River made Durham a center of maritime activity in the 19th century. Among the lures today are the water, farms that welcome visitors, and the University of New Hampshire, which occupies much of the town's center.

The **Art Gallery** at the University of New Hampshire occasionally exhibits items from a permanent collection of about 1,100 pieces but generally uses its space to host traveling exhibits of contemporary and historic art. Noted items in the collection include 19th-century Japanese woodblock prints and American landscape paintings. ⊠ *Paul Creative Arts Center, 30 College Rd.,* ☎ *603/862–3712,* WEB *www.unh.edu/arts/gallery.html.* ⊠ *Free.* ☉ *Sept.–May, Mon.–Wed. 10–4, Thurs. 10–8, weekends 1–5.*

Emery Farm, which has been in the same family for 11 generations, sells fruits and vegetables in summer (including pick-your-own raspberries, strawberries, and blueberries), pumpkins in fall, and Christmas trees in December. The farm shop carries breads and pies, as well as local crafts. Children can pet the resident goats and sheep and attend storytelling events on several Tuesday mornings in July and August. ⊠ *U.S. 4, 1½ mi east of Rte. 108,* ☎ *603/742–8495.* ☉ *Late Apr.–Dec., daily 9–6.*

Dining and Lodging

$$$$ ✕🏠 **Three Chimneys Inn.** This stately yellow house on more than 3 acres has graced a hill overlooking the Oyster River since 1649. Rooms in the house and the 1795 barn, mostly named after plants from the extensive gardens, are decorated with Georgian- and Federal-period antiques and reproductions, canopy or four-poster beds with Edwardian bed drapes, and Oriental rugs—most have fireplaces. Specialties in the Maples dining room ($$$–$$$$) include New England mussel salad and roast leg of farm-raised duckling. The ffrost-Sawyer Tavern ($$) serves simpler fare in a cozy setting, as does the outdoor Conservatory, which is open spring through fall. The inn is no-smoking. ⊠ *17 Newmarket Rd., 03824,* ☎ *603/868–7800 or 888/399–9777,* FAX *603/868–2964,* WEB *www.threechimneysinn.com. 23 rooms. 3 restaurants, in-room data ports, meeting room. AE, D, MC, V. BP.*

$$-$$$ ✕🖾 **New England Conference Center and Hotel.** In a lush wooded area on the campus of the University of New Hampshire, this contemporary hotel is large enough to be a full-service conference center but quiet enough to feel like a retreat. Acorns Restaurant specializes in American regional cuisine and is a favorite place for Sunday brunch. A signature dish is blackened red snapper with pineapple chutney. ✉ *15 Strafford Ave., 03824,* ☎ *603/862–2801 or 800/909–6931,* FAX *603/ 862–4897,* WEB *www.necc.unh.edu. 115 rooms. 2 restaurants, bar, in-room data ports, health club, meeting rooms. AE, DC, MC, V.*

Nightlife and the Arts

The **Celebrity Series** (✉ Memorial Union Building, 83 Main St., ☎ 603/ 862–2290) at the University of New Hampshire brings music, theater, and dance to Durham. The **UNH Department of Theater and Dance** (✉ Paul Creative Arts Center, 30 College Rd., ☎ 603/862–2919) produces a variety of shows. The University of New Hampshire's **Whittemore Center Arena** (✉ 128 Main St., ☎ 603/862–4000) hosts everything from Boston Pops concerts to home shows, plus UNH sports. In nearby Newmarket, UNH students and local yupsters head to **The Stone Church** (✉ 5 Granite St., ☎ 603/659–6321)—in an authentic 1835 former Methodist church—to listen to live rock, jazz, blues, and folk.

Outdoor Activities and Sports

You can take a picnic to or hike several trails at 130-acre **Wagon Hill Farm** (✉ U.S. 4 across from Emery Farm, ☎ no phone), overlooking the Oyster River. The old farm wagon, sitting on the top of a hill, is one of the most-photographed spots in New England. Park next to the farmhouse and follow walking trails to the wagon and through the woods to the picnic area by the water. Sledding and cross-country skiing are winter activities.

Dover

9 *6 mi northeast of Durham.*

Considered New Hampshire's oldest permanent settlement, Dover Point was settled in 1623 by fishermen who worked Great Bay. By the end of the century, the town center had moved inland to its present location. The falls on the Cocheco River made Dover a natural mill town. Many of the brick mill buildings still stand and have been converted to restaurants and shops that make the town worth a stop.

The **Woodman Institute** consists of three buildings: the 1675 William Damm Garrison House, the 1813 J. P. Hale House, and the 1818 Woodman House. Exhibits focus on early American cooking utensils, clothing, furniture, New Hampshire's involvement in the Civil War, and natural history. Abolitionist Senator John P. Hale lived in the Hale House from 1840 to 1873. ✉ *182–190 Central Ave.,* ☎ *603/742–1038,* WEB *www.seacoastnh.com/woodman.* 🎟 *$3.* ☉ *Apr.–Nov., Wed.–Sun. 12:30–4:30; Jan.–Feb., weekends 12:30–4:30.*

Dining

$-$$$ ✕ **Newick's Seafood Restaurant.** Newick's, which also has locations in Hampton and Merrimack, might serve the best lobster roll on the New England coast, but regulars cherish the onion rings, too. This over-size shack serves seafood and atmosphere in heaping portions. Picture windows allow terrific views over Great Bay. ✉ *431 Dover Point Rd.,* ☎ *603/742–3205. AE, D, MC, V.*

Shopping

Downtown Dover has a selection of crafts and specialty stores. **Downtown Dover Crafts** (✉ 464 Central Ave., ☎ 603/749–4952) showcases country-style crafts by local artisans who are part of a collective. **Just the Thing!** (⊠ 451 Central Ave., ☎ 603/742–9040) carries an engaging mix of vintage collectibles and contemporary handicrafts. **Salmon Falls Pottery & Stoneware** (⊠ Oak St. Engine House, ☎ 603/749–1467 or 800/621–2030) produces handmade, salt-glaze stoneware using a method that was favored by early American potters. Potters are on hand should you want to place a special order or watch them work. **Tuttle's Red Barn** (⊠ 151 Dover Point Rd., ☎ 603/742–4313) carries jams, pickles, and other farm products.

Rochester

⑩ *22 mi northwest of Portsmouth, 10 mi north of Dover, 21 mi south of Wakefield.*

This old mill factory city may lack the quaint factor of either the coastal communities or the lake hamlets, but it's an excellent base for exploring its fine Victorian architecture, both commercial and residential. Stroll around downtown's centralmost intersection at Main, Wakefield, and Congress streets to get a feel for the town's heritage, or drive up along the mighty Salmon Falls River, which once powered the towns many mills.

Dining and Lodging

$$–$$$ ✕🖼 **Governor's Inn.** Just north of downtown, this pair of neighboring early 20th-century Georgian Colonial mansions are the former homes of state governors (and brothers) Huntley and Roland Spaulding. Guests now make their way about the homes' stately marble fireplaces, elliptical staircases, sweeping garden patios, and lavishly furnished guest rooms. The restaurant (No lunch Jan.–Apr.) presents an often-changing menu of creative regional American dishes such as breast of duck with a port sauce, green figs, and local blue cheese. ⊠ *78 Wakefield St., 03867, ☎ 603/332–0107, ᖴᴀᕽ 603/335–1984, ᴡᴇᴃ www.governorsinn.com. 16 rooms. Restaurant, bar. D, MC, V.*

The Coast A to Z

To research prices, get advice from other travelers, and book travel arrangements, visit www.fodors.com.

AIRPORTS

Manchester Airport is a one-hour drive from the coastal region.

BUS TRAVEL

C&J Trailways, Concord Trailways, and Vermont Transit provide bus service to New Hampshire's coast from other regions. Coast and UNH Wildcat Transit provides limited access to towns in New Hampshire's coastal section.

➤ Bus Information: **C&J Trailways** (☎ 603/430–1100 or 800/258–7111). **Vermont Transit** (☎ 603/436–0163 or 800/451–3292). **Coast** (☎ 603/862–2328). **UNH Wildcat Transit** (☎ 603/862–2328).

CAR TRAVEL

The main route to New Hampshire's coast from other states is I–95, which runs from the Massachusetts to Maine borders. Coastal Route 1A has views of water, beaches, and summer estates. The more convenient U.S. 1 travels inland. The Spaulding Turnpike (Route 16) and U.S. 4 connect Portsmouth with Dover, Durham, and Rochester. Route 108 links Durham and Exeter. The quick route along the coast is I–95. The main route to New Hampshire's coast from other states is I–95, which travels from the border with Maine to the border with Massachusetts.

EMERGENCIES

➤ CONTACTS: **New Hampshire State Police** (☎ 603/271–3636 or 800/ 852–3411). **Portsmouth Regional Hospital** (✉ 333 Borthwick Ave., Portsmouth, ☎ 603/436–5110). **Exeter Hospital** (✉ 10 Buzell Ave., Exeter, ☎ 603/778–7311).

➤ PHARMACY: **Rite Aid** (800 Islington St., Portsmouth, ☎ 603/436– 2454).

OUTDOORS & SPORTS

FISHING

Companies on the coast offer rentals and charters for deep-sea fishing and cruises. For information about fishing and licenses, call the New Hampshire Fish and Game Office.

➤ CONTACTS: **New Hampshire Fish and Game Office** (☎ 603/868–1095).

HIKING

An excellent 1-mi trail reaches the summit of Blue Job Mountain, where a fire tower has a good view. The New Hampshire Division of Parks and Recreation maintains the Rockingham Recreation Trail, which wends 27 mi from Newfields, just north of Exeter, to Manchester and is open to hikers, bikers, snowmobilers, and cross-country skiers.

➤ CONTACTS: **Blue Job Mountain** (✉ Crown Point Rd. off Rte. 202A, Rochester, 13 mi northwest of Dover). **New Hampshire Division of Parks and Recreation** (☎ 603/271–3254).

TOURS

Portsmouth Livery Company gives narrated horse-and-carriage tours through Colonial Portsmouth and Strawbery Banke. The Isles of Shoals Steamship Company runs island cruises, river trips, foliage excursions, and whale-watching expeditions from April to January. Captain Jeremy Bell hosts these voyages aboard the M/V *Thomas Laighton*, a replica of a Victorian steamship and the smaller and more modern M/V *Oceanic*. Lunch and light snacks are available on board, or you can bring your own. Some trips include a stopover and historic walking tour on Star Island.

New Hampshire Seacoast Cruises conducts naturalist-led whale-watching tours and narrated Isles of Shoals cruises aboard the 150-passenger M/V *Granite State* from May to October out of Rye Harbor State Marina. From May to October, Portsmouth Harbor Cruises operates tours of Portsmouth Harbor, trips to the Isles of Shoals, foliage trips on the Cocheco River, and sunset cruises aboard the M/V *Heritage*.

➤ TOUR-OPERATOR RECOMMENDATIONS: **Portsmouth Livery Company** (✉ Market Sq., ☎ 603/427–0044). **Isles of Shoals Steamship Company** (✉ Barker Wharf, 315 Market St., Portsmouth, ☎ 603/431–5500 or 800/441–4620). **New Hampshire Seacoast Cruises** (✉ Rye Harbor, Rte. 1A, Rye, ☎ 603/964–5545 or 800/964–5545). **Portsmouth Harbor Cruises** (✉ Ceres Street Dock, Portsmouth, ☎ 603/436–8084 or 800/ 776–0915).

VISITOR INFORMATION

➤ TOURIST INFORMATION: **Exeter Area Chamber of Commerce** (✉ 120 Water St., Exeter 03833, ☎ 603/772–2411, WEB www.exeterarea.org). **Greater Dover Chamber of Commerce** (✉ 299 Central Ave., Dover 03820, ☎ 603/742–2218, WEB www.dovernh.org). **Greater Portsmouth Chamber of Commerce** (✉ 500 Market St. Extension, Portsmouth 03801, ☎ 603/436–1118, WEB www.portcity.org). **Hampton Beach Area Chamber of Commerce** (✉ 836 Lafayette Rd., Hampton 03842, ☎ 603/926–8718, WEB www.hamptonbeaches.com).

For further information on the region and links to numerous attractions, visit WEB www.seacoastnh.com.

LAKES REGION

Lake Winnipesaukee, a Native American name for "smile of the great spirit," is the largest of the dozens of lakes scattered across the eastern half of central New Hampshire. With about 240 mi of shoreline full of inlets and coves, it's the largest in the state. Some claim Winnipesaukee has an island for each day of the year, but the total actually falls well short: 274.

In contrast to Winnipesaukee's summer-long bustle, the more secluded Squam Lake has a dearth of public-access points. Its tranquillity no doubt attracted the producers of *On Golden Pond*; several scenes of the Oscar-winning film were shot here. Nearby Lake Wentworth is named for the first Royal Governor of the state, who, in building his country manor here, established North America's first summer resort.

Well-preserved Colonial and 19th-century villages are among the region's many landmarks, and you'll find hiking trails, good antiques shops, and myriad water-oriented activities. This tour begins at Laconia, just off I–93, and more-or-less circles Lake Winnipesaukee clockwise, with several side trips.

Laconia

⑪ *27 mi north of Concord; 94 mi north of Boston, MA.*

When the railroad reached Laconia—then called Meredith Bridge—in 1848, the formerly sleepy community became a manufacturing center. Laconia borders both Winnisquam and Winnipesaukee lakes and is easily accessible from I–93, making it the commercial hub of the Lakes Region. If you need a McDonald's or Rite-Aid, you'll find it here.

Belknap Mill (⊠ Mill Plaza, ☎ 603/524–8813), the oldest unaltered, brick-built textile mill in the United States (1823), contains a knitting museum devoted to the textile industry and a year-round cultural center that sponsors concerts, exhibits, a lecture series, and workshops.

Dining and Lodging

$$–$$$ ✕ **Le Chalet Rouge.** This yellow house with two small dining rooms recalls a country-French bistro. To start, try the house pâté, escargots, or steamed mussels. The steak au poivre is tender and well spiced, and the duckling is prepared with seasonal sauces: rhubarb in spring, raspberry in summer, orange in fall, creamy mustard in winter. ⊠ *385 W. Main St., Tilton (10 mi west of Laconia),* ☎ *603/286–4035. Reservations essential. MC, V.*

$$ ✕ **Hickory Stick Farm.** This restaurant, inside a 200-year-old Cape-style inn, is renowned for its roast duckling with herb stuffing and orange-sherry sauce. Other favorites from the mostly traditional Continental and American menu include prime rib and vegetarian lasagna. ⊠ *66 Bean Hill Rd., Belmont (4 mi south of Laconia),* ☎ *603/524–3333. Closed Mon. No lunch; call for winter hours. AE, D, MC, V.*

$$ 🏠 **Ferry Point House.** Built in the 1800s as a summer retreat for the Pillsbury family of baking fame, this red Victorian farmhouse has superb views of Lake Winnisquam. White wicker furniture and hanging baskets of flowers decorate the 60-ft veranda, and the gazebo by the water's edge is a pleasant place to lounge and listen for loons. A paddleboat and a rowboat await those eager to get in the water. The pretty rooms have Oriental rugs and Victorian furniture. ⊠ *100 Lower Bay Rd., Sanbornton 03269,* ☎ *603/524–0087, FAX 603/524–0959, WEB www.new-hampshire-inn.com. 6 rooms. Beach, boating, fishing. No credit cards. Closed Nov.–Apr. BP.*

Outdoor Activities and Sports

Bartlett Beach (✉ Winnisquam Ave.) has a playground and picnic area. **Opechee Park** (✉ N. Main St.) has dressing rooms, a baseball field, tennis courts, and picnic areas.

Shopping

The **Belknap Mall** (✉ U.S. 3, ☎ 603/524–5651) has boutiques, crafts stores, and a New Hampshire state liquor store. The **Bending Birch** (✉ 569 Main St., ☎ 603/524–7589) sells local crafts, including Laconia pottery, birdhouses made in Meredith, and lap robes in New Hampshire's official tartan. The 53 stores at the **Lakes Region Factory Stores** (✉ Exit 20 from I–93, Tilton, ☎ 888/SHOP–333) center include Brooks Brothers, Eddie Bauer, and Black & Decker.

OFF THE
BEATEN PATH

CANTERBURY SHAKER VILLAGE – Shaker furniture and inventions are well regarded, and this outdoor museum and National Historic Landmark helps illuminate the world of the people who created them. Established as a religious community in 1792, the village flourished in the 1800s and practiced equality of the sexes and races, common ownership, celibacy, and pacifism. The last member of the community passed away in 1992. Shakers invented household items such as the clothespin and the flat broom and were known for the simplicity and integrity of their designs, especially furniture. Ninety-minute tours pass through some of the 694-acre property's 24 restored buildings, and crafts demonstrations take place daily. The Creamery Restaurant serves lunch daily and candlelight dinners Friday–Saturday (reservations essential). A large shop sells fine Shaker reproductions. ✉ *288 Shaker Rd., 15 mi south of Laconia via Route 106, Canterbury,* ☎ *603/783–9511 or 800/982–9511,* WEB *www.shakers.org.* 🖭 *$10 for 2 consecutive days.* ☉ *May–Oct., daily 10–5; Apr. and Nov.–Dec., weekends 10–5.*

Gilford

🕐 *4 mi northeast of Laconia.*

One of the larger public beaches on Lake Winnipesaukee is in Gilford, a resort community. When the town was incorporated in 1812, the inhabitants asked the oldest resident to name it. A veteran of the Battle of the Guilford Courthouse, in North Carolina, he borrowed that town's name—though apparently he didn't know how to spell it. Quiet and peaceful, Gilford remains decidedly uncommercial but offers a variety of recreational opportunities.

Lodging

$$–$$$ 🏨 **B. Mae's Resort Inn.** All the rooms in this modern resort and conference center are large and have a deck or patio; some are suites with kitchens. Close to Gunstock ski area and within walking distance of Lake Winnipesaukee, B. Mae's is popular with skiers in winter and boaters in summer. ✉ *Rtes. 11 and 11B, 03246,* ☎ *603/293–7526 or 800/458–3877,* FAX *603/293–4340,* WEB *www.bmaesresort.com.* *60 rooms, 24 suites. 2 restaurants, bar, indoor and outdoor pools, hot tub, gym, recreation room. AE, D, DC, MC, V.*

$$ 🏨 **Gunstock Inn & Fitness Center.** The original building of this Colonial-style inn was built in the 1930s by Civilian Conservation Corps workers who cut the area's first ski trails. The inn has individually decorated rooms, with some large ones suitable for families. Many have views of the mountains and Lake Winnipesaukee. The tavern serves everything from fresh seafood to burgers in a cozy setting. In the fitness center, guests can take water aerobics and body-toning classes free of charge. ✉ *580 Cherry Valley Rd., 03246,* ☎ *603/293–2021 or 800/654–0180,* FAX *603/293–2050,* WEB *www.gunstockinn.com. 23 rooms,*

2 suites. Restaurant, indoor pool, sauna, steam room, health club. AE, MC, V. BP.

$ ⚕ **Gunstock Campground.** The campground at the Gunstock ski and recreation area has a pool and 300 tent and trailer sites. ⊠ *Box 1307, Rte. 11A, Laconia 03247,* ☎ *603/293–4341 or 800/486–7862. AE, D, MC, V.*

Nightlife and the Arts

The **New Hampshire Music Festival** (⊠ 88 Belknap Mountain Rd., ☎ 603/524–1000) presents award-winning orchestras from early July to mid-August. The outdoor stage (with 2,500 covered seats) at **Meadowbrook Farm** (⊠ Meadowbrook La., off Rte. 11B, ☎ 603/528–5550 or 888/563–2369) hosts top music acts, from Bonnie Raitt to 98°.

Outdoor Activities and Sports

Ellacoya State Beach (⊠ Rte. 11, ☎ 603/293–7821) covers just 600 ft along the southwestern shore of Lake Winnipesaukee. In season, there's a bathhouse, picnic tables, and a fee for parking.

Ski Areas

GUNSTOCK USA

High above Lake Winnipesaukee, this all-purpose area dates from the 1930s. It once had the longest rope tow lift in the country—an advantage that helped local downhill skier and Olympic silver medalist Penny Pitou perfect her craft. Gunstock allows patrons to return lift tickets for a cash refund for absolutely any reason within 75 minutes of purchase. Thrill Hill, a snowtubing park, has 10 runs, multipassenger tubes, and lift service. ⊠ *Rte. 11A (Box 1307, Laconia, 03247),* ☎ *603/293–4341 or 800/486–7862,* WEB *www.gunstock.com.*

Downhill. Clever trail cutting along with grooming and surface sculpting three times daily have made this otherwise pedestrian mountain good for intermediates. That's how most of the 44 trails are rated, with a few more challenging runs and designated sections for slow skiers and learners. Lower Ramrod trail is set up for snowboarding. Gunstock, which has one quad, two triple, and two double chairlifts and two surface tows, has the largest night-skiing facility in New Hampshire, with 15 lighted trails and five lifts in operation.

Cross-country. Gunstock has 50 km (30 mi) of trails for skiing and snowshoeing. Some 15 km (9 mi) are for advanced skiers, and there are backcountry trails as well.

Child care. The nursery takes children ages 6 months and up; the ski school teaches children ages 3–14.

Summer activities. In summer, Gunstock has a swimming pool, a children's playground, hiking trails, mountain-bike rentals and trails, a skateboarding/blading park, guided horseback trail rides, paddleboats, and a campground.

Weirs Beach

⑬ *10 mi northwest of Gilford, 8 mi north of Laconia.*

Weirs Beach is Lake Winnipesaukee's center for arcade activity. Anyone who loves souvenir shops, fireworks, water slides, and hordes of children will feel right at home. Several cruise boats depart from the town dock.

The period cars of the **Winnipesaukee Scenic Railroad** carry passengers along the lake's shore on one- or two-hour rides; boarding is at Weirs Beach or Meredith. Special trips that include certain meals are also offered. ⊠ *U.S. 3, Meredith,* ☎ *603/279–5253 or 603/745–2135.* 🎫 *$8.50–*

*$22.50. ☉ July–mid-Sept., daily; weekends only Memorial Day–late June
and late Sept.–mid-Oct. Call for hrs and for special Santa trains in Dec.*

☺ A giant **Water Slide** (⊠ U.S. 3, ☎ 603/366–5161) overlooks the lake.
For an aquatic experience, visit **Surf Coaster** (⊠ U.S. 3, ☎ 603/366–
4991), which has seven slides, a wave pool, and a large area for young
children. Day or night you can work your way through the miniature
golf course, 20 lanes of bowling, and more than 500 games at **Funspot**
(⊠ Rte. 11B, at U.S. 3, ☎ 603/366–4377).

Outdoor Activities and Sports
Thurston's Marina (⊠ U.S. 3 at the bridge, ☎ 603/366–4811 or 800/
834–4812) rents pontoon boats, power boats, and personal watercraft.

Meredith

⑭ *5 mi northwest of Weirs Beach, 41 mi north of Concord.*

Meredith, on U.S. 3 at the western end of Lake Winnipesaukee, has a
fine collection of crafts shops and art galleries. An information center
is across from the Town Docks.

At **Annalee's Doll Museum,** you can view a collection of the famous
posable felt dolls and learn about the woman who created them. Annalee Davis Thorndike began making the dolls after her graduation from
high school in 1933. Her dolls caught on with collectors, and the company has grown into an empire. ⊠ *Hemlock Dr. off Rte. 104,* ☎ *603/
279–3333.* WEB *www.annalee.com* ✉ *Free.* ☉ *Memorial Day–mid-
Oct.; call for hrs.*

Dining and Lodging
$$–$$$ ✕ **Mame's.** This 1820s tavern, once the home of the village doctor, now
contains a warren of convivial dining rooms accented by exposed-brick
walls, wooden beams, and wide-plank floors. Expect mostly traditional
American standbys of the seafood, steak, veal, and chicken variety; the
mud pie is highly recommended. ⊠ *8 Plymouth St.,* ☎ *603/279–4631.
AE, D, MC, V.*

$$–$$$$ ✕▥ **The Inns at Mill Falls.** Overlooking Lake Winnipesaukee and in-
★   corporating the historic sections of the 19th-century Meredith Linen
Mills, the Inns at Mill Falls offer the amenities and dining of a full re-
sort but on a manageable scale and with a wonderful sense of warmth
and personality. Choose from three different properties: the central-
most Inn at Mills Falls, which adjoins an 18-shop specialty market,
has the resort's indoor pool and 54 spacious rooms; Inn at Bay Point,
which faces a long and dramatic stretch of lakefront, has 24 rooms—
most with balconies, some with fireplaces and whirlpool baths; and
Chase House at Mill Falls, which has lake views and 23 rooms—all
with fireplaces, some with balconies and whirlpool baths. Dining is a
major activity here, among both inn guests and visitors from all around
the lake. The upscale Boathouse Grill ($$–$$$) sits directly on the lake
and serves such contemporary fare as Caesar salad with sea scallops
and pan-seared almond-and-cornmeal-crusted trout with apple butter.
Camp ($$–$$$) delights diners with cedar-plank salmon amid a rus-
tic cabin-inspired motif. Other options include the breakfast/lunch-ori-
ented Waterfall Cafe ($), which overlooks the old mill stream and 40-ft
cascades, and **Giuseppe's** ($–$$), a contemporary Italian eatery with
live cabaret many nights. ⊠ *U.S. 3 at Rte. 25, 03253,* ☎ *603/279–
7006 or 800/622–6455,* FAX *603/279–6797,* WEB *www.millsfalls.com.
101 rooms. 4 restaurants, bars, indoor pool, sauna, shops, meeting
rooms. AE, D, DC, MC, V.*

$ ⚠ **Clearwater Campground.** This wooded tent and RV campground on Lake Pemigewasset has 153 shady sites, a large sandy beach, a recreation building, a playground, basketball and volleyball courts, and boat rentals and slips. ✉ *26 Campground Rd., off Rte. 104, 03253,* ☎ *603/ 279–7761. Closed mid-Oct.–mid-May.*

Outdoor Activities and Sports

BEACHES

Wellington State Beach (✉ Off Rte. 3A, Bristol, 12 mi west of Meredith), on the western shore of Newfound Lake, is one of the most beautiful area beaches. You can swim or picnic or hike along the ½-mi shoreline, or use the boat launch.

BOATING

Meredith Marina and Boating Center (✉ Bay Shore Dr., ☎ 603/279–7921) rents power boats. **Wild Meadow Canoes & Kayaks** (✉ Rte. 25 between Center Harbor and Meredith, ☎ 603/253–7536 or 800/427–7536) has canoes and kayaks for rent.

GOLF

Waukewan Golf Course (✉ Off U.S. 3 and Rte. 25, ☎ 603/279–6661) is an 18-hole, par-71 course. Greens fees are $22–$28.

Shopping

About 170 dealers operate out of the three-floor **Burlwood Antique Center** (✉ U.S. 3, ☎ 603/279–6387), open May–October. The **Meredith League of New Hampshire Craftsmen** (✉ U.S. 3, ½ mi north of Rte. 104, ☎ 603/279–7920) sells works of area artisans. **Mill Falls Marketplace,** part of the Inns at Mills Falls, contains shops with clothing, gifts, and books. The **Old Print Barn** (✉ 1008 Winona Rd., ☎ 603/279–6479), the largest such gallery in northern New England, carries rare prints— Currier & Ives, antique botanicals, and more—from around the world.

Center Harbor

⑮ *5 mi northeast of Meredith.*

In the middle of three bays at the northern end of Winnipesaukee, the town of Center Harbor also borders Lakes Squam, Waukewan, and Winona. This prime location makes it popular in summer, especially with boaters who spend summer weekends on the water.

Dining and Lodging

$$–$$$$ ✕🏨 **Red Hill Inn.** The large bay window in the common room of this rambling late-19th-century inn overlooks the Sandwich Mountains. Guest rooms are furnished with Victorian pieces and country furniture— some of them in a neighboring 1850s farmhouse, just down the hill. Twenty rooms have fireplaces, some have claw-foot tubs, and 10 have two-person hot tubs. For dinner, try the Vermont goat cheese bruschetta, followed by the rack of lamb encrusted in rosemary and garlic. ✉ *Rte. 25B and College Rd. (Box 99M, 03226),* ☎ *603/279–7001 or 800/ 573–3445,* 🅵🅰🆇 *603/279–7003,* 🆆🅴🅱 *www.redhillinn.com. 16 rooms, 9 suites. Restaurant, pub, pool, outdoor hot tub, cross-country skiing. AE, D, DC, MC, V. BP.*

Outdoor Activities and Sports

Red Hill, a hiking trail on Bean Road off Route 25, northeast of Center Harbor, really does turn red in autumn. The reward at the end of the trail in any season is a view of Squam Lake and the mountains.

Shopping

Keepsake Quilting & Country Pleasures (✉ Senter's Marketplace, Rte. 25B, ☎ 603/253–4026), reputedly America's largest quilt shop, contains 5,000 bolts of fabric, hundreds of quilting books, and countless supplies.

Holderness

🔟 *8 mi northwest of Center Harbor, 8 mi north of Meredith.*

Routes 25B and 25 lead to the small and simple town of Holderness, perched between Squam and Little Squam lakes. *On Golden Pond,* starring Katharine Hepburn and Henry Fonda, was filmed on Squam, whose quiet beauty attracts nature lovers.

★ ⟳ The several trails at the 200-acre **Science Center of New Hampshire** include a ¾-mi path that passes by black bears, bobcats, otters, and other native wildlife in trailside enclosures. Educational events at the center include the "Up Close to Animals" series in July and August, at which you can study a species in an intimate setting. The Gordon Children's Activity Center has interactive exhibits. You can also tour the lake on 28-ft pontoon boats, especially useful for observing loons. ⊠ *Rtes. 113 and 25,* ☎ *603/968–7194.* 🌐 *www.sciencectrofnh.org* 🎟 *$9.* ⊙ *May–Oct., daily 9:30–4:30 (last admission 3:30).*

Dining and Lodging

$$$$ ✕🏠 **Manor on Golden Pond.** Built in 1903, this dignified inn with a British-
★ manor ambience has well-groomed grounds and a private dock with canoes, paddle boats, and a boathouse. You can stay in the main inn, the cottages, or, during summer and fall, the carriage house. Sixteen rooms have wood-burning fireplaces; eight have two-person whirlpool baths. Three-, four-, or five-course prix-fixe dinners (reservations required) may include cumin-molasses-charred beef tenderloin with lobster mashed potatoes. ⊠ *U.S. 3 and Shepard Hill Rd., 03245,* ☎ *603/968–3348 or 800/545–2141,* ꜰꜰ *603/968–2116,* 🌐 *www.manorongoldenpond.com. 20 rooms, 3 cottages, 1 carriage house. Restaurant, pub, pool, tennis court, beach, boating. AE, MC, V. BP.*

$$–$$$ 🏠 **Glynn House Inn.** Innkeepers Karol and Betsy Paterman run this swanky three-story 1890s Queen Anne home with a turret and wraparound porch. Many rooms have fireplaces and hot tubs; the bi-level honeymoon suite has a whirlpool tub and fireplace downstairs and a four-poster bed and skylights above. Breakfast usually includes fresh-baked strudel. Squam Lake is minutes away. ⊠ *43 Highland St., Ashland 03217,* ☎ *603/968–3775 or 800/637–9599,* ꜰꜰ *603/968–3129,* 🌐 *www.new-hampshire-lodging.com. 10 rooms, 6 suites. In-room VCRs. MC, V. BP.*

$$ 🏠 **Inn on Golden Pond.** This informal country home, built in 1879 and set on 50 wooded acres, is just up the road from Squam Lake. Rooms have a traditional country decor of hardwood floors, braided rugs, easy chairs, and calico-print bedspreads and curtains; the quietest rooms are in the rear on the third floor. The homemade jam at breakfast is made from rhubarb grown on the property. ⊠ *Box 680, U.S. 3, 03245,* ☎ *603/968–7269,* ꜰꜰ *603/968–9226,* 🌐 *www.innongoldenpond.com. 7 rooms, 2 suites. Hiking. AE, MC, V. BP.*

$–$$ ⛺ **Yogi Bear's Jellystone Park.** This family-oriented camping resort has wooded, open, or riverfront sites; basic and deluxe cabins; and trailers. There's also a pool, a water playground, a hot tub, mini-golf, a basketball court, canoe and kayak rentals, and daily supervised activities. ⊠ *R.R. 1, Box 396, Rte. 132, Ashland 03217,* ☎ *603/968–9000,* 🌐 *www.jellystonenh.com. 275 sites, 43 cabins, 7 trailers.*

Outdoor Activities and Sports

White Mountain Country Club (⊠ N. Ashland Rd., Ashland, ☎ 603/536–2227) has an 18-hole, par-71 golf course. Greens fees are $26 to $32.

Center Sandwich

★ ⑰ *12 mi northeast of Holderness.*

With Squam Lake to the west and the Sandwich Mountains to the north, Center Sandwich claims one of the prettiest settings of any town in the Lakes Region. So appealing are the town and its views that John Greenleaf Whittier used the Bearcamp River as the inspiration for his poem "Sunset on the Bearcamp." The town attracts artisans—crafts shops abound among its clutch of charming 18th- and 19th-century buildings.

The **Historical Society Museum** traces the history of Center Sandwich through the faces of its inhabitants. Works by mid-19th-century portraitist and town son Albert Gallatin Hoit hang alongside a local photographer's exhibit portraying the town's mothers and daughters. The museum houses a replica country store and local furniture and items. ⊠ *4 Maple St.,* ☎ *603/284–6269.* 🖭 *Free.* ☉ *June–Sept., Tues.–Sat. 11–5.*

Dining

$$ ✕ **Corner House Inn.** The restaurant, in a converted barn decorated with local arts and crafts, serves classic American fare. Before you get to the white-chocolate cheesecake with key-lime filling, try the chef's lobster-and-mushroom bisque or tasty garlic-and-horseradish-crusted rack of lamb. There's storytelling Thursday evenings. ⊠ *Rtes. 109 and 113,* ☎ *603/284–6219. AE, D, MC, V. Closed Mon. Nov.–May. No lunch.*

Moultonborough

⑱ *5 mi south of Center Sandwich.*

Moultonborough claims 6½ mi of shoreline on Lake Kanasatka, a large chunk of Lake Winnipesaukee, and even a small piece of Squam.

The highly browsable store that is part of the **Old Country Store and Museum** (⊠ Moultonborough Corner, ☎ 603/476–5750) has been selling maple products, cheeses aged on site, penny candy, and other items since 1781. Much of the equipment still used in the store is antique, and the museum (free) displays antique farming and forging tools.

The town's best-known attraction, the **Castle in the Clouds** is an odd, elaborate stone mansion built without nails; it has 16 rooms, eight bathrooms, and doors made of lead. Construction began in 1911 and continued for three years. Owner Thomas Gustave Plant spent $7 million, the bulk of his fortune, on this project and died penniless in 1946. A tour includes the mansion, and the Castle Springs Microbrewery and spring-water facility on this 5,200-acre property; there's also hiking, pony rides, and horseback-riding. ⊠ *Rte. 171,* ☎ *603/476–2352 or 800/729–2468,* WEB *www.castlesprings.com.* 🖭 *$12 with tour, $6 without tour.* ☉ *Early June–late Oct., daily 9–5; mid-May–early June, weekends 10–4.*

The **Loon Center** at the Frederick and Paula Anna Markus Wildlife Sanctuary is the headquarters of the Loon Preservation Committee, an Audubon Society project. The loon, recognizable for its eerie, haunting calls and striking black-and-white coloring, resides on many New Hampshire lakes but is threatened by boat traffic, poor water quality, and habitat loss. The center presents changing exhibits about the birds. Two nature trails wind through the 200-acre property; vantage points on the Loon Nest Trail overlook the spot resident loons sometimes occupy in late spring and summer. ⊠ *Lees Mills Rd.,* ☎ *603/476–5666,* WEB *www.loon.org.* 🖭 *Free.* ☉ *July–Columbus Day, daily 9–5; Columbus Day–June, Mon.–Sat. 9–5.*

Dining

$$–$$$ ✕ **The Woodshed.** Farm implements and antiques hang on the walls of this enchanting, romantic converted 1860 barn. The menu offers few surprises—mostly traditional New England fare such as sea scallops baked in butter and lamb chops with mint sauce—but exceptionally fresh ingredients and delightful ambience are sure to please. ✉ *Lee's Mill Rd.,* ☎ *603/476–2311. AE, D, DC, MC, V. Closed Mon. No lunch.*

Tamworth

19 *12 mi northeast of Moultonborough, 20 mi southwest of North Conway.*

President Grover Cleveland summered in what remains a village of almost unreal quaintness—it's equally photogenic in verdant summer, during fall foliage, or under a blanket of winter snow. Cleveland's son, Francis, returned to stay and founded the acclaimed Barnstormers Theater in 1931. Tamworth has a clutch of villages within its borders. At one of them—Chocorua—the view through the birches of Chocorua Lake has been so often photographed that you may feel as if you've been here before.

For 99 years, Dr. Edwin Remick and his father provided medical services to the Tamworth area and operated a family farm. At the **Remick Country Doctor Museum and Farm,** endowed by Dr. Remick, exhibits focus on the life of a country doctor and on the activities of the still-working farm. There are always hands-on activities, but try to visit when ice harvesting, stone wall building, or the like is scheduled. ✉ *58 Cleveland Hill Rd.,* ☎ *800/686–6117,* WEB *www.remickmuseum.org.* *Free.* ⏲ *Nov.–June, weekdays 10–4; July–Oct., Mon.–Sat. 10–4.*

Dining and Lodging

$$$–$$$$ ★ ✕🏨 **Tamworth Inn.** Owners Bob and Virginia Schrader spent two years completely renovating this 1833 Victorian inn anchoring the village, which is a great base both for exploring the lakes and also winter skiing in the eastern White Mountains. Common rooms range from the cozy beamed-ceiling pub to the formal dining room where tables are laid with white linen and crystal. Guest rooms have brass or antique beds, down comforters, and Caswell-Massey toiletries. The beautifully landscaped grounds border the Swift River. In the dining room (closed Sun.–Mon. in summer and Sun.–Wed. in winter), chef Jim Berry offers seasonal cuisine with specialties such as grilled salmon brushed with olive oil and cracked black pepper, with a balsamic reduction, sautéed baby spinach, and Yukon potato hash. ✉ *Main St., 03886,* ☎ *603/323–7721 or 800/642–7352,* FAX *603/323–2026,* WEB *www.tamworth.com. 16 rooms. Restaurant, pub, pool. MC, V. BP, MAP.*

$–$$ 🏨 **Mt. Chocorua View House.** This 1845 house began as a carriage stop and has been an inn almost continuously since then. Ideally located between the Lakes Region and the White Mountains, it draws many hikers and skiers. Guest rooms can be small, but all are welcoming with flowered wallpapers, quilts, ceiling fans, and other personal touches. Common areas include a guest kitchen and a screened porch that might make hiking nearby Mt. Chocorua seem like just too much work. ✉ *Box 348, Rte. 16, Chocorua 03817,* ☎ *603/323–8350 or 888/323–8350,* FAX *603/323–3319,* WEB *www.mtchocorua.com. 6 rooms, 3 with bath; 1 suite. Gym. AE, D, MC, V. BP.*

Nightlife and the Arts

The **Arts Council of Tamworth** (☎ 603/323–8104) produces concerts—soloists, string quartets, revues, children's programs—September–June and an arts show in late July. **Barnstormers** (✉ Main St., ☎ 603/323–8500) has performances in July and August. The box office opens in June.

Outdoor Activities and Sports

The 72-acre stand of native pitch pine at **White Lake State Park** (⊠ Rte. 16, ☎ 603/323–7350) is a National Natural Landmark. The park has hiking trails, a sandy beach, trout fishing, canoe rentals, two separate camping areas, a picnic area, and swimming.

Shopping

The many theme rooms—a Christmas room, a bride's room, a children's room, among them—at the **Country Handcrafters & Chocorua Dam Ice Cream Shop** (⊠ Rte. 16, Chocorua, ☎ 603/323–8745) contain handcrafted items. When you're done shopping, try the ice cream, coffee, or tea and scones.

The Ossipees

⑳ *6 mi southeast of Tamworth, 21 mi south of North Conway.*

Route 16 between West Ossipee and Center Ossipee passes Ossipee Lake, known for fine fishing and swimming. Around these hamlets you'll find several antiques shops and galleries.

Dining

$$ ✕ **Jake's Seafood.** Oars and nautical trappings adorn the wood-paneled walls at this seafood stop between West and Center Ossipee. The kitchen serves some of the freshest and tastiest seafood in eastern New Hampshire, notably lobster pie, fried clams, and seafood casserole; steak, ribs, and chicken dishes are also offered. ⊠ *2055 Rte. 16, ☎ 603/539–2805. Closed Mon.–Wed. MC, V.*

$–$$ ✕ **Yankee Smokehouse.** This down-home barbecue joint's logo depicting
★ two happy pigs ironically foreshadows the gleeful enthusiasm with which patrons dive into the hefty sandwiches of sliced pork and smoked chicken and immense platters of baby back ribs and smoked sliced beef. Ample sides of slaw, beans, fries, and garlic toast complement the hearty fare. Born-and-bred Southerners have been known to come away from this place impressed. ⊠ *Rtes. 16 and 25, ☎ 603/539–RIBS. Closed Tues.–Wed. No credit cards.*

Shopping

Local craftspeople create much of the jewelry, turned wooden bowls, pewter goblets, and glassware sold at **Tramway Artisans** (⊠ Rte. 16, West Ossipee, ☎ 603/539–5700).

Wakefield

㉑ *21 mi south of West Ossipee, 43 mi north of Portsmouth, 64 mi northeast of Concord.*

East of Lake Winnipesaukee, seven laid-back villages combine to form Wakefield, a town with 10 lakes. Wakefield's 26-building historic district, just off Route 16 near the Maine border, comprises a church, houses, and an inn that dates from the 18th century. A few miles down Route 153 in Sanbornville you'll find Wakefield's present-day commercial district.

☍ The **Museum of Childhood** displays a one-room schoolhouse, a child's room and a kitchen from 1890, model trains, antique sleds, teddy bears, 3,500 dolls, and 44 furnished dollhouses. Special events are scheduled most Fridays. ⊠ *2784 Wakefield Rd., ☎ 603/522–8073. ☒ $3. ☉ Memorial Day–Labor Day, Mon. and Wed.–Sat. 11–4, Sun. 1–4.*

Lodging

$–$$ ⌂ **Wakefield Inn.** The restoration of this 1804 stagecoach inn, a high-
★ light of Wakefield's historic district, has been handled with an eye for detail. The dining-room windows retain the original panes and shutters,

but the centerpiece of the building is the freestanding spiral staircase, which rises three stories. The large rooms, named for famous guests or past owners, have wide-board pine floors, big sofas, and handmade quilts. The 2-mi Wakefield Heritage Trail (for walkers) runs from the inn to the center of town. In late fall and early spring, you can learn how to quilt as part of the weekend Quilting Package. ⊠ *2723 Wakefield Rd., 03872,* ☎ *603/522–8272 or 800/245–0841,* WEB *www.wakefieldinn.com. 7 rooms. MC, V. BP.*

Wolfeboro

22 *21 mi south of West Ossipee, 28 mi northwest of Rochester, 49 mi northwest of Portsmouth.*

Quietly upscale and decidedly preppy Wolfeboro has been a resort since Royal Governor John Wentworth built his summer home on the shores of Lake Wentworth in 1763. The town center, bursting with tony boutiques and shops, fringes Lake Winnipesaukee and sees about a tenfold population increase each summer. Expect none of the exuberant commercialism of Weirs Beach—Wolfeboro marches to a steady, relaxed beat, comfortable for all ages. It maintains a small-town feel while still offering plenty of shopping and entertainment options.

Uniforms, vehicles, and other artifacts at the **Wright Museum** illustrate the contributions of those on the home front to America's World War II effort. ⊠ *77 Center St.,* ☎ *603/569–1212,* WEB *www.wrightmuseum. org.* 🖾 *$5.* ☉ *May–Oct., daily 10–4; Nov.–Apr., weekends 10–4.*

The artisans at the **Hampshire Pewter Company** (⊠ 43 Mill St., ☎ 603/ 569–4944 or 800/639–7704) use 17th-century techniques to make pewter tableware and accessories. Free tours are conducted at 10, 11, 1, 2, and 3 most days, Memorial Day–Columbus Day; the gift shop is open year-round.

Dining and Lodging

$$–$$$ ✕ **The Bittersweet.** This converted barn 2 mi north of downtown delights diners with its eclectic display of old quilts, pottery, sheet music, and china. Locals also love the nightly specials that range from a popular lobster pie to steak Diane. The upper level has antique tables and chairs and dining by candlelight. The lower-level lounge, decorated with Victorian wicker furniture, serves lighter fare. ⊠ *Rte. 28,* ☎ *603/ 569–3636. AE, D, MC, V.*

$–$$ ✕ **Wolfetrap Grill and Raw Bar.** The seafood at this festive shanty on Lake Winnipesaukee is guaranteed fresh—it comes from the Wolfetrap's adjacent fish market. You'll find all your favorites here, including a renowned clam boil for one that includes steamers, corn on the cob, onions, potatoes, sweet potatoes, and a hot dog. The raw bar has oysters and clams on the half shell. ⊠ *17 Bay St.,* ☎ *603/569–1503. MC, V. Closed mid-Oct.–mid-May.*

$$–$$$ ✕🏠 **Wolfeboro Inn.** Built in the early 1800s, this white clapboard house has later additions with views of the lakefront. The rooms have polished cherry and pine furnishings, armoires, stenciled borders, and country quilts but could stand a little updating, especially the bathrooms and toiletries. Pub fare and more than 70 brands of beer are available at Wolfe's Tavern ($–$$), where fireplaces make cool evenings cozy. The 1812 Steakhouse ($$–$$$) serves fresh seafood and a popular slow-roasted prime rib. ⊠ *Box 1270, 90 N. Main St., 03894,* ☎ *603/569– 3016 or 800/451–2389,* FAX *603/569–5375,* WEB *www.wolfeboroinn.com. 41 rooms, 3 suites, 1 apartment. 2 restaurants, bar, beach, boating, meeting room. AE, MC, V. CP.*

Outdoor Activities and Sports

BEACHES

Wentworth State Beach (⊠ Rte. 109, ☎ 603/569–3699) has good swimming, picnicking areas, and a bathhouse.

BOATING

Winnipesaukee Kayak Company (⊠ 17 Bay St., ☎ 603/569–9926) gives kayak lessons and leads group excursions on the lake. **Wetwolfe Boat Rentals** (⊠ 17 Bay St., ☎ 603/569–1503) rents motorboats and personal watercraft.

GOLF

Kingswood Golf Course (⊠ Rte. 28, ☎ 603/569–3569) has an 18-hole, par-72 course. Greens fees are $35–$48.

HIKING

A short (¼-mi) hike to the 100-ft post-and-beam **Abenaki Tower,** followed by a more rigorous climb to the top, rewards you with a vast view of Lake Winnipesaukee and the Ossipee mountain range. The trailhead is a few miles north of town on Route 109.

WATER SPORTS

Scuba divers can explore a 130-ft-long cruise ship that sank in 30 ft of water off Glendale in 1895. **Dive Winnipesaukee Corp.** (⊠ 4 N. Main St., ☎ 603/569–2120) runs charters out to wrecks and offers rentals, repairs, scuba sales, and lessons in waterskiing and windsurfing.

Alton Bay

㉓ *10 mi south of Wolfeboro, 20 mi southeast of Laconia*

Neither quiet nor secluded, Lake Winnipesaukee's southern shore is alive with visitors from the moment the first flower blooms until the last maple has shed its leaves. Two mountain ridges hold 7 mi of the lake in Alton Bay, which is the name of both the inlet and the town at its tip. The lake's cruise boats dock here, and small planes land here year-round, on both the water and the ice. There's a dance pavilion, along with miniature golf, a public beach, and a Victorian-style bandstand.

Mt. Major, 5 mi north of Alton Bay on Route 11, has a 2½-mi trail with views of Lake Winnipesaukee. At the top is a four-sided stone shelter built in 1925.

Dining

$$$$ ✕ **Crystal Quail.** This tiny (12-seat) restaurant, inside an 18th-century farmhouse, is worth the drive. The prix-fixe contemporary menu changes daily but might include saffron-garlic soup, a house pâté, quenelle-stuffed sole, or duck in crisp potato shreds. ⊠ *202 Pitman Rd., Center Barnstead (12 mi south of Alton Bay),* ☎ *603/269–4151. Reservations essential. No credit cards. BYOB. Closed Mon.–Tues. No lunch.*

Lakes Region A to Z

To research prices, get advice from other travelers, and book travel arrangements, visit www.fodors.com.

AIRPORTS & TRANSFERS
Manchester Airport is about an hour to 90 minutes away by car.

AIRPORT TRANSFERS

Greater Laconia Transit Agency has door-to-door service from Manchester Airport to anywhere within a 10-mi radius of Laconia.
➤ SHUTTLES: **Greater Laconia Transit Agency** (☎ 603/528–2496 or 800/ 294–2496).

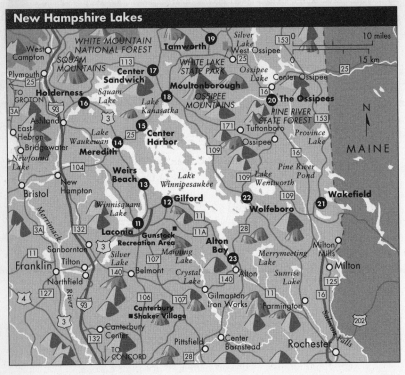

New Hampshire Lakes

BUS TRAVEL

Concord Trailways connects Boston's South Station and Logan Airport with Center Harbor, Chocorua, Laconia, Meredith, Moultonborough, Plymouth, Tilton, and West Ossipee.

➤ BUS INFORMATION: **Concord Trailways** (☎ 800/639–3317).

CAR TRAVEL

On the western side of the Lakes Region, I–93 is the principal north–south artery. Exit 20 leads to U.S. 3 and Route 11 and the southwestern side of Lake Winnipesaukee. Take Exit 23 to Route 104 to Route 25 and the northwestern corner of the region. From the coast, the Spaulding Turnpike (Route 16) heads to the White Mountains, with roads leading to the lakeside towns.

EMERGENCIES

➤ HOSPITAL: **Lakes Region General Hospital** (⊠ 80 Highland St., Laconia, ☎ 603/524–3211).

LODGING

For longer stays in the Lakes Region consider renting a lakeside house or condominium. Among the rental agencies are Preferred Vacation Rental, Inc. and Strictly Rentals, Inc.

APARTMENT & VILLA RENTALS
➤ LOCAL AGENTS: **Preferred Vacation Rentals, Inc.** (⊠ Box 161, Center Harbor 03226, ☎ 603/253–7811 or 800/639–4022). **Strictly Rentals, Inc.** (⊠ Box 695, Center Harbor 03226, ☎ 603/253–9800).

OUTDOORS & SPORTS

The Lakes Region Association provides boating advice. The New Hampshire Fish and Game office has information about fishing and licenses. The Alexandria headquarters of the Appalachian Mountain

Club has trail information. The Laconia Office of the U.S. Forest Service can provide trail advice and information.

➤ CONTACTS: The **Lakes Region Association** (☎ 603/744–8664 or 800/925–2537). **New Hampshire Fish and Game** office (☎ 603/744–5470). **Appalachian Mountain Club** (☎ 603/744–8011). **Laconia Office of the U.S. Forest Service** (☎ 603/528–8721).

TOURS

The 230-ft M/S *Mount Washington* makes 2½-hour scenic cruises of Lake Winnipesaukee from Weirs Beach, mid-May–late October, with stops in Wolfeboro, Alton Bay, Center Harbor, and Meredith. Evening cruises include live music and a buffet dinner.

The M/V *Sophie C.* has been the area's floating post office for more than a century. The boat departs Weirs Beach with mail and passengers Monday–Saturday, mid-June–Labor Day; call for stops. Sky Bright operates airplane and helicopter tours and provides instruction on aerial photography. From May to late October, Squam Lake Tours takes up to 48 passengers on a two-hour pontoon tour of "Golden Pond." The company also operates guided fishing trips and private charters. Moultonborough Airport operates chartered flights and tours.

➤ TOUR-OPERATOR RECOMMENDATIONS: **M/S *Mount Washington*** (☎ 603/366–5531 or 888/843–6686, WEB www.msmountwashington.com). The **M/V *Sophie C.*** (☎ 603/366–5531 or 888/843–6686). **Sky Bright** (✉ Laconia Airport, Rte. 11, ☎ 800/639–6012). **Squam Lake Tours** (☎ 603/968–7577). **Moultonborough Airport** (✉ Rte. 25, Moultonborough, ☎ 603/476–8801).

VISITOR INFORMATION

➤ TOURIST INFORMATION: **Lakes Region Association** (✉ Box 430, Rte. 104, just off exit 23 of I–93, New Hampton 03256, ☎ 603/253–8555 or 800/925–2537, WEB www.lakesregion.org). **Squam Lakes Area Chamber of Commerce** (✉ Box 65, Ashland 03217, ☎ 603/968–4494. **Wolfeboro Chamber of Commerce** (✉ Box 547-WT7, Railroad Ave., Wolfeboro 03894, ☎ 603/569–2200 or 800/516–5324).

THE WHITE MOUNTAINS

Sailors approaching East Coast harbors frequently mistake the pale peaks of the White Mountains—the highest range in the northeastern United States—for clouds. It was 1642 when explorer Darby Field could no longer contain his curiosity about one mountain in particular. He set off from his Exeter homestead and became the first man to climb what would eventually be called Mt. Washington, the king of the Presidential Range. More than a mile high, Mt. Washington must have presented Field with formidable obstacles—its peak claims the highest wind velocity ever recorded and it can see snow every month of the year.

More than 350 years after Field's climb, curiosity about the mountains has not abated. People come by the tens of thousands to hike and climb in spring and summer, to photograph the vistas and the vibrant foliage in autumn, and to ski in winter. In this four-season vacation hub, many resorts (some of which have been in business since the mid-1800s) are destinations in themselves, with golf, tennis, swimming, hiking, cross-country skiing, and renowned restaurants.

Roughly 770,000 acres of forested mountains, valleys, and notches (deep mountain passes) make up the White Mountain National Forest. Long popular with hikers, campers, and skiers, and easily accessible to Bostonians and New Yorkers, it is one of the most heavily used for recreation of the nation's protected forests. The forest includes the Presidential Range of the White Mountains: these peaks, like Mt. Washington, are all named after early presidents. Notorious for its foul weather, Mt. Washington is, nonetheless, a favorite with hikers. An auto road and a railway also lead to the top. The mountain scenery of Franconia Notch, Crawford Notch, and Pinkham Notch also fall within the forest's boundaries. Crawford and Franconia notches are doubly protected, since they are state parks, too.

This section begins in Waterville Valley, off I–93, then continues to North Woodstock, where it follows the **White Mountains Trail** (☎ 888/944–8368, WEB www.whitemountainstrail.com), a magnificent 100-mi loop designated as a National Scenic & Cultural Byway in 1998. For a detailed map that notes specific photo-ops and provides additional historic background, contact or visit the **White Mountains Visitors Bureau**. The tour breaks off from the White Mountains Trail in a few places, but you can easily follow this chapter in conjunction with the trail map.

Waterville Valley

㉔ *60 mi north of Concord.*

In 1835, visitors began arriving in Waterville Valley, a 10-mi-long cul-de-sac cut by one of New England's several Mad Rivers and circled by mountains. First a summer resort, then more of a ski area, and now a year-round getaway, Waterville Valley retains a small-town feel. There are inns and condos, restaurants, shops, conference facilities, a grocery store, and a post office. Hiking and mountain biking are popular summer sports, while ice-skating and snowshoeing supplement skiing and snowboarding in winter.

Dining and Lodging

$–$$ ✕ **Chile Peppers.** Southwest-inspired Chile Peppers caters to skiers with fajitas, tacos, enchiladas, and other Tex-Mex staples. The food here may not be authentic Mexican, but it's well priced and filling. If you're solely into Tex, the lineup includes ribs, steak, seafood, and chicken. ⊠ *Town Square,* ☎ *603/236–4646. AE, DC, MC, V.*

$$–$$$ ⌧ **Black Bear Lodge.** This family-oriented property has one-bedroom suites that sleep up to six and have full kitchens. Each unit is individually owned and decorated. Children's movies are shown at night in season, and there's bus service to the slopes. Guests can use the White Mountain Athletic Club. ⊠ *Box 357, Village Rd., 03215,* ☎ *603/236–4501 or 800/349–2327,* FAX *603/236–4114,* WEB *www.black-bear-lodge. com. 107 suites. Indoor–outdoor pool, hot tub, sauna, steam room, gym, recreation room. AE, D, DC, MC, V.*

$$–$$$$ ⌧ **Golden Eagle Lodge.** Waterville's premier condominium property recalls the grand hotels of an earlier era. The full-service complex, which opened in 1989, has a two-story lobby and a capable front-desk staff. Guests have access to the White Mountain Athletic Club. ⊠ *6 Snow's Brook Rd., 03215,* ☎ *603/236–4600 or 888/703–2453,* FAX *603/236–4947,* WEB *www.goldeneaglelodge.com. 139 condominiums. Kitchenettes, indoor pool, sauna, recreation room. AE, D, DC, MC, V.*

$$–$$$ ⌧ **Snowy Owl Inn.** The fourth-floor bunk-bed lofts at this inn are ideal for families; first-floor rooms, some with whirlpool tubs, are suitable for couples seeking a quiet getaway. The atrium lobby, where guests are treated to afternoon wine and cheese, contains a three-story fieldstone fireplace and many prints and watercolors of snowy owls. Four restaurants are within walking distance. Guests have access to the White Mountain Athletic Club. ⊠ *Box 407, Village Rd., 03215,* ☎ *603/236–8383 or 800/766–9969,* FAX *603/236–4890,* WEB *www.snowyowlinn.com. 85 rooms. Indoor and outdoor pools, hot tubs. AE, D, DC, MC, V. BP.*

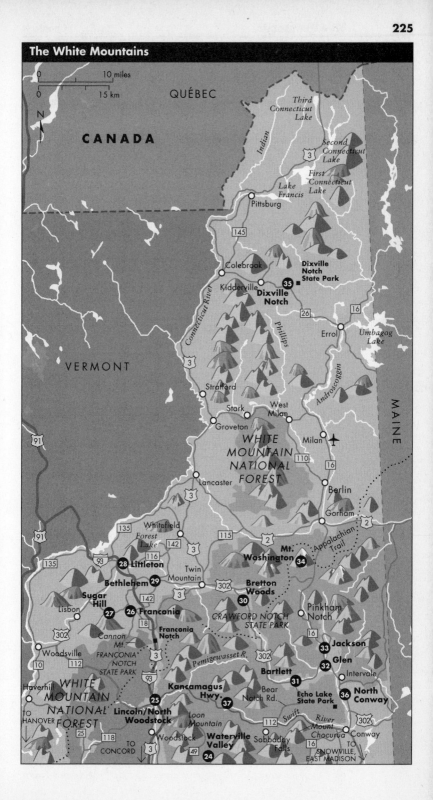

The White Mountains

QUÉBEC

CANADA

Third
Connecticut
Lake

Second
Connecticut
Lake

First
Connecticut
Lake

Indian

3

Lake
Francis

Pittsburg

145

Colebrook

Dixville
Notch
State Park

Kidderville

35

**Dixville
Notch**

26

16

Errol

Umbagog
Lake

Phillips

Connecticut River

3

Stratford

VERMONT

Stark

West
Milan

Androscoggin

91

Groveton

Lancaster

*WHITE
MOUNTAIN
NATIONAL
FOREST*

Milan

MAINE

110

16

3

Berlin

Gorham

2

Whitefield

Forest
Lake

135

142

115

2

Appalachian Trail

91

116

3

**Mt.
Washington**

34

93

135

28 **Littleton**

Twin
Mountain

Bethlehem **29**

302

**Bretton
Woods**

**Sugar
Hill**

142

3

30

Pinkham
Notch

Lisbon

27

26 **Franconia**

18

*CRAWFORD NOTCH
STATE PARK*

16

33 **Jackson**

302

Cannon
Mt.

**Franconia
Notch**

302

10

Woodsville

112

*FRANCONIA
NOTCH
STATE PARK*

3

Pemigewasset R.

Bartlett

32 **Glen**

Intervale

Haverhill

93

31

*WHITE
MOUNTAIN

NATIONAL
FOREST*

**Kancamagus
Hwy.**

Bear
Notch Rd.

Echo Lake
State Park

36 **North
Conway**

TO
HANOVER

25

**Lincoln/North
Woodstock**

37

Loon
Mountain

Swift

*River
Mount
Chocurua*

302

25

118

TO
CONCORD

3

Woodstock

**Waterville
Valley**

49

24

Sabbaday
Falls

112

16

Conway

TO
SNOWVILLE,
EAST MADISON

Outdoor Activities and Sports

The **White Mountain Athletic Club** (⊠ Rte. 49, ☎ 603/236–8303) has tennis, racquetball, and squash as well as a 25-meter indoor pool, a jogging track, exercise equipment, whirlpools, saunas, steam rooms, and a games room. The club is free to guests of many area lodgings.

Ski Areas

WATERVILLE VALLEY

Former U.S. ski-team star Tom Corcoran designed this family-oriented resort. The lodgings and various amenities are about one mi from the slopes, but a shuttle renders a car unnecessary. ⊠ *Box 540, Rte. 49, 03215,* ☎ *603/236–8311; 603/236–4144 snow conditions; 800/468–2553 lodging,* WEB *www.waterville.com.*

Downhill. Mt. Tecumseh has been laid out with great care. This ski area has hosted more World Cup races than any other in the East, so most advanced skiers will be adequately challenged. Snowboarders have a terrain park that includes a timed boardercross course, and lift-serviced snow tubing has been added. Most of the 52 trails are intermediate: straight down the fall line, wide, and agreeably long. A 7-acre tree-skiing area adds variety. Snowmaking coverage of 100% ensures good skiing even when nature doesn't cooperate. The lifts serving the 2,020 ft of vertical rise include two high-speed detachable quads, two triple, three double, and four surface lifts.

Cross-country. The Waterville Valley cross-country network, with the ski center in the Town Square, has 105 km (65 mi) of trails. About two-thirds of the trails are groomed; the rest are backcountry.

Child care. The nursery takes children 6 months to 4 years. SKIwee instruction accepts children ages 3 to 12. The Kinderpark, a children's slope, has a slow-running lift.

Summer activities. Hiking, mountain biking, tennis, and golf are popular activities. Mountain bikes are available for rent in the Town Square.

Lincoln/North Woodstock

㉕ *14 mi northwest of Waterville Valley, 63 mi north of Concord.*

Lincoln and North Woodstock, at the western end of the Kancamagus Highway or at Exit 32 off I–93, combine to make one of the state's liveliest resort areas—the area appeals more to the social set and families than to couples seeking a quiet, romantic getaway. Festivals, such as the New Hampshire Scottish Highland Games in mid-September, keep Lincoln swarming with people year-round, while North Woodstock maintains more of a village feel.

A ride on the **Hobo Railroad** yields scenic views of the Pemigewasset River and the White Mountain National Forest. The narrated excursions take 1 hour and 20 minutes. ⊠ *Rte. 112, Lincoln,* ☎ *603/745–2135,* WEB *www.hoborr.com.* ⌑ *$8.* ⊙ *June–Labor Day, daily, May and Sept.–Oct., weekends; call for schedule.*

⟲ At the **Whale's Tale Water Park,** you can float on an inner tube along a gentle river, careen down five water slides, take a trip down the multipassenger family tube ride, or body-surf in the large wave pool. Whale Harbor and Orca Park Play Island contain water activities for small children and toddlers. ⊠ *U.S. 3, North Lincoln,* ☎ *603/745–8810,* WEB *www.whalestalewaterpark.com.* ⌑ *$20.* ⊙ *Mid-June–Labor Day, daily 10–6.*

Dining and Lodging

$$–$$$ ✕🖫 **Woodstock Inn.** This social but laid-back inn, run by the Rice family since 1982, has rooms in three buildings, ranging from fairly simple to quite romantic (with canopy bed, whirlpool tub, and complimentary champagne). Many of them accommodate groups and families. The restaurants include the elegant Clement Room Grill ($$–$$$), where the Mediterranean seafood sauté or bison pot roast are favorite dishes; Woodstock Station ($), where the extensive menu lists everything from meat loaf to fajitas; and the Woodstock Inn Brewery. The complimentary country breakfasts (for overnight guests—are justly famous. ⊠ *Box 118, U.S. 3, North Woodstock 03262,* ☎ *603/745–3951 or 800/321–3985,* 𝐅𝐀𝐗 *603/745–3701,* 𝐖𝐄𝐁 *www.woodstockinnnh.com. 21 rooms, 19 with bath. 2 restaurants, bar, refrigerator, outdoor hot tub. AE, D, MC, V. BP.*

$$–$$$$ 🖫 **Mountain Club on Loon.** This first-rate slopeside resort hotel has an assortment of accommodations: suites that sleep as many as eight, studios with Murphy beds, and 117 units with kitchens. Many can be combined to form larger units. All rooms are within walking distance of the lifts, and condominiums are on-slope and nearby. Entertainers perform in the lounge on most winter weekends. ⊠ *Rte. 112, Kancamagus Hwy., Lincoln 03251,* ☎ *603/745–2244 or 800/229–7829,* 𝐅𝐀𝐗 *603/745–2317. 234 units. Restaurant, bar, lounge, indoor and outdoor pools, massage, sauna, tennis courts, aerobics, health club, racquetball, squash. AE, D, MC, V.*

$$–$$$ 🖫 **Indian Head Resort.** Views across the 180 acres of this resort motel near the Loon and Cannon Mountain ski areas are of Indian Head Rock Profile and the Franconia Mountains. Cross-country ski trails and a mountain-bike trail from the resort connect to the Franconia Notch trail system. The Profile Room restaurant ($$–$$$) serves a nice selection of standard American dishes. ⊠ *U.S. 3, North Lincoln 03251,* ☎ *603/745–8000 or 800/343–8000,* 𝐅𝐀𝐗 *603/745–8414,* 𝐖𝐄𝐁 *www.indianheadresort.com. 98 rooms, 40 cottages. Restaurant, bar, indoor and outdoor pools, lake, outdoor hot tub, sauna, tennis court, fishing, bicycles, ice-skating, cross-country skiing, recreation room. AE, D, DC, MC, V.*

Nightlife and the Arts

NIGHTLIFE

Skiers head to the **Granite Bar** at the Mountain Club at the Loon Mountain resort (⊠ Kancamagus Hwy., ☎ 603/745–8111). **Thunderbird Lounge** (⊠ Indian Head Resort, U.S. 3, North Lincoln, ☎ 603/745–8000) has nightly entertainment year-round and a large dance floor. The **Olde Timbermill Pub** (⊠ Mill at Loon Mountain, Kancamagus Hwy., ☎ 603/745–3603) brings in live dance music weekends.

THE ARTS

The **North Country Center for the Arts** (⊠ Mill at Loon Mountain, Kancamagus Hwy., Lincoln, ☎ 603/745–6032) presents theater for children and adults and art exhibitions from July to September.

Outdoor Activities and Sports

At **Lost River in Kinsman Notch** (⊠ Rte. 112, 6 mi west of North Woodstock, ☎ 603/745–8031, 𝐖𝐄𝐁 www.findlostriver.com), open from mid-May to mid-October, you can hike along the sheer granite river gorge and view geological wonders like the Guillotine Rock and the Lemon Squeezer, or pan for gemstones. A cafeteria, extensive nature garden, and gift shop round out the amenities. Admission varies according to the activity. **Pemi Valley Excursions** (⊠ Main St., Lincoln, ☎ 603/745–2744, 𝐖𝐄𝐁 www.i93.com/pvsr) offers moose and wildlife bus tours June–October, and guided snowmobile tours through the White Mountains in winter.

Shopping

CRAFTS

The **Curious Cow** (✉ Main St., North Woodstock, ☎ 603/745–9230) is a multidealer shop selling country crafts. **Sunburst Fashions** (✉ 108 Main St., North Woodstock, ☎ 603/745–8745) stocks handcrafted gemstone jewelry and imported gifts.

MALL

Millfront Marketplace, Mill at Loon Mountain (✉ Kancamagus Hwy., Lincoln, ☎ 603/745–6261), a former paper factory, contains restaurants, boutiques, a bookstore, and a post office.

Ski Areas

LOON MOUNTAIN

A modern resort on the Kancamagus Highway and the Pemigewasset River, Loon Mountain opened in the 1960s and underwent serious development in the 1980s. In the base lodge and around the mountain are many food-service and lounge facilities. There's day and nighttime lift-serviced snow tubing on the lower slopes. Loon's Equestrian Center runs horseback-riding trips along the east branch of the Pemigewasset River. ✉ *Kancamagus Hwy., Lincoln 03251,* ☎ *603/745–8111; 603/745–8100 snow conditions; 800/227–4191 lodging,* WEB *www.loonmtn.com.*

Downhill. Wide, straight, and consistent intermediate trails prevail at Loon. Beginner trails and slopes are set apart. Most advanced runs are grouped on the North Peak section farther from the main mountain. Snowboarders have a halfpipe and their own snowboard park, and an alpine garden with bumps and jumps provides thrills for skiers. The vertical is 2,100 ft; a four-passenger gondola, one high-speed detachable quad, two triple and three double chairlifts, and one surface lift serve the 43 trails and slopes.

Cross-country. The touring center at Loon Mountain has 35 km (22 mi) of cross-country trails.

Child care. The day-care center takes children from 6 weeks to 8 years old. The ski school runs several programs for children of different age groups. Children 5 and under ski free.

Summer activities. In summer and fall you can ride New Hampshire's longest gondola to the summit for panoramic mountain views. Among the daily activities at the summit are lumberjack shows, storytelling by a mountain man, and nature tours. You can also take self-guided walks to glacial caves. Other recreational opportunities include horseback riding, mountain biking, and in-line skating and skateboarding in a state park.

Franconia

㉖ *16 mi north of Lincoln/North Woodstock.*

Travelers have long passed north–south through the White Mountains via Franconia Notch, and in the late 18th century a town evolved just to the north. It and the region's jagged rock formations and heavy coat of evergreens have stirred the imaginations of such literary icons as Washington Irving, Henry Wadsworth Longfellow, and Nathaniel Hawthorne, who penned a short story about the Old Man on the Mountain. The town remains enchanting, if sleepy (especially compared with nearby bustling Lincoln/Woodstock), touched though it is by I–93—aka Franconia Notch Parkway—and modern ski resorts.

At **Frost Place,** Robert Frost's home from 1915 to 1920, the poet wrote one of his most-remembered works, "Stopping by Woods on a

Snowy Evening." Two rooms host occasional readings and contain memorabilia and signed editions of his books. Outside, you can follow short trails marked with lines from Frost's poetry. ✉ *Ridge Rd., off Rte. 116,* ☎ *603/823–5510.* ✉ *$3.* ⊙ *Memorial Day–June, weekends 1–5; July–Columbus Day, Wed.–Mon. 1–5.*

The **Old Man of the Mountain,** a granite profile high above the notch, defines New Hampshire; you can't easily—and shouldn't—miss glimpsing this icon. Nathaniel Hawthorne wrote about it, New Hampshire resident Daniel Webster bragged about it, and P. T. Barnum tried to buy it. Stop at the posted turn-outs from I–93 north- or southbound or along the shore of Profile Lake for the best views. There's also a small, free **Old Man of the Mountain Museum** administered by Franconia Notch State Park and located at the southbound viewing area (by the Cannon Mountain tram parking area); it's open daily 9–5.

The **Flume** is an 800-ft-long natural chasm with narrow walls that give the gorge's running water an eerie echo. The route through the flume has been built up with a series of boardwalks and stairways. The visitor center has exhibits on the region's history. ✉ *Franconia Notch Pkwy., Exit 2,* ☎ *603/745–8391,* WEB *www.nhparks.state.nh.us/parkops/ parks/franconia.html.* ✉ *$7.* ⊙ *May–Oct., daily 9–5.*

Dining and Lodging

$$–$$$ ✕🏨 **Franconia Inn.** At this 107-acre, family-friendly year-round resort, you can golf next door at Sunset Hill's nine-hole course, play tennis, swim in the pool, hike—even try soaring from the inn's airstrip. The cross-country ski barn doubles as a stable and horseback center in the warmer months. Rooms have designer chintzes, canopy beds, and country furnishings; some have whirlpool baths or fireplaces. The restaurant presents traditional American fare with some upscale twists, such as medallions of veal with apple-mustard sauce and filet mignon with green-chili butter and Madeira sauce. Meal plans are available. ✉ *1300 Easton Rd., 03580,* ☎ *603/823–5542 or 800/473–5299,* FAX *603/823–8078,* WEB *www.franconiainn.com. 34 rooms, 1 3-bedroom cottage. Restaurant, bar, pool, hot tub, 4 tennis courts, croquet, hiking, horseback riding, bicycles, ice-skating, cross-country skiing, sleigh rides. AE, MC, V. Closed Apr.–mid-May.*

$$–$$$ 🏨 **Horse and Hound Inn.** Off the beaten path yet convenient to the Cannon Mountain tram, this inn is on 8 acres surrounded by the White Mountain National Forest. Antiques and assorted collectibles provide a cheery atmosphere, and on the grounds are 65 km (39 mi) of cross-country ski trails. Pets are welcome (for a small fee). ✉ *205 Wells Rd., 03580,* ☎ *603/823–5501 or 800/450–5501. 10 rooms, 8 with bath. Restaurant, bar, cross-country skiing. AE, D, DC, MC, V. Closed Apr.–mid-May and mid-Oct.–Thanksgiving. BP, MAP.*

$ ⛺ **Lafayette Campground.** This campground has hiking and biking trails, 97 tent sites, showers, a camp store, a bike trail, and easy access to the Appalachian Trail. ✉ *U.S. 3 and I–93, Franconia Notch State Park, 03580,* ☎ *603/823–9513 information; 603/271–3628 reservations. No pets. MC, V.*

Nightlife and the Arts

Hillwinds (✉ Main St., ☎ 603/823–5551), a restaurant and bar, has live entertainment on weekends.

Shopping

Stores in the **Franconia Marketplace** (✉ Main St., ☎ 603/823–5368) include the Grateful Bread Quality Bakery and Magoons Natural Foods.

Ski Areas
CANNON MOUNTAIN

This state-run facility in Franconia Notch State Park gives strong attention to skier services, family programs, snowmaking, and grooming—all at a very sound value. It was one of the first ski areas in the country. The New England Ski Museum sits at the base of the tramway. ⊠ *Franconia Notch State Park, I–93, Exit 3, 03580,* ☎ *603/823–8800; 603/823–7771 snow conditions; 800/237–9007 lodging,* WEB *www.cannonmt.com.*

Downhill. The narrow, steep pitches off the peak of the 2,146 ft of vertical rise reveal the high level of skiing here. Intermediates will find newly recontoured cruising trails, and the Brookside learning slope serves beginners. Under a new fall of snow, Cannon's 42 trails present challenges rarely found elsewhere in New Hampshire. For additional fun, try the two glade-skiing trails, Turnpike and Banshee, or take to the lift-serviced tubing park. A 70-passenger tramway, two quads, three triples, and one surface lift move skiers upward.

Cross-country. Nordic skiing is on a 13-km (8-mi) multiuse recreational path.

Child care. Cannon's Peabody Base Lodge takes children one and up. All-day and half-day SKIwee programs cater to kids 4–12, and season-long instruction can be arranged.

Summer activities. A multiuse recreational path runs parallel to the Franconia Notch Parkway (I–93). For $9 round-trip, the Cannon Mountain Aerial Tramway (☉ daily Memorial Day–late Oct.) can lift you 2,022 ft for a sweeping mountain vista. It's a six-minute ride to the top, where marked trails lead to the observation platform.

Sugar Hill

㉗ *6 mi west of Franconia.*

Sugar Hill, a town of 500 people, is deservedly famous for its spectacular sunsets and views of the Franconia Mountains, best seen from Sunset Hill, where a row of grand hotels and summer "cottages" once stood. Quiet country charm and good-quality bed-and-breakfasts and small inns make Sugar Hill an ideal spot for a romantic getaway.

Sugar Hill may be small, but the surprisingly well-done **Sugar Hill Historical Museum** proves the town has a big history. Topics of the permanent and changing exhibits range from settlement through the resort era to the present day. ⊠ *Rte. 117,* ☎ *603/823–5336.* ☞ *$2.* ☉ *July–mid-Oct., Thurs. and weekends 1–4.*

Dining and Lodging
$ ✕ **Polly's Pancake Parlor.** This local institution, originally a carriage shed built in 1830, was converted to a tearoom during the Depression, when the Dexters began serving "all you can eat" pancakes, waffles, and French toast for 50¢. The prices have gone up some, but the descendants of the Dexters continue to serve pancakes and waffles made from grains ground on the property, their own country sausage, and pure maple syrup. ⊠ *Rte. 117,* ☎ *603/823–5575. D, MC, V. No dinner.*

$$–$$$$ ✕▥ **Sugar Hill Inn.** The old carriage on the lawn and wicker chairs on the wraparound porch set a nostalgic mood before you even enter this converted 1789 farmhouse. Many rooms have hand-stenciled walls, views of the Franconia Mountains, and rippled antique windowpanes; all contain antiques. There are 10 rooms in the inn and six (some with fireplaces) in three country cottages. Bette Davis visited friends in this house—the room with the best view is named after her. The restaurant ($$$; reservations essential) serves such haute American fare as

salmon baked with Dijon mustard and wine; the homemade desserts are always delicious. ✉ *Rte. 117, 03585,* ☎ *603/823–5621 or 800/ 548–4748,* FAX *603/823–5639,* WEB *www.sugarhillinn.com. 16 rooms. Restaurant, pub, cross-country skiing. AE, MC, V. BP, MAP required during fall foliage season.*

$$–$$$$ ⊞ **Sunset Hill House.** Since it opened in 1882, this sprawling compound
★ has been famous for having perhaps the best sunset views of any resort in New England—it lies along a 1,700-ft ridge with panoramic views not just west toward the sun but also east out toward the Presidential Range. The meticulously kept rooms have superb views, and some have antiques dating back to the inn's first years—gas fireplaces, double whirlpool tubs, and decks grace the top units. The restaurant ($$–$$$), even apart from its fabulous views, is among the most acclaimed in the White Mountains; you might start with pan-seared ostrich with a raspberry beurre-blanc, and then move on to roasted seasoned game hen with a lemon-spinach cream. A tavern ($–$$) serves lighter but still-excellent fare (blackened tuna, chicken sandwich with blue cheese–chipotle dressing). ✉ *Sunset Hill Rd., 03585,* ☎ *603/ 823–5522 or 800/786–4455,* WEB *www.sunsethillhouse.com. 28 rooms. 2 restaurants, bar, pool, hiking, mountain bikes, ice-skating, cross-country skiing. AE, D, MC, V. BP.*

$$–$$$ ⊞ **Foxglove.** Extensive gardens with hammocks for relaxing are just one of the sybaritic delights at this rambling turn-of-the-century home next to Lover's Lane. Common areas are decorated in country-French style with antiques, and guest rooms are thoughtfully furnished, each in a different motif. The Serengeti Room has animal-print linens, a chandelier with carnival glass shades, and black and brass fixtures in the bath. The inn is no-smoking. ✉ *Rte. 117, 03585,* ☎ *603/823–8840 or 888/343– 2220,* FAX *603/823–5755,* WEB *www.foxgloveinn.com. 6 rooms. BP.*

$$–$$$ ⊞ **Hilltop.** Staying with innkeepers Mike and Meri Hern is just like dropping by Grandma's—they even welcome pets. The rooms in their 1895 country farmhouse are done in a quirky mix of antiques with handmade quilts, Victorian ceiling fans, piles of pillows, and big, fluffy towels. The TV room has hundreds of movies on tape. Rockers on the porch are perfect for watching the sun set behind the mountains. The large country breakfast includes homemade jams, pancakes made with homegrown berries, soufflés, and smoked ham, bacon, or salmon. The no-smoking inn has a two-night minimum during foliage season, summer weekends, and on holidays. ✉ *Rte. 117, 03585,* ☎ *603/823– 5695 or 800/770–5695,* FAX *603/823–5518,* WEB *www.hilltopinn.com. 3 rooms, 3 suites. Bar, library. D, MC, V. BP.*

Littleton

❷❽ *9 mi northeast of Sugar Hill, 7 mi north of Franconia, 86 mi north of Concord.*

One of the largest towns in northern New Hampshire, Littleton sits along a granite shelf along the Ammonoosuc River, whose swift current and drop of 235 ft aided in the town's early flourish as a mill center. Later, the railroad came through and Littleton grew into the trade and commerce hub of the region. In the minds of many visitors to the White Mountains, Littleton is still more a place to stock up on supplies and basics than a bona fide tourist destination, but few New Hampshire communities have worked harder to revitalize themselves than Littleton. Today, a great wealth of engaging shops and several eateries line the town's Main Street, whose neatly kept rows of mostly 19th- and early-20th-century shopfronts suggest a scene from an old Jimmy Stewart movie.

Just off Main Street, stop by the **Littleton Grist Mill** (✉ 22 Mill St., ☎ 603/444–7478), a recently restored 1798 mill that contains a shop selling New England–made pottery, kitchenware, and home accessories, plus stone-ground flour products; you'll also find original mill equipment on display.

Dining and Lodging

$$ ✕ **Italian Oasis.** This homey spot on the second floor of Parker's Marketplace has red-checkered tablecloths, trellis wall dividers, and a separate brew pub up front, which produces a nice range of stouts and ales. You'll find an enormous menu of sandwiches, munchies, and pizzas, along with more substantial fare such as calamari platters, veal parmigiana, and spinach-and-roasted-garlic ravioli. ✉ 106 Main St., ☎ 603/444–6995. AE, D, MC, V.

$ 🛏 **Thayer's Inn.** Although this stately Greek Revival hotel, opened in
★   1843, hasn't been converted into a cushy luxurious property the way many old White Mountains inns have, it nevertheless offers among the most charming budget accommodations in the region. The clean, well-kept rooms (some share a bath) are quaintly old-fashioned, with creaky floorboards, exposed pipes, high ceilings, comfy wing chairs, and vintage steam radiators. The friendly staff welcomes passersby to drop in for a look at a small third-floor room set up as it would have appeared in the 1840s (you view it through a display window across the door), and to take in the 360-degree views from the cupola on the sixth floor. There's no elevator, something to keep in mind if booking an upper floor. ✉ 111 Main St., 03561, ☎ 603/444–6469 or 800/634–8179, WEB www.thayersinn.com. 38 rooms. MC, V.

Shopping

The **Village Book Store** (✉ 81 Main St., ☎ 603/444–5263) has a vast selection of both nonfiction and fiction titles—it's one of the most comprehensive bookshops in the state.

Bethlehem

㉙   *5 mi southeast of Littleton.*

In the days before antihistamines, hay-fever sufferers came by the bus load to the town of Bethlehem, elevation 1,462 ft, whose crisp air has a blissfully low pollen count. Today this quaint hamlet is notable for its distinctive arts and crafts, Victorian and Colonial homes, art deco movie theater, and shops and eateries on its main street.

Dining and Lodging

$$–$$$ ✕ **Tim-bir Alley.** This restaurant leases space from Adair and, for eight months of the year, serves dinner in Adair's elegant dining rooms. The menu, which changes weekly, utilizes regional American ingredients in creative ways. Main dishes have included southwestern spiced tournedos of beef with corn, smoked bacon, and black-bean relish; and cinnamon-scented pork tenderloin with cranberry vinaigrette and pear-pecan chutney. Desserts, like a chocolate-glazed espresso cheesecake, are well worth saving room for. ✉ 80 Guider La., ☎ 603/444–6142. *No credit cards. Closed Nov.–mid-Dec. and Apr.–May; Mon.–Tues. June–Oct.; Sun.–Tues. mid-Dec.–Mar. No lunch.*

$$$$ 🛏 **Adair.** In 1927 attorney Frank Hogan built this three-story Georgian
★   Revival home as a wedding present for his daughter, Dorothy Adair. Walking paths on the luxurious country inn's 200 acres wind through gardens. The rooms, which have garden or mountain views, are decorated with period antiques and reproductions. Many have fireplaces. One suite has a large two-person hot tub, a fireplace, a balcony, and a king-size sleigh bed. Tim-bir Alley, which leases space here, serves contem-

porary food part of the year. ✉ *80 Guider La., 03574,* ☎ *603/444–2600 or 888/444–2600,* FAX *603/444–4823,* WEB *www.adairinn.com. 7 rooms, 2 suites, 1 cottage. Restaurant, tennis court, billiards. AE, MC, V. BP.*

Outdoor Activities and Sports

The Society for the Protection of New Hampshire Forests owns two properties in Bethlehem open to visitors. **Bretzfelder Park** (✉ Prospect St., ☎ 603/444–6228), a 77-acre nature and wildlife park, has a picnic shelter, hiking, and cross-country ski trails. The **Rocks Estate** (✉ 113 Glessner Rd., ☎ 603/444–6228) is a working Christmas-tree farm (you can purchase a tree here for the holiday) with walking trails, historic buildings, and educational programs.

Bretton Woods

❸⓿ *14 mi southeast of Bethlehem, 28 mi northeast of Lincoln/Woodstock.*

In the early 1900s private rail cars brought the rich and famous from New York and Philadelphia to the Mount Washington Hotel, the jewel of Bretton Woods. The hotel was the site of a famous World Monetary Fund conference in 1944, which greatly affected the post–World War II economy. The area is also known for the cog railway and eponymous ski resort.

In 1858 Sylvester Marsh petitioned state legislature for permission to build a steam railway up Mt. Washington. A politico retorted that he'd have better luck building a railroad to the moon. Just 11 years later,
★ the **Mt. Washington Cog Railway** chugged up to the summit, and so it remains one of the state's most beloved attractions—a thrill in either direction. Allow three hours round-trip. ✉ *U.S. 302, 6 mi northeast of Bretton Woods,* ☎ *603/278–5404; 800/922–8825 outside NH,* WEB *www.thecog.com.* ☑ *$44 round-trip.* ☉ *Late May–mid-Oct., daily; late Apr.–late May and mid-Oct.–early Nov.; call for hours.*

En Route Scenic U.S. 302 winds through the steep, wooded mountains on either side of spectacular Crawford Notch, southeast of Bretton Woods, and passes through **Crawford Notch State Park** (✉ U.S. 302, Harts Location, ☎ 603/374–2272), where you can stop for a picnic and a short hike to Arethusa Falls or the Silver and Flume cascades. The visitor center has a gift shop and a cafeteria.

Dining and Lodging

$$–$$$$ ✕▥ **Bretton Woods Mountain Resort.** Comprising three distinct prop-
★ erties with rooms in a wide range of prices, Bretton Woods is most famous for the leviathan 1902 Mount Washington Hotel, one of the most ambitious projects of its day. It quickly became a top grand resort, most notable for its 900-ft-long veranda, which affords a full view of the Presidential Range. With its stately public rooms and large, Victorian-style bedrooms and suites, the hotel retains a turn-of-the-century formality. Jacket and tie are required in the dining room ($$$$). The regional cuisine highlights seasonal dishes such as lemon lobster ravioli with shrimp and scallops and roast pork with onions and mushrooms. Built in 1896, the restored Bretton Arms Country Inn predates the Mount Washington Hotel across the way and offers mid-priced rooms in a less dressy, country style. Reservations are essential in the contemporary dining room ($$–$$$) and should be made on arrival. Rooms at the newer Bretton Woods Motor Inn have contemporary furnishings, a balcony or patio, and mountain views. The Continental cuisine at the motor inn's Darby's Restaurant ($$) is served around a circular fireplace, and the bar is a hangout for skiers. ✉ *U.S. 302, 03575,* ☎ *603/278–1000 or 800/258–0330,* FAX *603/278–8838,* WEB *www.mtwashington.com. 281 rooms, 3 suites. 4 restaurants, 2 bars, 2 pools, sauna, driving range,*

18-hole golf course, 12 tennis courts, hiking, horseback riding, bicycles, downhill skiing, sleigh rides, recreation room, children's programs (ages 5–12). AE, D, MC, V.

$ ⚠ **Dry River Campground.** This rustic campground in Crawford Notch State Park has 30 tent sites and is a popular base for hiking the White Mountain National Forest. ⊠ *U.S. 302, Harts Location (Box 177, Twin Mountain 03595),* ☎ *603/271–3628,* WEB *www.nhparks.state.nh.us/parkops/parks/crawford.html. Closed mid-Dec.–mid-May.*

Ski Areas
BRETTON WOODS

This expansive and much-improved ski area has a three-level, open-space base lodge; a convenient drop-off area; easy parking; and an uncrowded setting. The views of Mt. Washington alone are worth the visit; the scenery is especially beautiful from the Top o' Quad restaurant and from the former Cog Railway car perched on the top of West Mountain. ⊠ *U.S. 302, 03575,* ☎ *603/278–3322; 800/232–2972 information; 800/258–0330 lodging,* WEB *www.brettonwoods.com.*

Downhill. The skiing on the 64 trails is novice and intermediate, with steeper pitches near the top of the 1,500-ft vertical and glade skiing to satisfy expert skiers. Skiers and snowboarders can try a terrain park with jumps and a halfpipe. The Accelerator halfpipe is for snowboarders only. One detachable quad, one fixed-grip quad, one triple, and three double chairlifts service the trails. The area has night skiing and snowboarding on Friday, Saturday, and holidays. A limited lift-ticket policy helps keep lines short.

Cross-country. The large, full-service cross-country ski center here has 100 km (62 mi) of groomed and double-track trails, many of them lift-serviced. You can also rent snowshoes.

Child care. The nursery takes children from ages 2 months to 5 years. The ski school has an all-day program for children ages 4 to 12, using progressive instructional techniques. There's also a snowboarding program for children 8 to 12. Rates include lifts, lessons, equipment, lunch, and supervised play.

Bartlett

③ *18 mi southeast of Bretton Woods.*

Bear Mountain to the south, Mt. Parker to the north, Mt. Cardigan to the west, and the Saco River to the east combine to create an unforgettable setting for the village of Bartlett, incorporated in 1790. Lovely Bear Notch Road (closed in winter) has the only midpoint access to the Kancamagus Highway.

Dining and Lodging

$$–$$$$ ✕⊡ **Grand Summit Hotel & Conference Center.** The gables and curves of this resort hotel at the base of Attitash Bear Peak mimic the mountain's peaks and slopes. The luxurious contemporary-style rooms have kitchenettes, VCRs, and stereo systems. Entrées in the Alpine Garden restaurant ($$–$$$) include grilled salmon with lobster sauce and baked stuffed pork with chestnut herb stuffing. ⊠ *Box 429, U.S. 302, 03812,* ☎ *603/374–1900 or 888/554–1900,* FAX *603/374–3040,* WEB *www.attitash.com. 143 rooms. 2 restaurants, bar, pool, hot tub, steam room, health club, downhill skiing, recreation room. AE, D, MC, V.*

$$–$$$$ ⊡ **Attitash Mountain Village.** The style at this condo-motel complex—across the street from the mountain via a tunnel—is alpine contemporary, and the staff is young and enthusiastic. Units, some with fireplaces, kitchens, and whirlpool tubs, accommodate from 2 to 14

people. The restaurant, with a varied and family-friendly menu, has unobstructed views of the mountain. ✉ *U.S. 302, 03812,* ☎ *603/374–6501 or 800/862–1600,* FAX *603/374–6509,* WEB *www.attitashmtvillage. com. 300 units. Restaurant, pub, indoor and outdoor pools, sauna, tennis court, gym, hiking, fishing, mountain bikes, downhill and cross-country skiing, recreation room, playground, laundry service, meeting rooms. AE, D, MC, V.*

Ski Areas

ATTITASH BEAR PEAK

This high-profile resort, which hosts many special events and ski races, continues to expand and improve its infrastructure. Lodging at the base of the mountain is in condos and motel-style units, away from the hustle of North Conway. Attitash has a computerized lift–ticket system that allows skiers to pay as they run. Skiers can share the ticket, which is good for two years. ✉ *Box 302, U.S. 302, 03812,* ☎ *603/374–2368 or 800/223–7669 snow conditions; 800/223–7669 lodging,* WEB *www. attitash.com.*

Downhill. Enhanced with massive snowmaking (98%), the trails now number 70 on two peaks, both with full-service base lodges. The bulk of the skiing and boarding is geared to intermediates and experts, with some steep pitches, glades, and good use of terrain. Beginners enjoy good terrain on the lower mountain and some runs from the top. The Attitash Adventure Center has a rental shop, lessons desk, and children's programs. Serving the 36 km (22 mi) of trails and the 1,750-ft vertical drop are two high-speed quads, one fixed-grip quad, three triples, three double chairlifts, and three surface tows.

Cross-country. Bear Notch Ski Touring Center (☎ 603/374–2277) has more than 70 km (43 mi) of cross-country trails, more than 60 km (37 mi) skate groomed and tracked. Backcountry skiing is unlimited. Guests staying at the Grand Summit Hotel can rent equipment, get trail passes, and connect to the trails from the hotel door.

Child care. The Attitash Adventure Center nursery takes children ages 6 months to 5 years. Other programs accommodate children up to 16.

Summer activities. Attitash Bear Park has two dry alpine slides, four water slides, Buddy Bear's Playpool for children, horseback riding, lift-serviced mountain biking, and a driving range. A chairlift whisks passengers to the White Mountain Observation Tower, which delivers 270-degree views of the Whites.

Glen

③② *6 mi northeast of Bartlett, 89 mi northeast of Concord, 71 mi northwest of Portland, ME.*

Glen is hardly more than a crossroads between North Conway and Jackson, but its central location has made it the home of a few noteworthy attractions and dining and lodging options.

☾ That cluster of fluorescent buildings on Route 16 is **Story Land,** a children's theme park with life-size storybook and nursery-rhyme characters. The 16 rides and four shows include a flume ride, a Victorian-theme river-raft ride, and a farm-family variety show. ✉ *Rte. 16,* ☎ *603/383–4186,* WEB *www.storylandnh.com.* ☏ *$18.* ☉ *Mid-June–Labor Day, daily 9–6; Memorial Day–mid-June and Labor Day–Columbus Day, weekends 10–5.*

☾ **Heritage New Hampshire** uses theatrical sets, sound effects, and animation to render the state's history. Visitors "sail" on the *Reliance* from a village in 1634 England over tossing seas to the New World and then saunter along Portsmouth's streets in the late 1700s. Exhibits continue through the present day. ⊠ *Rte. 16,* ☎ *603/383–4186,* WEB *www. heritagenh.com.* ⊠ *$10.* ☉ *Mid-June–mid-Oct., daily 9–5.*

Dining and Lodging

$$–$$$ ✕ **Red Parka Pub.** Practically an institution, the Red Parka Pub has been in downtown Glen for more than two decades. The menu has everything a family could want, from an all-you-can-eat salad bar to scallop pie. The barbecued ribs are local favorites, and you'll find hand-carved steaks of every type, from aged New York sirloin to prime rib. ⊠ *U.S. 302,* ☎ *603/383–4344. Reservations not accepted. AE, D, MC, V.*

$–$$ ✕ **Margarita Grill.** Après-ski and hiking types congregate here, in the cozy dining rooms in cold weather and on the covered patio when it's warm, for tasty southwestern fare. The menu includes a variety of homemade salsas, wood-fired steaks, ribs, burgers, and a smattering of Tex-Mex and Cajun specialties. Unwind at the tequila bar after a day on the mountains. ⊠ *U.S. 302,* ☎ *603/383–6556. AE, D, MC, V.*

$$ ✕🏨 **Bernerhof Inn.** This old-world–style hotel is right at home in its alpine setting. The rooms have hardwood floors with hooked rugs, antiques, and reproductions. The fanciest six rooms have brass beds and spa-size bathtubs; one suite has a Finnish sauna. The menu at the Prince Palace restaurant ($$$) includes Swiss specialties such as fondue and Wiener schnitzel, along with new American and classic French dishes. The Black Bear pub ($–$$) pours many microbrewery beers and serves sandwiches and pastas. ⊠ *Box 240, U.S. 302, 03838,* ☎ *603/383–9132 or 800/548–8007,* FAX *603/383–0809,* WEB *www.bernerhofinn.com. 9 rooms. Restaurant, pub. AE, D, MC, V. BP.*

$$–$$$ 🏨 **Best Western Storybook Resort Inn.** On a hillside near Attitash Bear Peak, this motor inn with large rooms is well suited to families. Copperfield's Restaurant has gingerbread, sticky buns, omelets, and a children's menu. ⊠ *Box 129, intersection of U.S 302 and Rte. 16, Glen Junction 03838,* ☎ *603/383–6800,* FAX *603/383–4678. 78 rooms. Restaurant, bar, refrigerators, pool, sauna, tennis court, playground. AE, DC, MC, V.*

Jackson

★ ㉝   *5 mi north of Glen.*

The village of Jackson just off Route 16 via a red covered bridge has retained its storybook New England character. Art and antiques shopping, tennis, golf, fishing, and hiking to waterfalls are among the draws. When the snow falls, Jackson becomes the state's cross-country skiing capital. The village's proximity to four downhill areas makes it popular with alpine skiers, too.

Dining and Lodging

$–$$ ✕ **Red Fox Pub & Restaurant.** Some say this restaurant overlooking the Wentworth Golf Club gets its name from a wily fox with a penchant for stealing golf balls right off the fairway. The wide-ranging menu has barbecue ribs, salads, burgers, and more sophisticated dishes such as chicken Florentine and seafood lasagna. The Sunday jazz breakfast buffet is popular with locals and visitors alike. ⊠ *Rte. 16A,* ☎ *603/ 383–6659. AE, D, MC, V.*

$$$$ ✕🏨 **Inn at Thorn Hill.** Architect Stanford White designed this 1895 Vic-
★   torian house, which is a few steps from cross-country trails and Jackson village. Practical vinyl siding now covers the house, but plenty of luxury lies within. Romantic touches in the main inn include rose-motif papers and antiques such as a blue-velvet fainting couch, and many

rooms have spa tubs and gas fireplaces. Rooms in the carriage house have a woodsy North Country feel, while the cottages provide extra privacy. The restaurant ($$$; reservations essential; closed mid-week in April) serves fine contemporary fare such grilled beef sirloin with a cabernet–roasted tomato–sweet garlic sauce, spiced bacon, and green-onion-mashed potatoes, garnished with a basil-gorgonzola cream. ⊠ *Box A, Thorn Hill Rd., 03846, ☎ 603/383–4242 or 800/289–8990, FAX 603/383–8062, WEB www.innatthornhill.com. 12 rooms, 4 suites, 3 cottages. Restaurant, pub, pool, hot tub, croquet, cross-country skiing. AE, D, MC, V. BP, MAP.*

$$$–$$$$ ╳🏠 **Christmas Farm Inn.** Despite its winter-inspired name, this 1778 village inn is an all-season retreat. Rooms in the main inn and the salt-box next door, five with whirlpool baths, are decorated in Laura Ashley and Ralph Lauren prints. The suites have beamed ceilings and fireplaces. Some standbys in the restaurant ($$–$$$) are grilled seafood bouillabaisse and vegetable *fra diavolo* with gnocchi. ⊠ *Box CC, Rte. 16B, 03846, ☎ 603/383–4313 or 800/443–5837, FAX 603/383–6495, WEB www.christmasfarminn.com. 41 units. Restaurant, pub, pool, sauna, hot tub, volleyball, cross-country skiing, recreation room. AE, MC, V. MAP.*

$$$–$$$$ ╳🏠 **Wentworth.** This pale-yellow 1869 Victorian charms guests with individually decorated rooms accented with antiques. All rooms have TVs and telephones; some have working fireplaces and two-person whirlpool tubs. The dining room ($$$) serves a five-course, candlelight dinner with a menu that changes seasonally. Good choices are the lobster bread pudding and the cider-poached salmon. ⊠ *Rte. 16A, 03846, ☎ 603/383–9700 or 800/637–0013, FAX 603/383–4265, WEB www. thewentworth.com. 60 rooms in summer, 52 in winter. Restaurant, bar, pool, tennis court, ice-skating, cross-country skiing, sleigh rides, billiards. AE, D, DC, MC, V. MAP.*

$$–$$$$ 🏠 **Inn at Jackson.** The builders of this 1902 Victorian, perched imperiously on a hill overlooking the village, followed a design by Stanford White. The inn has spacious rooms—six with fireplaces—with oversize windows and an airy feel. Other than an imposing grand staircase in the front foyer, the house is unpretentious, with hardwood floors, braided rugs, a smattering of antiques, and mountain views. ⊠ *Box 807, Thorn Hill Rd., 03846, ☎ 603/383–4321 or 800/289–8600, FAX 603/383–4085, WEB www.innatjackson.com. 14 rooms. Hot tub, cross-country skiing. AE, D, DC, MC, V. CP.*

$$–$$$$ 🏠 **Nordic Village Resort.** The light wood and white walls of these deluxe condos near several ski areas are as Scandinavian as the snowy views. The Club House has pools and a spa, and there is a nightly bonfire at Nordic Falls. Larger units have fireplaces, full kitchens, and whirlpool baths. The property is part of Luxury Mountain Getaways, which operates several additional upscale condos and hotels in the area. ⊠ *Rte. 16, 03846, ☎ 603/383–9101 or 800/472–5207, FAX 603/383–9823, WEB www.luxurymountaingetaways.com. 140 condominiums. 1 indoor and 2 outdoor pools, hot tub, steam room, hiking, ice-skating, cross-country skiing, sleigh rides. D, MC, V.*

$$–$$$ 🏠 **Eagle Mountain House.** This country estate, which dates from 1879, is close to downhill ski slopes and even closer to cross-country trails, which begin on the property. The public rooms of this showplace have a tycoon-roughing-it feel, and the bedrooms are large and furnished with period pieces. On a warm day, you can nurse a drink in a rocking chair on the wraparound deck. ⊠ *Carter Notch Rd., 03846, ☎ 603/383–9111 or 800/966–5779, FAX 603/383–0854, WEB www.eaglemt.com. 93 rooms. Restaurant, pool, hot tub, sauna, 9-hole golf course, 2 tennis courts, health club, playground. AE, D, DC, MC, V.*

$$–$$$ ⊞ **Wildcat Inn & Tavern.** After a day of skiing, you can collapse on a comfy sofa by the fire in this small 19th-century tavern in the center of Jackson village. The fragrance of home baking permeates into suite-style guest rooms, which are full of knickknacks and furniture of various periods. The tavern, where bands often perform, attracts many skiers. In summer, dining is available in the landscaped garden. ⊠ *Rte. 16A, 03846,* ☎ *603/383–4245 or 800/228–4245,* FAX *603/383–6456,* WEB *www.wildcatinnandtavern.com. 6 rooms, 4 with bath; 7 suites; 1 cottage. Restaurant, bar. AE, MC, V. BP, MAP.*

Outdoor Activities and Sports

Nestlenook Farm (⊠ Dinsmore Rd., ☎ 603/383–9443) maintains an outdoor ice-skating rink with rentals, music, and a bonfire. Going snow-shoeing or taking a sleigh ride are other winter options; in summer you can fly-fish or ride in a horse-drawn carriage.

Ski Areas

BLACK MOUNTAIN

Black Mountain draws families and singles with its fun, friendly, and informal atmosphere. The Family Passport, which allows two adults and two juniors to ski at discounted rates, is a good value. Midweek rates here are usually the lowest in Mt. Washington valley. ⊠ *Rte. 16B, 03846,* ☎ *603/383–4490; 800/475–4669 snow conditions; 800/698–4490 lodging,* WEB *www.blackmt.com.*

Downhill. The 40 trails and two glades on the 1,100-vertical-ft mountain are evenly divided among beginner, intermediate, and expert. There are triple and double chairlifts and two surface tows. Most of the skiing is user-friendly, particularly for beginners—although recent expansion has added trails geared toward experts—and the southern exposure keeps skiers warm. In addition to trails, snowboarders can use two terrain parks and the halfpipe.

Child care. The nursery takes children 6 months to 5 years. Kids 3–12 can take classes at the ski school.

JACKSON SKI TOURING FOUNDATION

One of the top four cross-country skiing areas in the country and by far the largest in New Hampshire, Jackson offers 157 km (98 mi) of trails. About 96 km (60 mi) are track groomed, 85 km (53 mi) are skate groomed, and there are 63 km (39 mi) of marked backcountry trails. You can arrange lessons and rentals at the lodge, in the center of Jackson village. ⊠ *Main St., 03846,* ☎ *800/927–6697,* WEB *www.jacksonxc.org.*

Mt. Washington

★ ③④ *20 mi north of Jackson.*

In summer, you can drive to the top of spectacular Mt. Washington, the highest mountain (6,288 ft) in the northeastern United States and home of the **Mt. Washington Observatory,** a weather station that has recorded the world's highest winds. The **Mt. Washington Auto Road,** opened in 1861 and said to be the nation's first manufactured tourist attraction, begins at the **Glen House,** a gift shop and rest stop 15 mi north of Glen on Route 16. Allow two hours round-trip and check your brakes first. Cars with automatic transmissions that can't shift down into first gear aren't allowed on the road.

If you prefer not to drive on a curving, narrow mountain road, you can choose a guided tour in one of the vans (aka "stages") that leave from Great Glen Trails Outdoors Center. In winter, the vans are refitted with snowmobile-like treads and become "SnowCoaches," which travel up the mountain to just above the tree line—you have the option of cross-country skiing or snowshoeing down. (In summer, you can also take the Mt. Washington Cog Railway to the summit.)

Up top, visit the **Sherman Adams Summit Building,** which contains a museum of memorabilia from each of the three hotels that have stood on this spot and a display of native plant life and alpine flowers. Stand in the glassed-in viewing area to hear the roar of that record-breaking wind. ☎ 603/466–3988, WEB *www.mt-washington.com.* ☞ *Auto road $16 per car and driver plus $6 for each adult passenger; van fare $22.* ☉ *Private cars, mid-May–late Oct.; van tours, year-round, daily. All tours/access are subject to weather conditions.*

Although not a town per se, scenic **Pinkham Notch** covers the eastern side of Mt. Washington and includes several ravines, including Tuckerman Ravine, famous for spring skiing. The **Appalachian Mountain Club** maintains a large visitor center here on Route 16 that provides information to hikers and travelers and has guided hikes, outdoor skills workshops, a cafeteria, lodging, regional topography displays, and a terrific outdoors shop.

Lodging

$ ⚏ **Joe Dodge Lodge at Pinkham Notch.** The Appalachian Mountain Club operates this rustic lodge at the base of Mt. Washington. Rooms are a combination of single-sex bunkrooms—rented by the bunk—for up to five people, and private rooms, all with gleaming wood, cheerful quilts, and reading lights. All share baths. The restaurant serves a buffet breakfast and lunch and a family-style dinner. Packages include breakfast and dinner, plus skiing at Great Glen Trails and/or Wildcat Ski Area. ✉ *Box 298, Rte. 16, Gorham 03581,* ☎ *603/466–2727,* FAX *603/466–3871,* WEB *www.outdoors.org. 102 beds without bath. Restaurant. MC, V. MAP.*

Ski Areas

GREAT GLEN TRAILS OUTDOOR CENTER

This center has a large, sunny base lodge that works as well for cross-country skiers in the winter as it does for hikers, mountain bikers, and backpackers in the summer. This facility, and the equipment rental shop inside, has helped turn Great Glen Trails into a year-round destination. ✉ *Box 300, Rte. 16, Gorham 03581,* ☎ *603/466–2333,* WEB *www. mt-washington.com/ggt.*

Cross-country. There are 40 km (24 mi) of cross-country trails, some with snowmaking, and access to more than 1,100 acres of backcountry. You can even ski or snowshoe the lower half of the Mt. Washington Auto Road. Trees shelter most of the trails, so Mt. Washington's famous weather shouldn't be a concern. The Great Glen Outfitters shop in the base lodge is the largest retailer of Nordic equipment in the state.

Summer activities. Great Glen Trails puts its extensive trail network to use for hiking, trail running, and mountain biking. The center also has programs in canoeing, kayaking, and fly-fishing. The base lodge has equipment for rent or sale.

WILDCAT

Glade skiers favor Wildcat, with 28 acres of official tree skiing. Wildcat's runs include some stunning double-black-diamond trails. Skiers who can hold a wedge should check out the 4-km (2½-mi) long Polecat. Experts can zip down the Lynx. Views of Mt. Washington and Tuckerman Ravine are superb. The trails are classic New England—narrow and winding. ✉ *Rte. 16, Pinkham Notch, Jackson 03846,* ☎ *603/466–3326; 888/SKI–WILD snow conditions; 800/255–6439 lodging,* WEB *www.skiwildcat.com.*

Downhill. Wildcat's expert runs deserve their designations and then some. Intermediates have mid-mountain-to-base trails, and beginners will find gentle terrain and a broad teaching slope. Snowboarders have several terrain parks and the run of the mountain. The 44 runs, with a 2,100-ft vertical drop, are served by a four-passenger gondola, one high-speed detachable quad, and three triple chairlifts.

Child care. The child-care center takes children ages 6 months and up. All-day SKIwee instruction, on designated slopes, is offered to kids ages 5–12.

Dixville Notch

③⑤ *63 mi north of Mt. Washington, 66 mi northeast of Littleton, 149 mi north of Concord.*

If you really want to get away from it all, Dixville Notch is the place to go. Just 12 mi from the Canadian border, this tiny community is known for two things. It's the home of The Balsams Wilderness, one of the oldest and most celebrated resorts in New Hampshire. And Dixville Notch and Harts Location are the first election districts in the nation to vote in the presidential primaries and general elections. At midnight on election day, the 30 or so Dixville Notch voters gather in the little meeting room beside a hotel service bar to cast their ballots and make national news.

One of the favorite pastimes for visitors in this area is watching for moose, those large, ungainly, yet elusive members of the deer family. Although you may catch sight of one or more yourself, **Northern Forest Moose Tours** (☎ 603/752–6060) offers bus tours of the region that have a 97% success rate for spotting moose.

OFF THE BEATEN PATH

PITTSBURG – Just north of the White Mountains, in the Great North Woods region, Pittsburg contains the four Connecticut Lakes and the springs that form the Connecticut River. The entire northern tip of the state—a chunk of about 250 square mi—lies within the town's borders, the result of a dispute between the United States and Canada. The two countries could not decide on a border, so the inhabitants of this region declared themselves independent of both countries in 1832. They named their nation the Indian Stream Republic, after the river that passes through the territory—the capital of which was Pittsburg. In 1835 the feisty, 40-man Indian Stream militia invaded Canada, with only limited success. The Indian Stream war ended more by common consent than surrender; in 1842 the Webster-Ashburton Treaty fixed the international boundary. Indian Stream was incorporated as Pittsburg, making it the largest township in New Hampshire. Canoeing, fishing, and taking photos are favorite pastimes up here; the pristine wilderness teems with moose. Contact the **North Country Chamber of Commerce** for information about the region.

Dining and Lodging

$$$$ ★ ✕⊡ **The Balsams Wilderness.** This lavish grande dame of the North Woods has been rolling out the red carpet since 1866, drawing families, golf-enthusiasts, skiers, and others for a varied slate of activities—from dancing to cooking demonstrations. The individually decorated rooms vary in size but are generally spacious and comfortably furnished; all have views of the 15,000-acre estate and the mountains beyond. In the dining room ($$–$$$; jacket and tie), the summer buffet lunch is heaped upon a 100-ft-long table. At dinner, a starter might be chilled strawberry soup spiked with Grand Marnier, followed by poached salmon with golden caviar sauce and chocolate hazelnut cake. If rates seem high, remember they include breakfast and dinner and unlimited

use of resort facilities, including skiing and snowboarding. ⌂ *Rte. 26, 03576,* ☎ *603/255–3400; 800/255–0600; 800/255–0800 in NH,* FAX *603/255–4221,* WEB *www.thebalsams.com. 204 rooms. 3 restaurants, bar, pool, driving range, 18-hole golf course, 6 tennis courts, hiking, boating, fishing, mountain bikes, ice-skating, cross-country skiing, children's programs (ages 1–12). AE, D, MC, V. Closed late Mar.–mid-May and mid-Oct.–mid-Dec. MAP.*

$$$ ⌂ **The Glen.** This rustic lodge with stick furniture, fieldstone, and cedar is on First Connecticut Lake, surrounded by log cabins, seven of which are right on the water. The cabins come equipped with efficiency kitchens and mini-refrigerators—not that you'll need either, because rates include meals in the lodge restaurant. ⌂ *77 Glen Rd., 1 mi off U.S. 3, Pittsburg 03592,* ☎ *603/538–6500 or 800/445–4536,* WEB *www.nhconnlakes.com/glen.htm. 8 rooms, 10 cabins. Restaurant, kitchenettes, lake. No credit cards. Closed mid-Oct.–mid-May. FAP.*

Outdoor Activities and Sports

Dixville Notch State Park (⌂ Rte. 26, ☎ 603/823–9959), in the northernmost notch in the White Mountains, has picnic areas, a waterfall, and many hiking trails.

Ski Areas

THE BALSAMS WILDERNESS

Skiing was originally provided as an amenity for hotel guests at the Balsams, but the area has become popular with day-trippers as well. ⌂ *Rte. 26, 03576,* ☎ *603/255–3400; 800/255–0600; 800/255–0800 in NH; 603/255–3951 snow conditions,* FAX *603/255–4221.*

Downhill. Slopes with such names as Sanguinary, Umbagog, and Magalloway may sound tough, but they're only moderately difficult, leaning toward intermediate. There are 14 trails and four glades from the top of the 1,000-ft vertical for every skill level. One double chairlift and two T-bars carry skiers up the mountain. There is a halfpipe for snowboarders.

Cross-country. The Balsams has 95 km (59 mi) of cross-country skiing, tracked and groomed for skating (a cross-country technique). Natural-history markers annotate some trails; you can also try telemark and backcountry skiing, and 29 km (18 mi) of snowshoeing trails.

Child care. The ski lodge nursery takes children ages 6 months to 5 years at no charge to hotel guests. Lessons are for kids 3 and up.

North Conway

❸ *76 mi south of Dixville Notch, 7 mi south of Glen, 41 mi east of Lincoln/North Woodstock.*

Outlet shopping is as big a sport as skiing in this bustling, attractive town—businesses line Route 16 for several miles. Before the arrival of the outlets, the town drew visitors for its inspiring scenery, ski resorts, and access to White Mountain National Forest.

The **Conway Scenic Railroad** operates scenic trips of varying durations in vintage coaches pulled by steam or diesel engines. The dome observation coach on the 5½-hour trip through Crawford Notch offers views of some of the finest scenery in the Northeast. Lunch is served aboard the dining car on the Valley Train to Conway or Bartlett. The 1874 Victorian train station has displays of railroad artifacts, lanterns, and old tickets and timetables. Reserve early during foliage season for Crawford Notch or Valley dining car. ⌂ *Rte. 16/U.S. 302 (38 Norcross Circle),* ☎ *603/356–5251 or 800/232–5251,* WEB *www.conwayscenic.com.* ☎ *$9.50–$46, depending on trip.* ☾ *Mid-Apr.–late Dec; call for times.*

At **Echo Lake State Park,** you needn't be a rock climber to glimpse views from the 700-ft **White Horse** and **Cathedral** ledges. From the top you'll see the entire valley, in which Echo Lake shines like a diamond. An unmarked trailhead another ⁷⁄₁₀ mi on West Side Road leads to **Diana's Baths,** a spectacular series of waterfalls. ⊠ *Off U.S 302,* ☎ *603/356–2672.* ☜ *$2.50.* ☉ *Mid-June–mid-Oct., daily dawn–dusk.*

The **Hartmann Model Railroad Museum** houses 14 operating layouts (from G to Z scales), about 2,000 engines, and more than 5,000 cars and coaches. A café, a crafts store, a hobby shop, and an outdoor ride-on train are on site. ⊠ *Rte. 16/U.S. 302 and Town Hall Rd., Intervale,* ☎ *603/356–9922 or 603/356–9933,* 〖WEB〗 *www.hartmannrr.com.* ☜ *$5.* ☉ *Mid-June–mid-Oct., daily 9–5; mid-Oct.–mid-June, daily 10–5.*

Weather junkies and anybody fascinated by the White Mountains' famously extreme climate conditions should check out the **Weather Discovery Center.** Its hands-on exhibits challenge visitors to understand how weather is monitored and how it in turn affects us. The facility is a collaboration between the National and Atmospheric Administration Forecast Systems lab and the nearby Mt. Washington Observatory—at the summit of Mt. Washington, the world's highest surface wind speed was clocked in at 231 mph. ⊠ *Rte. 16/U.S. 302, ⅛ mi north of rail tracks,* ☎ *603/356–2137,* 〖WEB〗 *www.mountwashington.org/discovery.* ☜ *$2.* ☉ *Daily 10–5.*

Dining and Lodging

$–$$ ✕ **Delaney's Hole in the Wall.** This casual restaurant has an eclectic decor of sports and other memorabilia that includes autographed baseballs. An early photo of skiing at Tuckerman Ravine hangs over the fireplace. The menu is varied, with entrées ranging from fish-and-chips to fajitas to mussels and scallops sautéed with spiced sausage and Louisiana flavors. ⊠ *Rte. 16, ¼ mi north of North Conway,* ☎ *603/356–7776. D, MC, V.*

$–$$ ✕ **Muddy Moose.** A fun and inviting place—especially popular with younger singles and families—the Muddy Moose has a rustic lodge ambience created with fieldstone walls, exposed wood, and dark lighting. Dig into a Greek salad, grilled chicken Caesar wrap, char-grilled boneless pork chops with a maple-cider glaze, or muddy moose pie. ⊠ *Rte. 16, just south of North Conway,* ☎ *603/356–7696. AE, D, MC, V.*

$$$–$$$$ ✕🛏 **Snowville Inn.** Journalist Frank Simonds built the main gam-
★   brel-roof house in 1916. To complement the inn's tome-jammed bookshelves, guest rooms are named for famous authors. The nicest of the rooms, with 12 windows that look out over the Presidential Range, is a tribute to native son Robert Frost. Two additional buildings—the carriage house and the chimney house—also have libraries. Snowshoe rentals are among the amenities. Menu highlights in the candlelit dining room ($$$; reservations essential) include fillet of salmon glazed with honey and mustard and roasted on a cedar board. The vegetarian selections include roasted eggplant and red peppers topped with goat cheese and served in puff pastry. ⊠ *Box 68, Stuart Rd., Snowville (5 mi southeast of Conway) 03849,* ☎ *603/447–2818 or 800/447–4345,* 〖FAX〗 *603/ 447–5268,* 〖WEB〗 *www.snowvilleinn.com. 18 rooms. Restaurant, sauna, cross-country skiing. AE, D, DC, MC, V. BP, MAP.*

$$$–$$$$ ✕🛏 **White Mountain Hotel and Resort.** The rooms at this hotel at the base of Whitehorse Ledge have mountain views. Proximity to the White Mountain National Forest and Echo Lake State Park makes you feel farther away from civilization (and the nearby outlet malls) than you actually are. Dinner at the Ledges restaurant ($$$) might include White Mountain venison in a cranberry currant sauce or beef Wellington. ⊠ *Box 1828, West Side Rd., 03860,* ☎ 〖FAX〗 *603/356–7100 or* ☎ *800/533–*

6301, WEB *www.whitemountainhotel.com. 69 rooms, 11 suites. Restaurant, bar, pool, hot tub, sauna, 9-hole golf course, tennis court, health club, hiking, cross-country skiing. AE, D, MC, V. BP, MAP.*

$$–$$$$ ✕⊞ **Darby Field Inn.** After a day of activity in the White Mountains, warm up by the fieldstone fireplace in the inn's living room or by the woodstove in the bar. Most rooms in this unpretentious 1826 converted farmhouse have mountain views, and three have fireplaces or double-whirlpool baths. The restaurant ($$$), renowned for its views, presents such haute regional American recipes as roast duckling with a raspberry Chambord sauce and rack of lamb with a burgundy sauce. The dark-chocolate pâté with white-chocolate sauce is a knockout dessert. ⊠ *Box D, 185 Chase Hill, Albany 03818,* ☎ *603/447–2181 or 800/ 426–4147,* FAX *603/447–5726,* WEB *www.darbyfield.com. 15 rooms. Restaurant, bar, pool, outdoor hot tub, cross-country skiing. AE, MC, V. Closed Apr. BP, MAP.*

$$–$$$$ ⊞ **Buttonwood Inn.** A tranquil 17-acre oasis in this busy resort area, the Buttonwood is on Mt. Surprise, 2 mi northeast of North Conway village. Rooms in the 1820s farmhouse are furnished in simple Shaker style. Wide pine floors, quilts, and period stenciling add warmth. Two rooms have gas fireplaces; one has a whirlpool bath. Innkeepers Peter and Claudia Needham supply many thoughtful extras, such as backpacks and picnic baskets. ⊠ *Box 1817, Mt. Surprise Rd., 03860,* ☎ *603/356–2625 or 800/258–2625,* FAX *603/356–3140,* WEB *www.buttonwoodinn.com. 9 rooms. Pool, hiking, cross-country skiing. AE, D, MC, V. BP.*

$$ ⊞ **Cranmore Inn.** This authentic gambrel-roof country inn opened in 1863, and many of its furnishings are antiques dating from the mid-1800s. The former stables have been rebuilt to house condo-style rooms with kitchens. A mere ⅓ mi from the base of Mt. Cranmore, the inn is within easy walking distance of North Conway village. Guests have privileges at a nearby health club. ⊠ *Box 1349, Kearsarge St., 03860,* ☎ *603/356–5502 or 800/526–5502,* WEB *www.cranmoreinn.com. 18 rooms. Restaurant, kitchenettes, pool. AE, MC, V. BP.*

Nightlife and the Arts

Horsefeather's (⊠ Main St., ☎ 603/356–6862), a restaurant and bar, often has music on weekends.

Mt. Washington Valley Theater Company (⊠ Eastern Slope Playhouse, Main St., ☎ 603/356–5776) presents musicals and summer theater from mid-June to Labor Day. The Resort Players, a local group, gives pre- and postseason performances.

Outdoor Activities and Sports

Snowvillage Inn conducts a llama trek up Foss Mountain. Your picnic will include champagne and fine food. Reservations are essential.

Shopping

ANTIQUES

The **Antiques & Collectibles Barn** (⊠ 3425 Main St., ☎ 603/356–7118), 1½ mi north of the village, is a 35-dealer colony with everything from furniture and jewelry to coins and other collectibles. **Richard Plusch Fine Antiques** (⊠ Rte. 16/U.S. 302, ☎ 603/356–3333) deals in period furniture and accessories, including glass, sterling silver, Oriental porcelains, rugs, and paintings. **Sleigh Mill Antiques** (⊠ off Rte. 153, Snowville, ☎ 603/447–6791), an old sleigh and carriage mill 6 mi south of Conway, specializes in 19th-century oil lighting and early gas and electric lamps.

CRAFTS

The **Basket & Handcrafters Outlet** (⊠ Kearsarge St., ☎ 603/356–5332) sells gift baskets, dried-flower arrangements, and country furniture. **Handcrafters Barn** (⊠ Main St., ☎ 603/356–8996) stocks the work of 350 area artists and artisans. The **League of New Hampshire Craftsmen** store (✉ 2526 Main St., ☎ 603/356–2441) carries the creations of the area's best artisans. **Zeb's General Store** (✉ Main St., ☎ 603/356–9294 or 800/676–9294) looks like an old-fashioned country store but sells food items, crafts, and other products, all made in New England.

FACTORY OUTLETS

More than 150 factory outlets—including L. L. Bean, Timberland, Pfaltzgraff, London Fog, Anne Klein, and Reebok—line Route 16.

SPORTSWEAR

A top pick for skiwear is **Joe Jones** (✉ 2709 Main St., ☎ 603/356–9411).

Ski Areas

KING PINE SKI AREA AT PURITY SPRING RESORT

King Pine, some 9 mi south of Conway, has been a family-run ski area for more than 100 years. Some ski-and-stay packages include free skiing for midweek resort guests. Among the facilities and activities are an indoor pool and fitness complex, ice-skating, and tubing. ✉ *Rte. 153, East Madison 03849,* ☎ *603/367–8896; 800/367–8897; 800/373–3754 snow conditions.*

Downhill. King Pine's gentle slopes are ideal for beginner and intermediate skiers; experts won't be challenged except for a brief pitch on the Pitch Pine trail. The 16 trails are serviced by two triple chairs, a double chair, and two surface lifts. There's tubing on Saturday and Sunday afternoons and night skiing and tubing on Friday and Saturday.

Cross-country. King Pine has 15 km (9 mi) of cross-country skiing.

Child care. Children from infants up to 6 years are welcome (8:30–4) at the nursery at base lodge. Children ages 4 and up can take lessons.

CRANMORE MOUNTAIN RESORT

This ski area on the outskirts of North Conway has been a favorite of families since it opened in 1938. Five glades have opened more skiable terrain. ✉ *Box 1640, Skimobile Rd., 03860,* ☎ *603/356–5543; 603/356–8516 snow conditions; 800/786–6754 lodging,* WEB *www.cranmore.com.*

Downhill. The mountain's 39 trails are well laid out and fun to ski. Most runs are naturally formed intermediates that weave in and out of glades. Beginners have several slopes and routes from the summit, but experts must be content with a few short but steep pitches. In addition to the trails, snowboarders have a terrain park and a halfpipe. One high-speed quad, one triple, and three double chairlifts carry skiers to the top. There are also two surface lifts. Night skiing is an option from Thursday to Saturday and during holidays.

Other activities. Other winter activities are outdoor skating, snowshoeing, and tubing.

Child care. The nursery takes children ages 6 months–5 years. There's instruction for children ages 3–12.

Summer and year-round activities. You can take a chairlift to the top for a panoramic view of the White Mountains or mountain bike on selected trails. The fitness center has an indoor climbing wall, tennis courts, exercise equipment, and a pool.

CROSS-COUNTRY

Sixty-four kilometers (40 mi) of groomed cross-country trails weave through North Conway and the countryside along the **Mt. Washington Valley Ski Touring Association Network** (✉ Rte. 16, Intervale, ☎ 603/356–9920 or 800/282–5220).

Kancamagus Highway

★ ㊲ *36 mi between Conway and Lincoln/North Woodstock.*

Interstate 93 is the fastest way to the White Mountains, but it's hardly the most appealing. The section of Route 112 known as the Kancamagus Highway passes through classic mountain vistas with some of the state's most unspoiled scenery. This stretch, punctuated by scenic overlooks and picnic areas, erupts into fiery color each fall, when photo-snapping drivers can really slow things down. Prepare yourself for a leisurely pace. There are also campgrounds off the highway. In bad weather, check with the **White Mountains Visitors Bureau** (☎ 800/346–3687) for road conditions.

Outdoor Activities and Sports

A couple of short hiking trails off the highway yield great rewards for relatively little effort. The **Lincoln Woods Trail** starts from the large parking lot of the Lincoln Woods Visitor Center, 4 mi east of Lincoln. You can purchase the recreation pass ($5 per vehicle, good for seven consecutive days) needed to park in any of the White Mountain National Forest lots or overlooks here; stopping to take photos or to use the rest rooms at the visitor center is permitted without a pass. The trail crosses a suspension bridge over the Pemigewasset River and follows an old railroad bed for 3 mi along the river. The parking and picnic area for **Sabbaday Falls,** about 15 mi west of Conway, is the trailhead for an easy ½-mi trail to the falls, a multilevel cascade that plunges through two potholes and a flume.

The White Mountains A to Z

To research prices, get advice from other travelers, and book travel arrangements, visit www.fodors.com.

AIRPORTS
Manchester Airport is about a 60- to 90-minute drive from the region. Charters and private planes land at Franconia Airport & Soaring Center and Mt. Washington Regional Airport.
➤ AIRPORT INFORMATION: **Franconia Airport & Soaring Center** (⊠ Easton Rd., Franconia, ☎ 603/823–8881). **Mt. Washington Regional Airport** (⊠ Airport Rd., Whitefield, ☎ 603/837–9532).

BUS TRAVEL
Concord Trailways connects Boston's South Station and Logan Airport with Berlin, Conway, Franconia, Gorham, Jackson, Lincoln/North Woodstock, Littleton, and Pinkham Notch.
➤ BUS INFORMATION: **Concord Trailways** (☎ 800/639–3317).

CAR TRAVEL
I–93 and U.S. 3 bisect the White Mountain National Forest, running north from Massachusetts to Québec. The Kancamagus Highway (Route 112), the east–west thoroughfare through the White Mountain National Forest, is a scenic drive. U.S. 302, a longer, more leisurely east–west path, connects I–93 to North Conway. From the seacoast, Route 16 is the popular choice.

EMERGENCIES
➤ HOSPITAL: **Memorial Hospital** (⊠ 3073 Main St., North Conway, ☎ 603/356–5461).

LODGING
Country Inns in the White Mountains handles reservations for a wide variety of B&Bs and inns throughout the region.

➤ LOCAL AGENTS: **Country Inns in the White Mountains** (☎ 603/356–9460).

White Mountain National Forest campground reservations has 20 campgrounds with more than 900 campsites spread across the region; only some take reservations. All sites have a 14-day limit.
➤ CONTACTS: **White Mountain National Forest** (✉ U.S. Forest Service, 719 N. Main St., Laconia 03246, ☎ 603/528–8721 or 877/444–6777).

OUTDOORS & SPORTS
River outfitter Saco Bound Canoe & Kayak leads gentle canoeing expeditions, guided kayak trips, and white-water rafting on seven rivers and provides lessons, equipment, and transportation.
➤ CONTACTS: **Saco Bound Canoe & Kayak** (✉ Box 119, Conway 03813, ☎ 603/447–2177).

For trout and salmon fishing, try the Connecticut Lakes, though any clear stream in the White Mountains will do. Many are stocked, and there are 650 mi of streams in the national forest alone. Conway Lake is the largest of the area's 45 lakes and ponds; it's noted for smallmouth bass and—early and late in the season—good salmon fishing. The New Hampshire Fish and Game Office has up-to-date information on fishing conditions. The North Country Angler schedules intensive guided fly-fishing weekends.
➤ CONTACTS: **New Hampshire Fish and Game Office** (☎ 603/788–3164). **North Country Angler** (✉ 3643 White Mountain Hwy., Intervale, ☎ 603/356–6000).

With 86 major mountains in the area, the hiking possibilities are endless. Innkeepers can usually point you toward the better nearby trails; some inns schedule guided day-trips for guests. The White Mountain National Forest (☞ Visitor Information) has information on hiking and parking passes ($5) required in the national forest. These are available at visitor centers; if you can't buy one in advance, you can park and you can buy a $3 day pass (exact change only) at the parking area.

The Appalachian Mountain Club headquarters at Pinkham Notch offers lectures, workshops, slide shows, and outdoor skills instruction year-round. Accommodations include a 100-bunk main lodge, a 24-bed hostel in Crawford Notch, and two rustic cabins. The club's eight trailside huts provide meals and dorm-style lodging, June–October, on several trails in the Whites. The rest of the year the huts are open, self-serve.

New England Hiking Holidays conducts scheduled guided hiking tours with lodging in country inns for two to eight nights. Hikes, each with two guides, allow for different levels of hiking and cover between 5 and 10 mi per day.
➤ CONTACTS: **White Mountain National Forest** (☞ Visitor Information).
Appalachian Mountain Club (✉ Box 298, Rte. 16, Gorham 03581, ☎ 603/466–2721; 603/466–2725 trail information; 603/466–2727 reservations, WEB www.mountwashington.com/amc/home.html).
New England Hiking Holidays (✉ Box 1648, North Conway 03860, ☎ 603/356–9696 or 800/869–0949, WEB www.nehikingholidays.com).

VISITOR INFORMATION

➤ TOURIST INFORMATION: **Mt. Washington Valley Chamber of Commerce** (⊠ Box 2300, North Conway 03860, ☎ 603/356–5701, WEB www.4seasonresort.com). **North Country Chamber of Commerce** (⊠ Box 1, Colebrook 03576, ☎ 603/237–8939 or 800/698–8939, WEB www.northcountrychamber.org). **White Mountains Visitors Bureau** (⊠ Box 10, Kancamagus Hwy. at I–93, North Woodstock 03262, ☎ 603/745–8720 or 800/346–3687, WEB www.whitemtn.org). **White Mountain National Forest** (⊠ U.S. Forest Service, 719 Main St., Laconia 03246, ☎ 603/528–8721 or 877/444–6777 campground reservations, WEB www.fs.fed.us/r9/white).

WESTERN AND CENTRAL NEW HAMPSHIRE

Western and Central New Hampshire mixes small-town charm with city hustle across three distinct regions. The Merrimack River valley includes the state's largest and fastest-growing cities of Nashua, Manchester, and Concord. Northwest of Concord, Dartmouth–Lake Sunapee—accessible from I–89—is home to the famous college in Hanover, year-round sporting activities at Lake Sunapee and its nearby mountains, and several well-preserved colonial villages. The least developed of the three areas, the Monadnocks region occupies the sleepy southwestern corner of the state. Here you'll find peaceful hilltop hamlets that appear barely changed in the past two centuries, plus many opportunities for hiking. Famous Mt. Monadnock, the largest peak in southern New Hampshire, stands guard over the area.

When you're done climbing and swimming and visiting the past, look for the wares and small studios of area artists. The region has long been an informal artists' colony where people come to write, paint, and weave in solitude. The towns in this region, beginning with Nashua, are described in counterclockwise order.

Nashua

38 *98 mi south of Lincoln/North Woodstock, 48 mi northwest of Boston, MA; 36 mi south of Concord; 50 mi southeast of Keene.*

Once a prosperous manufacturing town that drew thousands of immigrant workers in the late 1800s and early 1900s, Nashua declined like its Massachusetts neighbors Lowell and Lawrence following World War II, as many factories shut down or moved to where labor was cheaper. Since the 1970s, however, the metro area has jumped in population, developing into a charming, old-fashioned community. The low-key feel is most evident in its downtown, with classic redbrick buildings that line the Nashua River, a tributary of the Merrimack River, which skirts the east side of town. Though not visited by tourists as much as other communities in the region, Nashua has some good restaurants and an engaging house-museum.

Nashua's impressive industrial history is kept alive in the Federal-style **Abbot-Spalding House** (⊠ 5 Abbot St., ☎ 603/883–0015, ⊡ donation suggested, ☉ weekdays 10–4), which is run by the Nashua Historical Society and contains both permanent and changing exhibits on the region's past.

Dining

$$–$$$ ✕ **Michael Timothy's Wine and Jazz Bar.** Part hip bistro, part jazzy wine
★   bar (with live music many nights), Michael Timothy's is so popular that even foodies from Massachusetts drive here. The regularly chang-

ing menu might offer Atlantic salmon and Littleneck clams braised in a lemongrass-ginger broth with baby bok choy or semi-boneless game hen pan-seared with dried cranberries, shiitake mushrooms, port wine, and shallots over crisp-fried spinach. The menu also includes wood-fired pizzas, and a stellar wine list. ⊠ *212 Main St.,* ☎ *603/595–9334. AE, D, MC, V. No lunch weekends.*

$–$$ ✕ **Martha's Exchange.** A casual spot with copper brewing vats, original marble floors, and booth seating, Martha's appeals both to the after-work set and office workers on lunch breaks. Burgers and sandwiches, maple-stout-barbecued chicken and ribs, Mexican fare, seafood and steak grills, and salads—all in large portions—are your options here; there's also a sweets shop attached. You can buy half-gallon jugs of house-brewed beers to go. ⊠ *185 Main St.,* ☎ *603/883–8781. D, MC, V.*

Nightlife and the Arts

American Stage Festival (⊠ 14 Court St., ☎ 603/886–7000), the state's largest professional theater, presents Broadway-style and newer works, music concerts, and a children's-theater series from March through October.

Manchester

③⑨ *18 mi north of Nashua, 53 mi north of the Boston, MA.*

Manchester, with just over 100,000 residents, is New Hampshire's largest city. The town grew around the power of the Amoskeag Falls on the Merrimack River, which fueled small textile mills through the 1700s. By 1828, a group of investors from Boston had bought the rights to the Merrimack's water power and built on its eastern bank the Amoskeag Textile Mills, which became a testament to New England's manufacturing power. In 1906, the mills employed 17,000 people and churned out more than 4 million yards of cloth per week. This vast enterprise formed the entire economic base of Manchester; when it closed in 1936, the town was devastated.

Today Manchester is mainly a banking and business center. As part of an economic recovery plan, the old mill buildings have been converted into warehouses, classrooms, restaurants, museums, and office space. The city is also home to the state's major airport, and a new civic and convention center is under construction with a projected opening of late 2001—it will host concerts and minor-league hockey and basketball games.

The **Amoskeag Mills** houses both restaurants and museums. In 1998, the mills became home to the **SEE Science Center,** a hands-on science lab and museum that for now, unfortunately, is open only to groups. The **Millyard Museum,** which opened in spring 2001, contains state-of-the-art exhibits depicting the region's history, from when Native Americans lived alongside and fished the Merrimack River to the heyday of Amoskeag Mills. Additional features include an interactive Discovery Gallery geared toward kids, a lecture-concert hall, and one of the larger museum shops in the state. ⊠ *Mill No. 3, 200 Bedford St. (entrance at 255 Commercial St.),* ☎ *603/625–2821,* WEB *www.mv.com/org/mha.* ⊡ *Free.* ◔ *Weekdays 8–5:30.*

At the neoclassical redbrick (1931) headquarters of the **Manchester Historic Association,** you'll find a few exhibits on this city's long history and information on Amoskeag Mills. ⊠ *129 Amherst St.,* ☎ *603/622–7531,* WEB *www.mv.com/org/mha.* ⊡ *Free.* ◔ *Tues.–Fri. 9–4, Sat. 10–4.* The **Currier Gallery of Art,** in a 1929 Beaux Arts Italianate building, has a permanent collection of European and American paintings, sculpture, and decorative arts from the 13th to the 20th century, including works by Monet, Picasso, Edward Hopper, and Georgia O'Keeffe. Also part of the museum is the Frank Lloyd Wright–designed **Zimmerman House,** built in 1950. Wright called this sparse, utterly functional living space "Usonian." The house is New England's only Wright-designed residence open to the public. ⊠ *201 Myrtle Way,* ☎ *603/669–6144; 603/626–4158 Zimmerman House tours.* ☞ *$5; free Sat. 10–1; Zimmerman House $9 (reservations essential).* ⊙ *Sun.–Mon. and Wed.–Thurs. 11–5, Fri. 11–8, Sat. 10–5; call for tour times.*

ⓒ Salmon, shad, and river herring "climb" the **Amoskeag Fishways** fish ladder near the Amoskeag Dam during the migration period, from May to mid-June. The visitor center has an underwater viewing window, year-round interactive exhibits and programs about the Merrimack River, and a hydroelectric-station viewing area. ⊠ *Fletcher St.,* ☎ *603/626–3474.* ☞ *Free.* ⊙ *Mon.–Sat. 9:30–5.*

Dining and Lodging

$$$–$$$$ ✕ **Richard's Bistro.** Whether you want to celebrate a special occasion or you just crave first-rate regional American cuisine, head to this romantic and hip bistro by the downtown intersection of Lowell and Elm streets. The fare bridges traditional New England ingredients with worldly preparations: try the char-broiled filet mignon with gorgonzola, baked-stuffed potato, and strawberries, or broiled fresh haddock topped with shrimp and scallops on an herb-risotto cake with a honey-peach sauce. ⊠ *36 Lowell St.,* ☎ *603/644–1180. AE, D, MC, V. No lunch Sat.*

$$–$$$ ✕ **Cotton.** This swanky eatery—with mod lighting and furnishings, and
★ an arbored patio—occupies a dapper space inside one of the old Amoskeag Mill buildings. The kitchen churns out updated comfort food with a global spin. Start off with mussels in a red curry of coconut milk, lemongrass, and kafir-lime leaves. Stellar entrée picks include a tuna-noodle casserole updated with fresh yellowfin tuna, julienne vegetables, and pappardelle pasta tossed with wild-mushroom cream and toasted lemony crumbs. ⊠ *75 Arms Park,* ☎ *603/622–5488. AE, D, DC, MC, V.*

$–$$ ✕ **Siam Orchid.** This dark and attractive Thai restaurant serves fairly authentic spicy food. Try the fiery broiled swordfish with shrimp curry sauce or the pine-nut chicken in an aromatic ginger sauce. ⊠ *15 N. Main St.,* ☎ *603/228–3633. No lunch weekends. D, MC, V.*

$ ✕ **Red Arrow Diner.** A mix of hipsters and oldsters, including comedian and Manchester native Adam Sandler, favor this neon-streaked, 24-hour greasy spoon that's been going strong since 1922. Filling diner fare—such as the platter of kielbasa, French toast, and the diner's famous pan-fries—keep patrons happy. ⊠ *61 Lowell St.,* ☎ *603/626–1118. MC, V.*

$$$$ ✕ **Bedford Village Inn.** This luxurious 1810 Federal inn, just a few
★ miles southwest of downtown Manchester, was once a former farmstead that still shows horse-nuzzle marks on its old beams. Its old hayloft and the milking rooms now contain lavish suites with king-size four-poster beds, whirlpool baths, and three telephones. The restaurant, with a warren of elegant but rustic dining rooms with fireplaces and wide-pine floors—plus a casual tavern—presents an oft-changing contemporary menu that might include a starter of braised escargot in Chartreuse with chives and hazelnuts, followed by roast duckling with sage spaetzle, roast root vegetables, and vanilla-rum glaze. ⊠ *2 Village Inn La., Bedford 03110,* ☎ *603/472–2001 or 800/852–1166,* FAX *603/472–2379,* WEB *www.bedfordvillageinn.com. 12 suites, 2 apartments. Restaurant, bar, meeting room. AE, DC, MC, V.*

$$–$$$ 🏨 **Holiday Inn Manchester.** Of the many chain properties in Manchester, the 12-story Holiday Inn has the centralmost location—just steps from Amoskeag Mills and the great dining along Elm Street. Rooms are simple and clean, perfect for business travelers. ⊠ *700 Elm St., 03101,* ☎ *603/625–1000,* FAX *603/625–4595. 244 rooms, 6 suites. 2 restau-*

rants, bar, indoor pool, sauna, gym, meeting rooms, business services. AE, D, DC, MC, V.

Nightlife and the Arts

Revelers come from all over to drink and mingle at the **Yard** (⊠ 1211 S. Mammoth Rd., ☎ 603/623–3545), which is also a full steak house and seafood restaurant. **Club Merrimack** (⊠ 201 Merrimack St., ☎ 603/623–9362) is a popular lesbian/gay disco. The **Palace Theater** (⊠ 80 Hanover St., ☎ 603/668–5588) presents musicals and plays throughout the year. It's also host to the New Hampshire Philharmonic Orchestra (☎ 603/647–6476), the New Hampshire Symphony Orchestra (☎ 603/669–3559), and the Opera League of New Hampshire (☎ 603/429–9887).

Shopping

Bell Hill Antiques (⊠ Rte. 101 at Bell Hill Rd., Bedford, ☎ 603/472–5580) sells country furniture, glass, and china. The enormous **Mall of New Hampshire** (⊠ 1500 S. Willow St., ☎ 603/669–0433) has every conceivable store and is anchored by Sears and Filene's.

Concord

🟠 *20 mi north of Manchester; 67 mi northwest of Boston, MA; 46 mi northwest of Portsmouth.*

New Hampshire's capital (population 38,000) is a quiet, conservative town that tends to the state's business but little else. The residents joke that the sidewalks roll up promptly at 6. The **Concord on Foot** walking trail winds through the historic district. Maps are available from the **Chamber of Commerce** (⊠ 244 N. Main St., ☎ 603/224–2508) or stores along the trail.

The **Pierce Manse** is the Greek Revival home in which Franklin Pierce lived before moving to Washington to become the 14th U.S. president. ⊠ *14 Penacook St., ☎ 603/225–2068 or 603/224–5954. ⊡ $3. ☉ Mid-June–Labor Day, weekdays 11–3.*

At the gilt-domed neoclassical **State House,** New Hampshire's legislature still meets in its original chambers. The building dates to 1819 and is the oldest in the United States in continuous use as a state capitol. ⊠ *107 N. Main St., ☎ 603/271–2154. ☉ Weekdays 8–4:30; guided tours by reservation.*

Among the artifacts at the **Museum of New Hampshire History** is an original Concord Coach. During the 19th century, when more than 3,000 coaches were built in Concord, this was about as technologically perfect a vehicle as you could find—many say it's the coach that won the West. Other exhibits provide an overview of New Hampshire's history, from the Abenaki to the settlers of Portsmouth up to current residents. ⊠ *6 Eagle Sq., ☎ 603/226–3189, WEB www.nhhistory.org/museum.html. ⊡ $5. ☉ Jan.–June and mid-Oct.–Nov., Tues.–Wed. and Sat. 9:30–5, Thurs.–Fri. 9:30–8:30, Sun. noon–5; Dec. and July–mid-Oct., Mon.–Wed. and Sat. 9:30–5, Thurs.–Fri. 9:30–8:30, Sun. noon–5.*

☾ The high-tech **Christa McAuliffe Planetarium** presents shows on the solar system, constellations, and space exploration that incorporate computer graphics, sound, and special effects in the 40-ft dome theater. Children love seeing the tornado tubes, magnetic marbles, and other hands-on exhibits. Outside, explore the scale-model planet walk and the human sundial. The planetarium was named for the Concord teacher and first civilian in space, who was killed in the Space Shuttle *Challenger* explosion in 1986. ⊠ *New Hampshire Technical Institute campus, 3 Institute Dr., ☎ 603/271–7827. ⊡ Exhibit area free, shows $6. ☉*

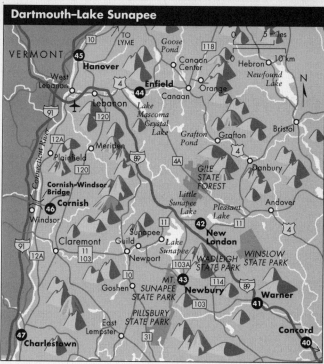

Dartmouth–Lake Sunapee

Tues.–Thurs. 9–5, Fri. 9–7, weekends 10–5. Call for show times and reservations.

Dining and Lodging

$–$$ ★ ✕ **Moxy Grill.** Concord lacked for much in the way of innovative eateries before this funky little bistro opened a couple years ago, just off Main Street. Although the dining room is small—with closely spaced tables, pumpkin- and raspberry-shaded walls, and several seats crowded around a cozy central bar—the exceptional contemporary fare, such as sage-and-wild mushroom gnocchi, burgers, and other light offerings, is worth enduring the tight quarters. ⊠ *6 Pleasant St. Ext.,* ☎ *603/229–0072. MC, V.*

$ ★ ✕ **Foodee's Pizzas.** A local chain with additional parlors in Keene, Dover, Lincoln, Milford, and Wolfeboro, Foodee's serves high-caliber, creative pizzas with especially delicious crusts (such as sourdough, six-grain, and deep-dish). The capital branch is in the heart of downtown and offers such pies as the Polish (with kielbasa, sauerkraut, and three cheeses) and the El Greco (with sweet onions, sliced tomatoes, olive oil, and feta). You can also order from a selection of pastas, salads, and calzones. ⊠ *2 S. Main St.,* ☎ *603/225–3834. MC, V.*

$$–$$$ ⊡ **Centennial Inn.** Built in 1896 for widows of Civil War veterans, this brick-and-stone building is set back from busy Pleasant Street. Much of the original woodwork has been preserved. Each room is decorated with antiques and reproduction pieces, and all have ceiling fans and VCRs. In the Franklin Pierce dining room, the menu leans toward contemporary cuisine. ⊠ *96 Pleasant St., 03301,* ☎ *603/225–7102 or 800/360–4839,* ℻ *603/225–5031. 27 rooms, 5 suites. Restaurant, bar, in-room data ports, in-room VCRs. AE, D, DC, MC, V.*

Nightlife and the Arts

The **Capitol Center for the Arts** (⊠ 46 S. Main St., ☎ 603/225–1111) has been restored to reflect its Roaring '20s origins. It hosts touring

Broadway shows, dance companies, and musical acts. The lounge at **Hermanos Cocina Mexicana** (⊠ 11 Hills Ave., ☎ 603/224–5669) has live jazz Sunday through Thursday nights.

Outdoor Activities and Sports

Hannah's Paddles, Inc. (⊠ 15 Hannah Dustin Dr., ☎ 603/753–6695) rents canoes for use on the Merrimack River, which runs through Concord.

Shopping

CRAFTS

Capitol Craftsman and Romance Jewelers (⊠ 16 N. Main St., ☎ 603/224–6166 or 603/228–5683), which share adjoining shops, sell fine jewelry and handicrafts. The **Den of Antiquity** (⊠ 2 Capital Plaza, ☎ 603/225–4505) carries handcrafted country gifts and accessories. The **League of New Hampshire Craftsmen** (⊠ 36 N. Main St., ☎ 603/228–8171) store exhibits crafts in many media. **Mark Knipe Goldsmiths** (⊠ 2 Capitol Plaza, Main St., ☎ 603/224–2920) sets antique stones in rings, earrings, and pendants.

MALLS

Steeplegate Mall (⊠ 270 Loudon Rd., ☎ 603/224–1523) has more than 70 stores, including chain department stores and some smaller crafts shops.

Warner

④ *22 mi northwest of Concord.*

Three New Hampshire governors were born in this quiet agricultural town just off I–89. Buildings dating from the late 1700s and early 1800s, and a charming library give the town's main street a welcoming feel.

★ **Mt. Kearsarge Indian Museum, Education and Cultural Center** gives guided tours of an extensive collection of Native American artistry, including moose-hair embroidery, quiltwork, and basketry. Signs on the Medicine Woods trail identify plants and explain how Native Americans use them as foods, medicines, and dyes. ⊠ *Kearsarge Mountain Rd., 03278,* ☎ *603/456–2600,* WEB *www.indianmuseum.org.* ☞ *$6.* ☉ *May–Oct., Mon.–Sat. 10–5, Sun. noon–5; Nov.–Dec., Sat. 10–5, Sun. noon–5.*

A 3½-mi scenic auto road at **Rollins State Park** (⊠ off Rte. 103) snakes up the southern slope of Mt. Kearsarge, where you can then tackle on foot the ½-mi trail to the summit. The road is closed November through mid-May.

New London

④ *16 mi northwest of Warner, 25 mi west of Tilton.*

New London, the home of Colby-Sawyer College (1837), is a good base for exploring the Lake Sunapee region. At the 10,000-year-old **Cricenti's Bog,** off Business Route 11 (Business Route 11 goes right through town; Route 11 goes around town), a short trail shows off the shaggy mosses and fragile ecosystem of this ancient pond.

Dining and Lodging

$–$$ ✕ **Peter Christian's Tavern.** Exposed beams, wooden tables, a smattering of antiques, and half shutters on the windows make Peter Christian's a cool oasis in summer and a cozy haven in winter. Tavern fare such as beef stew and shepherd's pie has been updated for modern tastes. ⊠ *186 Main St.,* ☎ *603/526–4042. AE, D, MC, V.*

$$–$$$ ✕ **Inn at Pleasant Lake.** This rambling 1790s inn lies just across Pleas-
★ ant Lake from majestic Mt. Kearsage. The country antiques-filled

rooms are spacious with modern bathrooms (some with whirlpool tubs). The restaurant ($$$$, reservations essential) presents a nightly changing prix-fixe menu that has drawn raves for such expertly executed dishes as pan-seared mahimahi with tropical-fruit chutney and Thai eggplant relish, and such desserts as white-chocolate mousse with a trio of sauces. ⊠ *Box 1030, 125 Pleasant St., 03257,* ☎ *603/526–6271 or 800/626–4907,* ℻ *603/526–4111,* WEB *www.innatpleasantlake.com. 12 rooms. Restaurant, beach, boating, gym. MC, V.*

$$–$$$ ✕ 🖼 **New London Inn.** The two porches of this rambling 1792 country inn overlook Main Street. Rooms have Victorian decor; those in the front of the house overlook the pretty campus of Colby-Sawyer College. The nouvelle-inspired menu in the restaurant starts with items such as butternut squash with a sun-dried cranberry pesto and includes entrées such as grilled cilantro shrimp with a saffron risotto. The inn is no-smoking. ⊠ *Box 8, 140 Main St., 03257,* ☎ *603/526–2791 or 800/ 526–2791,* ℻ *603/526–2749,* WEB *www.newlondoninn.com. 28 rooms. Restaurant. AE, MC, V. BP.*

$$ 🖼 **Follansbee Inn.** Built in 1840, this quintessential country inn on the shore of Kezar Lake is a perfect fit in the 19th-century village of North Sutton, about 4 mi south of New London. The common rooms and bedrooms are loaded with collectibles and antiques such as traveling trunks and a wooden school desk. You can ice-fish on the lake and ski across it in winter and swim or boat from the inn's pier in summer. A 3-mi walking trail circles the lake. The inn is no-smoking. ⊠ *Rte. 114, North Sutton, 03260,* ☎ *603/927–4221 or 800/626–4221,* WEB *www. follansbeeinn.com. 23 rooms, 11 with bath; 1 cottage. Lake, hiking, boating, fishing, ice-skating, cross-country skiing. MC, V. BP.*

$ 🏕 **Otter Lake Camping Area.** The 28 sites on Otter Lake have plenty of shade, and boating and fishing are available. Facilities include a beach, a playground, and canoe and paddleboat rentals. ⊠ *55 Otterville Rd., 03257,* ☎ *603/763–5600. No credit cards.*

Nightlife and the Arts

The **New London Barn Playhouse** (⊠ 209 Main St., ☎ 603/526–6710) presents Broadway-style and children's plays every summer in New Hampshire's oldest continuously operating theater.

Shopping

Artisan's Workshop (⊠ Peter Christian's Tavern, 186 Main St., ☎ 603/526–4227) carries jewelry, glass, and other local handicrafts.

Ski Areas

NORSK CROSS COUNTRY AND SNOWSHOE CENTER
The 70 km (43 mi) of scenic cross-country ski trails here include 45 km (28 mi) that are tracked and 24 km (15 km) skate-groomed. Snowshoers have 19 km (12 mi) of groomed and backcountry trails. ⊠ *Rte. 11,* ☎ *603/526–4685 or 800/426–6775,* WEB *www.skinorsk.com.*

Newbury

43 *8 mi south of New London.*

Newbury is on the edge of Mt. Sunapee State Park. The mountain, which rises to an elevation of nearly 3,000 ft, and sparkling Lake Sunapee are the region's outdoor recreation centers. The popular League of New Hampshire Craftsmen's Fair is held at the base of Mt. Sunapee each August.

Narrated cruises aboard the **M/V Mt. Sunapee II** (⊠ Main St., Sunapee, ☎ 603/763–4030) provide a closer look at Lake Sunapee's history and mountain scenery. Dinner cruises are held on the **M/V Kearsarge** (☎ 603/763–4030). Both boats leave from the dock at Sunapee Harbor.

John M. Hay, who served as private secretary to Abraham Lincoln and secretary of state for Presidents McKinley and Theodore Roosevelt, built **The Fells** on Lake Sunapee as a summer home in 1890. House tours focus on his life in Newbury and Washington. Hay's son is responsible for the extensive gardens, a mix of formal and informal styles that includes a 75-ft perennial border and a naturalized heather garden on the hillside. More than 800 acres of the former estate are open for hiking and picnicking. ⊠ *Rte. 103A,* ☎ *603/763–4789,* WEB *www.thefells. org.* ☜ *$4.* ☉ *House Memorial Day–mid-Oct., weekends 10–5; grounds daily dawn–dusk.*

Lodging

$ ⚠ **Crow's Nest Campground.** This campground has 100 sites, some directly on the Sugar River. The facilities include a recreation hall, a swimming pool, a children's wading pool, miniature golf in summer, and a warm-up room with fireplace for winter use. River swimming and fishing are summer pastimes; you can skate or sled in the winter, and area snowmobile trails connect to the campground. ⊠ *529 S. Main St., Newport 03773,* ☎ *603/863–6170. D, MC, V. Closed mid-Oct.– Nov. and Apr.–mid-May.*

Outdoor Activities and Sports

BEACHES

Sunapee State Beach has picnic areas, a beach, and a bathhouse. You can rent canoes here, too. ⊠ *Rte. 103,* ☎ *603/763–5561.* ☜ *$2.50.* ☉ *Daily dawn–dusk.*

FISHING

Lake Sunapee has brook and lake trout, salmon, smallmouth bass, and pickerel.

Ski Areas

MOUNT SUNAPEE

Although the resort is state-owned, the operation of Mt. Sunapee is now leased to Vermont's Okemo Mountain resort, known for its family-friendly atmosphere. The agreement brought a necessary influx of capital, and since 1998, lifts, equipment rentals, snowmaking (now at 97% coverage), parking, and trail grooming have all been vastly improved. ⊠ *Box 2021, Rte. 103, 03772,* ☎ *603/763–2356; 603/763– 4020 snow conditions; 877/687–8627 lodging,* WEB *www.mtsunapee.com.*

Downhill. This mountain is 1,510 vertical ft, tops in southern New Hampshire, and has 57 trails, mostly intermediate. Experts take to a dozen black-diamond slopes, including three nice double-black diamonds. The beginner's section is well away from other trails and has a new quad chairlift. Boarders have a 420-ft-long halfpipe and a terrain park with music. Two base lodges and a summit lodge supply the essentials. One high-speed detachable quad, one fixed-grip quad, two triple, and two double chairlifts, and three surface lifts transport skiers.

Child care. The Mother Goose Day Care takes children ages 1–5. Children's programs in skiing or snowboarding are available for kids 4 and up.

Summer activities. The Sunapee Express Quad zooms you to the summit. From here, it's just under a mile hike to Lake Solitude at the back of the mountain. Mountain bikers can use the lift to many trails, and an in-line skate park has beginner and advanced sections (plus equipment rentals).

Enfield

44   *33 mi northwest of Newbury.*

In 1782, two Shaker brothers from Mount Lebanon, New York, arrived at a community on the northeastern side of Mascoma Lake. Eventually, they formed Enfield, the ninth of 18 Shaker communities in this country, and moved it to the lake's southern shore, where they erected more than 200 buildings.

The **Enfield Shaker Museum** preserves the legacy of the Enfield Shakers, who numbered 330 members at the village's peak. By 1923, interest in the society was dwindling, and the last 10 members joined the Canterbury community. A self-guided walking tour takes you through 13 of the buildings that remain, among them the Great Stone Dwelling (now the Shaker Inn) and an 1849 stone mill. Demonstrations by craftspeople of Shaker techniques and numerous special events take place year-round. ✉ *24 Caleb Dyer La.,* ☎ *603/632–4346,* WEB *www.shakermuseum.org.* 🖃 *$7.* ☉ *Memorial Day–mid-Oct., Mon.–Sat. 10–5, Sun. noon–5; mid-Oct.–Memorial Day, Sat. 10–4, Sun. noon–4.*

Dining and Lodging

$$–$$$ ✕🛏 **The Shaker Inn.** Built between 1837 and 1841, the Great Stone Dwelling is the largest main dwelling ever built by a Shaker community. Adjacent to the Enfield Shaker Museum, it is now an inn, and the guest rooms in the original Shaker sleeping chambers have reproduction Shaker furniture and are decorated with the simplicity and style for which the religious community was known. The dining room serves Shaker-inspired cuisine such as pumpkin ravioli and maple-glazed baked ham. ✉ *447 Rte. 4A, 03748,* ☎ *603/632–7810 or 888/707–4257,* WEB *www.theshakerinn.com. 24 rooms. Restaurant. AE, D, MC, V.*

Outdoor Activities and Sports

Anglers can try for rainbow trout, pickerel, and horned pout in **Lake Mascoma.**

Hanover

45   *12 mi northwest of Enfield, 62 mi northwest of Concord.*

Eleazer Wheelock founded Hanover's Dartmouth College in 1769 to educate the Abenaki "and other youth." When he arrived, the town consisted of about 20 families. The college and the town grew symbiotically, with Dartmouth becoming the northernmost Ivy League school. Today Hanover is still synonymous with Dartmouth, but the attractive town is also a respected medical center and the cultural center for the upper Connecticut River valley.

Robert Frost spent part of a brooding freshman semester at Ivy League **Dartmouth College** before giving up college altogether. The buildings that cluster around the green include the **Baker Memorial Library,** which houses literary treasures including 17th-century editions of Shakespeare's works. The library is also well known for the 3,000-square-ft murals by Mexican artist José Clemente Orozco that depict the story of civilization on the American continents. If the towering arcade at the entrance to the **Hopkins Center** (☎ 603/646–2422) appears familiar, it's probably because it resembles the project that architect Wallace K. Harrison completed just after designing it: New York City's Metropolitan Opera House at Lincoln Center. The complex includes a 900-seat theater for film and music, a 400-seat theater for plays, and a black-box theater for new plays. The Dartmouth Symphony Orchestra performs here, as does the Big Apple Circus (in summer). In addition to African, Peruvian, Oceanic, Asian, European, and American art, the

Hood Museum of Art owns the Picasso painting *Guitar on a Table*, silver by Paul Revere, and a set of Assyrian reliefs from the 9th century BC. Rivaling the collection is the museum's architecture: a series of austere redbrick buildings with copper roofs arranged around a courtyard. Free guided tours of the museum are available on request. ⊠ *Museum: Wheelock St.*, ☎ *603/646–2808.* 🖃 *Free.* ☉ *Tues. and Thurs.– Sat. 10–5, Wed. 10–9, Sun. noon–5.*

OFF THE BEATEN PATH | **THE UPPER VALLEY** – From Hanover, you can make a 60-mi drive up Route 10 all the way to Littleton for a highly scenic tour of the upper Connecticut River Valley. You'll have views of the river from many points, as well as the mountains in Vermont. The road passes through groves of evergreens, over leafy ridges, and through some delightful hamlets. Stop at the bluff-top village green in historic **Haverhill** (28 mi north of Hanover) for a picnic amid the panorama of classic Georgian and Federal mansions and faraway farmsteads. Consider this as a scenic route to the White Mountains area, or loop back south through the mountains from Haverhill down Route 25 to Route 118 to U.S. 4 west, leading you back to Enfield—a drive of about 45 mi (and 75 minutes).

Dining and Lodging

$$ ✕ **Murphy's.** Students, visiting alums, and locals regularly descend upon this dark and pubby storefront eatery whose walls are lined with shelves of old books. The varied menu ranges from orange-chipotle– seared pork chops to buffalo chicken po' boys to Cajun salmon Caesar salads. For libations, try the extensive beer list. ⊠ *11 S. Main St.*, ☎ *603/643–4075. AE, D, DC, MC, V.*

$–$$ ✕ **Panda House/Bamboo Garden.** In a region with few decent Asian restaurants, these two-restaurants-in-one offer a welcome taste of Chinese and Japanese fare. They occupy a sedate basement space of the Hanover Park shopping arcade. Try the sashimi/sushi platters from the Bamboo Garden kitchen; Panda House favorites include tangerine beef, and whole crispy fish with a spicy Hunan sauce. ⊠ *3 Lebanon St.*, ☎ *603/643–1290. AE, D, DC, MC, V.*

$$$$ ✕🏠 **Hanover Inn.** Owned and operated by Dartmouth College, this
★ sprawling, Georgian-style brick building rises four white-trimmed stories. The original building was converted to a tavern in 1780, and this expertly run inn, now greatly enlarged, has been operating ever since. Rooms have Colonial reproductions, Audubon prints, and large sitting areas. The formal Daniel Webster Room ($$$–$$$$) serves regional American dishes such as braised rabbit leg and seared loin with watercress celery salad, spiced walnuts, and cumin vinaigrette. The swank Zins wine bar ($–$$) prepares lighter but still highly innovative fare and has a fine list of vintages by the bottle, glass, and half-glass. ⊠ *Box 151, The Green, 03755*, ☎ *603/643–4300 or 800/443–7024*, FAX *603/646–3744*, WEB *www.hanoverinn.com. 92 rooms. 2 restaurants. AE, D, DC, MC, V.*

$$–$$$$ 🏠 **Trumbull House.** This white Colonial-style house sits on 16 acres on the outskirts of Hanover. The sunny guest rooms are furnished with king- or queen-size beds, window seats, writing desks, and other comfortable touches. Breakfast, with a choice of entrées, is served in the formal dining room or in front of the fireplace in the living room. The inn is no-smoking. ⊠ *40 Etna Rd., 03755*, ☎ *603/643–2370 or 800/ 651–5141*, WEB *www.trumbullhouse.com. 5 rooms. Dining room, pond, basketball, hiking. AE, D, DC, MC, V. BP.*

Outdoor Activities and Sports

Ledyard Canoe Club of Dartmouth (☎ 603/643–6709) provides canoe and kayak rentals and classes on the swift-flowing Connecticut River, which is not suited to beginners and is safest after mid-June.

Shopping

Shops, mostly of the independent variety but with a few upscale chains sprinkled in, line Hanover's relentlessly cute and dapper Main Street—the commercial district blends almost imperceptibly with Dartmouth's campus. Goldsmith Paul Gross of **Designer Gold** (⊠ 3 Lebanon St., ☎ 603/643–3864) designs settings for gemstones—all one-of-a-kind or limited-edition.

West Lebanon, south of Hanover on the Vermont border, has many more shops. The **Mouse Menagerie of Fine Crafts** (⊠ Rte. 12A, ☎ 603/298–7090) sells its signature collector's series of toy mice, plus furniture, wind chimes, and other gifts. The **Powerhouse Mall** (⊠ Rte. 12A, 1 mi north of Exit 20 off I–89, ☎ 603/298–5236), a former power station, comprises three buildings of specialty stores, boutiques, and restaurants.

Cornish

46 *22 mi south of Hanover.*

Today Cornish is best known for its four covered bridges, but at the turn of the century the village was known primarily as the home of the country's then most popular novelist, Winston Churchill (no relation to the British prime minister). His novel *Richard Carvell* sold more than a million copies. Churchill was such a celebrity that he hosted Teddy Roosevelt during the president's 1902 visit. At that time Cornish was an enclave of artistic talent. Painter Maxfield Parrish lived and worked here, and sculptor Augustus Saint-Gaudens set up his studio and created the heroic bronzes for which he is known.

The 460-ft **Cornish-Windsor Bridge,** built in 1866, is the longest covered bridge in the United States. It spans the Connecticut River, connecting New Hampshire with Vermont.

★ The **Saint-Gaudens National Historic Site,** 1½ mi north of the Cornish-Windsor covered bridge, contains sculptor Augustus Saint-Gaudens's (1848–1907) house, studio, gallery, and 150 acres of grounds and gardens. Scattered throughout are full-size casts of his works. The property has two hiking trails, the longer of which is the Blow-Me-Down Trail. Concerts are held every Sunday afternoon in July and August. ⊠ *Off Rte. 12A,* ☎ *603/675–2175,* WEB *www.sgnhs.org.* ≊ *$4.* ☼ *Buildings mid-May–Oct., daily 9–4:30; grounds daily dawn–dusk.*

Dining and Lodging

$$$–$$$$ ✕▥ **Home Hill Inn.** This restored 1800 mansion set back from the river on 25 acres of meadow and woods is a tranquil place best suited to adults. The owners have given the inn a French influence with 19th-century antiques and collectibles. Rooms in the main house have canopy or four-poster beds, and four have fireplaces; a suite in the guest house can be a romantic hideaway. The dining room ($$$$; closed Mon.–Tues.) serves classic and Mediterranean French cuisine such as Vermont rabbit in a pastry crust. ⊠ *River Rd., Plainfield 03781,* ☎ *603/675–6165,* WEB *www.homehillinn.com. 6 rooms, 2 suites, 1 seasonal cottage. Restaurant, pool, tennis court, cross-country skiing. AE, D, MC, V. CP.*

$$–$$$ ▥ **Chase House Bed & Breakfast Inn.** Innkeepers Barbara Lewis and
★ Ted Doyle love sharing the history of this 1795 Federal-style house. It was the birthplace of Salmon P. Chase, who was Abraham Lincoln's secretary of the treasury, chief justice of the Supreme Court, and a founder of the Republican Party. Careful restoration with Colonial-style furnishings and Waverly wall coverings has recaptured early 19th-century elegance. Ask for a room with a canopy bed or one with a view of the Connecticut River valley and Mt. Ascutney. The inn is no-smoking.

✉ R.R. 2, Box 909, Rte. 12A, 03745 (1½ mi south of Cornish-Windsor covered bridge), ☎ 603/675–5391 or 800/401–9455, FAX 603/675–5010, WEB www.chasehouse.com. 5 rooms, 4 suites. Gym, boating. MC, V. Closed Nov. BP.

Nightlife and the Arts

The beautifully restored 19th-century **Claremont Opera House** (✉ Tremont Sq., Claremont, ☎ 603/542–4433) hosts plays and musicals from September to May.

Outdoor Activities and Sports

Northstar Canoe Livery (✉ Rte. 12A, Balloch's Crossing, ☎ 603/542–5802) rents canoes for half- or full-day trips on the Connecticut River.

Charlestown

47 20 mi south of Cornish, 63 mi west of Keene.

Charlestown has the state's largest historic district: 63 homes, handsome examples of Federal, Greek Revival, and Gothic Revival architecture, are clustered about the center of town; 10 of them were built before 1800. Several merchants on Main Street distribute brochures that contain an interesting walking tour of the district.

The **Fort at No. 4,** 1½ mi north of Charlestown, was in 1747 an outpost on the lonely periphery of Colonial civilization. That year fewer than 50 militia men at the fort withstood an attack by 400 French soldiers that changed the course of New England history by ensuring that northern New England remained under British rule. Costumed interpreters at the only living-history museum from the era of the French and Indian War cook dinner over an open hearth and demonstrate weaving, gardening, and candlemaking. Each year the museum holds full reenactments of militia musters and battles of the French and Indian War. ✉ Rte. 11, ☎ 603/826–5700, WEB www.fortat4.com. ⌧ $8. ☉ Late May–mid-Oct., Wed.–Mon. 10–4 (weekends only 1st 2 wks of Sept.).

On a bright, breezy day you might want to detour to the **Morningside Flight Park** (✉ Rte. 12/11, ☎ 603/542–4416), not necessarily to take hang-gliding lessons, although you could. You can watch the bright colors of the gliders as they swoop over the school's 450-ft peak.

Lodging

$$ 🏠 **MapleHedge.** The innkeepers live in the oldest section of this home, which dates from about 1755. Guest rooms, in the 1820 Federal-style part, are decorated with carefully chosen antiques. The Cobalt Room showcases an extensive collection of cobalt glass, stencil-pattern wallpaper in cobalt and burgundy, and mahogany furnishings. In Lt. R.A.D.'s Quarters, Marine Corps memorabilia and dark pine wainscoting give the room a masculine air. Freshly ironed linens and a three-course breakfast served in the formal dining room are among the amenities. ✉ Box 638, 355 Main St., 03603, ☎ 603/826–5237 or 800/962–7539, FAX 603/826–5237, WEB www.maplehedge.com. 5 rooms. MC, V. Closed Jan.–Mar. BP.

Walpole

48 13 mi south of Charlestown.

Walpole possesses one of the state's perfect town greens. This one, bordered by Elm and Washington streets, is surrounded by homes built about 1790, when the townsfolk constructed a canal around the Great Falls of the Connecticut River and brought commerce and wealth to the area. The town now has 3,200 inhabitants, more than a dozen of whom are millionaires.

OFF THE
BEATEN PATH **SUGARHOUSES –** Maple-sugar season—a harbinger of spring—occurs about the first week in March when days become warmer but nights are still frigid. A drive along maple-lined back roads reveals thousands of taps and buckets catching the fresh but labored flow of unrefined sap. Plumes of smoke rise from nearby sugarhouses where sugaring off, the process of boiling down this precious liquid, takes place. Many sugarhouses are open to the public; after a tour and demonstration, you can sample the syrup with traditional unsweetened doughnuts and maybe a pickle—or taste hot syrup over fresh snow, a favorite confection. Open to the public in this area of the state are **Bacon's Sugar House** (✉ 243 Dublin Rd., Jaffrey, ☎ 603/532–8836); **Bascom Maple Farm** (✉ Mt. Kingsbury, off Rte. 123A, Alstead, ☎ 603/835–6361), which serves maple pecan pie and maple milk shakes; and **Stuart & John's Sugar House & Pancake Restaurant** (✉ Rtes. 12 and 63, Westmoreland, ☎ 603/399–4486), which offers a tour and pancake breakfast.

Shopping

Walpole has a few shops that are well worth visiting. **Boggy Meadow Farm** (✉ River Rd. S, ☎ 603/756–3300) sells the farm's Fanny Mason Farmstead Swiss cheese in its store. A window overlooks the cheesemaking area. **Burdick Chocolates** (✉ Main St., ☎ 603/756–3701) is renowned for its chocolates, especially the chocolate mice, which are shipped to trendy restaurants in New York and other cities.

Keene

④⑨ *17 mi southeast of Walpole; 20 mi northeast of Brattleboro, VT; 56 mi west of Manchester.*

Keene is the largest city in the southwest corner of the state and the proud locus of the widest main street in America. Each year, on the Saturday before Halloween, locals use that street to hold a Pumpkin Festival, where they seek to retain their place in the record books for the most carved, lighted jack-o-lanterns—13,500 in 1997.

Keene State College, hub of the local arts community, is on the tree-lined main street. The **Thorne-Sagendorph Art Gallery** (☎ 603/358–2720) houses George Ridci's *Landscape* and presents traveling exhibitions. The **Putnam Art Lecture Hall** (☎ 603/358–2160) shows art films and international films.

Dining and Lodging

$–$$ ✕ **176 Main.** This grand old brick house near the campus of Keene College in the heart of downtown has a varied menu that runs the gamut from pad Thai noodles to blackened catfish. The bar stocks an extensive selection of beers on draught. Weekend brunch is a big event here. ✉ *176 Main St.,* ☎ *603/357–3100. AE, D, MC, V.*

$$$–$$$$ ✕🏨 **Chesterfield Inn.** Surrounded by gardens, the Chesterfield sits
★ above Route 9, the main road between Keene and Brattleboro, Vermont. The spacious rooms, decorated with armoires, fine antiques, and period-style fabrics, have telephones in the bathroom and refrigerators; many have fireplaces. The views from the dining room are of the gardens and the Vermont hills. Ragout of chicken with chorizo sausage and braised lamb shank with lemon and green olives are among the menu highlights. ✉ *Box 155, Rte. 9, Chesterfield 03443,* ☎ *603/256–3211 or 800/365–5515,* 📠 *603/256–6131,* 🌐 *www.chesterfieldinn.com. 13 rooms, 2 suites. Restaurant. AE, D, DC, MC, V. BP.*

Monadnock Region and Central New Hampshire

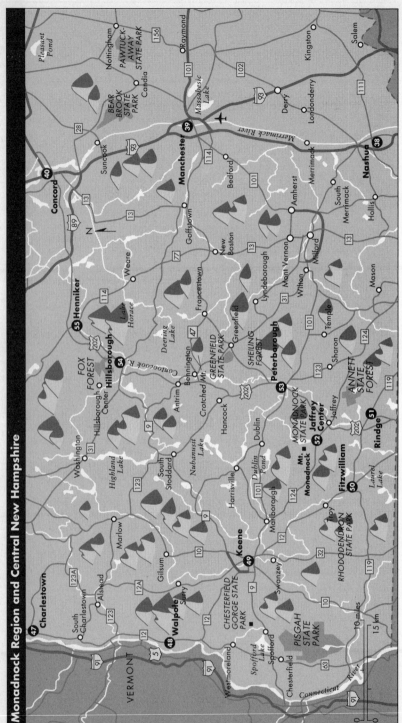

$$ 🏨 **Carriage Barn.** Antiques and wide pine floors lend this inn across from Keene State College a cozy charm. An expansive buffet is served each morning in the breakfast room, but many guests savor a second cup of coffee in the summerhouse. ⊠ *358 Main St., 03431,* ☎ *603/357–3812,* WEB *www.carriagebarn.com. 4 rooms. MC, V. CP.*

$ ⛺ **Swanzey Lake Camping Area.** This 82-site campground for tents and RVs has a sandy beach, a dock, a ball field, a recreation area, and boat rentals. ⊠ *88 E. Shore Rd. (Box 115, W. Swanzey 03469),* ☎ *603/352–9880,* WEB *www.swanzeylake.com.*

Nightlife and the Arts

The **Colonial Theatre** (⊠ 95 Main St., ☎ 603/352–2033) opened in 1924 as a vaudeville stage. It now hosts folk and jazz concerts and has the largest movie screen in town. The **Redfern Arts Center at Brickyard Pond** (⊠ 229 Main St., ☎ 603/358–2171) has year-round music, theater, and dance performances. **Elm City Brew Co.** (⊠ 222 West St., ☎ 603/355–3335), at the Colony Mall, serves light food and draws a mix of college students and young professionals.

Outdoor Activities and Sports

The Monadnock region has more than 200 lakes and ponds, most of which offer good fishing. Rainbow trout, smallmouth and largemouth bass, and some northern pike swim in **Spofford Lake** in Chesterfield. **Goose Pond** in West Canaan, just north of Keene, holds smallmouth bass and white perch.

Shopping

ANTIQUES

The more than 240 dealers at **Antiques at Colony Mill** (⊠ 222 West St., ☎ 603/358–6343) sell everything from furniture to dolls.

BOOKS

The extraordinary collection of used books at the **Homestead Bookshop** (⊠ Rtes. 101 and 124, Marlborough, ☎ 603/876–4213) includes biographies, cookbooks, and town histories.

SHOPPING CENTER

Colony Mill Marketplace (⊠ 222 West St., ☎ 603/357–1240), an old mill building, holds 30-plus stores and boutiques such as **Country Artisans** (☎ 603/352–6980), which showcases the stoneware, textiles, prints, and glassware of regional artists; the **Toadstool Bookshop** (☎ 603/352–8815), which carries many children's and regional travel and history books; and **Ye Goodie Shoppe** (☎ 603/352–0326), whose specialty is handmade chocolates and confections. There's also a food court, with excellent desserts, homemade soups, sandwiches, fish-and-chips, teas, and coffees.

Fitzwilliam

50 *14 mi southeast of Keene.*

A well-preserved historic district of Colonial and Federal-style houses has made the town of Fitzwilliam, on Route 119, the subject of thousands of postcards. Many show views of its landscape in winter, when a fine white snow settles on the oval common. Town business is still conducted in the 1817 meeting house.

The **Amos J. Blake House,** maintained by the Fitzwilliam Historical Society, contains a museum with period antiques and artifacts and the law office of its namesake. A town walking-tour pamphlet is available here, too. ⊠ *Village Green,* ☎ *603/585–7742.* 🎟 *Free.* ☾ *Late May–mid-Oct., Sat. 1–4 or by appointment.*

More than 16 acres of wild rhododendrons burst into bloom in mid-July at **Rhododendron State Park,** which has the largest concentration of *Rhododendron maximum* north of the Allegheny Mountains. Bring a picnic lunch and sit in a nearby pine grove, or follow the marked footpaths through the flowers. ⊠ *Off Rte. 12, 2½ mi northwest of the town common,* ☎ *603/532–8862.* 🎦 *$2.50 weekends and holidays; free at other times.* ⊙ *Daily 8–sunset.*

Lodging

$$–$$$ 🏨 **Inn at East Hill Farm.** At this 1830 farmhouse resort at the base of Mt. Monadnock, children are not only allowed but expected. If you don't have kids, you might be happier elsewhere. Children collect the eggs for the next-day's breakfast, milk the cows, feed the animals, and can try arts and crafts, storytelling, hiking, and games. The innkeepers schedule weekly sleigh, hay, and pony rides. Rates include most activities and three meals in a camplike dining hall. Twice weekly in July and August trips are scheduled to a nearby lake for boating, water-skiing, and fishing. ⊠ *460 Monadnock St., Troy 03465,* ☎ *603/242–6495 or 800/242–6495,* 🅵🅰🆇 *603/242–7709,* 🆆🅴🅱 *www.east-hill-farm.com. 65 rooms. Restaurant, 2 outdoor pools, indoor pool, wading pool, sauna, tennis court, hiking, horseback riding, sleigh rides, recreation room, baby-sitting. D, MC, V. FAP.*

$$ 🏨 **Amos Parker House.** The garden of this Georgian B&B is the town's
★   most stunning, complete with lily ponds, Asian stone benches, and Dutch waterstones that create a gently burbling waterfall effect. Two rooms have garden views; three have wood-burning fireplaces. One of the suites is decorated with hand-painted wall murals. In winter, breakfast is served in an elegant setting in front of a roaring fire. ⊠ *Box 202, Rte. 119, 03447,* ☎ *603/585–6540. 2 rooms, 2 suites. No credit cards. BP.*

$–$$ 🏨 **Hannah Davis House.** This 1820 Federal-style house just off the vil-
★   lage green has retained its elegance. The original beehive oven still sits in the kitchen, and one suite has two Count Rumford fireplaces. Pumpkin pine floors, antique quilts, and braided rugs give the rooms a cozy glow. Your host has the scoop on area antiquing. ⊠ *106 Rte. 119, 03447,* ☎ *603/585–3344. 3 rooms, 3 suites. D, MC, V. BP.*

Shopping

ANTIQUES

You'll find about 35 dealers at **Bloomin' Antiques** (⊠ Rte. 12, 3 mi south of Rte. 119, ☎ 603/585–6688). The wares of some 40 dealers comprise **Fitzwilliam Antiques** (⊠ Rtes. 12 and 119, ☎ 603/585–9092).

Rindge

🛇 *8 mi southeast of Fitzwilliam.*

The small town of Rindge sits on a hill overlooking the Monadnock region. Most diversions center on outdoor activities in this scenic setting.

Cathedral of the Pines is an outdoor memorial to American men and women, both civilian and military, who have sacrificed their lives in service to their country. There's an inspiring view of Mt. Monadnock and Mt. Kearsarge from the **Altar of the Nation,** which is composed of rock from every U.S. state and territory. All faiths are welcome to hold services here; organ meditations take place at midday from Tuesday to Thursday in July and August. The **Memorial Bell Tower,** with a carillon of bells from around the world, is built of native stone. Norman Rockwell designed the bronze tablets over the four arches. Flower gardens, an indoor chapel, and a museum of military memorabilia share the hilltop. ⊠ *75 Cathedral Entrance Rd., off Rte. 119,* ☎ *603/899–3300.* 🎦 *Free; donations suggested.* ⊙ *May–Oct., daily 9–5.*

Dining and Lodging

$$-$$$ ⊞ **Woodbound Inn.** This rustic inn was built as a farmhouse in 1819 and became an inn in 1892. A favorite with families and outdoors and fishing enthusiasts, it occupies 200 acres on the shores of Contoocook Lake. Accommodations are functional but clean and cheerfully decorated; they range from quirky rooms in the main inn to modern hotel-style rooms in the Edgewood building to cabins by the water. ⊠ *62 Woodbound Rd., 03461,* ☎ *603/532–8341 or 800/688–7770,* FAX *603/532–8341, ext. 213,* WEB *www.woodboundinn.com. 46 rooms, 42 with bath; 11 cottages. Restaurant, bar, lake, 9-hole golf course, tennis court, croquet, hiking, horseshoes, shuffleboard, volleyball, fishing, ice-skating, cross-country skiing, tobogganing, recreation room. AE, MC, V. BP, MAP.*

$–$$ ⊞ **Cathedral House Bed and Breakfast.** This 1850s farmhouse on the edge of the Cathedral of the Pines was the home of the memorial's founders. Rooms have high ceilings, flowered wallpapers, quilts, and well-stocked cookie jars, all of which help create the feeling that you've just arrived at Grandmother's house. Innkeepers Don and Shirley Mahoney are well versed in area history. ⊠ *63 Cathedral Entrance Rd., 03461,* ☎ *603/899–6790. 5 rooms, 1 with bath. MC, V. BP.*

Jaffrey Center

52 *8 mi north of Rindge, 7 mi northeast of Fitzwilliam.*

Novelist Willa Cather came to the historic village of Jaffrey Center in 1919 and stayed in the Shattuck Inn, which now stands empty on Old Meeting House Road. She pitched a tent not far from here in which she wrote several chapters of *My Antonia.* She returned nearly every summer thereafter until her death and was buried in the Old Burying Ground. **Amos Fortune Forum,** near the Old Burying Ground, brings nationally known speakers to the 1773 meeting house on summer evenings.

The oft-quoted statistic about **Mt. Monadnock** in **Monadnock State Park** is that it's the most-climbed mountain in America—second in the world to Japan's Mt. Fuji. Whether this is true or not, locals agree that it's never lonely at the top. Some days more than 400 people crowd its bald peak. Monadnock rises to 3,165 ft, and on a clear day the hazy Boston skyline is visible from its summit. The park maintains picnic grounds and a small campground (RVs welcome, but no hookups). Five trailheads branch into more than two dozen trails of varying difficulty that wend their way to the top. Some are shorter than others, but you should allow between three and four hours for any round-trip hike. A visitor center has exhibits documenting the mountain's history. Trail maps are available free of charge. ⊠ *Off Rte. 124, 2½ mi north of Jaffrey Center, 03452,* ☎ *603/532–8862.* ✍ *$2.50.* ☉ *Daily dawn–dusk.*

Dining and Lodging

$$ ✕⊞ **Inn at Jaffrey Center.** This delightful gambrel-roof inn was completely overhauled and reopened by new owners in June 2000. Rooms are done in lavenders, yellows, and peaches, with fluffy bedding and towels, fine toiletries, and period furnishings but with a hip sensibility (no phones or TVs, however). The restaurant ($$–$$$; no lunch Sat.) offers a mix of American (pot roast, lamb shanks), Asian (chicken with mild curry, ginger-and-chipotle-steak), and Italian (sole piccata, veal marsala) dishes. ⊠ *379 Main St., 03452,* ☎ *603/532–7800,* FAX *603/532–7900,* WEB *www.innatjaffreycenter.com. 9 rooms. Restaurant, bar. MC, V. CP.*

$–$$$ ⊞ **Benjamin Prescott Inn.** The working dairy farm surrounding this 1853 Colonial farmhouse makes guests feel as though they are miles out in the country rather than just minutes from Jaffrey Center. Stenciling and wide pine floors add to the country feel. A full breakfast of Welsh miner's cakes, baked French toast with fruit, and Jaffrey maple syrup prepares you for a day of antiquing or climbing Mt. Monadnock. ✉ *Rte. 124, 03452,* ☎ *603/532–6637 or 888/950–6637,* WEB *www. benjaminprescottinn.com. 10 rooms, 3 suites. AE, MC, V. BP.*

Peterborough

❺❸ *9 mi northeast of Jaffrey Center, 30 mi northwest of Nashua.*

The nation's first free public library opened in Peterborough in 1833. The town, which was the first in the region to be incorporated (1760), is still a commercial and cultural hub.

The **MacDowell Colony** (✉ 100 High St., ☎ 603/924–3886) was founded by the composer Edward MacDowell in 1907 as an artists' retreat. Willa Cather wrote part of *Death Comes for the Archbishop* here. Thornton Wilder was in residence when he wrote *Our Town*; Peterborough's resemblance to the play's Grover's Corners is no coincidence. Only a small portion of the still-active colony is open to visitors.

In **Miller State Park** (✉ Rte. 101, ☎ 603/924–3672), 3 mi east of town, an auto road takes you almost 2,300 ft up Pack Monadnock Mountain. The road is closed mid-November through mid-April.

Dining and Lodging

$$–$$$ ✕ **Acqua Bistro.** At this smartly decorated, stylish downtown bistro,
★ many patrons congregate at the long bar up front. You might begin a meal with cornmeal-crusted oysters, with white-wine-braised spinach and Emmanthal fondue, before moving on to seared wild Arctic char with roasted vegetable-dill toasted couscous and basil-walnut pesto. Seven thin-crust pizzas are also offered, including a delicious chicken sausage pie with garlic cream, caramelized onions, cured Moroccan olives, and fontina. Save room for the excellent bittersweet chocolate soufflé. ✉ *9 School St.,* ☎ *603/924–9905. MC, V. No lunch.*

$$–$$$$ ✕⌂ **Hancock Inn.** This Federal-style 1789 inn is the pride of the idyllic, well-preserved town it anchors. Common areas possess the warmth of a tavern, with fireplaces, big wing chairs, couches, dark wood paneling, and Rufus Porter murals. Rooms, done in traditional Colonial style, have antique four-poster beds. One suite has the original domed ceiling from the inn's 1800s ballroom. Updated Yankee fare is served by candlelight in the dining room ($$$); a specialty is pecan-crusted pork tenderloin with apples, maple-mustard glaze, and sweet-potato hash. ✉ *Box 96, 33 Main St., Hancock 03449,* ☎ *603/525–3318,* FAX *603/525–9301,* WEB *www.hancockinn.com. 11 rooms, 4 suites. Restaurant, bar. AE, D, DC, MC, V. BP.*

$$ ✕⌂ **Inn at Crotched Mountain.** This 1822 inn has nine fireplaces, four of which are in private rooms. The other five spread cheer in several common areas. The inn, whose rooms are furnished with early Colonial reproductions, is a particularly romantic place to stay when snow is falling on Crotched Mountain. The restaurant's multicultural menu lists Eastern specialties such as Indonesian charbroiled swordfish with a sauce of ginger, green pepper, onion, and lemon; cranberry-port pot roast is one of the regional entrées. Breakfast and dinner must be included in the rate on weekends. ✉ *Mountain Rd., Francestown 03043 (12 mi northeast of Peterborough),* ☎ *603/588–6840. 13 rooms. Restaurant, bar, pool, tennis court, cross-country skiing. No credit cards. BP, MAP.*

$ ✕⌂ **Birchwood Inn.** Thoreau slept here, probably on his way to climb Monadnock or to visit Jaffrey or Peterborough. Country furniture and handmade quilts outfit the bedrooms of this no-smoking inn, as they did in 1775 when the house was new and no one dreamed it would someday be listed on the National Register of Historic Places. Allow time to linger in the dining room ($$; reservations essential; BYOB; no lunch; closed Sunday and Monday), where Rufus Porter murals cover the walls and she-crab soup, roast duckling, and fresh-fruit cobblers are among the specialties. ⊠ *Box 197, Rte. 45, Temple 03084,* ☎ *603/878–3285,* FAX *603/878–2159,* WEB *www.birchwood.mv.com. 7 rooms, 5 with bath. Restaurant. No credit cards. BP.*

$–$$ ▥ **Apple Gate Bed and Breakfast.** With 90 acres of apple orchards across the street, this B&B is appropriately named. The four rooms and even the yellow labrador, Macintosh, are named for types of apples. Some rooms are small, but Laura Ashley prints and stenciling make them cheery and cozy. The house dates from 1832, and the original beams and fireplace still grace the dining room. A music and reading room has a piano and a television with VCR tucked in the corner. From June to October, there's a two-night minimum on weekends. ⊠ *199 Upland Farm Rd., 03458,* ☎ FAX *603/924–6543. 4 rooms. MC, V. BP.*

Nightlife and the Arts

Monadnock Music (☎ 603/924–7610 or 800/868–9613) produces a summer series of concerts from mid-July to late August, with solo recitals, chamber music, and orchestra and opera performances by renowned musicians. The concerts, at locations throughout the region, usually take place in the evening at 8 and on Sunday at 4; many are free.

In winter, the **Peterborough Folk Society** (☎ 603/827–2905) presents folk music concerts. The **Peterborough Players** (⊠ Stearns Farm, off Middle Hancock Rd., ☎ 603/924–7585) have performed for more than 60 seasons. Plays are staged in a converted barn. The **Temple Town Band** (☎ 603/924–3478) was founded in 1799. Members range from teenagers to septuagenarians. The band plays a selection of patriotic songs, traditional marches, and show tunes at the Jaffrey Bandstand, the Sharon Arts Center, and local festivals and events.

Outdoor Activities and Sports

Several types of trout swim in **Dublin Pond,** near Dublin.

Shopping

The corporate headquarters and retail outlet of **Eastern Mountain Sports** (⊠ 1 Vose Farm Rd., ☎ 603/924–7231) sells everything from tents to skis to hiking boots, gives hiking and camping classes, and conducts kayaking and canoeing demonstrations. **Harrisville Designs** (⊠ Mill Alley, Harrisville, ☎ 603/827–3333) sells hand-spun and hand-dyed yarn sheared from local sheep, as well as looms for the serious weaver. The shop also hosts classes in knitting and weaving. **North Gallery at Tewksbury's** (⊠ Rte. 101, ☎ 603/924–3224) stocks thrown pots, sconces, candlestick holders, and woodworkings. **Sharon Arts Downtown** (⊠ Depot Sq., ☎ 603/924–7256) has a gallery that exhibits locally made pottery, fabric, and woodwork and other crafts.

Hillsborough

54 *20 mi north of Peterborough, 23 mi west of Concord.*

Hillsborough comprises four villages, the most prominent of which lies along the roiling Contoocook River and grew up around a thriving woolen and hosiery industry in the mid-1800s. This section, which is really considered Hillsborough proper, is what you'll see as you roll through town along Route 9/U.S. 202.

Turn north from downtown up School Street, however, and continue 3 mi past Fox State Forest to reach one of the state's best-preserved historic districts, **Hillsborough Center,** where 18th-century houses surround the town green. For a wonderfully scenic drive, continue north 6 mi through the similarly quaint village of **East Washington,** and another 6 mi to reach the colonial town center of **Washington.** One of the highest-elevation villages in New Hampshire, this picturesque arrangement of white clapboard buildings made the cover of *National Geographic* several years back. You can loop back to Hillsborough proper via Route 31 south.

The nation's 14th president and arguably the least-liked of all of them, Franklin Pierce was born in Hillsborough and lived here until he married. The **Pierce Homestead,** operated by the Hillsborough Historical Society, welcomes visitors for guided tours. The house is decorated much as it was during Pierce's life. ⊠ *Rte. 31 at Rte. 9,* ☎ *603/478–3165,* WEB *www.conknet.com/~hillsboro/pierce.* ⌑ *$2.50.* ☉ *June and Sept., Sat. 10–4, Sun. 1–4; July–Aug., Mon.–Sat. 10–4, Sun. 1–4.*

NEED A   Families have been coming to **Diamond Acres Dairy Bar** (⊠ Rte. 9, ¼ mi
BREAK?   west of Rte. 31, ☎ 603/478–3121), an ordinary-looking short-order seafood shanty and ice cream stand attached to a gas station, for years to devour super-fresh clam platters, lobster rolls, and frozen sweets.

Dining and Lodging

$$–$$$ ✕ **Red Maples.** In tiny Bennington, about 10 mi south of Hillsborough, you'll find this tiny eatery in a Colonial Cape house in the center of town. Oil lamps, lace curtains, and white napery impart a romantic mood. The kitchen presents a short but ambitious menu of simply and elegantly prepared meals, such as filet mignon with wild mushroom sauce and a starter of clams in a mild Thai curry. ⊠ *12 School St., Bennington,* ☎ *603/588–3588. AE, D, MC, V. Closed Mon. and Jan.–Apr. No lunch.*

$$ ✕ **Rynborn Restaurant and Blues Club.** You may be surprised to find a blues club in such a quiet town as Antrim (8 mi south of Hillsborough), but this place serves up some vibrant sounds. The menu consists of mostly regional American fare such as blackened Cajun shrimp and pecan-crusted chicken in a honey mustard sauce. ⊠ *76 Main St., Antrim,* ☎ *603/588–6162. AE, D, MC, V. No lunch.*

Outdoor Activities and Sports

Fox State Forest (⊠ Center Rd., ☎ 603/464–3453) has 20 mi of hiking trails and an observation tower.

Shopping

At **Gibson Pewter** (⊠ 18 E. Washington Rd., ☎ 603/464–3410), Raymond Gibson and his son Jonathan create and sell museum-quality pewter in contemporary and traditional designs.

Henniker

⑤⑤ *7 mi northeast of Hillsborough, 16 mi west of Concord.*

Governor Wentworth, the first Royal Governor of New Hampshire, named this town in honor of his friend John Henniker, a London merchant and member of the British Parliament (residents delight in their town's status as "the only Henniker in the world"). Once a mill town producing bicycle rims and other light-industrial items, Henniker reinvented itself after the factories were damaged, first by spring floods in 1936 and then by the hurricane and flood of 1938. New England College was established in the following decade. One of the area's covered bridges can be found on campus.

Dining and Lodging

$$–$$$$ ✕⊞ **Colby Hill Inn.** The cookie jar is always full at this Colonial farmhouse, where guests are greeted by Delilah, the inn dog. There is no shortage of relaxing activities: you can curl up with a book by the par-

lor fireplace, stroll through the gardens and 5 acres of meadow, or play badminton out back. Rooms in the main house contain antiques, Colonial reproductions, and frills like lace curtains. In the carriage-house rooms, plain country furnishings, stenciled walls, and exposed beams are the norm. The frequently changing dining menu ($$$$) is excellent and focuses heavily on fish: one fine choice is spicy Malaysian pan-seared tuna with a chili relish, wasabi, and julienne gingered vegetables. ⊠ *Box 779, 3 The Oaks, 03242,* ☎ *603/428–3281,* FAX *603/428–9218,* WEB *www.colbyhillinn.com. 16 rooms. Restaurant, in-room data ports, pool, recreation room. AE, D, DC, MC, V. BP.*

$–$$ ╳🍴 **Meeting House Inn & Restaurant.** The owners of this 200-year-old farmhouse at the base of Pats Peak, who tout the complex as a lovers' getaway, start guests' days off with breakfast in bed. The old barn has become a restaurant ($$) that specializes in leisurely, romantic dining. Items such as lobster pepito are served in a heart-shape puff pastry, and the chocolate-raspberry frozen mousse also comes in the shape of a heart. ⊠ *Rte. 114/Flanders Rd., 03242,* ☎ *603/428–3228,* FAX *603/ 428–6334,* WEB *www.conknet.com/~meetinghouse. 6 rooms. Restaurant, hot tub, sauna. AE, D, MC, V. BP.*

Shopping

The **Fiber Studio** (⊠ 9 Foster Hill Rd., ☎ 603/428–7830) sells beads, hand-spun natural-fiber yarns, spinning equipment, and looms.

Ski Areas

PATS PEAK

A quick trip up I–93 from the Mass border, Pats Peak is geared to families. Base facilities are rustic, and friendly personal attention is the rule. ⊠ *Rte. 114, 03242,* ☎ *603/428–3245; 888/PATS–PEAK snow conditions,* WEB *www.patspeak.com.*

Downhill. Despite Pats Peak's short 710 vertical ft rise, the 20 trails and slopes have something for everyone. New skiers and snowboarders can take advantage of a wide slope and several short trails; intermediates have wider trails from the top; and advanced skiers have a couple of real thrillers. Night skiing and snowboarding take place in January and February. One triple and three double chairlifts and three surface lifts serve the runs. Pats Peak also has afternoon snowtubing on weekends and holidays.

Child care. The nursery takes children ages 6 months–5 years. Special nursery ski programs operate on weekends and during vacations for kids 4–12; all-day lessons for self-sufficient skiers in this age range are scheduled daily.

Western and Central New Hampshire A to Z

To research prices, get advice from other travelers, and book travel arrangements, visit www.fodors.com.

AIRPORTS

Manchester Airport is the main airport in western and central New Hampshire. Colgan Air offers flights to Rutland, Vermont, and Newark, New Jersey, from Keene Airport. Lebanon Municipal Airport, near Dartmouth College, is served by US Airways.

➤ AIRPORT INFORMATION: **Keene Airport** (⊠ Rte. 32 off Rte. 12, North Swanzey, ☎ 603/357–9835). **Lebanon Municipal Airport** (⊠ 5 Airpark Rd., West Lebanon, ☎ 603/298–8878).

BIKE TRAVEL

Eastern Mountain Sports (☞ Visitor Information) and the Keene Chamber of Commerce have information about local bike routes.

➤ Bike Maps: **Keene Chamber of Commerce** (✉ 8 Central Sq., Keene, 03431, ☎ 603/352–1303).

BUS TRAVEL

Concord Trailways runs from Concord to Boston. Dartmouth Coach connects Boston's South Station and Logan Airport with Concord and Manchester. Vermont Transit links the cities of western New Hampshire with major cities in the eastern United States. Advance Transit stops in Enfield and Hanover. Keene City Express buses run from 9 AM to 4 PM. Manchester Transit Authority has hourly local bus service around town and to Bedford from 6 AM to 6 PM.

➤ Bus Information: **Concord Trailways** (☎ 800/639–3317). **Dartmouth Coach** (☎ 603/448–2800 or 800/637–0123 out of state). **Vermont Transit** (☎ 603/351–1331 or 800/552–8737).

Advance Transit (☎ 802/295–1824). **Keene City Express** (☎ 603/352–8494). **Manchester Transit Authority** (☎ 603/623–8801).

CAR TRAVEL

Most people who travel up from Massachusetts do so on I–93, which passes through Manchester and Concord before cutting a path through the White Mountains. I–89 connects Concord, in the Merrimack Valley, with Vermont. Route 12 runs north–south along the Connecticut River. Farther south, Route 101 connects Keene and Manchester, then continues to the seacoast. On the western border of the state, Routes 12 and 12A are picturesque but slow-moving. U.S. 4 crosses the region, winding between Lebanon and the seacoast. Other pretty drives include Routes 101, 202, and 10.

EMERGENCIES

➤ Hospitals: **Cheshire Medical Center** (✉ 580 Court St., Keene, ☎ 603/352–4111). **Concord Hospital** (✉ 250 Pleasant St., Concord, ☎ 603/225–2711). **Dartmouth Hitchcock Medical Center** (✉ 1 Medical Center Dr., Lebanon, ☎ 603/650–5000). **Elliot Hospital** (✉ 1 Elliot Way, Manchester, ☎ 603/669–5300). **Monadnock Community Hospital** (✉ 452 Old Street Rd., Peterborough, ☎ 603/924–7191). **Southern New Hampshire Medical Center** (✉ 8 Prospect St., Nashua, ☎ 603/577–2000).

➤ 24-Hour Pharmacies: **Brooks Pharmacy** (✉ 53 Hookset Rd., Manchester, ☎ 603/623–1135). **CVS Pharmacy** (✉ 271 Mammouth Rd., Manchester, ☎ 603/623–0347; ✉ 240–242 Main St., Nashua, ☎ 603/886–1798).

LODGING

The Sunapee Area Lodging and Information Service can help with reservations.

APARTMENT & VILLA RENTALS

➤ Local Agents: **Sunapee Area Lodging and Information Service** (☎ 603/763–2495 or 800/258–3530).

OUTDOORS & SPORTS

FISHING

For word on what's biting where, contact the New Hampshire Fish and Game Office in Keene.

➤ Contacts: **New Hampshire Fish and Game Office** (☎ 603/352–9669).

VISITOR INFORMATION

➤ Tourist Information: **Concord Chamber of Commerce** (✉ 244 N. Main St., Concord 03301, ☎ 603/224–2508, WEB www.concordnhchamber.com). **Lake Sunapee Business Association** (✉ Box 400, Sunapee 03782, ☎ 603/763–2495 or 800/258–3530,

WEB http://sunapeevacations.com). **Manchester Chamber of Commerce** (⊠ 889 Elm St., Manchester 03101, ☎ 603/666–6600, WEB www.manchester-chamber.org). **Monadnock Travel Council** (⊠ Box 358, 8 Central Sq., Keene 03431, ☎ 800/432–7864, WEB www.monadnocktravel.com).

NEW HAMPSHIRE A TO Z

To research prices, get advice from other travelers, and book travel arrangements, visit www.fodors.com.

AIRPORTS

Manchester Airport, the state's largest airport, is rapidly becoming a cost-effective and hassle-free alternative to Boston's busier Logan International Airport. It has scheduled flights by Air Canada, American Eagle, Continental, Delta, Northwest, Southwest, United, and US Airways. Lebanon Municipal Airport has commuter flights by US Airways Small local airports that handle charters and private planes are Berlin Airport, Concord Airport, Laconia Airport, Nashua Municipal Airport, and, in Rochester, Skyhaven Airport.

➤ AIRPORT INFORMATION: **Manchester Airport** (⊠ 1 Airport Rd., Manchester 03103, ☎ 603/624–6539). **Lebanon Municipal Airport** (⊠ 5 Airpark Rd., West Lebanon, ☎ 603/298–8878). **Berlin Airport** (⊠ Rte. 16, Milan, ☎ 603/449–7383). **Concord Airport** (⊠ 71 Airport Rd., Concord, ☎ 603/229–1760). **Laconia Airport** (⊠ Rte. 11, Laconia, ☎ 603/524–5003). **Nashua Municipal Airport** (⊠ Borie Field, Nashua, ☎ 603/882–0661). **Skyhaven Airport** (⊠ 238 Rochester Hill Rd., Rochester, ☎ 603/332–0005).

BIKE TRAVEL

Bike the Whites, Monadnock Bicycle Touring, and New England Hiking Holidays organize bike tours.

➤ CONTACTS: **Bike the Whites** (☎ 800/448–3534), **Monadnock Bicycle Touring** (☎ 603/827–3925), **New England Hiking Holidays** (☎ 603/356–9696 or 800/869–0949).

BUS TRAVEL

C&J serves the seacoast area of New Hampshire. Concord Trailways links Boston's South Station and Logan Airport with points all along I–93 and, around Lake Winnipesaukee and the eastern White Mountains, along Route 16. Vermont Transit links the cities of western New Hampshire with major cities in the eastern United States.

➤ BUS INFORMATION: **C&J** (☎ 603/431–2424). **Concord Trailways** (☎ 603/228–3300 or 800/639–3317). **Vermont Transit** (☎ 603/228–3300 or 800/451–3292).

CAR TRAVEL

Interstate 93 is the principal north–south route through Manchester, Concord, and central New Hampshire. To the west, I–91 traces the Vermont–New Hampshire border. To the east, I–95, which is a toll road, passes through the coastal area of southern New Hampshire on its way from Massachusetts to Maine. Interstate 89 travels from Concord to Montpelier and Burlington, Vermont.

The official state map, available free from the New Hampshire Office of Travel and Tourism Development (☞ Visitor Information), also has useful telephone numbers and information about bike, snowmobile, and scenic routes.

Speed limits on interstate and limited-access highways are generally 65 mph, except in heavily settled areas, where 55 mph is the norm. On state and U.S. routes, speed limits vary considerably. On any given stretch, the limit may be anywhere from 25 mph to 55 mph, so watch the signs carefully. Right turns are permitted on red lights unless indicated.

EMERGENCIES

➤ CONTACTS: **Ambulance, fire, police** (☎ 911).

LODGING

CAMPING

New Hampshire Campground Owners Association publishes a guide to private, state, and national-forest campgrounds.

➤ CONTACTS: **New Hampshire Campground Owners Association** (✉ Box 320, Twin Mountain, 03595, ☎ 603/846–5511 or 800/822–6764, FAX 603/846–2151).

OUTDOORS & SPORTS

BIRD-WATCHING

Audubon Society of New Hampshire schedules monthly field trips throughout the state and a fall bird-watching tour to Star Isle and other parts of the Isles of Shoals.

➤ CONTACTS: **Audubon Society of New Hampshire** (✉ 3 Silk Farm Rd., Concord 03301, ☎ 603/224–9909).

FISHING

For information about fishing and licenses, call the New Hampshire Fish and Game Office.

➤ CONTACTS: **New Hampshire Fish and Game Office** (☎ 603/271–3211).

FOLIAGE AND SNOW HOT LINES

A fall foliage hot line is updated twice weekly from mid-September through October. Two snow hot lines provide updates on snow conditions at ski centers.

➤ CONTACTS: **Foliage hot line** (☎ 800/258–3608). **Snow hot lines** (☎ 800/258–3608 New Hampshire alpine ski conditions; 800/262–6660 cross-country ski conditions).

SKIING

Ski New Hampshire has information on downhill and cross-country snow sports in the state.

➤ CONTACTS: **Ski New Hampshire** (✉ Box 10, North Woodstock 03262, ☎ 603/745–9396 or 800/887–5464).

VISITOR INFORMATION

➤ TOURIST INFORMATION: **New Hampshire Office of Travel and Tourism Development** (✉ Box 1856, Concord 03302, ☎ 603/271–2343; 800/386–4664 for free vacation packet, WEB www.visitnh.gov). **Events** (☎ 800/258–3608 or 800/262–6660). **New Hampshire Parks Department** (☎ 603/271–3556). **New Hampshire State Council on the Arts** (✉ 40 N. Main St., Concord 03301, ☎ 603/271–2789).

5 PORTRAITS OF NEW ENGLAND

Skiing New England

Map of Maine, Vermont, New Hampshire Ski Areas

Books and Videos

SKIING NEW ENGLAND

Say the words New England, and a number of images will probably focus in your mind's eye: farmhouses and general stores, cheddar cheese and maple syrup. The traits Yankee stubbornness and idealism might also come to mind. Say the words *New England skiing,* and likely you'll think of narrow trails weaving down rugged terrain sheltered by birches and hardwoods. Or perhaps you'll think McSkiing—the corporate smoothness that unites areas from Maine to California, Québec to British Columbia. Given the predominance of corporate-owned areas in northern New England, you might think that if you've skied one New England area, you've skied 'em all. Wrong.

Rather than being carbon copies of areas across America, New England resorts reflect New England values: independence, resourcefulness, thriftiness. No two are alike. Although McSkiing may have changed the face of some resorts, it hasn't affected the charm of a New England village: the church on the town green, the barns and homesteads brimming with antiques for sale, the country inns.

Blending Old and New

New England areas have attitude and history on their side, and much of that history can be discovered at the New England Ski Museum, near Cannon Mountain in New Hampshire. Some of the first lifts in North America were located here: a shovel handle tow at Black Mountain, New Hampshire; single chairlifts at Stowe and Mad River Glen, Vermont. Many of these have given way to high-speed chairlifts, trams, and gondolas.

Sugar Hill, in Franconia, New Hampshire, was the site of America's first ski school, and Mt. Cranmore, in North Conway, New Hampshire, was where Austrian skimeister Hannes Schneider introduced the famed Arlberg technique. Today most areas offer instructional programs for adults and children, including clinics for women, tree skiers, bump bashers, and extreme skiers. First-timers should ask about Learn-to-Ski-or-Ride programs that package lessons with equipment and a lift ticket. Discovery Centers at Mt.

Snow and Killington, Vermont; Sunday River, Maine; and Attitash Bear Peak, New Hampshire, are excellent programs for families and beginners.

Perhaps nowhere is the blend of old and new more apparent than on the hill. Old-fashioned trails ebb and flow with the mountain's contours, weaving through woods, over knolls, and offering glimpses of the surrounding countryside. Newer trails were built to accommodate snowmaking and grooming equipment; they're usually wide and often follow the fall line. Often at the same mountain, you can cruise down a steep, wide, perfectly groomed slope; experience the thrills of linking tight turns on a narrow, bump-choked trail; or ramble along a trail that takes the least direct route from summit to base.

Advanced skiers have even more options: tree skiers can snake their way through glades at most resorts, with Stowe Mountain and Jay Peak, Vermont, and Sugarloaf/USA and Sunday River, Maine, providing some of the best tree skiing in the country. For the true expert, Tuckerman Ravine in New Hampshire is the Holy Grail. This hike-to-only terrain on Mt. Washington, New England's tallest peak, is a rite of passage.

Yes, New England's weather can be unpredictable: rain on the coast is often snow in the mountains, and sleet at lower elevations may be feathery powder at higher ones. For the most part modern snowmaking and grooming produce reliable conditions from early December into April. Nevertheless, New England snow is not western-style snow. What New Englanders consider hard-packed powder, Westerners often consider ice. While powder days are a rare treat here, grooming means top-to-bottom cruising runs are the rule. It can get cold, but if you dress in layers and wear a neck warmer and face mask, you'll be prepared. As a general rule, the farther north the ski area, the longer the season and the more natural snow you can expect.

Riding, Gliding, Shoeing

Snowboarding has changed American resorts as riders have come to share the lifts, slopes, and trails with skiers. Most resorts (the lone exception being feisty Mad River Glen, Vermont) have embraced snowboarding. Halfpipes and terrain parks are popular not only with riders but also with skiers. New snow toys, such as the giant Zorb ball, ski bikes, and Snow Blades, as well as tubing parks, provide alternative activities.

Off-the-hill activities abound. Cross-country centers such as Jackson, Bretton Woods, and the Balsams Wilderness, New Hampshire; Bethel, Maine; and Stowe, Vermont, have gained international recognition for their climate, terrain, and size. Bretton Woods and the Balsams are self-contained downhill and cross-country resorts anchored by historic grand resort hotels. In Jackson, you can ski from inn to inn, and Stowe has the Trapp Family Lodge. At many cross-country centers you can also snowshoe, a wonderful, easy-to-do sport.

Saving Big by Thinking Small

While day tickets at the bigger resorts approach $50, those at smaller areas can be as low as $20. Some independently owned areas are bona fide bargains for skiers who don't require the glitz of the high-profile resorts. Family pricing, multiday tickets, frequent-skier programs, junior and senior rates, Web site deals, and lift-and-lodging packages can all lower the price significantly. Midweek prices are often less expensive, and many areas offer incentives then, such as two-for-one days.

Most ski areas have a variety of accommodations—lodges, condominiums, hotels, motels, inns, bed-and-breakfasts—close to the action. For stays of three days or more, a package rate may be the deal. Packages vary in composition, price, and availability; their components may include a room, meals, lift tickets, ski lessons,

rental equipment, transfers to the mountain, parties, races, use of a sports center, tips, and taxes. In general, if you're willing to commute a few extra miles, off-site lodging offers good value.

Getting Practical

If you're traveling with children, ask about programs geared to their age. Areas renowned for their family emphasis include Smugglers' Notch, Vermont, and Waterville Valley, New Hampshire. Both have plenty of activities, both on the snow and off, for all ages.

Child-care centers can be found at virtually all ski areas and often accept children from ages six weeks to six years. Parents must usually supply formula and diapers for infants; reservations are advised at most, essential at some. Most programs also have instructional opportunities for children at least three years of age and older. Rental equipment is available at all ski areas, at ski shops around resorts, and even in cities far from ski areas. Shop personnel will advise you on equipment and how to use it.

Ski areas have devised standards for rating and marking trails and slopes that offer fairly accurate guides. Trails are rated Easier (green circle), More Difficult (blue square), Most Difficult (black diamond), and Expert (double diamond). Keep in mind that trail difficulty is measured relative to that of other trails at the same ski area. A black-diamond trail at one area may rate only a blue square at a neighboring area. Unless you're able to handle any type of terrain, your best bet is to start on green-circle trails and work your way up in difficulty until you find the terrain where you're most comfortable.

— Hilary M. Nangle

Maine, Vermont, and New Hampshire Ski Areas

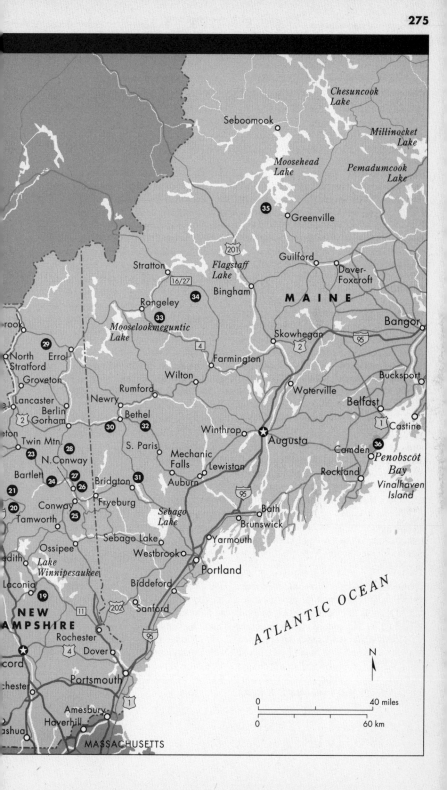

Chesuncook Lake

Millinocket Lake

Seboomook

Moosehead Lake

Pemadumpook Lake

35

Greenville

201

Guilford

Dover-Foxcroft

Stratton

Flagstaff Lake

16/27

Rangeley

34

Bingham

M A I N E

33

Mooselookmeguntic Lake

Skowhegan

Bangor

rook

4

Farmington

2

95

Bucksport

29

North Stratford

Errol

Wilton

Waterville

Belfast

Groveton

Rumford

Newry

1

Castine

Lancaster

Berlin

30

32

Bethel

Winthrop

Augusta

Camden

36

Gorham

2

eton

S. Paris

Penobscot Bay

Twin Mtn.

28

Mechanic Falls

Rockland

23

N.Conway

Lewiston

Vinalhaven Island

Bartlett

24

27

Bridgton

31

Auburn

21

26

Fryeburg

20

Conway

25

Sebago Lake

Bath

Tamworth

Brunswick

Ossipee

Sebago Lake

Yarmouth

edith

Lake Winnipesaukee

Westbrook

95

Portland

Laconia

Biddeford

ATLANTIC OCEAN

19

11

202

Sanford

NEW AMPSHIRE

95

cord

Rochester

cheste

4

Dover

N

ashua

Portsmouth

1

Amesbury

Haverhill

MASSACHUSETTS

0 _____ 40 miles

0 _____ 60 km

BOOKS & VIDEOS

New England has been home to some of America's classic authors, among them Herman Melville, Edith Wharton, Mark Twain, Robert Frost, Ralph Waldo Emerson, Henry Wadsworth Longfellow, and Emily Dickenson. Henry David Thoreau wrote about New England in *Cape Cod, The Maine Woods,* and his masterpiece, *Walden.* Modern New England literary voices have included that of Stephen King, the horrormeister of Bangor, Maine.

Among books written about the Maine islands are Philip Conkling's *Islands in Time,* Bill Caldwell's *Islands of Maine,* and Charlotte Fardelmann's *Islands Down East.* Kenneth Roberts set a series of historical novels, beginning with *Arundel,* in the coastal Kennebunk region during the Revolutionary War and also wrote *Trending into Maine,* a book of essays on traditional but rapidly changing Down East ways of life. Sarah Orne Jewett's 1896 novel, *The Country of the Pointed Firs,* describes the heart of small-town life with sympathy. Ruth Moore's *Candalmas Bay, Speak to the Winds,* and *The Weir* and Elisabeth Ogilvie's "Tide Trilogy" books capture both the romanticism and hardships of coastal life. Carolyn Chute's 1985 bestseller, *The Beans of Egypt, Maine,* offers a fictional glimpse of the hardships of contemporary rural life. The 1994 movie version of the book, starring Martha Plimpton, is in video stores with the title *Forbidden Choices.*

Charles Morrissey's *Vermont: A History* delivers just what the title promises; it's part of a series of bicentennial histories all published by Norton, in which the other five New England states are also represented. *Without a Farmhouse Near,* by Deborah Rawson, describes the impact of change on small Vermont communities, as does Joe Sherman's *Fast Lane on a Dirt Road.*

Real Vermonters Don't Milk Goats, by Frank Bryan and Bill Mares, looks at the lighter side of life in the Green Mountain state. Howard Frank Mosher, long a resident of Vermont's sparsely populated, bleakly beautiful Northeast Kingdom, has written works of fiction including *A Stranger in the Kingdom, Northern Borders,* and *Where the Rivers Flow North,* all dealing with the hard lives and bristly independence of the region's natives. *Where the Rivers Flow North* was made into an acclaimed independent film in 1993, with stars Rip Torn and Michael J. Fox. Another video with a Vermont locale—although in a vastly different, comic vein—is John O'Brien's 1996 *Man with a Plan,* about a retired dairy farmer who decides to run for Congress.

Visitors to New Hampshire may enjoy the classic 19th-century history-cum-travel guide *The White Mountains: Their Legends, Landscape, and Poetry,* by Thomas Starr King, and *The Great Stone Face and Other Tales of the White Mountains,* by Nathaniel Hawthorne. New Hampshire was also blessed with the poet Robert Frost, whose first books, *A Boy's Way* and *North of Boston,* are set here, as is his long poem *New Hampshire.* It's commonly accepted that the Grover's Corners of Thornton Wilder's play *Our Town* is the real-life Peterborough. The 1981 movie *On Golden Pond* was partially filmed on Squam Lake.

Also published by Fodor's, *Where Should We Take the Kids? The Northeast* provides ideas on what to do with the little ones while in New England. Fodor's Compass American Guides, handsomely illustrated with color photographs, provide topical and cultural essays and historical background. Look for *Vermont,* by Don Mitchell, and *Maine,* by Charles Calhoun.

INDEX

Icons and Symbols

★ Our special recommendations

✕ Restaurant

⊞ Lodging establishment

✕⊞ Lodging establishment whose restaurant warrants a special trip

☺ Good for kids (rubber duck)

☞ Sends you to another section of the guide for more information

⊠ Address

☏ Telephone number

⌚ Opening and closing times

🎟 Admission prices

Numbers in white and black circles ③ ❸ that appear on the maps, in the margins, and within the tours correspond to one another.

NOTES

NOTES